The Official Roster

— OF THE —

SOLDIERS OF THE AMERICAN REVOLUTION BURIED

IN THE

STATE OF OHIO

Compiled Under the Direction of

FRANK D. HENDERSON, *The Adjutant General,*

JOHN R. REA, *Military Registrar,*

DAUGHTERS OF AMERICAN REVOLUTION OF OHIO.

JANE DOWD DAILEY (MRS. O. D.),
State Chairman.

This volume was reproduced
from a personal copy located in
the Publishers private library

Please direct allcorrespondence and book orders to:
SOUTHERN HISTORICAL PRESS, Inc.
PO Box 1267
Greenville, SC 29602-1267

Originally printed 1929
Reprinted By: Southern Historical Press, Inc.
Greenville, SC 2022
ISBN #978-1-63914-046-6
Printed in the United Sattes of America

AUTHORIZATION

H. B. No. 101

Providing for the publication and distribution of the roster of the soldiers of the revolutionary war, buried in Ohio.

Be it enacted by the General Assembly of the State of Ohio:

SECTION 1. The adjutant general of Ohio is hereby authorized to secure the publication in book form of a complete roster of all the soldiers and sailors of the revolutionary war, buried in Ohio, the data for which has already been collected by the Ohio Daughters of the American Revolution, and presented to the state.

SECTION 2. Such roster shall contain the principal items of the record of each soldier or sailor of the revolutionary war who is buried in Ohio. All names in such roster shall be arranged in alphabetical order in such a manner as to render all information contained therein ready and accessible, and shall be thoroughly indexed. The binding shall be done at the state bindery under the direction of the superintendent of purchase and printing.

SECTION 3. Two thousand copies of such roster shall be printed, to be distributed as follows: three hundred copies shall be delivered to the state librarian for distribution by him, to the libraries of Ohio and other states, provided that one copy be sent to a library in each county; two hundred copies shall be delivered to the Daughters of the American Revolution for distribution among their own chapters; fifty copies to the adjutant general; and two copies to each member of the General Assembly.

In addition to the above free distribution, the remaining copies shall be delivered to the Ohio Archæological and Historical Society, to be sold by it at cost, and the proceeds thereof paid into the state treasury to the credit of the general revenue fund.

SECTION 4. For the printing, stock and binding of the roster as provided for in this act there is hereby appropriated out of any moneys in the state treasury to the credit of the general revenue fund, and not otherwise appropriated, not to exceed the sum of two thousand dollars. The appropriation herein made shall be for the use of the adjutant general in carrying out the provisions of this act.

Adopted by House Bill 502—Appropriation Bill.
Published by direction of Frank D. Henderson, Adjutant General.
John R. Rea, Military Registrar.

TO THE PIONEERS OF OHIO WHO SERVED THEIR COUNTRY IN THE REVOLUTIONARY WAR

This volume is respectfully and gratefully dedicated

FOREWORD

The records contained in this Roster were presented by the Daughters of the American Revolution to the State of Ohio as a tribute of respect to the hardy pioneers who transplanted to this State the noble ideals for which they fought from 1775 to 1783, and who now sleep the last sleep beneath its soil.

The 87th General Assembly of Ohio accepted the gift of these records from the Daughters of the American Revolution and provided an appropriation for their publication as a part of the Military records of the State. The Roster is not designed as a genealogical reference book, although it may be of service in tracing pioneer ancestry. Its primary object is to present an authetic and complete list of Revolutionary soldiers buried in this State. Research has extended over a quarter of a century, and had it not been for the patriotic service given gratis by Ohio men and women the compilation of these records would not have been possible. No detail was too insignificant for these searchers; county cemeteries were investigated by faithful Chapter chairmen of the D. A. R.; newspapers gave freely of their space; the U. S. Bureau of Pensions gave valuable aid and many persons were assiduous in searching the D. A. R. lineage books and the published lists of the Sons of the American Revolution.

Contained herein are many records of proven service, but there are some which may never be proved though the service given by the individuals is beyond question. Information in many instances was meager, but this, it is felt, can be corrected by adding to the Roster additional records which are now or will be in the future under investigation. The chapter or person who filed the data is responsible for the authenticity of the record and any communication should be carried on with them. Filing of the records was begun by Mrs. Eugene Kennedy, Dayton, Ohio, during her term as State Chairman of Historical Sites and Revolutionary Graves, 1920 to 1923, and the Roster was compiled by the present State Chairman who submits the work in answer to the toast of David Morris, Revolutionary soldier, who pleaded at a patriotic meeting held at Troy, Ohio, July 4, 1827—

> "May the precious blood that was spilt between the years '75 and '83 as a sacrifice for our liberty and independence be ever commenorated."

Lest the reader should wonder at the large number of Revolutionary soldiers buried in Ohio, it should be recalled that the present boundaries of Ohio were nearest the original colonies, and when land grants were given to the soldiers thither came the hardy New Englanders to the Western Reserve and the region of Lake Erie; sturdy Pennsylvanians crossed over into central Ohio and the Virginian and Carolinian took up his abode in the southern part of Ohio. Here in the Northwest Territory they lived and died; they were fathers of a race who inherited the invincible courage and sterling qualities of the Revolutionary soldier and who took up the burden of founding the Nation by pressing westward.

JANE FRANCES DOWD DAILEY, Albany, Ohio.
State Chairman of Historic Sites and Revolutionary
Graves, D. A. R., 1923-29.

MRS. HERBERT BACKUS,
State Regent, Ohio D. A. R.
1926-29.

ABBREVIATIONS

A

Apr ....April
Aptd ....Appointed
Amer ....Amer
Aug ....August

B

Bk ....Book
Bur ....Buried
Bn ....Battalion
Br ....Born
Brig ....Brigade
Brig Gen..........Brigadier General

C

Capt ....Captain
Cav ....Cavalry
Cem ....Cemetery
Chap ....Chapter
Col ....Colonel
Corp ....Corporal

D

D ....Died
Da ....Day
Dau ....Daughter
Dec ....December
Disch ....Discharged

E

Enl ....Enlisted
Enlmt ....Enlistment
Feb ....February
Fur Infor.....Furnished Information
Fr ....From

G

Gen ....General
GM ....Grave Marked

H

Hist ....History

I

Inf ....Infantry
Infor ....Information

J

Jan ....January
July ....July
June ....June

L

Lin ....Lineage
Lt ....Lieutenant
Lt Col...........Lieutenant Colonel

M

Maj ....Major
Maj Gen..............Major General
Mar ....Married
May ....May
Mch ....March
Mil ....Militia
MI ....Monument Inscription
Mo ....Month
Mos ....Months

N

Natl ....National
Nov ....November

O

O ....Ohio
Oct ....October

P

P ....Page
pp ....pages
Pens ....Pension
Pvt ....Private

R

Ref ....Reference
Reg ....Regular
Regt ....Regiment
Rev ....Revolution

S

Sec ....Section
Serv ....Service
Sept ....September
Sgt ....Sergeant

T

Tr ....Troops
Twp ....Township

V

Vol ....Volume

Y

Yrs ....Years

CHAPTERS OF THE D. A. R. ALPHABETICALLY

A-B

Chapter	Location
Akron	Akron
Ames, Nabby Lee	Athens
Avery, Temperance	Ellet
Bain, Jane (Now Freedom)	Alliance
Bellefontaine	Bellefontaine
Blanchester	Blanchester
Boyer, Lewis	Sidney
Byrd, Lieutenant	Decatur

C

Chapter	Location
Canton	Canton
Chesney, Mary	Warren
Chittenden, Molly	Geauga County
Cincinnati	Cincinnati
City, Delaware	Delaware
City, Plain	Plain City
Cleaveland, Moses	Cleveland
Cliff, Cedar	Cedarville
Clinton, George	Wilmington
Colony, French	Gallipolis
Columbus	Columbus
Connecticut, New	Painesville
Cops, Sarah	Ashland
Coshocton	Coshocton
Crawford, Hannah	Bucyrus
Crawford, Col. William	Upper Sandusky
Creek, Turtle	Lebanon
Croghan, Col. George	Tremont

D

Chapter	Location
Davis, Ann Simpson	Columbus
Dayton, Jonathan	Dayton
Defiance, Ft.	Defiance
De Forest, Sally	Norwalk
Devin, Amanda Barker	McConnelsville
Dew, Elizabeth Zane	Nelsonville
Dustin, Hannah Emerson	Marysville

E

Chapter	Location
Elyria	Elyria

F

Chapter	Location
Falls, Cuyahoga	Cuyahoga Falls
Findlay, Ft.	Findlay
Firelands	Willard
Fowler, James	Leroy

G

Gilead, Mt. .... Mt. Gilead
Grant, Eunice .... Jefferson
Granville .... Granville
Greene, Catherine .... Xenia
Greenville, Ft. .... Greenville

H

Hendricks, Capt. Wm. .... Marion
Hetuck .... Newark
Horney, William .... Jeffersonville

I

Industry, Ft. .... Toledo

J

James, Capt. John .... Jackson

K

Kokosing .... Mt. Vernon

L

Lagonda .... Springfield
Lakewood .... Lakewood
Laurens Ft. .... New Philadelphia
Lima .... Lima
London .... London

M

Madison, Dolly Todd .... Tiffin
Mahoning .... Youngstown
Mansfield, Jared .... Mansfield
Marietta .... Marietta
Massie, Nathaniel .... Chillicothe
Massillon .... Massillon
McArthur, Ft. .... Kenton
Meigs, Return Jonathan .... Pomeroy
Miami .... Troy
Muskingum .... Zanesville
Myers, Michael .... Toronto

N

Northwest, Old .... Ravenna

O

Oberlin (Now Nancy Squire) .... Oberlin
Olentangy .... Galion
Olmstead, Aaron .... Kent

P

Perry, Nathan .... Lorain
Piqua .... Piqua
Pitkin, Martha .... Sandusky
Plains, Pickaway .... Circleville
Portage, Cuyahoga .... Akron
Portage, Delery .... Port Clinton
Preble, Commodore .... Eaton

R

Redmond, Mary .... Conneaut
Reese, Elizabeth Sherman .... Lancaster
Reeve, Luther .... Rome
Reily, John .... Hamilton
Reserve, Western .... Cleveland
Ripley .... Ripley
Rucker, Ann .... Woodsfield

S

Scott, Oxford Caroline .... Oxford
Slagle, George .... Jamestown
Smith, Col. Jonathan Bayard .... Middletown
Southwick, Bethia .... Wellsville
Spencer, Joseph .... Portsmouth
Stanley, Mary .... Ashtabula
Sterling, Mt. .... Mt. Sterling
Steubenville .... Steubenville
Stone, Anna Ashbury .... Cambridge
Swamp, Black .... Bowling Green
Sycamore .... Winchester

T

Taliaferro .... Georgetown
Taylor .... Chardon
Tomepomehala .... New Concord
Trail, Moravian .... Cadiz

U

Urbana .... Urbana

V

Valley, Scioto .... Waverly
Van Wart, Isaac .... Van Wert

W

Washington, Jane .... Fostoria
Washington C. H. .... Washingeon C. H.
Washington, Mary .... Mansfield
Wauseon .... Wauseon
Waw-Wil-A-Way .... Hillsboro
Wayne, Wooster .... Wooster
Westervelt, Jacobus .... Westerville
White, Julianna .... Greenfield
Wolcott, Ursula .... Toledo
Worthington, Governor .... Logan

ABBOTT, JOSEPH, (Brown Co.)

Served in the Continental army during the Rev. Br May 29/1739. Mar Esther —, who was br Sept 17, 1746. Children: Mary, Chloe, John, Rebecca, Eunice, Silas, Jane, Joseph. D Franklin Twp, Brown Co. O. Bur Abbott family Cem in Franklin Twp. Moved fr NJ to Va and shortly after the war came to Straight Creek, Franklin Twp, Brown Co, O. With Greer Brown, located 1000 acres, each taking 500 acres. Ref: Brown Co Hist 1883 by Beers & Co., p 539. Malcolm Abbott, Georgetown, O, and Mrs. A. A. Wicoff, descendants. Fur infor Taliaferro and Lieutenant Byrd Chaps.

ABEL, JOHN, (Lake Co.)

Corp. Enl June 1777 for three mos under Capt Jonathan Penoyer; Oct 1 for one mo under Capt Ephriam Merimer; Dec 1778 for 3 mos under Capt Amos Chapel; July 1778 for 3 mos under Col Lawrence. Br 1756. D Dec 23, 1836 at Perry, Lake Co, O. Bur Perry, O. MI: "Died in Perry, Lake Co, O on Friday the 23rd of Dec 1836, Mr. John Abel, a Revolutionary Soldier, in the 80th yr of his age." GM by New Connecticut Chap. Fur infor New Connecticut Chap.

ACHOR, JOHN, (Clinton Co.)

Bur Smithson Cem, near New Vienna. Fur infor George Clinton Chap.

ACKERMAN, JOHN, (Knox Co.)

Pvt. Br 1757, Bergen Co, NJ. Mar: 1st wife (no date). 2nd wife: Amy Barton Roberts (a widow) Feb 1803. Children: Catherine b 1803, John Jr b 1805, Abraham b 1808, Mary b 1810. D Sept 8, 1841, Knox Co, Middlebury Twp. Bur in North Fork Cem in the western part of the county. MI: "John Ackerman died Sept 8, 1841, aged 83 yrs, 9 mos, 16 da. A soldier of 1776." Pioneer settler. A farmer. Ref: Wm. Ackerman, Mt Vernon, O. Fur infor Mt Gilead and Kokosing Chaps.

ADAIR, JAMES, (Mahoning Co.)

Pvt. Third Bn, NJ. Br 1740. Mar Mary McCord (1744-1824). Children: William, James, Alexander. D 1816. Bur Presbyterian Cem. Poland, O. GM by D. A. R. in 1915-17. Ref: N. J. Men in the Rev p 485; p 59 Vol 2, Hist of Trumbull and Mahoning Cos. Natl No. 51982 D. A. R. Lin. Mrs. J. Craig Smith, descendant. Fur infor Mahoning Chap.

ADAMS, ABRAHAM, (Delaware Co.)

Sgt in Sussex Co, NJ. Mil. Br 1755 Sussex Co, NJ. D 1822 Delaware Co, O. Natl No 96327, Vol 97, p 103 D. A. R. Lin. Fur infor Delaware Chap.

ADAMS, ASAHEL, (Trumbull Co.)

Enl fr Norwich, Conn in 1775, 7th Regt Continental Line May 5, 1777. Transferred to "The Guards" Apr 1, 1778 and served to close of war. Disch May 5, 1781. With Washington at Valley Forge, crossing Delaware river and Trenton battle. Br Sept 13, 1754 at Canterbury, Conn. Parents: Phineas and Lydia Fitch Adams. Mar Olive Avery 1779, (bur at his side). Children: Elizabeth, David Augustus, Asael, Frances Ursula, Susan, Mason, Olive, Jay, Adeline, Phineas. D May 25, 1821, Girard, O. Bur Miami Cem Liberty Twp. MI: "Asahel Adams formerly of Canterbury, Conn. Died 5/25/1821, aged 66 yrs." GM by family. Ref: Fred Adams, Warren, O. (S. A. R. on this line). Fur infor Mary Chesney Chap.

ADAMS, DAVID, (Delaware Co.)

Pvt under Col Seward, Capt Benj Kirkendall, NJ Tr. Bur in Harlem Twp. Pensioned. Fur infor Delaware Chap.

ADAMS, ELIJAH, (Licking Co.)

Enl at Enfield, Conn, May 1, 1775 as Pvt in Capt Hezekiah Parson's Company, Col Inman's Regt; also Col Motto's Regt. Was detached as a marine with Capt Murison on a row-galley on Lake Champlain, where he was captured, but shortly after was released on parole. On June 1, 1782 he enl as Sgt in Col Willet's Regt in New York. Br 1755 in Conn. Mar Sarah Vails, Feb 11, 1798, Otsego, NY. D Dec 7, 1843 Monroe Twp. MI: "Rev. War" GM by Hetuck Chap in 1910. Ref: Hist of Licking county by E. M. Brister. Fur infor Hetuck Chap.

ADAMS, GEORGE, (Darke Co.)

Served as a drummer boy in Capt Finley's Company, Pa Line in the Rev. Also served as an Indian spy under St Clair, and a coat worn by him is in the Smithsonian Institution, Washington, DC. A Maj in Mil at beginning of 1812 and commanded Ft Green. Br Oct 26, 1767 in Pa. Mar Elizabeth Ellis, Ft Washington (now Cincinnati). Children: Elizabeth Adams Worley (first white female child born in Cincinnati.) D Nov 28, 1832. Bur in Martin Cem, 3 miles east of Greenville, Adams Twp, near Bears Mills, formerly Adams Mill, built by him on land given him by the government. MI: Name, date of birth and age. His wife was a dau of Gen and Elizabeth Ellis. Ref: Ohio Archaeological and Hist Society, Vol 22, p 522. Fur infor Fort Greenville Chap, and S. A. R. of Dayton.

ADAMS, JOHN, (Coshocton Co.)

Died at West Bedford. Fur infor Mrs. Augustus Ripple, member Coshocton Chap.

ADAMS, MOSES, (Portage Co.)

Pvt in Conn Continental Line. Placed on pens roll Sept 6, 1819. Bur in Franklin, O. Drew pens at Ravenna, O, in 1840. Fur infor Old Northwest Chap.

ADAMS, SAMUEL, (Cuyahoga Co.)

On Ohio pens roll. Fur infor Western Reserve Chap.

ADAMS, THOMAS, (Greene Co.)

Was receiving a pens in 1840 at age of 83, for military serv thought to be Revolutionary. Record taken from census of 1840. Lived at Xenia, O. Fur infor Catherine Green Chap.

ADAMY, HENRY, (Cuyahoga Co.)

Served as Pvt New York Troops. D in 1836. GM by Western Reserve Chap. Fur infor Western Reserve Chap.

ADGATE, JOHN HART, (Trumbull Co.)

Surgeon. Br Sept 13, 1759. Parents: Thomas and Ruth Leffingwell) Adgate. (Mar Jan 25/1735). Mar Salley Fitch, probably in New London, Conn. Children: John, James, Charles, Ulises, Salley, Hoover, Bolinda, Leviett, Caroline, Anna. D Apr 23, 1809, Warren, O. Bur Old Cem, Mahoning Ave in family lot. Monument in good order. MI: John Hart Adgate. Born 1759. Died 1809. GM by family. Name also on monument erected in Old Cem for Revolutionary Soldiers. Ref: Family Hist in possession of Adgate family still living in Warren. Fur infor Mary Chesney Chap.

AGARD, JOHN, (Portage Co.)

Lived at Brimfield. Drew pens at age of 78 yrs. Fur infor Old Northwest Chap.

ALBAN, GEORGE, (Jefferson Co.)

Enl 1776 Va Continental Line, 8th Regt. Transferred 1777 to Commander-in Chief's Guard. In battles of Germantown and Brandywine. Br 1758, Winchester, Va. Mar 1783 Jane Green (1760-1839). D 1840, Steubenville, O. Bur Two Ridges Cem, Jefferson Co. GM by Steubenville Chap with official marker. Ref Natl No 102642, Vol 103, p 197 D. A. R. Lin. Fur infor Steubenville Chap.

ALBAUGH, ZACHARIAH, (Licking Co.)

Enl as Pvt and rose to rank of Major. Was at Germantown, Oct 31, 1777; served until close of war. Also at Brandywine. From Frederick county, Md. Br 1758 Shenandoah Valley, Va. D Nov 9, 1859 Newton Twp. Bur in Evans Cem near St Louisville. MI: "Rev. War." GM by Hetuck Chap in 1909. Ref: History of Licking County by E. M. P. Brister. Pension file 2902. Fur infor Hetuck Chap.

ALBIN, JOHN, (Clark Co.)

Br 1740, Virginia. Children: William, Gabriel, John, Joseph, Sarah. D 1820, Clark Co. Bur Ebenezer, 5 miles south on Yellow Springs pike, southeast corner. MI: Name, date of death. GM by family monument. Came to Ohio at close of war. A farmer. Ref: Family records. Fur infor Lagonda Chap.

ALDEN, DAVID, (Geauga Co.)

Pvt Mass State Mil. Enl 1780 in Capt Isaac Pope's Company. Br 1759. Williamsfield, Mass. Parents: David and Lucy (Thomas) Alden. Mar 1783 Susanna Ward. Children: Ezra, Lucy, Chandler, Mary, Lydia, Enoch, Susanna, Hannah, Sarah, Wheeler. D Jan 8, 1843. Bur Middlefield, O. cemetery, on lot of son Enoch Alden, which has monument. MI: 'David Alden, died Jan. 8, 1843, 84 years.' GM by family. Farmer. Descendant of John Alden of Plymouth. National number of Revolutionary Soldier in D. A. R. Honor Roll 21065, 14575. Ref: 90269, Vol 91, p 88 D. A. R. Lin. Fur infor Taylor Chap.

ALDRED, HENRY, (Adams Co.)

Br in Germany, date unknown. D in 1835. Bur McColm cemetery on Brush Creek. Was one of first settlers on Brush Creek. Fur infor Sycamore Chap.

ALEXANDER, JAMES, (Belmont Co.)

Br 1733, Campbellton, Scotland. Mar Margaret Wilson. Margaret Clark Ross, 2nd wife. Children: Jane, Margaret, James ,Andrew, Nancy, Mary, John, Robert, Peter, Jenetta, Thomas, Elizabeth. D May 9, 1817 Belmont Co, O. Bur Scotch Ridge, near Martins Ferry, O. A farmer. Ref: Mrs. Minteer, New Concord, O. Fur infor Wheeling, W. Va. Chap, by Mrs A. L. McFarland, St Clairsville, O.

ALEXANDER, JOSEPH, (Harrison Co.)

Served as a member of Capt Eleazer Williamson's company in 3rd Bn Washington Co, Pa. Mil 1782-84. Br 1752. Mar Elizabeth —— (1762-1833). D 1830. Bur in Cadiz Old graveyard. Ref: Pa. Archives, 6th Series, II, 124. Fur infor Moravian Trail Chap.

ALEXANDER, MARGARET CLARKE, (Belmont Co.)

Received into her home and nursed back to health four soldiers sick with fever. Br 1743 in Scotland. Mar James Ross. D 1809 in Belmont Co. O. Ref: Natl No. 99898, Vol 100, p 279, D. A. R. Lin.

ALEY, ABRAHAM, (Greene Co.)

Br Miami City, O. Buried in Aley Churchyard. Ref: Robinson's History of Greene County. Fur infor Catherine Greene Chap.

ALFORD, BENEDICT, (Geauga Co.)

Pvt 1776 Capt Prevr's Company, Conn. Tr. 1777. Capt Fassett's Company, Col Stafford's Regt 1780. Sgt in charge of guarding prisoners, Capt Clark's Company of Mass Mil. Br Mch 13, 1757, Windsor, Conn. Parents: Benedict and Jerusha (Ashley) Alford. Mar Huldah ———. Children: Annie, Benedict. D Feb 25, 1838, Welshfield, O. Bur North of Pope's Corners, Welshfield, O. MI: "Benedict Alford died Feb 25, 1835 aged 82." Came to Welshfield, Troy Twp, O. 1835. Ref: Ancient Windsor Record Vol 2, p 615. Pioneer Hist Geauga Co. Natl No in D. A. R. Honor Roll 75674. Fur infor Taylor Chap.

ALFORD, ELIJAH, (Portage Co.)

Lived at Windham. Drew pension. Fur infor Old Northwest Chap.

ALLBERRY, JOHN, (Licking Co.)

Has an authentic record which was investigated by Granville Chap. and verified by War records. Bur in Universalist cem., Jersey Twp., Licking Co. Fur infor Granville Chap.

ALLEN, ADAM, (Fayette Co.)

Pvt. Volunteered from Pa, later Washington's Aide. Br 1754, Pa. Mar Nancy ———— (2nd wife.) Children: Elizabeth, William, Adam, Ethan, Aaron, Betsy, Sarah. D Aug 27, 1851, near Milledgeville. Bur Coons Cem on Jamestown Pike in old part. MI: "Adam Allen a soldier of Revolution, entering Army of Washington in 1776. Fought at Monmouth and Brandywine." GM by family, in 1852. A farmer. Ref: Natl No. 109696. Fur infor Washington Court House Chap.

ALLEN, ELIHU, (Ashtabula Co.)

Enl Aug 4, 1778, Capt Olcott's Company, Col. Chapman's Regt, Conn Mil. Disch Sept 21. Enl July 23 in Col Webb's 2nd Regt 1780, Connecticut Line. Disch Dec 13. Br 1764. D 1836, Wayne Twp, Ashtabula Co. Bur Roberts Cem, Wayne. Ref: Connecticut Men in the Revolution. Fur infor Mary Stanley Chap.

ALLEN, JACOB, (Hamilton Co.)

Pvt in N. J. Militia. Br 1760, Essex Co, N. J. D 1840, Cincinnati, O. Ref: Natl No. 94374, Vol 95, p 121, D. A. R. Lin.

ALLEN, JOHN, (Trumbull Co.)

Bur Soaptown, Lordstown Twp, southeast of Lordstown. Administrator of estate ordered July 1843. Did not locate this grave. Name given in Yr Bk of S. A. R. Fur infor Mary Chesney Chap.

ALLEN, JOSIAH, (Harrison Co.)

Served as a ranger of the frontier in Richard Johnston's Company. Br Jan 17, 1761, Chester Co, Pa. Parents: David and Susannah (White) Allen. Mar Susannah Dickerson in 1798. Children: Susannah, Nancy, Elizabeth, John, George, Joshua, David. D Dec 28, 1842, Harrison Co, O Bur Dickerson Churchyard about 3 miles from Cadiz. MI: "Josiah Allen, Sr. d. Dec. 28, 1842; 81 years." GM by son David, stone slab, prior to 1847. Moved to Harrison county in 1818. A farmer. Pa Archives. Fur infor Moravian Trail Chap.

ALLEN, SILAS, (Fairfield Co.)

In 1780 aptd Surgeon in Conn Troops. Br 1754, Canterbury, Conn. Mar Mary Cleveland in 1776. D 1825, Royalton, O. Natl No. 75447, Vol 76, D. A. R. Lin.

ALLEN, WILLIAM, (Greene Co.)

1781 a Pvt in Capt George Sharp's Company, Washington Co, Pa Mil. Br 1750, Meadville, Pa. Mar Susan Ruckman. D 1822, Xenia, O. Ref: Natl No. 79808, Vol 80, D. A. R. Lin.

ALLERTON, JOHN, (Mahoning Co.)

Pvt in State Troops N. J. Mil. Br 1763. Bur in Mahoning Co. Ref: N. J. Men of the Revolution, p488. Fur infor Mahoning Chap.

ALLIS, MOSES, (Lorain Co.)

Pensioned for service as Sgt. Mass Continental Line (Lorain Co.) 1834. Br 1754, Mass. Mar Anna ——————. D 1842, Laporte, O. Natl No. 78258, Vol 79, D. A. R. Lin.

ALLISON, RICHARD, (Clermont Co.)

Served throughout Rev under Gen St Clair. Br 1744, Goshen, Orange Co, N. Y. Mar Apr 1794 at Ft Washington (Cincinnati) O. to Rebecca, dau of Col Strong of U. S. Army. D Mch 22, 1816. Southwest part Stonelick Twp, Clermont Co. Graduated 1776 from Jefferson Medical College, Philadelphia. Entered army 1777 as Surgeon. After war practiced in Philadelphia till 1788 when made Surgeon-General of Northwest, serving under Harmar, St Clair and Wayne. Was first physician in Cincinnati, O. and one of the most noted of his time—known over all U. S. Ref: A. S. Abbott, Bethel, O. Fur infor Cincinnati Chap.

ALLISON, RICHARD, (Hamilton Co.)

Br 1768, Pennsylvania. D 1816. Ref: S. A. R. Fur infor Cincinnati Chap.

ALLISON, WILLIAM, (Pickaway Co.)

Br 1748 (supposed to be in Va). Mar Miss Robertson in Va. Children: The only one we have record of was Dorcas Allison who on Sept 3, 1811 mar John Mills of Augusta, Va. Bur south end of cemetery. MI: "Soldier Pt Pleasant and American Revolution. William Allison died Aug 15, 1825 in the 75th year of his age." The grave stone was made of Free Stone and is in fair shape. GM re-marked by Dr. Edward C. Mills, Columbus, O. Was a soldier in Gen Andrew Lewis' Army of Virginians who on Oct 10, 1774 won the battle of Pt Pleasant Va. and marched with Lewis' army to join John Murry's army Camp Charlotte on Scippo Creek about 4 miles from its mouth in the Scioto river, in what is now Pickaway Co, O. Afterwards served in the war of the Revolution. Fur infor Mt Sterling Chap.

ALLYN, NATHAN, (County not stated)

Seaman on board privateer "Marquis de LaFayette." Br 1740, Groton, Conn. D 1814 in Ohio. Natl No. 99265, D. A. R. Lin.

ALSPAUGH, JOHN, (Fairfield Co.)

Bur in Betzor Churchyard. Fur infor Elizabeth Sherman Reese Chap.

ALSPAUGH, MICHAEL, (Fairfield Co.)

Bur in Betzor Churchyard. Fur infor Elizabeth Sherman Reese Chap.

ALSTON, (or Allston), THOMAS, (Hamilton Co.)

Ensign 1780, 7th Company, 1st Regt, Middlesex Co, N. J. Mil. Br 1753, N. J. Mar Rebecca Brown. One child was named Wallis. D 1833 in Ohio. (No 114421, D. A. R. descendant believes he is buried at Reading, Hamilton Co, O.) Natl No. 50459, Vol 51, D. A. R. Lin. Ref: Mrs. R. A. Alberts, Cincinnati, O. Fur infor Cincinnati Chap.

ALTMAN, WILLIAM, (Columbiana Co.)

Bur in Fairfield Cem, Columbiana Co, O. Lived in Fairfield Twp, Columbiana Co. Fur infor Bethia Southwick Chap.

AMES, MORDECAI, (Harrison Co.)

A Revolutionary pensioner living in North Twp, 1840, aged 90. U. S. Pens Rolls, 1940. Fur infor Moravian Trail Chap.

AMES, STEPHEN, (Lake Co.)

Enl in 1778 for three years, or the war, in Col Cilley's Regt. Br 1749, Hollis, N. H. One child was Jeremiah. D Nov 2, 1825, South Kirtland, O and buried there. GM by New Connecticut Chap. Selectman of Hollis, N. H., Treasurer of Kirtland Twp fr Jan 5, 1818. Fur infor New Connecticut Chap.

AMRINE, ABRAHAM, (Union Co.)

Pvt. Ranger on frontier. Br June 1, 1761, Bedford Co, Pa. Mar Mary Wolford June 25, 1785. Children: John, Henry Andrew, Moses, Frederick, Jeremiah, Abraham 2nd, Susannah. D Nov 14, 1849, Union Co, O. Bur Amrine Cem, Paris Twp. GM by family. He moved from Pa to Belmont Co, O. in 1801 and in 1817 to Union Co. A farmer and Justice of Peace. First settler of Union Co. Ref: Record of War Dept. Pa Archives. Mrs. James R. Marker, No 156227; Mrs. James E. Hall No 237038. Acceping this inform Jane Dailey, State Chairman.

AMRINE, ADRIAN, (Union Co.)

Bur in Amrine Cem, Paris Twp. Fur infor Hannah Emerson Dustin Chap.

AMSDEN, ABRAHAM, (Ashtabula Co.)

Pvt. Capt Farwell's Company, Mass Mil. Bur 1752, Southboro, Mass. D 1833, Ashtabula, O. D. A. R. descendant Mrs. Laura Frances Cumings White, Natl No. 32679. Vol 33, p 229, D. A. R. Lin.

ANDERSON, AUGUSTINE, (Morgan Co.)

Ensign Spencer's Additional Continental Regt in 1777. Pensioned Lieutenant 1818. Br 1750, N. J. D 1834, Morgan Co, O. aged 84. Natl No. 12173. Vol 13, p 65, D. A. R. Lin.

ANDERSON, ISAAC, (Butler Co.)

Br Sept 15, 1757, Ireland. Mar Euphemia Morehead. D Dec 18, 1809, Venice, Butler Co, O. (other authentic data says 1839.) Natl No. 43433, Vol 44, p 165. Fur infor John Reilly and Cincinnati Chaps.

ANDERSON, JAMES, (Highland Co.)

Pvt. Br Mch 25, 1763, Chester Co, Pa. Mar "Rachel Hopkins, May 2, 1801, Montgomery Co, Md. Twelve children. Philip Anderson, a son, living in Marshall Twp, Highland Co, O. in 1853 aged about 49 yrs. D Sept 6, 1850 in Highland Co, O." (from pension certificate of James Anderson). Bur in country graveyard near Belfast, O. Fur infor Waw-Wil-a-Way Chap.

ANDERSON, LEWIS, (Warren Co.)

Served as "minute man." Enl in Capt John Schenck's Company, Col Nathaniel Heard; reenlisted under Capt Peter Gordon, Col David Forman, 1776; taken prisoner at Kings Bridge. Br 1757, Monmouth Co, N. J. Mar Jane Gaston. (see No 722111 D. A. R.) D Mch 1838, Carlisle, O. Bur Old Baptist graveyard, near Carlisle, Warren Co, O. Came in 1832 to live with sons William, James and Kenneth at Carlisle. Pensioned 1833 for three years actual service. Pvt in N. J. line. Descendant; Gertrude Anderson, Franklin, O. who furnished this information to Jane Daily, State Chairman. Natl No 42242, Vol 43, p 93, D. A. R. Lin.

ANDERSON, ROBERT, (Butler Co.)

Name appears on the tablet erected at Hamilton, O. on the site of Ft Hamilton, as a Revolutionary soldier of that county. Fur infor John Reily Chap. (Unidentified by Chap.)

ANDERSON, THOMAS, (Mahoning Co.)

Pvt, Capt Well's Company, Col Well's Regt. Enl for nine mos, July 12, 1779, Disch 1780. Received at Springfield, July 19, 1779. Age 17 years, stature 5 ft. 6 in. Said (by Baldwin) to be buried in Oak Hill, Youngstown. Settled in Mahoning Co, early in 1800. Ref: Trumbull and Mahoning Co. History, Vol II, p 90, Fur infor Mahoning Chap.

ANDERSON, WILLIAM, (Ashland Co.)

Pvt in Rev. Br 1769, Lancaster Co, Pa. D Feb 2, 1847, Ashland Co, O. Bur in Ashland Cem in oldest section. MI: "In memory of William Anderson, who died February, 1847, aged 78 years." GM by Sarah Copus Chap. D. A. R. on Memorial Day, 1923. A farmer. Fur infor Sarah Copus Chap.

ANDERSON, WILLIAM, (Trumbull Co.)

Br 1743. D Jan 18, 1837 and bur in Old Cemetery, Mahoning Ave, Warren, O. MI: "In memory of William Anderson, d Jan 18, 1837, aged 94 yrs." GM: very old stone, carving nearly obliterated. At foot of grave new stone erected by George Anderson. Fur infor Mary Chesney Chap.

ANDREW, JOHN, (Hamilton Co.)

Br 1744, New Jersey. D 1816. Ref: S. A. R. Fur infor Cincinnati Chap.

ANDREW, JOHN, (Jefferson Co.)

Bur Annapolis, Jefferson Co, O. Fur infor Steubenville Chap.

ANDREWS, HUGH, (Montgomery Co.)

Pa Archives, Vol 7, p 957. Associators and Mil Company of Capt James McCreight, 9th Bn, Lancaster Co, Mil in 1782. Also commander of a Light Horse Company; 6th series, Vols 4 & 5. Capt in Dauphin Co, Mil Rolls dated Dec 29, 1792 and Dec 13, 1793. Br Aug 31, 1762, Hanover Twp, Dauphin Co. Parents: James and Jane (Strain) Andrews. Mar 1st ——— Spear, of Hanover Twp, Lebanon Co, Pa. 2nd Elizabeth Ainsworth, in Hanover Twp, Lebanon Co. Children: 1st wife: John, Isabelle, Margaret—all lived and died in Logan Co, O. 2nd wife: Nancy, James Hugh, Samuel Ainsworth, Eliza. D May, 1811, Dayton. Bur in Old Presbyterian Church burying ground, and the remains were not moved when the ground was abandoned. Came to Ohio, prospecting in 1797, by boat to Cincinnati, thence through the woods to Dayton. He brought his family in 1804. His father, James Andrews, was a private in Capt James McDowell's Company, 4th Bn of Chester Co Militia, Col Montgomery. Muster roll July 12, 1776. Pa Archives, 5th series, Vol 5, p 591. Fur infor Richard Montgomery Chap. S. A. R.

ANDRUS, DAVID, (Ashtabula Co.)

Pvt under Capt Ebenezer Brewster 1775. Enl Jan 1, 1781, term of War, from Southington, Conn, as fifer. Name appears on the roll of Capt Robinson's Company, Col Swift's 2nd Regt, Conn Line Feb 1, 1783. Br 1756 at Granby, Conn. Mar Abigail McDonald. D 1849, East Trumbull, Ashtabula Co, O. Bur East Trumbull. Grave sunken and stone gone. Ref: Connecticut Men in the Revolution, Lin Bk, Vol 41. Fur infor Mary Stanley Chap.

ANTHONY, GEORGE, (Jackson Co.)

D Aug 16, 1833. (Ancestor of the Coal Twp Anthonys.) Mar Elizabeth Redd Feb 2, 1833. Fur infor Cap John James Chap.

ANTISEL, SILAS, (Lake Co.)

From Willingon he served in the Lexington Alarm in the Revolutionary War in Capt Heath's Company in Apr, 1775. Br 1749, Norwich, Conn. Parents: Lawrence and Mary (Armstrong) Antisel. Mar Maria Bethiah Curtis, May 4, 1775. Children: Curtis, Thomas, Peres, Lawrence, Silas, Thankful, Sarah, Hannah, Betsy, Bethiah. D Sept 13, 1817, Madison, O. Bur on his farm located on the South Ridge, Madison, O. GM New Connecticut Chap. Ref: Natl No 60223, Vol 61, p 74, D. A. R. Lin. Fur infor New Connecticut Chap.

APPLEGATE, BENJAMIN, (Mahoning Co.)

Ranger in Thomas Moore's Company in Westmoreland Co, Pa. Bur in Mahoning Co. Came from Westmoreland Co, Pa. A farmer. Ref: Pa Archives, Series III, Vol 23, pp 224—322. Trumbull and Mahoning Cos. Vol 1, p 48. Fur infor Mahoning Chap.

APPLEGATE, JAMES, (Trumbull Co.)

Mar Mary ————. D Mch 20, 1820. Bur Seceeders Corner Churchyard, Liberty Twp. MI: "Died Mch 20, 1820. James Applegate." Came from Allegheny City to Youngstown, 1800. Ref: Pa Archives, Series III, Vol 23, pp 233, 236, 354; Mahoning and Trumbull Co History, pp 363-482. Historial Library, Cleveland, Revolutionary Soldiers buried in Trumbull Co. Fur infor Mary Chesney and Mahoning Chaps.

APPLEGATE, JOSEPH, (Mahoning Co.)

Teamster in New Jersey. Pensioned in 1834. Br in 1753. Bur in Mahoning Co. Came to Youngstown from New Jersey. A farmer. Ref: Old deeds in court house, Vol A. New Jersey Men of the Revolution, p 858. Fur infor Mahoning Chap.

APPLEGATE, ZEBULON, (Clermont Co.)

Enl as Pvt, 1776, Capts Perrin, Hulick and Vorheis. Br January, 1755, Middlesex Co, NJ. Mar Rebecca McCandless in Campbell Co, Ky. Children: Lydia, Zebulon, Nathaniel, Mary Glover, Nathan Loveberry, Julia Ann, Ruth Rowley, Susannah P and Hannah D. D Oct 20, 1840. At the age of 86 he was residing in New Richmond, when receiving pens in 1840. (From Census of Pensioners of Revolutionary Soldiers). Fur infor by A. S. Abbott, Bethel, O, to Blanchester Chap.

ARCHBOLD, THOMAS, (Harrison Co.)

A Revolutionary pensioner living in Harrison Co, in 1833, aged 80; served in Westmoreland Co Mil. U. S. Pension Rolls, 1835; Pa Archives, 5th IV, 428. Fur infor Moravian Trail Chap.

ARMSTRONG, ABEL, (Co. not stated.)

Pvt in Capt John McGuire's Company, Col William Grayson's Va Regt, Continental Line. Br 1758 in Virginia. D 1837 in Ohio. Fur infor Natl No 86161, Vol 87, p 50, D. A. R. Lin.

ARMSTRONG, DANIEL. (Mahoning Co.)

Ranger in frontier 1778-1783, Northampton Co. Pa Archives, Series 5, Vol VIII, p 684; Series III Vol 23, p 196. Br 1747, Lawrence Co. Mar Salley Harris (b 1760, d 1816). Children: Thomas, George, David, Rebecca, Polly, Roland, Archibald, Samuel (mar Jane Ervin), Betsey Ann. Grave not located, but he lived in Canfield, probably buried there. Came to Ohio from Northampton Co, Pa with Samuel Everett. Dr Truesdale's History of Canfield in Mahoning Dispatch 1895-96-97-98. History of Trumbull and Mahoning Cos, Vol II, p 177. Fur infor Mahoning Chap.

ARMSTRONG, GEORGE. (Sandusky Co.)

Dec 25, 1776, 2 mos, Sgt. Capt James Gibson; 1178—2 mos, Pvt. Capt Robert Matier; 1780, 2 mos. Pvt. Capt Hurl. Residence at enlistment Juniata, Pa. Application for pension Sept 28/1832. Allowed. Residence at application, Benton, Yates Co, NY. Age at date of application, 71. GM by L. M. Kelley, Commissioner. Fur infor Col George Croghan Chap.

ARMSTRONG, CAPT. JOHN. (Butler Co.)

Name appears on tablet in the Soldiers and Sailors monument at Hamilton, and supposed to be buried in Butler county. Fur infor John Reily Chap.

ARMSTRONG, WILLIAM. (Columbiana Co.)

Lived in Elk Run Twp, Columbiana Co, O. Fur infor Bethia Southwick Chap.

ARNER, HENRY, (Mahoning Co.)

Pvt, 8th class, 3rd Bn, Northampton Co Regt, Mil 1778. Children: Jacob, John (mar Susan, had ten children), Phillip (br Oct 17, 1773), David (br Mch 3, 1776 or 1778), Leonard, settled in NY State, Elizabeth (mar Matthias Lower). D 1828 or 1829. Bur Old Springfield Cem. Marker is destroyed. Came to Mahoning Co about 1812. Took up land in Springfield Twp. Came fr Northampton Co, Pa. Farmer. Ref: Pa Archives Series V, Vol V, p 230, and Church and family records. Fur infor Mahoning Chap.

ARNOLD, NORRIS. (Ross Co.)

Pvt in Maryland Mil. D in Deerfield Twp. Ross Co, in 1835-36. Bur in graveyard, many years abandoned, on the James M. Reeves farm, three-fourths mile southwest of Clarksburg. Fur infor Nathaniel Massie Chap.

ARNOLD, RICHARD. (Hamilton Co.)

1776. Corp. Col Hunter, Col Lacy and Capt Brooks commanding officers. Special mention for bravery at Seven Star Tavern, Chester Co, Pa. Br 1746, Pa. D 1843. Bur Family plot Harrison, O. where located after war. GM No. Dashing Scotch Highlander, grandson of Richard Arnold, Lord of Manor of Bagl—, Dorset Co, England. Ref: S. A. R. Mrs. Mary St Clair Blackburn, Org. Regent of Richard Arnold Chap, Washington, D. C. who gave above data, verified by Cincinnati Chap.

ARNOLD, THOMAS. (Athens Co.)

Pensioned in 1840, at age of 84 yrs, while residing in Canaan Twp, Athens Co, O. Br 1756. Lived in East Greenwich, Kent Co, RI. One child was Thomas, Jr. (who mar Rachel—). Bought Northeast quarter Sec. 5, Twp 5, Range 13, Canaan Twp, on Feb 7, 1818; sold same to Emory Daniels, Feb 7, 1828. (County Records Surveyors office, Vol 3, p 322). Sold the land he drew in the original allotment of the Ohio Company to David Putnam Mch 15, 1816 (County Records). Ref: Surveyors office, Athens Co. Pensioner of 1840. Accepting this infor Jane Dailey, State Chairman.

ARTHUR, JAMES. (Clermont Co.)

In 1840 was living in New Richmond Twp, Clermont Co, O. Age 76. Drawing pens for serv. Br 1764. Fur infor Census of Pensions, 1840. Copied by State Chairman.

ARTHUR, JOEL. (Jackson Co.)

D Sept 15, 1837, aged 69, and is bur in Arthur Graveyard near Clay. (Co records give a "Joel Arthur mar Letha Davis Nov 24, 1838." Fur infor Capt John James Chap.

ASHLEY, WILLIAM. (Darke Co.)

Capt. Parents: Thomas and Phoebe (Freeman). Bur Private cem 1½ miles south of Ithaca, (on farm now owned by J. Frazier). Lived at one time in Massachusetts and was present at Burgoyne's surrender, as a Revolutionary Soldier. Fur infor Fort Greenville Chap.

ASHLEY, WILLIAM S., (Morrow Co.)

Sgt 15th Vt Mil. Br 1758, Rochester, Mass. Mar Phebe Howe. D 1828, Preble Co, O. Bur Bloomfield Cem, Morrow Co. Ref: Natl No 70780, Vol 71, p 280, D. A. R. Lin and A. J. Sipe, Sexton Bloomfield Cem, Marengo, O. Fur infor Mt Gilead Chap. Compare with Ref: Natl No. 100216, Vol 101, p 66, D. A. R.

ATER, GEORGE, (German). (Ross Co.)

Served under George Washington in Va. Pvt. Br Dec 25, 1745, in Germany. Mar Mary Boyer, Harper's Ferry, Va, about 1777. Children: Abraham, Isaac, Jacob, Samuel, Thomas, George, William, Mary and Catherine. D June 18, 1820, Deer Creek Twp, Pickaway Co, O, or Deerfield, Ross Co. Bur Deerfield Twp, Ross Co, O. Little Zion Baptist graveyard Ross Co. MI: "George Ater born in Germany 1745. Emigrated to Va 1765. Soldier in Revolutionary War. Settled in Ohio 1799. Died—18, 1820." GM by funds left by Abraham his son. By Will. Monument put up about 1890. Came to Va 1765, to escape military duty and later came to Ohio and was given title to land at the Ohio Land office at Chillicothe by Gen Nathaniel Massie who helped divide up the northwest territory in 1784. Records destroyed by fire in 1853, at Chillicothe. Ref: Mrs. E. M. Ater, Williamsport, Ohio. R. F. D. 2. Fur infor Mt Sterling and Nathaniel Massie Chaps.

ATHERTON, JAMES. (Delaware Co.)

Served as a Pvt in Capt John Franklin's Company, Sullivan's expedition, 1779. Br 1751, in Connecticut. D 1828, Galena, O. Ref: Natl No 50489, Vol 51, p 223, D. A. R. Lin.

ATKINS, JOSIAH. (Ashtabula Co.)

Enl July 10, 1775 in the 6th Company, 7th Regt, Continental Regts. Capt Shipman, Col Webb. Served in several enlmts as Sgt. Was pensioner, Act 1818 in Ohio. Br 1757, Middletown, Conn. Mar Mary Gillett, 2nd wife. Children: Quintus F., one Josiah, 3rd son and 6th child erected his monument. D 1828, Jefferson, Ashtabula Co, O. Bur Oakdale, Jefferson, Ashtabula Co. MI: "In memory of Josiah Atkins, An * * * Sargent in the war of the Revolution. Br Nov 1, 1757, died Aug 28, 1828 at Conneaut in this county of Ashtabula and there lies buried. Mary Gillet, his wife." Ref: Connecticut Men of the Revolution, Vol 48, Line Bk. Fur infor Mary Stanley and Eunice Grant Chaps.

ATKINSON, CHARLES. (Monroe Co.)

Pvt, Capt McCoy's Company, Cumberland Co, Pa. Mil, during 1781-1782. Bur 1760. Mar second wife, Elizabeth Stephen. Br 1769. D 1841. Ref: Mrs. Edna Quick Acomb, Nelsonville. Tombstone standing. Fur infor by Elizabeth Zane Dew Chap.

ATWATER. (Summit Co.)

Indications point to serv as Revolutionary Soldier, but none found as yet (1928). Bur Coventry. Fur infor Cuyahoga Portage Chap and Records of Soldiers.

ATWATER, KALEB. (Mahoning Co.)

Continental Line. Enl July 25, 1779. Disch Jan 15, 1780. Birthplace unknown. D and bur Mahoning Co. Came fr Wallingford, Conn. to Mahoning Co, 1796. Ref: Conn men of the Rev, p 165. Fur infor Mahoning Chap.

ATWOOD, ICHABOD. (Mahoning Co.)

Pvt, Capt Churchell's Company, Ebenezer White's Regt. Marched Aug 1, 1780, disch Aug 9, 1780. Serv 9 days. Mass Men of the Rev, p 343. Bur Canfield Village Cem, Canfield, O. He came to Ohio in 1799. Bought a sawmill of John Scovill, completed it and ran it in 1802. Ref: Hist of Mahoning Co by Butler, Vol 1, p 669. Fur infor Mahoning Chap.

AUSTIN, ANDREW. (Portage Co.)

Enl as a Pvt in 1776, Served 11 mos; 1777, 3 mos; 1778, 3 mos; 1779, 3 mos; 1780, 3 mos. Engaged in battle of Trenton. Br Aug 11, 1751, Suffield, Conn. Mar Mary Griswold, in 1775. Children: Horace, Amos, Charles, Homer, Sophia. D Dec 11, 1838, Ravenna, O. Bur Charlestown, O. Pens applied for Aug 27, 1832. Allowed. Ref: Bureau of Pensions and Natl No 779970, Vol 78, D. A. R. Lin. Fur infor Old Northwest Chap.

AUSTIN, ELIPHALET. (Ashtabula Co.)

Conn State Tr, Marched June 12, disch Aug 3. Enl May 26, 1777, Conn Line 8th Regt, Col Chandler, Capt Munson's Company, 8 mos. Disch Jan 1, 1778. Capt Seymour's Company. Br 1761, New Hartford, Conn. Mar Sibyl Dudley. Children: Betsy, Chloe, Florilla, Sophia, Sibyl, Eliphalet. D 1828, Austinburg. Bur Austinburg. Ref: Conn Men in the Rev. Pioneer Women of the Western Reserve. See Vol 12, p 131. D. A. R. Lin. Mary Stanley Chap.

AUSTIN, NATHANIEL. (Ashtabula Co.)

Served in the Mil under Gen Gates. To the Northward 1777. Was wounded at Stillwater. Was on the Pens Roll of Ashtabula Co, O. 1831, for services in the Conn Continental Line. Br 1752, Torrington, Conn. Mar Annie Bidwell. D 1844, Austinburg. Bur Austinburg; center of the town. Ref: Conn Men in the Rev; Lin Bk, Vol 48. Fur infor Mary Stanley Chap.

AUTEN, THOMAS. (Hamilton Co.)

Served in Capt John Sebring's Company, 1st Bn Somerset Co, N J also Capt Vroom's Company, 2nd Bn Somerset Co. Br 1759, New Jersey, or 1761. Mar Elizabeth Vantule. Children: Amy (mar Cornelius Snyder, Jr.) Revolutionary soldier, settled on farm at Montgomery, Hamilton Co. D 1847 or 1849, Pleasant Ridge, O. Hamilton Co. Settled on farm at Montgomery in 1796. Date of death not found. Bur Montgomery, O. Ref: S. A. R. and Natl No. 44065,, Mrs. Effie Keys, Dayton. Fur infor Cincinnati Chap.

AYERS ———. (Clermont Co.)

Came fr New Jersey about 1800, and settled near mouth of Boat Run Creek, Monroe Twp Clermont Co where he died. Ref: A. S. Abbot, Bethel, O. Fur infor Cincinnati Chap.

BABBET, STEPHEN. (Mahoning Co.)

Pvt in Moor's Company, N J. New Jersey Men in the Rev. p 494. Mar Mary ———. Bur Cornersburg. Came to Mahoning Co, early in 1800. Fur infor Mahoning Chap.

BACKUS, ELIJAH. (Washington Co.)

Capt Conn Mil 1781. Br 1726, Norwich, Conn. D 1798, Bur Marietta. Ref: Natl No 16434, Vol 17, p 162, D. A. R. Lin.

BACKUS, SAMUEL. (Trumbull Co.)

Lived at Nelson, Portage Co. Enl at Ashford, Conn 1782 in a volunteer Matross Co under Capt Benj Durkee. Was at Fort Trumbull. Br 1764. D 1854. Pens 1832 fr Trumbull Co for services as Pvt Conn line. Ref: Natl No 43429, Vol 44, p 163, D. A. R. Lin.

BACON, GEORGE, (Lorain Co.)

Br 1751. D 1834. Bur Brownhelm Cem 1834. GM Government marker (stone slab) with words: "On the ship 'Warren' (Boston Tea Party.)" Ref: Natl No 99551, 85882, D. A. R. Lin. Fur infor Elyria Chap.

BACON, RICHARD. (Clark Co.)

Pvt in Capt H Well's Company. Col Erastus Wolcott Regt Conn Tr 1776; Pvt in Capt Wyllyn's Company. Col S. B. Webbs Regt Conn Tr 1777, Pvt in Capt Hopkin's Company same Regt 1781. Br Feb 1757, Middletown, Conn. Parents: Zaccheus, Bacon, Mercy Hubbard Bacon. Mar Annie Fosdick, Wetherfield, Conn, Dec 26, 1784. Children: Richard, Henry, George, Charles, Allyn, John, Samuel. D Nov 2, 1822. Dayton, O. Bur Ferncliffe, Springfield, O. on lot 20, Sec E. MI: "In memory of Capt Richard Bacon who died Nov 2, 1822 aged 65 years." GM by Family Monument. Was prisoner in Old Dutch Church, New York City. Ref: Records of Conn Men in Rev War. pp 248, 332, 383. Fur infor Lagonda Chap.

BADGER, JOSEPH REV. (Wood Co.)

Enl in Mass Mil at 19 yrs of age and served 4 yrs. Br Feb 28, 1757. D Apr 5, 1846. Bur Perryburg Cem Maumee, O. GM erected by Synod of Western Reserve. First Missionary upon the Western Reserve. Ref: Vol 2, p 662, Howe's Historical Coll. Ohion and "Ashtabula Sentinel" Ashtabula, O. by Mrs. Dana Jones, Erie, Pa. Fur infor Usula Wolcott Chap.

BAILY, DANIEL. (Miami Co.)

Bur Raper Chapel. GM: by Miami Chap with bronze marker in 1904. Fur infor Miami Chap.

BAILEY, DAVID, (Trumbull Co.)

Bur Hubbard, O. Unable to locate grave; many stones thrown out, and many inscriptions obliterated. Will probated Nov 1836. Ref: Baldwin Library, Youngstown, O., by Miss Kyle. Fur infor Mary Chesney Chap.

BAILEY, GEORGE. (Pickaway Co.)

Enl 1776, in Capt Zachariah Maccubins Company of Tr in Continental Line. Br 1750, Mar Nancy D Pickaway Co O. Ref: Natl No 68593, Vol 69, p 213, D. A. R. Lin.

BAILEY, JARED. (Guernsey Co.)

Pvt and Corp, Capt Benj. Hopkins' Company, Col John Topham's Regt and also in Sullivans Life Guard. Enl Apr 11, 1778. Br Aug 20, 1758, New London, Conn. Mar Elizabeth Apr 7/1758. Children: Sidney, Betty, John, Nancy. D Aug 26, 1839. Center Twp Guernsey Co, O. Bur on his farm in Center Twp Guernsey Co, O. He was granted military land in Center Twp Guernsey Co. described as follows: Part of Sec 17 Military Lot 20 south half, Range 2 Twp. 1. Farmer. Ref: Records of War Dept Washington D. C. State Records Providence R. I. Mrs. Alice Hutton, Byesville, O. Fur infor Anna Asbury Stone Chap.

BAILEY, SILAS COL. (Lake Co.)

Pvt in Capt Artemas Hows' Company, Apr 19, 1775. Served 24 days under Capt Jonathan Houghton during Oct and Nov 1776. Was second Lt in Col Josiah Whitney's Regt. Br 1754, Mass. Children: Rev Jacob Bailey. D July 9, 1845, Perry, Lake Co, O. Bur Perry, O. GM by New Connecticut Chap. Fur infor New Connecticut Chap.

BAIN, JERMIAH, (Butler Co.)

Bur Lehigh Center, Ross Twp. Fur infor John Reily Chap.

BAINTER, JACOB, (Muskingum Co.)

Bur New Hope Lutheran Cem, Salem Twp. GM Headmarkers give names and state: "Revolutionary". Fur infor Muskingum Chap.

BAIRD, GEORGE, (Summit Co.)

Name appears in Westmoreland Co, P Mil. Br 1750. Mar Hanah (D Sept 8, 1815.) D Apr 6, 1823. Bur White farm, Springfield Twp. Came to Springfield, Summit Co, O. 1809, with family; Charter member of Presbyterian Church. Fur infor Cuyahoga Portage Chap.

BAIRD, WILLIAM, (Clark Co.)

Guarded pioneer in Hessian Camps. Br Mch 16, 1762, Hagarstown, Md. Parents: Maj Wm Baird, member of Committee of Observation and delegate to convention Sept 14, 1775. Mar Dorothy Kammerrer. Children: Hester, Susannah, Elizabeth, Mary Ann, Peter C., John, William D. D Mch 9, 1837. Harmony, Clark Co., Bur Asbury Chapel 8½ miles northeast of Springfield. MI: William Baird, dates of birth and death. GM Family, marble slab. Came to Ohio in 1808. Attended the peace treaty with Kenton and Indians in 1809. Was personally acquainted with Daniel Boone. Ref: Family and Co Histories. Fur infor Lagonda Chap.

BAIRD, (or Beard), WM., (Brown Co.)

Pvt. Served in the Cumberland Co Mil in Pa under command of Gen Lacy and Capt Robert McCoy. Br Jan 26, 1758, Path Valley, Cumberland Co., Pa.

Parents: William Baird Sr., and Esther Smalley. Mar Nancy Moore Baird, 1789. Children: Esther, John, James David, Nancy, Margaret. D June 28, 1828, Russellville, Brown Co, O. Bur Baird, 2 miles east of Russellville, Brown Co, O. MI: "W. B." Government marker by D. A. R. GM: by son just a stone with above initials cut on it. Farmer, Lawyer, Justice of Peace. Ref: Natl No. 96436, Vol 97, p 38, D. A. R. Lin and Pa Archives, Hist of U. S. Hist of Montgomery Co Pa and "Churches of the Valley." Fur infor Talliaferro and Lieutenant Byrd Chaps.

BAKER, ABNER, (Huron Co.)

Pensioner. Bur Woodlawn Cem Norwalk. Fur infor Sally De Forest Chap.

BAKER, DANIEL, (Licking Co.)

Enl as fifer in Col Legard's Regt. Br Nov 8, 1763, Ellington, Conn. D Dec 19, 1836, Granville, O. Bur Old Cem Granville, O. GM by Granville Centennial Committee in 1901. Settled in Granville, O. about 1820. Granted Pens in 1833 fr Licking Co, O. Ref: Natl No 88908, Vol 89, p 286, D. A. R. Fur infor by Hetuck Chap.

BAKER, DANIEL, (Butler Co.)

Pvt Cavalry NJ Mil. Br 1755, Essex Co, NJ. Mar Hannah Halsey in 1779. One dau was Nancy. D 1845, Somerville, O. Ref: Natl No 101216, Vol 103, p 65, also Natl No 69007, Vol 70, p 4, D. A. R. Lin.

BAKER, MELYN, (Clark Co.)

Pvt Capt Harriman's Company 1st Regt Essex Co, N. J. also in NJ State Tr Enl for 9 mos in Capt Thomas Patterson's Company, 3 Bn 2 Establishment; wounded at Battle of Monmouth June 28, 1778. Br Jan 10, 1710, Conn Farmes, N. J. Parents: Daniel Baker and Abigail Miller. Mar Prudence Whitehead Feb 19, 1786. Children: Elizabeth, Dave, Ezra, Phoebe, Elias, Melyn. D Jan 20, 1826, Enon, Clark Co, O. Bur Enon Cem ¼ mile northeast of Enon. Grave not platted. MI: "Melyn Baker, a native of New Jersey. Died Jan. 20, 1826, aged 66 yrs, 10 das." GM by Family Monument and S. A. R. metal marker in 1906. Remained in serv until surrender of Cornwallis and was disch Mch 1, 1779. Farmer. Emigrated to northwest Territory and located in Knob Prairie, in 1805. Ref: Family histories and D. A. R. papers of Elizabeth Ann Supfer. Fur infor by Lagonda Chap.

BALDRIDGE, REV. WM., (Adams Co.)

Enl fr N. C. in the cavalry and is said to have served seven years. Br Feb 26, 1761. Lancaster Co, Pa. Parents were fr Ireland. Mar Rebecca Agnew 1st wife, July 17, 1792; Mrs Mary Logan Anderson 2nd wife May 16, 1820. Children: James R, Alexander H, John Y, William S, Samuel C, and Rebecca G, twins. David A, Wade, Agnew, Joseph G, Ebenezer W, William and Mary Jane; 2 by second wife Benjamin L, and Nancy M. D Oct 26, 1830, Cherry Fork, O. Bur Cherry Fork Cem. Grave unmarked and location lost. Ref: Hist of Adams Co. Fur infor Sycamore Chap.

BALDWYN, AMOS, (Mahoning Co.)

Pvt. Enl Sept 23, 1776 Capt Colley's Company, Col Moseley's Regt. Serv 2 mos, 1 da. Sgt. Volunteer Capt Barnes Company, Col Moseley's Regt. Serv June 12 and 17, 1782. Br 1764, North Milford, Conn. Parents: Simeon Baldwin and Rebecca Buck. Mar Sally Hicks. Children: Minerva, Jacob Hicks, John Murry, Asa, Garry, Eli, Amanda C, Ozro, Amander. D 1852, Boardman. Bur Boardman Center, Boardman Twp. Marched to quell mob in Northampton, Mass. Vol 8, p 516 Mass Soldiers and Sailors in the Rev. Learned shoemaker's trade and made shoes for the army. Ref: Mrs. C. H. Andrews Natl No 4649, D. A. R. p 85 Hist of Trumbull and Mahoning Co. Fur infor Mahoning Chap.

BALDWIN, CALEB, (Mahoning Co.)

Pvt. Capt Asher Randolph's State Tr. Was detailed to manufacture guns. Br 1752, Mendham, N. J. Mar Elizabeth Pitman (Pitney), Children: Eunice, Hannah, Phebe, Stephen, Elizabeth, Caleb, Byron, Benjamin, Nehemiah. D 1810, Youngstown, O. Bur Oak Hill Cem, Youngstown, O. GM by Mahoning Chap D. A. R. marker in 1915. Gunsmith. Ref: Natl No 3128 D. A. R. Etal. Hist Trumbull and Mahoning Cos, p 426; NJ Men in the Rev, p 496.

BALDWIN, DAVID, (Portage Co.)

Took oath of fidelity and detached for serv fr Wallingford as Pvt. Br 1739, Wallingford, Conn. Mar Parnall Clark in 1764. Children: Roswell, Benjamin, David, Noah, Rebecca, Lydia, Abigail, Joseph, Moses. D Sept 1808, Atwater, O. Bur Atwater, O. Ref: Copy of original MSS State Library Hartford, Conn. Fur infor Old Northwest Chap.

BALDWIN, ELEAZER, (Hamilton Co.)

Br Connecticut. Fur infor Cincinnati, Chap.

BALDWIN, JOHN CAPT., (Madison Co.)

Capt under Washington of a Mil Company equipped and raised by himself. Br Feb 21, 1749, Va. Mar Hannah Simmons. Children: Jonah, William, Thomas, John, Francis, Betsy, Hannah, Mary, Margaret, Rebecca, Martha. D Apr 18, 1820, Fayette Co, O. Bur Baldwin family burying ground near Mt Sterling, O. GM by Mt Sterling Chap with bronze marker in 1911. Fur infor by Mt Sterling Chap.

BALDWIN, JOHN, (Adams Co.)

Pvt. Br 1756, Frederick Co, Md. D Oct 4, 1848. Bur Kirker Cem, Liberty Twp. Enl in mil July 1776, served 4 mos and again in 1777 2 mos. Ref: Evans and Stivers Hist of Adams Co, O. Fur infor Sycamore Chap.

BALDWIN, JONATHAN, (Portage Co.)

Pvt in Pennsylvania Mil. Placed on pens roll Sept 2, 1833. Was drawing pens at Ravenna in 1840. Fur infor Old Northwest Chap.

BALDWIN, SAMUEL, (Portage Co.)

Lived at Aurora. Drew pens. Fur infor Old Northwest Chap.

BALDWIN, SETH C., (Cuyahoga Co.)

Pvt under Ethan Allen at Ticonderoga. Br England. D 1835, Cleveland, O. Ref: Natl No 29849, Vol 30, p 305, D. A. R. Lin.

BALL, SAMUEL, (Licking Co.)

Enl in Essex Company, June 1778, in Col Matthias Ogden's Regt; was at Monmouth. Br 1775, N. J. D Nov 2, 1844, Jersey Twp. Bur Jersey Cem. MI: "Rev War." GM by Hetuck Chap in 1909. Ref: Hist of Licking Co by E. M. P. Brister. Fur infor Hetuck Chap.

BALLENTINE, EBENEZER, (Marion Co.)

Surgeon's mate in Thomas Nixon's 6th Regt. Br 1756. D 1823. Bur Marion Cem. GM by Capt William Hendricks Chap with bronze marker. Came to Marion in the fall of 1820. Ref: Mass Soldiers and Sailors. Fur infor Capt William Hendricks Chap.

BANCROFT, JOHN, (Clark Co.)

Lt. Col Eben Learned's Regt. Capt Isaac Bolster's Company. Enl as Pvt in 8 mos tr at beginning of war. Br Sept 18, 1748, Reading, Mass. Parents: Moses and Mary Bancroft. Mar Anna Waters Dec 1, 1777. Children: Amasa, John, Nancy, Louis, Lawson. D Sept 26, 1837, Springfield, O. Bur Columbia St Cem, Springfield, O west of Central Park. Name plate has been removed. GM by Society S. A. R. Metal marker about 1906. Was commissioned by Council of Safety before there was any president. Commission sent to Washington for pens, and was not returned. Ref: Family records and Pens Claim. Fur infor Lagonda Chap.

BANTA, DANIEL, (Warren Co.)

Pvt. His serv prior to 1781 indicates a serv in the Classified Mil, a reserve for duty on alarm, patrolling a prescribed district guarding lines, etc. (Pens Bureau, Washington, D. C. S 2090). Br Sept 13, 1762, Bergen Co, N. J. Mar Mary Van Voorhes, Feb 21, 1784. Children: Charity, Albert, Mary, Magdalena, Daniel, Henry, (d in infancy), Margaret, Peter D, Henry, Rachel, Elizabeth. D Sept 1837, Warren Co, O. Exact location of grave not known, evidently he is bur in an ancient tomb on the farm in which rest the remains of 4 other pioneer members of the Banta family. While fighting in the Rev he was wounded in the leg while in NJ Mil. In 1786 he removed to Kentucky and in 1794 removed to Ohio, locating 3½ miles east of Lebanon, Warren Co, O. In 1788 he was in the Indian wars, and stationed at a blockhouse on the present site of Cincinnati. Ref: Natl No 223737, Mrs Edna Evans Hudson, Nelsonville, O. (Banta Genealogy by T. M. Banta, 1893, p 98). Fur infor Elizabeth Zane Dew Chap.

BANTA, PETER, (Warren Co.)

Br 1760. Mar Rachel Vanclefe. D 1829, Lebanon, O. Ref: Natl No 61911, Vol 62, p 314, D. A. R. Lin.

BANTUM, JOHN, (Coshocton Co.)

Bur Bethlehem Twp. Ref: Co Hist. Fur infor Coshocton Chap.

BARBEE, AMAZIAH, (Huron Co.)

Served in Rev, French and Indian Wars. Br 1738. D 1834, Townsend. Fur infor Salley De Forest Chap.

BARBEE, WILLIAM, (Miami Co.)

Pvt. Br 1759, Mecklenburg Co, Va. D 1813, Troy, O. Enl at 17 yrs in Col Burwell's Regt and d fr wounds received in war of 1812. Ref: Natl No 31385, Vol 32, p 149, D. A. R. Lin.

BARBER, URIAH, Scioto Co.)

3 mos as pvt, 8 mos as pvt, 6 mos 1779 served Indian skirmishes; Col Hosterman of Pa, Capt Champlin, Capt Morrow, Capt Grove. Enl fr Northumberland Co, Pa. Br 1761. Mar Barbara Clingman 1780 in Pa. Children: Polly, Barbara, Raynor, Barbara, Hannah, John, Samuel, Joseph, Nathaniel, James, Washington and Mary (twins). D June 26, 1846. Bur Kinney Graveyard on Wallie St. GM by Joseph Spencer D. A. R. Chap. Just lived on 60 acres farm, A Pensioner. Ref: W. H. Briggs Et al at Raynor, and Mrs. Sarah Briggs Smith, 1207 W Market, Greensboro, N. C. Vol 43, p 190, D. A. R. Lin. Fur infor Joseph Spencer.

BARDWELL, SIMEON, (Clark Co.)

Corp in Capt Jonathan Bardwell's Company, Col Warner's Regt which marched in response to the Lexington alarm; again in Capt Dwight's Company, Col Porter's Regt Aug 1777; also in Capt Bardwell's Company, Col Porter's Regt Sept 22 to Oct 17, 1777. Br Jan 10, 1749, Bardwell Hollow, Mass. Parents: Jonathan and Violet (Amsden) Bardwell. Mar Huldah Warner 1780; 2nd wife Dolly Childs 1782. Children: William, Azubah, Huldah, Seth, Leonard, Zebira. D Mch 25, 1837, at Vienna Cross Roads, South Vienna, O. Bur Thompson, on Old Columbus Road Pleasant Twp Clark Co. Location of grave south end near "Lingle" stone. MI: "Simeon Bardwell died March 25, 1837, aged 88 yrs 2 mo 15 days." Slab or marker down. GM by children in 1837. He was resident of Belchertown. Mass. Moved south 1749, settled near Vienna Cross Roads, O. Farmer. Ref: Family hist not published; Revolutionary War Serv Record in detail appears in Vol 1 of the official publication Mass Soldiers and Sailors in the Revolutionary War. Fur infor Lagonda Chap.

BARNES, ISRAEL, (Geauga Co.)

Pvt Capt Pendleton's Company; Col Crane's Regt artillery 1777—1783. Br 1762, New Hartford, Conn. Mar Lucy Gillet June 24, 1790. D June 5, 1832, Montville, O (age 77 yrs). Bur at Montville Center Cem at center front. MI: Israel Barnes, age 77, died June 5, 1832." GM by G. A. R. Date of enlmt Sept 4, 1777, term 3 yrs. Residence Farmington, Conn. Came to Montville, O. in 1832. Fur infor Taylor Chap.

BARNES, JACOB, (Highland Co.)

Bur Baptist Cem, at New Market. Grave marked. Fur infor Waw-Wil-a-Way Chap.

BARNES, JOHN, (Trumbull Co.)

Enl Watertown, Conn, as an Artificer, in the Conn Tr Revolutionary War. Served under Capt Lewis and Col Duglass. Br 1759, Litchfield Co, Conn. Mar Lucretia B. Children: Samuel Neuton, John Rodney, Evelin, Nancy, Fanny, Katy or Lucretia. D June 12, 1834, West Farmington, O. Bur West Farmington, Trumbull Co, O. First moderator of the Bristol and Bloomfield Church, Presbyterian Congregational Church and known as Deacon John Barnes. Was granted a pens as a Rev soldier under an act of Legislature. Our Ohio State Supreme Court Record Aug 1832. Fur infor Mary Chesney Chap.

BARNES, MARK, (Geauga Co.)

Pvt Capt Elijah Lewis' Company; Col Greene's (I. R. I.) Regt Jan, Feb, Mch 1778. Enl during War. Br Mch 12, 1764. Parents: Stephen & Sarah. Mar Sarah Roberts. Children: Sarah, Maria, Abigail, Martha, Mark. D Apr 19, 1831, Thompson, O. Bur in the pasture of Harry Webster's farm in twp, lot 11. Justice Peace, Aug 15, 1817. Moved to Southampton, Mass, 1806. Came to Thompson, O, in 1816. Ref: Mass Soldiers and Sailors, p 661. Fur infor Taylor Chap.

BARNES, MOSES, (Geauga Co.)

Pvt Feb 1, 1776, 2 mos Capt Selah's Company. Col Gray's Regt; Aug 1778; 2 mos Capt Hooker's Company Col Stanley's Regt, Summer 1779, 2 mos Capt Woodford's Company, Col Norton's Regt. Br Apr 9, 1746, (Old Style) Farmington, Conn. Lived with Jehiel Wilcox early settler of Montville in 1833. Pens June 11, 1833. Ref: Pens Dept File 2356, Vol 6, p 17. Fur infor Taylor Chap.

BARNETT, JOHN, (Montgomery Co.)

Served in Revolutionary War. Pvt Lancaster Co, Pa. Mil Capt James Murray's Company 3 yrs. Settled in Ky on land granted for serv (see Ky S. A. R. Yr Bk

1913) on pens roll of Bourbon Co, Ky. Br June 23, 1748-49 in Virginia. Parents: James and Sarah Barnett. Mar Elizabeth Flynn (br 1750, d July 17, 1824). Children: James, Abraham, Mary M, David Huston, Elizabeth M, Geo Davis, Rachel M, Wm Walton, Susan M, Luther, Bruen. D July 6, 1806, Dayton, O. Bur Woodland Cem, Lot 87-8-9-90 (Brady) Sec 51. Ref: Natl No of Rev Soldier in D. A. R. Honor Roll 30134, and Natl No 102216, Vol 103, p 67, D. A. R. Lin. Fur infor Jonathan Dayton Chap.

BARNHART, FRED B. (Wayne Co.)

Served for Pennsylvania. Br 1752. D 1848. Bur Wooster. GM by Western Reserve. His 5 brothers pensioners to Medina Co, O. Fur infor Western Reserve Chap.

BARNUM, JOHN, (Lorain Co.)

Capt Barnum's Company 16th Regt of Mil in Conn. Br 1758. D 1819. Bur Ridgeville Center Cem. Fur infor Western Reserve Chap.

BARR, ADAM, (BAER), (Muskingum Co.)

1st Lt of 4th Company, 2nd Bn York Co Mil. Br 1761. D 1833. Bur Lutheran Cem, near Stovertown, Muskingum Co. Ref: Pa Archives 6 series, Vol 2, p 462. Census 1790 Pa p 288. Under Col Wm Rankin, Capt Jacob Hiar Apr 5, 1778. Fur infor Muskingum Chap.

BARR, ALEXANDER, (Co. not stated.)

Served Westmoreland Co Mil in expedition to Indian country and was killed by Indians. D 1785. Killed on Ohio River. Ref: Vol 32, p 88, D. A. R. Lin.

BARR, ANDREW, (Fairfield Co.)

Pvt Pa Mil. Br 1740, in Ireland. Mar Jane Hamilton. D 1815, Fairfield Co. Bur Dutch Hollow Cem. Ref: Vol 61, p 4, D. A. R. Lin. Fur infor Elizabeth Sherman Reese Chap.

BARR, CHRISTIAN, (Brown Co.)

Bur Sardinia. Fur infor Ripley Chap.

BARR, CHRISTOPHER, (Brown Co.)

Served in the Rev. Br "On the Rhine," Germany. Children: Peter, mar Barbara Hoss, Lincoln Co, N. C. in 1806. D Aug 18, 1852, his wife in 1863. Bur near Higginsport. Came fr North or South Carolina in 1811 and lived in Lewis Twp the remainder of his life. Farmer. Ref: Brown Co Hist published in 1883 by Beers & Company p 463, and A. S. Abbott, Bethel, O. Fur infor Taliaferro Chap.

BARRE, IVA S. (Huron Co.)

Bur Greenwich Cem. Fur infor Salley De Forest Chap.

BARRETT, BENJAMIN, (Ashtabula Co.)

Enl fr Paxon, Mass. at the age of 16 yrs. Was wounded at the Battle of Bennington, Capt Earll's Company, Col Danforth Keyes' Regt 1777-78-79. Br 1759, Worcester, Mass. Mar Clarinda Barnes. D Feb 9, 1845, Kingsville, Ashtabula Co. Bur Kingsville. A soldier of 2 wars. Ref: Ashtabula Sentinel Feb 15, 1845; Vol 60 and Vol 34, p 53, D. A. R. Lin. Fur infor Mary Stanley Chap.

BARRETT, JONATHAN, (Butler Co.)

Pvt 1776 in Capt Stephen Crosby's Company, Col Comfort Sager's Regt Conn Line. Br 1760, Killingly, Conn. Mar Elizabeth Murdock 1786. One son was Don Carlos. D 1839, Hamilton, O. Applied for pens 1832, claim allowed. Ref: Natl No 101645, Vol 103, p 194, and 100544, Vol 101, p 166, D. A. R. Lin.

BARRETT, THOMAS, (Ashtabula Co.)

Pvt. One son was Lord Whatley Barrett. D Apr 1, 1845. Bur Solomon Durkee private cem. MI: "Died Apr 1, 1845, Aged 83." GM by slab erected by his son. Fur infor Mary Redmond Chap.

BARTHOLOMEW, JOSEPH DEACON, (Medina Co.)

Served fr Conn. Br 1756. D 1856. Bur Middlebury, O. GM by Western Reserve. Pensioned in 1840, age 82 yrs, while residing in Wadsworth Twp, Medina Co which is adjacent to Summit Co. Fur infor Western Reserve Chap.

BARTHOLOMEW, SAMUEL, (Brown Co.)

Pvt. Enl Jan 18, 1781, for 3 yrs in Capt Nemiah Rice's Company, 3rd Company 5th Conn Regt. His name appears last on Company Muster Roll for Sept 1783 dated Oct 14, 1783. Br 1762, Harwinton, Conn. Parents: Samuel Bartholomew and Martha. Mar Chloe Fancher, 1802. Children: Fancher, Samuel, Chester, Sylvanus, Silas, Chloe Ann, Martha. D Brown Co, O. Bur Old Brick Red Oak Cem, Union Twp. GM by a limestone rock. His father d when quite young, he was bound out and was promised his freedom if he enl in Rev War, which he did. Came to Ohio. Farmer. Bought a small pine tree in Vt and planted on farm which was made into lumber a few yrs ago. Ref: Mrs Louella Pittenges, Decatur, O. Fur infor Lieutenant Byrd Chap.

BARTLE, JOHN, (Hamilton Co.)

Br 1743, New York. D 1839. Ref: S. A. R. Fur infor Cincinnati Chap.

BARTON, DAVID, (Belmont Co.)

Soldier who defended Fort Henry when attacked by Simon Girty and Indians 1782; lived in Wheeling, W. Va. during Rev. Br about 1742, County Down, Ireland. Mar Peggy in Ireland about 1765. Children: Margaret. Br 1767 (mar James Patton); Sarah (mar Rev Archibald McElroy). D after 1796 in Belmont Co, O. Bur near St Clairsville, and Bartons Mills. Fur infor Mrs. Lowell Hobart fr Washington Records.

BARTOON, JOHN, (Fairfield Co.)

Bur United Brethren Church, Pleasant Run, known as Harmon Cem. Fur infor Elizabeth Sherman Reese Chap.

BARTOW, ZENAS, (Harrison Co.)

Said by family to have served as a Capt in the Rev. Br 1750. One dau Charity. Mar Jas Edgar Jr., about 1800 and settled at Conotton, O. D 1844. Ref: Miss Eloise Edgar, Delaware Co. Fur infor Moravian Trail Chap.

BARTRAM, DANIEL, (Lake Co.)

Pvt in Capt Hull's Company, Col Stearns Regt, Conn Mil in 1777. He saw active serv in the defense of Danbury against the raids of the British. Br Oct 23, 1745, Fairfield Conn. D May 17, 1817. Madison, Lake Co, O. Bur Unionville, O. GM by New Connecticut Chap. Fur infor New Connecticut Chap.

BASKERVILLE, SAMUEL, (Madison Co.)

Served as an officer of the 10th Virginia Regt Revolutionary War. Was made 1st Lt Sept 14, 1778, in Capt Hughes Woodson's Company. Served also as quartermaster fr May to Nov 1779. Br Dec 24, 1754, Virginia. Mar Statira Bently in 1790. Children: John, Judith, Edward, William, Samuel, George W, James, R. A. and Nancy. D Aug 29, 1830, Madison Co, O. Bur Baskerville family grave yard, Madison Co. Enl in Rev War at age of 21. Retired fr serv Jan 1, 1783. Lived in Virginia till 1795, coming to Ohio. Was a farmer and judge of Court in Chillicothe. Ref: Heitman's Historical Registers of Officers of Continental Army. Fur infor London Chap.

BASSETT, CORNELIUS, (Co not stated.)

Pvt in Capt Ebenezer Baker's Company, Col Freeman's Mass Regt. Br 1754, Sandwich, Mass. Mar Chloe Smith, in 1783. One son Abiram Bassett. D 1821. Ref: Natl No 75001, Vol 76, D. A. R. Lin.

BASSETT, NATHAN, (Lorain Co.)

Pvt in Capt Abram Washburn's Company, Col Cotton's Regt. Enl Mch 10, 1781. Disch Apr 1, 1781. Serv 22 days marched to Newport, R. I. Br Aug 12, 1763. Bridgewater, Mass. Parents: Joseph and Phebe Bassett. Mar Sarah Standish Apr 4, 1793, North Milford, Cecil Co, Md. Children: Thomas, Phebe, Sarah, Naomi, Betsy, Trulove, Amanda, Emily and Charles. D Apr 23, 1853, Russia Twp, Lorain Co, O. Bur South Amherst, Evergreen Cem, double lot situated north of vault 58. MI: "Nathan Bassett, born Aug 12, 1763, died Apr 23, 1853, (wife Sarah Standish)". GM by son, Charles Bassett. Spent 7 yrs in the serv of the West India Company. Soldier in War of 1812 later moved to Chili, Monroe Co, N. Y. when past 70 yrs of age migrated to Ohio arriving in 1834 settling on a farm of 67 acres in Lorain Co. Farmer and also filled several twp offices of his day particularly that of school examiner. Ref: Marion Jessie Bassett 115 Park Ave, Elyria, O.

BATCHELOR, GEORGE, (Greene Co.)

D May 15, 1827, Miami Twp. Bur Cedarville. Bath, 1813. Ref: Robinson's Hist of Greene Co. Fur infor Catherine Greene Chap.

BATES, BENJAMIN, (Lake Co.)

Enl 1777. Capt Benj Bonney's Company, Col Ezra May's Regt, which marched to Stillwater. Br Aug 3, 1733, Hingham, Mass. Mr Huldah Cudworth, Dec 1757 (d 1811). D May 8, 1815, Leroy, O. Ref: Natl No 72632, Vol 101, p 25, D. A. R. Lin. Fur infor New Connecticut Chap.

BATES, DANIEL, (Erie Co.)

Eastern Bn Morris Co, Capt Minard's Company, also with State Tr and Continental Army. Br Mch 27, 1762, Morris Co, N. J. Parents: Daniel and Jane (Reed) Bates. Mar Mary Kitchell dau of Moses Kitchell in 1787, Cincinnati, O. Second mar S. Osborne, in 1801, one dau Mary. Children: Eunice br 1788, Moses 1790, Infant 1793, Hervey 1795, Irena 1797, (Possibly other children were Rebekah, Uzal and Seth, who lived in Sycamore in 1808.) D 1845, Sandusky, O. On pens roll of Ohio in 1832. Bur Sandusky, O. Erie Co. GM by County Commissioners. With the earliest of settlers at Columbia. In 1808 his name is found on tax list in Sycamore and Symnes (Twp?). Name of Rebekah is on Charter Roll of Reading Presbyterian Church in Aug 29, 1823. Ref: Natl No 71379 and Mrs C. E. Hudson, Dallas, Tex. Fur infor Cincinnati and Col Geo Croghan Chap.

BATES, EPHRAIM, (Noble Co.)

With NJ Tr. D Jan 12 1834, near Sarahsville, aged 90. Bur McWilliams farm, grave located but not marked. Moved to Pa then to Ohio, near

Sarahsville. Early settler of Center Twp. See notes on his Pens Declaration; one son Isaac. In Mch 1833, at the age of 89 yrs 10 mos was drawing a pens. Ref: Mrs. L. B. Frazier, Caldwell, O.

BATES, HINSDALE, (or Hinesdale), (Summit Co.)

Enl at Hartford, Conn. Apr 1, 1776 to Apr 1, 1777, as Pvt in Capt Ozias Pettibones' Company, Col Meig's Regt. His father Oliver Bates was Lt of Company he served in battle White Plains. Br Dec 25, 1757, Durham, New Haven Co., Conn. Parents: Oliver Bates and Lois. Children: Nathan br 1782, D 1821, Lyman D 1871, aged 81 yrs, Dennis D 1832, Col Talcott D 1826 and Curtis D 1842, Norton. Bur Old Norton Cem, Norton Twp, Summit Co. Baptised Jan 1, 1758. Coat of arms given in Bates Bulletin in 1911. Minor Lee Bates, a president of Hiram College. Ref: Fur infor Cuyahoga Portage Chap.

BATES, ISAAC, (Hamilton Co.)

Br 1763. D 1831, Ref: S. A. R. Fur infor Cincinnati Chap.

BATHMAN, J., (Or Bathane), (Butler Co.)

Name appears on the tablet erected at Hamilton, O. on the site of Fort Hamilton, in memory of the Revolutionary Soldiers who are bur in that Co. Unidentified. Fur infor John Reily Chap.

BATTELLE, EBENEZER, Col., (Washington Co.)

Br 1752, Dedham, Mass. Parents: Ebenezer Battelle. Mar Anna Durant. D 1815. Bur Newport Cem, Newport, O. MI: "Col Ebenezer Battelle 1752—1815" GM by Marietta Chap with Rev marker in 1922. Came to Marietta in May, 1788. In 1789 he moved in Belpre, then in 1802 to Newport, which village he laid out on his land. Was a Harvard graduate; in business in Boston. Ref: Hist of Washington Co. Fur infor Marietta Chap.

BAUGHMAN, GEORGE, (Franklin Co).

Served in the Pa State Tr and was pensioned fr Franklin Co. Br Washington Co, Pa. Bur at Riverside Cem. GM Rev Grav Committee with bronze marker May 30, 1912. Came to Ohio in 1807 fr Washington, Pa and located on Big Lick. In 1812 he moved to Mifflin Twp and settled on Big Walnut Creek. He raised the first barn in the Twp. Fur infor Columbus Chap.

BAUM, CHARLES, W., (Clermont Co.)

1781, served in Capt James Douglas' Company, 2nd Bn Cumberland Co Mil. Br Poland. One son was Charles, br in Clermont Co. D 1817, Ohio. Presumably bur in Clermont Co. Ref: Natl No 90510, Vol 91, p 165, D. A. R. Lin.

BAXTER, SCHUYLER, (Hamilton Co.)

Col in Pa Bn of Flying Cp dated Nov 16, 1776. "Heitman," ref. Shot in left temple by Indian, Sept 1788. Bur near bluff, near river at mouth of Deer Creek. Grave dug by their tomahawks. 2 Amer Soldiers bur in Hamilton Co 40 yrs later, a skeleton with hole in skull, and bullet inside found by boys digging. He with Hall, a relative, 3 others came in 2 canoes fr Georgetown, Ky. Compare records in D. A. R. Lin Vol 26, p 42, Natl No 25117. Ref: Jones Hist p 31-33; Greves Hist p 126 of Cincinnati & Hamilton Co. Fur infor Cincinnati Chap.

BAY, ROBERT, (Guernsey Co.)

Age 86 yrs. Br Cumberland, Spencer Twp. Ref: S. A. R. Fur infor Anna Asbury Stone Chap.

BAYLEY, or BAILEY TIMOTHY, (Clark Co.)

Pvt in N. H. Rangers. Br 1749, N. H. Mar Zeremiah Blodgett, date not given. Children: Lewis Br Aug 25, 1784; Elvira, Benjamin, are the only ones of 13 given. Sept 19, 1825, Lisbon Clark Co. Bur Lisbon Cem. Grave not platted. Came to Clark Co, O, 1806, from Haverhill, Grafton Co, N. H. Blacksmith and Farmer. Pensioned in 1819, at the age of 70 yrs. Ref: Nat D. A. R. Natl No 26004 and War Dept Washington D. C. Fur infor Lagonda Chap.

BEACH, ELIHU, (Trumbull Co.)

Br 1761. D Aug 9, 1832, aged 71 yrs. Bur Old Cem south of center of Vernon. MI: "The wearied dust lies here at rest, the soul has fled through realms of space to those bright climes forever blest where mortals sing of pardoning grace." Fur infor Mary Chesney Chap.

BEACH, OBIL, (Madison Co.)

Enl 1777 in Capt Chapman's Company, Herman Swift's Regt. Br 1758, Goshen or Litchfield, Conn. Mar Elizabeth Kilbourne in 1782. D 1846, Plain City, O. Pensioned 1831. Pvt Conn Continental Line. Ref: Natl No 77468, Vol 78 and No 100945, Vol 101, p 292, D. A. R. Lin.

BEACH, REUBEN, (Summit Co.)

Sgt. Enl Mch 28, 1777, served to close of war; Corp in Samuel Granger's Company. Command of Col Chas Webb, 2nd Regt Conn line 1777-81. Br Dec 4, 1757, Stratford, Conn. D July 4, 1844 at Tallmadge. Bur Tallmadge, O. Ref: See Co Roster. Fur infor Cuyahoga Portage Chap.

BEALE, JOHN, (Muskingum Co.)

Bur Willis Farm Cass Twp between Dresden and Frazeysburg on the dirt road. Fur infor Muskingum Chap.

BEAM, ———, (Darke Co.)

Bur Beamsville. Fur infor Ft Greenville Chap.

BEAM, JACOB, (Hancock Co.)

Pvt. Helped to erect fort at Mansfield, O. Served under Capt Robert Clark, (West Moreland Co, Pa.) at Valley Forge. Br 1760, Weslmoreland Co, Pa. Mar Hulda Waldo. D Aug 1839. Bur Maple Grove Cem, Findlay, O. GM by Fort Findlay Chap. Miller, Beams Mill, (yet standing) also Old Fort in Central Park. Fur infor Fort Findlay Chap.

BEAM, MICHAEL, (Licking Co.)

Enl in George Washington's Body-Guard in N. J. Br 1755 Germany. Mar 1816. D Dec 12, 1850, Jersey Twp. Bur Universalist Cem. GM by Hetuck Chap in 1909. Ref: History of Licking Co by E. M. P. Brister. Fur infor Hetuck Chap.

BEARD, AMOS, (Geauga Co.)

Pvt Capt Peter Porter's Company, Col Patterson's Regt. Service 13 days. On pay roll for mileage dated Dec 1, 1776 same Co. Br Mendon, Mass. 1745. Mar Hannah Meedham, 1776. Children: Daniel. Amariah, Jedediah. D Burton, O. 1821. Bur Lower Cem Burton, O. MI: "In memory of Amos Beard who died at Burton Aug 7, 1821, age 76." Regt marched 1775 in response to alarm of Apr 1775 from Becket to Cambridge. Ref: Mass Soldiers and Sailors Vol 1, p 868. Natl No of Revolutionary Soldier in D. A. R. Honor Roll 40308. Fur infor Taylor Chap.

MRS. HERBERT BACKUS, STATE REGENT, D. A. R. OHIO, 1926-1929 AND MRS. JANE DOWD DAILEY, STATE CHAIRMAN FOR THE PRESERVATION OF HISTORIC SPOTS AND REVOLUTIONARY SOLDIERS' GRAVES--1923-1929.

BEARD, JOHN, (Licking Co.)

Enl in Mass, July 19, 1779. Pvt in Col Samuel McCobb's Regt. Br 1753 in Ireland. Mar Margaret Kirk. Children: Thomas. D Feb 15, 1814. Bur Beard family plot, Licking Twp. GM by Family and Hetuck Chap, in 1909. Ref: History of Licking Co, by E. M. P. Brister. Fur infor Hetuck Chap.

BEARD, JOHN, (Mahoning Co.)

Pvt Capt Neet's Company, Washington Co, Pa. Mar Agnes ——. Children: Thomas, Agnes, Polly, Peggie, Martha, James, John, High, maybe more. D 1805 Youngstown. Bur Youngstown, O. Mahoning Co desecrated Cem. Ref: Pa Archives, Series 6, Vol 2, p 98. Fur infor Mahoning Chap.

BEARD, WILLIAM SR., (Ross Co.)

Moved into Union Twp in 1809. A brief biographical memorandum in the possession of R. W. Bowdle, Esq., reads as follows: "William Beard, jr., br Dec 27, 1759, in Frederick Co (Since Washington), was at Gen Gates' defeat Aug 16, 1780; moved to Greenbrier Co, in 1798; emigrated to Ross Co, O. in 1809; was the father of fourteen children. N. B. He has ever been a true Whig, and a true friend of American liberty." Mr. Beard d in this twp in 1851, aged nearly ninety-three yrs. He is bur in Mt Union Cem and his grave has not been marked. His tombstone reads: "William Beard d Mch 24, 1851, aged 94 yrs. Marjery, wife of William Beard d Oct 11, 1821 aged 54 yrs." Several descendants live in Union Twp, Ross Co. Ref: p 262, History of Ross & Highland Cos. Fur infor Nathaniel Massie Chap.

BEARDSLEY, ELIJAH, (Clark Co.)

Pvt in Col Herman Swift's 7th Conn Regt, Capt Phineas Beardsley's Company. Enl Jan 1, 1777, for 3 yrs was disch Jan 1, 1780. Br May 16, 1760, Fairfield, Conn. Parents: Capt Phineas Beardsley and Ruth Fairchilds. Mar Sarah Hubbell in 1780. Children: Ezra, Patrick, Ruth, Darius, Herman, Clara, Sydia, Abby, Sara, Fanny, Laura, Marilla, Elijah. D Oct 2, 1826, Springfield, O. Bur Old Columbia Street northeast corner of cem (not Platted). MI: "Elijah Beardsley a member of Boston Tea Party." GM by S. A. R. in 1906. At close of war located in Danbury, Conn. Moved to Delhi, N. Y. in 1796, thence to Delaware, O. 1811, to Urbana, O. in 1815 thence to Springfield in 1821. He was a farmer. Ref: Natl No 28705, Vol 29, D. A. R. Lin. Fur infor Lagonda Chap.

BEARDSLEY, PHILO, (Mahoning Co.)

Pvt Continental Regt 9th Company, Capt Peter Perrett. Enl July 10, 1775, disch Dec 10, 1775. Br 1755. Mar Esther Curtis (br 1764, d 1836). Children: Birdsley (1785), Anna 1787, Joseph 1789, Sarah 1794, Philo 1794, Curtis 1797, Almus 1799, Agur 1801. Canfield. Came early to Canfield where son Almus was born. Trumbull and Mahoning Co History, Vol II, p 36. Fur infor Mahoning Chap.

BEASLEY, BENJAMIN, (Brown Co.)

Revolutionary Soldier of Va. Huntington Twp. Brown Co, O. Fur infor Cincinnati Chap.

BEATS OR BETZ, URBAN, (Mahoning Co.)

Pvt Capt Samuel Patton's Cumberland Co Mil, Col Culbertson's 4th Bn, Cumberland Co Mil. Br 1747, Franklin Co, Pa. Mar Dorothy Barker or Baker. 1822. Bur Washingtonville, O. Ref: Pa Archives 5 Series, Vol 6, p 279-288, Pa Archives 3 Series, Vol 23, Natl No 67133, Vol 68, p 47. D. A. R. Lin. Fur infor Mahoning Chap.

BEATTY, ANDREW, (Highland Co.)

Pvt Capt Matthews Mil Cumberland Co, Pa. Br Rye Twp, Cumberland Co, Pa. D Highland Co, 1828. Bur on farm owned by Mike Kelly (1912). Grave not marked. Fur infor Waw-Wil-a-Way Chap.

BEATTY, JOHN, (Fairfield Co.)

Sgt and Lt 1779-80 in Capt Gilbert McCoy's Company, Col Joseph Reed's Regt Cumberland Co Mil. Br 1749, Ireland. D 1824, Fairfield Co, O. Ref: Vol 89, p 212 Natl No 88672 D. A. R. Lin.

BEAVER, MICHAEL, SR. (Ross Co.)

Pvt Va. Br Va. Children 1 son, Michael, Jr. Was in war of 1812; 1 dau Mary mar Isaac Sperry and d June 23, 1863 aged 78 yrs, 5 mos, 23 days. D near Frankfort, O, 1821 or 22. Cem located on Chillicothe Pike. Came to Ross Co from Va in 1796. After about two yrs, went to Ky but returned to Ohio in 1800; bought 1100 acres in Chillicothe survey on Deer Creek. Ref: p 259, History of Ross & Highland Counties. Fur infor Nathaniel Massie Chap.

BEAVERS, SAMUEL, (Muskingum Co.)

Enl as pvt in 1780 under Capt Thomas Lewis, Col Merriwether; Enl again in 1781 under Capt Francis Russell, Col George West. Fought in battle of Yorktown and was present at capture of Cornwallis. Br Jan 18, 1762, Loudoun Co, Va. D June 23, 1833. Bur Sonora Cem. Fur infor Muskingun Chap.

BECKETT, HUMPHREY, (Franklin Co.)

Br Apr 19, 1758 Frederick Co, Va. Mar Susannah Blann Battott, Aug 29, 1778. Children: Richard M, Nelson W, James, Patsey, Ansel, Blan, Willey H, Jemina, William and Winson. D Sept 1839 near Dublin, Franklin Co, O. Bur Old Cem adjoining Dublin. Enl Jan or Feb 1777. Pensioned July 6, 1818. Mar in Albemarle Co, Aug 29, 1778. Pvt under Capt Chas. Porterfield and Col Morgan, State of Va. Three yrs in serv. In battles of Somerset C. H., Amboy & Monmouth. Ref: Margaret A. P. Dunlap, Williamsport, O. Fur infor Mt. Sterling Chap.

BECKETT, JOHN C. (Butler Co.)

Name appears on tablet at Hamilton, O. in memory of Revolutionary Soldiers bur in that Co. D near West Chester, Butler Co. Fur infor John Reily Chap.

BECKWITH, BENJAMIN, (Morgan Co.)

Pvt 1776. Jacob Young, Md Mil. Br 1751, Frederick Co, Md. Mar 1st Lavinia Crum, 2nd Martha Rogers. Children: William, Benjamin, Elizabeth, Mary, Lenor. 2nd Lorena, Lavinia, Matilda, George, Solomon, David, Rosanna. D Malta, Morgan Co, O. Apr 3, 1839. Bur Wiseman Graveyard, Malta Twp. MI: "Benjamin Beckwith's a soldier of the Rev. War" Ref: Mrs. Lena Tracy Barkhurst, Malta, O. Natl No 79047, 41262, Vol 80, D. A. R. Lin. Fur infor Amanda Barker Devin Chap.

BEDDOW, THOMAS, (Delaware Co.)

Pvt under Col Benjamin Skinner, Capt Thomas Truman, Md Tr. Bur Berlin Twp. Pensioned. Fur infor Delaware Chap.

BEEBE, DAVID, (Lorain Co.)

Quartermaster, Sgt Conn Tr. Br 1747. D 1840. GM by Western Reserve, bronze marker. Fur infor Western Reserve Chap.

BEEBE, EZRA, (Lake Co.)

1st Regt NY Line, under Col Goose Van Schaik. Br 1737. D Jan 15, 1813. Bur Perry, O. GM by New Connecticut Chap. Fur infor by New Connecticut Chap.

BEEBE, HOPSON, (Athens Co.)

Enl May 26 for 8 mos and disch Jan 1778. Pvt under Capt Kirtland. Br Feb 17, 1749. State of Conn. Mar Deliverance Curtis Sept 4, 1774. Children: Peter, Polly, Betsey, Charles, William. D 1836, Athens, O. Bur West State St., Athens, O. If the grave has ever been marked, the marker has disintegrated. Ref: Conn Men in the Rev. p 208. Walker's Hist of Athens Co p 516. Fur infor Nabby Lee Ames Chap.

BEEM, MICHAEL, (Licking Co.)

Placed in Pension Roll of Licking Co, O. 1832 for serv as pvt 1777-1778. Br 1755 Pa. D 1850 Licking Co, O. Ref: Natl No 65800, Vol 66, p 276.

BEER, JAMES, (Columbiana Co.)

Br 1758. Living in Hanover Twp, Columbiana Co in 1840. Aged 82 yrs. A pensioner. Fur infor Bethia Southwick Chap.

BEERS, MATTHEW, (Fairfield Co.)

Pvt and wounded. Br 1754, Stratford. Mar Sarah Curtis. On Pension Roll of Fairfield Co for 2 yrs serv. Ref: Natl No 13955, p 354, Vol 14, D. A. R. Lin.

BELAMY, ASA, (Trumbull Co.)

Bur Vienna. Ref: Baldwin Library, Youngstown. Fur infor Mary Chesney Chap.

BELKNAP, CALVIN, (Ashtabula Co.)

Calvin Belknap served as Pvt fr July 1 to Nov 27, 1781, 148 days. His name is also on the pay roll of Capt Blakesley's Company in Col Fletcher's Bn, Gen Enos Rodgers in service of the state of Vt, Adjutant Office State of Vt. Br Jan 30, 1761. Dummerston, Vt. Parents: Daniel and Polly Whipple Belknap. Mar Bathshua Larabee, Mch 28, 1786. Children: Asa, Daniel, Norton, Asenath, Elmira, Lucy, Polly, Eliza, Bathshua, Clarissa. D Mch 17, 1848. Austinburg, Ashtabula Co. Bur Hickok in Austinburg. MI: "Calvin Belknap, died Mch 16, 1848, aged 87 yrs. Saved by grace. Fletchers Vt Mil Rev War." GM with marble slab. Ref: Adj Gen, State of Vt. Fur infor Mary Stanley and Eunice Grant Chap.

BELKNAP, SAMUEL, (Muskingum Co.)

Br Newburg, N. Y. D May 19, 1815. Zanesville, O. Bur Woodlawn Cem, Zanesville, O. Fur infor Muskingum Chap.

BELL, JOHN, (Hamilton Co.)

Lt Cumberland Co, Pa. R. 279. Rangers on frontier. Bur on farm Montgomery, Hamilton Co, O. Came to Ohio with his brother and a sister. Settled on a farm east from Montgomery, O. Was judge in an early court of the territory. Fur infor Cincinnati Chap.

BELL, WILLIAM, JR., (Highland Co.)

Pvt. Served two enlmt in the Revolutionary War as a Pvt in Capt Silas Howell's Company 1st NJ Regt, Commanded by Mathias Ogden. Br May 28, 1763. Del. Parents: William Bell Sr. Ann Bell. Mar Mary Brady in 1782. Children: Joseph, Josiah, Charles, Mearia, Sarah. D Nov 18, 1801, Greenfield, O. Bur Greenfield Cem northeast of Greenfield Sec 3 Lot 2. MI: "William Bell br May 28 A. D. 1763, d Nov 18, A. D. 1801." GM by Juliana White Chap. Official marker with name plate, June 30, 1923. When very young he joined the first NJ Regt and with his father William Bell Sr served in the same company. Farmer and carpenter. Arrived in Greenfield, O. 1800. Being the first white man to be bur .in Greenfield, O. Ref: Jerseymen in the Revolution p 13, 505 and 707. Fur infor Juliana White Chap.

BELLESSELT, (or BELLESFELLER), PETER, (Trumbull Co.)

A soldier by name of Peter Bellesfeller granted a pens; he lived at the time in Farmington. Bur Eli Young Farm, in northeast corner Farmington Twp. Did not locate grave. Copied from S. A. R. Yr Bk. Fur infor Mary Chesney Chap.

BELLI, JOHN, Maj., (Scioto Co.)

Quartermaster Gen. Mar Cynthia Harrison. Children: Eliza, and four others names not given. D 1809, West Side Scioto Co. Bur Greenlawn Cem, Portsmouth, O. Lot 27, Sec 14. MI: "Maj John Belli." His body was moved from farm he owned and which was inherited by son, in 1911 to Greenlawn by grandson Judge Greagory of Calif. A close friend of Gen Washington. Recorder. He laid out town of Alexandri Northwest Territory. Alexandri was moved to Portsmouth 1798. Fur infor Joseph Spencer Chap.

BENMAN, MOSES, (Harrison Co.)

A Revolutionary pensioner living in Harrison Co, in 1833, aged 78. Served in Capt John Boyd's Company of Rangers, Bedford Co, Pa Mil 1781-83. Pa Archives, 5 series. Vol 108-9. 195 US Pension Roll in 1835. Fur infor Moravian Trail Chap.

BENEDICT, HEZEKIAH, (Trumbull Co.)

Br 1754. Mar Huldah, (D Mch 25, 1845. Aged 92 yrs.) D Nov 16, 1831. Bur Braceville. MI: "Hezekiah Benedict D Nov 16, 1831, aged 77 yrs, 8 mos." GM by relaives, kept in good condition. Will admitted to Probate 1832. Fur infor Mary Chesney Chap.

BENHAM, ROBERT, (Warren Co.)

Ens in Mil under Col Israel Ludlow. Br 1750. Pa. Children: Joseph, 1 dau Mrs John Torrence, later Mrs. John Wingate. D 1809 aged 59, in Cincinnati. (On farm 1 mile southwest of Lebanon, once a part of Hamilton Co, O.) Bur Cincinnati, O. Built first hewn log cabin in Cincinnati, O. 1789 on lot in the first assignment of lots after survey of the town; in Feb 1792 was given license to maintain a ferry across Ohio river at Cincinnati. Member of 1st Territorial Legislature. 1st Board of Commissioners of Warren Co. Ref: Howe's History, Vol II, p 741. Fur infor Cincinnati Chap.

BENHAM, THOMAS, (Ashtabula Co.)

Enl Mch 9, 1779, Capt Bradley's Company of Artillery. Disch Feb 1780. Enl Apr 3, 1789 Capt Bradley's Company. Disch Jan 1, 1781. Was among Sentries taken Sept 1, 1781 by 500 of the enemy in 5 armed vessels at West Haven. Br 1759, Cheshire, Conn. Mar Esther Bonnell; other data states Eliz Tuttle and Esther Bonnell as wives. Children: Samuel, Adnah, Thomas Jr. D July 2, 1842, Ashtabula, O. Bur "Old graveyard," now abandoned. Ref: Conn Men in the Rev, Pioneer Women of the Western Reserve, p 552, 560, 626. Family Bible, Mrs. Albert Goodwin, fr Conn; and Emma Benkam Crosby, Ashtabula, O. Fur infor Mary Stanley Chap.

BENJAMIN, ASA, (Ashtabula Co.)

Asa Benjamin was a soldier of the Rev and served as such through the whole war. D Pierpont, Ashtabula Co. Bur Old Burying Ground, Lot No. 16. There were evidently two Asa Benjamins in the Revolutionary War, and the ref below is all I dare use. Ref: Records Ashtabula Co Hist Society, p 397, written by Lampson Wright Esq., who settled in Pierpont 1801. Fur infor Mary Stanley Chap.

BENJAMIN, JONATHAN, (Licking Co.)

Enl Jan 1776, as Pvt in Col Long's Regt, Lycoming Co, Pa. Served 4 yrs and 6 mos. Br 1738 New York, Mar 1802. Children: Lillie, Mary, Jemina, Jane, Benoni. D Aug 26, 1841. Bur Old Cem Granville, O. GM Granville Centennial Committee. 1909. Fur infor Hetuck Chap.

BENNETT, ISHMAEL, (Co not stated)

Pvt. Capt John Franklin's Company organized at Wyoming, Pa. Br 1730. Rhode Island. D 1820 in Ohio. Ref: Natl No 96327, p 103, Vol 97, D. A. R. Lin.

BENNETT, OLIVER, (Delaware Co.)

Pvt under Col Zebulon Butler Capt Simon Spaulding Conn Tr. Bur Orange Twp. Pensioned. Fur infor Delaware Chap.

BENNETT, THADDEUS, (Scioto Co.)

Enl as Pvt 1776 in Capt Blaine's Company. Serv 18 mos, 12 mos, 2 mos, 8 weeks. Br 1754. Marwick, N. Y. Parents: Ethiram Bennett. Mar J. Bentlay. Children: Mollie, Thaddeus Jr., Joseph, Sallie, Rhoda, Quance, Hetty, Benjamin, Jael. D 1834, Scioto Co near Minford. Bur near Minford on a farm he once owned. Farmer. Ref: Mrs. Goldia Lants Wendelken. Fur infor Spencer Chap.

BENT, SILAS, (Washington Co.)

Pvt in Capt Eustis' Company which marched on alarm of Apr 1775 for Cambridge, Mass. Served 12 days. Ens in Capt Wheeler's Company; also 1st Lt in Capt Barnes Company Col Nixon's Regt. Br Rutland, Mass. Mar Mary ——. Children: Son Daniel who lived in Belpre, O. D Belpre, O 1818. Bur Belpre Cem Washington Co. GM Marietta Chap by Revolutionary marker in May 1923. Silas Bent and his wife, Mary Bent, came in Marietta in 1789. Remaining one yr they moved to Belpre, O. Ref: See Natl No 26915. Fur infor Marietta Chap.

BENTLEY, BENJAMIN, (Medina Co.)

Served fr R. I. Bur Sharon Cem. GM Western Reserve. Fur infor Western Reserve Chap.

BENTON, ZADOCK. (Geauga Co.)

Pvt 2nd Regt Conn Line; Chas Webb. Pensioned 1833. Br Tolland Conn, Mch 6, 1761. Parents: Samuel Benton. Mar Lydia Day (br Colchester, Conn about 1786) Children: Orrin, Ariel, Lyman, Sally, Horace, Elihu, Nancy, Zadock, Otis. D Nov 3, 1845, Chardon, O. Bur Village Cem, Chardon, O. Lot 102 east center sec. MI: "Zadock Benton a soldier of the Revolution died Nov 3, 1845, aged 84." GM family, granite marker. Enl July 1, 1780; Dec 9, 1780. Millwright. Ref: Conn Men of Revolution p 165. Pension Records. Fur infor Taylor Chap.

BERNARD, (or BANNARD), THOMAS, (Highland Co.)

Pvt in Capt Charles Fleming's Company Va. Participated in battles of Brandywine, Monmouth, Germantown and Stony Point. Served 4 yrs. Br 1757, Cumberland Co, Va. Mar Mary Hicks Dec 29, 1792, Va. (d 1847). Children: Elizabeth, John, Sarah, George W Thomas, Mary, Susanah. D Leesburgh, Highland Co, O. June 12, 1833. Bur Old Quaker Graveyard near Leesburg, O. GM by family many years ago. Received land warrant in 1784 for services. Farmer. Ref: Natl No 102813, Vol 103, and Natl No 100634, Vol 101, p 197, D. A. R. Lin and also Natl No 160277. Fur infor Waw-Wil-a-Way Chap.

BERRY, BARTHOLOMEW. (Greene Co.)

Pvt. Annual allowance $60.00; same received $447.68; on record Nov 20, 1792; commencement of pens Nov 7, 1809, under law of Mch 3, 1808; same Apr 24, 1816, under law of Apr 24, 1816. Fur infor Catherine Green Chap.

BERRY, THOMAS, (Butler Co.)

Pvt Va Continental Line. Name appears on tablet at Hamilton Soldiers and Sailors monument, (listed by John Reily Chap.) Br in Va. D Miltonville, O. 1832, aged 69. Ref: Natl No 18900, Vol 19, p 324, D. A. R. Lin.

BERRYHILL, ALEXANDER, (Greene Co.)

Pvt on roll of Sumter's Brig (Capt N. M. Martin) S. C. found in statehouse, Columbia, S. C. 1898. He served with this Brig in the battle of Guilford C. H. and received a saber or sword wound across his forehead, the scar fr which he carried to his grave. D 1823, Va. Bur Pioneer Graveyard, Bellbrook. Sugar Creek, 1815. Ref: Robinson's Hist of Greene Co and Mrs. S. O. Hale Xenia, O. Fur infor Catherine Greene Chap.

BEST, JOHN, (Mahoning Co.)

Pvt, 7th class, Northampton Co, Capt Frederick Kleinhantz, 1st Bn. Bur Berlin, Berlin Twp. Nothing was found in the Co records or in the Co Histories. Ref: Pa Archives, Vol 5, Series 5, p 90. Fur infor Mahoning Chap.

BEST, THOMAS, (Portage Co.)

Lived at Deerfield. Fur infor Old Northwest Chap.

BETHNAL, NORRIS, (Hamilton Co.)

Br N. J. 1757. D 1841. Bur Pisgah Cem Sycamore Twp. In 1840 was a pensioner at age 89. Fur infor Cincinnati Chap.

BETTES, NATHANIEL, (Summit Co.)

Minute man; Capt Soul's Company Col Fellow's Regt 1775. In 1776 under Capt Noah Allen, Col Wiggleworth's Regt. Full Serg 1777 at West Point, N. Y. Br West Springfield, Mass, 1747. Mar 1st Hannah Mills; 2nd Candice Ives. D Jan 15, 1840, Bettes Corner. Bur Bettes Corners. Full account of life in Co roll. Ref: See Vol 34, p 69, Natl No 33191 D. A. R. Lin. Fur infor Cuyahoga Portage Chap.

BEVIS or BEAVIS, ISSACHUR, (Hamilton Co.)

For serv, see Sons of Rev records of Howard Bevis, Cincinnati, O. who joined on this serv. Br 1739. D 1804. Bur Johnson's Cem near Venice, on Hamilton Co side. Came to Hamilton Co 1791, settled near Bevistown. Fur infor Cincinnati Chap.

BICKEL, CHRISTIAN, (Hamilton Co.)

Br 1753, Pa. D 1831. Ref: S. A. R. Fur infor Cincinnati Chap.

BIDLACK or BIDLOCK, PHILEMON, (Delaware Co.)

Pvt under Col Zebulon Butler, Conn State Tr. D 1844, age 84. Bur Sunbury. Pensioned. Fur infor Delaware Western Reserve Chap.

BIDWELL, WILLIAM, SR., (Lake Co.)

Joined the 8th Conn Regt in 1782 under Capt Joseph Jewett and Col Jedediah Huntington. His Regt protected the Boston Camps and took part at Roxbury. Br 1767. Children: William, Jr. D 1831. Bur Middle Ridge Cem, Madison, O. GM New Connecticut Chap. Fur infor New Connecticut Chap.

BIERCE, WILLIAM, (Portage Co.)

Sgt in Conn Continental. Served 7 yrs. Placed on pen roll Apr 16, 1833. Bur Nelson, O. Ref: See Natl No 12430, p 164, Vol 13, D. A. R. Lin. Fur infor Old Northwest Chap.

BIGELOW, TIMOTHY, (Trumbull Co.)

Pvt Conn State Tr. Pen granted Mch 4, 1831. D July 30, 1830. Bur Bloomfield, O. MI: "In memory of Timothy Bigelow who died July 30, 1830, aged 77 yrs." GM probably by family. Ref: Cleveland Historical Library, Revolutonary Soldiers bur in Trumbull Co. Fur infor Mary Chesney Chap.

BIGFORD, SAMUEL, (Washington Co.)

Location of grave in path in Greenlawn Cem Lowell, O. Fur infor Marietta Chap.

BIGGER, JOHN, (Montgomery Co.)

Pvt Capt Walter McVinnis' Company 4th Bn Cumberland Co. Br 1760, Ireland. D 1831 Centerville, O. Ref: Vol 55, p 407, Natl No D. A. R. Lin.

BILGEAR or BILGER, FREDERICK, (Columbiana Co.)

Pvt 4th class. Capt Adam Scott's Company Lancaster Co Mil. Br 1747. Mar Elizabeth (1766-1846). D 1822. Bur Washingtonville, O Columbiana Co. Ref: Pa Archives, 5 series, Vol 7, p 746. Fur infor Mahoning Chap.

BINCKLEY, CHRISTIAN, CAPT., (Fairfield Co.)

Bur Binckley Cem north of Rushville. Fur infor Elizabeth Sherman Reese Chap.

BINCKLEY, HENRY, (Fairfield Co.)

Bur Binckley Cem north of Rushville, O. Fur infor Elizabeth Sherman Reese Chap.

BINER, GEORGE, (Harrison Co.)

A Revolutionary Pensioner living in Harrison Co in 1833, aged 69. Served in a Va State Regt. U. S. Pension Rolls, 1835. Fur infor Moravian Trail Chap.

BINGHAM, ALVAN, (Athens Co.)

Was at Ft Schuvler, Apr 1, 1776. Disch Apr 1, 1777. Br Dec 20, 1754, Salisbury, Conn. Mar Elizabeth Dorsey Jones. D Feb 11, 1841, Athens, O. Bur W. State St., Cem. Athens, O. Came with his brother Silas to Marietta, O thence to Athens in 1797. First treasurer of Athens Co 1806. Served as associate judge several yrs. Ref: Natl No 55058, Vol 56, D. A. R. Lin. Walker's History Athens Co. Fur infor Nabby Lee Ames Chap.

BINGHAM, SILAS, SR., (Athens Co.)

Enl Aug-Sept 1775; June, July 1776; June July 1777; Sept 1777, 1778. Pvt. Belonged to Green Mountain Boys; was 10 days guarding part of Burgoyne's Army.

Was in the Canadian Expedition. Br July 24, 1758, Salisbury, Conn. Mar Irenah Royce, July 4, 1789. Children: Silas Jr. There were other children. D Oct 1840, Athens, O. Bur W State St, Athens, O east of main driveway. MI: "Silas Bingham Vt. Mil. Rev. War." GM Nabby Lee Ames Chap D. A. R. secured a Govt marker, white marble through Co Commissioners. Deputy Sheriff, Constable, a Millwright. Applied for a pens Oct 13, 1832. Claim was allowed. Ref: Bureau of Pensions; Walker's History of Ohio 75271, D. A. R. See 25570, Vol 33, p 116, D. A. R. Lin. Fur infor Nabby Lee Ames Chap.

BIRD, GEORGE, (Muskingum Co.)

A Pvt in Capt John Nilson's 3rd Company, 6th Bn, Northampton Co Mil. Col Jacob Stroud, p 431, Vol 8, Pa Archives 5 series. Br July 12, 1757, England Mar Deborah Thomas, 1788 in Pa, Chester Co. Children: John (br July 25, 1789), Jonathan, Joseph, Elizabeth, Jane, George, Deborah (twins), (br July 12, 1799). D 1840, Rural Dale, Muskingum Co, O. Bur Old Stone Church. Taken from his tailor's bench at the age of 19 yrs by British Authorities. Brought to British Camp on Brandywine July 1777, made his escape and joined American Army. Served until close of the Revolutionary War. Tailor. The Courier published at Zanesville, O under date of May 7, 1885, published a sketch of this pioneer, George Bird and his children and grand children. Pa Archives, p 431, Vol 8, 5 series. Ref: Miss Annie Laurie Bird, Route 1, Nampa, Idaho, Miss Minnie Bird, 1258 Euclid Ave., Zanesville, O. Fur infor Eed-ah-how Chap. Nampa, Idaho & Muskingum Chap.

BISHOP, DANIEL, (Huron Co.)

D Feb 5, 1848, aged 83 yrs. Bur M. E. Cem Clarksfield Twp. Fur infor Sally De Forest Chap.

BISHOP, JOEL, (Huron Co.)

Pvt. Br 1759 Guilford, Conn. D 1839, Huron Co. Ref: Natl No 23139, p 49, Vol. 24, D. A. R. Lin.

BISSELL, BENJAMIN, (Lake Co.)

In 1778 or 1779 in Capt Bliss' Company, Col Ledyard's Regt for 3 mos, again in 1781 for 9 mos in Capt Munson's Company. Col Zebulon Butler's Regt, Conn Tr. Br Mar 31, 1761, Lebanon, Conn. Mar Elizabeth Heath 1784. D Oct 1, 1841, Painesville, O. Bur Evergreen Cem, Painesville, O. GM New Conn Chap. Fur infor New Connecticut Chap.

BISSELL, JOSEPH, (Mahoning Co.)

Served as Pvt 1776 in Capt Walter Hyde's Company. Col Wolcott's Regt fr Lebanon, Conn. Br Lebanon, Conn. 1730. D 1814 Youngstown, O.

BISSELL, JOHN PARTRIDGE, (Mahoning Co.)

Pvt in the Lexington Alarm. 1775 at Bunker Hill; was in Capt Skinner's Company, Col Latimer's Regt at the battle of Stillwater. Br 1751 Conn. Mar Temperance Stark (1761—1850). Children: three sons, and six daughters, one dau Mary married a Kyle. D 1811, Coitsville, O. Bur Oak Hill Cem, Youngstown, O. GM Mahoning Chap D. A. R. marker 1915-17. Surveyor, Justice of Peace. Came to Ohio from Lebanon, Conn. Ref: p 165-166 Hist Trumbull and Mahoning Cos. Conn Men of the Rev, p 50, 313, Natl No 90103, Vol 91, p 34. Fur infor Mahoning Chap.

BISSELL, JUSTUS, (Portage Co.)

Pvt 2nd Regt, Col Buller's Conn Mil, Capt Wolcott's Company. Enl July-Aug 1776; Enl June 24, 1780. Disch Dec 9, 1780. 2nd Regt. Br Feb 16, 1759, East

Windsor, Conn. Parents: Justus. Mar Ann Blodgett, Dec 20, 1779. Children: Justus, Barber, Orris, Cephas, Eunice, Philena, Elvira, Anna, Ebenezer Blodgett. D Sept 16, 1882. Aurora. Ref: Conn Men of Rev. History of Twinsburg, O, p 255. Fur infor Taylor Chap.

BLACK, DAVID, (Hamilton Co.)

Br 1763, N. J. D 1832. Ref S. A. R. Natl No 100638, Vol 101, p 197. D. A. R. Lin. Fur infor Cincinnati Chap.

BLACK, DAVID, (Butler Co.)

Pvt in Col Philip Van Cortland's NY Regt. Br 1763, N. J. Mar in 1787 Catherine Cramer (1763-1849.) D 1832, Hamilton, O. Ref: Natl No 100632, Vol 101, p 197, D. A. R. Lin.

BLACK, ISAAC, (Delaware Co.)

Pvt under Col Jonathan Brown, Capt Daniel Whiting Mass Tr. Bur Africa Cem. Pensioned. Fur infor Delaware Chap.

BLACK, JAMES, (Harrison Co.)

Is said by family to have served in the Revolution from York (now Adams) Co, Pa. B 1756 in Ireland. D 1846 and bur at Beech Spring Church. Fur infor Moravian Trail Chap.

BLACK, JOHN, (Columbiana Co.)

Lived in Liverpool Twp, Columbiana Co, O. Fur infor Bethia Southwick Chap.

BLACK, WILLIAM, (Delaware Co.)

Bur Millcreek Cem, Concord Twp. Fur infor Delaware Chap.

BLACKBOURNE, MOSES, (Mahoning Co.)

Pvt in Revolutionary War. Pensioned Aug 8, 1830 age 83 yrs. Br 1752. D 1835. Bur Petersburgh Center, Mahoning Co, O. Location of grave about the center of burial ground which is in a very bad condition, and located between a church and a school house. Ref: Pa Archives Vol 23, Series 3, p 584. Fur infor Mahoning Chap.

BLACKBURN, JAMES, (Butler Co.)

Name appears on the tablet erected at Hamilton, O. on the site of Ft Hamilton, in memory of Revolutionary soldiers who are bur in that Co. Unidentified. Fur infor John Reily Chap.

BLACKBURN, JOHN, (Mahoning Co.)

Pvt Cumberland Co Mil in 1777, 1778, Lt 1779. Bur Poland, O. He was taxed in 1803 in Poland and bought land same yr. Ref: Trumbull and Mahoning Co Hist, Vol 2, p 61, Pa Archives, series 5, p 160, 168, 604, Old deeds, Vol A, p 61, Compare with John Blackburn. D. A. R. Lin Bk Vol 91, p 285. Fur infor Mahoning Chap.

BLACKMAN, ELIJAH, (Portage Co.)

Lived at Aurora. Drew pension.

BLACKWELL, JOHN, (Pickaway Co.)

Lt of 3rd Va Continental Tr; wounded at Brandywine; then promoted to Capt. Taken prisoner at Charleston Sept 15, 1777. Br Mch 22, 1775, Faquier Co, Va. Mar Agatha Ann Enstance, 1799. Children: Lucy Steptoe, Agatha Conway, Elouisa, John Enstance, William, Anna. D Apr 28, 1831, Pickaway Co, O. Bur Old Family Cem near Darbyville, Pickaway Co, O. Ref: Military District Survey Bk A, p 265 and 206. Fur infor Mt. Sterling Chap.

BLAIN, ALAM, (Delaware Co.)

Pvt in Capt John Heard's Company, Col Anthony White's Regt 4th Regt Continental dragoons, N. J. D Delaware Co, O. Bur Genoa Twp, Delaware Co, O. Ref: Natl No 94694. Vol 95, p 211. Fur infor Delaware Chap.

BLAIR, ABRAHAM, (Knox Co.)

Of Perth Amboy, N. J. Settled in 1811, upon the farm on which he d in his 90th yr on the 2d of October, 1846. He served as a Minute Man during the Revolutionary War and participated in the battles of Trenton and Monmouth. He settled in Franklin Twp, Knox Co, O. Ref: Norton's History Knox Co, p 289. Fur infor Kokesing Chap.

BLAIR, ANDREW, (Ross Co.)

D Apr 20, 1842, aged 84 yrs., Bur Bainbridge Cem. Grave will be marked. Mrs. J. Blosser Anderson descendant. Credentials approved by National Society for her supplemental paper. Fur infor Nathaniel Massie Chap.

BLAKE, NICHOLAS, (Adams Co.)

Bur Killinstown. Ref: History of Adams Co. Fur infor Sycamore Chap.

BLAKE, SIMEON, Capt., (Noble Co.)

As a soldier in Maine; also under Gen Wayne at Fallen Timbers, in Indian Wars 1794-95. Settled in Oliver Twp about 1806. Fur infor Mrs. L. B. Frazier, Caldwell.

BLAKELY, JAMES, (Vinton Co.)

Enl at 17 yrs of age. Served honorably. Children: Betsy, James. Bur Small lot on a farm, about 1½ miles south of Wilksville. GM by slab, erected in later yrs. Farmer. Ref: A great grand dau, Mrs. Henry David Grate, Wellston and Dr. C. B. Taylor, McArthur, O.

BLAZER, JACOB, (Gallia Co.)

Children: Philip, (six daus, names unknown), Peter. D Blazer farm. Bur near Centenary. On own farm. MI: Obliterated. GM by son Philip. Ref: Miss Maggie, Blazer, O. Fur infor Return Johnathan Meigs Chap.

BLICKENSDERFER, CHRISTIAN, (Tuscarawas Co.)

Pvt in Capt George Feather's 6th Company, 9th Bn, Lancaster Co, Pa. Mil 1778 to 1783. (See Pa Archives Series 5, Vol 7, pp 874, 896, 238, 284 and 608). Br Oct 6, 1753, Philadelphia. Parents: father's name was also Christian. Mar Barbara (br July 1, 1780). Children: John (br 1782, mar Elizabeth Friedrich) Christian (br 1787, mar Louise Salome Friedrich), George, (mar Marie Ricksecker), D Mch 3, 1820, Warwick Twp. Bur in Sharon (Moravian) Cem, near Tuscarawas. MI: "Christian Blickensderfer. Br Oct 6, 1753, Philadelphia, Pa. Departed Mar 3, 1820." GM with sandstone, lying flat, placed by family, marks his grave, probably erected soon after his death. In his infancy his family settled in Lancaster Co, Pa. where in 1784 he purchased a farm. Came to Ohio in 1812 and located on farm in Warwick Twp. Farmer. Name appears on Soldier's Memorial erected in Gnadenhutten Cem in 1927. Ref: Miss Lily Peter, Arkansas, a direct descendant entered the D. A. R. on his serv. Fur infor Charles L. Stocker, Esq., 609 Society for Savings Bldg., Cleveland, O.

BLISH, BENJAMIN, (Lake Co.)

Pvt Col Thomas Marshall's Regt from June 13, 1776 to Aug 1, 1776, at Castle Island, 25 days; 31 days in Col Williams' Regt in R. I; 6 days under Col Thomas Carpenter, 1780. Br Feb 22, 1753, Tolland Co, Conn. Mar Phebe Skinner 1774. D Mch 11, 1825. Bur Blish Cem, West Painesville, O. GM New Connecticut Chap. Fur infor New Connecticut Chap.

BLUE, JOHN, (Ross Co.)

Pvt in NY Continental Line. Bur Frankfort. Fur infor Nathaniel Massie Chap.

BLUE, MICHAEL, (Fayette Co.)

Br 1742. Mar Mary. Children: Elizabeth, Mary, Ann, Kziah, Daniel, John, Garnet, Isaac, Michael, Uriah. D Aug 25, 1821 near Bloomingsburg. Bur Bloomingsburg Cem old part unplatted. MI: "Michael Blue died Aug 25, 1821, aged 79 yrs. Iron star, 1776." GM by family and Cem Trustees. Marked in 1822. Farmer. Fur infor Washington C. H. Chap.

BLUE, URIAH, (Miami Co)

Served in Va Mil under Capt Wm M Morgan in company of volunteers fr Berkeley Co, Va. Br Aug 8, 1752, in Hampshire Co, O. Mar Ruth, (br Nov 6, 1752; d May 27, 1817.) Children: Michael (in war of 1812); James, Uriah Jr., Barnabas, Elizabeth, Sarah, Martha, Ruth, Hannah, John. D Miami Co, O. Mch 2, 1829. Bur on own farm near Troy, O. He was one of the first settlers of Miami Co, O. (1800) and lived in Bedford Co, Pa. for several yrs before coming to Ohio. Judge Ref: Howe's History O; Mrs. P. J. Blosser, Chillicothe, O. Fur infor Nathaniel Massie Chap.

BLUNDON, ELIJAH, (Fairfield Co.)

Enl Dec 9, 1776 for 3 yrs. Served as Pvt in Capt Edurn Hull's Company, Commander Lt Col Jas Innes and Maj Gustavis B Wallace. 15th Va Regt. Transferred in 1778 to Maj Wallace's Company 11th and 15th Va; Lt Col John Cropper and Col Daniel Morgan. Br 1740, Pope's Creek, Westmoreland Co, Va. Mar Mary Coulter, or Colton. Children: Elisah, Sarah, John, Thomas, Sophia. D 1820, Lancaster, O. Ref: Revolutionary Soldiers of Va p 50; Pens Record Vol 2, p 87. Soldiers of Va. Fur infor Mrs. C. H. Eversole, 267 Tibet Rd, Columbus, O.

BOATMAN, BARNERD, (Columbia Co.)

War soldier of Revolution. In 1840 at age 83, was a pensioner residing in Unity Twp. D Jan 12, 1843, aged 95 yrs, 17 days. Bur East Palestine, O. GM by stone. Fur infor Bethia Southwick Chap.

BOBENMEIR, GABRIEL (or Puppingmeyer)), (Fairfield Co.)

Br Dec. 2, 1749, near Zionsville, Upper Milford Twp, Northampton Co, Pa (now Lehigh Co). Parents: Philip Stephen and Maria Sophia (Thum) Bobenmeir. Mar Christenah Walter Apr 25, 1773. Children: John Adam, John Jacob, Catherine Elizabeth, Mary, Mary Charlotte, Barbara, Johannes, Johann George, Samuel, Philip. D Apr, 1817, Amanda Twp, Fairfield Co, O. Bur, not positively known. He is supposed to be bur in St Peter's Lutheran Church Cem (Dutch

Hollow) one mile south of his farm on the Circle-Lancaster pike. A visit to this cem in 1923 failed to reveal the grave. Was told by several who lived near that in building the new church in 1900 quite a few of the older gravestones were removed to make room for the new church. Lived in Northampton Co until 1790; moved to Cumberland Co; moved to Westmoreland Co, in 1810 and to Fairfield Co, O. in 1812. A farmer. Ref: Charles R. Roberts, Geneaologist, 520 N. Sixth St., Allentown, Pa. Fur infor Pa Archives, series V, Vol 8, p 33, Gabriel Bobenmyer; Pa Archives, series V, Vol 8, p 56 Gabriel Coppenmyer; Pa Archives, series V, Vol 8, p 105 Gabriel Puppingmeyer.

BODLEY, WILLIAM, (Richland Co.)

Pvt Va State Tr. Br 1764. D Nov 1843. Bur Adams Cem, 2 miles northeast fr London, O. on new state road. MI: Name and tr, bronze marker (large) GM by Mary Washington D. A. R. Chap, bronze marker in 1911. Pens 1840. Fur infor Mary Washington Chap.

BODMAN, SCAMON, (Muskingum Co.)

Revolutionary soldier. D Sept 5, 1816; aged 79. Bur Springfield Chapel Cem, Springfield Twp. Fur infor Muskingum Chap.

BOGGS, JOHN, Capt., (Pickaway Co.)

Received rank or title of Capt fr Col Couch of the 2nd Bn of Delaware Mil. (taken fr American Biography of Prominent Men). Br 1739, Penn Co, Pa. Parents: Dr. William Ellison Boggs, Scotch-Irish descent. Mar Jane Irwin. Children: Major John Boggs (b May 10, 1775, d 1861, mar Sally McMicken 1801); Lydia, d 1829. Bur near Logan Elm Park, Pickaway Co, on a hill. GM by sons with stone slab. Removed fr Delaware to W Va and settled near Wheeling Fort, now Fort Henry. In 1798 he came to Ohio with his son Maj John Boggs. He settled on Scipps Creek and his son on Congo Creek. Zane Gray's book, ("Betty Zane"). Logan Elm Park is a historical spot six miles below Circleville, O. Boggs family hist is connected with its hist. Ref: Miss Sara (Sally) Boggs Kingston, O. Fur infor Mt Sterling Chap.

BOLENDER, STEPHEN, (Clermont Co.)

Pvt 2nd class, Lancaster Company Mil. Muster Roll of Capt Geahrs Company 9th Bn, Commanded by Col John Huber, 1779. See p 899, Vol VII, Archives 5 Series. Br Oct 9, 1756, Lancaster Co, Pa. Mar 1st Margreta Shinkle; 2nd Mrs. Elizabeth Fitteman. Children: Peter, Catharine, Barbara, Henry, John, Jacob, Elizabeth, Christian, Stephen, Joseph, by 2nd mar: William H, Julia H, Julia Ann, Daniel, Margaret, Mary. D Feb 25, 1820. Bur Felicity, Clermont Co, O. Emigrated to Ohio in 1800. He was a farmer, blacksmith and Dunkard minister. Ref: Records fr Family Bible and Geneology compiled by a grandson of Shinkle ancestor while soldier was still living. Fur infor Cincinnati Chap.

BOLL, JOSEPH, (Miami Co.)

Bur Raper Chapel, old Country Cem. GM by Miami Chap. Fur infor Miami Chap.

BOLLIN, JOSEPH, (Miami Co.)

He fought at Saratoga and was at Warren's side when he fell at Bunker Hill. It is said that twenty of this name fell in the war of the Rev. Bur Raper Chapel North of Troy, O. GM Miami Chap with bronze marker in 1904. Fur infor Miami Chap.

BONHAM, JOHN, (Hamilton Co.)

Br 1760, N. J. D 1821. Ref: S. A. R. Fur infor Cincinnati Chap.

BONNEL, AARON, (Hamilton Co.)

Was an Artificer for the Government for which he drew a pens in latter yrs of life. This record is in 1898 S. A. R. Bk furnished by Col Samuel J. Cary. Br Mch 4, 1759, Essex Co, N. J. Parents: Benjamin and Rachel. Mar Rachel Clark who d in Harrison Twp, Hamilton Co. Children: six in all. Clark Bonnell only child's name given. D 1855, Harrison Twp. Bur in Park of Village of Harrison. Grave undisturbed to prevent the reversion of ground to donor's heirs. Name on bronze tablet on wall of soldiers Memorial Building in Cincinnati, Hamilton Co. GM by family. By S. A. R. in Memorial Building. Aaron Bonnell came to Hamilton Co 1805, with his brothers, Benjamin and Paul and his two mar sisters Rhoda and Abigail and their husbands. Ref: Natl No 52214 D. A. R. Lin. Vol 53. Infor given in Hamilton Co Hist published 1894 by Nelson Co. p 978. Fur infor Cincinnati Chap.

BONNELL, ISAAC, (Guernsey Co.)

Bur Winterset. Ref: S. A. R. Fur infor Anna Asbury Stone Chap.

BONNELL, JAMES, (Hamilton Co.)

Lt under Col Spencer; also in Continental Army 1777 to close of Revolutionary War. Settled at Columbia in beginning of settlement. Name occurs often in early local history. Family still in neighborhood. Fur infor Cincinnati Chap.

BONNELL, PAUL, (Butler Co.)

Enl 1782 fr Philadelphia for the war in the Light Horse and marched to Carlisle under Col Richard Butler. He guarded the British prisoners at Lancaster, 1783. He applied for a pens in Butler Co, O, 1819 and it was allowed for two yrs actual serv as Pvt, Pa line. Ref: D. A. R. Lin, Vol 26, p 97. Natl No 35265.

BONSER, NATHANIEL, (Clermont Co.)

Revolutionary soldier. D at Franklin, Clermont Co, O. Name also reported as one bur near Felicity, Clermont Co, O. as no Franklin now in Clermont Co, O. Fur infor Cincinnati Chap.

BOONE, SQUIRE, (Harrison Co.)

Pioneer of Ky who gave valuable service and was wounded in the defense of Boonesboro. After nine days siege the enemy was defeated. Br 1734, Bucks Co, Pa. D 1815. Natl No 27410. Vol 28, p151. D. A. R. Lin.

BOSSINGER, CONRAD, (Summit Co.)

Teamster in Pa. Br 1752 on Susquehanna river. Mar Barbara Yancer. Br Dec 18, 1753 in Pa. D Mch 16, 1816. (Bronsons history). Bur Tallmadge, private cem. 1801 came to Ravenna with his wife, Barbara Yancer. In 1809 settled in Tallmadge, and was father of the first settler of that place. Fur infor Cuyahoga Portage Chap.

BORING, ABSALOM, (Clinton Co.)

Bur New Antioch. Fur infor George Clinton Chap.

BOSS, ADAM, (Hamilton Co.)

Br Maryland. D 1833. Ref: S. A. R. Fur infor Cincinnati Chap.

BOSTWICK, DOCTOR, (Portage Co.)

Pvt in Connecticut Mil. Placed on Pens Roll Feb 25, 1833. Drew pens at Ravenna, O. Fur infor Old Northwest Chap.

BOSTWICK, EBENEZER, (Portage Co.)

Pvt in Conn Continental. Placed on Pens Roll Nov 13, 1818. Fur infor Old Northwest Chap.

BOSTWICK, ELEAZER, (Portage Co.)

Pvt in Conn Continental. Placed on Pens Roll Apr 2, 1883. Bur Edinburg. Fur infor Old Northwest Chap.

BOSTWICK, REUBEN, Capt., (Trumbull Co.)

Commanded 7th Company, 1st Bn Wadsworth Brig 1776. Mar Mabel Ruggles 1734. Bur Newton Falls, O. 1813. MI: An old headstone gives the name "Bostwick" but the first part was effaced. Came from New Millford, Litchfield Co, Conn. Ref: Baldwin Library, Youngstown, O. Kindness of Miss Kyle. See Natl No 61352, Vol 62, p 121. D. A. R. Lin. Fur infor Mary Chesney Chap.

BOSTWORTH, PETER, (Trumbull Co.)

Br 1763. D Aug 16, 1822. Bur Braceville Cem. Will probated 1823. Fur infor Mary Chesney Chap.

BOSWORTH, JOHN, (Portage Co.)

Pvt in Col Ashley's Regt at Saratoga and 1780 served as a Sgt, same Regt. Br 1751 Middletown, Conn. D 1832 in Rootstown, Portage Co, O. Ref: Vol 93, p 252, Natl No 92806 D. A. R. Lin.

BOSWORTH, JOHN, (Cuyahoga Co.)

Pvt R. I. Br 1760. D 1845. Bur Baptist Cem Churchyard (deserted). Fur infor Western Reserve Chap.

BOSWORTH, SALA, (Washington Co.)

Pvt in Capt Calvin Partridge's Company. Marched in Lt Col Samuel Regt Plymouth Company May 21, 1799; also in Capt Jesse Sturdevant's Company, Col John Jacob's Regt July 3-26, 1780. (Ref: Mass in the Rev Vol 2, p 382). Br Halifax, Mass. Mch 11, 1764. Mar Rebecca Perkins, Feb 21, 1788, Plymouth, Mass (d Mch 27, 1847 at McConnellsville, O). D Marietta, O, Oct 12, 1816. Bur Marker placed in Mound Cem. MI: "In memory of Sala Bosworth who died Oct 12, 1823, aged 58 yrs." About 1907 the original stone was replaced by the present stone and the discrepancy in dates may be due to lack of care in reading the dates on the old stone. GM Marietta Chapter D. A. R. in Apr 1925. Fur infor Marietta Chap.

BOUGHER, JOHN, BOWER, BOHER, (Mahoning Co.)

Pvt 3rd class Chester Co Muster Roll Capt Brumback's Company; also Flying Ranger 1776-1780. Capt Lockheart's Company Chester Pa. Br 1768. Children: Sarah (mar John Stambaugh). D 1856. Bur Old Four Mile Run, Austintown Twp, Mahoning Co, O. Ref: Pa Archives Vol 5, Series 5, p 532, Pa Archives, Vol 23, Series 3, p 421. Fur infor Mahoning Chap.

BOUGHNER, MARTIN, (Monroe Co.)

Ranger Northumberland Co, Pa. Record not verified by Ohio D. A. R. Br Sussex Co, N. J. Parents: Daniel, Catherine. First wife bur in Fayette Co, Pa. Mar twice. Children, 1st wife, Daniel, Pamilla, Anna; 2nd wife, Andrew, Joseph, Mary, Elsie Cristie, Ann. D about 1838 or 1840. Bur near Woodsfield. Mar in N. J. Lived in Northumberland Co, Pa. during war, lived in Fayette Co, Pa. 1790. See census record. Ref: Miss L. Ethel Boughner, Uniontown, Pa. Fur infor Great Meadows Chap, Uniontown, Pa.

BOUTON, JEHIEL, JR., (Knox Co.)

Pvt in Ebenezer Sharon's Company, Westchester Co, NY Mil, 1780-1782. Br 1775. D 1830, Knok Co, O. Natl No 25415, p 150, Vol 26, D. A. R. Lin.

BOUTON, NOAH, (Lorain Co.)

Lt in Capt Jos Lockwood's Company, Col Thomas Thomas' Westchester Co Regt; Capt in 7th NY Mil. Br 1743. Mar Deborah Hoyt. D 1812. Ref: Mrs. Nettie Richardson Young, Grafton, O. Natl No 51496 Vol 52 D. A. R. Lin.

BOWEN, THOMAS, (Hamilton Co.)

Serv recorded in Pa Archives Vol 4, 5. Settled on farm near Pleasant Ridge and bur on farm, perhaps Hamilton Co. Descendants still in region of Cincinnati. Fur infor Cincinnati Chap.

BOWER, HENRY, (Clinton Co.)

Served 7 yrs in Revolutionary War, fr Va, now in West Va, Hampshire Co, Romney the county seat. Deeds and records show land grants were given him for this service. Name spelled "Bowers" in Ohio. D in Clinton Co and reported to be bur in or near New Vienna, O. Ref: Mrs. Luella Caldwell, St Marys, O. Accepting this information, Jane Dailey, State Chairman.

BOWMAN, JOHN, (Montgomery Co.)

Ens fr Bedford Co, Pa, Capt Rhoades' Company, May 8, 1779, Brothers Valley Tr. Br 1763, Germany. (according to Bible record). D 1843, aged 80 yrs. Bur near Salem, Montgomery Co, O. Will names wife as Mary Magdalene (Will in Recorder's office Dayton, O.) Ref: fr Mrs. Etta Havens Carrithers, Hudson, Ill. Accepted by Mrs. Herbert Backus, State Regent 1928. Bible possessed by Mrs. Eli Helmick, Centennial Biography Record, Dayton, O. pp 1166, 1167. Pa Archives Series 5, Vol 5, pp 64, 79.

BOWMAN, PHILIP CASPER, (Mahoning Chap.)

Pvt 4th class Capt Lowrey's Company Lancaster Co Mil, Pa. Pensioner. Br 1755, Md. Mar Catherine Fast (Faust) p 230 Biog. E. O, Summers. Children: Elizabeth, John J, Christian, Joshua, Keziah, John Nicholas, Sarah, Rebecca, Catherine, Charlotte. D 1845. Bur Ellsworth Twp. Ref: Md Archives, Vol. 18, p 47, Pa Archives 5, series, Vol 7, p 327. Fur infor Mahoning Chap.

BOYD, ROBERT, (Muskingum Co.)

D 1853. Bur Newton Twp. Census pens list, 1840. No other found. Fur infor Muskingum Chap.

BOYER, LEWIS, (Shelby Co.)

Pvt Dragoon in Von Heer's Cav, Pa. Br 1756. Mar Rosetta Kerns. Children: John, Jacob, William, Rosanna Young, Mary Kiggins, Elizabeth Kiggins, Catherine Johnstown, Margaret Millhouse, Nancy Clawson. D Sept 19, 1843 on farm in Miami Co. Bur Wesley Chapel Cem, Shelby Co, near Miami Co, line. Location of grave near northeast corner of church; not platted. MI: See separate sheet too lengthy for this space. GM D. A. R. Piqua Chap; bronze marker. Enl from Rockingham Co, Va. Moved to Miami Co, O, where he was living when granted a pens by Certificate 620 issued Aug 3, 1829. Farmer.

On Mch 7, 1805, Warrant No 187 issued for 100 acres of land on account of services in war. Bureau of Pension's claim survey, File No 46370. See copy of disch attached. Original disch paper now owned by Murray Millhouse, R. F. D. Piqua, O. a great grandson of Lewis Boyer. Fur infor Piqua Chap.

BOYLES, TIMOTHY, (Harrison Co.)

A Revolutionary pensioner living in Harrison Co in 1820, aged 96. Served in Capt Samuel Smith's Company in Col John Haslet's Delaware Line Regt 1776. Del Archives 1, 54, 56, US Pens Rolls, 1835. Fur infor Moravian Trail Chap. Pvt in Capt Richard Peabody's Company, Col Edward Wigglesworth's Mass Regt. Br 1760, Rowley, Mass. D 1837, Haverhill, O. Fur infor Vol 88, p 52, Natl No 87177, D. A. R. Lin.

BOYNTON, ASA, (Scioto Co.)

Pvt in Capt Richard Peabody's Company, Col Edward Wigglesworth's Mass Regt. Br 1760, Rowley, Mass. D 1837, Haverhill, O. Fur infor Vol 88, p 52, Natl No 87177, D. A. R. Lin.

BRADFORD, JOSHUA, (Trumbull Co.)

Pvt in Capt Aaron Cleveland's Company 1776, served in Bacon's Company, Wadsworth Brig. Br 1751, Canterbury, Conn. Mar Anna Cleveland, 1775. D June 11, 1817, aged 66 yrs. Bur Braceville, O. MI: "Joshua Bradford died June 11, 1817, aged 66 yrs." GM by relatives; kept in good condition. Ref: Vol 84, Natl No 83726, D. A. R. Lin. Fur infor Mary Chesney Chap.

BRADFORD, ROBERT, MAJ., (Washington Co.)

His serv began with Bunker Hill and ended with the capture of Cornwallis. He saw active serv in nearly all battles fought in the Northern and Eastern states, retiring with the rank of Maj. Br 1750, Plymouth, Mass. Mar Keziah Little. With the exception of one, all of their children born prior to 1792 d in an epidemic of putrid sore throat at Farmers Castle. After 1792, Sarah, Robert, Samuel A, Otis L. D 1822, Belpre. Bur in Ohio Company burying grounds, Belpre, O. MI: "Maj Robert Bradford 1750-1822." GM Marietta Chap with Revolutionary marker in 1921. Was a direct descendant of Gov Bradford. With many American officers was presented with sword from Marquis LaFayette. Joined Ohio Company and came to Belpre in 1789. Was associated with Griffith Green in discovering salt springs on the Scioto River. Ref: Hildreth's History. Fur infor Marietta Chap.

BRADLEY, AREIL, (Lucas Co.)

When a lad, under pretense of going to a mill, brought back infor fr British camp whose lines he entered. Br 1767, Salisbury, Conn. Mar Chloe Lane. D 1852 or 1857. Bur Waterville, O. MI: Bronze Marker bearing letters S. A. R. Ref: Natl No 38181, Vol 39, p 67, D. A. R. Lin. Fur infor Ursula Walcott.

BRADLEY, JAMES, (Mahoning Co.)

Resident of Salisbury. Enl May 21 during the war. Corp in 1780, Sgt in 1781, Seldon Butler's Company, Lt Lee's Company, served 130 days. In 1780 stationed as a guard to the town of Milford. ("Conn Men of Revolution" pp 208, 355 and 560). Bur in Canfield, Mahoning Co, O. Grave not located. Came to Canfield early in 19th century, lived for 7 yrs on a farm afterward owned by Philo Beardsley. Ref: Trumbull and Mahoning Co Hist, Vol II, p 13; Truesdale's Hist of Canfield, O. Fur infor Mahoning Chap.

BRADLEY, JAMES, (Trumbull Co.)

Corp. Mar Asenath Bird (br 1752 Conn, d 1832). Children: Thaddeus, Dr. Jas Bird, Dr. Ariel (who d near Buffalo, N. Y. 1859). D Mch 3, 1817, aged 62 yrs. Bur Johnstown, O. Northwien Cem. Unable to locate grave. First resident of Johnstown. Pencil notes from Jas. K. Buell, 1926 Youngstown, O, at call for names. Ref: Miss Nellie Elder, Warren, O; name given by S. A. R. of Ohio. Fur infor Mary Chesney Chap.

BRADLEY, THADDEUS, (Geauga Co.)

Pvt 1775 at Ticonderoga, 1776 served under Capt Steffen Bradley, 1777 at Port Stanwix under Capt Jeremiah Parmley and Col Samuel Elmore in Conn Line. Pensioned 1832. Br 1756, Cheshire, Conn. Mar Parnal Whitmey 1783. Children: Hull, Gomer, Abigail, Betsey, Silah, Nabby. D Nov 16, 1840, Burton, O. Bur Williams Cem, Burton, O. MI: "Died Sept 19, 1840 age 84. Parnal his wife died Jan 16, 1861 age 95." GM by family. Shoemaker. Came to Burton, O, 1808. Ref: Conn Men 116. Pioneer History Geauga Co, History Cheshire Conn. Natl No 27521 Vol 28, D. A. R. Lin. Fur infor Taylor Chap.

BRAINARD, AMOS, (Cuyahoga Co.)

Corp Conn State. Br 1755. Bur Brooklyn, Brookmere Cem. Fur infor Western Reserve Chap.

BRAINERD, ANSEL, (Medina Co.)

Pvt Conn Tr. Br Chatham, Conn, 1765. D Westfield, O. Mar Mary Warren (1767 d 1859). Pensioned 1832 for serv as Pvt Conn Tr. Natl No 53397, Vol 54, p 172, 90583 D. A. R. Lin.

BRAINARD, JABEZ, (Cuyahoga Co.)

Fifer Conn Tr. Br 1758. D 1855. Bur Lake View, Euclid Ave, Cleveland, O. GM Western Reserve Chap. Fur infor Western Reserve Chap.

BRAKEMAN, JOHN, (Ashtabula Co.)

Bur Harpersfield Twp Cem (abandoned). Fur infor Eunice Grant Chap.

BRANCH, WILLIAM, (Lake Co.)

Enl Apr 1, 1777 in Capt Jedediah Hyder's Company, Col John Durkee's Conn Regt. Was at Germantown, Red Bank, Monmouth, Mifflin, Valley Forge and Yorktown. Was one of three to take Maj Andre from the gallows. Disch July 7, 1783, Received Badge of merit for faithful services for 6 yrs. Br Sept 3, 1760, Preston, Conn. Mar Lucretia Tracy, 1796. Children: William Witter. D Apr 13, 1849, Madison, O. Bur Middle Ridge Cem, Madison, O. GM by New Connecticut Chap. Ref: Natl No 33643 Vol 34, p232, D. A. R. Lin. and 81368, Vol 82, D. A. R. Lin.

BRANDON, BENJAMIN, (Miami Co.)

Pvt. N C Mil. Pensioned 1833 in Miami Co. Br 1759 Dowan Co, N C. D 1837 Miami Co. Ref: Natl No 55186, p 87, Vol 56, D. A. R. Lin.

BRANDT, ADAM, (Licking Co.)

Bur Near Licking Co line, in territory formerly Fairfield Co. Fur infor Elizabeth Sherman Reese Chap.

BRANNON, JOHN, (Harrison Co.)

Placed on Pens Roll 1818, for serv 1776, in Capt Abraham Smith's Company, Col William Irvine's Pa Bn. Br 1744. Mar Elizabeth Harborn (br 1755). D 1820, Cadiz, O. Ref: Natl No 67240, Vol 68, p 87, D. A. R. Lin.

BRANNON, JOHN, (Harrison Co.)

A Revolutionary pensioner living in Harrison Co in 1821, aged 89; served in the 2nd Pa Line Regt. Pa Archives, 5, 11, 865; U S Pens Rolls, 1835. Fur infor Moravian Trail Chap.

BRANSON, JONATHAN, (Clermont Co.)

Served in Capt Samuel Cochran's 10th Bn, Lancaster Co, Pa Associators. Br 1758 Utica, N. Y. Mar Hannah Willing. D 1822 Milford, O. Ref: Vol 59, p 336.

BRANT, STEPHEN, (Warren Co.)

Bur South Lebanon, Hamilton Twp. Ref: S. A. R. Yr Bk 1917.

BRASBRIDGE, JOHN, (Holmes Co.)

Reid's Regt. Bur Hopewell Cem, Holmes Co, O. Grave located in old part of cem. MI: "John Brasbridge, Reid's Regt. N. H. Revolutionary War." Fur infor Wooster Wayne Chap.

BRASHER, JOHN, (Hamilton Co.)

Br 1764, New York. D 1840. Ref: S. A. R. Fur infor Cincinnati Chap.

BRASS, GARRIT, (Lake Co.)

Enl from Westfield, Mass in 1781. Served until Dec 21, 1783, in Capt Banister's Company, Col Newel's Regt; also in Capt Smith's Company under Col Vose in the Mass Tr. Br 1763. Mar Lucy Matthews Apr 19, 1791; Pensioned in Chester, Geauga Co, Dec 6, 1843; also Feb 29, 1844. D Nov 25, 1837, Mentor, Lake Co, O. Bur old residents think on school property, since vacated as burial ground. Fur infor New Connecticut Chap.

BRATTON, ELISHA, (Brown Co.)

Bur Sardinia. Fur infor Ripley Chap.

BRATTON, JAMES, (Guernsey Co.)

Pvt Pa Mil. Br 1741 Butler Twp, Chester Co, Pa. Mar Bathsheba Ripley, 1783. Children: Edward, Robert, Elizabeth, John, William, Bathsheba, James, Rachel, Sarah, James, Joseph, Samuel. D Oct 6, 1844 Center Twp, Guernsey Co, O. Bur Pleasant Hill Cem, Center Twp. MI: "James Bratton, Revolutionary Soldier. Aged 88." GM by family. Farmer. Ref: Records in Pens Office Washington D. C. Mrs. Hazel Bratton French, Cambridge, O. Natl No 199548. Fur infor Anna Asbury Stone Chap.

BREHMER or BREMER, CONRAD, (Tuscarawas Co.)

Family tradition that he was a Hessian soldier deserted to, and later served with the Continental Armies. Service record not definitely identified, but I suggest that he may be the Conrad Beamer whose serv as 1st Lt with Capt Noah Abraham's 3rd Company, 1st Bn of Cumberland Co. Pa, Mil, is noted in Pa Archives, Series 5, Vol 6, p 17, 69, 79, 100. Br about 1742, probably in Europe. Mar Barbara Keener. Children: John, Conrad Jr., Elizabeth,—others. Cannot be sure of this list, but it is probably correct as far as it goes. D Aug 16, 1830, near Port Washington, O. Bur in Moravian Cem at Gnadenhutten (Re-interred here from Port Washington about 1880). Location of grave in special Bremer family lot in southwest corner of Monument lot. MI: "Conrad Bremer Died Aug 16, 1830, aged 88 yrs." GM Monument set up by family, about 1880. It is believed that his middle life was probably spent in Pa. He came to Tuscarawas Co in 1801. Farmer. Name appears on Soldier's Memorial erected in Gnadenhutten Cem in 1927. Fur infor Charles L. Stocker, Esq., 609 Society for Savings Building, Cleveland, O.

BREWSTER, WILLIAM, (Hamilton Co.)

Br 1762, New York. D 1834. Ref: S. A. R. Fur infor Cincinnati Chap.

BRICE, JAMES, (Athens Co.)

Lt. Served on several tours of duty in Pa Mil under Capt Zadock Wright 1781, 1783. Br Oct 11, 1751, Md. Parents: James and Mary Johnson. Mar Hester Johnson, Annie Grant. Children: Thomas, Barnett, Rachel, Nancy, Hester, Mary, John Grant, Anne Grant, Jane. D Dec 22, 1832, Athens, O. Bur West State St. Cem (near the gateway at the left of driveway). MI: "Sacred to the memory of James Brice who died Dec 22, 1832." GM by family long ago; sandstone marker which is disintegrating. Nabby Lee Ames Chap D. A. R. placed Jones marker Oct 1925. One of the incorporators of Washington College Pa and many yrs trustee resigning in 1824; Commissioner for Washington Co, Pa, 1791. Pa Legislature 1794; Com Wash Co 1797, Collector W. S. Internal Revenue for Washington and Greene Cos, Pa. 1798-1799-1800-1801-1802. Ref: Archives of Pa and W. S. War Dept. Fur infor Nabby Lee Ames Chap.

BRICKER, ADAM, (Clermont Co.)

Enl at age of 14 in 1776, at Redstone Fort Pa. Later was sent to Fort Pitt, to Marietta and to Fort Washington, (Cincinnati) and to the Falls of the Ohio (Louisville) where he was disch. Reenlisted under Gen St Clair, disch after battle of Fallen Timbers. Br Oct 6, 1762, Redstone Fort, Pa. Names of parents not known, both killed by Indians in 1770. Mar Rebecca Hartman, 1805. Children: John Hartman, Robert M., William, Thomas, Isaac, and 3 dau, names unknown. D Aug 31, 1843, on his farm 2 miles south of Williamsburg. Served during the Rev but only in the west. Farmer, noted hunter. Fur infor A. S. Abbott, Bethel, O. and Cincinnati Chap.

BRIDGE, BENJAMIN, (Clark Co.)

Served in War of 1842. Enl 1776 in Capt Joseph Lindley's Company, Col Baldwin's Regt Continental Artillery Artificers. Br Oct 13, 1748. England. D Apr 17, 1843. Bur Knob Prairie, Enon, Clark Co. MI: "Benjamin Bridge. Died Apr 17, 1843, at the age of 94 yrs., 6 mos, and 4 days." GM Metal Marker S. A. R. about 1906. In 1818 was a pensioner from Green Co, O; 1840, a pensioner in Bath Twp. Enl at the age of 21 yrs. Fur infor Lagonda Chap.

BRIDGMAN, ELISHA, (Geauga Co.)

Pvt. Capt Josiah Smith's Company, Col Whitney's Regt. May 25, 1776 to Dec 1, 1776. Company raised for defense of Boston. Capt Lyman's Company, Col Dike's Regt Dec 1, 1776 to Mch 1, 1777; Capt Clapp's Company, Col Wells' Regt May 10, 1777 to July 10, 1777; Capt Lyman's Company Aug 17, 1777, 7 days, 1778, 8 mos serv. Br Feb 18, 1760, Northampton, Mass. Parents: Noah and Mercy (Clark). Mar Sybil Burk, 1786. D about 1835, Huntsburg. Bur probably old cem, Huntsburg. Ref: Bridgman Genealogy p 26. Mass Soldiers and Sailors Vol 2, p 494. Fur infor Taylor Chap.

BRIGGS, JOHN, Muskingum Co.)

Pvt in Capt Ross Johnson's and Paxton's Companies. Lancaster Co, Pa Mil. (Col 7, p 1017, 5 Series, Pa Archives). Br Ireland. Parents: Scotch-Irish. Mar Mary Brown, at Lancaster, Pa, about 1764. Children: Jane, Thomas, Robert, John, James (br Jan 3, 1773), Sarah, Andrew, Mary, William, Esther. D Feb 1802, Muskingum Co, O. Bur Duncan Falls, O. John Briggs of Scotch Irish descent, mar Mary dau of James and Jane Brown of Lancaster Co, Pa. They sold their home in Lancaster and moved to Ohio about 1797-'98, bringing all their household goods in a flat boat up the Muskingum River. Settled the land on the East side of the Muskingum River from one mile below Duncan Falls to about the same distance above Gaysport, extending back fr below the river about ½ mile. Farmer. Ref: Miss Annie Louise Bird, Natl Member 143336, Route 1, Nampa, Idaho. Verified by Muskingum Chap. Fur infor Ead Ah How Chap Nampa, Idaho.

BRIGGS, JOHN, (Scioto Co.)

Fr Mch 1 to Apr 1, rank Sgt, Capt Churtiss, Col Craig. Parents: Samuel Briggs. Ref: Epworth Briggs Kinney, 978 East Eleventh Ave., Spokane, Washington. Fur infor Joseph Spencer.

BRISTOL, DANIEL, (Portage Co.)

Lived at Windham.

BROADWELL, JACOB, (Hamilton Co.)

3rd NJ Regt Col Barbee 1780. Commissioned a Lt by St Clair in Ohio Mil. Br 1766, NJ, near Elizabethtown. Mar Jane (Wells) or similar name. Children: Cyrus, Lewis, Jacob Jr, and perhaps Samuel. D 1836 or 1840, Hamilton Co, O. Settled near Mt Carmel, Union Twp in 1894, Clermont Co, but descendant 48088 D. A. R. states bur in Hamilton Co on line. Ref: S. A. R. and Natl No 207308 D. A. R. Fur infor Cincinnati Chap.

BROADWELL, SIMEON, (Montgomery Co.)

Pvt in Morris Co NJ Mil. May 7, 1778 (Record of Proceedings of a Commission at Thomas Gardner's Classings, Capt Lindley's Company according to role, appears his name as class No. 33). Br New Providence, N J. Parents: Josiah Broadwell; (sometimes spelled Brawdwell). Mar Rachael Lindsey, July 1, 1778, at Morristown, N. J. Children: Silas, Ephriam, Josiah, Lewis. D Apr 23, 1827. Bur probably in the old Presbyterian graveyard, and the remains were not removed when the cem was abandoned. Nothing is known of this soldier; families all disappeared. Fur infor Richard Montgomery Chap. S. A. R.

BROCKWAY, EDWARD, (Trumbull Co.)

Enl 1777 as Sgt in Capt Jonathan Calkin's Company Conn Serv. Br Lyme, Conn. Mar Sarah ——— (d Sept 8, 1838, in the 87th yr.) D Mch 1813, at Hartford, O. Bur Center of Hartford, tombstone worn off. Ref: See Natl No 54940. Vol 55, p 411. D. A. R. Lin. Fur infor Mary Chesney Chap.

BRODERICK, WILLIAM, (Belmont Co.)

Minute Man, Monmouth Co Mil, Corp in Indian campaign, 1777; also a Corp in campaign against Indians, 1777, and Sgt at battle of Springfield, where wounded. Br Burlington, N. J. Mar Esther ———. D St Clairsville, O. Ref: Natl No. 17789, p 287, Vol 118, D. A. R. Lin.

BROKAW, GEORGE, (Belmont Co.)

Pvt in Capt Peter Vroom's Company, Col Abraham Quick's Regt, 2nd Bn Somerset Co, NJ Mil. Br 1755, Germany. Parents: Abraham and Judith Davis Brokaw, Mar Jane—1752-1850.) D 1842 Flushing, Belmont Co, O. Bur Crabapple Church, Belmont Co. At age 80, was living in Harrison Co 1833. Ref: Hist Somerset & Hunterdon Co, N. J. 94687, Vol 86, p 80, Natl No 85216 D. A. R. Lin. Fur infor Moravian Trail Chap.

BROOKS, CHARLES, (Montgomery Co.)

Pa Archives, 5 series, Vol 4, p211. Received depreciation pay. In Aug 1780, he volunteered for 7 mos service in Pa York Co Mil. Capt Boyd and Lt Montgomery. Marched against the Indians. In Woodstock Valley, thence to Bedford, thence to N. J. under Gen Wayne. In Capt McClellan's Company, Col Chamber's Regt. Br 1756 Pa. (?). Have no knowledge of this soldier, supposed to have been one of the early German families in Germantown, Montgomery Co. He applied for pens Oct 3, 1832, a resident of Clear Creek Twp, Warren Co, O. Request for information fr that locality brought no response. Fur infor Richard Montgomery Chap S. A. R.

BROOKS, DAVID, (Geauga Co.)

Pvt and teamster 2nd Regt Conn line 1777. Pensioned. Br 1759. Mar Jane Durand May 1782, Cheshire, Conn. Children: Patty Hotckiss and Harriet Brown. D 1821 Burton. Bur Lower Cem. MI: "David Brooks died 1821, age 61 yrs. Jane his wife, died Apr 14, 1846, age 84." Stone broken. Ref: Pens Dept. Probate Record. Conn Men Rev. Fur infor Taylor Chap.

BROOKS, DAVID, (Trumbull Co.)

Br 1754. D Mch 5, 1841. Bur Braceville. MI: "David Brooks Died Mch 5, 1841, aged 87 yrs." GM by relatives; kept in good condition. Will probated 1841; given pens Aug 1832. Fur infor Mary Chesney Chap.

BROOKS, HANNANIAH, (Ashtabula Co.)

Was placed on the pens roll of Ohio for services in the Conn Mil. Br 1753. Mar Elizabeth Spooner. Children: John. D 1849. Ref: Lineage Bk Vol XXXVI p 91, Pens Roll of 1840. Fur infor Mary Stanley Chap.

BROOKS, JAMES, (Lorain Co.)

Pvt Capt Roger Buckley's Company, 2nd Conn Regt. Disch 1780. In 1777 in Capt Mill's Company, and in 1779 when the life guard of the Commander-in-Chief was increased, he was among those chosen and served in this capacity 3 yrs. Br Nov 1758 Haddom, Conn. Mar Lydia King. D Dec 29, 1837. Bur La Porte, O. GM Western Reserve Chapter in 1920. Ref: D. A. R. Lin 11099, p 39, Vol 12, and 75099 Vol 76. Fur infor Western Reserve Chap.

BROOKS, JOHN, (Erie Co.)

Pvt in 8th Regt NY State Tr. Br 1775, Ridgefield, Conn. Mar Rachel Blizzard D 1846, Florence, O. Bur Near Spragues Corners, Florence, O. Ref: 79556, Vol 80, D. A. R. Lin. Fur infor Martha Pitkin Chap.

BROOKS, OLIVER, (Trumbull Co.)

Br 1727. D Sept 6, 1821. Bur Old Cem Mahoning Ave, Warren, O. All that is left on the stone is "Died Sept 6, 1821, aged 94 yrs." Because of the stone on next grave marked "wife of Oliver Brooks" judge this grave to be that of Oliver Brooks. Fur infor Mary Chesney Chap.

BROUSE, SE. MICHAEL, (Medina Co.)

Served fr Pa. Br 1752 (or 1755) Lancaster Co, Pa. Mar—Duck. Children: Michael Jr., John, William, Curtis, Jacob and Frederick. D 1854 at the age of 102. Bur Wadsworth, Woodlawn. MI: "Michael Brouse Died Nov 6, 1851 or 1854, aged 102 yrs, 8 mos, 15 days." GM by Western Reserve. S. A. R. marker. (Official) Ref: Compare Vol 70, p 226, Natl No. 69641, D. A. R. Lin. and Edwin Brouse. Fur infor Western Reserve Chap.

BROWN, CAPTAIN, (Paulding Co.)

Beyond a reasonable doubt, there lies bur at the confluence of the Big Auglaize and Little Auglaize Rivers a Revolutionary soldier, Captain Brown, who was placed in command of the Fort at this location, named Fort Brown, in honor of its commander. A little town was platted by Miller Arrowsmith, in 1835 and was known as Ft Brown, I believe it was the first PO in Brown Twp, Paulding Co. Plat in the recorder's office. James Bobenmeyer, Oakwood, O, has a clear mind running back many yrs. He remembers old portions of the Ft. He says that not only Capt Brown, but two other soldiers possibly Rev. were bur there. He stated that the 3 graves were in evidence quite plainly until a granary covered the spot. Fur infor Albert Blakeslee, Treasurer of Paulding Co. 1928. Sent in by Ft Defiance Chap. Filed by State Chairman Jane Dailey, but not verified by her.

BROWN, BENJAMIN, CAPT., (Athens Co.)

Feb 1775 joined a regt of Minute Men; May, commissioned a Lt Col Prescott, Mass Line; June in battle of Bunker Hill; Jan 1777 Commissioned Capt 8th Regt Mass Line. A Lt and Capt. Br Oct 17, 1745, Leicester, Mass. Parents: Capt John Brown. Mar Jane or Jean Thomas, 1772, in Mass. (d June 14, 1840.) Children: Benjamin, Loring, Sally, William, Samuel, Joseph, John, Apphia, Patience, Hannah, Archibald, Green. D Oct 1, 1821, Athens, O. Bur W State St. east side of main walk. MI: "In Memory of Capt Benj Brown who died Oct 1st, 1821 in the 76 year of his age." GM by descendants; Brown stone. About 1789 he removed to Washington Co, N. Y. thence to Marietta, O, in 1797; 1799 to Ames Twp, Athens Co.; in 1817 he went to live with his son John in Athens." He was one of the prominent citizens of Ames Twp holding various township offices." In 1818 he applied for a pens. His claim was allowed. Ref: Walker's Hist of Athens Co.; Early Pioneers of Oho. S. P. Hildreth. Fur infor Nabby Lee Ames Chap.

BROWN, DANIEL JR., (Highland Co.)

Pvt Capt James Curtiss Company, Col James Cargills Regt. Br 1750 Kingstown, N. H. Mar Margaret Elliott. D 1818, Brush Creek, O. Ref: 24068 and 60540. Vol 61, p 177 D. A. R. Lin. p 25, Vol 25, D. A. R. Lin.

BROWN, EZEKIAL, (Delaware Co.)

Pvt under Col James Potter, Capt Cocksey Long, Pa Tr. Bur Sunbury. Pensioned. Fur infor Delaware Chap.

BROWN, FREDERICK, (Clark Co.)

Br Oct 29, 1753, Va. Children: Roland. D Jan 19, 1829. Bur Green Lawn, South Charleston, O. Grave not platted. MI: "Dingess. Frederick Brown." GM by Society S. A. R. Metal marker about 1906. Was one of the early settlers of Madison Twp but family has scattered and infor meagre. Farmer. Fur infor Lieutenant Byrd Chaps.

BROWN, GEER, (Brown Co.)

Br Va. Children: Lettie, Ann. D Franklin Twp, Brown Co, O. Bur Abbott Cem on Straight Creek. Came to Franklin Twp with Joseph Abbott after the Rev where they settled on 1000 acres of land, each taking half. (It may have been a grant or warrant). Hist of Brown Co pp 539 and 540. Fur infor Taliaferro and Lieutenant Byrd Chaps.

BROWN, HENRY, (Summit Co.)

"Served during entire seven years struggle", as told on inscription on marker. Br 1733. D Boston Twp, Ohio, Oct 17, 1837, aged 104 yrs. Bur in Cem at that place. Fur infor Cuyahoga-Portage Chap.

BROWN, HENRY JR., (Ashtabula Co.)

Served in NY Regt until after battle of Long Island. Corp in Capt Roe's Company and was at Valley Forge in 1777-1778. Br 1738. Oyster Pond, LI. Parents: Henry Brown, Sr. and Mary Paine Brown. Mar: Sarah Cobb (third wife). Children: David, Mary, Hepsibah, Mehitable, Bula, Henry, Easter, Elijah. D Jan 20, 1831. Bur Dodgeville Cem, New Lyme, O. west gate, about middle of eastern part of cem. GM by family, brown slate stone slab. Came to Ohio with his son in 1821. Fur infor Luther Reeve Chap.

BROWN, ISAAC, (Columbia Co.)

Pensioned in Columbiana Co, O for serv as Pvt Va Continental Line. Br 1756, Va. Mar Hester Williams, (1756-1840). D 1825, Ohio. Natl No 790033, Vol 80. D. A. R. Lin.

BROWN, JOHN, (Washington Co.)

Was at Lexington Alarm and Sgt at Bunker Hill, where wounded. Br 1734, Leicester, Mass. Mar Rebecca Baldwin 1757. D 1821. Bur in Cem on Schantz farm about 3 miles above Lowell on Muskingum River. MI: "He was a Revolutionary Soldier." GM by Marietta Chap with Revolutionary Marker in 1922. Ref: Natl No 77677, Vol. 78 D. A. R. Lin. Fur infor Marietta Chap.

BROWN, JOHN JR., (Scioto Co.)

Maj. Br Oct 30, 1760. Harrisburg, Pa. Parents: Adley Brown and Hannah Blue. Mar Charity Johnson. D Lucasville. Bur Lucasville Cem Scioto Trail. Lived on a farm. Market master, Justice of Peace. Ref: Mrs. Rardin, Miss Helen Rardin, 1206 Gallia St, Portsmouth. Fur infor Joseph Spencer Chap.

BROWN, NICHOLAS, (Licking Co.)

Ensign in Capt Heister's Company, Berks Co, Pa, Bn. Br 1756, Frederick Co, Md. D 1858 near Kirkersville, O. Natl No 83023, Vol 84. D. A. R. Lin.

BROWN, OLIVER, (Lake Co.)

Enl May 26, 1777; in serv until Nov 22, 1780. In battles of Brandywine and Germantown and endured the hardships of Valley Forge. Br 1760 at Stonington Point, Conn. Parents: Zebulon Brown. Mar Mrs Gracie Welch in 1780. Children: Oliver, Hosea, Dauphin, Lewis, Hannah (Bliss), Nabby (Searls) and Patience (Holcomb). D 1845. Bur Concord, Lake Co, O. GM by New Connecticut Chap. Fur infor New Connecticut Chap.

BROWN, PHINEAS, (Fulton Co.)

Bur Seward Cem, Amboy Twp, Fulton Co, O. Fur infor Wauseon Chap.

BROWN, SAMUEL, (Athens Co.)

Enl at Boston, Mass. Pvt. Br 1758, Leicester, Mass. Parents: John Brown & Elizabeth (1st wife and mother of all his children). Mar Lydia Thayer. Children: Samuel B., William F., Phoebe, Lydia, Betsey, Harriet, John. D Jan 15, 1841. Bern Twp, Athens Co. Bur West Union Cem Athens, O. Sec 4, Lot 30-31-48-49. Interment fr Bern Twp. MI: "Samuel Brown was born in Leicester, Mass. D Jan 16, 1841. Aged 82 yrs, 7 mos, 14 days. Foot stone Samuel Brown 1758-1841. GM by family of son John. Inscription on tall Scotch granite shaft. A family monument. Came to Northwest Territory in 1797. Lived in Washington, then Athens Co, O. Farmer. He received a pens. Ref: Bur of Pensions. Walker's History of Athens Co. Natl No. 79038, Vol 80. D. A. R. Fur infor Nabby Lee Ames Chap.

BROWN, SAMUEL, (Summit Co.)

Enl Continental Army Apr 1, 1778 at South Brimfield, Mass. Served several enlmts; disch Nov 1782. 1st Infantry under Capt Carpenter; then substituted for his father, Samuel Brown Sr in Capt Shaw's Company, Col Porter's Regt in Mch 1779. Member Capt Ballard's Company (First), Col Alden's Seventh Mass Regt. After he was killed, Col Brook took command. Br June 21, 1763, Pomfret, Windham Co, Conn. D 1845 while a resident of Springfield Twp. Bur cem Springfield Center, O. by second wife. 1781 joined tr at Union, Conn under Ensign Strong and

Col Mead. In fall of that year, joined Capt Solomon Wales Company, Col McClannahan's Regt at Union. From Mch 1 to Nov 1782 was under Capt Bowdwoin's Company. Fur infor Cuyahoga-Portage Chap.

BROWN, SAMUEL, (Belmont Co.)

Minute man and Lt under Capt Jas Hubbard in Arnold's Expedition to Quebec. Br 1749, Boston, Mass. D 1828 St Clairsville, O. Mar Mary Newkirk (see 63397) D. A. R. Ref: Natl No 29741, p 266, Vol 30. D. A. R. Lin.

BROWN, THOMAS, (Clermont Co.)

Pvt in Va Continental Line. Br 1730 Cardiganshire, Wales. Mar Mary Ball 1754 (see 74012 D. A. R.) D 1818, Bethel, O. Ref: Natl No 90613, Vol 91, p 196, and Natl No 27376, p 139, Vol 28, D. A. R. Lin.

BROWN, WHITE, (Ross Co.)

Served from Delaware. Br Mch 23, 1749. D Mch 25, 1842, aged 93 yrs. Bur Browns Chapel, Deerfield Twp. Ref: D. A. R. member, Mrs Wm Higley, Chillicothe. Fur infor Nathaniel Massie Chap.

BROWN, WILLIAM, (Darke Co.)

Served from Pa. Bur Old Cem at Greenville. Fur infor Ft Greenville Chap.

BROWN, WILLIAM, (Hamilton Co.)

Enl 1779 for the war, Capt Sam'l Comstock's Company Continental Line. Was standard bearer of the "Forlorn Hope" at Stony Point, 1870. Br 1759, Stamford, Conn. Mar Ruth Hanford. D 1808, Hamilton Co. Bur Hamilton Co. Ref: S. A. R. Natl No 13770; p 288, Vol 14. D. A. R. Lin. Fur infor Cincinnati Chap.

BROWN, WILLIAM, (Hamilton Co.)

Br 1737, New Jersey. D 1831. Ref: S. A. R. Fur infor Cincinnati Chap.

BROWN, WILLIAM, (Hancock Co.)

Pa Bedford Co. Pvt. Served 8 mos. Col Robert Cluggage, Capt Thomas, assisted to erect Lead Mine Fort. Br 1758. Mar Ruth Lane. D Apr 30, 1853. Bur Lee Cem, Amanda Twp, Hancock Co. GM by Fort Findlay Chap. Fur infor Fort Findlay Chap.

BROWSER, HENDRICK, (Adams Co.)

Pvt with NY Tr at age twenty. D Adams Co. Ref: Natl No 25231, p 82, Vol 26, D. A. R. Lin.

BRUEN, JABEZ, (Hamilton Co.)

Pvt Morris Co Mil NJ. Br 1750, Newark, N. J. D 1841, Hamilton Co, O. Ref: S. A. R. See Natl No 30134, Vol 31, p 49, D. A .R. Lin. Fur infor Cincinnati Chap.

BRYAN, ELIJAH, (Licking Co.)

Enl Apr 25, 1777, disch June 8, 1783. Br Sept 6, 1760, North Milford, Conn. D Jan 12, 1844, Granville, O. Bur Maple Grove. GM by Granville Chap in 1901. For the 6 yrs serv, he was honored by Gen Washington with a Badge of Merit. Ref: Natl No 87137, Vol 88, p 40, D. A. R. Lin. Fur infor Hetuck Chap.

BRYANT, ROSS, (Fayette Co.)

Bur Washington C. H. Cem Fayette Co, Lot 30, Sec 9. Fur infor Washington C. H. Chap.

BRYSON, JAMES, (Hamilton Co.)

Pvt in Cumberland Co. See "Rangers on the Frontier" p 281. D about 1819 at Cincinnati. Family removed to Indiana near Dunlapville, Union Co. Fur infor Cincinnati Chap.

BRYSON, SAUL, (Mahoning Co.)

1st Lt Mch 20, 1777. Continental Line. 234 wounded, Germantown. One son and three dau, maybe more. Bur Mahoning Co. Merchant. Owned 200 acres of land in 1875 in Cumberland Co. Ref: Pa Archives, Vol XX, p 712 Census,-152. Pa Archives, Vol III, p 775. Fur infor Mahoning Chap.

BUCHANAN, ALEXANDER, (Clermont Co.)

Br North of Ireland. Mar Margaret ——— in Washington Co, Pa. (She d 1814.) Children: Alexander (scout under Wayne). William, James, John, Andrew, Jane, Martha. D Washington Twp. Clermont Co O. 1803. Bur Calvary Cem. Came to America 1764; was 1st cousin of the father of President Jas. Buchanan; in 1792 came to Limestone, Ky. and in 1799 to Clermont Co. Abstract of Wills of Washington & Westmoreland Cos, Pa. Gen Magazine Grieve. Ref: A. S. Abbott, Bethel, O. Fur infor Cincinnati Chap.

BUCHANAN, GILBERT, (Mahoning Co.)

Pvt 3rd class Capt Robert's Company, Lancaster Co Mil. He furnished a substitute (James Carter in 1871, for which he received 200 acres of land. (Pa Archives Series 5, Vol VII, pp 578 and 599). Children: Walter, Isaac, James, John, (mar Rebecca Applegate). Came to Lowellville with his family in 1803. Pa Census of 1790 p 139 gives wife, 2 sons, 2 daus Britain Twp Lancaster Co, Pa. Ref: Trumbull and Mahoning Hist Vol II, pp 54, 60, Sanderson's p 630. Fur infor Mahoning Chap.

BUCK, —————, (Morrow Co.)

Bur Old Cem called Asbury, in Lincoln Twp north of Fulton. Fur infor Mt Gilead Chap.

BUCK, WILLIAM JR., (Mahoning Co.)

Pvt. Conn Men of the Rev. p 264. Bur Poland, O. Settled in Poland in 1800 or 1801. Trumbull and Mahoning Co History, Vol 11, p 59. Fur infor Mahoning Chap.

BUCKINGHAM, EBENEZER, (Athens Co.)

Was a pvt soldier in the 12th Regt of New Volunteers under Col Jacobus Con Schoonhaven, serving from 1779 to the end of the war. Br Nov 1, 1748, Greenfield, Conn. Parents: Stephen Buckingham (br 1703,) Elizabeth Sherwood (br 1708.) Mar Esther Bradley Oct 23, 1770. Children: Ebenezer, Rachel, Stephen, Ebenezer 2nd, Sarah, Esther, Brandley, Milton, Elizabeth, Alvah, John, Matilda, Parnelia. D—according to stone—Oct 24, 1824 Carthage Twp, Athens Co. Bur Cooley Burying Grounds Athens Co, Carthage Twp. Also called Glazier and Old Brick. MI: "Ebenezer Buckingham, who departed this life Oct 14 A. D. 1824 in the 76th year of age. He died at his residence in peace and in full faith and assurance of the Gospel of our Lord and Saviour Jesus Christ. Blessed are the dead who die in the lord." GM by his family. About 1779 he removed to N. Y. state, thence to Ohio arriving in the spring of 1800. Was living at the mouth of the Hockhocking in 1802, but soon removed to Carthage Twp where he died. Farmer. Ref: Buckingham family p18-19. Fur infor Nabby Lee Ames Chap.

BUCKINGHAM, LEVI, (Hamilton Co.)

New York p 162, Orange Co. Children: William L, Isaac, Elizabeth, Jane, Maria, Lydia H. D Hamilton Co. Bur Remington Cem. Settled farm. (Grieves Hist p 284). Was at Covalt's Sta when Abel Covalt was killed by Indians (pp 62, 63, Jones Hist Cincinnati O). Name on tax list 1808 Sycamore and Symmes Twp. Fur infor Cincinnati Chap.

BUCKLES, WILLIAM SR., (Greene Co.)

Br Mch 25, 1766. D Mch 29, 1846, aged 79 yrs. Bur Middle Baptist Cem near Bellbrook, Sugarcreek Twp, O. Sugarcreek, 1803, Soldier of 1812, also. Ref: Robinson's Hist. of Greene Co. Fur infor Catherine Greene Chap.

BUEL, JOHN, Maj., (Coshocton Co.)

Bur Adams Twp. Ref: Hist of Co. Fur infor Coshocton Chap.

BUELL, EPHRAIM, (Hamilton Co.)

Br 1741, Conn. D 1821. Ref: S. A. R. Fur infor Cincinnati Chap.

BUFFINGTON, DAVID, (Fairfield Co.)

Bur New Salem Cem. Fur infor Elizabeth Sherman Reese Chap.

BUGH, PETER, (Perry Co.)

Pvt, Capt Jacob Ring's Company of Col Mathias Glough's Bn Light Inf in Lancaster Co, Pa. Sept 9, 1776; belonged to "Flying Camp" at battles of Kings Bridge and Long Island. Br Dec 26, 1753, Whautensburg, Germany. Parents: Christian Bugh. Mar Catherine Haverstic, in Germany. Children Peter 2nd, Charlette Bugh Chidister. D Oct 11, 1819, Somerset. Bur New Reading Cem, Perry Co. (formerly Fairfield Co.) GM by Elizabeth Sherman Reese Chapter, a bronze marker Oct 14, 1927. Ref: Mary E. Stalter Peters, Lancaster, O. Also Natl No 26737, Vol 27, p 272, and Natl No 49414, Vol 50, p 182, D. A. R. Lin. Fur infor Elizabeth Sherman Reese Chap.

BUKER, ISRAEL, (Muskingum Co.)

Enl as Pvt under Capt Allen, 23rd Regt of Continental Tr; enl again under Capt Noah Allen, 13th Regt, as Pvt and Corp; and enl again as Sgt under Capt Abram Watson. Hon disch signed by Washington. Br Apr 17, 1756, Bridgewater, Plymouth Co, Mass. Mar Sarah Black, 3rd wife. D Nov 5, 1848, Otsego, O. Bur in Town Cem. Ref: Natl No 48257, Vol 49, p 121, D. A. R. Lin. Fur infor Muskingum Chap.

BULL, THOMAS JR., (Franklin Co.)

Pvt in Capt Silas Goodrich Company Mil, Col Allin's Regt. Br Nov 17, 1762, Manchester, Vt. D Oct 16, 1823 Clintonville. Bur Union Cem. MI: "Thomas Bull, Jr Born Nov. 17, 1762 died Oct. 16, 1823." GM by Revolutionary Grace Committee with bronze marker May 30, 1912. Moved from Manchester to Ohio and settled in Franklin Co in 1814 on the present site of Clintonville. Fur infor Columbus Chap.

BULL, WILLIAM SR. (Greene Co.)

Br 1740, Va. D Oct 11, 1811. Bur Massie's Creek (Stevenson). Xenia, 1803. Ref: Robinson's History of Greene Co. Fur infor Catherine Greene Chap.

BUNTIAN, WILLIAM, (Highland Co.)

Bur Fall Creek Cem. Fur infor Waw-Wil-a-Way Chap.

BUNTON, RAMOTH, (Clermont Co.)

Came fr Va to Cincinnati about 1790, and thence to Williamsburg, Clermont Co in 1796. Children: James, Mary, Hattie. Ref: A. S. Abbott, Bethel, O. Fur infor Cincinnati Chap.

BURDICK, JOHN, (Union Co.)

Bur Dover Cem, Dover Twp. Ref: Union Co History. Col W. L. Curry. Fur infor Hannah Emerson Dustin Chap.

BURGER, NICHOLAS, (Columbiana Co.)

Corp in Capt George Drines' Company, Lt Stephen Balliet's Regt, Northampton Co, Pa Mil. Br Oct 20, 1736, Switzerland. Mar Ann Maria in 1761. Children: Theresa, Daniel and Jacob. D Sept 20, 1828, Columbiana Co, O. Bur St. Jacob's Cem, north of Lisbon, O. GM Jane Bain Chap with metal marker in July, 1921. Fur infor Jane Bain Chap.

BURGIS, JOHN, (Champaign Co.)

Br 1754 in Va. D 1840. Bur Mt. Tabor Cem. Fur infor Urbana Chap.

BURGETT, VALENTINE, (Brown Co.)

Bur Pisgah Ridge. Fur infor Ripley Chap.

BURK, SYLVANUS, (Cuyahoga Co.)

Served 1777-78 in Capt Luke Day's Company, Col Alden's Regt of Mass Infantry. Pens granted 1818. Br 1763. Mar Achsa Webster. D 1825, Cleveland, O. Ref: Natl No 82827, Vol 83, D. A. R. Lin.

BURKE, JOSEPH, (Cuyahoga Co.)

Drum Maj, Mass Tr. Also in War of 1812. Bur Harvard Grove Cem, Lansing Ave & East 57th St. GM by Western Reserve Chap. Fur infor Western Reserve Chap.

BURKE, SYLVANUS, (Cuyahoga Co.)

Drummer Mass Tr. Br 1747. D 1835. Bur Harvard Grove Cem, Lansing Ave and East 57th St. GM Western Reserve Chap. Fur infor Western Reserve Chap.

BURKHARDT, JOHN, (Sandusky Co.)

Enl in Von Heer's Light Dragoons or Troop Marchause in 1778. Later reenlisted at Reading, Pa, and was a member of Washington's Life Guard through the war. Was in the Battle of Yorktown. Br in Switzerland; came to America 1753 or 1754. D 1842, aged 93 yrs; (br 1749?). Bur Hessville Cem, Washington Twp, Sandusky Co, O. MI: "A member of Washington's Life Guard." GM by L. M. Kelley, Commissioner. After surrender of Cornwallis, at Yorktown, came home to Reading, Pa, and was mar. He was twice mar. His wives were sisters. His family lived at Reading Pa, until about 1795, then they moved to Lancaster, Pa. Later to Perry Co, O. Name now spelled John Burkett. Moved to Sandusky, O. Ref: Natl No 18902, p 325, Vol 19, D. A. R. Lin. Fur infor Col. George Croghan Chap.

BURLINGAME, CHRISTOPHER, (Washington Co.)

Pvt. He was with Washington's Army at the time of crossing the Delaware at Trenton, Dec 1777. Br 1753, Providence, R I. Mar Susannah Putnam in 1787. Children: Susannah, Persis Maria, Martha, Elizabeth Putnam, Lucy, Sarah, Edwin, Rufus Putnam, John Bennet, Christopher, William. D July 12, 1841, at Harmar. Bur Harmar Cem across the Muskingum. MI: "Christopher Burlingame 1753-1841." GM Marietta Chapter with Revolutionary marker in 1906. At the close of apprenticeship as hatter, he embarked on a Privateer bound for the West Indies. Taken prisoner, finally returned to U. S. and then enl in the Revolutionary army proper. Hatter, seaman and farmer. Ref: Yr Bk of Ohio Society, 1897. Fur infor Marietta Chap.

BURNETT, DAVID, (Trumbull Co.)

Bur Hubbard, O. Ref: Name taken from the list of Revolutionary soldiers, Baldwin Library, Youngstown, O. Fur infor Mary Chesney Chap.

BURNETT, EDMUND, (Trumbull Co.)

Minute Man and Pvt, NJ Mil. Br Morris Co, N. J. 1756. Mar Sarah Smith. D Hubbard, 1840. Bur Old Cem at Hubbard. MI: All that is left of the inscription is "In memory of Edmund Burnett." Pen granted Oct 3, 1832. Ref: Natl No 72640, p 226, Vol 73, D. A. R. Lin. Fur infor Mary Chesney Chap.

BURNHAM, JEDEDIAH, DR. (Trumbull Co.)

Surgeon. Br 1755, Norwich, Conn. Mar Lydia Kent (d Dec 11, 1826). D Mch 11, 1840. Bur Old Cem, Kinsman. Grave in good condition. Fur infor Mary Chesney Chap.

BURRELL, NATHANIEL, (Athens Co.)

Pvt Capt Lemont, Col J. Allen, Oct to Dec 1777; in Capt Berry's Company, Col Gerrish Regt; Pvt-Capt Lemont; Maj Lithgow's detachment Sept 15 to Nov 1, 1779; Fifer, Capt Lemont May to Dec 1781. Br Apr 21, 1761, Abington, Mass. Parents not known to us, but a descendant of Count Burrelle who owned estates in France. Mar Rachel Springer, soon after close of Revolutionary War. Children: Nancy, Harriet R, Frances P, Nathaniel, Levi P, Almond H. D Oct 14, 1842, Athens, O. Bur West State St. Athens, O. West side near the fence. MI: "Nathaniel Burrell, born at Abington, Mass, May 21, 1761, died Oct 14, 1842. He served four terms of enlistment in the Revolutionary Army." GM first by youngest son, Almond H, sandstone, and fell to pieces; second, by descendent Almond Rochester Burrell, New Lexington, O. Date of marking; 1st unknown; 2nd Sept 19, 1922. When he first offered to enl, being but 4 ft. 4 in. tall he was refused. He put "rags" in his boots till his head touched the peg at 4 ft 4 in. He was accepted. Farming; received a grant of land. He came to Ohio in 1838 or 39 to live with his son, Almond H. the youngest. Ref: Mass Soldiers and Sailors in the Rev. Fur infor Nabby Lee Ames Chap.

BURROWS, JEREMIAH, (Hamilton Co.)

Br 1752, Maryland. D 1836. Ref: S.A.R. Yr Bk, 1898, has "Burroughs, Jeremiah came to Mill Creek Twp, Hamilton Co, O. 1827. Grave not located. Br 1752. D 1832". Fur infor Cincinnati Chap.

BURT, AARON, (Lorain Co.)

In Grafton Cem is a stone for "Hannah Burt, his wife, died Feb 17, 1850, age 90 yrs". It is reported Aaron lies beside his wife. At age of 82 yrs was drawing pens in Grafton Twp, Lorain Co. Fur infor Elyria Chap.

BURT, BENJAMIN, (Scioto Co.)

Artificer, Col Badwin, Capt Thomas Ralton, serv rendered 3 yrs. Capt Pete Mills. Children: Benjamin, Samuel Munsell, Mehitable. D 1849, Wheelersburg. Bur A&P Highway, Wheelersburg Cem. GM by descendants, old time stone. D.A.R. Joseph Spencer about 15 yrs ago. Disch at West Point, N. Y., 1782, a resident of N. J. Applied for pens, granted. Ref: Mrs. Ella P. Chase, 5838 Farney Ave, Scioto Station, Portsmouth, O. Fur infor Joseph Spencer Chap.

BUSH, LEONARD, (Fayette Co.)

Pvt in Capt John Harris Rangers Va. Br Mch 5, 1756, Pendleton Co, Va. Mar Catherine Stingley. Children: Catherine, Rachel, Mollie, Susan, Sarah, Elizabeth, Jemima, Mary, Rebecca, Amy, Jacob, Abraham, Leonard, and Daniel. D July 6, 1832, Fayette Co. Bur Bush Cem, Fayette Co in old part, unplatted. MI: "Leonard Bush, aged —". GM by family in 1832. Farmer. Ref: Pensioner. Fur infor Washington C. H. Chap.

BUSH, MICHAEL, (Ross Co.)

Pvt from Hardy Co, Va. Br Frederick Co, Va. Jan 10, 1750. Mar Magdalene — (br 1752 d 1821.) D Frankfort, O. Aug 10, 1825. Bur near Austin, Concord Twp, Ross Co, O. .Fur infor Nathaniel Massie Chap.

BUSHNELL, ALEXANDER, (Trumbull Co.)

Sgt 1776 under Capt Benj Hutchins and as Ensign, 1780, under Capt Benj Mills. Br 1739, Lyme, Conn. Mar Chloe Waite, 1st wife. D Mch 1818, age 77, at Hartford. Grave marked. Wife's tombstone not readable. Ref: Natl No 38428, Vol 39, p 175, D. A. R. Lin. Fur infor Mary Chesney Chap.

BUSHNELL, DANIEL, (Trumbull Co.)

Br 1764. Mar Rebeckah, (who died July 7, 1809, age 44 yrs.) D Aug 12, 1842, at Hartford. Bur Center of Hartford. MI: "The law produced precepts ten and then desolved in Grace. This vine produced as many buds, and then returned to rest." Will probated Nov. 1842. Fur infor Mary Chesney Chap.

BUSHNELL, JASON, (Hamilton Co.)

Br 1763, Conn. D 1848. Ref: S. A. R. Fur infor Cincinnati Chap.

BUSHNELL, THOMAS, (Trumbull Co.)

Br 1762. Mar Rebecca, (d Jan 12, 1842, age 76 yrs.) D Apr 10, 1817 Hartford. Bur Center of Hartford. Emigrated from Hartland, Conn, in 1804. Fur infor Mary Chesney Chap.

BUSHONG, JOSEPH, (Carroll Co.)

"A soldier of the war"—history of Carroll Co. p 360 Vol 1. Howe's Hist Coll O. Bur Carrollton, Carrol Co, O. Fur infor Jane Dailey, State Chairman.

BUTLER, BENJAMIN, (Columbiana Co.)

Bur Center of Goshen, Friends Cem. Lived in Butler Twp, Columbiana Co. Fur infor Bethia Southwick Chap.

BUTLER, BENJAMIN, (Mahoning Co.)

Pvt in Chester Co, 1778. Name appears in the U. S. Mil. Mar Hannah. Children: Ellen, Lawrence, Hannah, John, Anna, Sarah, Meribah. D 1828. Came from Philadelphia in 1811 to Goshen Twp. He was a member of the Society of Friends, was appointed on an Executive Court of Central Indiana Superintendency of the U. S. Farmer. Ref: Pa Archives, Series 3, Vol 12, p 122: Series 2, Vol 14, p 11. Trumbull and Mahoning Co. History, Vol. 2, p 437. Fur infor Mahoning Chap.

BUTLER, EBENEZER, JR.

Served in Light Dragoons. Br 1761, Harwinton, Conn. Mar Rebecca Davis. D 1829, in Ohio. First white settler, Pompey, N. Y. Came to Ohio in 1802 where he died. Natl No 42494, Vol 43, p 189. D. A. R. Lin.

BUTLER, GEN. RICHARD, (Butler Co.)

Distinguished officer of Rev. He fell in St. Clair's defeat Nov 4, 1791. Br Ireland; coming to America with his brothers, before 1760. Name appears on memorial tablet at Hamilton, Butler Co, O. named for him. Ref: See Ohio Historical Collection by Howe, p 342, Vol 1, Non resident of Butler Co. Fur infor John Reiley Chap.

BUTLER, STEPHEN, (Summit Co.)

1776, member of Conn Tr under Col Matthew Talcott and Samuel Selden, Capt John Cochran, and Elisha Chapman, served as Pvt, Corp & Sgt; was in battle of White Plains, Rhode Island, Jamestown, and taking of Cornwallis. In Capt John Hart's Company, Col Samuel Webb's Regt. 1777-1781; served as Sgt—ranked as Corp in company drafted from Third Conn Regt to serve at the southward under command of Marquis de Lafayette in 1781. Br Dec 10, 1758, Saybrook, Conn. D 1882 aged 64 yrs. So stone states. Bur Cem at Stow, where he was a pioneer. Presbyterian of the old school, a deacon; organized a class in this New Conn and conducted services. Fur infor Cuyahoga-Portage Chap.

BUTLER, THOMAS, MAJ. (Butler Co.)

Name appears on the tablet in the Soldiers and Sailors monument at Hamilton, and supposed to be a soldier of the Rev buried in Butler Co. Fur infor John Reily Chap.

BUTLER, ZEBULON, (Co not stated.)

Commanded forces at Wyoming 1778 and served to close of War. Original member of Cincinnati. Br 1731. D 1795. Tho not stated think possibly Hamilton or Butler Co. where the Cincinnati was organized. Ref: Natl No 20038 p 15, Vol. 21, D. A. R. Lin.

BYARD, GEORGE, (Clinton Co.)

Bur Mt Pleasant Cem. Fur infor George Clinton Chap.

BYENS, JOHN, (Miami Co.)

Bur McKendree Chapel, 4 miles east of Troy, O. GM Miami Chapter with bronze marker. Fur infor Miami Chap.

BYRAM, EDWARD, (Highland Co.)

Pvt Capt Stephen Bett's Company Conn Mil 1777. He removed to Pa where in 1779 he and dau Abigail were imprisoned by Indians at Ft Niagara 21 mos. Released to lead exchange prisoners to Amer Army. Br Bridgewater, Conn. 1742. Mar Phoebe Ann Coe. Children: Edward, Abigail. D Greenfield, O. 1824. Bur Rocky Spring Cem. GM by Juliana White Chap, 1924. Farmer. Will of Edward Byram on record in Highland Co. courts. Ref: Natl No 26301, Vol. 27, p 109 D. A. R. Lin. Fur infor Waw-Wil-a-Way and Juliana White Chaps.

BYRNS, LARRY, (LAWRENCE?) (Clermont Co.)

No doubt is "Lawrence Byrn," Pvt. Pa Continental Line. Pensioned Sept 6, 1719, allowance $96. Pvt. Capt Alex Grayton's Company 3rd Bn Pa Line, Col John Shay, again Capt Christy's Company, Col Thos Craig's Regt. In many battles. Imprisoned at Germantown; escaped. Br 1756. Mar Elizabeth, 1788 (about) in Philadelphia, Pa. D 1838, Cincinnati, O. Children: William K, George S. (br 1805). Philip (br 1791), Nancy (mar David Fisher,) Margaret (mar Jas. Hobbs), Sarah (br 1803 mar Edward Goudy), and John. D July 15, 1832, aged 78 yrs. Clermont Co. Bur Point Pleasant (1820 is given by Abbott). Came to Monroe Twp in 1797; settled at mouth of Big Indian Creek. Came to Pt Pleasant, Clermont Co about 1800. Ref: Natl No 87133 Vol. 88, p 39, D. A. R. Lin. A. S. Abbott, Bethel, O. and Pension R 1576. Fur inform Cincinnati Chap.

BYXBE, MOSES, (Delaware Co.)

Pvt in Col John Ashley's Regt, Capt Morton's Mass Tr. Bur Oak Grove Cem. Pensioned. Fur infor Delaware & Western Reserve Chaps.

CABLE, PHILIP, CAPT. (Jefferson Co.)

Br 1754. D 1812. Bur Union Cem, Steubenville, O. GM by D. A. R. with official marker Steubenville Chap. Fur infor Steubenville Chap.

CAHALL, JAMES, (Brown Co.)

Served through the Revolutionary War to its close and witnessed the surrender of Lord Cornwallis. Children: James, Thomas, Solomon. D Lewis Twp, Brown Co, said to be 105 yrs. Bur Shinkle Ridge. GM by Tombstone. The day he attained his one hundredth year he took a sickle in the field, leading his men in the work. Ref: Brown Co. Hist. p 8, A. P. Cahall. Fur infor Taliaferro Chap.

CAHOON, WILLIAM, (Lake Co.)

Oct 11, 1781 under Capt Samuel Sloan, Col Asa Barnes' Regt from Berkshire Co. He marched by order of Gen Stark to Saratoga on an alarm. Br 1765. D Oct 1, 1828, Kirtland, Lake Co, O. Bur Kirtland, O. GM by New Connecticut Chap. Fur infor New Connecticut Chap.

CAIN, HUGH, (Mahoning Co.)

Pvt in the Revolutionary War. Bur Poland Twp, Mahoning Co. (Reported by Henry Baldwin, former Regent of Ohio S. A. R.) Ref: Pa Archives, 3 Series, Vol 13, p 30. Fur infor Mahoning Chap.

CALDWELL, MATTHEW, (Miami Co.)

Ensign in Pa Tr. Br 1757, Ireland. Mar Mary Pinkerton. D 1810 Miami Co, O. Ref: Natl No 64064, p 24, Vol 65, D. A. R. Lin.

CALDWELL, ROBERT, (Hamilton Co.)

Pvt. 14th Regt Col Knicbacke's, p 125 on State Treas Pay Roll. Enl Men N Y. See N Y in Revolutionary War. Robert Caldwell contributed large amounts toward finances for war. Br 1720, Scotland, Hamilton Co. Children: Robert Jr., James, Samuel. D 1802. Bur west of Carthage, Hamilton Co in farm burial grounds, stone standing. Robert Caldwell was a "Pioneer" at Griffins Station, now Carthage, Hamilton Co. In 1790 he bought land; deed signed by Symmes. Built a large grist and saw mill. Fur infor Cincinnati Chap.

CALDWELL, ROBERT, (Noble Co.)

Teamster with Pa Tr. Bur Olive Cem, Caldwell. Grave marked. Came to land where Caldwell now is, 1809. Fur infor Mrs. L. B. Frazier, Caldwell, O.

CALDWELL, ROBERT, (Trumbull Co.)

Ranger, Washington Co 1778-1783 Pa Mil. Pvt. Pensioned July 20, 1823. Br 1762. D June 29, 1833. Bur Pricetown, Newton Twp. MI: "Robert Caldwell, died June 29, 1833, age 71 yrs. Farmer. Ref: Pa Archives, Series 3, Vol 23, p 592, and "Soldiers Pensioned and Bur in Trumbull Co." Fur infor Mahoning & Mary Chesney Chaps.

CALDWELL, WILLIAM, (Butler Co.)

Br Larue, Ireland, May 18, 1763. D Butler Co, Mch 1849. Bur Oxford Cem, Oxford, O. Ref: Natl No. 27835, Vol 28, p 305. Fur infor John Reily Chap.

CALHOUN, JOHN, (Muskingum Co.)

One of body guard of Geo Washington, p 573 Muskingum Co Hist, says served from Mass. D aged full 113 yrs. Bur Fairview Church Graveyard. Ref from unquestionable source to the Chap. Fur infor Muskingum Chap.

CALHOUN, SAMUEL, (Jackson Co.)

Bur near Davisville, Jackson Co. Fur infor Capt John James Chap.

CALHOUN, SAMUEL, (Mahoning Co.)

Pvt. Was pensioned. Br 1753. Children: Andrew, Samuel, Matthew, Nancy, Betsey, Isabella, Sally, Anna, Martha, Esther. D 1841. Resided in Youngstown in 1801, moved to Green Twp and settled in Jackson in 1803. Farmer. Ref: Mahoning and Trumbull Co Hist, Vol 2, p 147. Census of pensions 1841, p 179. Fur infor Mahoning Chap.

CALKINS, JOHN PRENTISS, (Lorain Co.)

Served at Lexington Alarm and siege of Boston. Br New London, Conn, 1753. D Avon, O 1836. Ref: Natl No 14801, p 300, Vol 15, D. A. R. Lin.

CALL, JOSEPH, (Lake Co.)

Served numerous calls in the Vermont Mil. Was in Zebulon Lyon's Company to guard the committee of safety to Windsor and Springfield, Vt. Children: Rufus Call, in War of 1812. Bur South Ridge Cem. West Madison, O. GM New Connecticut Chap. Removed from Vermont to Ohio in 1815. Ref: Natl No 31055, p 22, Vol 32 and Natl No 95142, Vol 96, p 48, D. A. R. Lin. Fur infor New Connecticut Chap.

CALLAHAN, JEREMIAH, (Mahoning Co.)

Pvt. Capt James Poe's Company Cumberland Co. Mil Ranger, Washington Co Mil. Br 1768. D 1865. Bur Greenford, O. Ref: Mentioned Hist Trumbull & Mahoning Co, Vol 2 p 197; Pa Archives Series 5, Vol 6, p 583. Fur infor Mahoning Chap.

FORT GOWER, THE SECOND PLACE OF IMPORTANCE THAT WAS MARKED BY D. A. R., NOVEMBER 10, 1923, IS LOCATED AT THE CONFLUENCE OF THE HOCKING AND OHIO RIVERS AT HOCKINGPORT, ATHENS CO., OHIO. IT WAS AT THIS SPOT IN ATHENS CO. THAT A DECLARATION OF INDEPENDENCE WAS MADE BY THE PIONEERS, ALMOST TWO YEARS BEFORE JULY 4, 1776, THUS GIVING OHIO A CLAIM TO A PART IN THE UTTERANCES OF THE PIONEERS FOR INDEPENDENCE.

CAMERON, ALEXANDER, (Hamilton Co.)

Pvt fr Cumberland Co, Pa. (See Rangers on Frontier, p 281). Children: Duncan (mar dau of C Felter, who was son of Jacob Felter, a Revolutionary soldier fr N. Y.) Bur near Montgomery (no dates found of death.) Settled near Montgomery early in 1800. Fur infor Cincinnati Chap.

CAMERON, LEWIS, (Columbiana Co.)

Rendered service to his country during the Revolutionary War as a Pvt Washington Co Pa. Mil Rangers on the Frontier 1778-1783. Pa Archives 3rd Series, Vol 23, p 216; also pp 35, 55, 239 Pa Archives, 6 Series, Vol 2. Lewis Cameron Pvt in Capt John Wall's Company, 2nd Bn Washington Co, Pa Mil ordered to rendezvous Mch 18, 1782. He appears in the same company ordered to rendezvous June 22, 1782. He also appears on the rolls as a Pvt in Capt Samuel Cunningham's Company Washington Co. Mil in service on the Frontiers 1782 to 1785. Lewis Cameron paid taxes in Washington Co, Pa in 1781 on 15 acres of land, a horse and a cow. Bur on the A. R. Hickman farm near Calcutta, O, Columbiana Co (near East Liverpool, O.) The grave is on a ridge marked by three trees which are visible for miles. This Hickman farm being the first burial place in Columbiana Co until the Longs Run Cem was established. (Above copied from papers of Mrs. Fannie B. Moriarty, 228 Miami Ave., East Logansport, Ind. Making application for membership in D. A. R. Papers pending for verification, Aug 28, 1928.)

CAMPBELL, ALEXANDER, (Mahoning Co.)

Pvt Capt Dixon's Company. Third Bn Wadsworth Brig. Reinforced Washington at N. Y. Served in New York City and Long Island. Engaged in Battle of White Plains. Among the first settlers of Milton Twp. Lived with John Johnson. Died in Lordstown. Ref: Trumbull and Mahoning Co Hist, p 181. Fur infor Mahoning Chap.

CAMPBELL, ENOS, (Butler Co.)

Name appears on the tablet erected at Hamilton, on the site of Ft Hamilton, and considered as a Revolutionary soldier who is bur in that Co. Unidentified. Fur infor John Reily Chap.

CAMPBELL, JAMES, (Greene Co.)

Pvt. New York State Tr. On pens roll Mch 4, 1831, age 71. Transferred fr Tioga Co, Pa, Sept 4, 1831. Annual allowance $74.43. Fur infor Catherine Green Chap.

CAMPBELL, JOHN, (Hamilton Co.)

Br 1750, Virginia. D 1839. Fur infor Cincinnati Chap.

CAMPBELL, JOHN, (Lake Co.)

Served in the NY State Tr. Pensioner. Br 1759. Children: James. D either in Willoughby, O or while visiting in N. Y. He was an early settler of Willoughby, O, being a prominent man there for many years. Fur infor New Connecticut Chap.

CAMPBELL, JOHN, (Warren Co.)

Served in Union District, S. C. Br probably in Scotland, Apr 3, 1742. Mar Hester Clark. D Mch 19, 1824. Bur Mt Holly, near Waynesville, O. GM Oct 3, 1928 with impressive ceremony. Moved to Ohio in 1803. Ref: Mrs. H. Backus, State Regent.

CAMPBELL, McDONALD, (Morrow Co.)

Fifer in 1775 in Middlesex Co, N. J. 1776 in Rangers under Capt Fitz Randolph with rank of Lt. 1778 express rider. In 1831 was placed on pens roll of Trumbull Co, O, for services as express rider and fifer. Pa Lines. Br 1754, Somerset Co, N. J. Mar Margaret Tingley. D 1845, Morrow Co. On pens roll of Trumbull Co, 1831, 1840, at age of 86, drawing pens in Gilead Twp, now Morrow Co. Ref: Natl No 53256. Copied by Jane Dowd Dailey, Vol 44, p 98, D. A. R. Lin.

CAMPBELL, MATTHEW, (Brown Co.)

Sgt Dec 8, 1776. Capt Thomas Paxton's Company of Mil. 1st Bn Bedford Co, Pa. Br Scotland. Mar Mary Shelby. Children: Evan (perhaps others). D June 18, 1819, Maysville, Ky. Bur Aberdeen's first cem on the upper river bank. Came to Maysville at an early date. Later was one of a party who left Maysville, Jan 1788 to settle Cincinnati, O. His descendants live in and near Aberdeen and his grave is pointed out by them. Ref: Pa Archives, 2 series, Vol 13, p 349; also 5 series, Vol 5, 19, p 61 and Collins Hist of Ky; Hist Brown Co, O. B Sketches, p 151 Mrs. Fred M. Power, Aberdeen, O, and Natl No 15545. Fur infor Taliaferro Chap.

CAMPBELL, WILLIAM, (Adams Co.)

Pvt from Va. Br 1754 Augusta Co, Va. Mar Elizabeth Wilson (1758-1832). D 1822, Adams Co, O. Natl No 79040, Vol 80. D. A. R. Lin.

CAMPBELL, WILLIAM, (Mahoning Co.)

Ranger, 1778-1783 Washington Co, Pa. Mar Mary Riddle, dau of Revolutionary Soldier. Children: John, Allen, William, James. Cem not located, probably in Poland. Br in Ireland. Came to Pa. Located in Washington Co. Removed to Poland, O about 1803. Fur infor Mahoning Chap.

CANADA, JAMES, (Mahoning Co.)

Ranger Cumberland Co, Pa. Bur Boardman. Was a resident of Boardman in 1801. Ref: Trumbull and Mahoning Cos Hist, p 48, Vol 1, Pa Archives, Series 3 Vol 23, p 289. Fur infor Mahoning Chap.

CANARY, CHARLES, (Brown Co.)

Served through entire war; in 1790 came to Washington Ky and thence to Lewis Twp, Brown Co, O, in 1804. Br Linningen, Germany. Mar Margaret Swyer at Philadelphia, Pa. Children: William (br 1797, Washington, Ky, mar Elizabeth Hoss, 1820), Ellen (mar Alex Love, br 1776 in Ireland). D on his farm, Lewis Twp, Brown Co, O. Justice of Peace 7 yrs. Ref: A. S. Abbott, Bethel, O. Fur infor Cincinnati Chap.

CANE, (or CAIN), DANIEL, (Greene Co.)

Br 1743, Harpers Ferry. D 1851, age of 108 yrs. Bur on Allen Farm. Sugar Creek Twp 1810. Ref: Robinson's Hist of Greene Co, O. Fur infor Catherine Greene Chap.

CANE, DANIEL, (Portage Co.)

Lived at Palmyra. Fur infor Old Northwest Chap.

CANFIELD, ELIJAH, (Portage Co.)

Pvt in Conn Continental. Placed on pens roll July 16, 1832. Bur Palmyra, O. Drew pens at Ravenna in 1840. Fur infor Old Northwest Chap.

CANFIELD, JUDSON, (Mahoning Co.)

Pvt. Was in "Danbury Raid" Apr 25-28, 1777. Conn Men of the Rev, p 492. Here he was marked lost but these records were all poorly kept and some were lost. Br in New Milford, Conn son of Col Samuel Canfield. Mar Mabel Ruggles, dau of Capt Ruggles, a Revolutionary soldier. Children: Henry (br 1789, mar Sally Ferris), Julia Elvira, Elizabeth H, Caroline Elena. D Canfield, O. Bur Canfield. Came to Canfield with a surveying party in 1782. Trumbull and Mahoning Co. Hist p 34, Vol. 1; Mahoning Co. Hist by Butler, p 557 Vol. 1, Graduate of Yale College in 1782. Fur infor Mahoning Camp.

CANFIELD, LEVI, (Summit Co.)

Bur Copley. Fur infor Cuyahoga-Portage Chap.

CANNON, JAMES, Lt., (Shelby Co.)

Joined Continental Army, served throughout the war. Was Commissioned 1st Lt for meritorious conduct. Part of the time was under the immediate command of Gen Washington. Br around 1759 in Ireland. Mar Miss Mary Long, shortly after the close of war. Children: Abraham, Catherine, Margaret, James, Susanna, Richard M, and Daniel. D 1828, Clinton Twp, Shelby Co, O. Came to this country from Ireland a lad of 15, was tanner's apprentice for 2 yrs. Then joined Revolutionary Army. At the close he settled in Shenuans Valley, Ligonier Co, Pa, where he was mar to Miss Long. Moved to Ohio 1795, in Warren Co, where he built a tannery operating it for 4 yrs. In 1806 moved his family to Shelby Co, O. Locating first in Orange Twp then on land near mouth of Loramie Creek. In 1808 he moved on land which afterwards became town site of Sidney, his family being first white settler making improvements on the same. In 1815 moved to Turtle Creek Twp, living here a number of yrs. Ref: Furnished by Sutton's Hist of Shelby Co. Fur infor Lewis Boyer Chap.

CANTER, WILLIAM, (Jackson Co.)

Bur somewhere in Hamilton Twp. This may be the same Canter who found refuge in the caves here that bears his name, after the Burr Conspiracy was found. A fugitive from justice but afterwards exonerated. Fur infor Capt John James Chap.

CARD, WILLIAM, (Lake Co.)

He was commissioned Master of "The Schooner Phoenix" bound for Cape Francois, Boston, Mass. Nov 21, 1776. By a petition to the council signed by Mrs. Card in behalf of Daniel Pierce and Aaron Malady, owners of the Phoenix, said vessel was ordered for service in the Revolutionary War. Br 1753. D 1820. Bur Willoughby, O. GM by New Connecticut Chap. Further infor New Connecticut Chap.

CAREY, (or CAREY), CHRISTOPHER, (Hamilton, O.)

Br 1763. D 1837. Ref: S. A. R. Fur infor Cincinnati Chap.

CARLE, EPHRAIM T., (Harrison Co.)

A Revolutionary pensioner living in Harrison Co, 1833, aged 76. Served in Capt John Baird's Company, 2nd Bn Somerset Co Mil, and in 1st Bn NJ Continental Line Regt. Stryker's NJ in the Revolutionary War, pp 162, 532; Hist Somerset and Hunterdon Cos, 94, US. Pension Roll, 1835. Fur infor Moravian Trail Chap.

CARLE, JOHN, (Hamilton Co.)

Br 1760, N. J. D 1833. Ref: S. A. R. Fur infor Cincinnati Chap.

CARLTON, CALEB, (Portage Co.)

Enl in 1776 at the age of 18; served as a Pvt in Capt Parker's Company, Col Sager's Bn. Gen Wadsworth's Brig. Br Conn in 1758. Children: Caleb, Peter, Elias, Dudley, Hannah, Sally, Lucy. D Oct 3, 1823, Mantua, O. Bur Mantua, O. Fur infor Old Northwest Chap.

CARLTON, DARIUS, (Geauga Co.)

Pvt 5th Company Conn Men May 5, 1776 to Dec 3, 1776. Capt Solomon Willes Company of Tolland, 2nd Regt, Col Spencer Aug 1, 1779 to Jan 15, 1780. Mar Anna Spencer, Oct 21, 1782. Children: Guy, John, Lydia. D Huntsburg. Came to Huntsburg in 1810. Ref: Hist of Tolland; Pioneer Hist of Geauga Co, p 743; Conn Men in Rev, pp 48, 165. Fur infor Taylor Chap.

CARLTON, FRANCIS, (Trumbull Co.)

Bur Union Cem, Girard, Trumbull Co. Could not locate grave. Obliterated. Names from S. A. R. Yr Bk. Fur infor Mary Chesney Chap.

CARNAGHEY, WILLIAM, (Columbiana Co.)

Lived in Liverpool Twp, Columbiana Co. Fur infor Bethia Southwick Chap.

CARNEY, JOHN, (Huron Co.)

Firelands Pioneer Vol 5, Old Series p 56. Fur infor Sally De Forest Chap.

CARPENTER, AMOS, (Meigs Co.)

Enl fr Green Brier, Va, 1777 under Capt Samuel Lapsliy. Wounded in battle of Germantown. Pensioned in Meigs Co, O 1832 for eighteen months service as Pvt. Br 1754. D 1837. Natl No 36566, p 200, Vol 37, D. A. R. Lin.

CARPENTER, JUDGE BENJAMIN, (Delaware Co.)

Bur Galena. Fur infor Delaware Chap.

CARPENTER, DANIEL, (Erie Co.)

Pvt Conn Continental. On pens list Feb 10, 1820, under Act of Congress Mch 18, 1818. Fur infor Martha Pitkin Chap.

CARPENTER, EMANUEL, SR., (Fairfield Co.)

Was member of Committee of Safety. Br in Switzerland 1702. Mar Caroline Line. D Lancaster Co, Pa 1780. Bur Carpenter Cem south of Lancaster, O. GM by Elizabeth Sherman Reese Chap. Bronze Marker. Judge. Natl No 48083, p 40, Vol 49, D. A. R. Lin. Ref: Mary Pearce Davey, Columbus, O. Fur infor Elizabeth Sherman Reese Chap.

CARPENTER, EMANUEL JR., (Fairfield Co.)

Pvt in John Rowland's Company, Lancaster Co, Pa Mil. Br 1744. Mar Mary Smith. D 182—. Bur Old Koontz burial ground south of Lancaster. Removed to Lancaster, O 1798 and named town in compliment to Lancaster, Pa. Ref: Pa Archives, Series 2, Vol 15, and Natl No 48083, Vol 49, p 40, D. A. R. Lin. Fur infor Elizabeth Sherman Reese Chap.

CARPENTER, EZRA, (Lake Co.)

Served at an Alarm in R I Dec 8, 1781 under Capt Jacob Ide, commanded by Col Daggett. Br 1764. D Aug 7, 1849. Bur Kirtland, Lake Co, O. GM New Connecticut Chap. Fur infor New Connecticut Chap.

CARPENTER, GILBERT, Rev., (Delaware Co.)

Brother of Benjamin Carpenter. Bur Galena. Fur infor Delaware Chap.

CARPENTER, HIRAM, (Delaware Co.)

Bur Liberty Twp. Fur infor Delaware Chap.

CARPENTER, JOHN, (Coshocton Co.)

Served fr Va. Quartermaster Sgt of State Garrison Rgt. Served 3 yrs. Disch given June 1, 1781 by Thomas W. Ewell, Capt Commanding. D 1800; bur near Prairie Chapel Church. (Infor by W. A. Carpenter, Freeport, O. to Coshocton papers). See No 198703, D. A. R. Hist. of the Valley (1833), Samuel Kercheval, p 290; Hist of Upper Ohio Valley, Vol 2, p 32. Fur infor Margaret Beer, 1243 23rd St., Washington, D. C.

CARPENTER, JOHN, (Fairfield Co.)

Lt 7th Bn Lancaster Co Mil Pa. Br 1735, Lancaster Co, Pa. D 1807, Lancaster, O. Bur Old Koontz burial ground south of Lancaster. Ref: Natl No 28737, p 269, Vol 29, D. A. R. Lin. Fur infor Elizabeth Sherman Reese Chap.

CARPENTER, JOSEPH, (Noble Co.)

Va Mil. Said to have had three terms of service. D 1849, Beaver Twp. Came to Belmont Co in 1806; to Noble Co 1812 and settled in Beaver Twp, where he died in 1849. Fur infor Mrs. L. B. Frazier, Caldwell, O.

CARPENTER, NATHAN, (Delaware Co.)

Pvt. Burgoyne Campaign. Conn Regt 1775. Br 1757, Rehobeth, Mass. Mar Irene Read, 1780, D 1814, Delaware, O. Bur Liberty Twp on Carpenter farm. Ref: Natl No. 31191, Vol 32, p 71, and Natl No. 74918. D. A. R Lin. Fur infor Delaware Chap.

CARPENTER, SAMUEL, (Licking Co.)

Ensign 1776, 4th Pa Regt. Br 1753, Orange Co, N. Y. Mar Sarah Smith. D 1834, Licking Co, O. Natl No 64886, p 313, Vol 65, D. A. R. Lin.

CARR, AQUILLA, (Tuscarawas Co.)

I have only the tradition in the family to support the claim that he rendered service, and I advise caution, as I can find no record of service. Br 1759 in Baltimore, Md. Mar Susanna Bond; year not known. Children: Richard, William, Thomas, Susanna (list probably not complete). D Apr 10, 1826, near Gnadenhutten. Bur in Beersheba Cem about 1 1/2 miles southwest of Gnadenhutten. About 1785-90 removed to Va. Came to Ohio in 1802. Farmer. Was Associate Judge of Common Pleas Court of Tuscarawas Co from 1808 to 1811. His name appears on soldiers memorial in Gnadenhutten Cem erected in 1927. Infor fur by Charles L. Stocker, Esq., 609 Society for Savings Bldg., Cleveland, O.

CARR, THOMAS, (Butler Co.)

With Capt Robert Jackson's Company of Va Mil for three months from Oct 1781, and with Capt Ford's Company Tenn Mil under Gen Wayne from Apr 3 to Nov 4, 1791. Br Cookton, Ireland 1762. Parents: James Carr. Mar Apr 11, 1787 Anne Gates (br Jan 9, 1765, bur in Oxford Cem) in Berkley, Va. Children: Jacob, Mary, James, Jane, John, Thomas, William, Enoch, Samuel, Elijah, Josiah. D 1838, Hanover Twp, Butler Co, O. Bur Ebenezer, Hanover Twp, Butler Co, O, near corner of church, but in 1860, after the death of his wife, remains were removed to Oxford, O beside his wife. He gave this burying ground off of his farm, and a church was built, but afterwards torn down. GM by descendants who are members of John Reily Chap 1925. After the Rev he lived at Berkley Co, Va then went near Cumberland Gap, Tenn; then to Glasco, Ky and then to Butler Co, O in 1805 or 1806 and died there in 1838. Was present at the surrender of Cornwallis at Yorktown, a minute man. Fur infor John Reily Chap.

CARRELL, WILLIAM B., (Logan Co.)

Pensioned 1840 while living in Monroe Twp, Logan Co, O, aged 73, which the Commissioner Pensions states was for Revolutionary service. Fur infor Bellefontaine Chap.

CARROLL, CHARLES, (Miami Co.)

Served seven yrs in the state of Md. Bur Dunhard Cem near Pleasant Hill, west of Troy, O. GM by Miami Chap with bronze marker. He was given 100 acres of land near Baltimore, Union Co. Fur infor Miami Chap.

CARROLL, GEORGE, (Noble Co.)

Pa Line at Battle of Brandywine. Early settler of Jackson Twp. D and bur in Jackson Twp. Grave not located. Fur infor Mrs. L. B. Frazier, Caldwell, O.

CARROLL, WILLIAM, (Hancock Co.)

Pvt. 1776 in Flying Camp under Capt Enos Campbell, Col Charles Griffen. Placed on pens roll of Ohio 1832 for serv in Md Line. Br 1758 in Md. D 1845 Hancock Co, O. Natl No 26621, Vol 27, pp 229, 230, D. A. R. Lin.

CARSON, JOHN, (Mahoning Co.)

Pvt in Abram Marshall's Company 1776; also in the Continental Line. Mar Catherine Wentz. Bur probably Berlin Twp. Came from Dauphin Co, Pa, about 1835 with his son to Berlin Twp. Farmer. Ref: Pa Archives Series 2, Vol 14, pp 482, 505; Vol 4, p 737, Trumbull and Mahoning Co Hist. Fur infor Mahoning Chap.

CARSON, ROBERT, (Crawford Co.)

D Cranberry Twp. Bur 3 miles north of New Washington, O. Fur infor Hannah Crawford Chap.

CARSON, ROBERT, (Seneca Co.)

Bur Swamp Cem, Venice Twp. GM by Mrs. G. A. Downey, 1927, bronze marker. Tradition says this was the first person buried in Swamp Cem when it was only a spot in the woods. Ref: Mrs. Eva Smith Sutton, Tiffin, O. Fur infor Dolly Todd Madison Chap.

CARSON, WILLIAM, (Ross Co.)

Br 1745. Mar Isabella Gilmore. Children: Hugh Carson (1782-1847), William Carson (1788-1840). D 1829 Chillicothe, O. Bur Grandview, Chillicothe, O. MI: "William Carson a soldier of the Revolutionary War 1745-1829. Isabella Gilmore his wife 1747-1811". Fur infor Nathaniel Massie Chap.

CARSWELL, DAVID, (Erie Co.)

Pvt in NY Continental Line. Br 1746. D 1844. Bur in Oakland Cem, Sandusky, O. Ref: Natl No 89117, Vol 90, p 37, D.A.R. Lin. Fur infor Martha Pitkin Chap.

CARTER, CHARLES, (Union Co.)

Bur New Dover Cem, Dover Twp. Ref: Col W. L. Curry, Hist Union Co. Fur infor Hannah Emerson Dustin Chap.

CARTER, EZEKIEL, (Muskingum Co.)

D 1833, aged 70 yrs. Bur in Dresden Cem. Inscription on stone: "He was a Revolutionary soldier and was present at the surrender of Cornwallis." No data Fur infor Muskingum Chap.

CARTER, JABEZ, (Lake Co.)

Enl in Capt John Walton's Company, Col David Green's Regt; was in the Lexington Alarm and served his country until Mch 10, 1780. Br 1750. D Aug 12, 1836, Kirtland, Lake Co, O Bur Kirtland, O. GM by New Connecticut Chap. Fur infor New Connecticut Chap.

CARTER, JAMES, (Clermont Co.)

In 1840 was drawing pens for serv while living in Wayne Twp, Clermont Co, O, aged 85. Br 1755. Fur infor Census of Pensions 1840. Copied by Jane Dailey, State Chairman.

CARTER, JONAS, (Geauga Co.)

Pvt Mass Continentals, 8th Worchester Co. Enl from town of Lancaster. Br 1762. D Sept 20, 1837. Bur Mumford Cem, Troy Twp, about middle of Cem, south of Wells monument. MI: "Jonas Carter, died Sept 20, 1837, aged 75 years. A soldier of '76." GM White marble slab monument; also G. A. R. marker. Enl from Lancaster (Lunenburg), enl 3 yrs. Farmer. Ref: Mass Soldier and Sailor, p 156, Vol 3. Fur infor Taylor Chap.

CARTWRIGHT, JOHN, (Mahoning Co.)

Ranger Northumberland Co, Pa. Mar Margaret ——, (1763-1818). Bur Old Four Mile Run Cem, Austintown Twp. Settled in Austintown in 1828. Ref: Pa Archives, Series 3, Vol 23, p 299. Mahoning and Trumbull Cos Hist Vol 2, p 149. Fur infor Mahoning Chap.

CASE, AUGUSTUS SR., (Wayne Co.)

Pvt. Was a carpenter, worked in shipyards in N. Y. harbor; in 1777 enl in Revolutionary Army, served to close of war. Was in no hard fought battles and in but one skirmish. Br July 17, 1759, Long Island. Parents: Joshua Case. Mar Elizabeth Bell, 1794. Children: Annar, Samuel Y, Elizabeth, Sarah, John Bell, Phoebe, Augustus Jr, Onesium Joshua. D Mch 12, 1852, Wayne Co, Plain Twp. Bur Maple Grove Cem, Plain Twp, near Church Building. MI: "Augustus Case, Sr. D Mar 12, 1852, aged 92 yrs. 7 mos and 26 days." Pvt in NJ

Tr. Served under Capt Peter Dickinson's Company, Col Sylcanua Seeley's Eastern Bn. Morris Co, NJ Mil during Revolutionary War. Farmer. Augustus Case drew a pens of ninety-six dollars per yr as a Revolutionary soldier. Fur infor Wooster-Wayne Chap.

CASE, ELIJAH, SR. (Greene Co.)

Br 1754. D Jan 14, 1842. Bur Woodland, Xenia. Living in Xenia in 1840. Ref: Robinson's Hist of Greene Co. Fur infor Catherine Greene Chap.

CASE, MESHEK or MESHEL, (Trumbull Co.)

Br Oct 19, 1752. Mar Magdalin Case (br Oct 6, 1761, d Apr 18, 1832). D Apr 29, 1841. Bur Oak Grove, Warren, O. MI: Dates of birth and death only. Monument in good condition. Ref: Baldwin Library, Youngstown, O. Fur infor Mary Chesney Chap.

CASS, JONATHAN, (Muskingum Co.)

Served as Pvt, Ensign, Lt, Capt and Maj in N H line. Took part in Battle of Bunker Hill, Siege of Boston, battles of Saratoga, Princeton, Germantown, Trenton, Monmouth; was at Valley Forge; also a member of Sullivan Expedition against the Six Nations. Br Oct 9, 1752, East Kingston, N. H. Mar Mary Gilman, dau of a noted Tory. Children: Charles, Lewis (Gov). D Aug 9, 1830. Bur on farm; later remains moved to family plat in Dresden, O. Cem. GM granite monument. United States Marshal of New Hampshire. Ref: Natl No 61132, Vol 62, p 46, D. A. R. Lin. and Vol II, p 348, Howe's Hist of Ohio. Fur infor Muskingum and John Reily Chaps.

CASTLE, AMASA, (Ashtabula Co.)

Enl June 26, 1776; served as a member of the 4th Company, Col Wm Douglas' Regt of new levies from Conn. Served as a Pvt over a period of 6 yrs. Br Apr 6, 1755, Waterbury, Conn. Parents: Isaac Castle and Lydia Scott (mar Dec 21, 1740). Mar Mary Stanley, 1776 (dau of Timothy and Mary Hopkins Stanley). Children: Lydia, Mary, Clarissa, Daniel, Eliza, Amasa, Pamela. D June 21, 1826. Ashtabula, O. Bur Edgewood. MI: Name and dates. After the close of the War, settled just over the border, in Canada. Threatened with draft into the British army, left home, fields, their all. Farmer. Came to Ashtabula, 1808. Ref: Ashtabula Co. Hist; Record and Pension Office Dept Natl No 58541. Fur infor Mary Stanley Chap.

CATLETT, JONAS, (Columbiana Co.)

Lived in Madison Twp, Columbiana Co, O. Fur infor Bethia Southwick Chap.

CATTELL, JONAS, (Mahoning Co.)

Pvt in N. J. Located in Goshen Twp, Mahoning Co, early in the nineteenth century. Ref: N. J. Men of the Rev. p 585; Trumbull and Mahoning Co. History, Vol. 1 p 193. Fur infor Mahoning Chap

CATTELL, WILLIAM, (Mahoning Co.)

Pvt in N. J. Located in Goshen Twp, Mahoning Co, early in the nineteenth century. Ref: N. J. Men of the Rev. p 585; Trumbull and Mahoning Co. History, Vol 1, p 193. Fur infor Mahoning Chap.

CATTERLIN, JAMES, (Butler Co.)

Name appears on the tablet erected at Hamilton, O on the site of Ft. Hamilton, and considered a soldier bur in that Co. Unidentified. Fur infor John Reily Chap.

CAUGHEY, THOMAS, (Preble Co.)

Bur Mound Hill Cem. Harrison Twp, O. Ref: Mary P. Mitchell, Eaton, O.

CAULKINS, ROSWELL, (Delaware Co.)

Pvt under Col Chandler, Capt Theophilus Munson, Conn Tr. Bur Blockhouse Cem, Berlin Twp. Pensioned. Fur infor Delaware Chap.

CAVAULT,—— (Miami Co.)

Bur at Old Stanton Cem, 2 miles north of Casstown. GM by Miami Chap. Fur infor Miami Chap.

CAVE, BENJAMIN, (Ross Co.)

Enl 1779. Served 3 mos. Capt Browning, Col Barber, Staff Va. Reenlisted 1780. Served 18 mos. Capt Fields, Col Fowler, Staff Va. Br Culpeper, Va. 1760. Parents: Benjamin Cave. Mar Keziah Cave (per pension record.) Children: Benjamin, Emanuel, Ezekiel, John Jonas, Nathaniel. D Feb 16, 1842, Harrison Twp. Ross Co, O. Bur Stanhope, Ross Co, O. After Revolutionary War moved to Montgomery Co, Ky. thence to Ohio in 1816. Minister of the Gospel. Organized and was pastor for several years of Baptist Church, South Perry, O. Pens granted 1833, rate $70 per year. Ref: Mrs. Josephine Cave Harper, Evart, Mich and Byron Cave, Lancaster, O. Fur infor Mt Sterling Chap.

CAVENDER, JOHN, (Hamilton Co.)

Br Delaware. D 1837. Ref: S. A. R. Fur infor Cincinnati Chap.

CECIL, ZACHARIAH, (or Zachy Cesil,) (Shelby Co.)

"Richmond, Mch 13, 1784, Sundry Accounts Va Mil. Abstract Warrant to Zachy Cecil for his service in the Mil under Lt Daniel Howe, from Montgomery in 1781, 1 lb. 16 S." Br about 1757, Montgomery Co, Va. Parents: Samuel W. and Rebecca (White) Cecil. Mar Nancy Ingram. Children: Samuel, John, Aaron, Ingram, Blueford, (or Beauford,) James, Rebecca, Mary, Calvin. D Aug 20, 1823, Shelby Co, O. Reported to have been bur in Hart Cem, southeast of Walnut Grove, near Grayson Station east of Troy, O. A search of this cem fails to disclose the grave, although there are other Cecils bur in this cem. Might have been old Hardin Cem. Came to Shelby Co, O from Montgomery Co, Va about 1812, where he lived until his death. Ref: Sutton's History of Shelby Co. mentions Zachariah Cecil as a taxpayer, 1820, in Turtle Creek Twp. Farmer. Lester L. Cecil, Judge of the Municipal Court, Dayton, O. Fur infor Lewis Boyer D. A. R. and S. A. R. Richard Montgomery Chap.

CHAMBERS, JAMES, (Clermont Co.)

Pensioned Mch 19, 1819, $96, at age of 72, for Pvt NJ Continental Line. Br New Jersey. D Batavia Twp, Clermont Co, O, where he settled in 1807. Ref: A. S. Abbott, Bethel, O. Fur infor Cincinnati Chap.

CHAMBERS, ROBERT, (Guernsey Co.)

Bur Old Cem, Cambridge, O. Ref: S. A. R. Fur infor Anna Asbury Stone Chap.

CHANNELL, JOHN, (Licking Co.)

Bur in field one-quarter mile north and one-quarter mile west along Pa R R on hill in field, second row of graves in corner of field near Bowling Green Church, east of Newark. GM by Hetuck Chap. 20 yrs ago stone then standing now broken and could only find footstone and part of head stone. There are stones standing of John Channell, Jr., br Dec 12, 1802, died Jan 31, 1825. Another "In memory of Jesse Channel, d Jan 16, 1828, aged 34 yrs." Fur infor Hetuck Chap.

CHAPIN, LUCIUS, (Hamilton Co.)

Br 1760, Mass. D 1842. Fur infor Cincinnati Chap.

CHAPMAN, CONSTANT, (Portage Co.)

Enl as Pvt in 1778 for 3 yrs. Enl again, served 3 yrs, when he was made Sgt and later was promoted to Sgt Maj. Br Dec 27, 1761 at West Brook, Conn. Mar Jemima Kelsey Jan 27, 1785. Children: Lydia, Thurot, John, Anna, Chloe, Mary, Joseph, Jemima, Henry. D Sept 24, 1850, at Brimfield, O. Bur Brimfield, O. Drew a pens. Ref: Adj Gen, Washington D. C. Natl No 105045. Fur infor Old Northwest Chap.

CHAPMAN, HERMAN, (Washington Co.)

Br 1764, D 1851. Bur Hoagland Cem, Barlow Twp, Washington Co. O. MI: "He was a Revolutionary soldier." GM by Marietta Chap with Revolutionary marker in 1922. Fur infor Marietta Chap.

CHAPMAN, LEMUEL, (Knox Co.)

Pvt in a Company designated at various times as Capt John St Johns', Capt David Strong's, Capt Humphrey's, Capt Colefax's, 7th and 8th Companies, 2nd Conn Regt, commanded by Col Herman Swift. He enl Apr 1, 1782 for 12 mos, and was disch Apr 1, 1783. (He enl when 17 yrs old.) Br 1765, Connecticut. D Mch 14, 1827, Brandon, Knox Co, O. Bur Brandon Cem, at edge of Brandon Village, just back of Church, 1st row on the north side of cem. MI: "In memory of Lemuel Chapman who died March 14th 1827 in the 62 year of his age. He was a soldier in the American Revolution and served during the war. He belonged to the army when General Washington marched in and took possession of New York, after the British army evacuated the city. He was a man of laborious industry during his life, and possessed a large share of friendship and good will to man. Low lies the warrior his battles are o'er, Mav the fame of his deeds last till time is no more." Ref: The Adj Gen of US gave this war record on the data contained in the above inscription which is an exact copy. Ref: Fur infor Kokosing Chap.

CHAPMAN, MICHAEL, (Erie Co.)

Pvt in Conn Continental Line. Br 1758, Bethlehem, Conn. D 1839, Huron, O. where he is bur. Ref: Natl No 39732, p 269, Vol 40, D. A. R. Lin. Fur infor Martha Pitkin Chap.

CHAPMAN, NATHANIEL, (Columbiana Co.)

Capt of Company of Wheelwrights. Br 1740, Springfield, Mass. Mar Lucy Cooley. D 1807, Salem, O. Ref: Natl No 59467 p 159, Vol. 60, D. A. R. Lin.

CHAPMAN, TITUS, (Summit Co.)

Enl May 1775, Conn Tr serving as Pvt in Capt Thomas Hobby's Company, (Third) of Greenwich and Stratford, Fifth Regt Col David Waterbury. D 1808. Bur Middlebury Cem Summit Co. Came to Summit Co with his son, Deacon Nathaniel Chapman, in 1806. Donated land for the cem and was first person bur there. Fur infor Cuyahoga-Portage Chap.

CHARLTON, JOHN, (Hamilton Co.)

Br 1759 N. J. D 1848. Bur M. E. Cem Newtown. At 78, drew a pen in Anderson Twp, in 1840. Ref: S. A. R. Fur infor Cincinnati Chap.

CHASE, BEVERLY, (Morrow Co.)

Pvt in Dutchess Co. NY Mil. Br 1759 in Ohio. Ref: Natl No 29602, p 216, Vol 30, D. A. R. Lin.

CHEADLE, ASA, (Morgan Co.)

Pvt. Br Dec 29, 1762, Ashford, Conn. Mar 1st, Sally Gray; 2nd, Nancy Hersey; 3rd, Sarah Divens. Children by 1st wife: Cyrus, Joseph, Sally, Martha, Asa, (twins) Tryfena, Tryfona; by 2nd wife: Olive, Parmelia, Martin, Clarissa, Eliza, John, Asa Jr., Louisa, Quincey. D Sept 13, 1836, Windsor Twp, Morgan Co, O. Bur near Big Bottom. Ref: Charlotte Hartzell a descendant. For infor Amanda Barker Devin Chap.

CHENEY, THOMAS, (Champaign Co.)

Noted Whig during the Rev. Carried valuable infor to Gen Washington at the Battle of Brandywine. Member Chester Co Council and Com of Safety; was Sub-Lt of Chester Co Mil under Robt Smith fr Mch 12, 1777 to Mch 21, 1785. Br Chester Co, Pa Dec 12, 1731. D Jan 12, 1811 Champaign Co, O and bur in small graveyard on farm in Union Twp. Was abandoned but now enclosed by wire fence. Ref: Mrs. Frank Harford, Springfield, O. Fur infor Urbana Chap.

CHENEY, THOMAS, (Champaign Co.)

Enl 1775 Capt Ephraim Manning's Company, Col Israel Putnam's Regt Connecticut Line. Br 1742, Ashford, Conn. Mar Keturah Owen, D 1828, Champaign Co, O. Ref: Natl No 102231, Vol 103, p 72, D. A. R. Lin.

CHENEY, WILLIAM, 5th, (Ashtabula Co.)

Enl as a drummer boy, at 16, in the 14th Albany Co, NY Regt. Served as Pvt in 1781 in Capt James Dana's Company, Col Samuel Wylly's Regt, Connecticut Line. Was placed on the Pension Roll of Ontario Co, N. Y. in 1832. Br 1765 in Ashford, Conn. Parents: Ebenezer and Priscilla (Lyon) Cheney. Mar: 1st Ruth Eastman; 2nd Delaliah Shipman. Children: one was Hannah, who married Lester Hulse. D 1851 Colebrook, Ashtabula Co, O. Bur East Cem. Ref: Natl No 45208, Vol 46, p 87, D. A. R. Lin. Also Natl No 101336, Vol 103, p 101. Fur infor Mary Stanley Chap.

CHENOWETH, WILLIAM I., (Allen Co.)

Sgt. Ent Revolutionary service fr Stafford Co, Va, in Washington's Army. Br Hartford Co, Md. 1st wife's maiden name was Rinkler. Children: 1st wife: John, Mary, Eleanor, Elizabeth, Catherine, Jacob, William, Birgilic, Casper, Sarah, Mason. By 2nd wife: Ann, Neda, Martha, Lewis. D near Lima, O. November 1838. Bur Tony's Nose, 2 miles east of Lima. No platted lots. Out of the way. Neglected cem. MI: "Sergeant William Chenoweth; War 1776." GM U. S. Government marker secured by Lima Chap. Came to Allen Co in 1827; remained about one year. Returned later and entered land 2 miles east of Lima. Built cabin on banks of Lost Creek in center of what is now Lima's principal reservoir for municipal water works purpose. Came through fr Virginia on horseback. Is said when 80 yrs of age he could split 100 rails in a day. Extensive land owner. Was of Welsh origin. Ref: Shelby Mumaugh, M D, a great-grandson. Fur infor Lima Chap.

CHERRY, HENRY, (Erie Co.)

Pvt. N. J. On pens list June 7, 1819 under act of congress Mch 18, 1818. Name on tablet, Sandusky, Erie Co Library, also. Huron Co was once a part of Erie Co, hence confusion arises when the exact burial spot is not known. Fur infor Martha Pitkin and Sally De Forest Chaps.

CHERRY, JOHN, (Mahoning Co.)

Ranger 1778-1783 Westmoreland Co. Mahoning Co Cem. Henry Baldwin. Ref: Pa Archives, Series 3, Vol 23, p 283. Fur infor Mahoning Chap.

CHERRY, JOHN, (Trumbull Co.)

Capt. Bur Niles Cem. Unable to locate. Many inscriptions obliterated. Ref: S. A. R. Yr Bk. Fur infor Mary Chesney Chap.

CHESNUT, DANIEL, (Ross Co.)

Was in the whiskey rebellion under Washington. Father came to this country fr Scotland; mother from Ireland. Children: Daniel (wife Isabella); William (wife Hannah); Margaret, Polly, Benjamin (d June 23, 1872, aged 75 yrs. 2 mos, 24 days—wife Ann d Apr 18, 1859, aged 65 yrs.) William (d July 7, 1879, aged 86 yrs, 5 mos, 18 days. Was in war of 1812, 90 days. His wife d Aug 12, 1845, aged 49 yrs.) D Huntington Twp, Ross Co, O. Bur on his farm, his stone gone. Those of above standing. Family lived at Portsmouth a short time and then came to Chillicothe in 1798. Lived in the town for four yrs, then three yrs on the nearby hill. Then bought a farm of 260 acres from Gen Massie, where he and his five children and wife lived. Was a hunter. One of first to keep sheep. Lost 40 at one time by wolves. Elected Justice of Peace in 1811, one of first three in the twp. Was captain of the mil for several yrs. Helped to cut the old Zane trace, now known as the limestone road. He and Wm Richie detailed a part of the time to watch Indians in upper end of the county. Ref: History of Ross and Highland Cos p 288. Fur infor Nathaniel Massie Chap.

CHEVALIER, ANTHONY, (Montgomery Co.)

Enl 1776 fr Va; served as Pvt until 1780. Capt Voss, Col Wood Va Tr. Br 1753 in France. Mar 1789 Rachel Scott Nelson (br 1755). Children: One dau was Charlotte who mar William McGrew. D in Montgomery Co. Pensioned in 1818. Ref: Natl No 100,000, Vol 100, p 311, D. A. R. Lin.

CHIDISTER, WILLIAM, (Mahoning Co.)

Pvt Capt Sedgwick's Company, Woodbridge, Conn. Enl Apr 25, 1777, disch Apr 25, 1780. Br 1758. Mar Martha Dean. Children: Hezikiah, Philo, Buell, Erastus, Rush, Velorus, Julius, Royal, Chloe, Betsey. D 1802. Bur Village Cem, Canfield, O. GM by D. A. R. in 1915-17. Ref: p 13 History Trumbull & Mahoning Co, Conn. Men in the Revolution, pp 63 and 221. Fur infor Mahoning Chap.

CHRISTIAN, WILLIAM, (Ross Co.)

Capt in Va Continental Line. Bur in small cem off Upper Twin Rd., Ross Co, O. (near Bourneville). Fur infor Nathaniel Massie Chap.

CHRISTIE, JESSE, (Clark Co.)

Lt in Col Daniel Moore's NH Regt in 1775. Bur Aug 8, 1736, Londonderry, N. H. Mar Mary Gregg. Of 12 children only Robert, 10th child, is mentioned. D Jan, 1823, Springfield. Bur Columbia St Cem Springfield, O. Not platted, northeast corner. Marker authorized and erected by Society S. A. R. Metal marker about 1906. Ref: Mrs. J. H. Cantrell, Vice Regent Tenn D. A. R., 821 Vine St., Chattanooga, Tenn. See 28705, Vol 29, p 257, D. A. R. Lin. Fur infor Lagonda Chap.

CHRISTOPHER, WALTER, (Guernsey Co.)

Pvt 2nd Pa Continental Line. Br Pa. Mar Mary Stutts or Stotts 1804-5 Pa. Children: Mary, William, Margaret, Katherine, Elizabeth, Rachel, Rebecca,

Hannah. D Guernsey Co, O. 1834. Bur on the Hawthorne Farm, Guernsey Co, O. Received a pens. Farmer. Ref: Pa Archives 5 series, Vol 2, p 892 Mrs. Blanche Walter Johnson, Mrs. Corda Walter Lofland, Cambridge, O. Fur infor Anna Asbury Stone Chap.

CHRISTY, ROBERT, (Fayette Co.)

Chaplain. Br Va 1756. D Washington C. H., Apr 13, 1856. Bur Washington C. H. Lot 195, Sec 8. MI: "Robert Christy, died Apr 13, 1856, aged 100 years." GM by family in 1856. Fur infor Washington C. H. Chap.

CHURCH, JOHN or JONATHON, (Erie Co.)

Pa Continental. On pens list Oct 18, 1819, under act of Congress Mch 18, 1818. A county divided into others since makes location of grave difficult. Fur infor Martha Pitkin and Salley De Forest Chaps.

CHURCH, PHILEMON, (Geauga Co.)

Drummer boy. Enl Boston Mass. Jan 1, 1776; served one yr 1777. Enl at Fish Hill, N. Y. Took part in battle at White Plains. Pensioned in 1818 for serv in Conn. Continental Army, Col Webb's 7th Regt, 1775, Capt Shipman's 6th Company July 11—Dec 18, 1775. Br Jan 6, 1752, Chester, Conn. Parents: Simeon and Eunice (Warner) Church. Mar Sarah Tryon, 1790 in Brandford. Children: Sally, Polly, Abigail, Asa, William, Timothy, Arminda, Hannah, Caroline. Br Nov 19, 1842, Huntsburg, O. The old cemetery in Huntsburg is in very bad condition. Family records would indicate Philemon Church was buried in this cem. Lived in Catskill, N. Y. when pensioned. Ref: Conn Men in Revolution; Church Genealogy, p 105, Natl No 46861. Fur infor Taylor Chap.

CILLEY, JONATHAN, (Hamilton Co.)

Pvt, Ensign and Lt in 1st NH Regt. Br 1763 in N. H. D 1807. Ref: S. A. R.; also Natl No 55425, Vol 56, p 196 D. A. R. Lin. Fur infor Cincinnati Chap.

CLANCY, JOHN, (Morgan Co.)

Enl Logtown Md, under Capt Levin Winder, Col John Stone and 1780 served under Capt Gaither. Was at Brandywine, Germantown, Stony Point and Paulus Hook. Br 1754. D 1841. 1818 pensioned in Morgan Co for serv as Pvt, Md Continental Line. Ref: Natl No 38189. Fur infor Jane Dowd Dailey, fr Vol 39. D. A. R. Lin.

CLAPPER, GEORGE, (Muskingum Co.)

Enl Pvt in Capt Irvine's Company of Pa Tr. Also in Capt Christian Stoke's Company. Col Michael Swope's Bn of the Pa Flying Camp. Was in battle of Trenton. Br York Co, Pa. Feb 1757. Mar Elizabeth Souders, 1781. D Aug 11, 1837. Bur Salt Creek Baptist Church Cem, six miles east of Zanesville. Pensioned in 1833, Muskingum Co, O. Ref: Vol 79, No 78699, D. A. R. Lin. Fur infor Muskingum Chap.

CLARK, DANIEL, (Hamilton Co.)

Serv 4th Regt Orange Co p 163 "NY Men in Rev War." D Columbia. Probably bur in Pioneer Cem here. Was first Baptist minister ordained in Ohio. Preached at Columbia, Hamilton Co, before 1795. Fur infor Cincinnati Chap.

CLARK, DENNIS, (Hamilton Co.)

Br Md 1756. D 1832. Ref: S. A. R. Fur infor Cincinnati Chap.

CLARK, EPHRAIM, (Trumbull Co.)

Bur Old Laird. This cem is north of Mesopotamia, is now used as a cornfield and has only one stone standing. Ref: Name fr S. A. R. Yr Bk. Fur infor Mary Chesney Chap.

CLARK, GEORGE, (Hamilton Co.)

Serv in 4th Regt Orange Co Mil, p 163 "NY Men in Rev War." D Cincinnati. Bur in Cincinnati. Name found in earliest Directory of Cincinnati, 1819. Listed as carpenter. Fur infor Cincinnati Chap.

CLARK, ISAAC, (Trumbull Co.)

Bur Old Laird; cem used as a cornfield. Only one stone standing. Name fr S. A. R. Yr Bk. Fur infor Mary Chesney Chap.

CLARK, ISRIAL, (Marion Co.)

Conn Pvt. Served 3 yrs. Capt John Hays, Col Durkee Hales, Col Ely Isaac Sherman, Elias Stillwell Butler, Res Delaware, O. Br Conn Mch 9, 1757. Mar Margaret Dye, 4th wife. Children: Elizabeth Clark (Little) a real D. A. R. D Feb 5, 1827, Richland Twp, Marion Co, O. Bur Smith Cem, Marion Twp, Marion Co, O. MI: Dates of birth and death. GM by Fort Findlay Chap in 1915. Ref: Natl No 61417, Vol 62, p 145. D. A. R. Lin. Fur infor Fort Findlay Chap.

CLARK, JAMES, (Delaware Co.)

Served 7 yrs. Bur Cem Marlboro Twp. Fur infor Delaware Chap.

CLARK, JAMES, (Hamilton Co.)

Served in 4th Regt Orange Co Mil p 161 "NY in Rev War." D Sycamore Twp. Settled on farm in Sycamore Twp. Lived, died and buried on farm. Descendants still in neighborhood. Fur infor Cincinnati Chap.

CLARK, JAMES, (Harrison Co.)

1753-1833; bur at Beech Spring Church; served as a Pvt in Capt John Clark's Company 6th Regt Pa Line and possibly as Capt 1st Company 2nd Bn Westmoreland Co Mil 1777. Pa Archives 6 series II, 303,347; Albert's Hist Westmoreland Co, Pa. 460. Fur infor Moravian Trail.

CLARK, JOHN, (Hamilton Co.)

Served in 4th Regt Orange Co, p 163 "NY in the Rev War." Was a tailor at 106 Main St, Cincinnati's earliest Directory 1819. Removed to Sycamore Twp. Name on tax list in Sycamore Twp. Fur infor Cincinnati Chap.

CLARK, NATHANIEL, (Hamilton Co.)

Br Mass, 1757. D 1832. Ref: S. A. R. Fur infor Cincinnati Chap.

CLARK, PERRY, (Clermont Co.)

Naval Officer in Revolutionary War. Br N. J. 12 children; one of whom, Perry F. G. lived to be 102 yrs old. Lived at Mt Carmel, Union Twp, Clermont Co, O. Ref: A. S. Abbott, Bethel, O. Fur infor Cincinnati Chap.

CLARK, THOMAS, (Gallia Co.)

Lt of the 13th Va Light Inf. Br Aug 10, 1759 Va. Children: William, James, Jeptha. D Mch 9, 1831, Sandfork, O. and bur in Sanford Cem Gallia Co, O; MI: "Lieutenant. Thomas Clark, Sr. Zanes Company 13th Va Light Infantry." GM by the Government, Sandfork Cem, Gallia Co, O. A farmer. Ref: Marbel Martt May, Tuscola, Ill. Fur infor French Colony Chap.

CLARK, THOMAS, (Hamilton Co.)

Served in 4th Regt, Orange Co Mil p 163 "NY Men in Revolutionary War." Bur in Hamilton Co near Pleasant Ridge. Was an attorney and land agent, office at 155 Main St, Cincinnati Directory of 1819. He was an efficient, upright leader in the early life of Cincinnati and community. Fur infor Cincinnati Chap.

CLARK, WILLIAM, (Hamilton Co.)

Lived in Cincinnati until his death. Date not found. Bur in Cincinnati. Served in Orange Co Mil 4th Regt (See 6163 "NY Men in Rev War.") Came to Cincinnati in 1795 as did five other Clarks, perhaps all brothers, as all served in Orange Co Mil. Listed as a mason (brick) 59 Front St., Cincinnati. Cincinnati Directory 1819. Fur infor Cincinnati Chap.

CLARK, WILLIAM, (Jackson Co.)

County histories name him as Revolutionary Soldier. Had a horse mill near Hewitt's Fork. Was bur in that neighborhood. Fur infor Captain John James Chap.

CLARK, ZELOTUS, (Summit Co.)

Pvt in Company fr Saybrook, Conn. Enl May 8, 1775. Disch Dec 18, 1775, having served in Capt John Ely's Company (9th) of 6th Regt under Col Samuel Holden Parsons. Bur 1747 Chester, Conn. D Dec 1834. Bur Twinsburg, O. Fur infor Cuyahoga-Portage Chap.

CLEMENT, LAMBERT, (Summit Co.)

Enl 1776 at Johnstown, N. Y.; served under Capt John Fisher, John Lefter, and John Wimple; Col Frederick Fisher and Marinus Willet. In battles of Oriskany, Stone Arabia and Johnstown. Br Johnstown, Herkimer Co, N. Y. 1757. Mar Mary Vedder, Schenectady, N. Y. Feb 28, 1787. D Coventry, Summit Co, O. Mch 31, 1842. Bur Middlebury Cem, East Akron by his wife. Fur infor Cuyahoga-Portage Chap.

CLENCY, GEORGE, (Montgomery Co.)

Enl in spring of 1776 under Capt Posey; Reenl in 1776, 77, 78, 79. Served 3 yrs and 6 mos under Col Morgan and many others, as a Pvt. In many battles, Brandywine, Valley Forge, Monmouth, and marched under Gen Petter Muhlenberg at Yorktown. Application for pens Sept 16, 1832 recites a very long list of serv. Pens granted Oct 8, 1833. Application supported by Elijah Mills of Dayton who served with him. Br Staunton Va 1747. Bur Old Cem Sunbury, O. GM by Richard Montgomery Chap in June 1922. Lived in the German settlement in German Twp, Montgomery Co. Has a descendant, Mrs. Pearl Emerick. Fur infor Richard Montgomery Chap S. A. R.

CLEVELAND, SAMUEL, (Geauga Co.)

Corp 1775, Capt Nathan Peter's Company. Col Timothy Danielson's Regt. Br Preston, Conn 1753. Parents: Moses and Mary Cleveland. Mar Mercy (or Marcy) Wilbur, May 22, 1777. Children: Ralph, Samuel, Moses, Samuel, Sarah,

Susanna, George, William, John, Polly, Maria, Laura. D Chardon, O. May 22, 1839. Bur Center Chardon. MI: Name, birth, age and epitaph "Soldier rest thy battle done, true in life and memory blest, all thy toil and marches o'er, Angels bear thee to thy rest." GM by family with stone marker. Settled in Chardon about 1828. Ref: Cleveland Genealogy, Vol 1, pp 238-116. Vol 49, No 48643, D. A. R. Lin. Fur infor Taylor Chap.

CLEVELAND, TRACY, (Lake Co.)

Pvt Capt Bacon's Company 6th Bn Wadsworth's Brig, Col John Chester commanding in 1776. Was in N. J. at the time of the battle of Trenton. Br Canterbury, Conn 1749. D Kirtland, Lake Co, O Feb 27, 1836. Bur Harmon farm Kirtland, O. GM by New Connecticut Chap. Ref: Natl No 25986. Vol 26, p 360. D. A. R. Lin. Fur infor New Connecticut Chap.

CLINGMAN, JOHN MICHAEL, (Scioto Co.)

Capt 7th Company 1778. Pa Mil Northumberland Co. Served throughout war. Br Oct 1734 Germany. Mar Anna Elizabeth Millar, Apr 13, 1756. Children; Mary Kinney. D Portsmouth, Scioto Co, O Jan 26, 1816. Bur Kinney Cem. East side of ground, head of Waller St. MI: "John Michael Clingman, died Jan 26, 1816, 81 yrs." Father of Mrs. Aaron Kinney Sr. GM by descendants. D. A. R. Joseph Spencer Chap. Owned many acres of ground in Scioto Co. Ref: Isabel Kinney, Janet Williams, Miss Anna Randal Ross, Mamie Reed. Natl No 27209, Vol 28, p 79. D.A. R. Lin. Fur infor Joseph Spencer Chap.

CLOUSE, JOHN (Franklin Co.)

Served in Rev fr Pa. Br Germany 1758. D in 1822, Plain Twp. Bur in Smith Cem near New Albany. MI: "John Clouse. Died Dec 26, 1822, aged 64 yrs." GM by D.A.R. with bronze marker, May 30, 1912. When a boy he ran away fr home and stole passage on a ship to America, where he was sold for his passage. When the Revolution broke out, he was offered his freedom if he would serve in the army. Fur infor Columbus Chap.

COBLER, MICHAEL (Wayne Co.)

He was a soldier fr the beginning to the end of the Revolutionary War. Children: Michael Jr, Isaac. D Shreve, O. Mch 24, 1842. Bur family cem 2 miles west of Shreve, O. MI: "In memory of Michael Cobler. Died Mch 24, 1842. Aged 87 years and 10 months". Fur infor Wooster-Wayne Chap.

COBURN, ASA (Washington Co.)

Lt 1776, Capt 1777 to close of war, Mass line. Br Sept 14, 1741, Dudley, Mass. Parents: Andrew and Jane (Allen) Coburn. Mar Apr 8, 1762, Mary McClure. Children: Sibyl, Asa, Phineas, Mary, Susannah, Nicholas. D Washington Co, O, 1789. Bur near Wolf Creek Mills, Waterford, Washington Co, O. Came to Ohio in company with Col Cushing and Maj Goodale Aug 19, 1788. The first families to settle in Northwest Territory. Owned 3 shares in Ohio Co. Farmer. Ref: p 256, Vol 45, D. A. R. Lin., Mass Rev records; Washington Co History. Fur infor Marietta Chap.

COCHRAN, WILLIAM (Brown Co.)

Served in Revolutionary War fr Pa in different Regts. Br County Antrim, Ireland, 1722. Mar Elizabeth Boethe, who died in Ky, 1823. Children: John, br 1781, supposed to be others. Sgt in 1812. D Brown Co O, Mch 1814. Bur on the farm where he lived, near the mouth of East Fork of Eagle Creek near Fitch Bridge. Lived in Pa later in Ky. About 1795 or 1796 came to Brown Co, O. D there at the age of 92. Ref: Robert Cochran, a descendant, Brown Co History; Adams Co Hist. Fur infor Taliaferro Chap.

QUINCY CHEADLE, SON OF ASA CHEADLE, REVOLUTIONARY SOLDIER, AT THE AGE OF 97, ROXBURY, OHIO.

FIRST MEMORIAL TABLET ERECTED BY D. A. R. OF OHIO.

COCHRUN, SIMON, (Allen Co.)

Enl in Monangalia Co, Va. in 1776, served as Pvt and Sgt under Capts David Scott and Berry in the Regt commanded by Col John Gibson. Disch Oct 28, 1780. Br July 3, 1755. Children: Wesley, Thomas. D June 9, 1845. Bur in Ash Grove, Allen Co, O. MI: "Reverend Simon Cochrun, Revolutionary Soldier, died June 9, 1845, aged 89 years, 11 mos, 6 days." Subsequent to Revolutionary War moved to Ky, then came to Ohio and settled on land grant in Franklin Co. Later moved to Allen Co. Methodist preacher. Ref: Eckemodis Rev soldier of Va, p 102, Register of Ohio Society S. A. R., p 83, Vol 3, Senate Doc 1st session, 23rd Congress, p 514. Fur infor Lima Chap.

COCK, MOSES, (Pickaway Co.)

An Associator in Westtown Company, Chester Co, Pa. Br 1742, Chester Co, Pa. Mar Hannah Evenson in 1766. D 1808 in Pickaway Co, O. Ref: No 99760, Vol 100, p 235, D.A.R. Lin.

COCKERILL, THOMAS, (Fayette Co.)

In Va Tr in West and paid off in Oct 1775 known as the "Romney & Winchester Payroll." Br 1760, Loudoun Co, Va. Mar Millien Lucas, Jan 10, 1786. Children: Newton, Wm. S, Thomas L, Jane, Elizabeth. D Fayette Co, O, July 9, 1842. Bur Walnut Creek Cem, about 2 miles below New Martinsburg, close to a fence near the road. MI: "In memory of Thos. Cockerill, who departed this life July 9, 1842, in the 82nd year of his age". Marker resembles a straight, flat rock. Lived in the country. Ref: Va State Library History of Fayette Co, and family Bible. Fur infor Washington Court House Chap.

CODDINGTON, WILLIAM, (County not stated.)

In 1779 served as Pvt in Capt James Humphrey's NY Mil. Br New York, 1754. D Ohio, 1839. Ref: Vol 50, p 70, Natl No 49158. D. A. R. Lin.

COFFINBERRY, GEORGE, (Richland Co.)

Pvt in the Va Mil. Br 1760. D Aug 13, 1851. Bur Springmill Cem, Springmill, O. MI: Name and State Tr. GM by Mary Washington D. A. R. Chap, bronze marker, in 1911. Fur infor Mary Washington Chap.

COKE, PHILIP, (Hamilton Co.)

Br 1753, North Carolina. D 1826. Ref: S. A. R. Fur infor Cincinnati Chap.

COLE, EPHRIAM, (Adams Co.)

Enl Nov 16, 1777, for three yrs, under Capt J. Drown; made prisoner while acting as spy; released. Br Maryland Children: James M, Leonard and Allaniah, Bur Collins Cem south of West Union. Ref: Evans and Stivers History of Adams Co. Fur infor Sycamore Chap.

COLE, JOHN, (Washington Co.)

Col John Dagget's Regt as Pvt. As aide to Capt Jas Hill, Col William's Regt. Br Sept 12, 1742, Swansea, Mass. Parents: John and Abigail (Butts Cole). Mar Mercy Wood, July 18, 1764, (1st wife); Susannah Salisbury, Mch 18, 1777 (2nd wife). Children: Asa, Nathan, Noah, Elizabeth, Candace, Philip, Icabod, John. D Oct 12, 1826, Warren Twp, Washington Co, O. Bur Gravel Bank Cem, Washington Co, O. Grave slightly north of center. MI: "A soldier of Rev. John Cole. Br Swansea, Mass, 1742, died Washingotn Co, O, 1826. Capt James Hill's Company, Col John Dagget's Regt, Bristol, R. I., 1777. This tablet erected by his descendants." GM by Marietta Chap with Revolutionary Marker Aug 22, 1918. John Cole was great-great grandson of James Cole, owner of Cole's Hill, first burial ground of Plymouth Colony and first individual owner of Plymouth Rock. Ref: Ernest B. Cole's Bk, Descendants of James Cole, Plymouth, Mass, 1683. Mortimer A. Cole's Bk, John Cole and his descendants of Swansea, Mass, 1742. Fur infor Marietta Chap.

COLE, JUSTIN, (Lake Co.)

Pvt 1775 Capt Israel Chapin's Company, Col John Fellow's Regt; 1779 enlist. 3 mo in levies. Br 1751 Hatfield, Mass. Mar Elizabeth Spofford (1765-1848). D 1829, Madison, O. Bur Madison Village Cem. Ref: No 77230, Vol 78, D.A.R. Lin. Fur infor New Connecticut Chap.

COLEMAN, JACOB, (Cuyahoga Co.)

Pvt Va Continental Tr. Br 1762. D after 1824 at Euclid. Bur Twp cem Stop 8, abandoned. GM by Western Reserve Chap. Fur infor Western Reserve Chap.

COLEMAN, JAMES, (Union Co.)

Bur Watkins Cem, Jerome Twp. Ref: Col. W. L. Curry Hist Union Co. Fur infor Hannah Emerson Dustin Chap.

COLEMAN, JOHN, (Fairfield Co.)

Bur Cem in Canal Winchester. Fur infor Elizabeth Sherman Reese Chap.

COLEMAN, LEONARD, (Belmont Co.)

Br Apr 14, 1754. D Mch 28, 1839. Bur Coleman cem at Dillies Bottom or Jacobsburg, both in Belmont Co. Ref: Mrs. Frank Bernhardt. Fur infor Mrs. A. L. McFarland, St. Clairsville, of Wheeling D.A.R.

COLEMAN, NATHANIEL, (Ashtabula Co.)

He took part in the Boston Tea Party and the battle of Bunker Hill; was among those stationed at "Horseneck" to intercept the landing of the British. Served in the Lexington Alarm, 4 mos in Continental Regts; was taken at the defeat of Quebec Sept 31, 1775. Pvt. Br 1754. Children: One was Nathaniel, Jr. D May 17, 1837, Wayne, Ashtabula Co, O, and bur in Wayne Cem. "He died honored and revered at the advanced age of 83 years." Ref: "Connecticut Men in the Revolution"; History of Ashtabula Co. Fur infor Mary Stanley Chap.

COLEMAN, NENIAD, (Hamilton Co.)

Br 1746, Virginia. Mar Susan, dau of Jacob Reeder. D 1823. Fur infor Cincinnati Chap.

COLLETT, DANIEL, (Warren Co.)

Served in 1778, Capt Chas. Porterfield's Company, Col Daniel Morgan's 7th and 11th Regts of Va. Br 1752 in Virginia. Mar Mary Haines. D 1835. Bur Friends Caesars Creek Meeting House Cem. Ref: No 65368, Vol 66, p 128, D.A.R. Lin.

COLLIER, JAMES, (Highland Co.)

Capt. He belonged to Flying Camp; was with Gen Washington through N. J.; terrible suffering at Valley Forge; took active part in battles of Long Island, White

Plains and Brandywine. Assisted in capture of Hessians at Trenton. Br Apr 20 (O S) May 1, (N S) 1752, Lancaster Co—now Dauphin, Pa. Parents: James and Susannah (Doughan) Collier. Mar Martha Rutherford, Apr 23, 1787. Children: Susannah, Margaret, Samuel, Eleanor, Thomas, Mary, John, James, William G, William, Rutherford. D Jan 3, 1844, Greenfield, O. Bur in Greenfield Cem northeast of Greenfield, Sec 1, Lot 18. MI: "James Collier br Apr 20th, 1752. Died Jan 3, 1844." GM by Julian White Chap. Official marker with name plate, in 1923. In 1778 he received a commission to raise a company to go up the Susquehannah river to guard the frontier. He built Fort Muncy. Received commission to enlist a company of Rangers. A farmer. For his gallant serv he was presented by La Fayette with a fine sword. Ref: Family record p 26; Pa Archieves, 5th series, Vol 7, p 362. Natl No 80311, D. A. R. Lin. Fur infor Juliana White Chap.

COLLINGS, JAMES, (Adams Co.)

Pvt in Capt John Lynch's Company, 5th Md Regt, Commanded by Col Wm Richardson, served Jan 18, 1777 to Aug 16, 1780. Bur in Collins Cem east of West Union. Ref: Evans and Stivers History of Adams Co. Fur infor Sycamore Chap.

COLLINS, BENJAMIN, (Morrow Co.)

1779 to 1783 a Pvt in NY Mil under Capts Peter Van Vort, Job Wright, and Dunham. His Col was Van Renssalaer. On Nov 22, 1832 pension claim allowed and paid to Apr 3, 1840. Br Sept 16, 1751 in RI. Mar 1st to Elizabeth Foster and 2d to Thankful ———. Children: Elizabeth (br in New York State dau of Thankful). D Apr 3, 1840 in Morrow Co. Bur in Stiner's Cem, Lincoln Twp, Morrow Co, O. Grave on edge of cem by side of road. Benj Collins removed fr RI to Conn then to Junius NY and later to Saratoga fr which place he enlisted in the NY State Mil. He brought with him to Ohio his only dau, Elizabeth Hubble, a widow. Ref: T. E. Buck, office of city surveyor, Mansfield, O, and Natl No 71685 Vol 72, D. A. R. Lin. Fur infor Mt Gilead Chap.

COLLINS, JAMES S., (Fairfield Co.)

Bur in Collins Chapel Cem. Fur infor Elizabeth Sherman Reese Chap.

COLLINS, JOHN, (Coshocton Co.)

D 1804-08 below Dresden. Bur Cem in Virginia Twp. Ref: Co History. Fur infor Coshocton Chap.

COLLINS, WILLIAM, (Montgomery Co.)

Enl Nov 1, 1780 as a substitute for his father who was drafted in Va under Capt James Legg, Col MacWilliams; served two mos and entered again May 6, 1781 as a substitute for Benj Stevens under Col Thomas Barber; again July 3 1781, substitute for James Porter, in company of Capt James Hawkins, Col James Matthews, disch Sept 3, 1781; served the 4th time under Capt James Jamison all in Pa line, having transferred thereto fr Va. Br 1764 in Va. Parent: John Collins. D Dayton. Very little is known of this patriot. Probably lived for a while in Chillicothe, O; and also lived for some time in Ripley, Ind. Fur infor Richard Montgomery Chap S. A. R.

COLSON, CHRISTOPHER, (Lake Co.)

Enl July 9, 1781 at age of 16 and served as a fifer throughout the war. Served under the command of Lt Col Calvin Smith 6th Mass Regt. Br May 10, 1765, Weymouth, Mass. D Willoughby, O. Bur on Daniel's farm just east of Willoughby village. GM by New Connecticut Chap. Came to Ohio in 1810. He was Willoughby's first Post Master and walked to Washington to secure his appointment. Ref: No 26245, Vol 27, p 89. D. A. R. Lin. Fur infor New Connecticut Chap.

COLVILLE, JAMES, (Licking Co.)

Enl Winchester Aug 1777. Pvt Col John Gibson's Regt. Apr 1 to July 1780 was government spy; Sgt last ten mos. Br Oct 7, 1757, Frederick Co, Va. D Dec 29, 1838. Bur Hilltop Cem, Bowers farm, Buena Vista Rd. MI: "Rev War." GM Hetuck Chap in 1909. Was a pensioner. Ref: History of Licking Co by E. M. P. Brister. Fur infor Hetuk Chap.

COMBS, JOHN, (Mahoning Co.)

Pvt Pa Mil. Br 1747. D 1822 and bur in Poland village Cem. Ref: S. A. R. Fur infor Western Reserve Chap.

COMPTON, JOSEPH, (Butler Co.)

Capt and Pvt under Washington at Valley Forge, and served in six Regts at Monmouth Co, N.J. Capt in two tr of Light Horse. Br Dec 29, 1759, Middletown, N. J. Mar Nancy Tapscott. Children: One was named Nancy. D Mch 13, 1841, Butler Co, O, and bur in Primitive Baptist Cem, Trenton, O. Was commissioned Adjutant of the 4th Regt. A farmer. Fur infor Col Jonathan Bayard Smith Chap.

CONAWAY, CHARLES, (Harrison Co.)

Enl Sept 1777 to Apr 1779; was a drummer boy in the Battle of the Brandywine in which battle his brother Samuel was wounded. Br June 30, 1752, Kent Co, Md. Mar Priscilla Barnes, widow of Jonathan Rees. Children: 1st died in infancy, Daniel, Sarah. D 1847, Harrison Co, O. Bur on the old Conway farm, about four miles from Scio, Harrison Co, O. Grave on the edge of a field, under an elm tree, by his brother Michael and wife. A minister in the M. E. Church as was his brother, Samuel. He was a close friend of and co-worker with Bishop Asbury, who in 1788 appointed him to the village of Pittsburgh, Pa. where he spent seven yrs as preacher and presiding elder. He applied for a pens in 1834. His claim was allowed. Has no descendants living. Fur infor Nabby Lee Ames Chap.

CONAWAY, MICHAEL, (Harrison Co.)

Serving as a Pvt on Ship Defense Sept 19, 1776. Br Jan 27, 1738, near Baltimore, Md. Mar Elizabeth Davis 1779. Children: Michael, John, Charles, Catherine, Susanna, Elizabeth. D at an advanced age in Harrison Co prior to 1847. Bur on a farm near Scio, O, once owned by Moses Conaway, in a field by his wife and brother, Rev Charles Conaway, also a Revolutionary soldier. None of these graves were marked a few yrs since. Ref: Archives of Md, Vol 18, p 606. Jessie F and Cora F Conway, York, Nebr. Fur infor Nabby Lee Ames Chap.

CONDON, REDMAN, (Ross Co.)

In 3d Company. Capt George Bush, New Eleventh Pa Continental Line May 17, 1777 to 1780. Br Ireland in 1755. D Jan 8, 1830 in Ross Co, O. Bur in field on his old farm on the Scioto Trail, south of Chillicothe and about three miles north of the Pike Co line. At the age of 22, when he enlisted, was a farmer, five feet four inches. Was in battle of Short Hills, Chemung and Elizabethtown. Allowed a pen Apr 20, 1818. Fur infor Nathaniel Massie Chap.

CONINE, JACOB, (Muskingum Co.)

Bur at Irville. Grave has a stone vault or box over it but the dates have not been placed thereon. Fur infor Muskingum Chap.

CONKEY, EZEKIEL, (Wayne Co.)

D Aug 17, 1837. Bur Knupps Cem one mile west of Rittman, O. MI: "Ezekiel Conkey died Aug 17, 1837, aged 75 yrs." Fur infor Wooster-Wayne Chap.

CONKLIN, DAVID, (Delaware Co.)

D 1858. Bur in cem in Orange Twp. Fur infor Delaware Chap.

CONKLIN, DAVID, (Licking Co.)

Lt under Capts Livingston and Todd, Col Dubois' Regt, NY Line. Br Dutchess Co, N. Y. D in Licking Co, O. Ref: Natl No 99235, D. A. R. Lin.

CONLEY, MICHAEL, (Brown Co.)

Bur Sardinia. Fur infor Ripley Chap.

CONNIE, JEREMIAH, (Ashland Co.)

Enl Martinsburg, Berkeley Co, Va in 1781, serving 3 mos in Capt Howell's Company, Col Gaskin's Regt, Va Tr; also Col White's Continental Dragoons, and served until Aug 23, 1783; also with Anthony Wayne at Fallen Timbers. D May 9, 1832, Richland Co (now Ashland Co.) Bur in Old Perrysville Cem Green Twp. Lot has no number. GM being marked by Sarah Copus Chap in 1927. He was a pioneer of Richland Co and was allowed a pens Oct 13, 1825. A farmer. Fur infor Sarah Copus Chap.

CONNER, JOSEPH, (Montgomery Co.)

Pvt in the Army of the Revolution for 18 mos. Berkley Co, Va about May 1777, Capt John's Company. Joined Regt commanded by Col Hunt at Winchester. About Nov 1778 again enl for the war in company of cavalry commanded by Col White. After a year was transferred to Col Washington's Regt and served until close of war in companies of Capts Grimes and Hughes. In battle of Guilford Court House and Monks Corner; also at Yorktown. Br 1754, Va. Grave not located, might be in Miami Co. Applied for pens at Troy, O, Mch 20, 1821 and it was granted. Lived then in Newberry Twp on a small lot of land. A farmer and laborer. No family. His wife, 69 years old at that time, very infirm and unable to work. Supported by neighborly charity. Granted a pens. Fur infor Richard Montgomery Chap S. A. R.

CONNOR, JOHN, (Muskingum Co.)

Bur in Pleasant Hill Cem near New Concord. MI: "Rev. Soldier." Fur infor Muskingum Chap.

CONRAD, CLINE, (Delaware Co.)

Buried in cem at Marlboro. Fur infor Delaware Chap.

CONVERSE, REV. JERMIAH, (Madison Co.)

Pvt soldier. Revolutionary War starting with the Lexington Alarm. Br Aug 5, 1761. Parents: Capt Paint and Mary Lee Converse. Mar Rhoda Converse (2nd cousin.) Children: One was Jeremiah. D June 26, 1837 Madison Co. Bur Darby Twp Cem near Plain City, O, near south end. MI: Name, birth and death. Also that he was a Revolutionary soldier. GM by London Chap 1928. Enl at age of 15 or 16 yrs. Returned in 1783. Came fr Vermont to Ohio. Farmer and M. E. Minister. Ref: p 14 Conn Men in the Revolution. Fur infor London Chap.

COOK ABSOLOM, (Clermont Co.)

Enlisted at age 16. D Sept 23, 1822, age 73 yrs. Bur Laurel, Clermont Co. Ref: Mrs. J. R. Hicks, Amelia, O. Fur infor Jane Dailey, State Chairman.

COOK, ASAPH, (Huron Co.)

At battle of Lexington, Mass. Certificate No 7827 L. U. (?) rest burned, dated Dec 1, 1780, Asaph Cooke Lieut in Capt Silas Child's Company of the Regt of Charlotte Co Mil commanded by Lieut-Col Alexander Webster and Major Thomas Armstrong. Was made Capt July 24, 1780. Br Mch 6, 1748. North Adams, Mass. Parents: Asaph and Sarah (Parker) Cooke. Mar Thankful Parker, June 17, 1776. Children: Asaph, Sarah, Chloe, Elutherus, Hannah, Thankful, Erastus, Israel, Aluima, Rhoda. D Sept 22, 1826, Cook's Corner, O, now North Monroeville, and bur there. MI: Name on soldiers monument. Fur infor Sally DeForest Chap.

COOK, CHAUNCEY, (Erie Co.)

Bur in Erie Co. Fur infor Martha Pitkin Chap.

COOK, EBENEZER, (Huron Co.)

Br 1759. D Sept 4, 1847. Bur in Fitchville Cem. MI: "Died Sept 4, 1847, aged 88 yrs." GAR Stone marker. Pensioner. Fur infor Sally DeForest Chap.

COOK, JAMES, "DEA," (Trumbull Co.)

Pvt NY State Tr. Pension 1831. Br 1762. Mar Diana, (wife of James, d Nov 23, 1850, aged 65 yrs.) D Apr 19, 1851. Bur East Mecca. MI: "James Cook, died Apr 19, 1851, age 89 yrs." GM probably by family. Fur infor Mary Chesney Chap.

COOK, JOHN, (Morrow Co.)

Bur North Fork Cem in eastern part of Co. Fur infor Mt. Gilead Chap.

COOK, JOSEPH, (Butler Co.)

Lt Enl as Pvt, served as Adjutant. 1778 was promoted to Lt to take the place of Peter Ferguson. Br 1750 in Granville, N. Y. D 1834, Oxford, O. Ref: Natl No 26184, Vol. 27, p 66, D. A. R. Lin.

COOK, JOSEPH, (Huron Co.)

1776 with expedition to Canada under Capt Hinman and Col Warner. 1777 and 1778 served under Capt William White and Col Warner. 1779 under Parmalee Allen and Seth Warner. 1782 under Wilp (looks like Wilp) and Warner. Engaged in battle of Bennington. Br Apr 13, 1758, Wallingford, Conn. Mar Rachel Langdon. Children: Charles L, Chancy, Electa, Rachel. D Aug 26, 1845, North Monroeville. Bur North Monroeville, O. MI: Name on soldiers monument. Fur infor Sally De Forest Chap.

COOK, MARIMAN, (Geauga Co.)

Pvt Conn Mil. Placed on pension roll 1833. Br Nov 12, 1761, Cheshire, Conn. Parents: Elam. Mar Dolly Bradley, Cheshire, Conn. Children: Loalma, Hiram, John, Clarissa, Elzar. D Aug 25, 1858, Burton, O. Bur Fox Cem, (Lower Cem). MI: "Mariman Cook died Aug 25, 1858, age 97." GM by granite marker and D. A. R. marker. A soldier in the Rev. He served in cooking for the officers and caring for sick. He was with Josiah Smith at Horse Neck, and saw his head trepanned after fight. Came to Burton about 1807. Ref: Pioneer History Geauga Co. p 455. Pension Records Vol. 3, p 514. Fur infor Taylor Chap.

COOK, NOAH, (Richland Co.)

Pvt and Sgt at Arms, Pa State Tr. Br 1755 Morrows Co, N. J. Mar 2nd wife, Sarah Baldwin. Children: Phoebe, Hannah, Lida, Jabes, Rachel, Lois, Thomas. D

Lexington O, Dec 30, 1831. Bur Lexington Cem Lexington, O. MI: Name and Company. GM by Mary Washington D. A. R. Chap in 1911. Ref: Mrs. Jennie Venum Cook, (Mrs. J. M.) Park Ave, West Mansfield, O., Miss Mary E. Blymyer, 35 Blymyer Ave., Mansfield, O. Fur infor Mary Washington Chap.

COOK, ROSWELL, (Delaware Co.)

Bur Oak Grove Cem. Fur infor Delaware Chap.

COOK, STEPHEN, (Knox Co.)

With his brother Noah, enl fr Washington Co, Pa. Rangers in Capt Eleazer Williams Company 1782. Br Morris Co, N. J. 1751. Mar Sarah McFarland in 1775. D 1829 Martinsburg, Knox Co, O. Ref: Natl No 43887. Vol 44, p 333 D. A. R. Lin.

COOK, CAPT. THOMAS B. (Guernsey Co.)

Made Lt 8th Pa Regt Aug 9, 1776. Made Capt July 25, 1777 under Col Daniel Brodhead 8th Pa. Went South and served under Gens. Marion, Sumpter, Pickens and Greene until the close of the war. Br Sept 4, 1749. Mar Elizabeth Smith in 1782, Spartansburg, S. C. Children: Joseph, William, John, Thomas, Elizabeth, Jane, Rebecca, Isaac. D Nov 5, 1831, Guernsey Co, O, and bur in Old Cambridge, Cambridge, O. First row of lots on west side. MI: "Capt Cook died Nov 5, 1831 aged 92 yrs, 2 mo, & 1 day." His wife's stone has "Relict of Capt Thos. Cook Rev Soldier." GM by the family with upright marble slab. He took up 200 acres of land on Cooks Run 3 miles east of Cambridge, O. A farmer, and was sent north with the Pa Tr. Is said to have been taken prisoner at the battle of Three Rivers, Canada; was taken out to execution, made Masonic sign of distress, was sent back to Guard House by young English officer and that night freed. Said to be on record of Masonic Lodge, Cambridge, O. Fur infor Anna Asbury Stone Chap.

COOK, ZACHARIAH, (Pike Co.)

Pensioned for service and in 1840 living in Beaver Twp age 96 yrs. Br about 1744. Bur Beaver Cem, Pike Co, O. Ref: C. M. Emory, Stockdale, O. who verified the burial place. Fur infor Census of 1840, copied by Jane Dailey, State Chairman.

COOLEY, LUTHER, SR., (Huron Co.)

D Jan 1, 1842. Bur Wm Bissell farm, Clarksfield Twp. Fur infor Sally De Forest Chap.

COOMBS, MAHLON, (Licking Co.)

Pvt in Va Line. Br Loudoun Co, Va, 1759. D Licking Co, O, 1834. Pensioned for one year actual service. Natl No 29431, p 159, Vol 30, D. A. R. Lin.

COOPER, EZEKIEL, (Belmont Co.)

Ensign in Mass Inf 1775. Lt 1777. Capt in Col Ebenezer Sprout's Vt Regt at close of war. Br 1745, Rowley, Mass. Mar Hannah Smith in 1776. Bur M. E. Cem, St Clairsville, O. MI: "Ezekiel Cooper Revolutionary Soldier." Came to Ohio in 1788, and in 1807 was living in Warrenton, O. Member of the Cincinnati of Mass. Ref: Natl No 36174, Vol 37, p 64, D. A. R. Lin. Fur infor Mrs. A. L. McFarland, St Clairsville, O, member of D. A. R. Wheeling, W. Va.

COOPER, JOHN, (Brown Co.)

Ensign. D 1835. Bur Liberty Cem, marked by stone. Fur infor Lieutenant Byrd Chap.

COOPER, OBEDIAH, (Cuyahoga Co.)

Corp NY Tr. Br 1759. D 1851. Bur Warrensville, East Cem. Fur infor Western Chap.

COOPER, SPENCER, (Hamilton Co.)

Capt served in Westmoreland and Greenbriar Cos Va. Br 1740. Mar 4th wife Nancy Crain, mother of these 12 children. Children: Spencer, Thomas, Benton, Sarah, William, Keziah, Polly, Nancy, Rebecca, Hiram, Joseph, Osborn, Cynthiana. D May 17, 1809. Bur Spring Grove, Cincinnati, O. Came to Ohio 1792; farm Sec 27 still in family hands. Children of other 3 marriages (36) remained in Va Natl No. 126968 etal. Ref: 8th Annual Report 1910-1911 Va State Library Assoc. Fur infor Cincinnati Chap.

COOPER, WILLIAM, (Brown Co.)

Pvt. Br Monmouth Co, N. Y. 1760. Mar Elizabeth Richmond, 1783. Children: John, Joanna, Margaret, Sydney, Thomas, Mary, Charles, Ellen, Zenas, Jacob, Eliza, Peter, David. D Brown Co, O. Bur Private Cem. He came to Ohio in 1812. Farmer. Ref: Brown Co Hist. Fur infor Lieutenant Byrd Chap.

COOSARD, VALENTINE, (Portage Co.)

Enl Amboy, N. J. in 1776. In battle at Ft Washington. Taken prisoner at that battle and confined in the Sugar House at New York for two mos. Pvt. Br Chambersburg, Pa. 1745. Mar —— Riefsnyder. D Rootstown, O. 1846. Bur Rootstown, O. Placed on pens roll Feb 28, 1833. Ref: Bureau of Pensions. Natl No 41059. Fur infor old Northwest Chap.

COPPLE, DANIEL, (Adams Co.)

Served as Pvt in German Bn of Continental Tr Revolutionary Army. Was member of Capt Daniel Burchart's Company between Oct 4, 1776 and July 1777. On the rolls of Capt Peter Boyer's Company fr Aug 1777 to June 1779. His name appears as Daniel Kettle on the rolls of Capt Michael Boyer's Company fr Nov 1779 to Dec 1780. Bur in Old Dutch Graveyard in Liberty Twp. Unmarked. Could speak only a few words of English and that with great difficulty. Fur infor Sycamore Chap.

CORN, GEORGE, (Jackson Co.)

Was father of 20 children. 10 came to this Co. Bur in country graveyard on the Phillips farm between Oak Hill and Samsonville, Jefferson Twp. A John R. Corn is mentioned as a voter in 1816 in the 1st election held in Bloomfield Twp, Jackson Co. This is probably a son. Fur infor Captain John James Chap.

CORTELYOU, HENRY, (Hamilton Co.)

Minute Man from Somerset Co, N. J. Br New Brunswick, N. J. 1760. D 1825, Reading, O. Ref: Natl No 11731, Vol 12, p 277, D. A. R. Lin.

COTTON, BENJAMIN, (Medina Co.)

Corp fr Conn in Gen Washington's Life Guard. Br 1758. D 1846. Bur Seville, Medina Co, O. GM by Western Reserve Chap. Dates of birth and death are same as Benjamin Cotton, Natl No 10180, Vol 11, D. A. R. Lin. We have recorded burial in Medina, as grave marked and record filed by D. A. R. Chap. Fur infor Western Reserve Chap.

COTTON, JOHN, (Mahoning Co.)

Ranger 1778-1783. Blacksmith Artillery artificer 1779 under command of Col Benj Flower. Pvt Washington Co Mil. Br 1746. Children: Joshua, Theophilus, John. D 1831. Bur pvt ground, Austintown, O. Farmer and merchant. Ref: p 129 Hist Trumbull and Mahoning Cos. Pa Archives Series 3, Vol 23, p 309, Series 5, Vol 3, p 1129. Series 5, Vol 4, p 704. For infor Mahoning Chap.

COULTER, JOHN, (Licking Co.)

Enl Pvt 1780 Capt John Lynn's Company, 5th Regt. Br Charlestown, Md. 1752. D Union Twp. Bur Union Station Cem. Was a pensioner. Ref: Hist of Licking Co by E. M. P. Brister. Fur infor Hetuck Chap.

COUNTRYMAN, GEORGE, (Mahoning Co.)

Pvt "NY Men of the Rev", p 172. 1st Regt Tryon Co Mil. Bur probably in Green Twp, O. In 1790 lived in Canajohara, N. Y. Came to Green Twp very early, settled in Sec 9 and 10. Trumbull and Mahoning Co Hist p 197. Fur infor Mahoning Chap.

COUNTRYMAN, JACOB, (Mahoning Co.)

Pvt. Enl Men 2d Regt "The Line" p 31, "NY Men of the Rev." D probably in Green Twp. Settled in Green Twp with his brother on sec 9 and 10. Trumbull and Mahoning Co Hist p 197. Fur infor Mahoning Chap.

COUNTS, JACOB, (Miami Co.)

Bur Raper Chapel, two miles north of Troy. GM Miami Chap with bronze marker in 1904. Fur infor Miami Chap.

COURTRIGHT, ABRAM VAN CAMPEN, (Fairfield Co.)

6th Bn 4th Company under Capt John Van Etten of Northampton Co, Pa Mil and also in Capt Weisenfeld's Company of N.Y. Br July 8, 1748. Baptized Walpeck, N. J. Reformed Dutch Church. Parents: Johannes (or John) Courtright and Margaret Dennemerken. Mar Affy or Effie Drake. Children: John, Jesse D, Abram Van Jr., Margaret, Christina. D Jan 12, 1825, Greencastle, Fairfield Co, O. Bur Greencastle Cem. MI: names and dates. GM by family years ago. Came to Ohio 1803 fr Pa taking six weeks to make journey; bought farm 1 mile east of Greencastle. Ref: Mrs. Jas Pallon, 2215 Bryden Rd., Columbus, O. who has original will made 1817, and deed 1803. Fur infor Elizabeth Sherman Reese Chap.

COUTS, CHRISTIAN, (Crawford Co.)

Liberty Twp. Bur Crall Cem, 5 miles east of Bucyrus. Fur infor Hannah Crawford Chap.

COVALT, ABRAHAM, (Hamilton Co.)

At 18 embarked on ship and was at storming of Martinico; later enlisted in Bedford Co, Pa; Rank, Captain to end of war. Br 1734, Pa. (Great Egg Harbor). Mar Lois Pendleton, (1738-1838, br in NJ, d Hamilton Co in 1838). Children: six sons and four daus. One dau Mary, mar Joseph Jones; one son, Cheniah, A. Covalt, Jr., and T. Covalt. D 1791. Killed by Indians, but body recovered by comrades. Bur at fort with honors. ("on his father's farm" stated by Mrs. Whallon, Cincinnati.) GM by monument. Established Colvalt Station east of Milford and settled near Columbia. Ref: S. A. R. Yr. Bk; this record copied from letter of his daughter, Mrs. Jones; see "Jones' History of Early Cincinnati," p 60-64, published in 1879, Cincinnati. Fur infor Cincinnati Chap.

COWDEN, JOHN, (Knox Co.)

Served as Pvt with his father in Capt James Dunn's Company of Chester Co, Pa Mil, Col Patterson Bell commanding Bn. (See Pa Archives Series II, Vol 14, p 112.) Br Jan 27, 1756, Faggs Manor, Chester Co, Pa. Parents: Robert Cowden Sr., and Jennett McChesney. Mar Mary Fletcher (br 1776, d 1820) in 1801. Children: Jane (br 1802), Sarah (1803), Robert (1805), David (1807), John (1809), William (1811), James (1813), infant (br Mch 30, 1815, d Apr 10, 1815), Mary (1818) and Catherine (1820). D 1840, near Mt Liberty, Knox Co, O. He is bur on the farm now (1929) owned by Leroy Squires situated on a crossroad leading fr the Three C's Highway at Mt Liberty, to the Delaware Road 1½ miles north of Mt Liberty. No tombstone at the grave. Farmer. Fur infor Kokosing Chap.

COWDERY, JACOB, (Meigs Co.)

Br 1761. D Apr 5,1846. Bur Keno, O. MI: "Revolutionary Soldier." Age 85 yrs. Ref: George Cowdery, Racine, O. Fur infor Return Jonathan Meigs Chap.

COWEN, WILLIAM, (Clermont Co.)

Enl in spring of 1776 fr Pa under Capts Samuel Davidson and Richard Dunlap, Col William Piper. Aptd 1st Sgt under Capt Solomon Adams. Lt under Capt James Clark and from May 1781 until fall 1781 under Capt James Irwin. Br Jan 1755, Donegal Twp, Pa. Mar Barbara Pelser. Children: Elijah and others; one was Michael (b Bedford Co, Pa, 1804; mar Mary Anne Roudebush 1831). D 1834 near Newtonsville, O. Bur in McCollum Graveyard near Newtonsville, O. A farmer. Came to Clermont Co 1805. He with parents came to Bedford Co, Pa at age of 9 yrs. Ref: Mrs. Cora C. Miller Greeley, 927 W. 76th St, Seattle, Wash. member of Blanchester Chap. Fur infor Blanchester Chap and A. S. Abbott, Bethel, O.

COWGILL, JOHN, (Logan Co.)

Pvt Capt Cooper's Company State Tr Burlington, NJ. "Men in the Rev" p 559. Bur Country Churchyard, between East Liberty and West Middleburgh, say Bellefontaine Chap. Since Mahoning could not locate grave, think they are records of same man. Settled in Smith Twp early in 19th century. Sanderson's Hist of Mahoning Co, p 225, Hist of Columbiana Co, p 309. Fur infor Bellefontaine and Mahoning Chaps.

COWLES, NOAH, (Ashtabula Co.)

Served Pvt and Marine under Capts Lacy, Thacker, Col Herman Swift. Br 1759 Norwich, Conn. Mar Ollie Mills. Children: One was Salmon. D 1840 in Geneva. Bur Old Cem Austinburg. MI: name and dates. Ref: Vol 46, p 364, Vol 51. D. A. R. Line. Fur infor Mary Stanley Chap.

COX, ANDREW, (Hamilton Co.)

Br 1761, Va. D 1852. Fur infor Cincinnati Chap.

COX, BENJAMIN, (Montgomery Co.)

1778, served 9 mos. Pvt under Capt Graham, Col Grimes, Gen Butler, fr Rowan, N. C. Br 1746, Hampshire Co, W. Va. Parents: Col Isaac Cox, Miss Morehead. Mar Rachael ————, (br 1760, d 1822.) Children: Elizabeth, Sarah, Susannah, William, John, Benjamin, Charles, Rachale, Lewis, Jesse. D Dayton, O. Montgomery Co. Bur Willow View. MI: "In memory of Benjamin Cox, died Dec 20, 1842, in 98th yr of his age. A native of Va." Emigrated fr Va to Nelson Co, Ky, 1779, to Cincinnati O 1788. Brothers: James, Friend, John, David, George, Michael, Gabriel, Joseph, Jonathan; Sisters: Nancy, Ann, Margaret, Polly. Fur infor Hetuck Chap and Richard Montgomery Chap S. A. R.

COX, JAMES, (Hamilton Co.)

Teamster. Bur Supposed to be Columbia. Cincinnati 1819, has brass foundry Ludlow St. Ref: Stryker's, "Men in Rev War," p 860; Mrs. E. P. Whallon, Cincinnati. Fur infor Cincinnati Chap.

COX, JOHN NEW, (Trumbull Co.)

Bur Center; unable to locate place of burial; tried several places. Name fr S. A. R. Yr Bk. Fur infor Mary Chesney Chap.

COX, MICHAEL, (Logan Co.)

Enl Washington Co, Pa. June 1779, served 6 mos Pvt in Capt Cross' Company, in Col Evans' Pa Regt. Enl July 1780, Pvt in Capt Levi Harrods' Company; Enl also July 1781, served 1 mo Orderly Sgt in Capt Gregg's Pa Company. Br Aug 27, 1752, Hampshire Co, Va. Application for pens executed July 23,1833, which was allowed, at which time he was living in Logan Co, Pens Claim S. 5020, which the commissioner of Pensions writes was for Revolutionary Serv. Fur infor Bellefontaine Chap.

COX, TUNIS, (Hamilton Co.)

Pvt fr New Jersey. Stryker's "Men in Rev War" p 462. D Columbia. Bur Pioneer Cem of Columbia. Settled in Columbia in the earliest colony. Was father of James Cox who had brass foundry on Ludlow St in 1819 Directory of Cincinnati; also of Christiana, who mar Solomon Ebersole, a Revolutionary soldier. A William Cox school master in 1819, was probably another son. Two great grandsons of Tunis Cox are still living at Indian Hill, Hamilton Co. Fur infor Cincinnati Chap.

COYKENDALL, HARMON, (Delaware Co.)

Pvt under Col Mickols, Capt John Little, New York Regt. Bur Kingston Twp. Pensioned. Fur infor Delaware Chap.

CRADLEBAUGH, OR (KREIDELBACH) JOHN, (Fairfield Co.)

Pvt Capt Martin Shutter's Company. Br Germany, 1750. Mar Dortha Mundshane (r or s) 1782. Children: Fred, John, Jacob, Andrew, Susan, Elizabeth, Mary, Catherine. D 1820. Bur Grandview Cem, Rushcreek Twp, Bremen, O. GM Elizabeth Sherman Reese D. A. R. 1927. First German Reformed Minister in County preached in homes, without compensation. Ref: Ida S. Freed, Lancaster, O. and Natl No 51782 D. A .R. Lin. Fur infor Elizabeth Sherman Reese Chap.

CRAFT, THOMAS, (Trumbull Co.)

Children: One was Thomas Craft Jr. Bur Hillside, Bazetta. Copied fr S. A. R. Yr Bk. Ref: Craft Jr. aptd administrator of estate Oct 14, 1841. Fur infor Mary Chesney Chap.

CRAIG, JOHN, (Butler Co.)

Name on memorial tablet at Hamilton O as Revolutionary soldier bur in that Co, Dec 4, 1840, Wayne Twp. Fur infor John Reily Chap.

CRAIG, JOHN, (Mahoning Co.)

Pvt D Berlin, Mahoning Co. Bur probably Berlin Center. Ref: Pa Archives series 2, Vol 13, p 46. Fur infor Mahoning Chap.

CRAIG, JOHN S., (Clark Co.)

Enl 1775. Disch 1780. Br Feb 15, 1750. Parents: Andrew Craig, who was born in Ireland 1710, and came to America in 1718. American serv 1776, was killed same year in the retreat fr Canada. Mar Mary Skillings. D Springfield Twp near Springfield O Mch 24, 1838. Bur Fletcher M. E. Cem. Harmony Twp, Clark Co. MI: "John S. Craig a soldier of the Revolution." GM by family, small marble slab. Came to Harmony Twp 1780. Was a man of moral wealth and sterling integrity. Cooper. An old painting of him holding a scroll with dates of enlmt and disch are only records of serv. Fur infor Lagonda Chap.

CRAIG, THOMAS SR., (Vinton Co.)

Enl 1776, Pvt in Capt Rezin Davis' Company, Col Rawling's Md Regt, taken prisoner at Ft Washington; Exchanged 9 mos later and returned to serv under Capt Lynn, same Regt, for three yrs; enl 1780-1784 as Sgt in Capt Spurrier's Md Company. Mar Elizabeth Fleming, Nov 9, 1786, Westmoreland Co, Pa. Children: Large family—only names stated. In 1821 as follows: Daniel, John, Fleming, Messer, a dau. D Aug 24, 1832. Bur near Hamden, though he was a Jackson Co soldier. Pens 1818 (W. 5255) while resident of Jackson Co, O, aged 65 yrs. Widow Elizabeth pensioned 1839, resident of Jackson Co, aged 68 yrs, while living with her son Thomas. Ref: Mrs O. D. Dailey, State Chairman, Albany, O. who holds Mil Rec. Fur infor Capt John James Chap.

CRAINE, ROGER, (Lake Co.)

Pvt fr Medway, Mass in 1781 and served until Dec 1783, under Capt John Fuller and Col Shepherd and was in the battle of White Plains. Br May 4, 1762, Mansfield, Conn. Mar Sarah Whiton, May 20, 1783, Ashford, Conn. Children: Abigail, Cyrus, Ahira, Eleazer, Tower, Horace, Alvin, Samuel, Alexis and Ruth. D June 3, 1841, Painesville, O. Bur 1857 removed to cem in Mentor, Lake Co, O. GM by New Connecticut Chap. Fur infor New Connecticut Chap.

CRAM, ROGER, (Lake Co.)

Pvt 3 yrs Conn Continental Line. Br 1762, Mansfield, Conn. Mar Sarah Whiton. D 1841 Painesville, O. Ref: Vol 100, D. A. R. Lin.

CRAMER, FREDERICK, Lt, (Trumbull Co.)

Lt 1777 in Capt James Anderson's Company. Br 1751. Mar Elizabeth Willett. D 1834 in Hubbard, O. Ref: Natl No 65905. Vol 66 p 312, D. A. R. Lin.

CRANDALL, AMARIAH, (Lake Co.)

Enl fr Stonington, Conn, Apr 1, 1779, for one yr under Capt Sheffield; enlisting again in June 1780 for two mos under Capt Elijah Palmer and Lt Col Richards. Bn Apr 2, 1759, Westerly, R. I. Mar Prudence Avery of Conn. Children: Elijah, Elisha, Sarah and Daniel. D Jan 18, 1861. Bur Middle Ridge Cem, Madison, Lake Co, O. GM New Connecticut Chap. Came to Ohio in 1820. Fur infor New Connecticut Chap.

CRANE, CALEB, (Hamilton Co.)

Lt in Morris Co, N. J. in 1778-82. Pensioned. Bur N. J. D Hamilton Co. Natl No 82836, Vol 83, D. A. R. Lin.

CRANE, CALVIN, (Mahoning Co.)

Pvt Abner Crane's Company, Feb 9, 1779 to May 4, 1779 in Mass. Capt Joseph Richard's Company Aug 14, 1779. Served one mo and two days. Ralph

Thompson's Company served one mo and 18 days. Bur Mahoning Co. Came to Canfield early in 19th Century. Farmer. Ref: Mass Soldiers and Sailors Vol 5, p 14-80. Old Deeds p 66 A. Fur infor Mahoning Chap.

CRANMER, JOHN, M. D., (Hamilton Co.)

Revolutionary soldier. (No serv stated.) D 1832, Cincinnati, O. Fur infor Cincinnati Chap.

CRANSTON, JOHN, (Champaign Co.)

Pvt in RI Mil. Br Newport, R. I. 1775. D Woodstock, O. 1825. Ref: 25550. p 202, Vol 26, D. A. R. Lin.

CRARY, CHRISTOPHER, (Union Co.)

Pvt in Capt John Williams' Company, detached to serve under Lt Col Nathan Gallup at Fort Griswold, July 11, 1779. In marine serv; was twice taken prisoner, the first time he escaped fr the Halifax prison, second time was imprisoned on the British ship, Jersey, but was finally liberated. Br 1759, New London, Conn. Grandson of Oliver Crary, native of Conn. D 1848. Bur Union Co, O. He was the first actual settler in Kirtland, Lake Co, O. In 1837 removed to Union Co, O. Fur infor New Connecticut and Bellefontaine Chaps.

CRARY, JOHN, (Hamilton Co.)

Br 1748. D 1838. Ref: S.A.R. Fur infor Cincinnati Chap.

CRAWFORD, JAMES, (Franklin Co.)

Enl Amherst, Nova Scotia, Nov 6, 1776, and while in command of a whale boat was captured by the British Aug, 1777, and carried to Halifax; kept 9 mo, when he escaped and returned to Boston. Br Ireland Apr 10, 1757. Mar Martha Dickey July 4, 1876. D June 14, 1838, Reynoldsburg. Bur Old Seceeder Graveyard, 1½ miles south of Reynoldsburg. GM by Revolutionary Grave Committee with bronze marker, May 30, 1912. Emigrated to Nova Scotia in 1763. Moved to Ohio in 1802 and settled in Reynoldsburg. Fur infor Columbus Chap.

CRAWFORD, JOHN, (Highland Co.)

D Dec 1, 1846. Bur Auburn Cem north of Hillsboro. MI: "John Crawford, died Dec 1, 1846, aged 101 yrs 3 mo 4 da. A Soldier of the Revolution." GM with substantial head stone. Fur infor Waw-Wil-a-Way Chap.

CRAWFORD, JOHN, (Madison Co.)

Pvt Croghan's Company, 8th Va Regt. Enl 1776. Fought at Brandywine, Germantown, Monmouth and Newton. Br Mch 1759, Va. D later than 1840. Bur Baldwin family burying ground near Mt Sterling, O. GM by Mt Sterling Chap with bronze marker, 1911. Fur infor Mt Sterling Chap.

CRAWFORD, WILLIAM, COL., (Wyandotte Co.)

Ensign, Lt, Capt, Lt Col, then commanded his Regt at battle of Long Island. Retreat through NJ, crossing Delaware with Gen Washington on Christmas Day, 1776. Br Berkeley Co, Va, 1732. Parents were Scotch-Irish. D June 11, 1782. Bur on high bank south of Lymochtee Creek, near the east line of southwest quarter of Sec 26. MI: "In memory of Col Crawford who was burned by Indians in this valley June 11, 1782." GM Pioneer Assn Wyandot Co, O. Aug 30, 1877. Col Crawford was put in command of expedition against the Indian town at or near

Sandusky. Acquired knowledge of surveying fr Washington. George Washington said, "He was known to me as an officer of much care and prudence; brave, experienced and active." Fur infor Mrs. H. H. Sears, Org Regent, Harpster, O.

CREED, MATTHEW, (Highland Co.)

Mar Elizabeth Carlile. Children: Matthew Creed, (Mar Margaret Creed) D Highland Co, O. Bur on farm owned in 1927 by William Ballentine about 3 miles southeast of Hillsboro. Ref: Mrs. Evans, Hillsboro. Fur infor Waw-Wil-a-Way Chap.

CRIBBS, JOHN, (Co. not stated)

Pvt 8th Pa Continental Line. Mar Katharine Harrold. D Ohio 1791. Natl No 68350, Vol 69, p 128 D. A. R. Lin. Ref: Mrs. Maude Lauffer Sommers, Westmoreland Co, Pa.

CRIST, CHRISTIAN, (Hamilton Co.)

Pvt in Capt Hendrick Van Keuren's Company, Col Jonathan Hasbrouck's Regt which was stationed at Montgomery (Fort). Was in battle of Stony Point July 16, 1779; in Col Malcolm's Regt also (War Dept). Br 1745 Orange Co, N. Y. near Stony Point. Parents: Family known to have come from Holland (or possibly Germany) many yrs before Revolutionary War. Mar Elizabeth Weller in 1765, dau of Wm Weller, Revolutionary soldier. Children: Moses, Joseph, Peter, Cornelius, Abraham, and George. D 1814 near Montgomery, Hamilton Co, O, at home of son Moses. Bur Hopewell, near Montgomery. Bur on lot of Moses Crist at whose house he died. No stone at grave. Flag stone marker removed a few yrs ago. Pioneer ancestors of Crist family were Henry and Stephanus, his son, who established a settlement opposite Ft. Montgomery, Orange Co, N. Y. fr Holland, or Germany, many years before 1760. He came to join colony at Montgomery O, founded by his former neighbors fr N. Y. in 1800. His grown up sons all coming at the same time. Farmer. Ancestors were Pioneers and early Colonists of Orange Co, N. Y. and founders of town and of the earliest church in Montgomery, N. Y. Pew holders record in Hist. (Headley's Orange, N. Y. p 305 and 323.) Ref: Natl No 34924 D. A. R. Fur infor Cincinnati Chap.

CRITCHFIELD, JOHN, (Holmes Co.)

Pvt Va Continental Line. Br 1758 in State of Delaware. D 1851 Nashville, O. Bur M. E. Cem Nashville, Holmes Co, O. Bur in old part of Cem north end. MI: "A Soldier of the Revolution. Service—Brandywine, Sept 11, 1777—Germantown, Oct 2, 1777—Stoning of Stony Point, July 16, 1779—Cowpens, Jan 17, 1781." He spent the notable winter of 1777-78 at Valley Forge, which privation, suffering and hardships is without parallel in the history of the U. S. Ref: Mrs. Maude Miley, Shreve, O. Compare Vol. 45, p 267 with Natl No 101233, Vol. 103, p 70, D. A. R. Lin. Fur infor Wooster-Wayne Chap.

CRITCHFIELD, JOSEPH, (Knox Co.)

Soldier. Mar Peggy Sapp. Children: Mary Greer, Elizabeth Waddle, Catherine Lybarger, Phoebe Beckwith, Alvin, William, Isaac, John and Joseph. D 1843. Emigrated from the neighborhood of Cumberland, Md, to Howard Twp, Knox Co, O. Farmer. Ref: Banning Norton's History of Knox Co, O, p 322-323. Fur infor Kokosing Chap.

CRITCHFIELD, JOSHUA, (Fairfield Co.)

Bur Hocking Twp. Fur infor Sherman Reese Chap.

CRITCHFIELD, NATHANIEL, (Knox Co.)

Soldier, drew pens until his death 1837. Mar Christina Welker at an early age. Children: William, Susannah, (Lepley,) Joseph, Catherine, (Sprague), Jesse, Sally

(Lybarger), Benjamin, Mary (Casteel), Isaac. D about 1837. Bur Old Cem at Jelloway, Howard Twp. Came into Howard Twp in 1806 fr Washington Co, Pa. He had come up the Potomac and stopped at Cumberland Md thence to Mt Pleasant, thence to Washington Co. Farmer. Ref: p 322, Banning Norton's Hist of Knox Co. Published 1862. Hill's Hist Knox Co, p 476, Mr. Lyman Critchfield, Wooster, O. Fur infor Kokosing Chap.

CRITCHFIELD, WILLIAM, (Knox Co.)

Soldier. Mar Widow Barcus, 2nd wife. Children: Reuben, Samuel, Betsy, Thatcher, Drusilla Thomas, Keziah Magers, Sally. D 1848. Emigrated fr the neighborhood of Cumberland, Md to Howard Twp, Knox Co, 1806. Farmer. Ref: Banning Norton's Hist of Knox Co, O, p 322-323. Fur infor Kokosing Chap.

CROCKER, DAVID, (Portage Co.)

D Oct 25, 1849, Streetboro, O. Bur Streetboro, O. MI: "He was a soldier of the Revolution." Placed on pens list in Portage Co, 1840. Fur infor Old Northwest Chap.

CROCKER, JEDEDIAH, (Cuyahoga Co.)

Sgt Mass State Tr. Br 1761. D 1811. Bur Evergreen Cem Dover. Fur infor Western Reserve Chap.

CRONINGER, JOSEPH, (Stark Co.)

Pvt in several Regts, served Northumberland Co, Mil. Br 1753, Germany. Mar Elizabeth Hill. D 1842, Stark Co. Natl No 80106, Vol. 81, D. A. R. Lin.

CROOKS, JAMES, (Mahoning Co.)

Pvt. In 1792 he served as ensign. Bur Mahoning Co. Came to Mahoning Co fr Franklin Co Pa 1805. Ref: Pa Archives Series 6, Vol 4, p137. Fur infor Mahoning Chap.

CROOKS, WILLIAM, (Portage Co.)

Pensioned 1840. Lived at Aurora. Listed in S. A. R. 1917 yr bk. Fur infor Old Northwest Chap.

CROSBY, ELIJAH, (Ashtabula Co.)

Enl Capt Hungerford's Company of Conn Mil on Nov 14, 1781, and served in Arnold's attack upon New London. Disch Jan 12, 1781. Br 1764 East Haddam, Conn. Mar Phebe Church. Children: Phebe, Lucinda, Calvin, Lovena, Elial, Elijah, Joseph, Levi, Anna, Larissa, Henry. D 1835 Rome, Ashtabula Co. Land agent for Henry Champion and held the office of Post Master fr 1785 to 1829. Built the first school house. The first sermon heard in Rome was delivered in his house. Ref: Conn Men in the Rev; Hist of Ashtabula Co. Fur infor Mary Stanley Chap.

CROSBY, OBED, (Trumbull Co.)

Br Hartland, Conn. 1753. D Jan 13, 1813, aged 60 yrs. Bur Old Cem south of center of Vernon. Monument good; erected by John I. King M. D. Came to Vernon in 1800. The first Methodist minister in this township. Formed a church class of five members in 1801, the first M. E. organization upon the Western Reserve. Fur infor Mary Chesney Chap.

CROSLEY, MOSES, (Warren Co.)

Pensioned in Warren Co, O. 1831 as Pvt in Md Mil Br 1764 D 1843 (Warren Co) O. Natl No 25493, Vol 26, p 180, D. A. R. Lin.

CROUSE, JOHN SR., (Ross Co.)

Pvt in Capt Jacob Good's Company. 1st Bn of Md Flying Camp, enlisting June 1776, at Fredericktown, Md. Br Jan 13, 1759 in Carroll Co, Md. Parents: John and Nancy (Smith) Crouse. Mar Catherine Umpstead, Mch 20, 1780. Children: David, Nancy, Ruth, Pheraby, John, Daniel, Jeremiah and Eliza. D Sept 5, 1847 Ross Co, (Kingston), O. Bur Crouse's Chapel Cem, Green Twp, Ross Co, O. 1st sec east side. MI: "John Crouse Sr. Sept 5, 1847, aged 88 yrs. 7 mo. 22 da." GM Monument by children, 1847. He enlisted as a Pvt at Frederick, Md, on or about June 1, 1776, in Capt. Jacob Good's Company of Inf in Col. Chas G. Griffith's 1st Bn of the Md Flying Camp, commanded by Brig Gen Reazei Beall. This command joined Gen Washington's army on York Island and took part in the engagements known as Battles of Harlem Heights, White Plains. Was Justice of Peace, State Rep. Enlmt was for 6 mos and he was honorably disch Dec 1, 1776, at the age of 17 yrs. Ref: Nellie Crouse Black, Kingston. Fur infor Nathaniel Massie and Mt Sterling Chaps.

CROSS, JOHN, (Fairfield Co.)

Pvt in Dragoons under Gen Wm Washington, Va Line. Br 1762, Berkeley Co, Va. D 1847, Royalton, O. Natl No 31805, Vol 32, p 296. D. A. R. Lin.

CROW, WILLIAM, (Jackson Co.)

Fur infor Capt John James Chap.

CROWELL, MATHEW, (Trumbull Co.)

Bur Bloomfield, village cem. MI: Has a marker, "M. Crowell; no dates of birth or wife's name. Fur infor Mary Chesney Chap.

CROWERCILER, (Fairfield Co.)

Bur St Peters Cem. Fur infor Elizabeth Sherman Reese Chap.

CROWL, GEORGE, (Columbiana Co.)

Fur infor Bethia Southwick Chap.

CROZER, JOHN, (Columbiana Co.)

Placed on pens roll of Ohio 1833 for serv as Pvt and Sgt Pa Tr. The official Register of the New Jersey Adj Gen "N J in the Rev" p 563 gives John Crozer, Pvt Jerseyman in the line, also State Trs. Br Philadelphia, Pa Mch 20, 1755. Parents: Robert and Susannah (Woodward) Crozer. Mar Eleanor Bradfield, 1783. Children: Susannah, James, Hannah, (died in infancy) Mary, Thomas, Elizabeth, John, Eleanor, Hannah, Reason. D East Fairfield, Columbiana Co, O. Feb 21, 1846. Bur East Fairfield. MI: "John Crozer, died Feb 21, 1846. 90 yrs. 11 mos. 8 days." Left a will, naming his children, in Court House at Lisbon, Columbiana Co. The village of East Fairfield, O was founded in 1803 by John Crozer and John Bradfield. John Crozer was the first Postmaster and kept the office at his home. Natl No 177458 and 49302. Vol 53, p 290 D. A. R. Lin. Ref: Pension office, Washington D. C. Fur infor Nabby Lee Ames Chap.

CROZIER, JOHN, (Cuyahoga Co.)

Minute Man. Corp, Sgt, Lt, Mass Mil. Pvt, Ensign and Lt at battles of Lexington, Germantown, Yorktown, Monmouth, Valley Forge. Br 1751. Dorchester, Mass. Mar Fannie Whiting. D 1823, Cuyahoga Co, O. Bur Euclid Ave. GM by Western Reserve Chap. Ref: Natl No 60193, Vol 61, p 65 D. A. R. Lin. Fur infor Western Reserve Chap.

CULBERTSON, ALEXANDER JR., (Muskingum Co.)

In the 1st Company of the 4th Bn of the Cumberland Co Pa Associators, commanded by Lt Samuel Culbertson. Br 1747 in "Culbertson Row" near Chamberland, Pa. Parents: Alexander Sr. Mar Mary Sharpe. Children: One was Elizabeth. D Dec 13, 1822, near Zanesville, O. Bur Old Town Cem on old high school hill. Tanner. Ref: Pa Archives, 3 series, Vol 23, p 699. Fur infor Muskingum Chap.

CULBERTSON, ROBERT, (Franklin Co.)

Lt Col 1st Bn Cumberland Co Pa Associates. Br 1738. D 1820, Franklinton, O. Natl No 77678, Vol 78. D. A. R. Lin.

CULVER, BEZALIEL, (Athens Co.)

One of the enl men in the Albany Co NY Mil, 16th Regt during the Revolutionary War. Pvt. Br Dec 24, 1755, Ireland. Mar Ann Caldwell, 1783. Children: Gardner, James, Joseph, Ann, Elizabeth, Deborah, Samuel, Mary, Andrew, John, Lucinda, Achsah, Levinia, Thomas McGee. D Aug 29, 1821, Athens, O. Bur West State St., Athens, O. East of main driveway. MI: "Bezaliel Culver." GM Family, small old fashioned brown stone. Came with his family fr NY State to Athens, O, 1816. Joseph, Samuel, Andrew, Levinia and Thomas McGee died in childhood or early youth. Ref: "New York in the Rev War" p 131. Fur infor Nabby Lee Ames Chap.

CULVER, DAVID, (Logan Co.)

Enl Jan 10, 1778 in Capt Daniel Dewey's Company, in Col Johnson's Regt. for serv in RI. Sgt in Capt John Harmon's Company, 4th Regt, Col John Durkee. Enl July 1, 1780. Disch Dec 10, 1780. Br July 26, 1764. D Oct 26, 1847. Bur Curl Cem, near East Liberty, O. Logan Co. Fur infor Bellefontaine Chap.

CULVER, SOLOMON, (Co. not stated.)

Pvt 17th NY Regt. Br Litchfield, Conn. 1760. Mar Lodamia Burr, 1781. D 1855. In 1790 removed to Plymouth Twp, Pa; in 1812 to Ohio (said Richmond) Co., where he died. Fur infor Vol 65, p 307, 64871.

CUMMINGS, JOHN, (Monroe Co.)

Was in Capt John Randolph's Company under Col Henry Lee; was with Washington when Benedict Arnold deserted. Enl in the Spring of 1778 in State of Md. Br Sept 12, 1755. Mar Areminta Short, (who was born Sept 9, 1761, D Sept 15 1851). Children: William, Thomas, John and Robert. D Apr 28, 1852. Age 96 yrs., 7 mos. 16 days. Bur Presbyterian Cem, Beallsville, Monroe Co, O. MI: "John Cummings died Apr 28, 1852. Age 96 yrs, 7 months, 16 days. A Soldier of the Revolutionary War. Areminta, wife of John Cummings, died Sept 15, 1851, age 90 yrs, 6 days." Farmer. The writer's mother remembered him quite well as he wore his blue soldier coat until he died. Ref: Mrs. Anne Orlena Hill Bartholomew, 115 N. Summit St., Dayton, O.; also 57476, Vol 58, D. A. R. Lin. Accepting this infor Jane Dailey, State Chairman.

CUMMINS, JAMES, (Co not stated)

Enl 1782 in Capt Alex People's Company, 1st Bn Cumberland Co, Pa Mil, Col James Dunlap. B 1755, Va. D 1835, Janesville, O. (May mean Zanesville, O.) Name "James Cummins" appears on Pioneer tablet, Butler Co, O. Ref: 88593, Vol 89, p 187, D. A. R. Lin.

CUMMINS, PETER, (Butler Co.)

Name appears on the tablet erected at Hamilton, O., on the site of Ft Hamilton as one of the Revolutionary Soldiers buried in that Co. Unidentified. Fur infor John Reilly Chap.

CUNNINGHAM, JAMES, (Greene Co.)

Pvt on roll of Sumter's Brig, S. C. Capt Isaac Ross. Served with this Brig in the battle of Guilford Court House. Bur in Cem north of Bellbrook, Sugarcreek Twp. Fur infor Catherine Greene Chap.

CUNNINGHAM, JAMES, (Hamilton Co.)

Lt Col 3rd Bn Lancaster Co Mil. Br Scotland, 1740. Parents: was descended fr Sir James Cunningham of Ireland, who left Scotland or removed his Manor in 1615. Mar Janet Park (Scotch ancestry, d 1835). Children: Robert, James, Samuel, Arthur, Jesse, Francis, Mary, Ann, Sarah, Janette. D June 1812. Bur on farm, 1 mile north of Reading, O. He with two brothers John and Robert came to "London Lands," now Lancaster Co, Pa. Col James came to Ky 1787, and 1789 to Cincinnati, O. First white man to break forest in Syracuse Twp. Paid 37 cents per acre for 800 acres, built stockade Cunningham Sta, built first brick house of brick he burned, 1801. Ref: Natl No 50187. Vol 51, p 85, D. A. R. Lin. Fur infor Cincinnati Chap.

CUNNINGHAM, RICHARD, (Greene Co.)

Pa Mil. Bur Sugarcreek Twp. Bellbrook. Pensioned May 4, 1831, age 77 yrs. Annual allowance $80.00 same received $240.00. On pens roll May 4, 1833. Fur infor Catherine Greene Chap.

CUPPY, JOHN, (Greene Co.)

In 1778 he enl as a Pvt in Capt McManus' Company of Va. Reenl in 1781 as Pvt in Capt Robert Mean's Company. Fr 1791 to 1794 was a scout in Capt Samuel Brady's Company. Was a Capt in Va Mil 10th Brig 3rd Div. Br Mch 11, 1761 in Morristown, N. J. but when a yr old moved with his parents to Hampshire Co, Va. Mar 2nd time to Lydia Oiler Russell, Oct 1824. (Br Morrow Co, now Greenbrier Co, Va, Feb 8, 1798). Children: Elizabeth, Henry and several others. D June 28, 1861, Wayne Twp, Montgomery Co, O. Bur Fairfield Cem near Fairfield Air in. Depot on the line of Greene and Montgomery Cos. Lot No 154. MI: "John Cuppy, soldier of the Revolutionary Continental Army. Br Mch 11, 1761, died June 28, 1861, aged 100 yrs, 3 mos, 17 days." It is a tall granite shaft, and has a powder horn and flint lock musket chiseled on same. There are other inscriptions on the other sides of monument. In 1788 he removed to Ohio Co, Va, settling on the Ohio River near New Cumberland where he was a farmer in Va until 1821, when he went to live with his oldest daughter in Ind. In 1823 he settled in Wayne Twp, Montgomery Co, where he lived until his death. He was buried in Wayne Twp, but after the death of his son Henry was reinterred in a family lot at Fairfield, Green Co, O. Fur infor Richard Montgomery Chap, S. A. R.

CURL, WILLIAM, (Logan Co.)

Enl Capt James Parsons' Company, Va Mil. Br Sept 1754 Va. Mar Sarah Brown in 1776 (b Feb 1758). Children: Mary, Jeremiah, Rachel, Elizabeth, Thomas, Nancy, Sarah, William, Charity, Isaac, John. D 1841, near De Graff, Logan Co, aged 88 yrs. Bur Mt Olive Chapel Cem. Ref: Natl No 60542, Vol 61, p 179, D. A. R. Lin. Fur infor Mt Sterling Chap.

CURRIER, Sgt., (Cuyahoga Co.)

Sgt Continental serv N. H. Br 1756. D 1823. Bur First Presbyterian Church Yard Euclid Ave, Cleveland, O. Fur infor Western Reserve Chap.

CURRY, JAMES, (Union Co.)

Col of Va line, served in battle of Point Pleasant Oct 10, 1774. GM by Curry family, large stone. An officer in Va line. Ref: Mrs. Jane Randall, Plain City, O. Fur infor Hannah Emerson Dustin Chap.

CURRY, JOHN, (Preble Co.)

Received pension in 1832 for serv as Pvt in Pa line. Br 1750, Lancaster Co, Pa. D 1835, Preble Co, O. Ref: Natl No 92965, Vol 93, p 302, D. A. R. Lin.

CURRY, ROBERT, (Brown Co.)

Pvt in Continental line. Enl July 22, 1777; disch Sept 5, 1777. Br 1759, Rockingham Co, Va. Mar Phoebe Sample. Children: Abigail, William, Mary, Lucinda, Phoebe and Rebecca. D 1804, Georgetown, O. Bur on one of the 6 farms which he owned. MI: "Robert Curry died 1804." He and his brother came to Ky to settle; afterward moved to Ohio and settled on a 1000 acre farm of their uncle. Farmer. Ref: Brown Co, O, Hist. Fur infor Lieutenant Byrd Chap.

CURTIS, ELEAZER, (Washington Co.)

Enl Pvt May 4, 1775. Disch Dec 18, 1775. Served at seige of Boston. Fought at Germantown, 1775; wintered at Valley Forge, 1777-1778; battle of Monmouth. Br Oct 20, 1759, Warren, Litchfield Co, Conn. Parents: Maj Eleazer Jr., and Mary (Carter) Curtis. Mar Nov 7, 1782, Eunice Starr. Children: Eleazer Starr, Jason Ralph, Walter, Mary, Benajah, Horace, Clarissa, Lucy. D Sept 7, 1801, Belpre, Washington Co, O. Bur Newbury Cem near Little Hocking, Washington Co, O. MI: "Capt Eleazer Curtis, D Sept 7, 1801, 42 yrs of his age." GM Marietta Chapter with Revolutionary marker, 1921. Removed with family fr Litchfield Co. Conn to Washington Co, O, 1791, settled on a farm lower Belpre. Farmer. Ref: Conn Men in the Rev. Fur infor Marietta Chap.

CURTIS, ISAAC (Curtis or Custis,) (Huron Co.)

Pvt NY State; Pensioned 1833, special act. Were early settlers of Fitchville. Curtis family in Norwalk until 1850. Fur infor Sally De Forest Chap.

CURTIS, CAPT. JOHN, (Washington Co.)

Bur Marietta, O. Ref: Lytle's Hist of Delaware Co, p 378, (Mrs. Dailey.) Fur infor Delaware Chap.

CURTIS, REUBEN, (Geauga Co.)

Pvt 10th Company Capt Parsons: Col Hinman's Regt. Br 1754, Middlesex Co, Conn. Mar Johana. D 1839. Bur South Cem in Parkman Village, near north fence, about half way back fr road. MI: "In memory of Reuben Curtis, who died April 3, 1839, aged 85 years. Also Johana, his wife, who died Aug 1, 1841, aged 81 years." GM Old white marble slab. Col Hinman's Regt disch Sept 1, 1777. 13th Regt arrived in camp Aug 16, disch Sept 9 Capt Hicock's Company. Ref: p 62, 467 Conn Men in Rev. Fur infor Taylor Chap.

CURTIS, ZARAH, (Knox Co.)

Pvt in Revolutionary War, Capt Webb's Tr. Also designated 1st Tr, 2nd Rgt, Light Dragoons, Continental Tr, commanded by Col Elisha Sheldon. He enlisted Jan 1, 1781. Transferred to 6th Tr same Regt. Br Litchfield Co, Conn, May 2, 1761. Parents: Jonham and Elizabeth (Barnes) Curtis. Mar 1st wife: Phalley Yale, Oct 22, 1784; 2nd wife: Mrs. Abigail Edwards. Children: Violette Davis, Eunice Eaton, Eliza Graham, Sally Curtis, Samuel Ryan, Henry Barnes, Homer. D June 7, 1849, Licking Co, O. Washington Twp. Bur Mound View Cem, Mount Vernon, O, Henry B. Curtis lot, Block 3, lot 1. MI: "Zarah Curtis, born Litchfield, Conn., May 2, 1761. Died June 7, 1849, aged 88 yrs." GM by family and Hetuck Chap, 1909 or before. He was a pioneer in the States of Vermont, New York and Ohio and during the last years Elder and Minister in Christian Church. Ref: Brister Co History. Fur infor Kokosing and Hetuck Chaps.

CUSBOTT, ROBERT, (Greene Co.)

Pvt. Pa. Continentals. Pensioned Mch 4, 1831. Age 80 yrs. Annual allowance $80.00. Same received $240.00. On Pension Roll Sept 27, 1832. Fur infor Catherine Green Chap.

CUSHING, NATHANIEL, (Washington Co.)

1st Lt in Capt Lemuel Trescott's Company, Col Jonathan Brewer's Regt; Capt in Col John Patterson's Regt and Col Joseph Vose's Regt; Brig Inspector, Brig Maj at New Windsor, Camp Philadelphia. Br Apr 8, 1753, Pembroke, Mass. Mar Elizabeth Heath. D 1814, Belpre, O. Bur Belpre, O. Was the original proprietor of lot 27 on the site of Farmer's Castle. After the capture of Maj Goodale by the Indians, Col Cushing was chosen to command the garrison at Farmer's Castle. Fur infor Marietta Chap.

CUSTARD, JACOB, (Perry Co.)

Drafted in 1775, while living in Rockingham Co, Va. serving in Va Mil. Pensioned 1832 for this serv. Br 1750, Germany. D 1833, Perry Co, O. Ref: Natl No 95474, Vol 96, p 154. D. A. R. Lin.

CUTTER, JOHN, (Hamilton Co.)

Br 1737, Massachusetts. D 1793. Ref: S. A. R. Natl No 30285, Vol 31, p 99, D. A. R. Lin. Fur infor Cincinnati Chap.

CUTTER, SETH, (Hamilton Co.)

Br 1760 Mass. D 1805. Ref: S. A. R. Fur infor Cincinnati Chap.

DAGUE, MATHIAS, (Franklin Co.)

Pvt in Pa Mil. Pensioned Oct 12, 1833. Br 1761 in Pa. D Feb 16, 1847 in Plain Twp. Bur in cem 2 miles fr New Albany. MI: "Mathias Dague. D Feb 16, 1847. Aged 86 years." GM Rev Grave Committee with bronze marker, May 30, 1912. Came fr Pa in 1810 and settled in the southwestern part of Plain Twp. Fur infor Columbus Chap.

DAILEY, DAVID, (Athens Co.)

Pvt in Capt Chittenden's Company Vt. Br 1750. Vt. Mar: His will dated June 9, 1826 mentions wife, Nancy. Children: He had two daughters and five sons, one of the latter was Benonah H. D prior to Jan 19, 1828. Bur Carthage Twp. Removed to NY after his disch fr the army, thence to western Pa fr here to the Northwest territory in 1797. Farming. He was a famous hunter. Pensioned Ref: Probate Court record; Walker's Hist of Athens Co., p 502-503. Bureau of Pens, Washington. Fur infor Nabby Lee Ames Chap.

DAILEY, JOHN, (Summit Co.)

On tablet erected in Glendale Chapel 1916 by Cuyahoga-Portage Chap. D. A. R. as a memorial to Revolutionary Soldiers buried in Summit county. His name heads the list as Bailey but is an error. Fur infor Cuyahoga-Portage Chap.

DAILY, WILLIAM, (Jackson Co.)

Spoken of in county historical research; (not yet secured.) Mar Lucinda Tripp, June 21, 1832. Fur infor Captain John James Chap.

DAINS, ASA, (Meigs Co.)

Pvt in Conn State Tr fifteen months. Pension fr Meigs Co, O, for this serv. Br 1764 in Conn. Mar Jane Hasson. D 1842 near Pomeroy, O. Children: One son was Hasson Dains (mar Esther Burroughs). Ref: Natl No 26400, Vol 27, p 145, D. A. R. Lin.

DAVID, DALYRYMPLE, (Sandusky Co.)

Pvt June, 1780 to Nov 1, 1780, Capt Taylor, Pvt Mch 1781 to Nov 1783, Capt Mason. Residence of soldier at enlmt, Petersham, Mass. Date of application for pens Oct 1832; allowed. Residence at date of application, Walworth, Wayne Co, NY. Age 67. GM L. M. Kelley, Commissioner. Fur infor Col George Croghan Chap.

DAMON, ABRAHAM, (Geauga Co.)

Pvt Mass State Trps Capt Hooker Company. Br 1858. Mar Anna. Children: Patty, Joel, Hosea. D Hambden, O. June 5, 1845. Bur Hambden Center, Lot 46. MI: "Abraham Damon died June 5, 1845 aged 87." Anna Damon died Mch 9, 1845 aged 84. GM family stone. Enl Aug 18, 1777, disch Nov 30, 1777. Pens granted 1833. Came to Hambden 1817. Ref: Mass Soldiers and Sailors Vol 4, p 665. Fur infor Taylor Chap.

DANA, DAN, (Trumbull Co.)

Br 1759. D Nov 8, 1839. Bur Old Cem Mahoning Ave., Warren, O. MI: D Nov 8, 1839, aged 80 years. Fur infor Mary Chesney Chap.

DANA, WILLIAM, Capt., (Washington Co.)

Was chosen Capt of Artillery at time of Bunker Hill Battle. Served 2 yrs. attached to Dept of Gen Knox Artillery Corp. Br 1744, Cambridge, Mass. Mar Mary Brancroft, 1770. Children: Luther, William, Stephen, Edmond, Augustus, Elizabeth, Mary, George, Fanny. D Oct 30, 1809, Belpre, O. Bur Burying ground at Belpre, O. MI: Capt William Dana, a Revolutionary soldier, born in Mass. Emigrated to west in 1788. Settled in Belpre. Died in 1809 aged 65 years. GM Marietta Chap with Revolutionary Marker, 1921. Farmer. Ref: Mass War records; Andrew Hist. Fur infor Marietta Chap.

DANFORTH, JOHN, (Lake Co.)

Washington Records say he was granted a bounty and land claim for Revolutionary serv. Children: Sally, Samuel and Polly. D 1810, Painesville, O. Fur infor New Connecticut Chap.

DANHAEFFER, CHRISTOPHER SR., (Guernsey Co.)

Bur Old Cemetery, Cambridge, O. Ref: S. A. R. Fur infor Anna Asbury Stone Chap.

DANIEL, DAVID, (Portage Co.)

Pvt 1776, Capt Prior's Company, Walcutt's Regt; Sgt 1778 in battles of Monmouth, Trenton, Stony Point, Brandywine and Yorktown. B 1759. Mar Lucina Meigs. D 1813, Palmyra, O. Ref: Natl No 57490, Vol 58, p 168, D. A. R. Lin.

DANIELS, AMARIAH, (Portage Co.)

Musician in 6th Regt, Mass Line. Placed on Pension Roll Aug 8, 1831. Bur Palmyra, O. Drew pens at Ravenna, O. 1840. Fur infor Old Northwest Chap.

DANIELSON, LUTHER, (Meigs Co.)

Br 1756. D Dec 12, 1841. Bur Weldon Cem, Racine, O. GM erected by family. Fur infor Return Jonathan Meigs Chap.

DARBY, WILLIAM, (Vinton Co.)

Pvt. Musician, Drummer. Br 1760 at or near Philadelphia, Pa. Mar Hannah 1781. Children: Samuel, Darby, John Darby, Barbara. D Allensville, O. Apr 30, 1836. Bur family graveyard at a point about ¾ mile fr Allensville, O, but remains removed to Allensville, O. Grave 2 rods northeast of entrance. MI: Granite monument; Top "Darby." "William Darby 1760-1836. Revolutionary War Drummer 1777-1783. Carberry's Co, Hubey's Regt. Princeton, Brandywine, Germantown, Monmouth." GM relatives monument erected in 1915, Marker 1915 and unveiled at a Darby reunion at Allensville, O. After war serv came to O as a pioneer. Farming, Hunting. He was a Pensioner, application made May 22, 1819, and drew pens to death April 30, 1836. Ref: Ethel Darby, Los Angeles, Calif. D. A. R. J. W. Darby, McArthur, O. Fur infor Jane Dailey, State Chairman.

DARKE, WILLIAM, Col., (Butler Co.)

Name appears on the tablet in the Soldiers and Sailors Monument at Hamilton as a soldier of the Rev. Bur in Butler Co, although a non-resident. Was in NY 1774. D Apr 15, 1851. Fur infor John Reily Chap.

DAVENPORT, ANTHONY SIMS, (Ross Co.)

Pvt in Va Mil, Berkeley Co. Br Maryland, 1757. Mar Mary Brazil. D 1835, aged 78 yrs. Bur in Davenport family burying ground near Yellowbud, Ross Co, O. Body was removed to Pleasant Valley Cem about 1922. Was placed on Pension Roll July 8, 1833, but never drew a pens. Natl No 18914, p 329, Vol 19. D. A. R. Lin. Natl No 102645, p 98 Vol 198. Fur infor Nathaniel Massie Chap.

DAVENPORT, E. SQUIRE, (Geauga Co.)

Pvt 2nd Regt Conn line, 1781-1783. Capt Converse 2nd Regt 1783, Capt Richards, Col Swift's Regt. Enlmt Mch 1, 1781-1784. Mar Lucy. Children: Betsey and Levi. Bur Hamblen Center, O., (supposedly). Enl fr town of Milford, Conn. Mch 1, 1781 for 3 yrs. Estate administered June 27, 1843, Courts Geauga Co. Ref: Conn Men of Rev 324-361-369. Fur infor Taylor Chap.

DAVIDSON, ABIGAIL, (Trumbull Co.)

Name given in S. A. R. directory as one of the sufferers at Wyoming massacre in 1778; she was the wife of Douglas Davidson. D Nov 13, 1824, aged 75 yrs. Bur East Farmington cem Farmington Twp. Fur infor Mary Chesney Chap.

DAVIDSON, JAMES, (Mahoning Co.)

Pvt Capt Walter's Tr Light Dragoons, Monmouth, N. J. Men of the Rev. p 567. Came to Youngstown early in 1800. Butler's Mahoning Co Hist p 215, p 607 records. He was an elder in Liberty Associate Presbyterian Church. Fur infor Mahoning Chap.

DAVIDSON, JAMES, (Stark Co.)

Pvt in Capt Wm Houston's Company, 4th Bn Cumberland Co Mil, under Col Samuel Culbertson. Br Carlisle, Pa. Mar Jane Hudson. D Canton, O. Natl No 54252, Vol 55, p 108, D. A. R. Lin.

DAVIDSON, JOHN, (Mahoning Co.)

Pvt Capt Humphrey's Company May 1, 1778 Conn. Br 1765. Mar Charlotte. Children: 1 dau 2 sons, one named Norman. D 1855. Bur Center of Boardman Twp, O. First shoemaker in Boardman. p 84, Vol 2, Hist Trumbull and Mahoning Cos p 210, Conn Men in the Rev. Fur infor Mahoning Chap.

DAVIDSON, JOHN, (Wayne Co.)

Bur Old Cem in Smithville, north east corner of cem, near road. MI: "Jno Davidson 9th Pa Inf. Revolutionary War." Fur infor Wooster-Wayne Chap.

DAVIDSON, JOSHUA, (Brown Co.)

Lt. Served 7 yrs. Crossed the Trenton, was at Valley Forge, Brandywine and with Lafayette at Yorktown, also Stony Point. Br 1754. Parents: William Davidson. Br in Scotland. Children: John, Joseph, William, Joshua, Ruth, Mary, Ellen, Betsey, Nancy. D 1844, aged 90 yrs, White Oak, Brown Co, O. Bur Cem Higginsport, O. Came to Bracken Co, Ky, 1790; in 1807 moved to Lewis Twp, Brown Co. By A. S. Abbott, Bethel, O. Ref: Brown Co, Hist, p 462. Fur infor Taliaferro Chap.

DAVIDSON, WILLIAM, (Mahoning Co.)

Ranger of the Frontier 1778-1783, Westmoreland Co. Pensioned in 1819, age 71 yrs. Br 1747. D July 29, 1831. Bur Eckis Cem, Milton Twp. Ref: Pa Archives, Series 3, Vol 23, p 284 and 316. Fur infor Mahoning Chap.

DAVIES, MARMADUKE S., (Belmont Co.)

Enl June 16, 1781 at Elbridge Landing, Md. A Corp of Capt Washington's Company, 4 Va Regt. At the surrender of Cornwallis at Yorktown attached the 22 Regt of Regulars. Disch Mch 1782, Richmond, Va. Br Mch 11, 1760 York Co, Pa. Parents: John and Jane (Underwood) Davies. Mar: Drusilla Forrest, 2nd Eleanor Wilson, Jan 30, 1816. Children: Joshua, Zadock, Betsey, Julia Ann, Margaret Davies Happer, Ellen J, Frazier, David M, Mary A. D Mch 13, 1855, St Clairsville, O. Bur M E Cem St Clairsville, O. MI: Name and date of birth and death with the words "A soldier and patriot of the Revolution." GM by son, David M; marble marker, soon after burial. July 7, 1790, at Green Castle Pa enl in Capt James Powers' Company of Inf at St Clair's Defeat on St. Mary's River, in serv under Gen Wayne until disch July 1793. Apprenticed as a tailor, he resumed the occupation. Received pens under Act of 1832. Fur infor Grace Allen McFarland, St Clairsville, O. D. A. R. Wheeling.

DAVIS, ANN, (Franklin Co.)

Was a messenger and carried orders fr Gen Washington to the other commanders in the Revolutionary War in 1779 and 1780. Br 1763, Bucks Co, Pa. Mar John Davis. D June 6, 1851, Perry Twp. Bur Old Davis Cem 1 mi below Dublin, east side of Scioto River. She is buried under the same monument with her husband. MI: "Ann Davis died June 6, 1851, aged 88 years, 5 months, 8 days. Ann Davis was a messenger and carried orders from General Washington to the other commanders in 1779 and 1780." GM D. A. R. bronze marker, June 14, 1916. Ann Davis was a revolutionary heroine. Her maiden name was Ann Simpson and she was a cousin of the mother of General Grant. Columbus D. A. R. Chap, "Ann Simpson Davis" honors her name. Ref: Natl No 89528, Vol 90, D. A. R. Lin. Fur infor Columbus Chap.

DAVIS, AZARIAH, (Licking Co.)

Pa. Br 1756. Mar Eliza Van Meter (1st wife), Mary Harrington Smith (2nd wife). 19 children. D Sept 22, 1838, near Utica, O. Bur Old Cem, 6th St., Newark, O. Grave near small mound. Has nearly 2000 decendants. Natl No 25494, Vol 26, p 181, D. A. R. Lin. Fur infor Hetuck Chap.

DAVIS, DANIEL, (Hamilton Co.)

Br 1753, N. Y. D 1851. Fur infor Cincinnati Chap.

DAVIS, DANIEL, (Washington Co.)

Lt. Daniel Davis was deputy for Killingly in Gen Assembly. Served as Capt of a Company in Mass Mil Rufus Putnam. Br Oct 12, 1742, Killingly, Conn. Parents: Daniel and Tamer (Town) Davis. Mar Elizabeth Whittemore Dec 2, 1762. (Br 1740, d 1806). Children: Willard, Tamer, Walter, Elizabeth, William, Daniel, Hezekiah, Jesse, Asa, Luena. D 1807, Waterford, O. Bur supposedly near Waterford, O. GM by Marietta Chap with Revolutionary marker. He was stationed at Boston for a time collecting funds for the poor and for families of soldiers. Came to Marietta with Putnam in 1788. Ref: G. M. Cole, Adjutant Gen, State of Conn. Natl No 102639, Vol 103, p 196, D. A. R. Lin. Fur infor Marietta Chap.

DAVIS, HENRY, (Tuscarawas Co.)

Pvt in Capt John Van Etten's Company of Volunteers of Northampton Co, Pa in 1780 and 1781. See Pa Archives series 5, Vol 8, p 374, 375, 571, and 574; also series 3, Vol 23, p 298. Br 1760, England. D 1836 Warwick Twp, Tuscarawas Co, O. Bur Beersheba Cem, 1½ miles southwest of Gnadenhutten. Came to Ohio in 1806. Farmer. Was Sheriff of Tuscarawas Co, 1808 to 1810. Name appears on Soldier's Memorial erected in Gnadenhutten Cem in 1927. Fur infor Charles L. Stocker, Esq, 609 Society for Savings Bldg, Cleveland, O. Secured by Jane Dailey, State Chairman.

DAVIS, JOHN, (Franklin Co.)

Enl Henry Darrah's Company, Bucks Co, Pa, 1778. Capt in Pa Regt. Served fr 1777 to 1781. Br Montgomery Co, Md. 1761. D 1832 Perry Twp. Bur Old Davis Cem 1 mile below Dublin. MI: "John Davis died Jan 25, 1832, aged 71 years. 4 months and 18 days. John Davis was a soldier in the Revolutionary War and served from 1777 to 1781 in Pennsylvania Reg." On the side of the monument is the following: "Buck S. S. I do hereby certify that John Davis hath voluntarily subscribed to the oath of allegiance and fidelity as directed by an Act of the General Assembly of Pennsylvania passed the 1st day of October, 1779. Witness my hand and seal this 18th day of October, 1779. John Chapman." GM Rev Grave Committee with bronze marker, May 30, 1912. He came fr Montgomery Co, Md to Ohio in 1816 and settled in Delaware Co, where he remained for two years. In 1818 he moved to Perry Twp, 1 mile below Dublin on the east side of the Scioto River and lived here until his death. Natl No 99430, Vol 100, p 136, D. A. R. Lin. Fur infor Columbus Chap.

DAVIS, JOHN, (Jackson Co.)

Bur Graveyard on Chillicothe pike near Willis farm. Fur infor Capt John James' Chap.

DAVIS, JOHN, (Montgomery Co.)

Wagoner. Br Aug 19, 1758, near Amsterdam, Holland. Mar Mrs. Jane——— (a widow). Date not known. 2nd wife Nancy Lee (date unknown). Children: 1st wife, Ruth Doll, Catherine (mar Mr. Davis), Nancy Furguson, Mary (mar Wyatt Lee Daves), Charlotte Nickum. D Feb 24, 1842, Dayton, O. Bur Old Cem where Union Station now stands. Removed to Woodland Cem., in Lot 934, Sec. 65. GM by S. A. R. Bronze Marker in 1919. Presumably farmer. Lived near Zanesville, O. Ref: Natl No 181916. Fur infor Jonathan Dayton Chap.

DAVIS, JOHN, (Muskingum Co.)

Revolutionary Soldier. Pensioner in 1840 while residing in Nashport, Muskingum Co, O. Children: Benjamin (br Oct 20, 1797, Hardy Co, Va.), (Benjamin's son, B. F. Davis, br Sept 17, 1841.) Came to Ohio in 1814, settling in Muskingum Co. John and Hannah Davis were married in Wales and emigrated to America during the Revolutionary War. Mr Davis was taken into the army and served during the remainder of the war." Ref: Biographical and Historical Memoirs of Muskingum County, printed in 1892 by the Goodspeed Publishing Co, p 426. Fur infor Muskingum Chap.

DAVIS, JOSEPH, (Montgomery Co.)

Name secured fr old Dayton newspaper years ago, but no other data kept; papers lost in 1913 flood. One Capt Joseph Davis was receiving a pens in 1840 while residing in Butler Twp. (Montgomery Co Census 1840). Ref: Richard Montgomery Chap S. A. R.

DAVIS, JOSHUA, (Hamilton Co.)

From Middlesex, N. J. Br 1760, N. J. D 1839. Name appears on tablet for "Pioneers," Butler Co, O. Ref: S. A. R. 1898 record. Fur infor Cincinnati Chap.

DAVIES, MARMADUKE S. (Co not stated.)

Pvt in Capt Horatio Johnston's Company, Col George Snell's Regt. Md Line. Br 1760 Warrenton, Pa. Mar Eleanor Wilson (2nd wife) in 1816. D 1855 in Ohio Widow was pensioned. Ref: No. 101369, Vol. 103, p 111, D. A. R. Lin.

DAVIS, NATHANIEL, (Summit Co.)

Enl May 1782. Served 6 mos. under Capt Bazaleel Bristol at Killingsworth to guard the coast. Br 1766, a native of Killingsworth, Conn. Mar Electa Palmer (died Feb 3, 1826.) Children: Of nine but three lived more than a short time. D Mch 20, 1846. Bur Copley, O. In 1807 moved to N. Y. In 1818 came to Stow, thence to Copley. Purchased 320 acres of land here and cleared it. Fur infor Cuyahoga-Portage Chap.

DAVIS, NEHEMIAH, (Athens Co.)

Pvt in Capt Moses Whiting's Company of Minute Men, Col. John Greaton's Regt, which marched on the Alarm of Apr 19, 1775. Served at Nantasket in June under Lt. James Morton, driving ships fr Boston Harbor. Br Apr 22, 1755, Mass. Mar 1st wife: Mary—2nd wife: Phoebe Dorr, July 15, 1793. Children: Nehemiah, Jr. James Dorr, Rufus P. Isaiah, Reuben, Susan (?). D Aug 23, 1823, Dover Twp, Athens Co, O. Bur Nye Cem, Chauncey, Athens Co, O. MI: "Erected in memory of Nehemiah Davis, Elder of Baptist Church, who died August the 23rd, A. D. 1823, aged 68 yrs 3 mo 20 da. He entered the ministry in the 27th year of his age and planted the first Baptist church in Ohio." GM by family—sandstone marker. Also by metal marker placed by Nabby Lee Ames Chap D. A. R. in 1925. Moved to Marietta, O. from the East in 1797. Removed to Dover Twp. Athens Co. in 1808. In Washington Co, Elder Davis organized a Baptist church believed to be the first Baptist church in Ohio. Ref: Mass. Soldiers and Sailors in the Rev, Vol IV, p 531. Walker's Hist of Athens Co, p 470. History of the Hocking Valley, p 733. Fur infor Nabby Lee Ames and Elizabeth Zane Dew Chaps.

DAVIS, NOAH, (Portage Co.)

Lived at Randolph. Fur infor Old Northwest Chap.

DAVIS, SAMUEL, (Franklin Co.)

Enl July 1776, 6 mo; in 1777 for 1 mo, in 1778 for 6 mo; in 1779 for 4 mo; in 1781 for 6 mos. Br Litchfield, Conn, Jan 15, 1762. D May 31, 1849 in Norwich Twp. Bur Dublin Cem. MI: "Samuel Davis. Br Jan 15, 1762 in Litchfield, Conn. Done service in the Revolution. Emigrated to Kentucky at the age of 19 years, employed as a spy to guard the infant settlement. Captured by the Indians, served in the war of 1812 as a Capt. Embraced religion at an early age and died in the Christian faith May 31, 1849." GM Rev Grave Committee with bronze marker, May 30, 1912. During the War 1812, he served in two expeditions to the Northwest. He came to Ohio soon after Wayne's Treaty and settled below Chillicothe. In 1814 he removed to Franklin Co and settled in Norwich Twp. After the Revolutionary War he was captured by the Indians near Hamen's Sta, Ky, 1786 and remained captive for 7 years. Fur infor Columbus Chap.

DAVIS, SILAS, (Greene Co.)

Bath, 1820. Ref: Robinson's Hist of Greene Co. Fur infor Catherine Greene Chap.

DAVIS, THOMAS, (Montgomery Co.)

Name secured from old Dayton Newspaper, years ago, but no other data kept; papers lost in 1913 flood. Ref: Richard Montgomery Chap, S. A. R.

DAVIS, THOMAS, (Greene Co.)

Pvt in 2nd Virginia Continentals. Pensioned Apr 27, 1818, age 78 yrs. Transferred fr Ky. Annual allowance $96. See Pension Roll Mch 5, 1819. Fur infor Catherine Greene Chap.

DAVIS, WALTER, (Jackson Co.)

Enl Dec 10, 1776 for 3 yrs. Transferred in Oct 1778 to Capt James Williams' Company. Pvt in Company designated at various times as Capt Thomas West's Company, Capt-Lieut James Williams and Lieut Thomas Pierson's Company, 10th Va Regt—also designated 6th Va Regt. Commanded at different times by Col Edward Stevens, Maj Samuel Hawes, Col John Green and Col William Russell. Enl for the war in Dec 1778; transferred May 1779 to Capt Nathan Lamme's Company, same Regt, and his name last appeared on the Company muster roll for Nov 1779. Br 1754. Mar Mary ——. D Jan 8, 1844. Bur about 9 miles north of Jackson, in Jackson Twp, one-fourth mile south of Pleasant Valley church. A Mr Simons owns the land where the graves are. Milton S. and George E. Davis, grandsons, live near, at Ray, O. MI: "Walter Davis, a patriot and soldier of the Revolution. Died Jan 8, 1844 in 90th year of his age. Mary, consort of Walter Davis, died Feb 26, 1854 in the 90th year of her age." Fur infor Captain John James Chap.

DAVIS, WILLIAM, (Muskingum Co.)

Revolutionary Soldier. Bur Greenwood Cem, Zanesville, O, 60 ft fr Main entrance. Fur infor Muskingum Chap.

DAVIS, WILLIAM, (Fairfield Co.)

Pvt Conn Continental line. Br 1761. D 1830. Descendant 31043. Placed on the Pension Roll of Fairfield Co 1818 in Ohio. Ref: p 17, Vol 32. D. A. R. Lin.

DAVIS, WILLIAM, (Pike Co.)

In 1776 served as guide under Col Samuel Forman. Pensioned 1832 from Clark Co. B 1754, Middletown, N. J. Mar ———— Havens. D 1834, Pike Co, O. Ref: Natl No 56932, Vol 57, p 322, D. A. R. Lin.

DAVIS, WILLIAM, (Trumbull Co.)

Bur Hillside, Bazetta. Copied fr D. A. R. Yr Bk. Fur infor Mary Chesney Chap.

DAVIS, WILLIAM, (Vinton Co.)

Enl June 3, 1777. Disch June 3, 1780. Fifer. Br 1759. Parents: John. Mar Mary Rathburn. Ref: Mrs. J. Hugg, Wellston, O. Children: John, Polly, William, Eunice, Reformer Dyer. D May 2, 1826. Bur family burying ground on farm, Yankee St Cem, 2 miles south of Wilkesville, O, on Gallipolis Rd. GM old style slab with name and date of death. Battles: Monmouth and Newport. Enl Providence, R. I. Date of application for pens May 8, 1818; brought home a musician's note book, taken in hand combat with Hessians; came fr Coventhy, N. Y. 1818 to Vinton Co, O. Farmer. Record at Washington is given under 3F44120. Ref: Great Granddaughter, Clara Davis Grate. Mrs. Henry Grate, Wellston. Fur infor Jane Dailey, State Chairman.

DAVIS, WILLIAM R., (Greene Co.)

Pvt in Maryland Mil. On Pension Roll Mch 4, 1831, age 71 yrs. Annual allowance $33.33. Fur infor Catherine Green Chap.

DAVISSON, ISAAC, (Clark Co.)

19½ mos as Indian Spy and Orderly Sgt in his brother's, Maj Daniel Davidson, Harrison Co, Va Tr. Applied for a pens Nov 12, 1832, which was allowed. Br 1746, East New Jersey. Parents: Obediah Davidson. Mar Isabella Anderson, May 25, 1779. Children: Hezekiah, James, Obediah, Daniel, Sarah, Mary, Jane, Isaac Jr., Nancy, Jesse, Jacob, Matilda, Thomas. D Oct 17, 1842, South Charleston, O, and bur in Green Lawn Cem. Lot 93, Sec 5. MI: "Davisson." GM by J. C. Davisson about 1844. His captains were James Booth and Christopher Carpenter. Ref: Bureau of Pensions; Family Bible; Census of Va 1790. Fur infor Lagonda Chap.

DAWSON, HENRY, (Clarke Co.)

Lieut QM Col John Gibson's Western Dept from Jan 1, 1780 to Dec 6, 1781 (the time he surrendered the command of the Dept to Brig-Gen William Irvine). Mar Constantine. Children: Ellen, George, John, Richard, Harriet, Elizabeth. D Pleasant Twp, Clark Co, O. Bur Asbury M. E. Chapel Cem, 9 miles northeast Springfield, O. Not platted. MI: "Lieut Henry Dawson. A soldier of the Revolution." GM by S. A. R. about 1906. Came fr Kentucky to Pleasant Twp, Clark Co, O, in 1804; brought first fruit trees to the county. A cooper; treasurer of Pleasant Twp, Clark Co, O. Body was moved from Dawson farm to present place in 1906. Ref: History of Clark Co. 1886; W. T. R. Saffrell's Records of Revolutionary Soldiers. Fur infor Lagonda Chap.

DAWSON, JAMES, (Jackson Co.)

Served 3 yrs, 7 mos in 13th Va Regt in battles against Indians at Coshocton, O, and at White Woman's Creek and Big Beaver, besides many other battles. D Jackson, O. Bur west side of Franklin Twp, perhaps at Four Mile. This man with Thomas Oliver was a guest of honor at the Jackson Fourth of July celebration, 1843. Applied for pens at Jackson Oct 6, 1820. Was receiving one in 1840. Fur infor Captain John James Chap.

DAY, GEORGE, (Jefferson Co.)

Enl 1776 as Pvt in Capt John Ogilvie's Company. 1783 was in the Flying Camp Mil. Br 1752, Cecil Co, Md. Mar Sarah Catherine Rogers (d 1828). D 1838 Bur Island Creek Cem Jefferson Co. GM by Steubenville D. A. R. with official marker. Ref: Natl No 102436, Vol 103, p 136, D. A. R. Lin. Fur infor Steubenville Chap.

DAY, JEHIAL, (Hamilton Co.)

Br 1758, New Jersey. D 1833. Ref: S. A. R. Fur infor Cincinnati Chap.

DAY, JOHN, (Miami Co.)

Bur Old Stanton Cem, 2 miles east of Troy. GM by Miami Chap. Fur infor Miami Chap.

DAY, LEWIS, (Portage Co.)

Pvt and Sgt Mass State Tr. Placed on Pension Roll May 13, 1833. Br 1754, Deerfield, Mass. Mar Sebra Ward. 1778. D 1847, Deerfield, O. Bur Deerfield, O. Drew pens at Ravenna in 1840; applied 1832. Ref: Natl No 80100, Vol 81, D. A. R. Lin. Fur infor Old Northwest Chap.

DAY, SAMUEL, (Ross Co.)

Pvt in Capt John Winston's Company, 14th Va Regt, 1778, 1779, 1780. Br 1757, Exter, Berks Co, Va. Parents: John Day and (Nichols) Day. Mar Margaret Cohague, North Carolina, 1780. Children: Hedgman, Demovil, Ransom, Addison, Allison, Ovington, Dorcas, Rebecca and Samuel. D May 4, 1820, Concord Twp, Ross Co, O. Bur Day Cem on Day farm near Good Hope, O. GM Marker placed by L. M. Day, a descendant, May 1922. Born in Pa. At early age went to North Carolina with parents. After war went to the Upper Tract in Pendelton Co, Va. In 1805 moved to Ohio, near Frankfort, Ross Co. Farmer. Was a first cousin of Daniel Boone and a brother of John Day of the Lewis-Clark expedition. Samuel Day was wounded in shoulder at Battle of Cowpens and later crippled by shot. Sons in War of 1812 Hedgman, Addison, Allison and Ovington. Fur infor by L. M. Day, Chillicothe, O., for the Nathaniel Massie Chap.

DEAM, HENRY, (Montgomery Co.)

Pvt in Capt Parker's Company, Chester Co Mil commanded by Col Thomas Hockley, Aug 5, 1776. 5 series Pa Archives Vol 5, p 510. Br Pa. Children: Henry. D Wayne Twp, Montgomery Co, O. Went to Va then came to Wayne Twp in 1802, with his family. No further infor available at this time. Richard Montgomery Chap S. A. R.

DEAN, AARON, (Seneca Co.)

Pvt soldier of 1776. Bur Omar Cem, Reed Twp. GM Bronze marker in 1927. Fur infor Dolly Todd Madison Chap.

DEAN, ABRAHAM, (Ross Co.)

Pvt 3rd class, 7th Company, 1st Bn, Cumberland Co Mil, Aug 18, 1780, Lt Col James Johnson, Capt John Woods, Lt Jacob Statler. See Pa Archives, 5 series, Vol 6, p 91 and 103 under May 17, 1781. Br 1763-1764. D May 10, 1806, Ross Co. Bur South Salem. GM Nathaniel Massie Chap D. A. R. Ref: 199980. Fur infor Nathaniel Massie and Juliana White Chap.

DEAN, BENJAMIN, (Mahoning Co.)

Pvt NY State Revolutionary War. Enl men 7th Regt Dutchess Co, N. Y. Col Henry Ludenton. Br 1740. Mar Ruth ——— (1741-1812). D 1815. Bur Canfield Cem. GM D. A. R. 1915-17. Ref: pp 23-66-150 "NY Men in the Rev." Fur infor Mahoning Chap.

DEAN, SAMUEL, (Cuyahoga Co.)

Minute man, Pvt Mass Line. Br 1755. D 1840. Bur Fair View Cem, Rockport. Fur infor Western Reserve Chap.

DEANE, WALTER, (Ashtabula Co.)

Capt. D 1814. Bur Kelloggsville, O. Fur infor Mary Redmond Chap.

DEATS, HENRY, (Hamilton Co.)

Br 1749, New Jersey. D 1823. S. A. R. Fur infor Cincinnati Chap.

DeCAMP, JAMES, (Clermont Co.)

Ensign 3rd Regt Continental Tr. (Stryker's "NJ Men of Rev" p 55). Served entire period of war. Present at Washington's farewell address to soldiers. Settled in Hamilton Co. Br Westfield, N. J. Mar Sarah Ross, in New Jersey (1746-1835. Bur Bethel Cem.) Children: One son, Ezekiel (1779-1860 mar Mary Baker), one son David. D 1827 Bethel, Clermont Co, O where he is buried. Came to Butler Co, 1812, Reily Twp, 4 miles south of Oxford. Was one of first to step from ranks and grasp Washington's hand, to show he stood by him, at his famous speech. Refused to receive a pens. History of DeCamp family, owned by Jas M DeCamp, mentions other brave deeds. Not able to find offical record. Ref: Mrs Rebecca Hand Wustin, Woods Station, who has his flintlock musket. Fur infor Cincinnati Chap, by Mrs. Whallon, Wyoming, O.

DEEDS, GEORGE, (Greene Co.)

Pvt Va Continental Line. Pensioned 1831, on roll Apr 11, 1833, age 71 yrs. Annual allowance $26.66. Br 1762. Mar Mary———. Children: Had seven daughters. D Oct 8, 1846. Bur Zoar's Churchyard, Caesar's Creek Twp. Living at Caesar's Creek in 1819. Ref: "Robinson's History of Greene County." Fur infor Catherine Greene Chap.

DeFORD, John, (Fayette Co.)

Served 1778 as Pvt in Capt John Hawkins' Company, 5th Regt, Queens Co, Md under Col William Richardson. Br 1750 in Kent Co, Md. Mar Lydia Hopgood. D 1800 in Fayette Co, O. Ref: Natl No 53961, Vol 54, p 432, D. A. R. Lin.

DeFORD, JOHN, (Fayette Co.)

Minute man under Capt Frederick Frelinghuysen. Served as Sgt and Ensign under different commands, short periods NJ Mil; Pensioned 1832. Br Mch 3, 1749, Readington, N. J. Mar Margaret Vandenburg. Children; Catherine. D Dec 11, 1847 Brookfield. Bur Brookfield Center. Ref: 43268, V 44, p 102, D. A. R. Lin. Fur infor Mary Chesney Chap.

DeFREES, JOSEPH HUTTEN, (Miami Co.)

Served all through the war. Pa Archives, 6 series, Vol 1, p 564. Pa Archives, 2 series, Vol 13, p 712-13. Br New York City 1753. Parents: Joseph DeFrees and Mary Hutten. Mar Mary Start in Old Swedes Church Philadelphia Sept 10, 1777. Children: John, James, Anna, Joseph. D Aug 1826, farm north of Piqua, O. Bur Johnson Cem (private) Piqua, O. GM Miami Chap, Bronze marker, May 29, 1925. Ref: D. A. R. Lin. Vol 49, p 50, Natl 48104. Fur infor Miami Chap.

DEITRICK, JOHN BALSAR (JOHANN BALTSH) SR., (Muskingum Co.)

Enl in York Co as Pvt under Capt John Paxton, Cols Robert McAlister, succeeded by John Kennedy. Took part in a skirmish on Long Island with the Picket Guard of Hessians. Br Dec 1753 in Lancaster Co, Pa. D Mch 18, 1838, Stovertown and bur in Lutheran Cem Stovertown. Annual allowance $20.00 as a Pvt. Ref: Pa Archives, 6 series, p 164; U. S. Pension Roll 3, p 150. Fur infor Muskingum Chap.

DELZELL, WILLIAM, (Hamilton Co.)

Br 1755, Pa. D 1837. Ref: S. A. R. Fur infor Cincinnati Chap.

DELONG, JOHN (Mahoning Co.)

Pvt 4th class Northampton Co Mil Pa. Pensioned 1819. Br 1738. Children: Names of only two given, John and Aaron. D in 1835 near Milton Dam, O. Bur in Ickes Cem. Ref: History of Trumbull and Mahoning Co. Vol 2, p 180; Pa Archives, Vol 8, Series 5, p 443, Ser 3. Vol 23, p 581. Fur infor Mahoning Chap.

DEMING, SIMEON, (Washington Co.)

Enl 1780 and again in 1781 in Capt Herman Smith's Company, Col Collen's Regt. Br May 4, 1763 Sandisfield, Mass. Parents: David and Elizabeth Robbins. Mar Lucy Wolcott, Mch 12, 1789. Children: Honor, Elizabeth, David, Sarah, Simeon, Joel, Daniel, Julius, Lucy, Polly. D July 30, 1850, Watertown, O. Bur near Watertown 2½ miles east on farm which was his. MI: "Simeon Deming a native of Berkshire Co, Mass. Died July 20, 1850 in the 88th year of his age." He with two other men cut the first wagon road west fr Marietta. Fur infor Marietta Chap.

DEMUTH, CHRISTOPHER, (Tuscarawas Co.)

Pvt in Capt Jacob Heller's 3rd Company of the 2nd Bn of Northampton Co, Pa. Mil in 1780-1781 (See Pa Archives series 5, Vol 8, pp 123-5, 161, 172 and 195.) Br Aug 2, 1775 at Allemaengel, Pa. Parents: Son of Gottlieb Sr and Eva. Mar Susanna Marie Klein, Apr 8, 1777. Children: John Frederick (1779), Susanna Catherine Anna Rosina, Anna Marie, Rachel Elizabeth, Margaretha, Sarah Catherine, Abagail, Lydia. D 1823 Gnadenhutten, O. Bur Moravian Cem, Gnadenhutten. MI: "Christopher Demuth. Born August 12, 1755. Died January 27, 1822. Aged 67 yrs, 5 mos, 15 days." GM by small stone, probably erected by family years ago. Resided in Plainfield Twp, Northampton Co, Pa, until 1805, when he came to Gnadenhutten, O. Farmer. Name appears on Soldiers' Memorial erected in Gnadenhutten Cem 1927. Fur infor Jane Dailey, State Chairman. Ref: Charles L. Stocker, Esq, Cleveland, O.

DEMUTH, GOTTLIEB, (Tuscarawas Co.)

Pvt in Capt Jacob Heller's Company of the 2nd Bn of Northampton Co, Pa Mil in 1780, 1781 and 1782. (See Pa Archives, Series 5, Vol 8, p 123-5, 161, 172 and 195.) Br Nov 18, 1750, Allemaengel, Pa. Parents: Gottlieb Sr., and Eva. Mar Marriet Anna Maria Allemann, Nov 16, 1773. Children: Joseph, John, Christian, Anna Maria, Frederick, Renatus, Wm Gottlieb, Abraham, Jonathan, Gottfried, Benjamin. D Jan 29, 1825 at Gnahenhutten, O. Bur Moravian Cem, Gnadenhutten, O. MI: "Gottlieb Demuth, Born November 18, 1750, Lynn Township, Northampton Co, Pa. Departed January 29, 1825. Aged 74 yrs 2 mo 11 days." GM by small stone, evidently erected by family years ago. Lived during Revolutionary War period and for some yrs afterward in Plainfield Twp, Northampton Co, Pa; came to Ohio about 1810. Carpenter and farmer. Name appears on Soldiers' Memorial erected in Gnadenhutten Cem in 1927. Fur infor Jane Dailey, State Chairman. Ref: Charles L Stocker, Esq, Cleveland, O.

DENISON, JOHN, (Trumbull, Co.)

He receipted for several sums of money for services rendered in defense of the territories of Westmoreland Co, Pa. Br 1748, Ireland. Mar Mary McCullough, 1782. D Oct 28, 1821. Bur Seceeder Corners, Liberty Twp. MI: name, date of birth and death. Ref: Pa Archives, 6 series, p 352, 357 and Natl No 101950, Vol 103, p 289; 78861, Vol 79. D. A. R. Lin.

DENISON, WILLIAM, (Muskingum Co.)

Pvt and Corp in 3rd Conn Regt. His company was detached to resist army of Cornwallis engaged in devastating country around Tide Water Va. Br Apr 1756, Stonington, Conn. Mar Ann Slack. Children: William S. D July 21, 1820. Bur family plat near former dwelling. Came to Ohio in 1810 and settled in Salem Twp near present Village of Adamsville. Fur infor Muskingum Chap.

DENMORE, JOHN, (Franklin Co.)

Drummer Boy. Enl Mch 1, 1780 in 6th Md Regt in command of Maj Landsell at Prince George's Co, Md. Was in the Battle of Guilford Court House, Camden, Entaw Springs and was wounded in the hand in the service. Br Prince George's Co, Md, 1751. D Nov 28, 1838, Mifflin Twp. Bur Old Cem Mifflin Twp. MI: "John Denmore died Nov 28, 1838, aged 87 years." GM Rev Grave Committee with bronze marker, May 30, 1912. Fur infor Columbus Chap.

DENNIS, JOHN, (Clermont Co.)

Several enlmts as Pvt to 1776-1778. Pension Roll of Clermont Co, O, 1840. Br Gloucester Co, N. J. 1760. Mar Sarah Highbee, 2nd wife. D 1850. Clermont Co. D. A. R. 60281, p 93, Vol 61, D. A. R.Lin.

DENNY, SAMUEL, (Pickaway Co.)

Chester Co. Pa Mil. Capt William Witherow, Col Patterson Bell's 8th Bn, Chester Co Mil. Br 1738. Mar Janet Sterling. D 1822, Pickaway Co, O. Ref: 15303 and 78909 D. A. R. Fur infor p 121, Vol 16, D. A. R. Lin.

DENUNE, JOHN, (Franklin Co.)

Drummer boy and soldier. Enl Mch 1, 1780 in 6th Md Regt in command of Maj Landsell Prince George's Command. Was in the battle of Guilford Court House, Camden, Eutaw Springs and Siege of Ninety Six. Was wounded in the hand in the serv. Served until June 1783. Br 1761, France. Mar Sarah Burrell. One child was Alexander Burrell Denune. D Nov 28, 1838, Franklin Co, O. age 77 yrs. Bur Riverside Cem, Mifflin Twp, Sunbury Pike, near Linden Heights, O, in Franklin Co. MI: "John Denune died Nov 28, 1838, aged 77 yrs." GM by descendants and D. A. R. Oct 16, 1927. Was from Prince George Co, Md. His name is on the marble tablet of Rev Soldiers of Franklin Co in Memorial Hall Lobby, Columbus. Was pensioned in 1819 for serv as Pvt in Md Continental Line. Ref: Natl No 93797, Vol 94, p 247. Fur infor Columbus Chap.

DEPOY, CHRISTOPHER, (Ross Co.)

Pvt in Va Line. D Apr 17, 1843. Bur in Concord Twp, Ross Co, O. on Waugh's Hill, west of Austin. MI: name, death and "aged 81 yrs, 7 mos, 19 days." GM Mch 24, 1928. Ref: Pens list. Fur infor Nathaniel Massie Chap.

DEPUE, DANIEL, (Mahoning Co.)

1st Lt Capt Manuel Hover's Company 3rd Bn NJ. Children: Joseph and Margaret. Bur Milton Twp. One of first schoolteachers. Ref: p 184, Vol 2, Hist Trumbull and Mahoning Cos. NJ Officers and Men in Revolution. Fur infor Mahoning Chap.

DEVER, JOHN (DEAVOR), (Scioto Co.)

Br Oct 20, 1746 in Va. D Oct 10, 1827. Bur near Lucasville, but in Scioto Co. 1827. D. A. R. Lin, Vol 9. Grace Hoch, Marion, O. Descendant. Fur infor Capt Wm Hendricks Chap.

DEVIN, MICHAEL, (Washington Co.)

Br 1749. D 1822. Bur Waterford Twp, Washington Co. Fur infor Marietta Chap.

DEVOL, JONATHAN, (Washington Co.)

Lt in Continental Serv. Br 1755. Mar Nancy Barker, 1776. Children: Henry, Charles, Baker, Frances, Salley and Nancy. D 1824. Bur Putnam Cem near

Marietta. MI: "Capt Jonathan Devol—1755-1824." GM Marietta Chap with Rev Marker, 1922. Shipbuilder. Fur infor Marietta Chap.

DEVON, DAVID, (Perry Co.)

Entire period of War. Pvt. Br New Jersey. Mar Mary Morgan. Children: David, Morgan, Alexander, Martha, Mary. D 1837, Perry Co. Bur Cem on Monroe Twp on his own farm. At close of war was in Gen Proctor's Tr (Pa Tr) record is in Pa Archives. Later served under Anthony Wayne. Natl No 225742 (on another ancestor). Fur infor Elizabeth Zane Drew Chap.

DEVOSE, NICHOLAS, (Brown Co.)

Pvt in Van Swearengen's Company, Morgan's Rifle Regt, Continental Tr. Br 1732, France. Mar Sarah Dicker. D 1815. Red Oak, O. Natl No 64591, p 206, Vol 65, D. A. R. Lin. Fur infor Ripley Chap.

DE WEESE, JOSHUA, (Miami Co.)

Served in Richard Dalinas' Company fr Kent Co, Del. Br Kent Co, Del, Aug 14, 1742. Mar 1st Elizabeth Bowman; 2nd Hannah Birch; 3rd Elizabeth New. Children: Anna, Thomas, Lewis, Samuel, William, James, Jethro, Joshua, Elizabeth, Mary. D Miami Co, O. Jan 25, 1819. Bur Staunton Cem, Troy, O. Fur infor Nathaniel Massie Chap.

DEWEY, OLIVER, (Summit Co.)

Pvt in Capt John Carpenter's Company Sept 30 to Dec 30, 1779; as guard at Springfield; also in Col Mosely's Regt Oct 26, 1780; also served July 20 to Oct 22, 1780, Capt Levi Ely's Company, Col John Brown's Regt. Br Westfield, Mass, Aug 12, 1763. Mar Hulda Morley, Oct 4, 1787, 1st wife; 2nd wife Mrs. Davis. D Jan 20, 1845, Cuyahoga Falls, O. Bur Northampton. Natl No 29850, Vol 30, p 305, D. A. R. Lin. Fur infor Cuyahoga Portage Chap.

DEWOLF, BENJAMIN, (Licking Co.)

Enl at age of 13. Pvt 1 yr in Col Samuel Parson's Regt. In Apr 1778, with Capt John B. Hopkinson on US Frigate "Warren." Br 1763, Conn. D Harrison Twp. GM by Hetuck Chap 1909. In 1779 with Capt Rathbone on sloop "Providence." Pensioner. Across fr the Smith farm is one upon which Joseph De Wolf settled when in 1799 he came fr Granby, Conn. with Gen Smith and in June 1800 brought his wife, Sarah Couch, formerly of Granville, Mass, and their 11 children to their new home. Ref: Hist of Licking Co by E. M. P. Brister. Fur infor Hetuck Chap.

DEWOLF, JOSEPH, (Trumbull Co.)

Corp Mass Continental Lines. Br 1762. Mar Sarah Gibbons. D Aug 15, 1846, 84 yrs, 11 mos, 20 days, at Mt Vernon, O. Bur Old Cem south of center of Vernon. MI: "A soldier of the Revolution and one of the first settlers of Trumbull County." GM Monument flat on the ground. On Ohio Pension Roll. Ref: See Natl No 70138, Vol 71, p 51, D. A. R. Lin. Fur infor Mary Chesney Chap.

DEWOLPH, ABDA (DOLPH), (Ashtabula Co.)

Served as Pvt in the 17th Regt Albany Co, NY Mil. He had served 3 yrs in the French War. Br 1743, Middletown, Conn. Mar Mary Coleman, 1766. Children: Joseph. D 1833 Andover, Ashtabula Co, O. Bur West Andover. MI: "Abda Dolph Died Oct 26, 1833 aged 90 yrs. He served three yrs in the French War, and was a soldier of the Revolution." Ref: Lin Bk Vol 15, p 158; and 74591 D. A. R. Fur infor Mary Stanley Chap.

DICKERSON, GEORGE, (Harrison Co.)

A Revolutonary Pensioner in Rumley Twp, 1840, aged 94. US Pens Rolls, 1840. Moravian Trail Chap.

DICKERSON, THOMAS, (Washington Co.)

Pvt in Capt Van Swearingen's Company, Col Aneas Mackey's 8th Pa Regt. Br Oct 15, 1757. Mar Margaret Davis. Children: Joseph, Frederick, Rebecca, Rachel, Isabella, Eleanor, Elizabeth, Thomas and Sarah. D 1836 in Ohio. Settled on a farm in Grandview Twp in 1795 where he lived until his death. Ref: Washington Co Hist; list of pensioners. Natl No 58066, Vol 59, p 25, D. A. R. Lin. Fur infor Marietta Chap.

DICKEY, HUGHEY, (Clermont Co.)

Settled in Jackson Twp, Clermont Co, O. 1798. Br near Chambersburg, Franklin Co, Pa. Children: William, Benj, Samuel, Hughey, Elizabeth, Jane. Ref: A. S. Abbott, Bethel, O. Fur infor Cincinnati Chap.

DICKEY, MOSES, (Columbiana Co.)

Bur Bowman Cem, Elk Run. Lived in Elk Twp, Columbiana Co, O. Fur infor Bethia Southwick Chap.

DICKEY, ROBERT, (Clermont Co.)

Franklin Co, Pa. Served in Col Bowman's expedition against old Chillicothe in 1779. He died in 1840 Jackson Twp, Clermont Co, O. Fur infor Cincinnati Chap.

DICKEY, ROBERT, (Ross Co.)

Light horseman and member of 2nd Provincial Congress, 1775-1776. Br November 25, 1745, near Rockfish (now Rockbridge) Gap, Albemarle Co, Va. Parents: John and Martha McNeely. Mar 1st Margaret Hillhouse, Mch 24, 1772; 2nd Mary Henry Jan 1780. D South Salem, O. May 24, 1817. Bur on farm now owned by Will Stinson. Moved to South Charleston before the Rev. Was a light horseman in Capt Thomas Kirkpatrick's Company, Col Tom Bratton's Regt in South Carolina. Ref: Journal of Gen Assembly of SC p 161 and Genealogical Magazine, Vol 7, p 107. Was very prominent in his community, as have been his descendants. Descendant Mrs. Edward Gore Miller, Greenfield, O. Fur infor Nathaniel Massie Chap.

DICKEY, SAMUEL, (Butler Co.)

1777 Pvt in Col John Patton's NC Regt and Sgt in Capt John Redmond's Company. Br 1753, North Carolina. Mar Catherine Saxton (br 1756 d 1812). Children: One son was George. D Dec 1, 1812, Butler Co, O. Name on Bronze tablet at Hamilton, O. Bur Elk Creek Cem, Madison Twp. Ref: Natl No 61930, Vol 62, p 319, and Natl No 102880, Vol 103, p 271 D. A. R. Lin.

DICKSON, CHRISTOPHER, (Butler Co.)

Teamster in Capt Munson's Team Brig, NJ Mil. Br New Jersey. D Butler Co, O. Mar Phebe Lewis Bayless, 1775. Natl No 70551. p 200 ,Vol 71, D. A. R. Lin.

DICKSON, GEORGE, (Harrison Co.)

Revolutionary Pensioner living in Harrison Co in 1833; served in Col Thomas Price's 2nd Md Regt of Mil; Hist of West Md, I Vol, p 150. U. S. Pension Rolls 1835. Fur infor Moravin Trail Chap.

DIERDORF, ABRAHAM, (Ger) (Deardorf), (Franklin Co.)

8th Company 3rd Bn of Lancaster Co, Pa. 1780 under Capt Smuller, (p 284 yr 1787, 6th class). Br Germany. Parents: Abraham and Catherine. Children: David, Daniel, Joseph Samuel, Elizabeth, Paulina Catherine. D 1805, killed on the border line between Pa and Ohio while carrying mail. Bur on the border line between Pa and Ohio. Next to Lucas Sullivant was Pioneer settler of Franklinton, 1798. Farmer and carried mail on horseback to Baltimore for US Government. Ref: Franklin Centennial Hist, p 20; also p 101, p 122. Fur infor Columbus Chap.

DILDINE, JOHN, (Columbiana Co.)

D Oct 15, 1837, 68 yrs, 1 mo, 10 days. Bur New Waterford Cem, Columbiana Co, O. Fur infor Bethia Southwick Chap.

DILL, THOMAS, (Columbia Co.)

Br 1744. D 1833 in his 83rd yr. Bur Yellow Creek Churchyard. Lived in Madison Twp, Columbiana Co, O. Fur infor Bethia Southwick Chap.

DILLE, DAVID, (Cuyahoga Co.)

Lt Va Mil; served 2 enlmts; with Crawford vs the Indians. Pensioned 1832, Euclid, O, for serv as Lt in Va Mil. Br 1753. D 1855. Ref: 25203, Vol 26, p 71, D. A. R. Lin. Fur infor Western Reserve Chap.

DILLEY, EPHRAIM SR., (Guernsey Co.)

Pvt soldier Sussex Co, N. J. Enl Oct 1776, Companies Henry Countryman, Capt Jacob Stull, Capt Matthia Bethwith, Capt Christian Longstreet, 2nd Regt, 1779, Br Nov 6, 1755, N. J. Parents: Aaron Dilley and Hannah Perry. Aaron said to have been Revolutionary soldier. Mar Lucy Ayres. Children: Abraham, Hannah, Anna, Robert, William, Ephraim, Samuel, Joseph. D Senecaville, O. GM family. Farmer. Ref: Natl No 65031 and others. Fur infor Anna Asbury Stone Chap.

DILLEY, SAMUEL, (Trumbull Co.)

Bur Hubbard, O. GM by many stones; Inscription is obliterated; many were broken and thrown out when cem was cleaned up. Will probated Oct 7, 1839. Ref: Baldwin Library, Youngstown, O. Fur infor Mary Chesney Chap.

DIMICK, MOOR, (Summit Co.)

Enl in Mass line at Ashford, Conn, in 1781 at age of 13, and was at Yorktown surrender of Cornwallis. Name appears in a newspaper of 1840, as one of the Revolutionary soldiers too feeble to march to polls and vote a presidential election that yr. Br Ashford, Windham Co, Conn. 1768. Mar Betsy. D Dec 21, 1841. Bur Talmadge, O. Previous to coming to Talmadge lived for some time in N. Y. Fur infor Cuyahoga Portage Chap.

DISBROW, HENRY, (Medina Co.)

Pvt in Capt Albert Chapman's Company 1777. D Medina, O. 1838. Natl No 61427, p 148, Vol 62, D. A. R. Lin.

DITTO, FRANCIS, (Seneca Co.)

Bur in an old private burying ground lot on the McHelheny farm in Eden Twp. Fur infor Dolly Todd Madison Chap.

DIVER, DANIEL, (Portage Co.)

Lived at Deerfield. Fur infor Old Northwest Chap.

DIXON, ALEXANDER, (Morrow Co.)

Bur Westfield Cem, Westfield Twp. Fur infor Mt Gilead Chap.

DIXON, ANDREW, (Dickson), (Belmont Co.)

Pvt in Capt Samuel Kearsley's Company of Independents, annexed to 6th Va Regt. Col James Hendrick's Command, also Capt Samuel Kearsley's Company, Col Wm Malcolm's Regt, Continental Tr of Cumberland Co, Pa. Br 1750, Ireland. Mar Rachel Bryson. Children: Mary, Lucy, Hannah, Margaret, Rebecca. D June 9, 1804, Pultney Twp, Belmont Co, O. Bur Cem at Neffs, near the home he established in 1796. Prominent man and trusted; first settled in Cumberland Co, Pa, thence to West Liberty Va, thence to Belmont Co. Ref: Dr. M. T. Dixon, 576 S. 3rd St., Columbus, O. Fur infor Mrs. Lowell Hobart, Washington Records.

DIXON, JOSHUA, (Columbiana Co.)

Pvt Chester Co, Pa Mil. Br 1750. D 1830, Columbiana Co, O. Ref: 85334, Vol 86, D. A. R. Lin.

DIXON, WILLIAM, (Brown Co.)

Served in the Revolutionary Army 7 yrs fr Va. Br Ireland. Mar Grizzy A. Bell. Children: William, one of 10 children. D Brown Co, O. Bur Red Oak. He founded a settlement in Mason Co, Ky. 1789 crossed the Ohio River with Neil Washburn, in 1793 at Logans Gap, built a cabin on Eagle Creek a mile fr the river and lived there 7 yrs. Was the first white settler to locate in Brown Co. Ref: Hist of Brown Co, O published by Beere & Co, 1883, Miss Eleanor Johnson, Ripley, O., R. F. D. 3. Fur infor Taliaferro Chap.

DOANE, RICHARD, (Washington Co.)

Served in the Revolutionary War in Capt Thomas Converse's Company and drew a pens for his military serv. Br Saybrook, Conn. D Salem, Washington Co, O, Aug 27, 1823. GM Marietta Chap D. A. R. ordered a marker, May 1923. In 1805 or 1806 Richard Doane moved fr Saybrook, Conn with his wife and children and settled on a farm at Lower Salem, Washington Co, O. Ref: John Doane, Marietta, O. Fur infor Marietta Chap.

DODDS, JOSEPH, JR., (Montgomery Co.)

Ensign 1778; Lt 1779 of York Co, Pa Mil to end of war. Br 1753 York or Adams Co, Pa. D 1833, Dayton, O. Natl Nos 35433 and 70773 Vol 71, p 278, D. A. R. Lin.

DODDS, WILLIAM, (Montgomery Co.)

Capt 1st Company Sept 3, 1777, Col Thompson Bn Apr 5, 1778, York Co, Pa. Capt of 6th Company 6th Bn York Co, Mil. June 17, 1778. Br 1753, England. Mar Isabel McGrew. (Br 1762; d Apr 19, 1842). Children: James, William, Thomas, Jack, Polly, Margaret, Martha. D July 16, 1831; West Carrollton. Bur Presbyterian Church Yard, Centerville & Miamisburg Pikes. MI: "In memory of Gen. William Dodds of York Co, Pa. Died July 16, 1831, aged 78 years 9 months. Blessed are the Dead who die in the Lord." GM by Richard Montgomery Chap, S. A. R. with bronze marker in 1919. Came to Ohio in early 1800 with his family and settled in what is now West Carrollton, where they lived and died. Farmer. See p 423, 554, 612, 638, Vol 2, Pa Archives. Ref: Natl No 33174, S. A. R. Fur infor Richard Montgomery Chap, S. A. R.

DODGE, JEREMIAH, (Ashtabula Co.)

Pvt in the 3rd Company in the 7th Regt under Col Chas Webb in Capt Nathan Hale's Company, Conn. Br May 23, 1742, East Haddam, Conn. Mar Elizabeth Chapman, 1770. Children Eusebrius Dodge. D Oct 9, 1825, Rome, O. Bur Dodgeville Cem, New Lyme, O. MI: "Jeremiah Dodge, D Oct 12, 1825, aged 82 yrs." Ref: Natl No 190369, D. A. R. Lin. Fur infor Eunice Grant Chap.

DODGE, JOHN JR., (Washington Co.)

Officer fr Beverly Mass. Served until close of war. Br 1748, Beverly, Mass. Mar Susanna Marsters. D 1806, Marietta, O. Member Ohio Company of Associates. Ref: Natl No 99410 and 56206, Vol 57, p 71 D. A. R. Lin.

DODGE, NATHANIEL, (Washington Co.)

Enl as a soldier in New Hampshire in 1780 at the age of seventeen. Br July 3, 1763. Hampton Falls, N. H. D May 13, 1838. Bur Mound Cem, Marietta, O. MI: "Nathaniel Dodge 1763-1838." GM Marietta Chap with Revolutionary marker. Nov 30, 1906 marker stolen and replaced in 1920. Ref. History of Washington Co. Fur infor Marietta Chap.

DODGE, SHADRACH, (Ashtabula Co.)

Served in Capt McGregor's Company of Inf. Col Cortland's Regt and under the immediate command of Washington. He was a pensioner for 27 years. Fought in Divisions of Gates, of Lafayette and under immediate Command of Washington. Br 1762, Brookfield, Mass. "Died in Ashtabula. Mehitable, Widow of the late Shadrach Dodge, aged 86 yrs." Ashtabula Sentinel, Feb 1844. D July 23, 1845, Ashtabula, O. Bur Edgewood. "The spirit which called to the field at the age of 16 burned within him to the last......He was a patriot by constitution and lived and died engrossed with one idea—the glory of serving and saving his country." At Ashtabula July 23, 1845. Ref: "Ashtabula Sentinel." Natl No 28863, Vol 29, p 314, D. A. R. Lin. Fur infor Mary Stanley Chap.

DODSON, JOHN, (Hamilton Co.)

1st Company 2nd Bn Chester Co, Md. under Col Thomas Bull Md Mil. Br 1752 Chester Co, Md. Mar Eleanor Howard, Baltimore, Md. 1778. Children: John, Margaret, Edward, William, Beal W., Samuel, Ann, Charles, Thomas. D 1825 Hamilton Co. Miami Twp. (Now Springfield Twp) Finneytown. Bur Finneytown now in limits of Cincinnati, O. MI: Name, Date, placed by family. Now crumbling. Was given farm as land grant for Revolutionary Services. Farmer. Ref: Two sisters. Natl Nos 3449 and 3448, also 134210, and 134211. Fur infor Cincinnati Chap.

DOHRMAN, ARNOLD HENRY, (Jefferson Co.)

Br 1749. D 1813. Bur Union Cem. GM by Steubenville D. A. R. with official marker. Fur infor Steubenville Chap.

DONLEY, JAMES, (Clermont Co.)

Came to Washington Twp, Clermont Co, O. in 1805. Bur Calvary Cem. Ref: A. S. Abbott, Bethel, O. Fur infor Cincinnati Chap.

DORR, MATHEW, (Athens Co.)

Capt in battle of Saratoga in Col Jonathan Latimer's Regt, Conn Mil. Br June 14, 1724-5 Lyme, Conn. Parents: Edmund and Mary (Griswold) Dorr. Mar 1st Elizabeth Palmer (d about 1775) Nov 4, 1747. 2nd Mrs. Lydia (Wood) McClean in 1776. Children: Edmund, Baruch, (mar Phoebe Ward) Lydia, William, Rhoda. There were other children. D Sept 18, 1801, Wolfs Plains, Athens

Co, O. Bur probably Wolfs Plains cem. MI: Tombstone evidently decayed. There are a number of disintegrated tombstones in the cem. His oldest son and wife, Ermund and Anna Dorr, were bur in same cem. Tombstones intact. Capt. Mathew Dorr, clothier, of Lyme, Conn, removed to East Haddam, Conn, where his first wife died. In 1795 he removed with his second wife to Athens Co, O. Ref: Natl No 38230, and 225740, and 101102, Vol 103, D. A. R. Lin. Fur infor Elizabeth Zane Dew Chap.

DORSEY, CHARLES, (Champaign Co.)

Br in Virginia. D July 14, 1811. Bur in family cem Grafton, now the Fromme farm, in Jackson Twp. Fur infor Urbana Chap.

DORSEY, JOHN HAMMOND, JR., (Butler Co.)

Soldier and Sgt, 2nd Company, 3rd Regt Md; Also served in Harford Co. Md, Mil Company No 6, Benj Rumsey Sept 16, 1775. Br Maryland, Feb 14, 1754, Parents: John Hammond and Frances (Watkins) Dorsey. Mar Ann Maxwell, Jan 20, 1772. Children: James Maxwell, Frances Rebecca. D Mch 1826 Oxford Butler Co, O. Supposed to be bur where he died. Fur infor Fort Greenville Chap.

DOTY, PETER, (Morrow Co.)

Bur Chester Cem, Chester Twp. Fur infor Mt Gilead Chap.

DOUD, ISAAC, (Crawford Co.)

Pvt Capt Herrick's Company, 1775, Capt Ball's Company, 1776, Col Shepard Mass Line. Br 1754. Mar Ellen Osborne. D 1824, Bucyrus, Natl No 48386, p 182, Vol 49, D. A. R. Lin.

DOUD, JAMES, (Mahoning Co.)

Capt in the Rev; later data says Pvt Enl Mch 20, 1781; disch Dec 31, 1781; Enl 1781 for 3 yrs from Windham, and Mch 1, 1784 in Swift's last Regt. Mar Lydia (1745-1808, bur Canfield, O.) Children: Herman, James, William, Samuel, Lydia, Anna. Bur unknown. Was a drover; came to Sanfield about 1800; Pres Trustee. Ref: Conn Men in Rev. pp 239, 363, 369. Hist Trumbull and Mahoning Co, Williams p 13, List of Revolutionary soldiers bur in Mahoning Co. Henry Baldwin, Historian S. A. R. Fur infor Mahoning Chap.

DOUGLAS, JAMES, (Pickaway Co.)

Seaman, Virginia State Navy (1776 to 1779). Served 3 yrs during Revolutionary War (Journal, House Delegates 1833-34 Doc 12); Served on Brig Liberty (Virginia State Library (N) N-8-20). Br Aug 27, 1740, probably Scotland or Connecticut. Parents: Father probably Hugh Douglas of Connecticut. Mar Hannah Huston 1765 in Scotland. Children: Margaret, Elizabeth, Jane, Mary Ann, James David, Hugh, George, Andrew, John, Nathaniel. D probably 1816, Madison Co. Bur Alkire graveyard, Pickaway Co, near Mt Sterling, north side of graveyard, north of grave of Hannah his wife which has a marker, no marker has been found for grave of James. Ref: Zoa Van Ness of Columbus Chap. Fur infor Mt Sterling Chap.

DOUGLASS, RANDALL, (Hamilton Co.)

Br 1763, South Carolina. D 1844. Ref: S. A. R. Fur infor Cincinnati Chap.

DOUGLASS, WILLIAM, (Highland Co.)

Br 1765. D Dec 23, 1853. Bur Greenfield. GM by Juliana White Chap, 1926. Fur infor Juliana White Chap.

DOWD, CONNER, (Vinton Co.)

Pvt in cavalry of NC. Served nearly through the war. Present at the surrender of Cornwallis at Yorktown. Br Oct 18, 1757, Ireland. Parents: Owen and Judith (Judah) Dowd. Mar Hannah Graves, 1796 or 7 (dau of Wm and Amy). Children: Jesse, Alex, Nancy, Owen, William, Charles, Conner, Hannah, John. D Mch 31, 1839, Zaleski, O. Vinton Co. Bur Oak Grove, Zaleski, O. east side of cem. MI: "Conner Dowd, born Oct 18, 1757. D March 31, 1839, aged 81 yrs. 5 mo. 13 days." GM by old style slab, many years ago. Pensioned 1834, Athens Co. Widow pensioned and received bounty land. Farmer. Genl C. H. Grosvenor furnished data from Washington records 25 years ago that he served repeatedly during war. Travis and Raper being two of his superior officers. Ref: Mrs Jane Dowd Dailey, Albany, O. D. A. R. State Chairman. Fur infor Nabby Lee Ames Chap, Athens, O.

DOWNEY, SAMUEL, (Clermont Co.)

Under Gen Washington. Br New Jersey. Bur. Statement of bur place not clear. Fur infor Cincinnati Chap.

DOWNING, WILLIAM, (Highland Co.)

In a Va Regt. Br 1761. D June 4, 1842. aged 81. Bur New Petersburg, Highland Co, O. On his stone J. M. Boyd, Md. 219 S. W. 6th Ave., Miami, Fla. Fur infor Waw-Wil-a-Way Chap.

DOWNS, JESSE, (Hamilton Co.)

Br 1764, Mass. D 1826. Ref: S. A. R. Fur infor Cincinnati Chap.

DOWNS, JOHN SR., (Ross Co.)

Fr Virginia, service being proven. Br Virginia. Children: John, James, Susannah (mar Davis), Jane (mar Covert), Rebecca, David, Thomas. Named in his will, signed June 2, 1805. D 1805, Green Twp., Ross Co., O. Came to Ohio from Virginia about 1801, bought land in Green Twp. Was a farmer and very religious. All of his sons served in the war of 1812; all are buried at Hopetown, Green Twp. p 47 and 109, Roster of Ohio Soldiers 1812. Fur infor Nathaniel Massie Chap.

DOXSEE, THOMAS, (various spellings), (Stark Co.)

Br Aug 2, 1742. Presumably in Ulster Co, N. Y. D Dec 28, 1821, Massillon, Stark Co, O. Bur Levers Cem, near village of Brookfield, ¼ mile north of Lincoln Highway, top of hill near center of cem. MI: "Thomas Doxsee. D Dec 28, 1821, age 79 yrs. 4 mo 26 days." GM by insignia of G. A. R. Appearance of the monument indicates that it was set soon after the decease of Thomas Doxsee. Descendants in Canterbury, Morrow Co, O, and Massillon, O. Fur infor Massillon Chap.

DRAKE, ABRAHAM, (Trumbull Co.)

Bur Niles. Unable to locate grave; unable to read many markers. Will admitted to probate 1818. Ref: S. A. R. Yr Bk. Fur infor Mary Chesney Chap.

DRAKE, BENJAMIN, (Huron Co.)

Enl as Pvt at 13. Pension Roll of Norwalk, O. Br 1765, England. Mar Miss Dean. Children: Frederick, James, Joshua. D Dec 22, 1844. Bur North Monroeville, O. MI "Revolutionary Soldier." Ref: Natl No 49979, Vol 50, D. A. R. Lin. Fur infor Sally DeForest Chap.

DRAKE, ISAAC, (Hamilton Co.)

Br 1756, New Jersey. D 1832. Ref: S. A. R. Fur infor Cincinnati Chap.

DRAKE, JOSUA, (Hamilton Co.)

Served in 4th Regt Orange Co. (See p 163, NY in Rev War). Fur infor Cincinnati Chap.

DRAKE, WILLIAM, (Mahoning Co.)

Ranger, from Northampton Co., Pa. Pa Archives series 3, Vol 23, p 300. Was a property owner in Boardman, O in 1806. Fur infor Mahoning Chap.

DRAPER, JONATHAN, (Summit Co.)

Apr 17, 1775, as Pvt for 8 days under Capt Moses Draper: May 1, 1775, enl for 13½ mos under Col Gardner and Capt Moses Draper; Aug 27, 1776 for 3 mos under Col Brewer and Col Cowel; 1777 Capt William Proctor of NH. Br Dec 18, 1750 in Roxbury, Mass. Children: Asa. D Feb 2, 1845. Bur Hudson, O. Old Cem on College St. West side. MI: "Jonathan Draper br Dec 18, 1750, D February 1845." GM by S. A. R. His name appears on roll of the 2nd Company in Roxbury commanded by Capt Wm Draper in Col Wm Heather's Regt, Apr 19. Fur infor Cuyahoga Portage and Cuyahoga Falls Chaps.

DRAPES, NATHAN SR., (Trumbull Co.)

Bur Niles. Unable to locate grave. Many markers letters obliterated. Ref: S. A. R. Yr Bk. Fur infor Mary Chesney Chap.

DRAY, EDWARD, (Trumbull Co.)

Br 1742. D Apr 5, 1828. Bur Casterline, South of Cortland. MI: "In memory of Edward Dray, who departed this life April 5 A. D. 1828, aged 86 yrs 5 mos." GM good condition. Fur infor Mary Chesney Chap.

DRYDEN, WILLIAM, (Hamilton Co.)

Soldier. Br 1739, Nova Scotia. Mar Lydia Jester (1786-1846) 2nd wife, in 1803. To this union, Lydia Dryden was br in 1810. D 1832, Cincinnati, O. Received land grant Clermont Co, O, for serv. Ref: Natl No 28253 Vol 29, p 93, also 36111 Vol 37, p 41, D. A. R. Lin.

DUC, HENRY, (Vinton Co.)

Officer in French Fleet; founder of Wilkesville, Ohio, and considered a Revolutionary soldier; on his stone is the following inscription: "To the memory of Henry Duc who departed this life June 27, 1827, aged 64 years. He was born in France, came to America an officer in the French fleet, was the founder of this town and endeared to all his acquaintances. He is now "where the wicked cease from troubling, and the weary are at rest." Record given by Dr. Charles B. Taylor, McArthur, O. Fur infor Jane Dailey, State Chairman.

DUDLEY, ISAAC, (Summit Co.)

Served in Continental army under Gen. Gates, and Arnold, Capt. Joseph Blake's Company July to Nov. 1777, and fought in 1st battle of Saratago. July 1779 to Mch 1780 served under Cols. John Mead and Matthew Weed; from Jan to July 1782, in Capt. Abner Smith's Company of Conn Volunteers. Br 1761, a native of Middletown, Conn. Mar Anna Woodhouse, of Wethersfield, Conn. Jan 25, 1786. Parents of 5 daughters three of whom were early settlers of Tallmadge, Mrs. Jesse Neal, Mrs. Harvey Spafford, and Mrs. Amos Seward. Died

Sept 1843. Bur Middlesbury. Lived in Oneida Co. N. Y. for a time, before coming to Tallmadge, in 1818. Ref: Natl No. 27681, Vol. 28, p 248. Fur infor Cuyahoga Portage Chap.

DUER, JOHN SR. (Mahoning Co.)

Pvt. Bucks Co Mil. Col. McElcane's Bn 2nd Company. Br 1748. Died 1831. Bur Covenanter's Cem. Jackson, O. Mahoning Co. Ref: Pa. Archives. Series 3. Vol 6 p 183. Fur infor Mahoning Chap.

DUGAN, HENRY, (Hamilton Co.)

Br 1736, Pennsylvania. D 1833. Ref: S. A. R. Fur infor Cincinnati Chap.

DUGAN, JAMES, (Darke Co.)

Maj. Body removed from old cem to the soldier lot in Greenville Cem. Fur infor Fort Greenville Chap.

DULIN, JOHN SR., (Wayne Co.)

Br May 21, 1760. Children: John Dulin, Jr. D May 21, 1845. Bur Congress Cem, Congress Twp, old cem near Congress village. MI: "John Dulin A Soldier of the Revolution Died May 21st 1845 Aged 85 years and 15 days. Job XIV All the days of my appointed time will I wait, till my change comes." Fur infor Wooster Wayne, Chap.

DUMM, PETER, (Ross Co.)

Br Sept 27, 1754. Mar Catherine ———. D Apr 20, 1837, Colerain Twp, Ross Co, O. Oldest Adelphi—downtown. MI: "Peter Dumm died Apr 20, 1837, aged 82 yrs, 6 mos, 23 days. Catherine wife of Peter Dumm died Aug 3, 1854, aged 92 yrs, 4 mos, 25 days." His widow received a pens as given in 1840 census, then 78 yrs. Fur infor Nathaniel Massie Chap.

DUNHAM, JONATHAN, (Washington Co.)

Enl as Pvt in Capt Robert Cliver's Company of Minute Men under Col Samuel William. Also Corp in Capt Samuel Taylor's Company, Col Nicholas Dike's Regt. Disch Aug 12, 1777. Br 1753, Sharon, Conn. Parents: Rev. Jonathan Dunham. Children: Amos and Betsey. D 1823. Bur in Dunham Cem, Dunham Twp, Washington Co, O. MI: "Jonathan Dunham born 1753, died 1823." GM Marietta D. A. R. with Revolutionary marker in 1922. Farmer. Ref: Mass. Soldiers and Sailors. Fur infor Marietta Chap.

DUNLAP, ALEXANDER, (Brown Co.)

Pvt Col Patterson Bell's Regt 5th Company 8th Bn Chester Co Mil 1778. Br 1743, Philadelphia, Pa. Mar Agnes Guy in 1768, (Br 1745). D 1828, Brown Co, O. Bur Red Oak. Ref: Natl No 66929 and 100276, Vol 101, p 85, D. A. R. Lin. Fur infor Ripley Chap.

DUNLAP, JOSEPH, (Delaware Co.)

Pvt under Col John Scott, Capt Walter McKinnie, 4th Bn Cumberland Co. Pa. Mil. Br 1754, Cumberland Co, Pa. D 1831, Delaware Co, O. Bur Oak Grove Cem. Pensioned. Ref: Natl No 86287, Vol 87, D. A. R. Lin. Fur infor Delaware Chap.

DUNLAP, ROBERT, (Lucas Co.)

Was under Capt Galick, Capt Cornelius Gearheart, Capt Jacob Gearhart, Capt Beaver, and Col Geo Ely in state of N. J. Br New Jersey, July 28, 1752. Mar

Nancy Giles 1783. Children: Sarah (br Aug 8, 1786, mar Daniel Scott). D July 25, 1838 Maumee, Wood Co. O. He was on detail to keep fires burning to deceive the enemy while Washington marched to Brunswick. Was in battle of Milltown. Applied for a pension Middletown, O. 1834, aged 82. Ref: Natl No. 63002, Vol. 64, p 2, D. A. R. Lin. Fur infor Nathaniel Massie Chap.

DUNLAP, WM. SR. (Mahoning Co.)

Pvt and Sgt. Pensioned in 1833 at age of 80. Br 1753. Mar Rachel Frazer. Children: Six sons and four daughters, maybe more. D 1835 Liberty Twp. at home of Mrs. Carlton. Came fr Washington Co, Pa, to Poland, O, in 1802. Went to Weatherfield in 1806. First Session of 23rd Congress. Supervisor of Highways. Ref: Vol 1, p 47, 363 Trumbull and Mahoning co. Hist. and Vol 11, pp 69-242; Sanderson Hist. p 216. Fur infor Mahoning Chap.

DUNLEVY, FRANCIS, (Warren Co.)

Pvt and Sgt, Pa. Mill. Br 1761, Winchester, Va. D 1839, Lebanon, O. Ref: Natl No 27,929 and 22,356, p 122, Vol. 3, D. A. R. Lin.

DUNN, ABMER MARTIN, (Hamilton Co.)

Ensign, later a Lt. Br 1755. D 1795, Cincinnati, O. Natl No 34,641, Vol 35, p 223, D. A. R. Lin.

DUNN, DUNCAN, (Hamilton Co.)

Br 1753, Massachusetts. D 1834. Ref: S. A. R. Fur infor Cincinnati Chap.

DUNN, REUBEN, (Greene Co.)

Fought in Battle of Monmouth, N. J. Aug 1778. "Stryker's Men of N. J. In Rev. War." Official Roster, State Tr and Mil p 582; "Pvt. Reuben Dunn, Middlesex Co." D Apr 2, 1824, aged 74. Bur Cost graveyard, on farm 1½ miles southeast of Franklin, O. on brow of hill, (recently visited 1923). Lived in Bath Twp. 1809; son of Simeon; a proven record. Ref: Sarah Prouty, Columbus, O. Robinsons Hist. of Green Co. p 299. Fur infor Columbus Chap.

DUNWELL, STEPHEN, (Cuyahoga Co.)

Pvt 1777, Capt Wm Converse, Col Heman Swift Regt Conn State Tr. Pensioned in 1833. Was from Phelps, N. Y. served 3 yrs. Br 1762, R. I. Mar Deborah Witter, 1780. (d 1842.) D Nov 21, 1840, Solon, O. Bur on a farm. Moved from Wayne Co. N. Y. to Solon, Cuyahoga Co. Ref: Pension Dept 2128. Natl No 81635, Vol 82, D. A. R. Lin. Fur infor Taylor Chap.

DURHAM, JOHN, (Pickaway Co.)

Served as a musician of the 10th Regt, N. C. Tr. Br Apr 13, 1760, North Carolina. Mar Mary Ann Durham. D June 16, 1852, Pickaway Co. O. Bur Cedar Grove Cem, about 3 miles below New Holland, O. GM by Mt Sterling Chap. with bronze marker in 1911. Came to Ohio from Virginia in 1816. Fur infor Mt. Sterling Chap.

DURKEE, EBBE, (Portage Co.)

Lived at Freedom, age 72 yrs. Fur infor Old Northwest Chap.

DURKEE, SOLOMON SR., (Ashtabula Co.)

Sgt. Br Sept 13, 1762. Children: Solomon, William, Alanson, David, Betsey, Sylvia, Lucy. D Dec 29, 1833, Monroe Twp. Bur private cem on farm. MI:

"Solomon Durkee Died Dec 29, 1833." GM Marble slab erected by his son. Shoemaker. Fur infor Mary Redmond Chap.

DUSENBERRY, WILLIAM, (Perry Co.)

Enl in Apr 1776, in Continental Army, when only 19 yrs of age, nearly 3 mos before the Declaration of Independence was signed, and served as Quartermaster, with rank of Sgt under Col Joseph Beavers, during the War. Engaged in the battles, of Amboy, Farm Road, Second River, Short Hills, Millstone, White Mills, and a number of others, his Regt frequently being under the direct command of Gen George Washington. Br Apr 6, 1757, near Bethlehem, Sussex Co., N. J. Mar Catherine Compton, at Bethlehem, N. J. Children: Henry, John, Benjamin, Mary, Rebecca, Catharine and Abigail. In 1800 he brought his family to Ohio and located where the Village of Sego now is, and where he lived until his death. D Mch 23, 1846, aged 89 yrs, on his old home farm, at Sego. Bur on summit of hill, about 7 hundred yards south of the Zanesville and Maysville pike, midway between Somerset and Fultonham. Around this grave, in the old family burying ground near the center of the thousand acre farm originally granted to him on account of his services in the war of the Rmer Rev, are grouped the graves of other members of his family, including his wife, Catherine Compton Dusenberry. GM by grave stones which are perfectly legible. Traditionally known as the first settler in Madison Twp. Was the first man buried in the honors of war in this Twp. Was a member of the first petit jury in the Co. Ref: p 209 Hist of Perry Co. Fur infor Muskingum Chap.

DUTTON, JAMES, (Washington Co.)

Pvt. Brandywine, 1777. Capt Seth Oak's Company of Artificers. Br 1740, Va. Mar Martha Kimbler, (d 1800). D 1839, Marietta, O. Ref: Natl No 43381, Vol 44, p 144, D. A. R. Lin. Copied by Jane Dowd Dailey, State Chairman.

DUVAL, JACOB, (Morgan Co.)

Ens in Capt McGill Company Md Line. Br Prince Georges Co. Md. about 1748. Mar ——— Taylor. D Morgan Co. Ref: Natl No 69213, p 79, Vol 70, D. A. R. Lin.

DYE, ANDREW SR., (Miami Co.)

Service in Pa. Mar Sarah Minor. Bur Pleasant Hill Cem. Miami Co., O. GM by Miami Chap with bronze marker. In Troy, O. July 4, 1827 at a patriotic meeting several Revolutionary Veterans gave toasts at a banquet; he gave this one: "The Fourth of July, 1776, a day ever to be remembered: health and prosperity to all who assisted in delivering the present generation from the weight of the yoke of British tyranny.' Fur infor Miami Chap.

DYE, (or Dey), EZEKIEL, (Noble Co.)

With NJ Tr at battle of Monmouth; saw other service. Br New Jersey. Bur Old Cem Renrock. Marked by stone. Army service and land patent under spelling of Dey. Settled in Brookfield Twp in 1804. Judge C. O. Dye has the disch. Fur infor Mrs. L. B. Frazier, Caldwell.

DYE, JOHN, (Brown Co.)

Served through the Rev with Washington. Br Md. Mar Ruth Applegate. Children: Rachel (perhaps others). D Brown Co., O. Bur on the Day farm, 3 miles east of Georgetown, O. Farmer. He mar a sister to the wife of Edward Evans who served in Capt Samuel Dawson's Company; Col Richard Humphreys Regt 11th Pa, and it is quite likely that he was in the same company. Came to Brown Co 1795 and lived near the said Evans. Ref: Brown Co. Hist. by Beers & Co., 1883; Adams Co. Hist of Evans and St. Stivers, Mrs. Nevin Chapman, a descendant. Fur infor Taliaferro Chap.

EARL, GRANTHAM, (Seneca Co.)

A soldier of the Rev of 1776. D Sept 1, 1838, 80 yrs, 8 mo, 9 days. Bur Egbert's Cem or Pleasant Ridge. GM D. A. R. with an iron marker (76) on May 30, 1922. Fur infor Dolly Todd Madison Chap.

EARL, THOMAS, (Ross Co.)

Enl in Flotilla, Chesapeake Bay, under Commodore Frazer. Reclaimed fr serv because of minority. In Dorchester Co, Md Mil 1781, Col Stapleford's Bn. Br at sea (Atlantic), 1762. Mar Rhoda Busic, Oct 29, 1791, Cambridge, Dorchester Co, Md. Children: James, (mar Mary Adams. In War of 1812). Nancy, Joseph, Thomas, Betsey, Sarah (mar William McClarey) and Jane. D Feb 15, 1844, Union Twp, Ross Co, O. Wife died Dec 10, 1810. Bur in field on farm, now part of Camp Sherman, northwest of Chillicothe on Egypt Pike. A farmer and weaver. Ref: Miss Linda Earl, Attica, Ind. Hist of Dorchester Co, Md p 238 by Jones. Scioto Gazette 1844. Fur infor Nathaniel Massie Chap .

EATON, ALEXANDER, (Hamilton Co.)

Serv fr Orange Co, p 164 N. Y. in Revolutionary War. Settled on a farm near North Bend, O, at present site of Cleves, Hamilton Co, O. Buried there. Fur infor Cincinnati Chap.

EATON, JOSEPH, (Guernsey Co.)

Pvt in Companies of Capt James Chambers and Thomas Buchanan, Col James Chambers and Thompson, Pa Regt. Was at battles of Trenton, Brandywine, Germantown and Monmouth. Disch Feb 25, 1779. Granted pens on application executed Mch 12, 1829 at Morristown, Belmont Co, O. (Pa archives Oct 1912, N. Y. Biog and his record). Br Mch 18, 1756, Franklin Co, O. Parents: see Eaton Genealogy. Mar Jeanet Ramsey. Children: John and others. D Guernsey Co after 1832. A Va and Pa family and came to Ohio early. Ref: Vol 27, D. A. R. and 42668 S. A. R. Fur infor Richard Montgomery Chap, S. A. R.

EBERSOLE, JACOB. (Clark Co.)

Pvt in 8th Pa Tr. Mar Salome Kellar. Children: John, Jacob, Abraham, Elizabeth, Eve, Kate, Mary and Christie. D 1828 near Northampton, O. Bur Myers Cem, North Hampton, O. MI: "Jacob Ebersole, a soldier of the Rev." GM Metal marker by S. A. R., 1901. Came to Ohio fr Botetourt Co, Va., 1810. Farmer and Carpenter. Ref: Pa Archives. Fur infor Lagonda Chap.

EBERSOLE, SOLOMON. (Hamilton Co.)

Mar Christiana Cox, dau of Tunis Cox. Lived, d and bur at Columbia, Hamilton Co. Fur infor Cincinnati Chap.

ECKMAN, HIERONIMOUS. (Mahoning Co.)

Took oath of allegiance July 2, 1778. Committee of Observation 1775; Committee of Observation 1774. Removed fr old courthouse cem to Oak Hill and marker lost. Gunsmith. Lived in Fayette Co, Pa. Hist Trumbull and Mahoning Co, Pa Archives series , Vol 13, p 292, Vol 1, p 337; 435, William Eckman, Youngstown, O. Fur infor Mahoning Chap.

EDDY, WILLIAM R. (Lake Co.)

Fr Mass serving in Capt John Wood's Company, Col Paul Dudley Sargent's Regt. Br 1760. D Dec 14, 1841, Concord, Lake Co, O. On farm 1½ miles northeast of Little Mountain. Fur infor New Connecticut Chap.

EDGAR, WM. (Union Co.)

Bur Liberty Twp. Ref: Col W. L. Curry Hist Union Co. Fur infor Hannah Emerson Dustin Chap.

EDGINGTON, JOSEPH. (Adams Co.)

Bur Adams Co, grave not marked. Revolutionary soldier and also served in the War of 1812. Ref: Mrs. Ora Ellis Leka, Marion, O. Fur infor Capt Wm Hendricks Chap.

EDMAN, SAMUEL. (Licking Co.)

Enl at New Mills, N J. July 1776, Pvt in Col Reed's Regt. Served 2 yrs under Cols Reynolds and Hait. "Retook a vessel laden with supplies of the enemy." Was at Battle of Bordentown and Crosswick Creek. Br Aug 16, 1758, Burlington Co, N. J. Mar 1779 to Dolly Paul. Nine Children. D Oct 29, 1847. Burlington Twp. Bur Family lot on 240 acre farm Utica, O. MI: "Rev War." GM Hetuck Chap, 1909. Settled in Burlington Twp 1808. Pensioner. Ref: Hist of Licking Co by E. M. P. Brister. Fur infor Hetuck Chap.

EDMONDS, PETER. (Wayne Co.)

Pvt in Capt William Meyer's Company, 6th Bn Northampton Co Mil, Pa, Col Nicholas Kearn, Br Aug 1, 1760, Pa, of English descent. Mar 1st Phoeba Davis, 2nd Elizabeth Warner and 3rd Mrs. Martha Anstrew Becktel. Children: 1st Margaret, David, Nathaniel; 2nd Edward, Benjamin, Simon, Elizabeth, Catherine, Rosan, Rebecca, Peter, 3rd Mrs. Emeline Edmonds Walton. D July 30, 1854, Wayne Co. Bur Warner Cem, 2 miles west of Wooster, along Lincoln Highway. MI: "Peter Edmonds Died July 30/1854. Aged 94 years. Elizabeth, wife of Peter Edmonds, died Jan 24, 1830 aged 60 yrs., 9 mo., 18 days." Farmer. Ref: Mrs. Emiline E. Walton, Maple Grove Twp, Barry Co, Mich. A real Daughter. 84827, D. A. R. Fur infor Wooster Wayne Chap.

EDWARDS, ADONIJAH, (Cuyahoga Co.)

Pvt Vt Line. Br 1741. D 1831, Bur East Cleveland, Euclid Ave opposite 123rd St. GM by Western Reserve Chap. Fur infor Western Reserve Chap.

EDWARDS, JAMES, (Brown Co.)

Pvt Capt Thomas Hamilton Company, 1st Va Regt commanded by Col George Gibson. Br Aberdeen, Scotland. Parents: Robert Edwards and Eleanor Laws. Mar Sarah Everett, after 1750 in NY. Children: William Everett, James, Alexander, Jacob, George, Eleanor, Jane, Nancy. D 1804 Aberdeen, Brown Co, O. Bur Old Cemetery, Aberdeen, O. Came to Ohio early; bought 1000 acres and laid out town of Aberdeen, O named it for his birth place, Aberdeen, Scotland. Ref: Mrs. Clara Manns, J. R. Williams, Misses Sarah & Ella West, Decatur, O. Fur infor Lieut Byrd Chap.

EDWARDS, JESSE, (Scioto Co.)

Pvt. Enl May 1776, disch July 17, 1781. Br 1754 or 1756 Bucks Co, Pa. Mar Catherine, (Beetman) Skillman. Children: Elizabeth. D 1856 Rarden. Bur Newman 1¼ miles below Rarden. Ref: See Natl No 70364, Vol 71, p 130, D. A. R. Lin. Fur infor Joseph Spencer Chap.

EDWARDS, JOHN, (Licking Co.)

Served 6 yrs, 3 mos in Va Continental Line, Stephen Southall Artillery. Br Va, 1750. Mar Ruth. D Union Twp, 1833. Bur Union Sta Cem. Settled in Union Twp in 1802, sold land. Vol A of Co Records. State papers of 1783 granted him his proportion of land for services. Ref: Brister's Hist. Fur infor Hetuck Chap.

EDWARDS, THOMAS, (Miami Co.)

Pvt in Capt Jas Stuard's Company, Col Zachariah Morgan's Regt, Va line. Br 1764, Bucks Co, Pa. D 1846, Miami Co, O. Ref: 86029, Vol 87, p 10, D. A. R. Lin.

EGGERS, GEORGE, (Butler Co.)

Name appears on tablet erected at Hamilton, O on the site of Ft Hamilton and considered as one of the Revolutionary soldiers bur in that Co. Unidentified. Fur infor John Reily Chap.

EGGLESTON, BENJAMIN, (Portage Co.)

Pvt Capt Shepard's Company, Col John Moseley's Regt, Hampshire Co, Vt. Br 1747, Aurora, O. Mar Mary Gordon (1754-1817) D 1832, Aurora, O. Ref: Natl No 100202, Vol 101, p 62, D. A. R. Lin. Fur infor Old Northwest Chap.

EGGLESTON, ELIAB, (Geauga Co.)

Drummer boy under Col Weston, Col Willett, Col Livingston, Col Van Cortland NY Mil. Enlmts Apr 1776, 4 mos; May 1776, 6 mos; Apr 1778, 9 mos; Mch 1779, 9 mos. Br Stonington, Conn. Mch 23, 1762. Mar Lucy Ingraham, Feb 20, 1798. Second wife (br 1777 d 1853). Children: Erastus, David, Darius, Almira, Eliab, Olive, Reuben, William, Lucy, Ann. D Mch 2, 1838, Newbury, O. County and family records would indicate that Eliab Eggleston was bur in cem adjoining the last farm he owned, but there is no marker and early graves are unplatted. Maple Hill Cem, Munson, O. Note by Mrs. H. H. Sears Harpster, O. states he is bur at Munson Cem. Enl at Stephentown NY, was at battle of Benis Point; at surrender of Burgoyne; wounded in head at Stony Point. Pensioned in 1833. Settled in Auburn 1823, came fr Middlesex, Yates Co, N Y. U. S. Pens Roll of Ohio 1832. Mr. Pool, a grandson. Ref: Natl No 33071, Vol 34, p 35, D. A. R. Lin. Fur infor Taylor Chap.

EGGLESTON, TIMOTHY, (Medina Co.)

Corp Conn in Gen Washington's Life Guard. Br 1759. Bur Bennetts Corners, Brunswick Twp. GM Western Reserve Chap. Fur infor Western Reserve Chap.

ELAM, JOSHUA, (Greene Co.)

Br 1752. D Feb 28, 1821. Bur on his farm. Sugar Creek, 1802. Ref: Robinson's Hist of Greene Co. Fur infor Catherine Greene Chap.

ELDRED, SAMUEL, (Lorain Co.)

Sgt, Ensign, 1st Lt, Mass Line. Br 1742. D 1826. GM Western Reserve bronze marker. Fur infor Western Reserve Chap.

ELDRIDGE, ————, (Clermont Co.)

Came fr NJ to mouth of Boat Run Creek, Monroe Twp 1800. Ref: A. S. Abbott, Bethel, O. Fur infor Cincinnati Chap.

ELLENWOOD, BENJAMIN, (Washington Co.)

Served in NH Line. Br New Hampshire. Mar Abigail Lawson. D Belpre, O, 1834. Ref: Natl No 18174. p 66, Vol 20, D. A. R. Lin.

ELLIOT, DR. JOHN, (Montgomery Co.)

Surgeon in Revolutionary War. Also in West under St. Clair and Wayne. Mustered out in 1802. Served fr 1776-1796. Hon disch June 1, 1802, Heitman Hist

Register p166. Br New York State. Children: Julia Ann, (mar Joseph H Crane) Harriet (mar Joseph Pierce). D Mch 26, 1809, Dayton, O. Bur Woodland, lots 16-22, (Pierce) Sec 77. Ref: Hist of Dayton (1889) U. B. Pub Co; Grieves Hist of Cincinnati p 366, p 91-2. Pioneer Life Dayton Edgar p 143. Fur infor Jonathan Dayton Chap.

ELLIOT, JOHN, (Geauga Co.)

Pvt Mass Continental, Capt Abner Pomeroy Company, 8th Regt. Enl Sept 20, 1777, disch Oct 14, 1777. Br 1749, East Hampton. Mar Rebecca, (as widow pens 1840, residing Claridon bur Hambden.) Children: Lewis and Chester. Bur Hambden, O. Farmer, fence viewer. Pensioned 1831. 1840 Census of pensioners living in Hambden, O. Ref: Mass Soldiers and Sailors, Vol 5, p 273. Fur infor Taylor Chap.

ELLIOTT, REUBEN, (Ross Co.)

Pvt. Enl fr Fauquier Co, Va. 1780 was at Yorktown Siege. Br 1764. Prince William Co, Va. Mar Reushaw. D 1841, Ross Co, O. where his widow received a pens. Ref: Natl No 39296, Vol 40, p 107, D. A. R. Lin.

ELLIOTT, ROBERT, (Franklin Co.)

Adjutant in Mil 1778 in the Pa Mil. Br Pa. D 1794. Killed by roving band of Indians. Bur in Ohio. Ref: S. A. R. Natl No 49684, in Ohio Vol 50, D. A. R. Lin. Fur infor Cincinnati Chap.

ELLIOTT, SAMUEL, (Licking Co.)

Enl Lancaster Co, Pa. Capt 2nd Co, 5th Bn of Mil Dec 26, 1781. Br 1751, Ballymena, County Antrim, Ulster, Ireland. Mar in Northampton, Pa. Children: one mar Dr Noah Harris, another Gen J. Taylor. D May 24, 1831. Bur Pataskala, O. Old quarter. MI: "A soldier of the Revolution." GM Hetuck Chap 1909. In 1880 purchased land in this county of Gen Schenck. Opened trading post with Indians in Bowling Green in 1800. p 490, Vol 7, Pa Archives, 5 series, Hist of Licking Co by E. M. P. Brister. Fur infor Hetuck Chap.

ELLIOTT, SAMUEL, (by some, Now Ellet), (Summit Co.)

Served 3 yrs in 4th Md Regt Capt John Sellman's Company, Col Carvil Hall, name appearing on roll dated Sept 8, 1778. Br 1757, England. Mar Kezia Webb, Maryland; she is bur in Kent Cem, Suffield Twp, Portage Co. Children: William br 1777, youngest, Jehu 1794. At least five of the sons came to Ohio, John, Thomas, Edward, David, and Jehu. D 1841. Bur on his farm, on Little Cuyahoga River. Came to Maryland, U. S. A. in 1770; Came to Liberty Trumbull Co about 1802; and to Summit Co 1806 or 1807 purchasing 538 acres land of Col Simon Perkins, in Springfield Twp. Part of Hull's army camped on his land and ate of his corn. Fur infor Cuyahoga Portage Chap.

ELLIS, ABRAHAM, (Clinton Co.)

Pvt in Pa State Tr. At Long Island, Germantown, Valley Forge and Yorktown. Br 1750, Hanover, Pa. Mar Katherine Joel (d 1840). D 1837, Clinton Co, O. Bur Miller Cem, near Lumberton. Ref: Natl No 61,419, Vol 62, p 146; Natl No. 102,211, Vol 103, p 66, and Natl No. 102,282, Vol 103 p 88, D. A. R. Lin. Fur infor George Clinton Chap.

ELLIS, JESSE, (Brown Co.)

Enl in Washington Co, Pa. Apr 1, 1776, Oct 4, 1776, a Pvt under Capt Matthew Richey; Spring 1778, 6 mos under Capt Andrew Swearingen and Col John Stephenson; Aug 1, 1779, 6 mos under Capt Nathan Ellis and Col Brodhead. Br Oct 15, 1756, Frederick Co, Md. D after 1845, as interviewed by Dr Draper. See

Draper MSS Wisconsin Historical Society. Bur near Aberdeen, family cem. A brother of Capt Nathan Ellis and Samuel Ellis. Pensioned. Bureau of Pensions. Fur infor Capt William Hendricks Chap.

ELLIS, LEMUEL, (Lake Co.)

Fr Dec 11 to Dec 30, 1776, he served under Capt Ebenezer Battle, and Col William McIntosh, later with Col Weld at Castle Island. Br 1764. Mar Polly Call. D Feb 20, 1859, Perry, Lake Co O Bur River Rd, Perry, O. 1810. In 1815 was overseer of the poor, and held that and other twp offices until 1831. Fur infor New Connecticut Chap.

ELLIS, NATHAN, (Brown Co.)

Capt Commanding Company in the Regt of Washington Co, Pa Mil. Col Daniel Broadhead. Br 1749, Wales. Parents: James and Mary Veatch. Mar 1770 Mary Walker, Brownsville, Pa. Children: Margaret, Mary, John, Jeremiah, Jesse, Samuel, Nancy, Nathan, Nelly, Elander. D 1819, Aberdeen, O. Bur on hill overlooking Aberdeen. Ref: 1890. "A town in Western Co." Dr Fortescue Cumming. Jesse Ellis application claim allowed, showing elmt under Capt Nathan Ellis. Bureau Washington D. C. file 8,402, Revolutionary War Hist and Archeological Col of Ohio, Vol 13, p 332, Howe's Hist of Ohio 1880, p 341, 18 Rep Natl Society S. A. R. (1914-1915) p 192. Fur infor Taliaferro Chap.

ELLIS, SAMUEL, (Brown Co.)

Sgt in Capt Andrew Swearengen's Co, Col Wm Slevenson's Regt, Pa Line. Br 1754, Md. D 1848, Brown Co. O. Bur Higginsport, O. Fur infor Ripley Chap.

ELLSWORTH, JOHN (Summit Co.)

Pvt at Torrington, Litchfield Co, Conn. Served under Col Starr, Capt Shubael Griswold and Alexander Catlin. Served Sept 1779, 2 mos, May 1780, 6 mos, Sept 1781 signed for 2 mos longer. Br Dec 7, 1762, Springfield, Mass. Mar Ann———; 2nd Ruth ———. Bur Maple Grove Cem, Stow, O. Fur infor Cuyahoga- Portage Chap.

ELLSWORTH, WILLIAM, (Geauga Co.)

Pvt and Sgt N. Y. State Mil. Pens 1833, under Capt Kosso 1778. Disch Jan 1789. Br Poughkeepsie, 1760. Mar Barbara Hitt, Aug 1789. D Mch 23, 1852. Bur Quirk Cem, Chester, Geauga Co. MI: "William Ellsworth died Mch 23, 1852, Aged 92." Ohio Pension roll 1840, as living in Cuyahoga Co, Mayfield Twp, which adjoins Chester Twp, Geauga. Ref: Pension Dept. Fur infor Western Reserve and Taylor Chaps.

ELSTUN, ELI, (Clermont Co.)

Br Essex Co, N J. Parents: William also Revolutionary Soldier captured by British, and died of cold and hunger. Mar Mary Payne (widow d 1820). Children: Isaac, John, William, William, Eli, (Moses mar Lydia Potter), Ralph (br 1802) Freeman, Fanny mar E Osborne) Mary (mar John Eppert) Hannah (mar John Van Zant; also one mar John Mann. In 1802 came fr New Jersey to Redstone settlement in Western Pa. In 1803 to Columbia (Cin) thence 1805 to Miami Twp Clermont Co, O. on Harner's Run. Ref: A. S. Abbott, Bethel, O. and Natl No 193911 D. A. R. Lin. Fur infor Cincinnati Chap.

ELY, DARIUS, (Portage Co.)

Minute man, Lexington Alarm fr West Springfield, Mass. Pvt in Capt John Morgan's Company Mass Continental Line. Enl Jan 7, 1778; disch July 1, 1778. Served 5 mos 14 das. Capt Preserved Leonard's Company; Col Elisha Porter Hampshire Co Regt. Enl July 28, 1779; disch Sept 2, 1779. Served 1 mo 10 das.

Also on descriptive list of men raised to reinforce Continental Army of the term of 6 mos. Age at enl 18 yrs status 5 ft 11 in. Complexion Light. Pensioned July 20, 1833. Ref: Natl No 43682, Vol 44, D. A. R. Lin. Fur infor Old Northwest Chap.

ELY, LEWIS, (Portage Co.)

Minute Man in Lexington Alarm fr West Springfield, Mass. Br 1756, West Springfield, Mass. Mar Anna Granger, 1777. Children: Asher (br 1778, d 1860) Hanson Asher (br 1813, d 1884) Eugene Hanson (br 1839, d 1910). D 1826, Deerfield, O. Ref: Natl No. 99,233, Vol 100, p 71, and Natl No. 99,769, Vol 100. p 238 D. A. R. Lin. Fur infor Old Northwest Chap.

EMERSON, JESSE, (Lake Co.)

Pvt in Ebenezer Gordale's Company of Minute Men. Col Woodbridge's alarm; also Sgt in Capt John King's Company. Col Benj Ruggels Woodbridge's 25th Regt and other short periods. Br Mch 6, 1749. Parents: Mark and Abigail Ingalls. Mar Lucy Warner, Mch 28, 1776. Children: Jerry Jr., Iva, Timothy, George, Elijah and Minerva. D Aug 8, 1820. Bur Painesville, early cem, abandoned. MI "Jesse Emerson, died Aug 8, 1820, age 71 yrs." Pensioned. Fur infor New Connecticut Chap.

EMERSON, JONATHAN, (Butler Co.)

Pvt soldier under Capt Woodbury and Col John Stark, New Hampshire Tr. Volunteered at the taking of Burgoyne. date on enlmt May 1755, under Col Johnson, Mass, served 1 yr and 8 mos. Was at battle of Bunker Hill. Frequently out in short campaigns. Br May 1, 1755, at Haverhill, Mass. Parents: Jonathan and Elizabeth (Mitchell) Emerson. Mar Rhoda Bailey, Jan 11, 1781, Boston. Children: Sally, Joshua, Elizabeth, Rhoda, Paul, Andrew, Harriet, Calista, Jonathan. D Sept 15, 1823, Hamilton, O. Bur Old Cem in Hamilton, O, Butler Co. This cem has been turned into a park. His body and his wife's body were not removed, so that the exact spot is not known. Br Haverhill, Mass. Mar and moved to Vermont. lived at Barre, at Salem, N. H. Moved to Ohio 1816. Cincinnati. Moved to Fairfield Twp, Butler Co. Received pension Oct 4, 1919. Ref: Miss Jean Rowland, London, O. Fur infor London Chap.

EMERSON, JOSEPH, (Lake Co.)

Apr 16, 1775 under Capt James Sawyer and Col Frye of the Mass Tr. Was in the battle of Bunker Hill. 2nd enlmt July 1777, 2 mos under Capt Aaron Osgood and Col Lyman. Pensioner. Br Feb 1754, Haverhill, Mass. Mar (1st wife) Lydia Foster; Mary Hilton (2nd wife). D Jan 23, 1850. Bur South Madison, Lake Co. MI "I have a house not made with hands, Eternal and on high. Here my spirit waiting stands, 'Till God shall bid it rise." GM New Connecticut Chap. Fur infor New Connecticut Chap.

EMERY, JOHN, Capt. (Lake Co.)

He served many enlmts throughout the war, ranking as Capt at the close. Br 1758, Mass. D Dec 27, 1831. Bur Unionville, O, which contains the first authentic grave on the Western Reserve. GM New Connecticut Chap. Fur infor New Connecticut Chap.

EMMS, JOSHUA, (Lake Co.)

Corp in Continental Line in Capt Solomon Higgin's Company July 13, 1775. Br 1751, Boston, Mass. D Dec 1, 1845. Bur Perry, Lake Co, O. GM New Connecticut Chap. Fur infor New Connecticut Chap.

ENEMS, JOHN, (Hamilton Co.)

Enl 1777 for 3 yrs in Capt Ross' Company, Col Elias Dayton's NJ Regt. Br 1755, Monmouth Co, N. J. Mar Joanna Hampton, 1834. D 1821, Hamilton Co, O. Natl No. 74022, Vol 75, D. A. R. Lin.

ENGART, BENJAMIN, (Hamilton Co.)

Br 1759, New Jersey. D 1842. Ref: S. A. R. Fur infor Cincinnati Chap.

ENOCHS, ENOCH, Capt. (Noble Co.)

Enl June 1, 1774, served 4 mos as Ensign in Capt Henry Enoch's Company on Ten Mile Creek, Pa. Apr 1, 1775; was Capt of Company under Col Dorsey Penticost; also Capt under Col Henry Enochs June 7, 1777, Br Hampshire Co, Va. Sept 29, 1750. Parents: Henry Enoch. Mar Rebecca Morris. Children: Rebecca Phoebe, Henry, Elisha, Enoch Jr., Jess, Rachel, Ama, Lydia, Elizabeth, Sally and Rohada. D 1835, Harrietsville, Noble Co. Bur Harriettsville, Noble Co. O. Ref: Mrs. J. R. Harvey, Athens, O. Fur infor Nabby Lee Ames Chap.

ENSIGN, WILLIAM, (Lake Co.)

Enl 1777, Pvt Capt John Strong's Company, Col John Brown's Berkshire Company, Mass Regt. Br West Hartford, Conn. 1748. Mar Mary Madham, 1777. D Madison 1833. Natl No 63482, p 159, Vol 64, D. A. R. Lin.

ENSMINGER, JOHN, (Meigs Co.)

Enl as Pvt in Oct 1776 under Capt William Gircus. Reenlisted about Jan 1781 under Capt Alexander Hanley and was in an engagement near Salisbury, N. C. Br Sept 1, 1757, Va. Mar Jane Reese, Feb 15, 1787. Children: David, John L, Margaret, Mary, Jane, Sarah and Elizabeth. D Oct 10, 1830, Langsville, O. Bur Miles Cem near Rutland, O. Ref: Pens Dept Sur File 42708; 76932, D. A. R. Vol 77. Fur infor Return Jonathan Meigs Chap.

ERNST, CHRISTOPHER, (Pickaway Co.)

Pvt 4th Bn, Lancaster Co, Pa. Capt Jacob Findley's Company, Present at Princeton. Trenton (Pa Archives gives dates). Br Aug 23, 1748, Lancaster Co, Pa. Parents: William and Eve (Bach) Ernst. Mar Anna Margaret Sichele Aug 6, 1768. Children: William, John, Elizabeth, David and Jacob. D 1818, Pickaway Co, O, near Circleville. Natl No 96115, D. A. R. Margaret E. Hill, 4041 Walnut St., Philadelphia, Pa. Fur infor Jane Dailey State Chairman.

ERUMAN, FREDERICK, (Fairfield Co.)

Came to this country with Lafayette in 1777 and served with him until close of war. Br France, Alsace. Mar Mary Evans. D 1824, Fairfield Co. Ref: Natl No 34423, Vol 35, p 149, D. A. R. Lin.

ERVIN, CHRISTOPHER, (Mahoning Co.)

Pvt muster roll of the 5th, 6th, 7th classes 10th Bn Lancaster Co, Mil. Came under head of persons who performed a tour of duty, Pa Archives Series 5, Vol VII, p 921, Pensioned. Br Cushandell, Ireland. 1741. Mar Mary Foulk fr New Jersey. Children: John (mar Louise Kincaid), William (mar Johanna Launterman) Margaret, (mar Robert Kincaid), Elizabeth (mar James White), Joseph (mar Mary Osborn). D 1836, in Austin Twp. Bur Four Mile Run. Came to Mercer Co, Pa and settled, early in 18th century came into Mahoning Co, O where he took up land. Ref: Hist of Mercer Co, Pa and Mahoning Co, O. Fur infor Mahoning Chap.

ERVIN, JOHN, (Greene Co.)

Bur New Burlington Cem. Fur infor Catherine Greene Chap.

ERVING, PETER, (or Ervin), (Richland Co.)

NJ Line 1779 to close of war. Br 1762. Mar Elizabeth Armstrong. D 1846, Plymouth, O. Bur old Cem Plymouth, O. MI: Soldier in Rev 7 yrs., stone records. GM by Mary Washington D. A. R. Chap, bronze marker in 1925. Ref: Natl No 25925, Vol 26, p 10 and Natl No 99894, Vol 100, p 278, D. A. R. Lin. Fur infor Mary Washington Chap.

ESPY, JOSIAH, (Green Co.)

A member of the committee of safety. Br Lancaster Co, Pa. 1727. Mar Elizabeth Patterson. D Greene Co, O. 1891. Natl No 61584, p 200, Vol 62, D. A. R. Lin.

ESSIG, SIMON, (Stark Co.)

Bur Waerstler Church Cem, Plain Twp. Authority: Hist of Stark Co, edited by William Henry Perrin. Fur infor Massillon Chap.

EVANS, EDWARD, (Brown Co.)

Served in Capt Samuel Dawson's Company of Col Richard Humphrey's 11th Regt, Pa. Was at Valley Forge, Brandywine and other engagements. Br 1760, Pa. Mar Jemima Applegate (d 1840) after June 28, 1778. Children: Elijah, William, Joseph, Robert, John, Hugh, James, Mary, Sarah, Isabel, Elizabeth, Rachel and Margaret. D 1839, Jefferson Twp, Brown Co, O. Bur Linwood Cem, Russellville. GM N. W. Evans a descendant, government marker. Left the serv on account of illness soon after the battle of Monmouth; soon mar and settled in Westmoreland Co, Pa, later moved to Washington, Ky, lived there 1785 to 1799, came to Brown Co, where he lived until death. Indian Scout, farmer. Ref: Hist of Adams by Evans and Stivers published 1900; also Brown Co, Beers Hist of Adams Co, 1883, also a family hist. Fur infor Taliaferro Chap.

EVANS, EVAN, (Morrow Co.)

D Chester Twp, Morrow Co, O. Fur infor Mt Gilead Chap.

EVANS, EVAN, (Highland Co.)

Bur Fairfield Twp. Fur infor Waw-Wil-a-Way Chap.

EVANS, HUGH, (Highland Co.)

Pvt. Associators and Mil in the Company of Cumberland 7th Bn 1st class in serv July 1777, Capt James Fisher. Br near Hagerstown, Md. Oct 7, 1730. Parents: Samuel. Mar 1st Sarah Harden, 1760; 2nd Lavinia Simpson 1763. Children: Sallie, Richard, Nancy, Samuel, Amos, Daniel, Sophia. D Highland Co, 1808. Bur farm where he settled. Grave obliterated. Migrated to Highland Co, O., 1800 fr Bourbon Co, Ky. Farmer. Fur infor Waw-Wil-a-Way Chap.

EVANS, JOSEPH. (Muskingum Co.)

Pvt served under Capt John Cotton, and under Capt Thomas Saskill in the Chester Co Bn. Br Apr 24, 1857 in Berks Co, Pa. Parents: Peter Evans. Mar Ruth Sayre, 1791. Children: John, Phoebe, Joseph, Jr., Caleb, Mary William, Reuben, James, Elizabeth and Anna. D July 1829, Muskingum Co. Bur Old Baptist Salt Creek Cem a short distance from Zanesville. Grave in the rear right hand corner as you approach the cem close to the graves of James Evans and wife, Sarah Comstock, and close to the graves of David Comstock and wife. Susannah Steenrad. MI: "Joseph Evans, born Apr 24, 1757. Died July 18, 1824. Ruth, wife of Joseph Evans, born Aug 11, 1765. Died Mch 26, 1836." Served 5 yrs. In 1805 purchased two farms about four miles east of Zanesville and brought wife and family and mother thru in 1806 in what is now Washington Twp. Came fr Washington Co. Pa. Joseph Evans was a widower with one son when he married his wife who was a widow with a son also. She was Ruth Sayre in Salem, N. J. but mar in Washington Co, Pa the second time. Ref: Pa Archives 6 series, Vol 2, p 237, Pa Archives, 5 series, Vol 5, p 485, 490, 545. Pa Archives, 3 series, Vol 23, p 348. Muskingum Co Hist, p 346. Fur infor Jane Washington Chap.

EVANS, NATHAN, (Washington Co.)

Pvt under Col Van Schoonhoven, NY Tr. Br 1742. D 1820. Marietta, O. Bur Marietta Cem. Ref; Vol 87, p 115, Natl No 86361, D. A. R. Lin. Mrs. H. R. Shafer, Cedar Rapids, Mich. Fur infor Jane Dailey, State Chairman.

EVANS, MOSES, (Logan Co.)

Listed as Revolutionary soldier, p 142, Antrim's Hist of Logan Co. Bur near Middleburg, Logan Co, O.. Fur infor Bellefontaine Chap.

EVANS, ORA, (Lake Co.)

At the Lexington Alarm, father and son responded and served as Minute Men through the 7 yrs war, their last engagement being at Harlem Heights. Br Apr 1760, North Adams, Mass. Parents: Moses Evans. His mother was a nurse in the army. D Feb 1845. Bur Madison, Lake Co, O. Was a pioneer of Madison, O. settling on the Co line in 1812. Tall, florid, silver haired and erect at 85 yrs. Fur infor New Conn Chap.

EVENS, EDWARD, (Mahoning Co.)

Served under the Land Bounty Act in 1841. List of Enl men. Br 1767. Bur Boardman. Came to Boardman early in 1800. Ref: "N. Y. Men in the Rev" p 94. Fur infor Mahoning Chap.

EVERETT, JOHN, (Mahoning Co.)

Bur Village Cem, Canfield. Ref: S. A. R. Fur infor Western Reserve Chap.

EVERETT, JOHN SR., (Mahoning Co.)

Pvt 1st Company Capt Adam Stohler, Col Henry's 6th Bn Northampton Mil 1780. Br 1727. Mar Sarah ——— (1731-1820). Children: 1 child, dau (mar ——— Sprague). D 1820. Bur Cem Canfield, O. GM D. A. R. in 1915-17. Ref: Vol 2, Hist Trumbull and Mahoning Cos. Pa Archives, Series 5, Vol 8, p 443. Fur infor Mahoning Chap.

EVERETT, SAMUEL, (Trumbull Co.)

Sgt in Northampton Co Regt in 1780-1782. One dau mar Jacob Oswold, another mar Christian Wannemaker. Bur Liberty Twp. Came from Northampton, Pa. and settled first in Canfield, later removed to Liberty Twp. At that time it was all Trumbull Co. Ref: Pa Archives, Series 5, Vol 8, p 443, Hist of Canfield "Early Settlers" p 68. Fur infor Mahoning & Mary Chesney Chaps.

EVERETT, SAMUEL SR., (Licking Co.)

Enl at Torrington, Conn. Br Feb 6, 1789, Torrington, Conn. Mar Mindwell Strong. D Nov 1, 1821, Granville, O. Fur infor Hetuck Chap.

EVERETS, AMBROSE, (or Evarts), (Washington Co.)

Enl 1776 and served till close of war. (Public Records of Conn. Vol 2, p142). Br Aug 1759 at Guilford, Conn. Mar Achsa Bingham. D 1799, Marietta, O. Grave unknown. GM by Marietta Chap, D. A. R. marker 1925. Ambrose Everts (Evarts) was the 4th of six sons of Silvanus Everts of Guilford, Conn. Silvanus Everts moved from Guilford to Salisbury then in 1770 to Vermont. Natl No 18052. Fur infor Marietta Chap.

EVERSOLE, ABRAHAM, (Fairfield Co.)

7th Bn, 5th Regt, Lancaster Co, Pa, Mil. Capt Noah Ceasey and Col Alexander Lowery. Br Lancaster Co, Pa. Mar Mariah ———— before 1788. Children: John, Henry, George, Jacob, Joseph. D May 31, 1836, Fairfield Co, O. Bur Delmont, 4 miles east of Lancaster, O in Eversole family graveyard, used 1834 to 1845. MI: "In memory of Abraham Eversole who died May 31, 1836 aged ———yrs." Ref: Pa Archives, 5th series VII 745,749; VII 794.

EVERSOLE, JACOB, (Stark Co.)

Pvt. Capt Andrew Scott's Company, 7th Bn, Lancaster Co, Pa Mil 1781. Br 1765, Lancaster Co, Pa. D 1848, Navarre, O. Ref: Natl No 101940, Vol 103, p 286, D. A. R. Lin.

EWALT, JOHN JR., (Knox Co.)

Pvt in Capt William McCall's Company, Bedford Co. Mil 1783 as testified by the custodian of Records Harrisburg, Pa. Br 1760 in Bedford Co, Pa. Parents: John Sr., Sarah Ewalt. Mar about 1790 to Elizabeth Bonnet (br 1775 d 1847). Children: John, Sophia, Henry, Anna, Richard, Sarah, Isaac, Samuel James, Robert, Eliza. D Aug 19, 1828, on farm west of Mt Vernon, O. Bur Mound View Cem, Mount Vernon, O. Lot 7, Block 2, Grave 2. MI: A large "Ewalt" family monument with a small headstone at John Ewalt's grave with J. E. on it. GM by Kokosing D. A. R. Chap in Dec 1927. After the war he came to Ohio, settled in Knox Co, near Mt Vernon; bought a big farm on which he lived until his death. Ref: Natl No 117,925. Fur infor Kokosing Chap.

EWING, JOSEPH, (Muskingum Co.)

Br 1753. D 1817, aged 84 yrs. Bur Ark Springs Cem in Meigs Twp, Muskingum Co, three miles southeast of High Hill on the Zanesville and Marietta road. Fur infor Muskingum Chap.

EWING, THOMAS, (Hamilton Co.)

Pvt. Enl 1777, Capt Matthew Gregg's Company, 2nd Bn Cumberland Co. Mil, Br 1748 NJ. (one record gave Pa). Mar Mary Ann Leeper, June 27, 1781, near Harrisburg, Pa. Children: Mary, Jane, Rebecca, John, Thomas. D 1823, on the bank of the Miami River near Cleves O at his farm. Bur Berea Cem near Cleves, O. GM by a fair sized boulder Mr. John Chidlaw placed there, as the original tombstone was gone. Since, Thomas Ewing's bones were taken from his farm, where he was first buried, to Berea Cem. After the Rev he was kept on for special services, serving in the army, then came to the banks of the Miami River, where he lived as a farmer and reared his family of four children. Ref: Thomas Ewing's name appears in Pa Archives, 5 Series, Vol 6, p 157, and Natl No 89327. Fur infor Cincinnati Chap.

EWING, WILLIAM, Lt. (Gallia Co.)

Lt battle Pt Pleasant W. Va. 1774, under Gen Lewis. Br 1756, Bath Co, Va. Parents: Capt James Ewing and Margaret Sargent. Mar Mary McNeal, 1785. Children: Elizabeth, Thomas, Jonathan, William, James, John, Sarah, Enoch, Jacob, Abram McNeil and George. D Sept 1822, Ewington, O. Bur family cem.

on his own farm, one mile east of village. MI: Name, dates. GM by family slab. Farmer. Founded Ewington in 1810. Ref: Nina Ewing Rothgeb and Price's Hist of Pocahontas Co, W. Va. Fur infor French Colony Chap.

EXLINE, JOHN, (Jackson Co.)

Listed in Co history as Revolutionary Soldier. Has descendants in this county. Fur infor Captain John James Chap.

EYMAN, HENRY, (Fairfield Co.)

Capt George Graff's Company; Col Cunningham's Regt; Capt. Samuel Haine's Company; same Col in Capt Samuel Henry's Company, 1st Bn, Lancaster Co, Pa Mil. Capt Geo. Stewart. Br 1758. Mar Mary Sager Eyman (1761-1843). D 1850. Ref: Florence Eyman Thomson, Columbus, O. Fur infor Elizabeth Sherman Reese Chap.

FAIRCHILD, ELEAZER (or Ezekiel,) (Mahoning Co.)

Pvt in The Danbury Raid, from New Milford, Conn. Br New Milford, Conn. Bur unknown, but somewhere in the Co. He came from Milford, Conn. about 1802 and settled in or near Canfield. Ref: "Conn Men of the Revolution." Fur infor Mahoning Chap.

FALKNER, JOHN, (Co. not stated)

Pa Continental Line. Pensioner in Ohio. Br 1739. D Ohio. Ref: Natl No 14608, p 227, Vol 15, D. A. R. Lin.

FALLEY, FREDERICK, (Erie Co.)

Drummer Boy. Fifer in father's company at Battle of Bunker Hill. Br 1764, Westfield, Mass. D July 3, 1828. Bur Castalia, O. Fur infor Martha Pitkin Chap.

FALLS, WILLIAM, (Adams Co.)

Bur near Cedar College School House, on hill just opposite the mouth of Beasleys Fork. Fur infor Sycamore Chap.

FANSHIR, ISAAC, (Fayette Co.)

Br 1760, Cook Co, Tenn. Children: David, John, Rebecca. D Mch 4, 1837. Bur Fanshir Farm, Marshall (near Hagler's Station.) MI: "Isaac Fanshir March 4, 1837, age 77." GM by family in 1837. Farmer. Fur infor Washington Court House Chap.

FARLEY, DAVID, (Noble Co.)

Served fr SC. Bur on farm of R. W. Horton near Carlisle. Came to Noble Co, early. Fur infor Mrs. L. B. Frazier, Caldwell.

FARNHAM, (FARNUM) JOHN, (Clarke Co.)

Corp in NH Line under Col Thos Stickney. Br Sept 9, 1763. Mar Minda Atkins. One dau was Permilia. D Apr 8, 1822, Clarke Co, O. Bur Fletcher Chapel, 100 feet east of Chapel. MI: "John S. Farnum born Sept 9, 1763, died April 3, 1822." GM by family and S. A. R. No trace of family or any one who knew him. Ref: Natl No. 36,649, Vol 37, p 229, D. A. R. Lin. Fur infor Lagonda Chap.

FARNUM, ELISAH, (Portage Co.)

Lived at Deerfield, where pensioned in 1840. Fur infor Old Northwest Chap.

FARNUM, JOHN, (Summit Co.)

Promoted from rank of Pvt to Corp. Enl 1777, at Litchfield, Conn, served 6 yrs. Disch June 9, 1783; Capt Joseph Allyn Wright's Company, 2nd Regt Conn Line, 1781-1783 commanded by Col Herman Swift. Also under Capt Robertson Company in 2nd Regt and was in battles of Red Bank and Monmouth. Br 1760. Litchfield, Conn. (See Natl No. 86111, D. A. R. Lin. Vol. 87) Mar. at Bethlehem, Conn. Apr 1786. Wife was living at time of his death D May 21, 1834, Richfield. Bur Richfield, O. Came from Conn in 1812 to North of Richfield Center; was supervisor of roads for 2 yrs, being one of first body of supervisors elected Apr 1816. Widow pensioned on his claims, 1828. Fur infor Cuyahoga Portage Chap.

FARLEY, DAVID, (Noble Co.)

Served from S. C. Bur on farm of R. W. Horton near Carlisle. Came to Noble Co. early. Fur infor Mrs. L. B. Frazier, Caldwell.

FARRALL, WILLIAM, (Columbiana Co.)

Br 1755. D 1827. Lived in Fairfield Twp, Columbiana Co. Fur infor Bethia Southwick Chap.

FARRAND, JARED, (Cuyahoga Co.)

Pvt fr Vt. in Capt Joe Safford's Company. Br 1756. D 1862. Bur Fair View Cem, Rockport. Fur infor Western Reserve Chap.

FAST, CHRISTIAN, (Ashland Co.)

Pensioned 1832 Richland Co, O. (now Ashland Co.) Pvt 1778-79, Capt Neek's Company, Col Zacharah Morgans Va Tr. Br 1762, Frederick Co, Md. Mar Anna Barbary Mason in 1783. D 1841 Orange Twp, now Ashland Co, O. Ref: Natl No 82312. Vol. 83, D. A. R. Lin. Fur infor Sarah Copus Chap.

FAULKNED (or FALKNER,) WILLIAM, (Adams Co.)

Capt. Br Ireland. Bur near former residence near mouth of Brugh Creek, Ref: Evans and Stivers Hist of Adams Co. Fur infor Sycamore Chap.

FAUST, PHILLIP, (Mahoning Co.)

Pvt. Luzerne Company; also drummer Northampton Co Mil. Pensioned Aug 16, 1833. Br 1759. Bur Middleton Cem. Ref: Pa Archives, series 3, Vol 23, p 534; Series 5, Vol 18, p 179, Series 3, Vol 23, p 534; Elias Foust Audt. Mahoning Co. Descendant. Fur infor Mahoning Chap.

FAY, AARON, (Huron Co.)

Enl from Hardwick 1775 in Capt Samuel Billings' Company. Br 1759. Mar Rebecca Winslow. D Norwalk, O. Bur Bronson Cem, now abandoned. Ref: Natl No. 58,389, Vol 59, p 135, D. A. R. Lin. Fur infor Sally De Forest Chap.

FEAGIN, DANIEL, (Brown Co.)

Served during the Revolutionary War as Capt. Br Virginia. Mar Violet ————. Children: (19) Susan, Daniel, Fielding. D 1815, Brown Co. Bur by family, on the farm near Georgetown now owned by Dr. Adamson. Emigrated from Loudoun Co, Va 1786 to Washington Ky in 1807, came to Brown Co, O, where he located on a tract of land in Lawson's survey. Ref: Hist of Brown Co. pub 1883, p 372, C. D. Thompson, Asst. Cashier First Natl Bank, Georgetown, O, who was a descendant. Fur infor Taliaferro Chap.

FEIGLE, JOHN, (Mahoning Co.)

Teamster in NJ Hunt's Team Brig. Mar Mary ——. D 1806. Bur Poland, O. Farmer. Ref: "New Jersey Men of the Rev" p 861. Fur infor Mahoning Chap.

FELLOWS, PARKER, (Geauga Co.)

Pvt. Enl Sept 10, 1780 term 3 mos. Northampton, Mass. Capt Kirtland's Company. Mustered July 1780, Capt Shelden's Company; Col Murray's Regt. Returned by Noah Goodman, Supt for said Company, aged 18 yrs. terms 3 yrs. Br 1762, Middletown, Mass. Mar Dorcas Meadham. Children: John M, Sophronia, Lyman, Isaac. D 1820, Chester, O. Bur Chester Center Cem. Charter member Congregational Church, Chester, O, 1919. Estate was administered June 26, 1820 in Georgia Co Court. Ref: Mass Soldiers and Sailors Vol. 5, p 596. Natl No of Revolutionary Soldier in D. A. R. honor roll 33,947. Fur infor Taylor Chap.

FELTER, CRONYMUS, (Hamilton Co.)

Orange Co, Mil NY. Br 1823. Parents: Mathias Felter. D 1835. Bur at Montgomery, Hamilton Co. Fur infor Cincinnati Chap.

FELTER, ISAAC, (Hamilton Co.)

Orange Co. Mil NY. Was partner with Joel Williams, who obtained 1st license for operating ferry boat on Ohio River. Bur in Hamilton Co, at Montgomery. Fur infor Cincinnati Chap.

FELTER, JACOB, (Hamilton Co.)

Orange Co. Mil, p 161, "NY in Revolutionary War.' Was with the other four men who founded town of Montgomery, Hamilton Co. Farm adjoining town, name on tax list 1808, Symmes Twp. Also names of Cronymus, David, William. Two or three daughters mentioned as wives of others of the colony. Fur infor Cincinnati Chap.

FELTER, MATTHIAS, (Hamilton Co.)

Capt in 4th Regt, Orange Co. Mil. (p161. N Y in Rev by Roberts.) Mar 1st Rebecca (1791-1830); 2nd Barbara (1795-1855) bur near his grave. Children: One son, by Rebecca, was Cronymus (1823-1835). Bur near Mt. Carmel of Madisonville, Hamilton Co, O. One of early colonists settling Montgomery, Sycamore Twp, Hamilton Co. Owned land at Columbia. Ref: Natl No 34924, D. A. R. Lin. Fur infor Cincinnati Chap.

FENNEL, STEPHEN, (Clermont Co.)

Pvt. Md line. Pensioned 1818. Served under Gen Nathaniel Greene. At beginning of war, his mother, a Quaker said to him "If thee will go to defend the liberties of thy country, never let thy mother hear that her son was wounded in the back." Mar Mahala ———. Lived in New Richmond, Clermont Co, O. Ref: A. S. Abbott, Bethel, O. Fur infor Cincinnati Chap.

FENT, PHILIP, (Fayette Co.)

Fought seven yrs in the Rev. Br Virginia. Mar Catherine Parret, in Va. Children: (5) James. D 1835, near Jeffersonville. Bur Higbee Cem on Jeffersonville Pike, center of cem. MI: "Philip Fent, a Revolutionary soldier." GM by family, granite monument. Given a grant of land for services in Ohio. Farmer. Ref: Dill's Hist of Fayette, 1881. Family records. Fur infor Washington C. H. Chap.

FENTON, GAMALIEL, (Cuyahoga Co.)

Pvt Conn Mil. Br 1763. D 1849. Bur Erie Street Cem, Cleveland, O. GM by Western Reserve. Fur infor Western Reserve Chap.

FENTON, SAMUEL, (Adams Co.)

Capt of 2nd Company 1st Bn, Cumberland Mil. May 14, 1778. He was also Capt of a company, Sixth Bn Cumberland Co Mil May 14, 1780. Br Virginia. Parents: Jeremiah Fenton Sr. Mar Elizabeth Dix. Children: Jeremiah, John Michael, Enoch, Hannah, Sarah, Mary. D near Gift Ridge in Adams Co. Bur Gift Ridge, Adams Co. GM by his family, granite monument. Ref: Mrs. Wilma Fenton Salisbury, Vincennes, Ind. Fur infor Sycamore Chap.

FENTON, SOLOMON, (Hamilton Co.)

2nd Conn Regt 1777, Ensign 2nd Lt in 1778 and 1st Lt in 78. Resigned in 1780. Br Conn. D Cincinnati, Hamilton Co. Came to Columbia and to Cincinnati before 1800; Name on tax list of 1794. Ref: "Oldest History of Hamilton Co" gives this infor; also "Heitman's Officer's in Revolutionary War" p 225; Fur infor Cincinnati Chap.

FERGUSON, HENRY, (Harrison Co.)

Pvt in 1st Company 4th Bn Cumberland Co, Pa. Mil. Br 1755, Washington Co, Pa. Mar Elnor Palmer (br 1758, d 1858). One son was John. Ref: Natl No 102707, Vol 103, p 218, D. A. R. Lin.

FERGUSON, ISAAC, (Clermont Co.)

Scout in Revolutionary War; in Kentucky was a companion to Boone, Kenton, et al. Br Brownsville, Pa. Parents: Thomas Ferguson, a Revolutionary soldier. Mar Eliz Leedom. Children: Isaiah, (br Brownsville, Pa. 1777. Mar Mary Johns; he was a Major in 1812 war; D 1852) Zachariah Hugh. (mar Mary Arthur, 1805); Isaac, James, Thomas, Elizabeth, (mar Abel Lonham), Nancy, (Mar Wm Lindsley). Ruth, (Mar Robert Donham). D 1818. Came to Limetone (Maysville) Ky. 1784, thence in 1794. to Campbell Co, Ky; thence 1796 to Ohio Twp, Clermont Co, O. at New Richmond. Ref: A. S. Abbott, Bethel, O. and Pa Archives, Vol 15, A see Vol. 4 5 Series p 399 & 708. Fur infor Cincinnati Chap.

FERGUSON, JAMES, (Hamilton Co.)

5th Regt Col Duboy's (N. Y. in Rev p 56). Mar Jane. Bur in Hamilton Co, O. Merchants; brought drugs from East for use of early doctors of Cincinnati. Ref: Grieves Hist; Recorders Office Book. p 266. Yr 1815.

FERGUSON, JAMES, (Ross Co.)

Enl in the Revolutionary War in Cumberland Co, Pa. Br County Antrim, Ireland; came to America in 1750. Parents: James and Rachel (Walker) Ferguson. Mar Margery Denny about 1776 in Franklin Co, Pa. Children: James, Margaret, John, Rachel, Creaghead. D Sept 11, 1806. Bur Grandview Cem, Chillicothe, O. McFarland lot. Justice of Common Pleas in 1798 Chillicothe. Member of 1st Council in Chillicothe. Fur infor Mt Sterling Chap.

FERGUSON, JOHN, (Hamilton Co.)

N. Y. 15th Regt Albany Mil. Came early to Cincinnati where he lived and died in Hamilton Co. Fur infor Cincinnati Chap.

FERGUSON, JOHN SR., (Highland Co.)

Capt in Noah Aleralianis' Company of Cumberland Co, Minute Men. Bn not known. Col James Dunlap commander. D Highland Co. Bur Fall Creek Presbyterian Church Cem. GM by Waw-Wil-a-Way Chapter. Fur infor Waw-Wil-a-Way Chap.

FERGUSON, JOHN, (Forgeson and Furguson), (Lake Co.)

Capt first under Capt Job Wright, Col Van Schaick's NY Bn. Saratoga, Dec. 17, 1776. Later in Col Morris Graham's Regt of NY Mil in 1778. Later he was made Captain of Mil. Br Dec 25, 1757. West Farms, Westchester Co, N. Y. Came from Scotland, settled in Hackensack, N. J. Mar Mary Campbell. D Apr 4, 1841, Willoughby, O. Bur Willoughby Ridge Cem. GM New Connecticut Chap. Pensioned in 1840, Willoughby. Ref: Natl No 43263, Vol 44, p 101, D A. R Lin. Fur infor New Connecticut Chap.

FERGUSON, MATTHEW, (Ross Co.)

Enl in Capt John Williams' Company of the 1st Bn of Cumberland Co, Pa. Mil Flying Camp, Revolutionary War 1777. Was at the battles of Brandywine and Germantown and acquired the title of Capt. Br 1749 County of Antrim, Ireland, Came with his parents to Cumberland Co, Pa in 1750. Parents: James and Rachel (Walker) Ferguson. Mar Ann Chestnut 1782. Children: John, James, Rachel, William, Catherine, Matthew, Ann, Margaret, James. D Nov 2, 1848 at home near Kingston, O. Bur Mt Pleasant Cem near Kingston, O. near south end of cem. MI: "Matthew Ferguson, A Soldier in the Revolution. Born in County of Antrim Ireland. Died Nov 2, 1848, aged 99 yrs." GM with new marker, by grandson, Matthew Ferguson, about the year 1895. Farmer; one of first Justices of Peace in Pickaway Twp, Pickaway Co. Two older brothers also served in Rev. James bur Chillicothe; William, bur Monongahda Co. Ref: Nellie Crouse Black, Kingston, O. Fur infor Mt Sterling Chap.

FERGUSON, WILLIAM, (Hamilton Co.)

Pa Capt. Lt 4th Continental Artillery 1777. Taken prisoner at Bound Brook Apr 13, 1777. Exchanged 1780; Capt 1778; retired 1783. Gave service later in army. Killed Nov 1791 near Ft Recovery, O in action with Indians, at time of St Clair's defeat. Fur infor Cincinnati Chap.

FERGUSON, WILLIAM, (Harrison Co.)

1748-1832; Bur in Cadiz Old Graveyard. Served as a member of Capt James Scott's Company, 3rd Bn Washington Co Mil in May 1782, and in Capt William Leets' Company of Washington Co Mil in 1782 in Crawford's Expedition against the Sandusky Indians. There was also a William Ferguson in the Westmoreland Co Mil in 1782. Pa Archives 6, 11, 105, 351, 394, 882. Fur infor Moravian Trail Chap.

FERREL, JOHN, (Licking Co.)

Enl at Red Stone, Fayette Co, Pa. Aug 1776, as Pvt in Capt James Piggott's Company, Col Enos McCoy's Regt. Served under Capt John Finley and Col Daniel Brodhead; was at Brandywine and Paoli. Br 1755. D 1840, Perry Twp. Applied 1838 for pens. Service file No 3354. Ref: Licking Co Hist by E. M. P. Brister. Fur infor Hetuck Chap.

FERRIS, ISAAC, (Hamilton Co.)

Mar 1st Mary (d after 1812, burial place not located); 2nd Elty (d 1855, bur Mt Carmel, Hamilton Co). D 1842, Bur Mt Carmel, Hamilton Co. GM of Isaac and Elty Ferris. Was in first group to land at Columbia, 1788; Deacon and Charter member of 1st Baptist Church; on tax list in Sycamore Twp 1808. Deed at court house Bk 1, p 76, signed by Isaac and Mary Ferris. Fur infor by Cincinnati Chap.

FERRIS, JOHN, (Lorain Co.)

Enl at Bedford, N. Y. 1776 in Capt Daniel Mills' Company, Col Van Schaick's Regt for Canadian expedition where he took smallpox. Servèd substitute 1777, 1778. Br 1760, Pond Ridge, N. Y. Mar Jerusha Lockswood. D 1811. Bur Huntington, O. (Some data also S. A. R. Bk). MI "In Revolutionary War." Applied for pens 1834, Portage Co, O and was allowed for 2 yrs actual service as Pvt NY Line. Ref: Natl No 42214, Vol 43, D. A. R. Lin.

FERRIS, JOHN, (Hamilton Co.)

4th NY Regt Col Jas Holmes. Br about 1757, England. Mar Elizabeth Deuton, (1758-1814). Children: John, Sarah, Elizabeth, Phoebe, Rachel, Solomon, Susan. D Sept 23, 1800. Bur near Montgomery, O. Came to Columbia, O. 1790. Ref: NY in Rev. p 48, Roberts: Court House Rec. Fur infor Cincinnati Chap.

FIELDS, CHARLES, (Adams Co.)

Entire war. Br in Ireland 1739. Mar Grizzel Hemphill. D 1822, place unknown. Bur Miller Farm, Monroe Twp, Adams Co. Ref: Evans and Stivers Hist of Adams Co. Fur infor Sycamore Chap.

FIGHT, JACOB, (Hancock Co.)

Frontier Ranger of Northumberland Co, Pa. Br 1760, Lancaster Co, Pa. D 1849, Hancock Co, O. Ref: Natl No 78861, Vol 79, D. A. R. Lin.

FIGHT, JACOB, SR., (Trumbull Co.)

Bur Seceeders Corners, Liberty Twp. Unable to locate grave. Ref: S. A. R. Yr Bk. Fur infor Mary Chesney Chap.

FIKE, HENRY, (Wayne Co.)

Bur Zion Church Cem at northwest corner under pine tree. MI: "Henry Fike, soldier of 1775." GM Plain marble slab at head of grave. Fur infor Wooster Wayne Chap.

FILSON, JOHN, (Hamilton Co.)

Ensign Montgomery's Pa Bn of the Flying Camp. Taken prisoner near Fort Washington Nov 16, 1788. Ref: Heitmans p 226. Br 1746, Chester Co, Pa. D 1788. Killed by Indians. Spot unknown. Surveyor; he with Matthias Denman and Robert Patterson were 3 original proprietors of Cincinnati. He suggested "Losantiville" as name of town, which in 1790 was changed by Gov St Clair to Cincinnati. Ref: Hist of Cincinnati by C. F. Goss, 42-45; 23-25. Fur infor Cincinnati Chap.

FINCH, WILLIAM, (Hamilton Co.)

Br 1759, Connecticut. D 1849. Fur infor Cincinnati Chap.

FINDLEY, DAVID, (Muskingum Co.)

Br Allegheny Co, Pa. Mar Jennie Mitchell in Pa. Pensioner in 1840 at age of 75 yrs, while residing in Union Twp on a large tract of land where the town of New Concord now stands. Reared a family of eight children of whom all married and deceased at time of this writing (1892) except the wife of the son John, who was born in 1802. John was the fourth child. David Findley was related to Gov. Findley and Dr. Findley of Pa. He lived to be over 90 yrs of age and died in Muskingum Co. Was Judge at one time. Judge David Findley, coming in 1806, purchased lands of Henry Reasoner, who had located in Sec 1 in 1804. In 1827 the establishing of the National road through his place prompted him to lay out a town which was accomplished Mch 24, 1828. The location of the town of Concord and description of the town is recorded as follows: "P 298. Judge David Findley's large brick house was erected in 1828. It was the first brick house in New Concord. Ref: Biographical and Historical Memoirs of Muskingum County" printed in 1892 by the Goodspeed Publishing Co. Fur infor Muskingum Chap.

FINDLEY, ROBERT W., (Hamilton Co.)

Pvt. Br 1750. D 1840, Germantown. Ref: Natl No 21637, p 232, Vol 22, D. A. R. Lin.

FINK, GEORGE HANS, (Mahoning Co.)

Ranger, Northampton Co. Served from Feb 10, 1781 to June 1, 1782. Capt Shrowder's Company. Br 1752. Mar Catherin Barbara K——— (1753-1829). Children: Roy, William. D 1838. Bur Old Church Cem Petersburg, O. Ref: p 202 Hist Trumbull and Mahoning Cos, Vol 2; Pa Archives, Series 2, Vol 14, p 581. Fur infor Mahoning Chap.

FINK, JOHN, (Mahoning Co.)

Pvt in Continental Army, Pa. Bur Old Springfield Cem. Ref: Pa Archives, Series 5, Vol 4, p 320; Vol 8, p 467, 599. Fur infor Mahoning Chap.

FINLEY, JOSEPH LEWIS, Maj., (Adams Co.)

He entered the Revolutionary War Apr 1, 1776, as a 2nd Lt in Capt Moorhead's Company of Miles' Pennsylvania Rifle Regt. Was transferred to the 8th Pa July 1, 1778 and was made a Maj July 20, 1780. He served until Nov 1783, more than 2 yrs after the surrender of Cornwallis. Br Feb 20, 1753, near Greensburg, Westmoreland Co, Pa. Mar dau of Rev Samuel Blair. Children: Hannah, Mary, Margaret, James and John. D May 23, 1830. Bur Old Cem, West Union, O. in center of Old Cem. MI: "Joseph L. Finley was born Feb 20, 1753 and died May 23, 1839." Was in Battle of Long Island, White Plains, Brandywine, Germantown and Battle of Monmouth. After that he was sent with Gen Broadhead to the western part of Pa. He lost his eye in serv and was otherwise much disabled. Ref: Hist of Adams Co and Natl No 29232, Vol 30, p 83 D. A. R. Lin. which gives date of death 1839. Fur infor Sycamore Chap.

FINNEY, MAJOR, (Hamilton Co.)

Bur at Finney Town, named for donor of grounds. Location of graves; now within city limits of Cincinnati, Hamilton Co. Name on p 68 "Janes Hist of Cincinnati," published 1879. In a letter of Rev. John Hindman, explorer, he states that Maj Finney was with Clark, Butler & Parsons (Gens) at North Bend (site) in 1785 seeking to make treaties with the Indians as missionary.' His farm was a Grant from Gov for Revolutionary services. Fur infor Cincinnati Chap.

FINNEY, EBENEZER W. (Hamilton Co.)

Br 1755, Connecticut. D 1822. Ref: S. A. R. Fur infor Cincinnati Chap.

FINNEY, JOHN, (Harrison Co.)

A Revolutionary pensioner living in Harrison Co, in 1834, aged 73; served in Capt Samuel Watson's company in 2nd Pa Line Regt. Pa Archives 5 series 11, 113. U. S. Pension Rolls 1835. Fur infor Moravian Trail Chap.

FINNEY, JOSIAH, (Trumbull Co.)

Br 1755, Warren, Litchfield Co, Conn. Parents: Josiah Finney and Sarah Carter Finney. Mar Joanna Phelps, Jan 21, 1779. Children: Laura, Josiah, Seth C, Welthy, Polliana, Sally, Lucinda. D Johnston, O. Dec 18, 1844. Bur Old Cem, Johnson, O. MI: Name, date of death, "age 89 yrs." GM by relatives, shortly after death. During his active years he followed farming. His war services is not recorded, but his name appears as a Revolutionary pensioner. Ref: D. J. Finney, Niles, O. Fur infor Mary Chesney Chap.

FINNEY, MAJOR, (Hamilton Co.)

Bur Finney Town, named for donor of grounds, now within city limits of Cincinnati, Hamilton Co. Name on p 68 "Janes Hist of Cincinnati" published 1879 In a letter of Rev. John Hindman, explorer, he states that Maj Finney was with Clark Butler and Parsons (Generals) at North Bend (site) in 1875 seeking to make treaties with the Indians as commissioner. His farm was a Grant fr Government for Revolutionary services. Fur infor Cincinnati Chap by Mrs. Whallon.

FISH, EBENEZER, (Co. not stated.)

Taken prisoner in defense of Ft Griswold, 1781. Br 1757, Groton, Conn. Mar Lydia Fish. D 1827, Ohio. Ref: Natl No 57,679, p 233, Vol 58, D. A. R. Lin. and Mrs. Eliz Jane Hatheway, Fall River, Mass.

FISH, EPHRAIM, (Huron Co.)

Pvt. Br 1760, Washington Co, N. Y. Children: Stephen, Joshua, John, Benjamin, Wilson, Sarah, Thryza. D Oct 5, 1838. Bur North Monroeville. MI: Name on Soldiers Monument. Fur infor Sally De Forest Chap.

FISHER, ADAM, (Clermont Co.)

Adjutant Lancaster Co Mil. 1777. Lt 6th Company 1779. D 1829 aged 79 yrs, Clermont Co, O. Ref: Natl No. 11,286, p 110, Vol 12, D. A. R. Lin.

FISHER, ADAM, (Stark Co.)

Bur Mud Brook Cem, Jackson Twp, Stark Co, O. Ref: Authority: Hist of Stark Co edited by William Henry Perrin. Fur infor Massillon Chap.

FISHER, DANIEL, Col., (Washington Co.)

Pvt and Corp in Capt Joseph Guild's Company; Lt in Capt Abel Richard's Company, Col MacIntoch's Regt. Disch Apr 6, 1778. Br 1743. D 1824. Bur Old Belpre, Washington Co, O. GM by Marietta Chap with Revolutionary marker, 1921. Ref: Mass Soldiers and Sailors. Fur infor Marietta Chap.

FISHER, ENOCH, (Union Co.)

Bur Milford Center Cem, Union Twp. Fur infor Hannah Emerson Dustin Chap.

FISHER, HENRY, (Columbiana Co.)

Br 1757. Lived in Fairfield Twp, Columbiana Co, in 1819, aged 62 yrs. A pensioner. Fur infor Bethia Southwick Chap.

FISHER, JACOB, (Delaware Co.)

Pvt under Col Jacob Hoover, Pa Tr. Bur Berkshire Twp. Fur infor Delaware Chap.

FISHER, HENRY, (Columbiana Co.)

Br 1757. Lived in Fairfield Twp, Columbiana Co in 1819, aged 62 yrs. Pensioner. Fur infor Bethia Southwick Chap.

FISHER, JOHN, (Hancock Co.)

Bur Hancock Co but grave not located. No descendants here. Fur infor Ft Findlay Chap.

FISHER, JOHN C., (Jefferson Co.)

Br 1756. D 1809. Bur Union Cem, Steubenville, O. GM by Steubenville D. A. R. Fur infor Steubenville Chap.

FISHER, PAUL, (Columbiana Co.)

Pvt 7 mos under Lt Peter Groves, Pa lines. Br Sunbury, Pa. Mar Kathrine Kishter. D 1828, Calcutta. Ref: Natl No 72133, p 49, Vol 73, D. A. R. Lin.

FISTER, JOHN, (Mahoning Co.)

Fifer. Capt Gobins Company, 6th Bn, Berk Co Mil. Col Joseph Huster's Regt. Served fr Aug 10, 1780 to Sept 9, 1780. Br 1746. D 1813. Bur Boardman, O. Ref: Pa Archives, Series 5, Vol 5, pp 136, 239. Fur infor Mahoning Chap.

FITCH, ANDREW, (Warren Co.)

Commanded a Company in 4th Conn Regt 1771-81. Br 1747, Preston, Conn. Mar Abigail Mason in 1781, (Br 1755 D 1842). D 1811, Lebanon, Warren Co. Ref: Natl No 56620, Vol 57, p 214, D. A. R. Lin.

FITCH, HAYNES, (Mahoning Co.)

Served in Conn in the Revolutionary War. Capt Jabez Gregory's Company 1777. Given land grant on Western Reserve. Br 1734, Conn. Mar Ann ——— (1740-1814). Children: Jedidiah, David. D Aug 11, 1815. Bur Cem, Canfield, O. Came fr Conn to Canfield, O in 1802. Ref: Conn Men in the Rev, p 601; Biog E. Ohio Summers, Descendant was Principal Thorne of Delason School, Youngstown, O and Natl No 12612, Vol 13, p 234, D. A. R. Lin. Fur infor Mahoning Chap

FITCH, JAMES, (Mahoning Co.)

Pvt in Capt Jabez Gregory's Company, Conn. Bur Elsworth Cem. Lived in Youngstown in 1826. Ref: Conn Men in the Rev, p 48. Fur infor Mahoning Chap.

FITHIAN, ISAAC, (Trumbull Co.)

Pvt NY State Tr. Pensioned Mch 4, 1831. Record in Cleveland Historical Library. Children: One daughter, Rebecca, mar Matthew Scott. D Jan 16, 1834. Bur Old Cem, Warren, O. Name placed on bronze tablet 1927 by local D. A. R. Descendant Isaac Fithian, Warren, O. Fur infor Mary Chesney Chap.

FLANAGAN, JOHN, (Columbiana Co.)

Pvt 1777 in John Eccleston's Company, 2nd Regt under Col Thomas Price. Br 1761, Port Deposit, Md. D 1820, Columbiana Co, O. Ref: Vol 94, p 32, Natl No. 93094, D. A. R. Lin.

FLEEHARTY, AMASSA, (Richland Co.)

Pensioned in Richland Co, O. 1819, for services as Pvt Pa Continental Line. Br 1755, Md. D 1841, Ohio. Living in Worthington Twp in 1840. Ref: Natl No. 79,834, Vol 80, D. A. R. Fur infor Mary Washington Chap.

FLEMING, JAMES, (Preble Co.)

Pvt. Capt James Halls Company, Light Horse Brig. Capt Wm. Stewarts' Company, Lincoln Co, N. C. Br 1742, Liedell Co, N. C. D 1835, Preble Co, O. Mar Elizabeth Mitchell. Ref: Natl No. 70,834, p 229, Vol 71, D. A. R. Lin.

FLEMING, THOMAS, (Preble Co.)

Bur Harrison Twp. Fur infor Grace Miller, Org. Regent Eaton, O.

FLETCHER, SHEREBIAH, (Washington Co.)

Enl at Chelmsford as Pvt in Capt John Ford's Company, Col Robinson's Regt; Capt James Varnum's Company, Col Michael Jackson's Regt. Br Lowell, Mass. D Belpre, O. Bur Belpre, O. GM Marietta D. A. R. Ref: Mass Soldiers and Sailors. Fur infor Marietta Chap.

FLINN, BENJAMIN, (Hamilton Co.)

Br 1763, New Jersey. D 1837. Ref: S. A. R. Fur infor Cincinnati Chap.

FLINT, HEZEKIAH, (Hamilton Co.)

Pvt in Mass Line, Capts. Upton and Green, Cols. Gerrish and Howe. Br Mass, but accepted record Natl No. 76,062, Vol 77, D. A. R. Lin gives birth 1748, N. C. D 1810 or 1811, Cincinnati, O. Fur infor Cincinnati Chap.

FLINT, JOHN, (Medina Co.)

Bur Beach Cem. GM by Western Reserve. Residence Hinckley. Fur infor Western Reserve Chap.

FLORA, ABIJAH, (Ross Co.)

Served in war of Revolution as Lt of his company. Emigrated from Va. to Haller's Bottom, O. D at age of 70 yrs. Ref: p 293, Hist of Ross and Highland Co. Fur infor Nathaniel Massie Chap.

FLOWER, ISAAC, (Trumbull Co.)

Pct. Hartford Conn Regt. Br 1755, Hartford, Conn. D 1813, Vienna, O. Mar Freelove Hopkins. Natl No. 70,314, p 112, Vol. 71, D. A. R. Lin.

FLOYD, WILLIAM, (Adams Co.)

Recruit under Gen Dan Morgan. Prisoner, confined in Quebec, but escaped. Br 1739, Virginia. Mar Elizabeth Goodie, date not given. Children: one dau name not given. D Dec 9, 1833. Bur on P. Morgan's farm near Cedar College School. Ref: Evans and Stivers History of Adams Co. Fur infor Sycamore Chap.

FOBES, LEMUEL, (Lake Co.)

Served with Minute Men who marched to Lexington Alarm, later in the battle of Bennington. Br 1754, Mass. Mar Anna Bills of Mass. D 1835. Bur Evergreen Cem, Painesville, O. GM by New Connecticut Chap. Treasurer of Painesville Twp in 1813. Fur infor New Connecticut Chap.

FOBES, NATHAN, (Ashtabula Co.)

Br Bridgewater, Mass. Parents: Capt Simon Fobes, Thankful Ellis. Mar Rebecca Parsons, Aug 29, 1727. Children: David, Jabez, Sally, Justus, Rebecca (Dean), Nathan, Loton, Oshea. D Nov 23, 1833, Wayne. Bur Center Cem near Wayne Center. Seventh Row. MI: "In Memory of Nathan Fobes." GM by family, sandstone slab. Came to Wayne from Chester, Mass in 1806, where he owned a small rocky farm. Farmer. Fur infor Eunice Grant Chap.

FOBES, SIMON, Capt., (Ashtabula Co.)

Was a Capt in the French and Indian War prior to the Rev. Commissioned by the General Assembly of Conn Colony as Capt of the 19th Company of Ft Trumbull. Br Feb 22, 1722, Preston, Conn. Parents: Caleb and Abigal (Gates). Fobes. Mar Thankful Ellis. Children: Lt Simon, Caleb, Nathan, Sarah, (Lt Simon and Nathan were both in Revolution). D Feb 7, 1808. Bur Wayne Center Cem. Seventh Row. MI: "In memory of Capt. Simon Forbes." GM old sandstone slab, erected by family. Came to Wayne in 1807. Pioneer Farmer. See p 198 Wayne History p 108 and 109. Mahoning Valley Historical Coll 345-394. Fur infor Eunice Grant Chap

FOBES, SIMON, Lt., (Ashtabula Co.)

Held rank of Lt at close of war. First enl under Capt Smith, Lt Ward and Gen Ward; 2nd enl under Capt Noah Smith; 3rd enl under Capt Shapley in 1780. "From a private he was promoted through the lower grades of office to a Lt Command." Br Apr 5, 1756, Canterbury. Parents: Capt Simon Fobes. Mar Elizabeth Jones. Children: Thankful, Joshua, Bethia, Simon, Nathan, Ellis, Eunice. D Jan 30, 1840, Wayne. Bur Center Wayne Cem, seventh row. MI: "In memory of Simon Fobes Esq., who was Lieutenant in the Revolutionary War." GM old sandstone slab. Came to Wayne in 1804 from Somers, Mahoning Valley. Farmer. He represented the town Somers in the Conn Legislature during three successive sessions, was a Justice of the Peace and Selectman of the town. Ref: See Mahoning Valley Historical Coll. (1876) pp345, 394. Fur infor Eunice Grant Chap.

FOOS, JOHN, (Franklin Co.)

Served in Capt Eyre's Company, 8th Company Pikeland Infantry, Chester Co Mil commanded by Lt Col Thomas Ball (Bell)? Br Pikeland Twp, Chester Co Pa in 1767. D Franklinton in 1803. Bur Old Franklinton Cem. GM by Revolutionary Grave Committee with bronze marker. May 30, 1912. Fur infor Columbus Chap.

FOOT, DAVID, (Cuyahoga Co.)

Minute Man. Pvt Mass. 1777-80. Bur 1760, Lee, Mass. Mar Betsy Hamblin. D 1851, Dover, O. Bur Lake Shore Cem, Bay Village. Fur infor Western Reserve Chap and Vol 56, p 133, D. A. R. Lin.

FOOT, TIMOTHY, (Huron Co.)

Bur on John Hard Farm, Peru Twp. Data not found. Listed in S. A. R. 1917 Bk. Fur infor Sally DeForest Chap.

FORD, ANDREW, (Lake Co.)

Marched in response to alarm at Lexington in Lt Joseph Warner's Company. Was in battle of Bennington; also in the expedition to Stillwater and Saratoga. Pensioner. Br 1752, Mass. D 1837, Madison, Lake Co, O. Bur Middle Ridge Cem, Madison, O. GM New Connecticut Chapter. Fur infor New Connecticut Chap.

FORD, BARNABAS OR BERNARD, (Mahoning Co.)

Pvt fr Bedford Co, 1783, Pa Archives Sec 6, Vol III, p 36. Br 1743, D Mahoning Co 1822. Bur Pleasant Grove, Youngstown, Northwest side of cem. MI: "Barnabas Ford, Born 1743. Died 1822." Came to Ohio from Bedford Co, Pa, about 1802. Fur infor Mahoning Chap.

FORD, HEZEKIAH, (Cuyahoga Co.)

Pvt Conn Line. Capt Wm Ward's Hampshire Co. Regt 1779 repelled Arnold's attack. Br 1759, Abbington, Mass. Mar Huldah Cobb. D 1848. Bur East Cleveland, Euclid Ave. Opposite E. 123rd St. GM Western Reserve Chap. Ref: Natl No 43466 Vol 44, p 177, D. A. R. Lin. Fur infor Western Reserve Chap.

FORD, JOHN, (Geauga Co.)

Pvt Conn Line, 2nd Regt July 1, 1780 to Dec 6, 1780. Maj Skinner's Tr stationed at New York, 1776. Br Oct 19, 1763, West Mountain, Cheshire, Conn. Mar Easter Cook, Cheshire, Conn, Sept 20, 1790. Children: Lydia, Stephen, John, Anson, Seabury, Henry, Esther, Eliza. D Aug 6, 1842, Burton, O. Bur Lower Cem, Burton, O. MI: "John Ford, died Aug 6, 1842, age 79. Esther Cook his wife died Dec 26, 1851." Came to Burton fr Cheshire, Conn. 1804. Ref: Conn Men Rev Pioneer History of Geauga Co. Fur infor Taylor Chap.

FORD, NATHAN, (Geauga Co.)

Pvt Conn Mil. Pens claim allowed 1833. Br July 14, 1761. Cheshire, Conn. Parents: Nathan Ford, Sarah (Hine) Ford. Mar Dec 25, 1785 Catharine Williams at Cheshire, Conn. Children: Electa, Philo, Miles, John, Sally, Luther, Sebra. D Apr 4, 1840. Bur East Claridon, O. Cem Lot 200. MI: "In memory of Nathan Ford who died Apr 4, 1840, aged 79 years." GM family, very old stone. Farmer. Served town of Cheshire 1769. Came to Geauga Co 1815, settled in southeast corner of Claridon Twp. Pioneer History pp 399, 465. "Pens Records" Vol 5, 514. Fur infor Taylor Chap.

FORD, WILLIAM, Capt., (Washington Co.)

Served 5 days under Capt William Francis as Pvt. Capt under Capt William Francis in 2nd Berkshire Co Regt of Mass Mil. Br 1745. D 1823. Bur Waterman's grave near Waterford, Washington Co, O. GM by Marietta Chap with Revolutionary marker, 1923. Ref: Mass Soldiers and Sailors in Revolution. Fur infor Marietta Chap.

FORMAN, DANIEL SR., (Miami Co.)

Pvt in Capt Roger's Company, 8th Bn Cumberland Co, Pa Mil. Bur Covington, O. Reported to have been marked by Troy D. A. R. Is a marble headstone as fur by the Army Quartermaster Department. Fur infor Richard Montgomery Chap. S. A. R.

FORNEY, ABRAHAM, (Harrison Co.)

D 1824; Bur at Cadiz; one family account states that he came from Germany after the Rev; another, that of R. L. Timmons, that he served from Georgia in the Rev. Fur infor Moravian Trail Chap.

FORSMAN, HUGH, (Ross Co.)

D Green Twp. Bur Mt Pleasant, near Kingston, Ross Co, O. MI: Obliterated. Name gone—wife of Hugh Forsman died March 12, 1814, aged 45 yrs, 6 mos, 27 days. Fur fr a 1913 S A. R. list. Fur infor Nathaniel Massie Chap.

FORSYTHE, JOHN, (Muskingum Co.)

D Aug 11, 1838. Bur Crooked Creek Cem, 1 mile south of New Concord. Fur infor Muskingum Chap.

FORT, JOSEPH, (Scioto Co.)

Pvt in the Somerset, NJ Mil in the American Rev. Br Mch 13, 1751, Somerset, N. J. Parents: Francis and Mary Fort. Mar Mary Davison in 1777. Children: Benjamin, Gabriel, Mrs. Mary Reeves, George, Mrs. Susanna, Noel, Mrs. Mercy Noel, Bartholomew, Thomas. D Aug 1, 1806 in Scioto Co on Pond Creek. Bur near Lomardsville, Scioto Co on Pond Creek, Old Country Graveyard. Came with his family from N. J. in 1796, and settled first at Alexandria at mouth of Scioto River, afterward moved to Pond Creek, where he died. Justice of the Peace for a time. Ref: Mrs. Mary Feurt Royse, Miss Edith Royse, Mrs. Sarah Feurt Black. Fur infor Joseph Spencer Chap.

FOSTER, ——— (Medina Co.)

Br 1754. D 1848. Bur in Sharon. GM by Western Reserve Fur infor Western Reserve Chap.

FOSTER, ALBIO, (Lorain Co.)

Fur infor Western Reserve Chap.

FOSTER, ASA, (Hamilton Co.)

Br 1758, Connecticut. D 1827. Ref: S. A. R. Fur infor Cincinnati Chap.

FOSTER, EPHRAIM, (Washington Co.)

Pvt in New Haven Continental Tr. In Capt John Cushey's Company of Minute Men, Col Samuel Johnson's Regt. Br 1750, Boxford. D Sept 25, 1823, Marietta, O. Bur Mound Cem, Marietta, O. MI: "Ephraim Foster, 1750-1823." GM by Marietta Chap by marker and gateway Nov 30, 1906; marker stolen and replaced in 1920. Ref: "Mass Soldiers and Sailors of the Revolutionary War." Fur infor Marietta Chap.

FOSTER, JAMES (Mahoning Co.)

Pvt in 10th Va Regt Col William Davis, Capt Overton's Company. Br Lancaster Co, Pa. 1753. D Poland, O. 1814. Ref: Natl No 20314, p 110, Vol 21, D. A. R. Lin.

FOSTER, JOHN 1ST, (Pike Co.)

Pvt in Capt Peter Mantz's Company, Maryland. Br Cumberland, Md. 1731. Mar Elizabeth Lewis in 1758. Children: Lewis, Casander, Thomas, Rachael, Rev. John 2nd, (Capt in War of 1812) Benjamin, Joseph, Richard. D Jan 1, 1800, Waverly, Pike Co. Fur infor Nathaniel Massie and Joseph Spencer Chap.

FOSTER, NATHANIEL, (Adams Co.)

Enl in 1776 in Capt Tom Broeck's Company, again in 1777, again in 1781; served short terms. Br Feb 7, 1760, in Morris Co, N. Y. Mar: first wife, name not given; second, named Cleveland. Children: Samuel, Isaac, Nathaniel, Mary and Anna; Nathan, Moses, Jeddiah, Asa. Daughters names not given. D 1842. Bur on banks Brush Creek in Foster grave yard. Ref: Evans and Stivers History of Adams Co. Fur infor Sycamore Chap.

FOSTER, PEREGRINE, (Washington Co.)

Pvt in Capt Daniel Gilber's Company, Col Job Cushing's Regt. Br 1749, New England. D 1804, Belpre, O. Bur Belpre, O. Peregine Foster and Mary, his wife, settled in Belpre Twp in 1796. He was one of the surveyors in the company of pioneers who landed at Marietta, Apr 7, 1788. In 1796 secured a franchise for a ferry across the Ohio River. Fur infor Marietta Chap.

FOUGHT, JOHN MORRIS, (Coshocton Co.)

Bur Baptist Cem, West Lafayette, O. MI: "An officer of the Revolution April 2, 1826, aged 87 years." Fur infor Coshocton Chap.

FOUST, JAKOB, (Morrow Co.)

Bur Fousts Cem, old country, north of Westfield. Fur infor Mt. Gilead Chap.

FOWLER, CALEB, (Geauga Co.)

Pvt Conn Continental Line, Capt Humphrey's Company. Enl Dec 2, 1777 for 3 yrs. Disch Corp Nov 23, 1780. Pensioned 1818. Br Dec 31, 1755, Guilford, Conn. Mar 1st, Mollie Chittenden, (br Mch 28, 1760 in Guilford, Conn.); 2nd, Oline Miegs (br Oct 16, 1767, d Apr 27, 1848). Children; Mollie, Clarinda, Rhoda, Harriet, Desire, Phebe. D Oct 12, 1822, Burton, O. Bur Burton Cem, new gate, right hand side. MI: "Caleb Fowler died Aug 27, 1880, age 93 yrs. 8 mos. 4 days. Soldier of Revolutionary War." GM by D. A. R. Was at the battle of Monmouth and the musket captured from the British is in possession of the family. Farmer. Came to Burton, Oct 21, 1812. Ref: "Pioneer Hist Geauga Co." p 432; Conn Men Rev. p 216, 388, 646, and Natl No. 92,249, Vol 80, D. A. R. Lin. Fur infor Taylor Chap.

FOWLER, RICHARD, (Coshocton, O.

Bur Bacon Run. Fur infor Mrs. A. Ripple, member Columbus Chap.

FOX, FREDERICK, (Montgomery Co.)

Drummer boy, in Lt Col Hay's Company of the 10th Pa, Regt Continent Line, Apr 20, 1777, and served until 1781. Br May 10, 1751, Providence of Hesse-Nassau, Germany. Parents: John Frederick Fox and wife, Christina, en route to America, came on Ship "Anderson" to Philadelphia, Sept 27, 1752. Mar Catherine Booker Mch 1, 1773; (br 1748, Frederick Co, Md. d Nov 1, 1800, Bur Sharpsburg, Frederick Co, Md.) Mar 2nd Mrs. Young. No children by second wife. Children: Christina, Rosanna, Mary Magdalena, George, Daniel Booker, Joseph, Elizabeth; all br in Maryland, and all came to Ohio, with their father in 1807, excepting Rosana. D Feb 27, 1837, near Miamisburg, O. Bur Gebhart Church, Miamisburg, on northeast side of church yard. MI: "To the memory of Frederick Fox, born May 10, 1751. died February 27, 1837, aged 85 years, 9 months, 17 days." GM by Richard Montgomery Chap, S. A. R. in 1919. Settled in Maryland, altho served from Pa.; was a planter, farmer and tavern keeper. Ref: Natl No 38391, D. A. R. Lin. Fur infor Richard Montgomery Chap.

FOX, ISRAEL, (Lake Co.)

Enl for three months with Col Talcott; in 1777 for three months with Col Woodbridge and another three months in 1779; in June 1780 for six months with Capt Phelps. Pensioner. Br 1755, Glastenbury, Conn. D Mentor, Lake Co, O. Fur infor New Connecticut Chap.

FOX, JACOB, (Hancock Co.)

Served for Pa. Pvt under Col Joseph Hirstner, Capt Sebastain Miller. Br Mch 12, 1764. Mar Mary Flick, Nov 18, 1821. D Aug 16, 1849. Bur Flick Cem.

Hancock Co, O. (Located by Mrs. A. Zugschwert.) GM Ft Findlay in 1915. Ref: Mrs. Anna Gibson, Findlay. Fur infor Fort Findlay Chap.

FRANKS, HENRY, (Washington Co.)

Pvt under Capt John Miner, Capt Jesse Pigman, Capt John Welsel, Capt Thomas Swann, Capt William Crawford and Col Evans. Br 1751, Piscataway, Md. Mar Margaret Van Buskirk in 1803. Children: Owen. D 1846, Grandview Twp Washington Co, O. Bur Grandview Twp. GM by Marietta Chap D. A. R. Pension allowed 1833. Ref: Pens. Department at Washington; also Natl No 77903 Vol 78, D. A. R. Lin. Fur infor Marietta Chap.

FRANKS, HENRY, (Wayne Co.)

Served from Pa. Br 1764. D 1836. Bur Chippewa. GM Western Reserve. Fur infor Western Reserve Chap.

FRANTZ, ADAM, (Tuscarawas Co.)

Sgt Col Lord's Regt 1777 at battle of Ft Washington and Trenton. Br Lancaster Co, Pa, 1755. Mar Sallie Shirk. D 1836, Tuscarawas Co. Ref: Natl No 55635, p 287, Vol 56, D. A. R. Lin.

FRAZEE, JONAS, (Hamilton Co.)

Pvt. Br Aug 4, 1759, Westfield, Essex Co, N. J. Soon after the war came with his wife and several children to the Northwest Territory and squatted near North Bend, O. D Oct 7, 1858 at his home in Miamitown, Hamilton Co, O. Bur Berea Cem, near Cleves, O. Lots No 158 and 159. MI: "Jonas Frazee A Soldier of the Revolution. Born in Westfield, N. J. 1759. Died 1858." GM erected by the citizens. Tombstone erected by subscription of citizens in 1859. He first enl at Westfield in Capt Craig's Company and again at Rahway in Capt Scudder's Company. He was several times engaged in bloody skirmishes with maurauding parties of tories and bandits, encouraged by the enemy to pillage and destroy. He served three years and was honorably discharged at the disbanding of the army. He was always poor, never owned a home until J. Scott Harrison, M. C. from this district secured him a land warrant, which he sold for a humble home in Miamitown, O. where he lived until his death. He was strictly an honest man and a good neighbor. Ref: Fur by Jessie H. Kayser D. A. R. Natl No 89327. Fur infor Cincinnati Chap.

FRAZEE, JONATHAN, (Mahoning Co.)

Pvt 2nd Pa Regt 1776 under Col Walter Stewart. Br 1750. Mar Mary ———. (1749-1834). D 1829. Bur Pleasant Grove, south of Youngstown, O. Ref: Pa Archives Series 5, Vol 2, p 837. Fur infor Mahoning Chap.

FRAZEE, MOSES, (Co not stated)

Served as Pvt in Middlesex Co, NJ Mil. Br 1762, N. J. Mar Priscilla Morris in 1785. D 1840 in Ohio. Ref: Natl No 100026, Vol 101, p 9, D. A. R. Lin.

FRAZIER, GEORGE, (Trumbull Co.)

Pvt in Capt Robert Cruickshank's Company 13th Bn, Col Richard Graves, Kent Co, Md Mil (1778-1779). D 1813. Bur Frazier Farm, Hubbard Twp. A small plot on farm where many of the family are buried. Stones are broken or down but the burial plot positively located by old residents of the town. Ref: L. B. Frazier, Caldwell, O. whose daughter belongs to D. A. R. tracing from George Frazier. Fur infor Mary Chesney Chap.

FREDERICK, THOMAS, (Columbia Co.)

Lived in Elk Run Twp, Columbiana Co. Fur infor Bethia Southwick Chap.

FREEMAN, JOHN, (Butler Co.)

Bur in Oxford Twp. On his stone is recorded "John Freeman, a soldier of 76, Died Sept 21, 1846, in the 85th year of his age." Fur infor Oxford Caroline Scott Chap.

FREEMAN, NATHAN, (Portage Co.)

Enl as a Pvt Mch 1777, served 3 mos; June, 1777, 5 mos; Mch, 1778, 8 mos; Mch 1779, 9 mos. Capt Edward Hodges, Capt Whipple, Capt John Hastings. Br May 30, 1762, Hardwick, Mass. Mar Polly Rice, 1790. Children: Clark, George, Hollis, Sally, Nathan, Elizabeth, Stephen. D Sept 10, 1849, Ravenna, O. Bur Maple Grove, Ravenna, O. MI: "Nathan Freeman." GM by Ida Freeman Britton (Grand-daughter). Marker. 1917. Applied for pension July 10, 1832. Claim allowed. Ref: Bureau of Pensions. Fur infor Old Northwest Chap.

FREEMAN, ROBERT, (Trumbull Co.)

Bur near Braceville, east of Phalanx Mills. Ref: Baldwin Library, Youngstown, O. Fur infor Mary Chesney Chap.

FREEMAN, RUFUS, (Medina Co.)

Pvt fr N. H. Br 1762. D 1847. Bur Seville. GM by Western Reserve. Fur infor Western Reserve Chap.

FREEMAN, SOLOMAN, (Licking Co.)

Enl at Lancaster, Mass. July, 1777, as Pvt in Elisha White's Company. Served in Col Tyler's and Col Malcolm's Regt New York; also 1779, Capt Merrick's (3 mos); and Capts Ruggs and Blakely's Companies of NY. Br 1762 at Lancaster, Mass. Parents: Adam Freeman. D Aug 23, 1847. Granville Twp. Bur at Alexandria. MI: "Rev War." GM Hetuck Chap in 1909. Was a pensioner; granted at Milford, Knox Co, 1735. Ref: Brister's Hist of Co. Fur infor Hetuck Chap.

FRENCH, NATHAN, (Lake Co.)

Enl July 20, 1777, and served until Aug 7, 1780. Pensioner. Br Feb 1760, Mass. D Aug 30, 1847, Leroy Twp, Lake Co, O. Aged 87 yrs, 6 mos, 27 days. Bur Southeast Leroy. GM New Connecticut Chap. Fur infor New Connecticut Chap.

FRENCH, SEBA, (Lake Co.)

Pvt in Capt Joseph Franklin's Company, Col John Daggett's Regt in an alarm at Tiverton, R. I. Pensioner 1833 (which was transferred to his widow at his death). Br 1761, Mass. Mar about 1779 to Mary Ide. Children: Daniel I, Warren, Aremas, William, Ezra. D Dec 28, 1836. Bur Washington St Cemetery, Painesville, O. GM New Connecticut Chap. Fur infor New Connecticut Chap.

FRENCH, WILLIAM, (Geauga Co.)

Sgt in Capt Malcolm Henry's Company, Col David Brewer's Mass Regt. Br 1744. Mar Elizabeth Avery. D 1834, Bundysburg, O. "Came to Geauga Co about 1815 with 3 sons, Wareham, William and Avery, from Otsego Co, N. Y." p 685. Pioneer History Geauga Co. (Copied by Taylor Chap D. A. R.) Ref: Mrs Rupert Ford, Oneonta N. Y. and Natl No 57439, Vol 58, p 149.

FRESHOUR, JOHN, (Ross Co.)

Enl Dec 1776 for 3 mos, and Mch 1778 for 1 yr, under Capts Scott and Steed, Col Neville. Br Virginia, May 13, 1756. D Ross Co, Oct 13, 1841. Bur on the Lou Metcalf farm near Bourneville. GM Stone D. A. R. marker in 1924. Engaged in battle Mch 1777 near Boundbook and Middlebrook. Filed application for pens Oct 12, 1832. Allowed. Fur infor Nathaniel Massie Chap.

FRISHBY, LUTHER, (Trumbull Co.)

Served 1777-83 as Artillery Artificer under Capt Wilcox, Conn. Br 1760, Branford, Conn. Mar Rachel F. —— (d Oct 21, 1834, aged 92.) D Nov 19, 1842, aged 82 yrs, Mesopotamia, O. Bur Center Johnston. Ref: Natl No 87268, Vol 88, p 83, D. A. R. Lin. Fur infor Mary Chesney Chap.

FRITZ, MARTIN, (Wayne Co.)

8th Bn Pa Mil. D Shinersburg, Aug 17, 1844. Bur Shinersburg, near Rittman. O, east end of cem. MI: "Martin Fritz died Aug 17, 1844, aged 94 years." 8th Bn Pa Militia. Fur infor Wooster Wayne Chap.

FRYBACK, GEORGE, (Pickaway Co.)

Battle of Long Island. In list of Capt Edward Burgess Company of Mil in lower district of Frederick Co Archives of Maryland Vol 18, p 42. Br 1759, Germany. Mar Susannah Steed. Children: Mary, Sarah, Lydia, Katherine, Ann Susannah, Elizabeth, George, John. D Dec 1, 1833 Pickaway Plains Farm. Bur Family burial ground on home farm. MI: "George Fryback Dec 1, 1833, aged 74 years." Came to America just prior to Rev, enl at 16 yrs. Married in Cumberland Co, Pa. Came to Ohio 1798, receiving land grant. Farmer. Ref: Mrs. A. W. Fleming, 44 Woodland Ave, Columbus, O. Fur infor Mt Sterling Chap.

FULLER, BENJAMIN, JR., (Clinton Co.)

Bur Sugar Grove Cem, Wilmington. Fur infor George Clinton Chap.

FULLER, JAMES, DR., (Athens Co.)

Pvt. Served one month at Providence, R. I. and re-enl in Mass Regt under Col Mason, Capt John Morgan's Company. Disch dated July 1, 1778. He drew a Revolutionary War pens. Claim S. 226, Bureau of Pensions, Washington D. C. Br Sept 1, 1760. Parents: Capt James and Abigail (Rue) Fuller. Mar Mollie May, Apr 22, 1781. Children: Porter, Lorinda, Orilla, Elbridge, James, Augustus, Polly. D Athens Co, O. Location of grave not known. He was born in Thompson, Conn, went to South Brimfield (now Wales) about 1781, removed to adjoining town of Holland about 1795. He was living in Canaan Twp, Athens Co. O when he applied for a pens. (Descendants of Thomas Fuller of Woburn, by Wm H. Fuller, p 150-152). His pens application executed Oct 13, 1832, while a resident of Canaan Twp, Athens Co, O., to which county he moved from South Brimfield, Mass in 1817. Ref: Natl No. 215,411. Fur infor Elizabeth Zane Dew Chap.

FULLER, JOSEPH, SR., (Lake Co.)

Enl Apr 21, 1777; was appointed Corp in Sept, 1779, and Sgt in 1780, 4th Mass Regt in Capt Kepps Company commanded by Col William Shepard. Br May 27, 1758, Munson, Hampshire Co, Mass. Parents: Nathaniel Fuller. Mar Rachel Miller, Nov 2, 1783. D Sept 26, 1846. Bur on the north Ridge Road, Madison, O. GM by New Connecticut Chap. Fur infor New Connecticut Chap.

FULLER, WILLIAM, (Cuyahoga Co.)

Pvt. Mass. Continental. Br 1745. Alive in 1818. Ohio pension roll. Fur infor Western Reserve Chap.

FULLERTON, ROBERT, (Mahoning Co.)

Pvt in Pa. Children: Andrew, Samuel, Joseph, Robert. Bur Mahoning Co. Ref: Pa. Archives, Series 2, Vol. 13, p 77; Trumbull & Mahoning Co. History, Vol 2, p 129. Fur infor Mahoning Chap.

FUNK, ADAM, (Perry Co.)

Battle of Yorktown and was with Washington when he crossed the Delaware. Possible foreign birth. D 1835. Bur Roseville, O. This lies in the neighboring part of Perry Co. To our knowledge this man did not enlist as a regular, but came over to this country from a foreign country and enlisted. Settled in Brownsville, Pa. after the war. Old family Bible in the hands of the Pemberton-Brown families of Roseville, O. Fur infor Muskingum Chap.

FUNK, MARTIN, (Scioto Co.)

Pvt Capt Williams, Alex Pomeroy, John Hopkins, Pa Regt 4 mos in Capt J. Pomeroys, Col Loughry. Many skirmishes with Indians. Enl 2 mos, Capt Barr, 2 mos as Pvt. Capt Williams. Br 1762, Frederick Co, Va. Parents: John Funk. Mar Elizabeth Studebaker, 1789. Children: Martin, John, Elizabeth, Jacob, Catherine, Barbara. D Oct 16, 1838, Scioto Co. Bur Greenlawn, city of Portsmouth, northeast corner, Section B. MI: "Martin Funk, soldier of Revolution—1762-1838." Money from his estate, granite marker (the D. A. R. marker of Joseph Spencer Chap was stolen). He was quiet and orderly, the men met on his farm for the war of 1812, his son was fifer in Morgan Co. Distillery, the lands of Scioto yielded such crops of corn, there was no other use for corn. Came from Chamberlin Co, Pa. 1798, to Alexandria. Ref: Natl No 49162, Vol 50, p 72, D. A. R. Lin. Fur infor Joseph Spencer Chap.

FURNACE, WILLIAM, (Huron Co.)

Served 4 yrs. Br Mch 20, 1759, Marblehead, Mass. D Mch 4, 1843. Bur Olena. Fur infor Sally De Forest Chap.

FUSON, WILLIAM, (Campaign Co.)

See Revolutionary War Records, Bureau of Pensions service S 4,291; Beers History of Champaign Co. Br Apr 16, 1762 in Hanover Co, Va. Parents: John Fuson and Miss Wheeler. Mar Hannah Bates, 1785. Children: John, Jesse, Obadiah, William, Elizabeth, Joel, Hannah, James, Isaiah, Samuel, Jeremiah. D 1835. Bur in Glady Creek Cem near Springhills. Ref: Mrs. Sylvia Fuson Ferguson, Cincinnati, O. Fur infor Urbana and Cincinnati Chaps.

GABRIEL, ABRAHAM, (Athens Co.)

Served in Capt. Sam'l Roger's Company, 1st Bn, Cumberland Co., Mil Commanded by Col J. A. Dunlap of Pa. Pvt. July 31, 1777. Br Oct 18, 1746 in Virginia. Mar Nancy J. Bartlett 1786. Children: Abraham, Elias, Reason, Polly, Henry, Dorcas, Basil, Nathaniel. D Athens Co, O., Apr 13, 1845. Bur Union Cem. (Pres. Churchyard) Hebbardsville, Athens Co, O. Order for a marker has been sent to the Government by the Nabby Lee Ames Chap. of the D. A. R. 1925. Ref: unpublished records of the descendants, Pa. Archives, Third Series, Vol. 23, p 613 and 640. Fur infor Nabby Lee Ames Chap.

GADDIS, THOMAS, (Clinton Co.)

Bur Gaddis Cemetery, near Wilmington, O. Fur infor George Clinton Chap.

GAGE, ABNER, (Ashtabula Co.)

Crippled for life at Battle of Bunker Hill. Br Pelham, N. H. 1753. Parents: Capt Daniel Gage and Ruth Kimball. Mar 1st wife: Susan Ober. Children:

John, Joshua, Stephen, Eliphalet, Polly, Ruth. D 1814, Gagesville, Ashtabula Co. Bur in Edgewood, Ashtabula, O. Ref: V 36, p 357 D. A. R. Lin, Hist of Ashtabula Co. Fur infor Mary Stanley Chap.

GAGE, REUBEN, (Hamilton Co.)

Br Mass. 1766. D 1849. Ref: S. A. R. Fur infor Cincinnati Chap.

GALL, GEORGE JR., (Highland Co.)

Served from Rockbridge Co, Va. 1781; and several shot enlmts. Present at surrender of Cornwallis. Br 1766, Berks Co, Pa. Mar: 1st wife: Susannah Nicholas. Children: Susan. D 1852, Highland Co, O. Bur Old Dutch Cem, Brushcreek Twp. GM by 316 descendants, monument unveiled Aug 26, 1905. After war, went to Pendleton, Vt. thence to Highland Co.O., where pensioned, 1832. Ref: No 45144, Vol 46, p 59. Fur infor Waw-Wil-a-Way Chap.

GALLOWAY, JAMES, (Clark Co.)

Pvt in Samuel Halliday's Company, 1778 and later in Clarke's Expedition against the Indians. Gave valuable service in Pa. and Ky. Pvt in Capt John Hatton's Company, Watt's Regt, 1776. Br Oct 16, 1756. Parents: William and Isabella Galloway. Mar 1st wife: Rebecca Junken. 2nd wife: Mary Barton, Sept 29, 1795. Children: James, 1st wife. D Apr 21, 1832, on farm 1 1-4 miles south of Enon, O. Not platted. MI "The grave of James Galloway—a soldier of the Revolutionary War." GM by S. A. R. and family; James Galloway D Apr 21, 1832, aged 75 yrs, p mos, 5 das, about 1910. Came to Ohio 1798, from Ky to take up land grant of 400 acres 1½ miles south of Enon, given him for Revolutionary War service; brought his anvil on a sled from Cincinnati. Blacksmith. Body was moved from farm to present location Enon Cem 1-4 miles northeast of Enon, O. by D. A. R. and S. A. R. Ref: Family Bible; Histories of Clark Co. Natl No D. A. R. 5209 and 6612. Fur infor Lagonda Chap.

GALLOWAY, JAMES SR., (Greene Co.)

Pvt.. In 1778 was in Capt Samuel Holliday's Company, Cumberland Co, Pa. Mil. and later served in Clark's Expedition against the Indians. Pensioned 1831, age 84. Br May 1, 1750 in Pa. Parents: George Galloway. Mar Rebecca Junkin, 1778. Children: George, James Jr., Joseph William, Rebecca, Andrew, Ann, Anthony, John. D Aug 6, 1838, Xenia. Bur Massie's Creek graveyard. MI "A soldier of the Revolution." Living at Beaver Creek, 1797. Ref: Pennsylvania Archives; Robinson's History of Greene County. Natl No 62,525, Vol 63, p 175, D. A. R. Lin. Fur infor Catherine Greene Chap.

GALLOWAY, JOSEPH, (Greene Co.)

Pvt. Br Pa 1757. Parents: George Galloway. Mar Isabelle Orr. Children: George, William, John, Jane Isabelle, Joseph, Jr., James, Sophia, Ann Eliza, Elizabeth. D Aug 18, 1838, Wolf Lake, Ind. Pa Archives; Robinson's History of Greene Co. Fur infor Catherine Greene Chap.

GALPIN, DANIEL, (Summit Co.)

Pvt and Corp fr Mch 3, 1777 to June 1783. Member of 4th Tr, Col Elisha Sheldon's Light Dragoons, Captains were Epaphras Bulland George Hurlburt. Conn records show he also served in Col Erastus Wolcott's State Regt at Boston Jan to Mch, 1776. Br Dec 31, 1757, Berlin, Hartford Co, Conn. Mar Mehetable Dorr. Children: Father of four daus and a son; one dau, Hettie, mar Seth Sacket, Yale man and Congregational minister from Warren, Conn., Oct 19, 1831. D July 9, 1844, Akron. Bur Glendale. After death of wife and children in Conn came to Akron to live with Hettie. So dearly beloved that house in which he lived was torn down at his death and memorial church built for him, where he had consecrated it with prayer. Fur infor Cuyahoga-Portage Chaps.

GAMBLE, JAMES, (Richland Co.)

Corp in N. Y. Mil. Br Dec 30, 1759. D June 1, 1841. Bur Old Cem Shelby. MI: name and state Tr. GM Mary Washington D. A. R. Chap, bronze marker in 1811. Pensioned 1840, age 81, Vernon Twp. Fur infor Mary Washington Chap.

GANER, PETER, (GAINER, GARDNER), (Tuscarawas Co.)

Enrolled in 1779 for the term of the war in Capt James Lee's Company, Second Continental Artillery (see Pa Archives, Series 5, Vol 3, pp 1047, 1051, 1052, 1080). Name appears Gainer and Gardner in some of these records. D at Ragersville Bur at Ragersville. MI: "Peter Ganer, 2nd Art, Cont. Troops, Rev. War." U. S. Government furnished grave marker about 12x4x36 inches in recent yrs. Dr. H. J. Peters, Civil War Veteran, was instrumental in having grave marked. Little is known about him. Not known that he had any descendants. Local report is that "after his death, his widow and adopted dau returned to Pa." His name appears on Soldiers' Memorial in Gnadenhutten Cem erected in 1927. This infor fur by Charles L. Stocker, Esq., Cleveland, O. on request of Jane Dailey, State Chairman.

GANSON, NATHAN, (Geauga Co.)

Mass Continental Line. Placed on pens roll 1818. Br New Salem, Miss. 1755. Mar Rebecca Childs. Children: Mary (Mrs. Jonah Johnson), Joseph. D Newbury, O. 1827. Bur South Newbury Cem No. 1 Grave has been marked by flag by patriotic citizens. Estate administered by Geauga Co Court June 4, 1827. Ref: Natl No D. A. R. Roll 55909. Fur infor Taylor Chap.

GARD, GERSHOM, Hamilton Co.)

Was in Morris Co Mil. Br 1736 Morristown, N. J. D 1807 (1818) North Bend, O. Ref: S. A. R. See Vol 32, p 154, D. A. R. Lin. Fur infor Cincinnati Chap.

GARD, BENJAMIN, (Brown Co.)

Served as Pvt 1778. Entered Rev about 17 yrs of age. Sgt 1779. Member Capt Jas Denison's Company, Col John Beekman's 4th Regt N. Y. Mil. Br Sept 13, 1760, Exeter, R. I. Mar 1783 2nd wife Lucy Hawk (or Hanks, br 1762 Conn. Other data gives Hawks). Children: Charlotte, Phineas, Simeon, Rodman, Clarissa, Matthew, Lucy, Benjamin. D Mch 1, 1840, Russellville. Bur Family Cem on farm south of Russellville. Government marker for grave by Taliaferro Chap. Mover to Rensselaer Co about 1770; about 1800 moved to Ohio, Brown Co, Union Twp. Farmer. Pensioned 1833. Served in War 1812; pioneer minister of "New Light" Church. Ref: Hist of Brown Co by Beers & Co, 1883, p 101, Mrs. C. A. Lieberman. Natl No 100924 and 78130, Vol 101, p 286, D. A. R. Lin Fur infor Taliaferro Chap.

GARLOUGH, JOHN II, Jr., (Clark Co.)

Pvt 5th Pa Regt. Records show he received $40.00 from Late Pa Line certificate 70565 for pay to Jan 1, 1782; $89.00 for pay to Nov 4, 1783, certificate 88296. Br Washington Co, Md. Parents: John Hunrich Gerlach and Magdalene Schluyzdun. Mar Ann Patton, first wife; and second wife, Margrette Eichelberger. Children: 1st wife, John, Katherine. 2nd wife, Mary, Margaret, Eve, Salome Ann, Jacob, Henry. D 1823 on farm, Pitchin, Clark Co, O. Bur Garlough near Pitchin. Private burial ground, grave not platted. MI: "Garlough." Farmer. Ref: Will in Clark Co court. War department, Washington, D. C. Fur infor Lagonda Chap.

GARNER, HENRY, (Butler Co.)

Name appears on the tablet erected at Hamilton, O. on the site of Ft. Hamilton, and considered as one of the Revolutionary soldiers buried in that county. Lived in Reily Twp. Fur infor John Reily Chap.

GARRIGUS, DAVID, (Butler Co.)

Served 1777 as Pvt in Capt Josiah Hall's Company, Col Ford's Bn of Morris Co, N. J. Tr under command of Brig Gen Williamson. Br 1748 Morris Co, N. J. D 1815 Butler Co, O. Ref: Vol 51, p 315, Natl No 50701, D. A. R. Lin.

GASKILL, SAMUEL, (Clinton Co.)

Lt in N. J. Line. Enl fr Burlington Co, N. J. Br N. J. Jan 2, 1750. Mar Catherine Rea, 1781. Children: Elizabeth, Eli, Thomas, Rea, Samuel Jr., Isaac. D 1821 at Wilmington, Clinton Co, O. Bur in old cem in Wilmington which afterwards became part of the village. The bodies being removed to the new village cem. Here they were all placed in rows. Perhaps the county records would show the number given to each one. Authority quoted "Stryker's "Jerseymen in the Revolution," also Pliny A. Durant's "History of Clinton County." Ref: Natl No 126196 D. A. R. Lin. Fur infor London Chap.

GASTON, THOMAS, (Meigs Co.)

Pvt. Served seven yrs. Br New England, settled in Ohio 1807. Children: Jared, Anson, William, Jonathan, John. D 1823, Rutland. Bur Miles Cem, near Rutland, O. MI "He was a man highly esteemed by all." Millwright, Farmer, Preacher. Fur infor Return Jonathan Meigs Chap.

GATES, DAVID, (Athens Co.)

Served under Capt Wylley 2nd Regt Conn Tr 1775. Br 1723, England. D 1808, Athens Co, O. Ref: Vol 88, p 272, 87877, D. A. R. Lin.

GATES, FREEMAN, (Trumbull Co.)

Br 1767. D Mch 6, 1845. Bur East Farmington Cem, Farmington Twp. MI: "Freeman Gates, died March 6, 1845, aged 78." GM by relatives; an old-fashioned white marble stone. Ref: Frank Housel, East Farmington, O. a descendant. Fur infor Mary Chesney Chap.

GATES, JOHN, Sr., (Richland Co.)

Enl under Gen Washington. Br Feb 14, 1756. D July 11, 1845. Bur Village of Windsor, O. MI: dates and Revolutionary Soldier. GM by Mary Washington D. A. R., bronze marker, 1925. Fur infor Mary Washington Chap.

GATES, TIMOTHY, (Washington Co.)

Pensioned Washington Co, 1818 as Pvt. Mass Continental Line. Br 1747 Stow, Mass. Mar Susanna Marsters. D 1822 Marietta. Ref: No 56206, Vol 57, p 71, D. A. R. Lin.

GAULT, ANDREW, (Mahoning Co.)

Pvt Sept 18, 1776. Br 1764, Ireland. Mar Eleanor Chesney, (1764-1829) 1788. Children: Ebenezer, Robert, Andrew, Rachel, Betsey, Ann. D 1852. Came to Ohio in 1803. Ref: p 147, Vol 2, Hist Trumbull & Mahoning Cos; N. H. Rev Doc Vol 30, p 210. Fur infor Mahoning Chap.

GAUMER, JACOB, Sr., (Muskingum Co.)

Drum Maj in Washington's Army. Mar Catherine, bur by husband. D 1820. Bur New Hope Cem near Adamsville, Salem Twp. Monument placed by great grand-son, C. N. Gaumer, 1927. 1806 he and family came from Pa. to Ohio at Gilbert. He sold ground to New Hope for cem. Two acres for $4.00. Was present at the surrender of Cornwallis army at Yorktown. Fur infor Muskingum Chap.

GAVITT, WILLIAM, (Licking Co.)

Enl as a sailor in 1781 at New London, Conn. Served on Brig "Favorite", sloop "Randolph," schooner "De Crops" and brig "Martin." Prisoner twice on the "Jersey." Br Apr 2, 1766, Westerly, R. I. Mar Sarah Babcock, Oct 9, 1785. D Jan 6, 1854, Ashley, Delaware Co, O. Bur Old Cem, Granville, O. GM by Granville 1901. In spring of 1788 he became a resident of Granville, Mass. Emigrated to Granville, O, in 1805. Never pensioned. Ref: Natl No 58557, Vol 59, p 189, D. A. R. Lin. Fur infor Hetuck Chap.

GAYLORD, JOEL, (Summit Co.)

Enl Goshen, Conn. Aug 15, 1777. Pvt; Capt. Albert Chapman's Company Served to end of war. 1778, Musician 7th Reg. Conn. line. Col. Herman Swift at Germantown; at Monmouth. See "Conn. Men of Rev." for further service. "1801 he returned to Conn. and his wife and 6 children (3 sons, 3 dau.) made journey back to Ohio." p 33 Revolutionary Soldiers of Summit Co. D July 24, 1827. Bur College St., Hudson. GM by S. A. R. 1800 came to Hudson, bought 640 acres land (now the Public Square). Influential man, holding civic and church offices. Ref: For data see p 33 Rev. Soldiers of Summit Co. Fur infor Cuyahoga-Portage and Cuyahoga Falls Chaps.

GAYLORD, JOHN, (Portage Co.)

Pvt in Massachusetts Continental line. Placed on pens roll Apr 28, 1818. Bur Franklin, O. Drew pens at Ravenna, O., in 1840. Fur infor Old Northwest Chap.

GAYLORD, JOHNATHAN, (Summit Co.)

Sgt. Capt. Return Jonathan Meig's Company from 1775; from 1776-77 served as carpenter on Frigate "Trumbull" commanded by David Saltonstall. Br Oct 29, 1747, Upper Houses, Middletown, Conn. (See p 150, Vol 71, D. A. R. Lin. for Ref). Mar Elizabeth Goodwin, May 9, 1773, (d 1809). D 1819. Bur Stow Cem. MI: S. A. R. emblem. He and brother Samuel with families came to Ohio, 1808. Fur infor Cuyahoga Falls and Cuyahoga Portage Chaps.

GAYLORD, JUSTUS, (Delaware Co.)

Served through war from Litchfield, Conn. Br 1732. Wife, Elizabeth ———. D 1820, Delaware Co, O. Ref: No 70737, p 265. Vol 71, D. A. R. Lin.

GAYLORD, LEVI JR., Maj., (Ashtabula Co.)

Enl Mch 1776, as artificer in Capt. Gamaliel Painter's Company. Br Mch 30, 1760, Farmington, Conn. Parents: Levi Gaylord. Mar Lydia ——— (She died May 18, 1846). Emigrated to Hartford, N. Y. and in 1806 came on to Geneva, O. At Geneva, O. June 3, 1846. Age 86 yrs. Ref: Natl No 23742, Vol 24, p 260, D. A. R. Lin. "Ashtabula Sentinel."

GAYLORD, SAMUEL, (Summit Co.)

Pvt. under Capt Ebenezer Hill, Col. Webb; 9th Reg; Col. Thos. Belden Regt, Col Increase Mosley Regt; Col Mosley and Enos. See service, p 34 "Rev Soldiers Summit Co." Br Sept 20, 1754, Upper Houses, Middletown, Conn. Mar Azubah Atkins, (dau of James and Rebecca (Stone) Atkins). D Sept 7, 1813 at home of son, John Jennison. Bur at Stow cem. MI: S. A. R. emblem. Only frame building in Cleveland when he and brother Jonathan and families passed through 1808, was Post Office 12 ft. square. Fur infor Cuyahoga Falls and Cuyahoga Portage Chaps.

GEBHART, (GEBHARD), NICHOLAS, (Montgomery Co.) .

Pvt in David Krause's 4th Company, 2nd Bn, Lancaster Co Mill and Pa. Continental Line. Last date of service, July 8, 1782. Br May 30, 1751, Lancaster Co, Pa. Parents: John Peter Gebhardt and Catharina (Meyer) Gebhart. Mar 1st wife, Anna Appolina Kornmann, Dec 8, 1771. Mar 2nd wife ——————? Children: Ann Elizabeth, George, John, Barnhard, Emmanuel, Noah, Anna Margaretha; By 2nd wife, Barbara. D July 15, 1829, Miamisburg, O. Bur Hill Grove Cem, Miamisburg, O. Government marker, 1925, Nicholas Gebhart, Revolutionary War. Pa. mil. GM by Richard Montgomery Chapter S. A. R., by Montgomery Co., bronze marker, 1919. Ref: No 38391 Vol 39, p 143 and No 102239, Vol 103, p 74, D. A. R. Lin. Fur infor Richards Montgomery Chap S. A. R.

GEER, GUERDON, (Summit Co.)

Enl Lebanon, Windham Co., Conn. Mch 20, 1777; served 3 yrs. Pvt under Col. Samuel B. Webb, Capt. Thomas Wooster's Company; in battle of Rhode Island, known to have served as Sgt in Col McClellan's Regt., Capt Eleazer Prentice's Company from Oct 1, 1782 to Nov 29, 1782. Br 1756. Mar Ruth ———. D June 27, 1828. Bur Transferred to Glendale, Sec 1, lot 81. MI: "Capt Guerdon Geer. In Memory of, Died June 27, 1828, age 72 yrs." GM by D. A. R. and 1812 markers. He and wife made journey to Ohio in covered wagon, with team of oxen, settling on what is now known as West Market, Akron, O. Enterprising citizen, aided in buying a printing press, for "The Portage Journal," first paper printed in Summit Co. Undoubtedly he is same man as Capt. Nathaniel Geer, as date of death on stone are same. Fur infor Cuyahoga-Portage Chap.

GEOHEGAN, ANTHONY, (Warren Co.)

Pvt in Capt Benj Brook's 3rd Regt Md Line. Br 1764. Mar 1792, Ann Lilley (Br 1765). D 1837, Lebanon, O. Widow received a pens. Ref: Natl No 100211, Vol 101, p 65, D. A. R. Lin.

GEOHEGAN, JOHN EDMUND, (Warren Co.)

Bur Old Methodist Cem Lebanon, Turtle Creek Twp. Infor fur by S. A. R. Yr Bk, 1917. Filed by Jane Dailey, State Chairman.

GEORGE, JESSE, (Noble Co.)

Served from Pa. Southern part of Brookfield twp. where he lived and died; grave not located. Was pensioned in Morgan Co where living in 1840 (S. A. R.) Fur infor Mrs. L. B. Frazier, Caldwell, O.

GEORGE, JOHN, (Harrison Co.)

Revolutionary pensioner. Lived in Harrison Co in 1833, aged 81; Served in Cumberland or Bedford Co, Pa. Mil. Pa. Archives, 5th series, Vols IV and VI. U. S. Pens Rolls, 1835. Fur infor Moravian Trail Chap.

GERARD, JOHN, (Miami Co.)

Bur Stanton, two miles east of Troy, O. GM by Miami Chap with bronze marker. Fur infor Miami Chap.

GERLACH, (also Henry Gerlough) JOHN HEINRICH, (Clark Co.)

Pvt and Corp in Capt. Bartholemew Van Heer's Independent Tr Light Horse Dragoons. Enl July 1, 1778, Potts Grove, for duration of War. Br Deuchland, Oct 7, 1728. Mar Magdalene Schluyzdum, (born in Switzerland, Jan 16, 1717) Children: John and Adam, only ones mentioned in will. D 1810, Pitchin, Clark Co, O. Bur Garlough, near Pitchin. Private Cem. MI: "Garlough." GM by family name. Farmer. Will in court—War Dept Washington D. C. Fur infor Lagonda Chap.

GIBBS, DANIEL, (Morrow Co.)

Bur in country cem at Shawtown, near Cardington. Ref: Fur infor Mrs. Addie Slack, Delaware, O. Fur infor Mt Gilead Chap.

GIBSON, GEORGE, (Co not stated)

Served as Lt Col in Virginia Line. Br 1740 Lancaster, Pa. D 1791 in Western, O. (May mean western Ohio). Ref: Vol 51 p 48 No 50105. D. A. R. Lin.

GIBSON, JAMES, (Mahoning Co.)

Pvt. Ranger, Lt. and Capt. of 4th Bn. Continental Line Cumberland Co. Mil Pa. Br 1747, Ireland. Mar: Arabella (Anna Belle) (1748-1836) 1777. Children: John, James, Robert, Samuel. D 1817 Youngstown, O. Bur Oak Hill Cem., Youngstown, O. GM by D. A. R. marker, 1915-17. Ref: 436 Vol 1, Hist. Trumbull and Mahoning Co. Pa. Archives, series 3, D. A. R. No 50981. Fur infor Mahoning Chap.

GIBSON, JOHN, (Mahoning Co.)

Pvt. James Coe's 3rd Company 8th Bn, Cumberland Co., Mil. Bur Mahoning Co., probably Poland. Came to Poland. Ref: Pa. Archives, Series 3, Vol 23; p 452. Fur infor Mahoning Chap.

GIBSON, SAMUEL, (Highland Co.)

Served three yrs as spy and Pvt in Va Mil. Br 1761, Cumberland Co, Pa. D Feb. 19, 1835 Highland Co., O. Bur Hillsboro, O, Sec. D, Lot 56. MI "Samuel Gibson died Feb 19, 1835, in 74th yr. Revolutionary Soldier." GM by D. A. R. official marker May 1925. See No. 26,332, Vol 27, p 120-121. Ref: Dr. J. C. Larkin (S. A. R. Cincinnati, O.) Fur infor Waw-Wil-a-Way Chap.

GIFFIN, STEPHEN, (or Griffin) (Knox Co.)

Pvt. 1776 Capt Hugh Campbell's Company; Col Robt McPherson's Regt. Pa. Served 5 enlmts. Br 1753, Lancaster Co, Pa. Mar Mary Donegen 1780. D 1839, Knox Co. Pensioned 1832. Ref: Natl No 75,090 and No 31,271, Vol. 76, D. A. R. Lin.

GIFFORD, JAMES, SEN., (Medina Co.)

Served from Maryland. Br 1755. D Oct. 16, 1829. Aged 74 yrs. Bur Wadsworth-Woodlawn. GM by Western Reserve. Fur infor Western Reserve and Cuyahoga Portage Chaps.

GILBERT, GEORGE (Mahoning Co.)

Ranger Frontier, 1778-1783, Northampton Co. Children: Charles, Jacob, only ones given. Bur Mahoning Co. Came from Pa to Ohio with his son Jacob who was an early settler in this county. Ref: Trumbull and Mahoning Co. History 135. Pa Archives Series 23, Vol 23, p 294. Fur infor Mahoning Chap.

GILBERT, HENRY (Trumbull Co.)

Bur East of center Bazetta. Copied from S. A. R. Yr Bk. Did not look up this grave. Fur infor Mary Chesney Chap.

GILBERT, SEWELL, (Licking Co.)

Enl at Cavendish, Vt in 1780 under Capt Jonathan White and Capt Green. Br Dec 9, 1765, Cavendish, Vt. D St. Albans Twp. Was living 1838. Sept 28, 1832, while living at Springivats, Livingston Co. N. Y. Applied for pension. Allowed. Fur infor Hetuck Chap.

GILBERT TRUMAN, (Portage Co.)

Enl as Pvt Conn State Tr. Apr 1775, served for 2 mos; 1776, 4 mos; 1778, 4 mos; 1778 3 mos 1779, 2 mos; 1782, 2 mos; Capt Beebe, Capt Joseph Carter, Capt Samuel Carter. In battle of New York City. Br 1756, Warren, Conn. Mar Eunice Phippany 1780. Children: Charles, Marvin, Champion, Benjamin, Walter, Lyman, Ezra, Rebecca. D June 15, 1841, Palmyra, O. Bur Palmyra Twp, O. Placed on pension roll on July 6, 1833. Ref: Bureau of Pensions. Fur infor Old Northwest Chap.

GILL, DANIEL, (Vinton Co.)

Enl Baltimore, Md. Mch 1, 1777, under Capt Eichelberger in Col Hartley's Regt, Gen Anthony Wayne's Brigade. Br Aug 18, 1756. Mar Marcy ———— or Nancy ———— who in 1820 was 57 yrs old. D Nov 8, 1843. Bur Old Cem McArthur, O. MI. Name, death and age. At 83 yrs age, pensioned in Elk Twp, Vinton Co. In battle of Iron Hill where he was taken prisoner and held nine months when he escaped from the enemy at Charleston, S. C. Again entered service for 18 mos under Col Wade, at Cheran Hills in N. C., where he served out his time. Pensioned 1818 while residing in Montgomery Co, O. Descendant, C. S. Gill, Athens, O. Ref: War Pensions claim S 42,745—only Daniel Gill in Revolutionary War records. Accepting this infor, Jane Dailey, State Chairman.

GILLESPIE, JAMES, (Montgomery Co.)

D Jan 14, 1840, aged 76 yrs 10 mos. Bur Woodland Cem, Lot 1533, Sect 16. On first Grand Jury, 1804, Montgomery Co. Fur infor Jonathan Dayton Chap.

GILLETT, NATHANIEL, (Summit Co.)

Served as teamster and fife Maj in Revolutionary War. Native of Conn. Br 1755. Mar Lucy Harrison, Apr 16, 1779; she d Sept 5, 1825. Had 9 children. D July 6, 1835. Bur Tallmadge. Native of Conn. Came from Torrington, Conn. with Hosea Wilcox another Revolutionary soldier in 1811, settled in Tallmadge; a wise counselor and Christian. Fur infor Cuyahoga-Portage Chap.

GILLETTE, JOSEPH (Marion Co.)

Pvt in Capt May's Company. Br 1754, Hartford, Conn. D 1836, Marion Co., O. Bur Wyatt graveyard near Waldo. Ref: "Connecticut in the Revolution." Fur infor Capt William Hendricks Chap.

GILLISPIE, WM. (Richland Co.)

Major Pa Tr. Br 1737. D 1841. Bur Bellville Cem, Bellville, O. MI: Name and company. GM by Mary Washington D. A. R. bronze marker, 1911. Pensioned in 1840, age 104, living in Jefferson Twp. Fur infor Mary Washington Chap.

GILMAN, JOSEPH, (Washington Co.)

Member of Board of War for New Hampshire during the Revolution. Br Exeter, N. H., Washington Co. 1738. Mar Rebecca Ives 1746. D in Washington Co. Ref: No. 71,301, p 111, Vol 72, D. A. R. Lin.

GILMORE, JAMES, (Geauga Co.)

Pvt. Lt. Josiah Wilson's Company, Col Porter's (Hampshire Co.) Regt, enl Sept 23, 1777; disch Oct 17, 1777; service 1 mo 2 days; travel included. Company marched northward to re-enforce army under Maj Gen Gates. Br 1754 or 1752, Pelham, N. H. Parents: James and Mary. Mar Nancy ————. Children: Silas, Molly, Susannah, Ashel, Asa, James Jr., Nancy, Reuben; all born in Chester, Mass. D Chester, Geauga Co. O. Bur Old Settlement Cem. MI:

"James Gilmore, died Aug 23, 1829, age 75. Nancy his wife died Nov. 10, 1833, age 77." GM by family. Came to Geauga Co. in 1812. Ref: Vital records Chester, Mass. Gilmore Gen Pioneer; Hist Geauga Co. Probate Record, Geauga Co. Hist. Women of Western Reserve; Mass. Soldiers and Sailors. Fur infor Taylor Chap.

GILSON, DANIEL (not David) SR. (Trumbull Co.)

Pvt State Tr Capt Morse's Company, Putnam's 5th Degt. Pension allowed 1833. Br 1761, Groton, Mass. Mar 2nd wife Rachel ———— 1823. Children: Isaac, Daniel Jr., Eli, Willard and Deborah; by second wife, Joseph, Thomas. D Aug 11, 1845, Middlefield, Geauga Co. Bur Mesopotamia Cem Trumbull Co, O. MI: "Daniel Gilson, died Aug. 11, 1845 aged 83." Continental pay accounts service May 2, 1777, also return dated Oct 24, 1777. Pension and probate records give first name as Daniel, not David. Will probated Sept 13, 1845, Chardon, O. Ref: Pioneer Hist. Geauga Co., p 729, Mass. Soldiers and Sailors, p 468, Natl No 71,599, D. A. R. Vol 72. Fur infor Taylor and Mary Chesney Chap.

GILSON, DANIEL, JR., (Trumbull Co.)

"Served from Mass. Was in Middlefield. Was a pensioner," stated by Western Reserve Chap. Ref: Mary Chesney gives ref to Baldwin Library for "Mesoptamia, Trumbull Co. as place of burial" where we record him, with his father, Daniel Gilson, who lived in Geauga Co. and bur in Trumbull Co. Fur infor Mary Chesney and Western Reserve Chap.

GILSON, DAVID, JR., (DANIEL, JR.,), (Trumbull Co.)

Bur Mesopotamia. Ref: Baldwin Library, Youngstown, O. Fur infor Mary Chesney Chap.

GILSON, ELEAZAR, (Mahoning Co.)

Pvt. Enl Feb. 21, 1777, Capt Strong's Company Conn. Pensioned 1818. Br 1754, Conn. Children: Samuel, Isaac, Lizzie, Cynthia, Marie. Died 1841. Bur Cem in Canfield, O. GM by D. A. R. 1915-17. The following statement was made at time Mr. Gilson applied for pens: "I declare on the honor of an old Revolutionary Officer that I know Eleazar Gilson to be a private soldier in the 5th Conn Regt, 2nd Brig in the army of the U. S. from the year 1777 to 1780, and personal acquaintance with him to be a man of truth. Signed Tryal Tanner, late Lieut and Adj in Conn Regt." Settled 1801 in Canfield, O. Ref: p 198, Conn "Men in the Revolution." Fur infor Mahoning Chap.

GINTHER, PETER, (Tuscarawas Co.)

Pvt Capt Stone's 6th Company, 2nd Bn Lancaster Co Pa Mil, in 1781 and 1782. (See Pa Archives, Series 5, Vol 7, pp 159 and 180). Also served in 1776 and 1777. (See diary of Hebron Moravian Church at Lebanon, Pa). Br Jan 12, 1740, probably in Berks or Lebanon Co, Pa. Parents: Probably son of John Peter Ginther of Oley Hills, Berks Co, Pa. Mar 1st Maria Catherine Williams 1761 or 1762; 2nd Elizabeth Schwarz 1791 or 1792. Children: Christian Frederick, (1764); Susanna (1769); John Peter (1771); Anna Maria (1773); Justina Juliana (1779); Catherine; John Adam (1800); Abraham (1802. Others died in infancy. D Jan 11, 1814 at Gnadenhutten, Tuscarawas Co, O. Bur Moravian Cem. GM by small stone marker, probably erected by family probably soon after his decease. Early life in Lancaster (now Lebanon) Co, Pa. Removed to Bedford Co, Pa. in 1795 and to Gnadenhutten, O. in 1802. Potter and farmer. Name appears on Soldiers' Memorial erected in Gnadenhutten Cem in 1927. D. A. R. Descendant Miss Jennie E. Stewart, Boulder, Colo. Infor Fur by Charles L. Stocker, Esq., Cleveland, O. on request of Jane Dailey, State chairman.

GLANCY, JESSE, (Clermont Co.)

Under Washington; at Brandywine and Monmouth; under immediate command of Lafayette at Yorktown. Br 1756 York Co, Pa. Children: William (b 1784, mar Elizabeth Metcalf); John (br 1786, mar 1st Elizabeth Shields, 2nd Elizabeth Frybarger); Joseph; Elizabeth (mar Judge Pollock); and Mary. D 1831, Clermont Co, O. Came to Williamsburg 1805; bought 1000 acres near Owensville, O. where lived till he died; wounded by a bear and made cripple. D. A. R. descendant 124410. Ref: Index Vol 15 Pa Archives, Vol 4, p 468, 5th Series. Fur infor Cincinnati Chap; fr A. S. Abbott, Bethel, O.

GLASS, MATTHIAS, (Mahoning Co.)

Said by Baldwin to have served as soldier, found record of Freeman in Pa. Came to Pa from Germany. Moved from Beaver Twp to Berlin and named twp after home city. Farmer. Came to Mahoning about 1800. Ref: Pa Archives, Series 3, Vol 23, p 100, Lancaster Co; Series 3, Vol 21, p 68, York Co; Mahoning and Trumbull Co Hist, Vol 2, pp 199-115-116. Fur infor Mahoning Chap.

GLAZE, BASIL, Brown Co.)

Bur Russellville. Fur infor Ripley Chap.

GLAZE, GEN. JAMES LAWRENCE, (Washington Co.)

Served under Lafayette. Br Aug 10, 1757. D June 1825. Bur Harmar Cem, grave moved and tombstone lost, but it told on the tombstone he was a Revolutionary Soldier. Fur infor Marietta Chap.

GLOYD, ASA, (Hamilton Co.)

Br 1757, Mass. D 1833. Ref: S. A. R. Fur infor Cincinnati Chap.

GOFF, JAMES, (Geauga Co.)

Br Middlesex Co, Conn. 1762. Bur Lower Cem. Burton, O. MI: "Died, Feb 8, 1849, age 87. Mary, his wife, died April 1, 1851." Name found in list of pensioners in Census of 1840, as living in Burton, O. Fur infor Taylor Chap.

GOFORTH, WILLIAM, (Hamilton Co.)

Served fr N. Y. Elected Capt 1775; Promoted to Maj for serv in Canada; served on committee of "One Hundred." Br 1731, N. Y. Mar Catherine —— D 1807, Columbia, O. age 76. Attorney, Judge in early courts. One of the founders of the Baptist Church at Columbia, which town he helped organize. Religious leader in early life of Cincinnati and state of Ohio. Aptd by Pres Thos Jefferson Receiver of Public Moneys. Ref: p 273, Vol 11, D. A. R. Lin; Bk L, p 35, Jan 1803, Recorder's office, Hamilton Co. Fur infor Cincinnati, O.

GOLDSBERRY, JOHN, (Ross Co.)

Pvt in Va Continental Line. D Ross Co. His wife is bur in a small cem beyond Greenlands on the Egypt pike, and there is an unmarked grave next hers which we think is his. Fur infor Nathaniel Massie Chap.

GOLDSMITH, BENONI, (Washington Co.)

Pvt in Capt Samuel Jordan Cabell's Company, 6th Va Regt; also Morgan's Rifles Regt Continental Tr; also Capt Benj Taliaferro's Company. Br Jan 9, 1756, Hampshire Co, Va. Mar Angelina ———. Children: William Burfet, John, Angelina, Elizabeth. D Mch 30, 1822. Bur Spindler Farm, formerly Hobby farm, near Caywood, O MI: "Benoin Goldsmith was born Jan 9, 1756. He served 6 yrs and 7 mos in the American Revolution and died Mch 30, 1822. Aged 66 yrs." In 1812 sold property in Hampshire Co, Va, moved family to Ohio. Farmer. Had part of chin shot away. Ref: Adj Gen Office, Washington, D. C. Fur infor Marietta Chap.

GOLDTRAP, JOHN, (Hamilton Co.)

Strykers "N. J. Men in Rev" p 608 says: "1st Bn Capt Ten Eyck's Company." Mar dau of Jas Cuningham (a Revolutionary Soldier). Children: John Jr., (mar Margaret Kitchell, a grand dau of 2 Revolutionary Soldiers). D 1791. Bur near Reading, Hamilton Co, O. Purchased Section 22 in Sycamore Twp. Ref: Mrs. Whallon, Cincinnati D. A. R. Fur infor Cincinnati Chap.

GOODALE, EBENEZER, (Ashtabula Co.)

D Nov 15, 1832, age 79 yrs. Bur in Jefferson, O. Cem. GM by marble slab, and June 14, 1925, metal marker by Eunice Grant Chap D. A. R. Fur infor Eunice Grant Chap.

GOODALE, MAJ. NATHAN, (Washington Co.)

Minute Man in Rev. Capt of Mil in Marietta. Lt 1775; Capt 1777. Br 1743 Brookfield, Mass. Parents: Josiah and Phoebe (Strode) Goodale. D 1793, Belpre Garrison. A Revolutionary marker for him has been placed in the spot in Mound Cem dedicated to those Revolutionary soldiers of the vicinity, the place of whose burial is unknown. Date 1923. Farmer and Bricklayer. Ref: Natl No 32,430, Vol 33, p 143, D. A. R. Lin. Fur infor Marietta Chap.

GOODALL, (Summit Co.)

D July 4, 1843. Bur Copley. Fur infor Cuyahoga-Portage Chaps.

GOODRICH, ABNER, (Monroe Co.)

Pvt 1776 under Capt David Downs; Col Chas Burrall; 1782 under Capt Moody, Col John Lamb's 2nd Continental Artillery. Br 1735, Conn. D 1825, Monroe Co, O. Ref: Vol 86, p 288, Natl No 85750, D. A. R. Lin.

GOODWIN, MAJOR SETH, (Medina Co.)

Pvt New Hartford, Conn. Maj War 1812. Granger served from Md. Br 1758. D 1829. Bur Reed Hill Cem. MI: "Goodwin General." GM by Western Reserve. Fur infor Western Reserve Chap.

GORDON, GEORGE, (Butler Co.)

Pvt Capt William Reppey's Company, Col William Irvine's Pa Regt; also Corp in Canadian campaign. Br 1755, Cumberland Co, Pa. Mar Mary McLean (McClean). D 1826, Butler Co, O. Natl No 42524 and 79476, Vol 43, p 200, D. A. R. Lin.

GORDON, JOHN, (Trumbull Co.)

Bur Champion Cem. Ref: Baldwin Library, by Miss Kyle. Youngstown, O. Fur infor Mary Chesney Chap.

GORDON, THOMAS, (Trumbull Co.)

Br 1766. D Oct 12, 1841. Bur Wilson Cem about 2 miles south of Warren. MI: "D Oct 12, 1841, aged 75 yrs, 7 mos, 12 days." Fur infor Mary Chesney Chap.

GOSS, EBENEZER, (Portage Co.)

Pvt in Pa Continental Line. Placed on pens roll Nov 4, 1819. D Aug 5, 1832. Bur Randolph. Fur infor Old Northwest Chap.

THIRD MEMORIAL ERECTED BY OHIO D. A. R. INSCRIPTION: FORT DEFIANCE WAS ERECTED UPON THIS SITE BY GEN. ANTHONY WAYNE, AUG. 9-17, 1794 AND THUS THE GRAND EMPORIUM OF THE HOSTILE INDIANS OF THE WEST WAS GAINED WITHOUT LOSS OF BLOOD. FROM THIS POINT GEN. WAYNE ADVANCED AGAINST THE INDIANS AND DEFEATED THEM IN THE BATTLE OF FALLEN TIMBERS, AUG. 20, 1794. AT THIS STRATEGIC CENTER IN OCTOBER, 1792, CONVENED THE LARGEST INDIAN COUNCIL EVER HELD ON THE AMERICAN CONTINENT. FORT DEFIANCE WAS AN IMPORTANT MILITARY POST IN THE WAR OF 1812.

GOUGAN, ALEXANDER M., (Belmont Co.)

D Sept 16, 1833, age 86. Bur Union Cem, St Clairsville, O. MI: "Soldier of Revolution." Fur infor Wheeling, W. Va. Chap by Mrs. A. L. McFarland, St. Clairsville, O.

GOWDY, JAMES, (Hamilton Co.)

Br 1758. Pa. D 1849. Ref: S. A. R. Fur infor Cincinnati Chap.

GRAFTON, THOMAS, (Champaign Co.)

Br 1759, Va. D Aug 12, 1851. Bur on Fromme Farm. Fur infor Urbana Chap.

GRAHAM, JAMES, (Jackson Co.)

Mar Susan Cassady, Mch 22, 1842, Jackson Co, records. Fur infor Capt John James Chap.

GRAHAM, JAMES, (Meigs Co.)

In Col Richard Buthle's Regt 9th Pa, in battles of Brandywine, Paoli, Germantown. Served in Commissary at Valley Forge as Capt. Br Carlisle, Pa. Oct 4, 1756. Mar Elizabeth Black. Children: Harvey and Mary. D Rutland, O. Sept 2, 1834. Bur Rutland, old part (Meigs Co.) MI "James Graham born 1756 died 1834." GM by marble head stone, placed by family. Was granted papers to be Justice of the Peace by Gov St. Clair before Ohio was a state, possessed by Pearl Graham Thompson. Ref: Pa Archives Sec Series, Vol 15—p 487. War records of Pa—War Dept Washington D. C. Fur infor Cincinnati Chap.

GRAHAM, JOHN, (Adams Co.)

Pvt in Capt Abel Westfall's Company. Col Abraham Bowman's Va Regt. Br 1751, Norfolk, Va. D 1845, Adams Co, O. Ref: Vol 85 p 87 No 84217, D. A. R. Lin.

GRAHAM, WILLIAM, (Franklin Co.)

Fought at Ticonderoga under Ethan Allen; Pvt N Y Mil Col John Williams. Br 1750 near Belfast, Ireland. D 1822. Bur near Reynoldsburg, O. Came to Ohio 1817. Ref: Natl No 66565 Vol 67 D. A. R. Lin. Fur infor Columbus Chap.

GRAHAM, WILLIAM, (Warren Co.)

Lt in Capt Christopher Crawford's Company. 1st Bn Lancaster Co Pa Mil 1776. Br 1758, County Down, Ireland. Mar 2nd wife, Phoebe Frazie. D 1858 Waynesville, O. Ref: Natl No 70759, Vol 71, p 274, D. A. R. Lin.

GRANGER, JULIUS, (Portage Co.)

Lived at Aurora, where pensioned 1840. Fur infor Old Northwest Chap.

GRANGER, THADDEUS, (Summit Co.)

1781 Sheffield Company, Capt Jeremiah Hickok, Col Elisah Porter's Regt, Berkshire Co, Mass Mil. Br 1765. D Akron, O. 1825. Ref: Natl No 19855. p 315, Vol 20, D. A. R. Lin.

GRANGER, THOMAS, (Summit Co.)

Enl at age of 13 under Col Samuel Brewer and Ebenezer Sprout and Capt Stone. Entered army May 15, 1777 at Sandisfield, Berkshire Co, Mass, as fifer, and at disch June 10, 1783, won rank of Fife Major. Seven yrs serv. Active witness in battles of Bemis Heights, Saratoga, Monmouth, Jamestown and capture of Cornwallis. Br 1764 or 1765, Suffield, Conn. Mar Jemima Kingsbury. Had at least three children—one was Lemuel. D Jan 4, 1848 or 1849 at Middlebury, Summit Co. Bur Mt Hope Cem South Akron. Before coming to Portage Co lived in Steuben Co, N. Y. Ref: Natl No 45978, Vol 46, p 411, D. A. R. Lin. Fur infor Cuyahoga-Portage Chap.

GRANT, ISAAC, (Clinton Co.)

Ohio Pens Roll 1832, for serv as Pvt 1776, in Capt Joseph Coomb's Company, Col Levin Powell's Va Regt. Br 1759 Prince William Co, Va. Mar Elizabeth East. D 1837, Clinton Co., O. Ref Natl No 56962, Vol 57, p 331, D. A. R. Lin.

GRANT, JOHN, (Meig Co.)

Br 1746. Mar (1) Agnes Reed, (br 1749; d 1780.) in 1774; (2) Sarah Boltwood, (br 1761; d Mch 20, 1825). Both marriages Burwick Co., Me. D June 15, 1820. Bur Niles Cem, Rutland, O. Slabs. John-Sarah, Beneath old elm. MI: "John Grant departed this life June 15, 1820 in the 74th yr of his age." Ref: of (1st mar) Mrs Della Smith Windsor of Middleport, O; of (2nd mar) Mrs A A Hugg. Fur infor Return Jonathan Meigs Chap.

GRANT, NOAH, Capt., (Columbiana Co.)

Lived in Liverpool Twp, Columbiana Co. Fur infor Bethia Southwick Chap.

GRANT, WILLIAM, (Hamilton Co.)

Br 1751, Virginia. D 1827. Fur infor Cincinnati Chap.

GRAY, DANIEL, (Warren Co.)

Served 2nd Essex Regt, New Jersey; also Capt Craig's State Tr. Br 1749 Morris Co, NJ. Mar Phoebe ———. Children: Catherine, (br 1791 in NJ came to Ohio with parents; mar Hervey Munger 1812). D 1843 Warren Co, O. Natl No 28958, Vol 29, p 350, D. A. R. Lin. Fur infor Mrs. Stanley C. Cash, Oakland, Coles Co., Ill. Ex Vice Regent Sallie Lincoln Chap, on request of Jane Dailey. State Chairman.

GRAY, FRAZIER, (Marion Co.)

Pvt in Capt George Smith's Company, 2nd Regt Delaware Mil. Enl at the age of 18 as a substitute for his brother-in-law for a term of 6 months, at the expiration of which time he re-enlisted for the duration of the war. Br 1761 NJ. Mar Elizabeth Lockwood, 1796. D 1849, Marion Co, O. Bur Union Cem. MI: "A soldier of the Revolution from the state of Delaware, Frazier Gray died in Oct 1849, aged 89 yrs. After a life of integrity and honor he quietly passed away from earth without a murmur or a struggle, content alike with life and death." Ref: Sec 55, 914 Vol 56, p 406, D. A. R. Lin. Fur infor Capt William Hendricks Chap.

GRAY, JOHN, (Noble Co.)

His father fell at White Plains, where John, age 16 took up the musket and served rest of war. Was at Williamsburg, Yorkstown, and on Maj Ramsay Expedition. Mustered out Richmond, Va. Br Jan 6, 1764, Mt. Vernon, Va. Mar twice in Va. once in Ohio, by his stone is one, reads "Catherine Gray, br May 28, 1779, died July 6/1764, aged 85 yrs, 1 mo, 8 da." Had Children (no names given). Lived his last yrs with a dau. D Mch 29, 1868 at Hiramsburg O; aged 104 yrs. Bur Hiramsburg, O. in family graveyard, near his old home. MI: Name, dates, and "The last of Washington's companions." "The hoary head is a crown of glory." His first day's work after the war was for Gen Washington. In 1795 left Mt Vernon, for Grave Creek. About 1803 came to Noble Co., O. Could read and write. Quiet, kindly, generous, good Christian. Farmer. In 1866 Congress granted him a pens of $500. Said to be the Last Surviving Soldier of the Revolutionary War. Ref: pp 356 and 357 Howe's Historical Collection of Ohio. Infor fur by Jane Dailey, State Chairman.

GRAY, NATHANIEL, (Medina Co.)

Pvt in Charlotte Co Mil. Br 1760, Pelham, Mass. D 1853 Seville, O. Ref: Natl No 52,921, Vol 59, p 315. D. A. R. Lin.

GRAY, ROBERT, (Warren Co.)

Mil under Gen Putnam and Gen Watts. Attached to Reg. Tr. who attacked British landing at Sandy Hook; served against Indians up Juanita River. Capts Sweilertt and John Robinson. Br 1747, Moneagle, near Londonderry, Ireland. Parents: Rev. Wm. Gray, (son of Rev. Neil Gray) (Pres) Mar Agnes Gray, Mifflin Co., Pa. (not relation, tho same name) D 1831. Children: Two named James, d soon; William, Richard, Robt. Marg, James, John G., Hugh, Jonathan, Martin. D 1843 near Franklin, Warren Co. An uncle who reared him gave him passage to America where he landed at Philadelphia, 1764. In 1806 moved to Ohio, taking up a farm in Butler Co. S. A. R. descendants, J. Edwards Ritchie, Cincinnati. Fur infor Cincinnati Chap.

GRAY, WILLIAM, (Preble Co.)

Entered American army as Capt of a Cav Company under Gen Francis Marion. Bore for short time the post of Maj under Gen Washington. Br 1755, Pa. D Mch 8, 1849, Dixon Twp. Bur Friendly Church Cem. Enl 1778. Served 3 yrs under Col John Colyer and James Degan, North Carolina. Descendants: Rhea family, Eaton, O. Fur infor Grace C. Miller, Org Reg, Eaton, O.

GRAY, WILLIAM, (Washington Co.)

Enl as Pvt in 1778 at 17 yrs of age and served to the close. At the attack of Stony Point was promoted to Lt. Br Mch 26, 1761, Lynn, Mass. Mar Mary Diamond, of Salem. D July 1812, Beverly, O. Bur near Waterford, O. GM Marietta D. A. R. In autumn of 1787 he joined the Ohio Company and had charge of one of the wagons that transported the first band of pioneers to Ohio. Joined settlement at Waterford; 1791, command of Ft. Tyler. Ref: Hildreth's Pioneer History. Fur infor Marietta Chap.

GREEN, BENJAMIN, (Licking Co.)

Enl as Pvt. Loudoun Co. Va, June 1777. Was at Yorktown. Served 3 enlmts. Was at surrender of Cornwallis. Br 1757, Allegheny Co, Md. Mar Catherine Beam (first wife); Mrs. Lewis (second wife). D 1835, Bowling Green Twp. Bur Green family cem. MI: "Revolutionary War." GM Hetuck Chap. 1909. Emigrated to this county in 1800. Was a pensioner. Ref: History of Licking Co. by E. M. P. Brister. Natl No 31,314, Vol 32, p 133,134 D. A. R. Lin. Fur infor Hetuck Chap.

GREEN, DUTY, (Washington Co.)

Enl from Lanesborough, Mass. Discharged Dec 12, 1781. Br 1761. D 1842. Bur in graveyard between Barlow and Watertown, Washington Co. O. GM Marietta Chap. with Revolutionary marker, 1922. Ref: Mass Soldiers and Sailors in Revolution. Fur infor Marietta Chap.

GREEN, GRIFFIN, (Washington Co.)

Quartermaster and paymaster. Served as commissary to the R. I. Tr in 1775. In 1777 was paymaster in Christopher Green's Regt. Br Feb 20, 1749, Warwick, R. I. D 1804 Marietta, O. Bur Mound Cem, Marietta, O. GM Marietta Chap with Revolutionary marker and on gateway, Nov. 30, 1906. Fur infor Marietta Chap.

GREEN, JOEL, (Hamilton Co.)

Br 1757, Conn. Ref: S. A. R. Fur infor Cincinnati Chap.

GREEN, JOHN, (Ottawa Co.)

Mass State Tr. Pensioned 1833. Age 78. D Ottawa Co, O. Fur infor Taylor Chap.

GREEN, JOHN, (Washington Co.)

Enl July 13, 1775 as Pvt in Capt Seth Washburn's Company. Br 1759 Leicester, Mass. D Apr 11, 1832, Marietta, O. Bur Mound Cem, Marietta, O. MI: "A soldier from his youth, first in the cause that freed our country from a tyrant's laws, and then through manhood to his latest breath, in the best cause which triumphs over death." GM Marietta Chap with Revolutionary marker. Replaced in 1920. Fur infor Marietta Chap.

GREEN, JOSEPH, (Lake Co.)

Enl from Muncy, Pa. in Aug, 1779 under Capt Samuel Brady. In May 1782, he enl for the war in a company of Rangers, commanded by Capt Thos. Robinson in Col Samuel Hunter's Regt. Pensioner. Br Feb 26, 1767 in Sussex Co., N. J. Parents: Ebenezer Green. Children: Ebenezer Jr killed by Indians Apr 16, 1782. D 1853. Bur Madison, O. Came to Madison in 1817. A large man of excellent character and proud that he could give some service to his country. The statement was made at the time of his death that he was the youngest Revolutionary Soldier. Fur infor New Connecticut Chap.

GREENWAY, JEREMIAH, (Washington Co.)

Br May 7, 1758, Newport, O. D Nov 15, 1828, Waterford, O. Bur about 3 1/2 miles fr Waterford, O. MI: "In memory of Jeremiah Greenway, Esq. An officer in that army which bid defiance to Britain's power and established the independence of the United States. Who was born at Newport, Rhode Island, May 7th, 1758 and died at Waterford, O. Nov 15, 1828 in the 71st yr of his age." GM Marietta D. A. R. Fur infor Marietta Chap.

GREERY, JOHN, (Harrison Co.)

Rev pensioner. Served in the Pa Mil. U S Pension Rolls, 1835. Living in Harrison Co in 1833, aged 82. Fur infor Moravian Trail Chap.

GREGG, JOHN SR., (Greene Co.,)

Lt 13th Regt Pa Line. Pensioned 1826. Br Pa. D June 15, 1834. Bur Massie's Creek churchyard (Stevenson's) Living in Xenia, 1806. Ref: Robinson's History of Greene Co. Fur infor Catherine Greene Chap.

GREGORY, JACOB, (Mahoning Co.)

Pvt 5th Bn, Philadelphia Pa 1787. Mar Katherine ————. Bur Ellsworth Cem. Settled in Ellsworth Twp. Farmer. Ref: Pa Archives, Series 6, Vol 3 p 1160. Fur infor Mahoning Chap.

GREGORY, NEHEMIAH, (Fayette Co.)

Served as Pvt in Westchester Co, NY Regt, under Gen Thomas. Br 1755 Gregory Point. D 1818 Fayette Co, O. Ref: No 93975 Vol 94, p 301. D. A. R. Lin.

GREINER, GEORGE, (Greene Co.)

Pvt. Br 1764. Mar Catherine Whitfel. Children: John, Jacob, Catherine, Jane. D 1828. Bur Bath Twp. Living in Greene Co about 1810. Ref: Pa Records. Fur infor Catherine Greene Chap.

GRIFFIN, DANIEL, (Hamilton Co.)

Pvt under Capt Deams (or perhaps name was Beams) Dec 23, 1776, 7th Regt. Found on muster roll. See p 305 Archives Md Hist Society. D Hamilton Co. Daniel Griffin was commissioned by St Clair as Lt in State Mil. He entered warrant No 147 in Registrar's Office and located Sec 7, Twp 3, now Springfield Twp and established a station named Griffin's Station 1/2 mile west of White Station. His brother Robert was associated with him later. Was a Cincinnati Officer. Ref: Entered warrant July 23, 1792. See p 41 "Teetor's Hist." Fur infor Cincinnati Chap. Sent by Mrs. E. P. Whallon.

GRIFFIN, ROBERT, (Hamilton Co.)

Served as Sgt Eastern Bn, Morris Co, N. J. Bur Hamilton Co. Brother to Daniel. p 465 "Strykers." Fur infor Cincinnati Chap.

GRIFFIS, DAVID, (Butler Co.)

Lived north of Princeton, Butler Co, O. Name appears on the tablet erected at Hamilton, O. on the site of Ft Hamilton, and considered as one of the Revolutionary soldiers bur in that county. Fur infor John Reily Chap.

GRIFFITHS, SAMUEL, (Fayette Co.)

Capt 3rd Md Regt. Commissioned Dec 10, 1776 and resigned Aug 1778. Pay roll shows time as 12 days. Wounded at Monmouth, June 28, 1778. Mar 1780 Mary ———. Children: Elijah. D 1833. Bur Old Hidy Cem near Bookwalter in Fayette Co, O. near grave of Elijah Griffith and Susannah. Infor received from a descendant who has the old Bible. Natl No 203141. Ref: War Dept. Hietman's Hist Regt. Fur infor William Horney Chap.

GRIGGS, DEACON ICHABOD, (Muskingum Co.)

Represented Holland in the Assembly 1775-77. Br 1718. D 1790, Norwich, O. Natl No 22978, p 345, Vol 23, D. A. R. Lin.

GRIMES, JAMES REV., (Butler Co.)

D Mch 16, 1846 Middletown, O. Bur Union twp. Name appears on the tablet erected at Hamilton, O. on the sight of Ft Hamilton and considered as one of the Revolutionary soldiers bur in that county. Fur infor John Reily Chap.

GRIMES, JOHN, COL., (Montgomery Co.)

3½ yrs Pa line, Col Chamber's Regt. Several other services; honorably discharged by Lt Col Robinson at Trenton, N .J. Br 1755 Lancaster Co, Pa. Parents: Samuel Grimes. Mar Susanna Martin (br 1761 Lancaster Co, Pa. and d Dec 14, 1827 dau of Alexander Martin). Children: Samuel, Alexander (br Apr 27, 1790, d Jan 12, 1860); John; Eliza (mar 1830 Samuel Bacon). D May 13, 1836, Dayton, O. Bur Woodland Cem, lot 135-36 Sec 77. MI: Names and dates. GM: S. A. R. bronze marker by Richard Montgomery Chap. July 2, 1921. From Lancaster Co Pa to Ky near Marysville, then to Ohio 1804 to Chillicothe; 1808 to Dayton. Kept tavern. Ref: Edgar's Early Dayton p 109. Fur infor Jonathan Dayton Chap and S. A. R. of Dayton.

GRISWALD, ALEXANDER, (Summit Co.)

Entered Revolutionary army in 1776, and was one of the force with Washington which undertook to protect New York City. Was one of the American prisoners placed on board the prison ship "Jersey," after battle of Long Island. Served under Capts Peter Curtis and Alex Catlin, and Col Beebe, Conn Line; prisoner in 1782. Br Oct 1760, Goshen, Conn. Mar Lucy Humphry Oct 30, 1790. (Wife d Dec 6, 1821, bur at Tallmadge). D April 26, 1850, Norton Twp. Bur Western Star Cem. MI: "A soldier of the Revolution." Early settlers of Tallmadge Twp; of great physical strength and eccentric in dress and habits. Natl No 13252. Vol 14, p 95, D. A. R. Lin. Fur infor Cuyahoga-Portage Chaps.

GRISWOLD, ZACHEUS, (Trumbull Co.)

Br Windsor, Conn. 1731. D May 12, 1819. Bur Braceville. MI: "Zacheus Griswold, by Windsor, Conn. D May 12, 1819. Age 88." GM by relatives, and kept in good condition. Will probated 1819. Fur infor Mary Chesney Chap.

GROSCOAT, DANIEL, (Seneca Co.)

Pvt Pa Line. Br about 1730, Pa. D 1811, Seneca Co, O. Bur Old Cem on Kilbourne Road north of Republic, O. GM in 1927. Ref: Vol 86, p 333, No. 85871 D. A. R. Lin. Fur infor Dolly Todd Madison Chap.

GROVE, WINDLE (or WENDELL), (Mahoning Co.)

Ranger, Northampton Co, Pa. also Pvt Northampton Co Continental Line. Pensioned Apr 1833. Br 1750, Northumberland Co, Pa. Mar 1st May ——; 2nd Jane Coon (d 1857). Children: 1st wife: Catherine, David, Benjamin, Susan, Elizabeth; 2nd wife: Jacob, Andrew, Maria, Eve, John, Orlando, Joseph, Abraham, Reuben. D Dec 19, 1849, Austintown, Bur Springfield, Mahoning Co. Farmer, carpenter by trade. Came to Ohio 1805-06. Ref: p 137, Vol 2, Hist Trumbull and Mahoning Co. Pa Archives, Series 3, Vol 23, p 242; Series 3, Vol 23, p 592; Series 5, Vol 4, p 279. Fur infor Mahoning Cap.

GUEST, MOSES, (Hamilton Co.)

Ensign in Capt Voorhees Company, 3rd Regt Middlesex, N. J. Sept 8, 1777. Capt 2nd Regt Middlesex. (p 392, Strykers Men from N. J.), Br Nov 7, 1755, New Brunswick, N. J. Parents: Henry (1727-1815) and Ann (Maddock) Guest (br 1722). Mar Lydia Dumont, (1778-1822). Bur by husband. Children: Henry Cornelius, Mary Ann, Lydia Jane, Elizabeth, Sarah Amelia, Sophia Hay. D Mch 22, 1828, Cincinnati, O. Bur Presbyterian Cem near corner of Park near Race St. Elder 1st Presbyterian Church, Cincinnati. Early at Cincinnati. An old street in Cincinnati still bears name Gest. Ref: T. M. Reynolds, Norwood, Cincinnati, O., son of Revolution. Fur infor Cincinnati Chap.

GULIC, FERDINAND, (Pickaway Co.)

Pvt under Capt Shenard, Col Chambers. In battles at Millstone Creek and Monmouth. Br Nov 15, 1756, Sussex Co, N. J. Mar Hannah Lee, 1789. Children: Eliahs, John, William, Amos, Daniel, Stephen. D Oct 1832, Pickaway Co, O. Bur Coleman Hill Cem, Pickaway Co, O. Fur infor Mt Sterling Chap.

GUMP, WILLIAM (Champaign Co.)

D 1842. Bur in Old Ward St Cem, Urbana. Fur infor Urbana Chap.

GUNSALUS, HENRY (Hamilton Co.)

Br 1759, New York. D 1839. Ref: S. A. R. Fur infor Cincinnati Chap.

GUSEMAN, JOHN, (Fairfield Co.)

Bur Guseman Burial Ground. Fur infor Elizabeth Sherman Reese Chap.

GUSTIN, AMOS, (Adams Co.)

Served fr Va in Gen Morgan's famous riflemen; at Cowpens he was wounded in shoulder. Br Florida, Orange Co, N. Y. Sept 7, 1753. Mar Susannah Jones (br 1770 Pa, d 1825) in Ky. Children: Sarah (mar Jos Gray), John (mar Susannah Scott), Thomas (mar Mary ——), Amos, William, Grizella (mar Geo Shelby), Alpheus Jones, Jeremiah W, Rebecca (mar Ramsey), Susan Jones, Jacob Jones, Samuel Jefferson, Benejah. D 1821, Adams Co, O. Bur on Squire" Enos Reed farm at Marble Furnace. Moved to Adams Co, O, 1795, in Bratton Twp. Ref: A. S. Abbott, Bethel, O. Fur infor Cincinnati Chap.

GUSTIN, BENAJAH, (Warren Co.)

Pens roll 1832, Warren Co, O. for serv. Pvt 1779-82. Capt Jacob Steele, Emanuel Blanford and James Bunnell, Sussex Co, N. J. Mil. Br 1766, Sussex, N. J. Mar Eleanor Bunton 1789. D 1835, Warren Co, O. Natl No 79409. Ref: Vol 80.

GUTHERIE (GUTHERY), JOHN, (Pike Co.)

Capt of Washington Co, Pa Mil. 1780 to 1790; Capt of 2nd Company, 4th Bn Washington Co, 1783 to 1790; also a return of same service. Aug 19, 1793. Br Apr 14, 1744, Pa. Parents: Scotch-Irish. Mar Lydia Baldwin, Mch 13, 1771. Had twelve children. One was Rebecca, wife of James Daniels, br Jan 21, 1786, d June 16, 1819, was the mother of Eliza D Stewart, known as "Mother Stewart" the originator of the Woman's Crusade, and 1st President of W. C. T. U. D June 1, 1823, on his farm, Pike Co. Bur Mound Cem on his original land. He is buried on the mound in center. GM Bricks and stones around the grave. Will be marked soon by Nathaniel Massie Chap D. A. R. Traveled down the Monongahela and Ohio Rivers to Portsmouth in 1798, thence up the Scioto to what is now Pike Co. Claimed land several miles south of where he afterwards laid out the town of Piketown. Was instrumental in making it the county seat of Pike Co. Was known as Col Gutherie and very prominent. Ref: Natl No. 172,874, et al. Fur infor Nathaniel Massie Chap.

GUTHRIE, JOHN, (Mahoning Co.)

Adj, Lt, Capt. Mar Sarah Davis. Children: Robert, William, John Prudentialis, Sarah. Bur Presbyterian Cem, Poland, O. Ref: Pa Archives Series 2, Vol 13, p 89; Series 3, Vol 23, p 14; Series 4, p 43. D. A. R. No. 77,619. Fur infor Mahoning Chap.

GUTHRIE, WILLIAM, (Mahoning Co.)

Ranger, Capt of Westmoreland Co Company of Rangers. Br 1766. D 1808. Bur Poland, O. Ref: Pa Archives, Series 3, Vol 23, p 547; Series 3, Vol 23, p 231; Series 5, Vol 5, p 443. Fur infor Mahoning Chap.

GWIN, JOHN, (Holmes Co.)

Enl 1776 as drummer under Capt Sullivan, Va Tr; served till 1779. Br 1763. D Apr 7, 1844, Holmes Co, O. Bur Salem Cem Holmes-Coshocton Co line, Killbuck and Clarke Twp. MI "John Gwin, Apr 7, 1844, age 82 yrs, 1 mo, 23 das. A soldier of the Revolution under Gen Washington, who fought for freedom's cause." Ref: Vol 90, p 131, No. 89,403 D. A. R. Lin. Fur infor W. C. Chapman, Millersburg, O, on request of Jane Dailey, State Chairman.

GWINNUP, GEORGE, (Hamilton Co.)

Br 1754, N. J. D 1840. Ref: S. A. R. Fur infor Cincinnati Chap.

HACKETT, ALLEN, (Ashtabula Co.)

D Oct 17, 1841. Aged 84 yrs. Pensioned. Bur Jefferson, O Cem. GM by marble slab, and June 14, 1925, metal marker by Eunice Grant Chap. Fur infor Eunice Grant Chap.

HADDEN, WM., (Muskingum Co.)

Soldier in Revolutionary War and served five yrs. Ensign. Date of commission Apr 25, 1758. Bn of Hon Wm Denny Ince of Pa. Col in chief. Ref: Pa Archives, Series 5, Vol 1, p 129; p 180-202-266. Family data in Muskingum Co. History, p 473. William Haden came from Pa to Ohio, settling in Muskingum Co about 1820. Fur infor Muskingum Chap.

HAGEMAN, ADRIAN, (Hamilton Co.)

Br 1747, N. J. D 1821. Ref: S. A. R. Fur infor Cincinnati Chap.

HAHN, MICHAEL, (Hamilton Co.)

Br 1757, Pa. D 1792. Ref: S. A. R. Fur infor Cincinnati Chap.

HAIN, (HANES) CHRISTOPHER, (Medina Co.)

Served from Mass. Bur Spencer Cem. GM D. A. R. Fur infor Western Reserve Chap.

HAINES, BENJAMIN, (Ashtabula Co.)

Pvt. D Feb 22, 1844. Fur infor Mary Redmond Chap.

HAIR, JOHN, (Clermont Co.)

In 1840, was drawing a pens in Jackson Twp, Clermont Co, O. for service. Aged 86 yrs, while living with Arthur Clark. Br 1754. In 5th Series, Vol 7, Pa Archives; On Muster Roll of Lancaster Co, Mil, 1781, 3rd Bn 7th Company, name of "John Hair" is found. This given for investigation, and may prove to be this record. Fur infor Cincinnati Chap.

HAKE, FREDERICK, (Trumbull Co.)

Bur Union Girad, O. MI: Old stones standing, inscription effaced. Name from S. A. R. Yr Bk. Fur infor Mary Chesney Chap.

HALE, ISRAEL, (Union Co.)

Bur Richmond Cem, Claiborne Twp. Fur infor Hannah Emerson Dustin Chap.

HALE, P., (Union Co.)

Bur Richmond Cem, Claiborne Twp. Fur infor Hannah Emerson Dustin Chap.

HALE, WILLIAM, (Montgomery Co.)

Teamster at battle of Cowpens, S. C. in 1781. Br Mch 29, 1763 in Newberry District, S. C. Mar Mary Kammack (br Oct 11, 1775, d 1837.) Children: James, John, Dorothy, Juanna, Mary, Hannah, Samuel, Sarah Ann and Dr William Hall. D Mch 3, 1858 in Butler Twp, Montgomery Co, O. Bur Quaker Cem just east of Fidelity on Montgomery-Miami Co line in southeast corner of cem. MI: "William Hall, born March 29, 1763, died March 3, 1858. GM by marble stone erected probably by some of the James Hall family. Date not known. Marked by Richard Montgomery, S. A. R. Chap, July 2, 1927. Montgomery Co. bronze marker.

Was a farmer in S. C. until towards the close of the Revolution and participated as teamster in the Battle of Cowpens. Farmer in Ohio after emigration here in 1804 until death in 1858. He came with the great influx of Quakers from the Carolinas in the early 1800's to avoid slavery. S. A. R. descendants, Charles J. Hall, 1212 N. Main St., Dayton, O. Fur infor S. A. R. Richard Montgomery Chap.

HALEY, THOMAS, (Harrison Co.)

Served in Capt Lansdale's Company, in Col Josias Carvel Hall's 4th Regt, Md. Line, 1776-1778. Revolutionary Pensioner living in Harrison Co, 1820, aged 74. Br 1746. D 1832. U. S. Pension Rolls, 1835. Ref: Md Archives 18, p 124. Fur infor Moravian Trail Chap.

HALIDAY, ELI, (Erie Co.)

Pvt in Conn Mil. Bur Erie Co. Fur infor Martha Pitkin Chap.

HALL, HEZEKIAH, (Lake Co.)

Br 1755. D Aug 1, 1832. Bur Willoughby, O. MI: "A soldier of the Revolution." Grave marked. Fur infor New Connecticut Chap.

HALL, JOHN, (Butler Co.)

D 1836. Bur on his farm, Hanover Twp. Name appears on the Tablet of Sailors and Soldiers Monument at Hamilton, and supposed to be Revolutionary soldier bur in that Co. Fur infor John Reily Chap.

HALL, JOHN, (Cuyahoga Co.)

Apprentice on frigate "Dean" Mass. Br 1763. D 1849. Bur North Royalton. Fur infor Western Reserve Chap.

HALL, PETER, (Union Co.)

Bur Amrine Cem, Paris Twp. Ref: A great granddaughter, Mrs. James Meidman, 822 W. 5th St., Marysville, O. Fur infor Hannah Emerson Dustin Chap.

HALL, REUBEN, (Jefferson Co.)

Enl from Chester Co, Pa. 1778, under Capt Matthew Saddler, Proctor's Artillery, as an artificer. In 1832 received pens in Jefferson Co, O. for one year's service, Pa line. Br 1755. After war resided for 30 yrs in Berkeley Co, Va. Ref: Vol 37, D. A. R. Lin. No. 36,489, p 174.

HALSEY, JOHN, (Warren Co.)

Pvt in Capt Isaac Gillman's Company, 2nd Regt, Essex Co, NJ Mil. Br 1756, Springfield, N. J. D 1827, Warren Co, O. Natl No 80513, Vol 81, D. A. R. Lin.

HALSEY, JOSEPH, JR., (Hamilton Co.)

Sgt Eastern Bn Morris Co, NJ. Br Springfield, N. J., 1751. Mar Mary Armstrong. D Cincinnati 1796. D. A. R. No 63994, p 335, Vol 64, D. A. R. Lin.

HALSEY, LUTHER, (Hamilton Co.)

Adj 1776, Morris Co, NJ Mil. Br 1758, Morriston, N. J. Mar Sarah Foster, D 1830, Cincinnati, O. Ref: S. A. R. and Vol 71, p 26, No 70070 D. A. R. Lin. Fur infor Cincinnati Chap.

HALSTEAD, EDWARD, (Lake Co.)

Pvt 3rd Regt, NY Mil. Capt John Acker, Hays' Regt. Pensioned. Br 1750, Ulster Co, N. Y. Mar Martha Ferguson. D 1837. Bur Willoughby, O. Ref: p 35, Vol 44, D. A. R. Lin. Natl No 43093. Fur infor New Connecticut Chap.

HALSTEAD, JACOB, (Trumbull Co.)

Pvt NH State Mil. Br July 4, 1757. Mar Charity ———, (d Mch 11, 1856.) D Sept 15, 1837. Bur Township Cem, Johnson. MI: Above dates. His will was probated in Nov 1837 at Warren, Trumbull Co. Fur infor Mary Chesney Chap, Warren.

HALSTEAD, JOHN, (Hamilton Co.)

Br 1754, N. J. Mar Ruth Richardson ——. (See Howes Hist. O. Vol I p 352.) D 1841. Ref: S. A. R. Fur infor Cincinnati Chap.

HAMAKER, JOHN, (Summit Co.)

Pvt 1778, Capt Duncan's Company, Pa. Volunteers. Br 1734, Pa. Mar Mary Pugh. D 1811, Hudson, O. Natl No 77701, Vol 78.

HAMILTON, ALEXANDER, (Preble Co.)

Bur Israel Twp. Fur infor Org. Regent, Mrs. Miller.

HAMILTON, ANDREW, (Preble Co.)

Bur Israel Twp. Fur infor Mary P Mitchell, Eaton, O.

HAMILTON, EDEN, (Medina Co.)

Drummer boy, served from Conn. Br 1762. D 1850. Bur Hamilton Corners. GM Western Reserve. Fur infor Western Reserve Chap.

HAMILTON, JONATHAN, (Co not stated.)

Pvt in Capt Robert Samuel's Company, 8th Bn Cumberland Co. Mil. Br 1761, Washington Co, Pa. Mar Susan Dilts. D 1852, Ohio. Ref: Natl No 99787, Vol 100, p 243, D. A. R. Lin.

HAMILTON, ROBERT, (Warren Co.)

Enl Dec 12, 1776. He was a member of Capt Henderson's Company, 9th Pa Line, commanded by Col Richard Butler and was in Gen Anthony Wayne's command. In 1778 he was a Corp in same company. Br 1757, Ireland. Mar Susanna Kean 1781, Apr 30. 2nd Mar Ann Hayes, Feb 23, 1792. Children: Ist wife: Elizabeth, Joseph, Robert Jr.; 2nd wife: William Hays. D Feb 24, 1841, Lebanon, O. Bur Methodist Cem, Lebanon, Warren Co, O. GM by son William Hays Hamilton. Farmer. Fur infor Taliaferro Chap.

HAMILTON, WILLIAM, (Jefferson Co.)

Br 1747. D 1840. Bur Richmond, Jefferson Co, O. GM Steubenville D. A. R. Fur infor Steubenville Chap.

HAMMITT, GEORGE, (Scioto Co.)

Enl July, 1775 as Pvt for one yr, Capt McClanahan, Col Stephens 2 mos. Capt Ruban Slaughter, Battles Great Ridge. Br Jan 13, 1756, Fanquier Co, Pa. D 1836,

Clay Twp. Not sure which burying ground, Kinney Lane. Enl at Culpeper, Va. Ref: William Burt, Mary Barton, Buffington, Price, Flowers. Fur infor Joseph Spencer Chap.

HAMMOND, ISAAC, (Butler Co.)

Br Apr 4, 1763. D Feb 21, 1847. Bur Greenwood Cem, Hamilton, O. MI: "John Hammond, born April 4, 1763, died Feb 21, 1847." Name appears on tablet under heading Revolutionary soldiers, in Soldiers and Sailors Monument, Hamilton, O. Fur infor John Reily Chap.

HAMMOND, JASON, (Summit Co.)

1779, Pvt in Capt Coon's Company, Col J. Well's Regt. Conn Line. Br 1762, Bolton, Conn. D 1830, Bath, O. Ref: Vol 87, p 83, Natl No 86266, D. A. R. Lin.

HAMPTON, MOSES, (Trumbull Co.)

Br Nov 25, 1762. Mar Hannah, (br Dec 19, 1769; d Sept 7, 1856.) D Nov 26, 1825. Bur Casterline Cem, south of Courtland. MI: "Br Nov 25, 1762, died Nov 26, 1825." Fur infor Mary Chesney Chap.

HAMRICK, DAVID, (Clinton Co.)

Enl 1777 in Fauquier Co, Va for 3 yrs under Col William Washington. Br 1760 in Virginia. Mar Lettice Wyatt, in 1788. D 1839, Clinton, O. Ref: Natl No 100832, Vol 101, p 258, D. A. R. Lin.

HANCHETT, JONAH, (Cuyahoga Co.)

Orderly Sgt under Capts Beebe and Bolen. Cols Strong and Wadsworth, Conn Line. Br 1768, Salisbury, Conn. Mar Sarah Squares 1782. One son was Ebenezer. D 1860, Cleveland, O. Ref: Natl No 101397, Vol 103, p 119, D. A. R. Lin.

HAND, ABRAHAM, (Huron Co.)

Lt in Capt Horton's Company. Enl Feb 26, 1777 or 1779. Sgt Dec 1, 1778. Lt Nov 1, 1779. Br Sept 22, 1760. Mar Mary West, Oct 21, 1784. (daughter of Abner West Revolutionary soldier.) Children: Roxana, Abner, James (?), Harvey, Clarinda, Nelson, Experience, Marcus. D Nov 4, 1840, Fitchville, O. Bur Old Cem northwest of Fitchville. Ref: "Conn Men in Revolution." P 291. Mrs. Ella C. Smith, 56 Buena Vista Ave, Highland Park, Mich; Mrs. Nellie A. Cressner, 40 N. Plum St, Plymouth, Ind.; Sally De Forest Chap.

HANKINS, RICHARD, (Hamilton Co.)

Br 1749, North Carolina. D 1823. Ref: S. A. R. Fur infor Cincinnati Chap.

HANKS, ELIJAH, (Lake Co.)

Served in Conn Line for 8 mos. Enl Mch 10, 1778 in Capt Allen's Company, 3rd Conn Regt under Col Samuel Wylly. Br Aug 30, 1761, Mansfield, Conn. Mar Mary Walker, Aug 14, 1782. (Received pension). Children: Joseph, Elijah twins. (Benjamin and John), Esther, Clarinda and Patty. D Feb 11, 1839. Bur Madison, O. GM D. A. R. marker. Sept 9, 1811, left Willington, Conn for Madison, O., arriving Oct 3rd. Fur infor New Connecticut Chap.

HANNA, JAMES, (Montgomery Co.)

Was in Capt Jacob's Company 1776 and same yr served under Capt James Young. Col Thomas Ewing's Bn Maryland Flying Camp. Br 1752, Ireland. Mar Hanna Bayles in 1782. (br 1761, died 1804). D 1805, Dayton, O. Ref: Natl No 102216, Vol 103, p 67, D. A. R. Lin.

HANNA, JOHN, (Jackson Co.)

In Continental Line, Va. Was with Washington at Monmouth (heard him reprimand Gen See profanely and justly.) Also served under Gen Andrew Lewis in the Dunmore War. Br Greenbriar Co, Va. Mar —— Graham (Grimes). Children: James, Nancy, John, Robert, Christopher, Joseph, Jane, Elizabeth, Martha. D April 11, 1845, aged about 90 yrs at Madison Furnace. Bur Callahan graveyard, near Madison Furnace. GM by D. A. R. Sept 1927. Came to Ohio with son Robert who was one of the county organizers. Applied for and received pens of $96 a yr from July 6, 1825 to his death. Was an old man when he came to live with son Robert and granddaughter Mrs. Martha Callahan in Jackson Co. Ref: Mrs. Ada Carrigan, Jackson, O.; D. W. Williams in articles Jan 29, 1926, Jackson Sunday Journal Fur infor Captain John James Chap.

HARBINSON, ROBERT, (Greene Co.)

Pvt in Pa Mil. Pensioned Mch 4, 1831, aged 76 yrs. Annual allowance $56.67. On roll July 27, 1833. Fur infor Catherine Green Chap.

HARDEN, RICHARD, (Brown Co.)

Bur Aberdeen. Fur infor Ripley Chap.

HARDENBROOK, LODWICK, (Morrow Co.)

Enl as Pvt Col Abraham Quick's 2nd Regt, Somerset Co, NJ Mil, June 1776; Pvt in Capt Peter D Vroom's Company 2nd Regt, Somerset Co, NJ Mil, Mch 20 to Apr 3, 1777. In battles of Germantown Oct 4, 1777 and Monmouth June 28, 1778. Br Apr 16, 1775, Somerset Co, N. J. Mar Elizabeth Waldron in 1780. Children: Jerome, John, Ralph, Lydia, Lewis, Samuel, Magdalene, Abraham, Francis, Elizabeth, William. D in Knox (now Morrow) Co, Feb 14, 1845. Bur Old Presbyterian Cem Mt. Gilead, O. MI: Name, date of birth and death. Soldier's Grave. GM by township trustees with government marker. First owner of all the land which the town of Mt Gilead now stands; entered the land at government lands office in 1816. Farmer; affidavit for pens taken in Knox Co, O. 1833. Ref: Mrs Carl V Beebe, Mt Gilead, O. Fur infor Mt Gilead Chap.

HARDESTY, RICHARD, (Belmont Co.)

1st Pa Rifle Regt. Pensioned 1840 while living in Richland Twp. Br 1751, England. Mar Mary ————. Children: Richard, Samuel and John. D Mch 1847, age 96 yrs, Wheeling Creek. Bur private cem on Wheeling Creek, Belmont Co. MI: "Richard and Mary Hardesty. Richard born 1751, died Mch 1847, age 96 yrs." He and his wife went to housekeeping after being married in Mch 1792. and was buried on the farm (same) at Wheeling Creek. Sons Richard and Samuel served in 4th Ohio Mil Mch 1812. His son John served in 1st Ohio Inf in War of 1812. Fur infor Mrs A. L. McFarland, St. Clairsville.

HARDIN, JOHN, (Hamilton or Shelby Co.)

2nd Lt, 8th Pa 1776; 1st Lt 1777. Wounded at Stillwater 1777. Lt in rifle corps of Gen Morgan. Later promoted to Colonel doing special work gaining information and receiving thanks from Gen Gates for capturing 3 British soldiers. Br 1753, Va. Murdered by Indians in message of peace from Ft Washington in 1792. Cincinnati Chap sends for his service: "10th Regt, Pa Cont Line as Brig Drum Maj with a ref to Heitman, p 273. Officer's Register, which see. After the Revolutionary War Col Hardin distinguished himself in several Indian expeditions up to 1786, where he settled in Washington Co, Ky. Was with Gen Hamar in his campaign against the Indian villages of St. Josephs, helping make it a success. April 3, 1792, was appointed by President to negotiate a treaty with Western Indians. Proceeded to Ft Washington, then north with his escort of three men, while carrying a flag of truce, they were all treacherously murdered in the spot where the present village of Hardin, Shelby Co stands. Ref: Heitman, p 273, Officers Registers, and Suttons History Shelby Co. Fur infor Lewis Boyer and Cincinnati Chap.

HARDIN, THOMAS, (Clinton Co.)

Pvt in Delaware Mil. Br 1755, in Ireland. Mar Mary Mager. One daughter was Jane (br 1779, died 1866.) D 1847, Clinton Co. Bur Sewells graveyard, Clarksville. Pensioned in 1834, Clinton Co. Ref: Natl No 27091, Vol 28, p 35. And Natl No 101527, Vol 103, p 159, D. A. R. Lin. Also compare "Rangers on Frontier Westmoreland Co 227 Fur infor George Clinton and Mrs. Whallon, Cincinnati Chaps.

HARDING, GEORGE, (Mahoning Co.)

Ranger, Bedford Co, Pa. 1778-1783. Br 1761. Bur Canfield, O. GM D. A. R. 1915-17. Ref: Pa Archives Series 3, Vol 23, p 264. Fur infor Mahoning Chap.

HARDING, JACOB, (Mahoning Co.)

Pvt. Buck's Co Mil 1783, 3rd class 4th Company, Capt Thomas. Bur Mahoning Co. Ref: Pa Archives, series 5, Vol 5, p 446. Fur infor Mahoning Chap.

HARDING, JOHN, (Mahoning Co.)

Ranger, Westmoreland Co, Pa. Br 1758. Mar Magdeline Nier. Children: John, Crumrine, George, Jacob, Mrs. Mollie Harroff, Mrs. Katherine Ohl, Mrs. Mary Neff, Mrs. Betsey Kline, Mrs. Sarah A. Oswald, Mrs. Rebecca Hood. D 1838. Bur Canfield, O. GM D. A. R. 1915-17. Came to Ohio 1805. Ref: p 129 and 52, Vol 2, History Trumbull and Mahoning Cos. Pa. Archives, Series 3, Vol 23, p 221. Fur infor Mahoning Chap.

HARDY, NATHANIEL (unable to verify) (Summit Co.)

Also a soldier reported to be bur in the old O'Brien cem, but unable to verify. Thought to be bur in Northhampton Cem. Fur infor Cuyahoga Falls Chap..

HARLISON, ROBERT, (Preble Co.)

Bur Mound Hill Cem. Fur infor Grace Miller, Org Reg, Eaton.

HARLOW, SAMUEL, (Clermont Co.)

Enl 1778, took part in Cowpens and Yorktown; was under Lafayette. Br Va near Richmond. Mar Sarah Washburn. Children: Cornelius (br 1795, enl War 1812 Capt Lockhart's Co.; taken prisoner at Detroit.) Came to Jackson Twp. Clermont Co, O. in 1815. Ref: A. S. Abbott, Bethel, O. Fur infor Cincinnati Chap.

HARMAN, JOHN, (Mahoning Co.)

Pvt Capt Thomas Ashley's Company Oct 23, 1777; Samuel Henry's Company, Lancaster Co, Mil. Pensioned Mch 3, 1834. Br 1748. Mar Margaret ——— (1760-1835) D 1842. Bur North Lima, Mahoning Co, O. Ref: Mentioned p 189, Vol 2, History Trumbull and Mahoning Cos., Pa Archives series 3, Vol 23, p 620; Series 5, Vol 7, p 91. Fur infor Mahoning Chap.

HARMON, JACOB, (Morgan Co.)

Served with Pa Tr; wounded at battle of Germantown. He was of Pa Dutch extraction. D and bur in Morgan Co, O. Left many descendants in Noble Co. Fur infor Mrs. Frazier, Caldwell, O.

HARMON, OLIVER, (Lake Co.)

Was one of the Green Mountain Boys of Vt, serving in Capt Williams' Company of Mil, in Col Thomas Lee's Regt, commencing the 21st of Oct, 1781. Pensioner. Br 1756, Rutland, Vt. Mar Mary Plumb, 1782. D Jan 9, 1843, Kirtland, O. Bur on farm in Kirtland, O. Fur infor New Connecticut Chap.

HARMON, RUBEN G., (Trumbull Co.)

Bur Warren "Oak Grove." Name taken from the S. A. A. Yr Bk. Fur infor Mary Chesney Chap.

HARNER, JAMES, (Hamilton Co.)

Br 1753, N. J. D 1837. Ref: S. A. R. Fur infor Cincinnati Chap.

HARNIST, JOHN, (Champaign Co.)

Bur Myrtle Tree Cem in St Paris. (First person bur in this cem.) Fur infor Urbana Chap.

HARP, (HERB) FREDERICK, (Montgomery Co.)

Pvt 5 mos in Capt Henry Knaus' Pa Company. Gen Bower's Brig about the beginning of the war. About 2 yrs later he enl and served 10 mos as Pvt in Capt Nathan Hatfield's Company, Col Barney Hart's Regt, Gen Anthony Wayne, and was in battle of Brandywine. Br Berks Co, Pa, Sept 17, 1756. Parents: Jacob and Mary Catherine Harp. Mar 1st wife Christina, 1778. 2nd wife, Catherine Egold, 1799. Children: Jacob and others. D Nov 21, 1835, German Twp. Montgomery Co, O. Bur county graveyard on Zeller's farm. Grave washed out by a flood in Twin Creek. An early settler that came with other Germans from Pa at an early date. He was a Pensioner and it was granted his widow, after his death. S. A. R. descendants, David Harp, Germantown, O. Fur infor Richard Montgomery S. A. R. Chap.

HARPER, ALEXANDER, (Ashtabula Co.)

Commissioned Lt and promoted Capt of Tyron Co, NY Mil 1777. Captured by Tories and Indians, held prisoner over 2 yrs at Ft. Niagara. Commissioned Colonel 1782. Br 1744, Middletown, Conn. Mar Elizabeth Bartholomew, 1771. Children: James A., William A., Elizabeth, Mary, Alexander, Robert, Margaret (1772-1856) D July 10, 1798, Harpersfield, Ashtabula Co. Bur Unionville. MI: "Col Alexander Harper, died July 10, 1798." GM by S. A. R. with their marker. Ref: Ashtabula County Historical Society Records; Lin Bk Vol 42, N. S. D. Fur infor Mary Stanley and New Connecticut and Eunice Grant Chaps.

HARPER, JOHN, SR. (Greene Co.)

Br Harpers Ferry, Va. D 1820, Ross Twp. Ross, 1804. Ref: Robinson's History of Greene Co. Fur infor Catherine Greene Chap.

HARPER, JOHN, (Trumbull Co.)

Br 1758. Bur Champion. MI: "John Harper, from Essong Co, N. Y. Died June 21, 1850, age 92 yrs." GM by relatives and kept in good condition. Ref: Mabel Harper Gibbons, D. A. R. Cleveland, O. Fur infor Mary Chesney Chap.

HARPER, JOHN W. (Highland Co.)

Br 1759. D Mch 1, 1844. Bur Hillsboro Cem, Hillsboro, O, Sec C, Lot 16. MI: "John W. Harper, died Mar 1, 1833, aged 85." GM D. A. R. official marker placed on stone at grave, May, 1925. Ref: Mrs. Layton Holmes, Hillsboro, O. Fur infor Waw-Wil-a-Way Chap.

HARPER, SAMUEL, (Wyandot Co.)

Wounded in Battle Bunker Hill. Br Ireland, 1748. Mar Catherine Grimes, Chester Co, Pa. Children: William, James, Samuel and George, and 3 daughters. D Oct 18, 1821. Sycamore Twp, Wyandot Co. Bur on A. Butz farm. First house in Sycamore Twp. erected by Samuel Harper about 1821; of hewed logs, 18x18 feet, 1½ stories high; stood until 1834 or 35. His death the first in Twp. Moved to Sycamore Twp. Mch 1821. Came to America previous to Revolutionary War, enl toward the beginning. After marriage settled in Northumberland Co, Pa. Fall 1818 moved to Ross Co, thence to Wyandot, as above. Was a farmer. Ref: Wyandot Co. History, 1884. Fur infor Col. Wm. Crawford Chap.

HARRIFF, JACOB, (Mahoning Co.)

Pvt. Pensioned. Mar Kitty Kline. Children: Holly, Jacob, Andrew, William, Lewis, Leah, Rachael. Bur Mahoning Co. Came from Pa early in the nineteenth century. Shoemaker. Ref: Pa. Archives, Series 3, Vol. 23, p 592; Trumbull and Mahoning Co. History, Vol 2, p 139. Fur infor Mahoning Chap.

HARRIMAN, STEPHEN, (Clark Co.)

Pvt in 3rd Continental Regt. Cōmpany 5. Also member of Gen Stark's Brig, Col Stickney's Regt, Capt Joshua Bailey's Company, Col Squanell commanding. Br Mch 10, 1757, Haverhill, Mass. Parents: Stephen Harriman Sr, and Sarah Mascroft. Mar 1st Lucy Story; 2nd Bridget Abbott Ames. Children: Betsy, Esther, Anna, Polly, Lucy, (1st wife's children). George, Folsom, Putney (2nd wife's children). D Feb 25, 1828, Lisbon, Clark Co, O. Bur Lisbon Cem. south of village 1-4 mile, near center. MI: "Stephen Harriman, a soldier of the American Revolution." GM Metal marker erected by S. A. R. about 1904. Farmer. Ref: Vol 93, No. 92,553; D. A. R. Lin and Miss Orpha Chamberlain, New Carlisle, O. Fur infor Lagonda Chap.

HARRINGTON, JONATHAN, (Ashtabula Co.)

Served as Pvt. under Capt Allen, Col Jermiah Olney, R. I. Regts, eleven mos. Br Lancaster, R. I. Mar Patience ———. Children: Sally, Pardon, Alexander, Jesse, Agnes, Robert, Clott, Bethiah, Dexter, Daniel. D May 4, 1847. Came to Monroe, Ashtabula Co. in 1801. Ref: History of Ashtabula Co. Fur infor Mary Stanley Chap.

HARRINGTON, RICHARD, (Summit Co.)

Bur Northampton, O. MI: S. A. R. Emblem. Fur infor Cuyahoga Falls Chap.

HARRIS, ELISHA, (Noble Co.)

Served in Fauquier Co, Va, Tr. D Duck Creek, at old age. Came to Ohio early date and settled in Enoch Twp. on Middle Fork of Duck Creek. Fur infor Mrs. L. B. Frazier, Caldwell.

HARRIS, JOSEPH, (Hamilton Co.)

(Known as Maj Harris, possibly in the Indian War.) p 319, 135. Pvt. with state Tr, 1776, in Capt Blagues Co. at Cambridge, N. J. Br North Ireland. Mar (1st) Rachael Drake, (2nd) Jemima Drake, daughters of John Drake at Hopewell, N. J. Children: (1st): Robert, John D., Nancy, Elizabeth, James B., Andrew, Susan, Eleanor, Cornelius, Julia, Joseph, Abijah and Prudence (13) For mar of children see Mrs. Whallon.) Owned large tract land West Springfield Pike. Built home (burned) and sawmill; owned Hamilton House, near Glendale, built 1807. The headstone was seen marked "Major Joseph Harris" on the farm owned by his son Andrew, but now destroyed and grave obliterated. Farm was on Compton Road, northwest of Wyoming. His name appears with the names of the incorporaters of Glendale, and with church and other interests. See "History of

Mill Creek Valley," by Teetor, p 295 and 221. Fur infor Cincinnati Chap. (Mrs Whallon.)

HARRIS, WILLIAM, (Clermont Co.)

Pvt. 4th Bn, Cumberland Co, Pa. 7th Bn, same county, Mil. Was called to make a town by order of council, dated June 27, 1781. Recorded in Archives of Pa, Series 5, Vol 6, p 244, 258, 502, 639. Br N. J. 1763. Mar Sarah Rich, 1788, in Ky. Children: John, Otho, William, Elizabeth, Nancy, Sarah. D Apr 15, 1833, at Edenton, O. Bur Old Cem at Edenton. MI: "William Harris, died Apr 15, 1835, aged 70 years." Farmer. Will on file in Probate Court office, Batavia, O. Vol. papers pending for Irene and Dorothy Curless. Blanchester, O. (1928). Fur infor Blanchester Chap.

HARRIS, WILLIAM, (Hamilton Co.)

Served in Capt Carle's Tr. of Light Horse from Hunterdon Co, N. J. Br 1746, Hunterdon Co, N. J. Mar Sarah Runyon, 1770. D 1797, Cincinnati, O. Ref: Natl No. 67,524, Vol 68, p 186. D. A. R. Lin.

HARRIS, WILLIAM, (Seneca Co.)

Br 1760, Harrisburg, Pa. Parents: Samuel and Betsy Boner Harris. Mar Mary Mead. Children: Betsey, Hettie, Augustus, Nancy, Polly, Samuel, John, Minerva, Tabitha, Jane. D 1834. Bur in a private cem, now only a field and the gravestones are piled against fence, Pleasant Twp. Ref: Mrs. Stanley (Elizabeth Kanp)? Fur infor Dolly Todd Madison Chap.

HARRIS, WILLIAM, (Licking Co.)

Enl Sept 25, 1776, Ohio Co, Va. Pvt in Col Crawford's Regt under Capts Wall, Tomlinson, Ogle, Severingen and Winter. Br Oct 2, 1755, Frederick Co, Md. Mar Martha Smith (1754-1838.)· Children: Son, William, (mar Mary Meyers, June 3, 1803.) D 1840, Bowling Green Twp. Bur on farm. Arrived in this county in 1804. Pension allowed on Oct 30, 1832. Ref: History of Licking Co, by E. M. P. Brister; see Natl No. 50,083 D. A. R. Fur infor Hetuck Chap.

HARROD, LEVI, (Knox Co.)

Pvt. Ranger on the Frontier. Sgt in the Washington Co Pa Mil. Pa Archives 6th Series, Vol 2, p 253. Br Jan 22, 1750, Bedford Co Pa. Parents: James Harrod. Mar Rachel Mills (br Oct 22, 1752, d Sept 28, 1834). Children: Levi, Michael, James, William, Samuel, Jemina, Rachel, Elizabeth and Sarah. D Oct 2, 1825, in Pleasant Twp, Knox Co, O. Bur Union Grove Cem, Harrison Twp, Knox Co, O, south central part of Cem. MI: "Levi Harrod Died Oct 2, 1825, aged 75 yrs 8 mo 10 da." Sgt. Ref: Pa Archives Series 5, Vol 4, pp 402 and 711. and also Series 6, Vol 3, pp 237, 1702, 85. Fur infor Kokosing Chap.

HARSCH, HENRY, (Trumbull Co.)

Br 1738. Children: Jacob, Margaret, John, Henry, Elizabeth. D 1828, Warren, O. Bur Old Cem, Warren, O. MI "Henry Harsh, d 1828 age 70 yrs." GM by family; also name on bronze tablet, 1927. Fur infor Mary Chesney Chap.

HART, BLISS, (Trumbull Co.)

Entered the Continental Army in 1777, serving under Gen Washington until 1780. Br Mch 6, 1761 in Conn. D Mch 6, 1831, Brookfield, O. Bur Brookfield Center. MI: all data on this record. Was a member of State Legislature of Conn fr 1811 to 1813. Was a member of the Convention to form the Constitution of Conn. Fur infor Mary Chesney Chap.

HART, JOSIAH, (Washington Co.)

Surgeon's mate. Enl at New Britain, Conn as Surgeon's Mate on staff of Col Samuel Holden Parsons, commissioned July 1775. Disch Dec 1775. Reentered 1776, 6th Regt Col Parson's first call of Tr April and May 1775. Recruited from New London, Hartford and Middlesex Cos, ordered by Governor's council to Boston camps. Took part at Roxbury, Mass in Gen Spencer's Brig. Was at siege of Boston then marched under Washington to N. Y. Assisted in fortifying the city July 24, 1776; ordered to Brooklyn; engaged at White Plains Oct 28. The 6th Brig of Mil in state of Conn for defense of sea coast until Mch 1780. 1st Regt commanded by Col Noah Hooker and Josiah Hart of Farmington. Br April 28, 1742, Kensington, Conn. Mar 1st Abigail Shuman (or Sluman). D Aug 1812, Lowell, O. GM Marietta Chap D. A. R. marker. Marker placed in unknown plot in Mound Cem in 1925. Ref: Natl Nos 36342 and 30747. Fur infor Marietta Chap

HART, RALPH, (Miami Co.)

Bur Knoops Cem 3 miles east of Troy. GM by Miami Chap with bronze marker, 1904. Fur infor Miami Chap.

HARTER, HENRY, (Miami Co.)

Volunteered in Va. Spent the winter at Valley Forge with Washington. Bur McKendree Chapel east of Troy, O. GM by Miami Chap with bronze marker, 1921. Fur infor Miami Chap.

HARTMAN, CHRISTOPHER, (Clermont Co.)

Pvt N. J. Mil. Pensioned 1831, $80 annually. Capt Samuel Stout's Company, 2nd Regt, Middlesex Co Mil. Also Heard's State Tr. Ref: Certificate fr N. J. Adj Gen Stryker's Nov 19, 1897. Br Swintzburg, Germany, May 6, 1750. Mar Mary Hutchinson Aug 1776 in Mercer Co, N. J. Children: William (mar Nancy Cullen, d 1858); Isaas (mar Mary Daughters 1807, d 1837); Samuel (mar Sarah Donham in 1814, she d 1841 and he mar Elizabeth Browning); Rebecca (mar Adam Bricker 1805); Elizabeth (mar Jacob Roudebush); Catherine (mar Ephraime McAdams); Rachel (mar John Page 1817). D Mch 16, 1833. Bur Marathon, O. family group. Came to Jackson Twp, Clermont Co, O. 1801 at Pleasant Run, 2 miles west of Marathon. Ref: 237994, and A. S. Abbott, Bethel, O. History of Clermont Co, gives service in Smallwood's Regt. Fur infor Cincinnati Chap.

HARTZELL, JOHN, Jr., (Portage Co.)

Lived at Deerfield, where pensioned 1840. Fur infor Old Northwest Chap.

HASELTINE, JOHN, (Preble Co.)

Bur Mound Hill, Eaton, O. Fur infor Grace Conger Miller, Org Reg.

HASFORD, ISAAC, (Trumbull Co.)

Br 1756, Vt. D May 28, 1826. Bur Brookfield Center. MI Name, date of birth and death. Fur infor Mary Chesney Chap.

HASKELL, JONATHAN, (Washington Co.)

Maj in reg serv. Stationed at Marietta in 1791. He entered Revolutionary Army at the age of 20 and served until the close. Commissioned Maj in 1795. Reenlisted in Indian War. Br 1754, Rochester, Mass. Mar Phoebe Green. D 1814, Belpre, O. Bur Belpre, O. GM by Marietta Chap with Revolutionary marker, 1921. Came to Marietta in 1788 and settled at Belpre near Farmers Castle. Returned to Belpre after war, where he lived the rest of his life. Ref: Williams Hist of Washington Co. Fur infor Marietta Chap.

HASKELL, PRINCE, (Huron Co.)

Enl as drummer under Capt Hazelton, Mass. Mil, 1775. Taken prisoner by Indians and given to the British. Released in about a yr. Br Rochester, Mass. 1758. D Peru, O. 1841. Fur infor Sally De Forest Chap.

HASKIN, ENOCH, (Montgomery Co.)

Enl 1776, Capt William France's Company under Gen Schuyler. Br Norwich, Conn. 1765. Mar Lydia Ackley, Pittsfield, Mass. D Dayton, O. 1838. Ref: 55335, p 156, Vol 56, D. A. R. Lin.

HASSAN, HUGH. (Trumbull Co.)

Br 1736. Mar Rosannah (d Jan 11, 1844, aged 91 yrs). D July 13, 1832. Bur Seceeders Corners, Liberty Twp. MI: Name, date of birth and death. Fur infor Mary Chesney Chap.

HATCH, ABNER, (Hamilton Co.)

Br 1753 Conn. D 1819. Ref: S. A. R. Fur infor Cincinnati Chap.

HATCH, ELIJAH, Sr., (Athens Co.)

Sgt on Muster Roll of Capt John McKinstry's Company, Col Patterson's Regt, dated Aug 1, 1775. Enl May 5, 1775. He was of Nobletown, N. Y. Br April 27, 1730, Rochester, Mass. Parents: Elisha and Patience Cane (or Keen) Hatch. Mar Kesiah Barrows 1757. Children: James, John, Elijah, Abezer, Obed, Olive, Comfort, Lydie, Kesiah. D 1809 Rome Twp, Athens Co, O. Bur Pioneer Cem, Rome Twp, Athens Co at the mouth of Federal Creek, one mile fr Stewart, O. Came to Rome Twp, Athens Co, O. in the yr 1801 fr State of N. Y. About the year 1885 the Marietta-Mineral R R (which afterward became Marietta, Columbus and Cleveland) was being built. It surveyed through the Hatch family burying lot in this old Pioneer Cem. The graves were removed to another cem, but to date have not been able to locate them. Fur infor Nabby Lee Ames Chap.

HATFIELD, THOMAS, (Montgomery Co.)

Drummer boy probably in Delaware Tr. Br Delaware of Welsh descent. Mar Sarah Allen, a native of Culpeper Co. Va. Had a son John br Nov 1793, who with his father enl in Capt Perry's Rangers in war of 1812 doing excellent serv as scouts and guides. Served a yr and both disch at Vincennes, Ind. Thomas Hatfield and 2 brothers were in Rev. John and Samuel, one killed at Cowpens and the other at Greenbrier C. H. After the war he went to the south and finally settled in Kentucky, where he mar; son John br in Mason Co, Ky. Came to Montgomery Co, O in 1801 and settled on land now owned by his grandchildren. Fur infor Richard Montgomery Chap S. A. R.

HATHORN, JAMES, (Hamilton Co.)

Br 1739, Pa. D 1835. Ref: S. A. R. Fur infor Cincinnati Chap.

HAUGHEY, THOMAS, (Greene Co.)

Br 1760 Va. D Apr 17, 1847. Bur Hussey graveyard. Lived at Silver Creek, 1818. Ref: Hist of Greene Co Fur infor Catherine Greene Chap.

HAUGHTON, HENRY, (Trumbull Co.)

Enl as Henry Horton. (Pvt, record of Military serv not hand.) Br Sharon, Conn, 1764. Children: Samuel, Aretus, Chauncey, Alonzo, Lois, Lovica, Mary Ann. D Southington, O. 1845. Bur Center Cem, Southington, about center of cem. MI: Name, date of death and age, also that of his wife. GM by estate. He came to Southington, Western Reserve in 1808, bought 200 acres of land, cleared 10 acres and returned to N. Y. Returned one yr to Ohio. Farmer. Lester Haughton of Southampton, O. is the only living grandson of Henry Haughton. Fur infor Mary Chesney Chap.

HAUN, JOHN, (Harrison Co.)

Served in 4th Va Regt, Col John Nelville, in the Rev; also in the 8th and 12th; Eckenrode, Va. Revolutionary Lists, II, 143. Bur in Zion graveyard at Germano. Came from Washington Co, Md. Fur infor Moravian Trail Chap.

HAWKS, JACOB, (Columbiana Co.)

Bur Lisbon, Old Cem south of Creek. Living in 1840. Aged 81 yrs. Center Twp. Pensioner. Fur infor Bethia Southwick Chap.

HAWKINS, JOSEPH, (Summit Co.)

In 1779, in May, enrolled in Capt Ephraim Buell's Company, Col Warren's Regt, which did scouting for security of frontiers. Later served in Capt Isaac Clark's Company of Volunteers for a mo, in Oct 1780. Enrolled in Capt John Hawkin's Company, Minute Men of Woodstock, for service in the alarm of Royalton, Oct 1780. Served in Mil under Lt Abisha Samson on 10 days duty at Barnard, Oct 1780. In Mch 1781 and Aug 10, 1781, member of Capt Jesse Safford's Company. Served as Corp in Capt Isaac Hurlburt's Company, Thos Lee's Regt, under Maj Gideon Brown on northward expedition. Br Nov 3, 1760, Providence, R. I. D Nov 17, 1848, Copley Twp, and Bur in Montrose Cem. Fur infor Cuyahoga-Portage Chap.

HAWKINS, SAMUEL, (Preble Co.)

Pvt in Inf, Va State Line. Br Botetourt Co, Va. Mar Christena Worthington. D Eaton, O. Ref: Natl No 72,496, p 175, Vol 73. D. A. R. Lin.

HAWLEY, EBEN RICE, (Hamilton Co.)

Think this is "Ebenezer" whose record is: Pvt. 1776, Capt. Matthew Mead's Company, Col David Waterbury's Regt. Conn. Tr. Br 1758 or 1760 at Hartford, Conn. D Hamilton Co, or might be confused with Hamilton city, (Butler Co.) See Vol 97, p 215, No. 96,689, D. A. R. Lin. Ref: S. A. R. Fur infor Cincinnati Chap.

HAYDEN, SAMUEL, (Lake Co.)

Enl at Goshen, Conn in 1755. Was Sgt under Capt Sedgewick and Col Hennian for nine mos. Was also with Lt Col John Mead's Regt. Marched Aug 12, 1776, was at the battle of Ticonderoga. Br 1749. Parents: Residents of Winstead, Conn. D 1838. Bur Concord Center, O. GM New Connecticut Chap. He received a pension. Fur infor New Connecticut Chap.

HAYES, SETH, (Geauga Co.)

Pvt. Capt Burr's to Col Moseley's Regt. Arrived in camp, July 13. Stationed along Hudson River. Br Russell, Mass. Mar Elizabeth ————. Children: Ira, Enos, Lorin, Olive, Betsy, Marilla, Martin, Riley. Bur probably in Lower Cem, as rest of family are buried there. Administrator of his estate aptd Mch 10, 1816, Chardon, O. Brought family to Burton in 1800. Was member of First M. E. Church. Came to Burton prior to Aug 2, 1799, fr Russell, Hampton Co, Mass. Ref: Pioneer History Geauga Co, p 436; Conn. Men Revolution," 366. Fur infor Taylor Chap.

HAYES, TITUS, (Trumbull Co.)

1777 was at Germantown, Valley Forge and Monmouth. Br 1748 or 1746, Lyme, Conn. Mar Deborah Beckwith, (d Jan 15, 1819, age 68 yrs.) Children: One son was Richard. D June 1811, aged 63 yrs, Hartford, O. Bur Burghill, Hartford Twp. GM Good condition. Will approved 1811. Ref: Natl No. 45,523, Vol 46, p 222. Fur infor Mary Chesney Chap.

HAYNES, DANIEL, (Warren Co.)

Pvt. Capt James Sherman's Company, Col Pynchon's Regt. at Lexington Alarm. In 1779 Capt Joshua Shaw's Company, Col Elisha Poster's Regt. Br Hampden, Conn, 1741. Mar Sarah Horton. D Franklin, 1802. Ref: Natl No. 62,619. p 206, Vol 63, D. A. R. Lin.

HAYS, OLIVER, (Hamilton Co.)

Ref: S. A. R. Fur infor Cincinnati Chap.

HAYWARD, SOLOMON, (Gallia Co.)

Record being verified (1928). Br Aug 2, 1755, Easton, Mass. Parents: Edward Hayward, Hannah Kingsley Hayward. Mar Martha Burr, 1780. Children: Edward, Adah, Patty, Caroline, Solomon, Royal A. D Sept 29, 1831, Gallipolis, O. Bur Pine St. Cem, Gallipolis, O. MI: "Solomon Hayward Sr." (Words worn very much.) GM Family. Farmer. Ref: Catherine Hayward, Gallipolis, O. Fur infor French Colony Chap.

HAZELTON, JOHN, (Perry Co.)

Pvt. on pay roll Continental Line, Westmoreland Co, (Pa) Mil. Pa. Archives, 5th Series, Vol 4, p 289-440-744. Br Apr 11, 1758, Laurel Hills, Pa. Mar Barbara Slaughter. Children: James, Joseph, Lot, Samuel, William, John, Henry, Betsey, Katie, Polly, Sarah, Jane. D Oct 17, 1834, Perry Co, O. Bur near New Lexington. Tombstone intact. GM unmarked by patriotic society. Natl No. 207,343. Fur infor Elizabeth Zane Dew Chap.

HAZELTON, JOHN, (Preble Co.)

Bur Mound Hill Cem. Fur infor Mary P. Mitchell, Eaton, O. and Org. Regent, Mrs. Miller.

HEADLEY, JOSEPH, (Licking Co.)

Enl in Sussex Co, N. J. in spring of 1777, as Pvt in Col Seeley's Regt. Served 3 yrs under Capts Belty, Hill, Westbrook and Ribble. Br 1758, N. J. D Mch 27, 1849, Jersey Twp, age 91. Bur at Jersey. MI: "Revolutionary War." GM Hetuck Chap, 1909. Emigrated to this county in 1815. Pension allowed on Oct 31, 1832. Ref: Hist. of Licking Co, by E. M. P. Brister. Fur infor Hetuck Chap.

HEADLEY, JOSEPH, (Trumbull Co.)

Mar Abigail ——— (d June 16, aged 86 yrs, 2 mos, 21 das.) D Feb 22, 1840, aged 94 yrs, 19 days. Bur by E. J. Cortland, Casterline Cem. GM Marker. Fur infor Mary Chesney Chap.

HEAGAN, PATRICK, (Montgomery Co.)

Entered service as Pvt at York, Pa, spring of 1775, as volunteer for 1 yr to go to Canada. Company of Capt Church, Lt Reed. Mustered at Chester, marched to and joined Regt of Col Harkley at York. Later enlisted in Reed's Company, in army of Gen Wayne. Was at Paoli when attacked by Hessians. At Stony

Point, Brandywine, and Saratoga. Many minor engagements mentioned in application for pension. Served in all about 5 yrs. Br Mch 5, 1749 (or 50) at York, Pa. Bur Minnich Cem, Randolph Twp, Montgomery Co., exact location of grave unknown. GM Richard Montgomery Chap S. A. R. July 2, 1923. Applied for pension at Darke Co, Nov 6, 1832. A resident of Adams co until 1826, when he came to Miami co, but no details are available. Mentioned as a pensioner in Miami Co Memorial History. Fur infor Richard Montgomery Chap S. A. R.

HEATH, ELEAZER, (Ashtabula Co.)

Br 1754, Conn. D 1850, aged 96. Bur Williamsfield Center, O. MI: "A soldier of the Revolution." Ref: F. A. Butler, Andover, O. Fur infor Eunice Grant Chap.

HEATON, DANIEL, (Butler Co.)

Name appears on the tablet of Sailors and Soldiers Monument at Hamilton, as a Revolutionary soldier buried in that co. Bur at Middletown, O. Fur infor John Reily Chap.

HEATON, ISAAC, (Seneca Co.)

Bur Buckeye Cem in Eden Twp. GM Bronze marker in 1927 by Mrs. G. A. Downey. Fur infor Dolly Todd Madison Chap.

HEATON, THOMAS, (Brown Co.)

Pvt. Capt Valentine Peyton's Company, Col Wm Heth's 3rd Va. Regt, 1777. Br 1761 Harpers Ferry. Mar Susan Taylor. Children: One was Joseph. D 1858, Brown Co, O. Natl No. 48,392, Vol 49, p 184, D. A. R. Lin.

HECK, PETER, (Mahoning Co.)

Pvt. served in Chester Co Mil, 1783. Br Aug 10, 1765. Mar Barbara (br 1767, died in 1841) D Mch 23, 1843, Springfield Twp. Bur Old Forney Church Yard. Ref: Pa. Archives, Series 5, Vol 5, p 888, Church Records. Fur infor Mahoning and Bethia Southwick Chaps.

HEGEMANN, PETER, (Montgomery Co.)

Bur from Eastern Heights, Dayton, in 1838. Name secured from Old Dayton newspaper, yrs ago, but no other data kept; papers lost in 1913 flood. Ref: Richard Montgomery Chap S. A. R.

HEIFFNER, JACOB, (Ashland Co.)

Pvt 3 yrs in Md Inf. Engaged in battles of Trenton and Princeton, Dec 27, 1776 and Jan 3, 1777. In Aug of 1777 in Battle of Birmington, Vt, also fought at Monmouth in June 1778. Was at surrender of Burgoyne at Saratoga. Br Hesse Darmstadt, Germany. D 1848 Orange Twp, Ashland Co, O. Bur on the Heiffner farm, one mile north of Nankin, Ashland Co, O. GM Sarah Copus Chap, 1927. Came from Hesse when 16 yrs old, located in Md. near Pa. State line; came to Ohio at close of Revolution. Settled in Orange Twp as a Farmer, 1817. Fur infor Sarah Copus Chap.

HEIZER, JOHN, (Brown Co.)

Soldier in war of Rev. Was wounded in the thigh. Br Mch 17, 1746 in Germany. Parents: Valentine Heizer. Mar Elizabeth Mowery, 1783. Children: Lewis, John (d), Mary, Andrews, Sarah, Christine, Samuel, George, John 2nd, Elizabeth, Jessie, Edward (d), Polly. D June 26, 1837. Bur Normand Cem, Brown Co. GM by son, Edward, ordinary tombstone. Farmer. Ref: Adams Co Hist, by Evans & Stiver 1900, Hist of Brown and Clermont Co by Buron Williams 1913. Mrs. Mary Grimes. Fur infor Taliaferro and Lt Byrd Chaps.

HELLER, HENRY, (Fairfield Co.)

Pvt in Capt George Hudson's Company Pa Line. Br 1755, York, Pa. Mar Catherine Seitz, D 1838, Fairfield Co, O. Ref: Natl No 99286, Vol 100 D. A .R. Lin.

HELLER, JOHN, (Richland Co.)

Pvt in Capt Richard Shaw's Company, 5th Bn Northampton Co, Pa Mil. Br Pa. Mar Susan Hammond. D Richland Co, O. 1824. Ref: Natl No 72187, p 68, Vol 73, D. A. R. Lin.

HELMICK, NICHOLAS, (Harrison Co.)

Served in a Va State Regt. U. S. Pens Rolls 1835. A Revolutionary pensioner living in Harrison Co in 1833, aged 74. Eckenrode's Va Rev Lists, 1. (No date to prove this is not same as Hancock Co. or a different one). Fur infor Moravian Trail Chap.

HELMICK, NICHOLAS, (Hancock Co.)

Winchester, Va. Pvt, served 3 yrs, 9 mos. Enl Sept 1777. Pvt Col Crocket, Capt John Shapman. Br 1760, Winchester, Va. Mar Sarah Ward. D McComb, Hancock Co, O. Bur Pleasant Hill Cem, Hancock Co, O. MI: dates of birth and death. GM Ft Findlay Chap, 1915. Fur infor Ft Finday Chap.

HEMINWAY, SAMUEL, (Geauga Co.)

Mass State Tr. Pensioned 1833 at age of 78. Fur infor Taylor Chap.

HEMPLEMAN, GEORGE, (Clark Co.)

Pvt Capt Wm Johnson's Company 4th Bn, Lancaster Mil 1781. At close of war was honorably disch. Br 1732 Castle Hessie, Germany. Parents, Lord Hempleman, a German nobleman. Mar Margarette Duffy, 1756, Richmond, Va. Children: Elizabeth, George, Katherine, Nancy. D 1842 near South Charleston, O. Bur Old M. E. Chapel Cem (body was moved to Charleston Cem). Lot 31, Sec 3. South Division. MI: "Hempleman." GM by S. A. R. metal marker about 1906. "George Hempleman. A soldier of the Revolutionary War. Born 1732—Died 1842." about 1906. Sold himself into slavery to pay for transportation to America, served 4 yrs to a cruel master and was broken in health at end of servitude. Farmer. Was mar in church of Patrick Henry fame (Settle Old St John's). After war went to N. C.; to Va., to Ohio in fall of 1808. Ref: Effie Hempleman's D. A. R. credentials and history of Hempleman family. Fur infor Lagonda Chap.

HEMPSTEAD, HALLAM, (Scioto Co.)

Capt John Hempstead, Lt Doglas, Ensign Mason. Parents: Nathaniel Hempstead, Hannah B. Hempstead. Mar Polly Barron, Marietta, Aug. Children: Hallam, Clarissa, Maria, Jane. D July 1833, Portsmouth, O. Bur Greenlawn Cem, Portsmouth, southeast corner old Methodist Lot. GM by family, old fashioned tall white marble. Shortly after death. Ref: Mrs. Jennie Lodwick Carson. Fur infor Joseph Spencer Chap.

HEMROD, ANDREW, (HIMROD), (Delaware Co.)

Pvt under Capts John Nelson and Robinson, Pa Mil. Bur Berkshire. Pensioned. Fur infor Delaware Chap.

HENDERSON, WILLIAM, (Warren Co.)

Enl Col Tootal's Md Regt to serve 3 yrs. Br 1753, Baltimore, Md. Mar Nancy Milbern. Children: One son was James. D 1829, Carlisle, O. Ref: 70480 and 75092, Vol 76, D. A. R. Lin.

HENDRICKSON, CORNELIUS, (Mahoning Co.)

Served as Pvt and also as nurse. Br 1746. Mar Ann ———. D 1832. Bur Old Springfield Cem. Came to Ohio in 1798. Ref: Pa. Archives, 5 Series, Vol 8, p 414, Church Records. Fur infor Mahoning Chap.

HENRY, FRANCIS, Sr., (Mahoning Co.)

Pvt Capt Bratton's Company, Washington Co. 4 yrs Pa Mil. Br 1753. Mar Agnes ———. D 1834, Poland Twp. Bur Mahoning Cem. Ref: Pa Archives, Series 2, Vol 13, p 99. Trumbull and Mahoning Co History. Fur infor Mahoning Chap.

HENRY, JOHN, (Richland Co.)

D 1828. Bur Adams Cem, 2 miles northeast fr London, O. on New State Road. GM Mary Washington D. A. R. marker, bronze marker, 1911. Fur infor Mary Washington Chap.

HENSEL, MICHAEL, (Fairfield Co.)

Enl Jan 1776 to July 1777. Pvt under Capt William Morgan, State of Va. Battle at Brunswick. Pens allowed to both himself and wife. Br Nov 9, 1753 in Berks Co, Pa. Mar Margaret Harsh of Washington Co, on the 17th day of Mch, 1778. (She was br Mch 9, 1765.) Children: Henry, George, John, Catherine, Anna, Maie, Sarah, Elizabeth, Magdaline, Maria, Susanah. D Fairfield Co, July 15, 1836. Bur Stuckey Cem, Fairfield Co. MI: Date of birth and death. GM by Elizabeth Sherman Reese Chap, a bronze marker, Sept 1, 1927. Farmer. Ref: Rebecca Hood Gresy, Lancaster, O. Fur infor Elizabeth Sherman Reese Chap.

HERRICK, LIBBEUS, (Geauga Co.)

Pvt Capt Elderkin's Company, Feb 9, 1777 for 3 yrs. 7th Regt Col Swift. Br 1749, Preston. Parents: Robert Herrick, Preston, Conn. and Abiah Hill. Mar Priscilla ———. Name found in Conn list of pensioners residing in Ohio. Conn Men in the Revolution, pp 223-646. Ref: Conn Rolls, Vol 2, 233, Herrick Gen 109. Fur infor Taylor Chap.

HERSHBERGER, JOHN, (Summit Co.)

Served 1781, Pvt Capt Michael Oberly's Company, Col George Feether's Regt, 4th Bn, Pa Mil. Br Pa 1759. Mar Christina E. Fehler. D Summit Co 1847. Ref: Natl No 63474, p 156, Vol 64, D. A. R. Lin.

HESS, BOLSER, (Franklin Co.)

Served 7 yrs in Revolutionary Army fr N. Y. and Pa. Br Bedford Co, Pa. in 1741. D Dec 27, 1806. MI: "Bolser Hess. Born 1841 died Dec 27, 1806, aged 65 years." GM Revolutionary Grave committee with bronze marker, May 30, 1912. Came to Ohio in 1796 and settled in Ross Co where he lived 4 yrs, then came to Clinton Twp and settled in 1800. Was a shoemaker and tanner by trade. Fur infor Columbus Chap.

HESS, PETER, (Fayette Co.)

Pvt Capt Isaac Adam's Company, Col Peter Grubb's Bn Lancaster Co, Pa. Associators, 1776. Br 1757, Lancaster Co. D 1825. Ref: Natl No 56623, Vol 57, p 215, D. A. R. Lin. Miss Elvisa Hess, Washington C. H., O.

HIBBARD, OZIAS, (Union Co.)

Pvt. Br Dec 1, 1763 Windham, Conn. Mar Mary Flower, 1791. Children: Eliza (mar John Makemson); Mary (mar J. Stuart); Lucy (mar Warren Ross);

Nancy (mar Harrison King). D May 19, 1851, Union Co, O. Bur Irwin Cem Union Twp, near Milford Center, O. Ref: 141523 D. A. R. Pens Bureau. Fur infor Hannah Emerson Dustin and Bellefontaine Chaps.

HICKMAN, JOSEPH, (Franklin Co.)

Served through Revolutionary War. Br Va. about 1740. D 1821. Bur at Ebenezer near Galloway. MI: "Joseph Hickman died 1821." GM by Revolutionary Grave committee with bronze marker, May 30, 1912. Came to Ohio fr Va in 1806 and settled near Galloway, Prairie Twp. Fur infor Columbus Chap.

HICKOK, DURLIN, (Ashtabula Co.)

Brewer's Mass Mil Revolutionary War. Br Mch 22, 1759, Sheffield, Mass. Mar Betsey Fletcher. Children: Juresta, Ezra, Eben, Durlin, Olive, Clarissa, Betsey, Maria. D July 30, 1837. Bur Hickok Cem, Jefferson, O. MI: "Durlin Hickok Born Mch 22, 1759, Died July 30, 1837." Brewer's Mass Mil Rev War." GM Marble slab, family. Farmer and Miller. Ref: Mrs. Ida Baylor, Mrs. Emily Jerome, Jefferson, O. Fur infor Eunice Grant Chap.

HICKOX, NATHANIEL, (Geauga Co.)

Pvt and Dragoon, Conn Continental Army. Pension allowed 1832. Br 1758, Conn. Mar Mary Ann Mallory, (d 1830.) D Hambden, 1848. Tradition, that he is bur in Hambden, O. Hickok, spelling on pension papers; Hickox, in history later generations, Hickok, and Hicok. Came from Otsego, N. Y. to Hambden. Name found in list of pensions in Census of 1840, living in Hambden, O. Ref: p 514, Vol 5, Pension Records. Vol 91, p 11, Natl No. 90,029, D. A. R. Lin. Fur infor Taylor Chap.

HICKOX, EBENEZER, (Portage Co.)

Served as drummer and Pvt 3 or 4 yrs. Was twice wounded and given a furlough, after which he served as Minute Man during the rest of the war. Was in Conn Mil. Bur Maple Grove Cem Ravenna, O. Placed on pension roll Oct 28, 1833. Fur infor Old Northwest Chap.

HIGGINS, DAVID, REV. (Huron Co.)

Soldier. Br Aug 6, 1761, Haddam, Middlesex Co, Conn. Parents: Capt Cornelius Higgins and Sarah (Hawes) Higgins. Mar Eunice Gilbert, Jan 17, 1788, New Haven, Conn. Children: David, James, Gilbert, Mary Bethiah, Myra, Lucius, Cornelius, Eliza, William. D June 19, 1842, Norwalk, O. Bur Woodlawn Cem Norwalk, O. main drive, Lot 239. MI: "Rev. David Higgins died June 19, 1842, in the 81st year of his age, and the 55th of his ministry. As a preacher he was solid and instructive, as a pastor devoted and faithful, as a Christian consistent and humble. Servant of God well done. Rest from thy loved employ. The battle fought, the victory won, Enter thy Master's joy." Erected by the First Presbyterian Church, in Norwalk, 1842? Graduated at Yale College in 1783. Founded Presbyterian Church at Auburn, N. Y. 1801. Presbyterian minister. Fur infor Sally De Forest Chap.

HIGGINS, JOHN (Hamilton Co.)

2nd Lt 2nd Bn, 6th Company, Somerset Co, N. J. (Stryker's Men from N. J. p 16.) Mar a daughter of Abraham Voorhees, in N. J. Bur Reading, O. Came to Ohio with father-in-law and family; settled on farm in Sec 33, Symmes Twp, 1794. Fur infor Cincinnati Chap.

HIGGINS, ROBERT, (Brown Co.)

Raised company soon after the beginning of the Revolution and soon rose to the rank of Col. Taken prisoner at the battle of Germantown and confined in N. Y. Harbor. Returned to his home in Va about the time of Cornwallis surrender. Br Westmoreland Co, Pa. Parents: Robert Higgins and Hannah Vanzant. Mar, 1st, Miss Wright; 2nd, Mary Jolliffe in Va, (d 1806.) Children: Robert, John J., Lydia, and a daughter. (Mar Trautwine,) 8 by 1st wife, none came to Ohio. D Higginsport, 1825. Bur Higginsport. In 1798 he moved and lived a yr in Ky opposite his survey in Lewis Twp, Brown Co, O. 1799, crossed the Ohio and lived in a cabin on the site of Higginsport, which town he founded. Ref: "Brown Co History" published by W. H. Beers & Co., 1883, p 460. Fur infor Taliaferro Chap.

HIGGINS, WILLIAM, (Highland Co.)

Br 1745, London, England. D 1842, Highland Co, O. Pensioned in 1840, at age of 97, while residing in Liberty Twp. (Fr Census 1840). Ref: Natl No. 24,295, p 106, Vol 25, D. A. R. Lin.

HIGLEY, BREWSTER, (Meigs Co.)

Br Simsburg, Conn, Mch 14, 1759. Mar Naomi ————. Children: Brewster Jr., Cyrus, Lucius, Joseph, Harriet, Theresa, Susan. D June 20, 1847. Bur Rutland. Justice of the Peace for Washington Co, appointed by Gov. St. Clair. Date of commission 1801, associate Judge for Gallia Co. Justice at Rutland. Bought share in Ohio Company for $1,000 and settled on farm in 1799. First settlement in Rutland, also 2nd postmaster of Rutland. Justice of the Peace, Postmaster, Farmer. Removed to Castleton, Rutland Co, Vt. then to Beesville, W. Va. before coming to O. Ref: Numerous Higley's at Rutland, Dr. A. A. Hugg, Middleport, O. Fur infor Return Jonathan Meigs Chap.

HIGLEY, JOEL, (Meigs Co.)

Lt, Commissioned 1778. Br Jan 1, 1739, Simsbury, Higleytown, Conn. Parents: Brewster Higley, 2nd Lt Revolutionary War (br Dec 12, 1709, Simsbury, Conn. D Mch 1, 1794.) Mar 1st Esther Holcombe, Mch 13, 17—; 2nd Mindwell Bull, Jan 5, 1775. Bur Rob't McElhinney Farm, Rutland, O. Old cem abandoned. 1803 he came with his family to what was known as Gallia Co. (now Meigs). Located on a farm south of Rutland, where he passed away few yrs later. Ref: Infor received from Bernard Higley, Rutland, O. "Higley Genealogy." Fur infor Return Jonathan Meigs Chap.

HILDEBRAND, MICHAEL, (Stark Co.)

Served in Lancaster Co, Pa. 1718. Company 8, Bn 5, Maj Henry Marbley, Capt James McConnell. Br Borles Co, Pa. Nov 17, 1766. Parents: John George Nicholas Hildebrand and Anna Maria Hill. Mar Elizabeth Schlenger, 1791. Children: Maria, Josiah, Adam, Samuel, Nicholas, Charles, Rebecca, John G., Elizabeth. D Jackson Twp, Stark Co, O, Oct 8, 1850. Bur Mud Brook Cem, Jackson Twp, Stark Co, O, McDonaldsville, O, not far from church. MI: Names, dates of both and death. GM Canton Chap D. A. R. Nov, 1922. Dr. A. K. Largman made the address, marker unveiled by 3 grandchildren. Ref: "History of Stark Co," edited by William Henry Perrin. Fur infor Massillon Chap.

HILDRETH, SAMUEL, (Washington Co.)

Surgeon. Br Townsend, Mass, 1750. D 1823, Belpre, O. Ref: Natl No. 34,426, Vol 35, p 150, D. A. R. Lin.

HILL, ALEXANDER, (Brown Co.)

Bur Pisgah Ridge. Fur infor Ripley Chap.

HILL, AMASA, (Lake Co.)

Enl from Spencertown, N. Y. in Mch 1780, for 9 mos in Capt Walter Vrooman's Company, Col John Harper's Regt. He was in the battle of Cherry Valley. Br Oct 1763, Stillwater, N. Y. D 1847, Madison, O. Bur near "Turney's Corners" in Madison. GM New Connecticut Chap. Came to Ohio in 1810. He received a pension. Fur infor New Connecticut Chap.

HILL, CALEB, (Licking Co.)

Enl Spring of 1776, as Pvt, in Capt William Faulkner's Company, Col Hornbeek's Regt. Was in skirmishes in the retreat from N. Y. to King's Bridge. Br 1756, Duchess Co, N. Y. Mar Rebecca ————. D Monroe Twp, 1842. Bur Old Cem, Johnstown. GM Hetuck Chap 1910. Pension granted Oct 31, 1832, this Co. Ref: "History of Licking Co." by E. M. P. Brister. Fur infor Hetuck Chap.

HILL, GEORGE, (Fairfield Co.)

Bur Walnut Twp. Fur infor Elizabeth Sherman Reese Chap.

HILL, IRA, Capt, (Washington Co.)

Enl July 18, 1778, as Pvt in Capt Enos Parker's Company, Col Jacob Gerrish's Regt of guards. Disch Aug 28, 1778; service, 1 mo 13 days; also 6 mos with Berkshire Company at Springfield. Br July 17, 1755, Goshen, Conn. Parents: Zenas Hill and Kerzia Hill. Mar Esther Post, Feb 2, 1786. Children: Ira Jr., Harry, Sally, Urania, Spedy, Guy and Dan. D Oct 13, 1841, Lower Salem, O. Bur Mt. Ephraim, Washington Co, O. MI: "Ira Hill, Esq. b July 17, 1775, Goshen, Conn, died Oct. 13, 1841." GM Marietta Chap, with Revolutionary marker, 1922. Removed from Tinmouth, Vt, with wife and six children to Marietta, O, in 1800. The following yr settled at Lower Salem. Occupation, Farmer. Ref: "William's History of Washington Co." "Andrews History;" Family Records. Fur infor Marietta Chap.

HILL, ROBERT, (Jefferson Co.)

Was in Capt Abner Howell's Company 3rd Bn Washington Co, Pa. He enl Sept 4, 1782. See Pa. Archives, Series 6, Vol 2 p 112, 119 and 244. Br Feb 15, 1761, near Hillsborough, County Down, Ireland. Parents: George Hill and Ann (mar in 1760, County Down, Ireland.) Mar Rosamond Welsh, late in 1789, Washington Co, Pa. She was br in Md Feb 26, 1770, died Mch 20, 1838, on Hill farm; bur by her husband. Children: Ann, George, John, Thomas, Eleanor, William, Robert, Stephan, Margaret, James, Joseph Welsh, Samuel, two died in infancy. D June 20, 1845, on the Hill farm, 3 miles south of Steubenville, O. Bur Hill Family Graveyard, on said farm, in center of graveyard. MI: "Robert Hill died June 1845, in his 85th yr." GM By Steubenville D. A. R. with bronze tablet, in 1923, marker put in place by his grandson, Robert S. Hill and wife Mary Mears Hill. Came to America in 1768 with his parents; lived for a while in Harford Co, Md; came into Washington Co, Pa, 1780; bought farm of 551 acres, Apr 12, 1806 in Jefferson Co, O, where he lived until his death. Farmer. The land for Hill's Sch District No. 2, was given by Robert Hill. Ref: Mrs. Robert Hill. (Mary Mears Hill), Natl No 175,759. Fur infor Steubenville Chap.

HILL ZIMRI, (Delaware Co.)

Pvt under Col Bebee, Gen McDouglas' Conn Tr. Bur Genoa Twp. Pensioned. Fur infor Delaware Chap.

HILLMAN, BENJ., (Delaware Co.)

Lt under Capt John Clingman's Company, Col James Morrow's Pa Tr. Bur Kingston Twp. Pensioned. Fur infor Delaware Chap.

HILLMAN, JAMES, Col., (Mahoning Co.)

Pvt in Capt Benj Smith's Company. Serv fr June 1, 1776 to Sept 1, 1776, 3 mos. Company stationed at Martha Vinyard in defense of the seacoast. Br 1762. Mar

Catherine (1772-1855. D 1843. Bur Oak Hill Cem, Youngstown, O. GM by D. A. R. 1915-17. A leader in all public enterprises. Ref: p 922, "Mass. Soldiers and Sailors." Fur infor Mahoning Chap.

HILLMAN, JOHN, (Delaware Co.)

Bur Stark Cem, near Olive Green. Fur infor Delaware Chap.

HILLYER, JAMES, (Hamilton Co.)

Br 1761, N. J. D 1846. Ref: S. A. R. Fur infor Cincinnati Chap.

HILTON, WILLIAM, (Fulton Co.)

Ref: The Military Record of Fulton Co, O. 1885, p 305. Fur infor Wauseon Chap.

HINES, RUDOLPH, (Harrison Co.)

Came from Allegany Co, Md, and settled in Nottingham Twp, 1814; said by family to have served in the Revolutionary War. Br 1733. D 1823. Fur infor Moravian Trail Chap.

HINEY, GEORGE, (Clinton Co.)

Pvt Pa Mil; Pensioned 1831. Br 1764. D May 21, 1849. Bur Miller Cem near Lumberton. Living in Sugar Creek, 1820. Fur infor George Clinton and Catherine Greene Chaps.

HINKLE, JOSEPH, (County not stated.)

Pvt in Capt Conrad Karner's Company, Lt Adam Fisher's Regt, Lancaster Co Mil. Br Lancaster Co, Pa. D Ohio. Ref: Mrs. Olive Dickey, Gelham, Butler Co, O. Natl No 61930, p 319, Vol 62, D. A. R. Lin.

HINSDALE, ELISHA, (Medina Co.)

Capt in Revolutionary War 3 yrs, wintered at Valley Forge. Also with Conn Tr. Br Harwinton, Conn. Feb 28, 1761. Mar 1st Asenath Barnes, 2nd Elizabeth Holcomb. Children: Elisha Jr., Julius, Sherman, Asenath, Albert, George. D June 22, 1827, Norton, O. Bur Woodlawn, Wadsworth. MI: "Elisha Hinsdale, Revolutionary Soldier. Died June 22, 1827, aged 86 years." Removed from Western Star Cem 1899. Blacksmith. Elected Justice of Peace several times of Norton Twp, where he then lived. Moved to Ohio in 1816 from Torrington, Conn. Ref: Mrs. Arthur Anbort, Wadsworth, O.; Natl No 82852, D. A. R. Fur infor Cuyahoga-Portage Chap.

HINSEY, CORNELIUS, (HINSLY), (Butler Co.)

Name appears on the Tablet of the Sailors and Soldiers Monument, Hamilton, O. Supposed to be a Revolutionary soldier. Lived in Milford Twp. Not identified. Fur infor John Reily Chap.

HIPSHER, ANDERSON, (Hamilton Co.)

Br 1763, Va. Fur infor Cincinnati Chap.

HISEL, FREDERICK, (Meigs Co.)

Served 2 yrs as Pvt under Capts John Roberts and James Sumption, Col Taylor, State of Va Tr. Afterwards Hostler under Maj Strode. D June 27, 1838. Bur Lower Cem, Middleport, O. MI: "Frederick Hysell Born —— Died 1838." GM: D. A. R. with government marker. Pens applied for June 22, 1818. Ref: Bureau of Pensions, Washington, D. C. Fur infor Return Jonathan Meigs Chap.

HITE, JOHN, (Ross Co.)

Bur Concord Presbyterian Cem, Concord Twp, Ross Co, O.

HOAGLAND, JOHN, (Trumbull Co.)

Bur Hillside Cem Bozetta Twp. Copied from S. A. R. Yr Bk. Fur infor Mary Chesney Chap.

HOBART, WILLIAMS, (Portage Co.)

Pvt in N. H. Continental Line. Placed on Pens Roll Sept 6, 1819. Bur Windham. Fur infor Old Northwest Chap.

HODGES, SIMEON, (Lake Co.)

When a mere youth he went with his uncle, Capt Isaac Hodges, in Col John Daggett's Regt on an alarm call for 8 days. Br 1768, Mass. D June 12, 1838, Mentor, O. Bur Mentor, Lake Co, O. GM by New Connecticut Chap. He made several Trips to "New Connecticut" as a traveling merchant. Fur infor New Connecticut Chap.

HOFFMAN, DETRICH, (Mahoning Co.)

Laborer, Pa. Berks Co. Br 1757. D 1862. Bur Washingtonville, O. GM: This grave has a D. A. R. marker but no one seems to know who placed it. Bronze. Ref: Pa Archives, Series 3, Vol 18, p 179. Fur infor Mahoning Chap.

HOFFMAN, JOHN, (Mahoning Co.)

Pvt. Ranger fr 1778 to 1783. Br 1769. Bur Old Springfield Cem. Ref: Pa Archives, Vol 4, p 231, Vol 4, p 606, Series 5, Old Springfield Church Records. Fur infor Mahoning Chap.

HOGUE, JAMES, (County not stated.)

Enl in Capt Hendrick's Rifle Company. In battle Quebec, taken prisoner sent to England. Br 1754, Ireland. Mar Margaret Irvin, 1783. D 1827, Ohio. Ref: Natl No 83742, Vol 84, D. A. R. Lin.

HOLCOMB, JESSE, (Trumbull Co.)

Br 1758. Children: Jesse Holcomb II (d Aug 18, 1827, aged 23 yrs). D July 22, 1827 aged 69 yrs. Bur Center of Mesopotamia. MI: "Jessie Holcomb, died July 22, 1827, aged 69 yrs." GM by relatives. The head-stones are falling down. Fur infor Mary Chesney Chap.

HOLCOMB, JOEL, (Lake Co.)

He served in regular Conn Line under Samuel Wylly fr Apr 26 to Dec 31, 1778. Br 1760, Granby, Hartford Co, Conn. Mar Sarah Warner. Children: Sally, Seymour, Fanny, Nancy and Marcus. D 1847. Bur Paine Hollow Cem, Leroy Twp, O. GM New Connecticut Chap. Made the journey to Ohio in 1820 with an ox team. Fur infor New Connecticut Chap.

HOLCOMB, JONATHAN, (Warren Co.)

Enl fr Sheffield, Mass. fifer, age 15. Pensioner when he died. Br 1762. Mar Hannah Everest. D 1847, Warren Co, O. Ref: Natl No 13304, p 114, Vol 14, D. A. R. Lin.

HOLDEN, NEHEMIAH, (Brown Co.)

Served 1781-83. Capt P. Wade's Company, Col Michael Jackson's Company, Mass. Tr. Br 1763, Fairlie, N. H. Mar Abbie Bassett, 2nd wife. Bur Higginsport, O. 1849. Ref: See 60, 557, Vol 61, p 184, D. A. R. Lin. Fur infor Ripley Chap.

HOLDEN, S. RICHARD, (Hamilton Co.)

Br 1762 Mass. D 1821. Ref: S. A. R. Fur infor Cincinnati Chap.

HOLE, DR. JOHN, (Montgomery Co.)

Commissioned Asst Surgeon and was at Bunker Hill. Was at Cambridge when the army was reorganized by Gen Washington. Was on medical staff of Gen Richard Montgomery at Quebec, where for want of lights he dressed the wounds of soldiers beneath the walls of the fort by the flashes of muskets and cannon. Went with the first Va Mil to Mass and continued in service until the close of war. Br 1754, Va. Parents: Youngest of 11 children of Jacob Hole, a grandson of Daniel Hole who came from England and settled in New York late in the 17th century. Mar Massie Ludlow, of N. J. Aug 14, 1778. (Br Feb 28, 1759, D July 25, 1842). Children: John Ludlow, Nancy, Jeremiah, Elizabeth, Jane, David, Matilda, Phebe, Mary, William, Polly. D Jan 6, 1813, Washington Twp, Montgomery Co, O. Bur Baptist Cem, Centerville, O. on ridge in center of cem near other Revolutionary soldiers. MI: "A large chiseled weeping willow tree. Dr. John Hole, died January 6, 1813, in the 58th year of his life." His wife is buried at his side. GM Richard Montgomery Chap, S. A. R., with official bronze Montgomery Co marker July 1, 1919. In 1796 he moved west in covered wagon and located at Cincinnati, but after prospecting up the Miami Valley in 1797 he moved his family to Silver Creek where he finally (about 1799) located 1440 acres of land, paying for it in military bounty land warrants for his Revolutionary services. He came fr a family of Baptists and was the first person baptized in Silver Creek. Here he built his cabin and reared his family of six children. The creek was renamed "Hole's Creek" and retains the name at this time. His long army service indicates that he was the peer of his contemporaries in the medical profession. Traditions of the neighborhood testify that his pretentious log cabin was long the center of pioneer hospitality and culture. He was the first physician in the locality, and although his practice extended over many miles of territory he found time to build and run two mills south of Dayton. He received his literary and medical training in Germany where he was sent in 1766. Socially he entertained Washington, Jefferson, and the best, socially, in the Revolutionary times in his NJ home. It was at the suggestion of Dr. Hole that this county was named "Montgomery" for Gen Richard Montgomery, who fell mortally wounded at Quebec, while leading his troops on Dec 31, 1775. Fur infor Richard Montgomery S. A. R. Chap.

HOLIDAY, ROBERT, (Ross Co.)

Entered serv under Gen Washington 1777. Br 1747, Cumberland Co, Central Pa. Children: John Hollyday. D Oct 11, 1823, near South Salem. Bur South Salem, Ross Co, O GM by Nathaniel Massie Chap D. A. R. Fur infor Nathaniel Massie Chap.

HOLLAND, GABRIEL, (Harrison Co.)

Served in Rev as a member of the 6th Regt Md Line, Col Otho H. Williams. Settled in Archer Twp before 1814. Ref: Md Archives XVIII, 214, 231. Fur infor Moravian Trail Chap.

HOLLAND, DR. WILLIAM, (Fulton Co.)

Bur Winameg Cem, Pike Twp. Fur infor Wauseon Chap.

HOLLAND, WILLIAM, (Mahoning Co.)

Pvt, 9th Volunteer Regt. Children: Benjamin, Sarah, Solomen, Samuel, Catherine. D Youngstown. Bur Oak Hill Cem, Youngstown, O. Removed from old Courthouse Cem and marker lost. Tavern keeper. Ref: p 454, Vol 1, Hist Trumbull and Mahoning Cos; p 152, "Virginia in the Revolution." Fur infor Mahoning Chap.

HOLLENBACH, GEORGE, (Muskingum Co.)

Served as Pvt 1780 in Capt Mathias Probst's Company, Pa Line. Br 1748, Lebanon Co, Pa. D 1824 near Zanesville, O. Ref: Vol 86, p 371, Natl No 85710, D. A. R. Lin.

HOLLISTER, ASAHEL, (Lake Co.)

Served fr Conn in Capt Elijah Wright's Company, Col Roger Enos' Regt, stationed on Hudson River at West Point in 1778. He was a pensioner. Br 1763. D Feb 12, 1839, Kirtland, O. Bur Waite Hill Cem. Left Methodist Church and joined the Mormons. Fur infor New Connecticut Chap.

HOLLISTER, NATHAN, (Monroe Co.)

Pvt in Mass. Continental Line. Br 1759, Catskill, N. Y. D 1843 Woodsfield, O. Placed on Monroe Co Pens Roll in 1831. Ref: D. A. R. Lin, Vol 32, p 155, Natl No 31399.

HOLMAN, THOMAS, (Ashtabula Co.)

Br 1754. D June 27, 1850. Bur Rays Corners Cem, Lenox, Ashtabula Co, O. GM Marble slab. MI: "Thomas Holman died June 27, 1850, aged 96. A soldier of the Revolution." Fur infor Eunice Grant Chap.

HOLMES, FRANCIS, (Harrison Co.)

A Francis Holmes was a member of 2nd Company, 6th Bn, Cumberland Co, Pa Mil, Capt Wm Moorhead, in 1781. Br 1739. D 1825. Settled in Green Twp about 1802, posisbly from Nottingham Twp, Washington Co, Pa. Ref: Pa Archives, 5th Series, Vol VI, p 413. Fur infor Moravian Trail Chap.

HOLMES, JAMES SR., (Licking Co.)

He was 3rd Lt in the 1st Bn of Miles Pa. Rifle Regt of Capt Richard Bevine's Company. Bur Georges Graveyard in Union Twp. GM Granville Chap. Enl in Bedford Co, Pa. on Apr 15, 1776, and retired on Dec 31, 1776, being incapacited from further service because of a gun wound in his hip, which made him a cripple for life. Fur infor Granville Chap.

HOLMES, JEDEDIAH, (Seneca Co.)

Bur Shock's Cem in Eden Twp. GM Bronze marker, 1927. Fur infor Dolly Todd Madison Chap.

HOLT, AARON, (Meigs Co.)

Br Hartford, Conn. Children: Horace, Mary. Died and bur Rutland, O. Farmer. Fur infor Return Jonathan Meigs Chap.

HOLT, EVAN, (Morrow Co.)

Served 6 yrs as a Revolutionary soldier. Was a native of Chester, Pa. Emigrated to Knox Co in 1808 and lived for 39 years on land received for his services. He was, pensioner until his death in his 84th yr, leaving a large family, married and settled, around him in Chester Twp, now Morrow Co. Only the name of his son, Evan, is given. Ref: Norton's History Knox Co, p 288. Fur infor Kokosing and Mt. Gilead Chaps.

HOOD, GEORGE, (Trumbull Co.)

Mar Catherine ———. (d May 18, 1845). Bur Union Cem Girard. MI: Stone with name only. Ref: Name in list S. A. R. Yr Bk. Fur infor Mary Chesney Chap.

HOOPES, BENJAMIN, (Columbiana Co.)

Lived in Butler Twp, Columbiana Co, O. Fur infor Bethia Southwick Chap.

HOOVER, JOHN (Franklin Co.)

Served as Pvt in Pa Mil was pensioned Apr 5, 1833. Br about 1742 in Pa. D near Grove City, 1840. Bur on old Hoover farm near Grove City. MI: "John Hoover, died 1840, aged nearly 100 years." GM Revolutionary Grave Committee with bronze marker, May 30, 1912. Came from Pa to Ohio in 1807. Fur infor Columbus Chap.

HOOVER, MANUEL, Capt., (Trumbull Co.)

Capt 3rd Bn, Sussex Co. Bur Pricetown, Newton Twp, Trumbull Co. MI: "Capt Manuel Hoover died 1824." Resided in North Hampton Pa in 1790. Farmer. Ref: "Jerseymen of the Revolution," p 395; Census, Pa, 1790, p 170, and "Soldiers Buried in Trumbull Co." Cleveland Historical Library. Fur infor Mahoning and Mary Chesney Chaps.

HOPKINS, ARCHIBALD, (Brown Co.)

Bur Red Oak. Fur infor Ripley Chap.

HOPKINS, EBENEZER, (Geauga Co.)

Pvt Vt State Tr. Capt Sawyer's Company. Pensioned 1834. Br 1761, Pittsford, Vt. Mar Rachel Mead, Dec 2, 1783. Children: Achsah, Josiah, Bradley, Charlotte, Hannah, Timothy, Ebenezer, Sophia. D Welshfield, July 16, 1838. Bur Welshfield Center Cem. MI: "Ebenezer Hopkins died July 16, 1838, aged 77. A Revolutionary soldier." GM by family. Was held prisoner May 12, 1779 up to June 9, 1782, being 36 mos and 28 days. Gen Assembly of Vt passed resolution to pay Ebenezer Hopkins $5 for loss of gun in service of State when taken prisoner. Ref: Pioneer History Geauga Co, p 632, Vermont Rolls, p 751, 775, 799, Vol 86, Natl No 85,616, D. A. R. Lin. Fur infor Taylor and Oberlin Chaps.

HOPKINS, TIMOTHY, (Morrow Co.)

Pvt 2 yrs under Col Zebulon Butler, Capts Ransom, Spaulding and Mitchell, Conn Tr. Br Nov 25, 1750. Parents: Timothy and Jemima Scovill Hopkins. Mar Phebe Marvin, Wilkesbarre, Pa, Jan 15, 1780. Children: Timothy, Abram, Isaac, Phebe, Jemima, (mar the father of Gen Rosecrans.) D Oct 10, 1803. Bur Westfield Twp, Westfield, O. GM by tall monument. Pensioned. Ref: O. D. Dailey, Albany, O Fur infor Mt. Gilead and Delaware Chaps.

HOPPLE, CASPER, (Hamilton Co.)

Served in Northampton Co, Pa. (Rangers on Frontiers p 327.) Mar (1st Anna Marie) and 2nd Mary ———, (signed with his to landsale.) Children: Dr. James, a son of 2nd wife, no doubt, and possibly Andrew. D Cincinnati, O. Bur Spring Grove Cem, Cincinnati. Came to Cincinnati in 1804; see Goss History of Cincinnati, p 98, from Philadelphia, Pa. Ref: Biographical Dept Nelson and Co. Pub 1894, Cincinnati, O. Fur infor Cincinnati Chap.

HORN, FREDERICK, (Hamilton Co.)

Br 1756, Pa. D 1838. Ref: S. A. R. Fur infor Cincinnati Chap.

HORN (OR HORNE), GEORGE, (Licking Co.)

Enl in Hampshire Co, Va, June, 1781 as Pvt in Capt Edward McCartey's Company, Col Drake's Regt. Br Feb 28, 1765, Germany. D Mch 10, 1844, Jersey Twp. Bur village cem of Jersey. MI: "Revolutionary War" GM Hetuck Chap, 1909. Pension allowed Oct 30, 1832. Ref: History of Licking Co, by E. M. P. Brister. Fur infor Hetuck Chap.

HORN, HENRY, (Preble Co.)

Pvt. Capt John Smith's Company, 4th Va Regt. Br Oct 8, 1755, Rockbridge Co, Va. D Nov 17, 1839, in Lewisburg, O. Bur Roselawn Cem. Emigrated to Ohio 1812. Founded the city of Lewisburg. Ref: Vol 85, p 338, Natl No. 84,877, D. A. R. Lin. Fur infor Organizing Regent, Mrs. Miller.

HORN, JOSEPH, (Highland Co.)

Bur New Market. Fur infor Waw-Wil-a-Way Chap.

HORNEY, WILLIAM, (Greene Co.)

Pvt in Muster Roll of the 5th Md Regt, Capt William Rie Cup's Company, Aug 1780, Jan 1781. Also 1778-1789. Fur semdries from N. C. Br 1752, Caroline Co, Md. Parents: Jeffrey and Deborah Horney. Mar Harriet Hannah Chipman, 1772. Children: Margaret, James, Paris, Deborah, Mary, Lydia, William, Daniel, Hannah, John, Chipman, Sarah, Jeffery. D 1829, near Spring Valley and Bellbrook, O. Bur Old Bellbrook, Greene Co, O. Br in Md, mar in Md, moved to N. C. then came to Ohio about 1800. Planter and Farmer. Quaker by faith. Ref: Maryland Archives; N. C. Army. Accounts, records and old Bibles Fedythe Horney Whitaker, 199 N. Main St, London, O. Fur infor William Horney Chap.

HORTON, JOSEPHUS, (Jackson Co.)

Enl 1779, Augusta Co, Va. Capt Tate Company, Maj George Morford Va. Tr; Mch 1781, Capt Alexander Telford's Company, Col Samuel McDowell's Va. Regt. Taken prisoner at Guilford, escaped July 8, 1781. Served several short periods. Br England, came over on ship Potomac. Mar July 4, 1824, Mary Jenkins of Scioto Co. A son John first official elected. D June 11, 1833. Bur on south end of Backus farm near Banner Station. Pensioned Sept 18, 1832, (War pensions claim W 7777). Living in Jefferson Twp. aged 73, where he died. Farmer. Ref: Prof. Tom Horton (S. A. R.) Milford Center, O. Fur infor Capt. John James Chap.

HOSBROOK, JOHN, (Hamilton Co.)

Sgt 1st Regt NJ Continental Line (p 116 Stryker's Men from N. J.) Br Ireland. Mar Lydia Kitchell, dau of Moses and Phoebe Hedges Kitchell, in 1780. Children: Archibald, Hannah, and Daniel, all born in N. J. Daniel (1785-1868). D 1798, on his farm which adjoins the present town of Maderia, Hamilton Co, O. Land in Symmes Purchase. No stone or marker. The chronicler states that a rail pen was placed around his hillside grave for a time. Many yrs ago in excavating, a walled rectangle was uncovered which is supposed to have been his grave. Farm is still owned by descendants. Came to America shortly before Revolutionary War, it is supposed. Lived in N. J. and mar in N. J. and here his children were born. Came to Cincinnati 1794. Farmer. Entered a large farm. It is probable that he was a surveyor as his son became a surveyor, and a son in each generation has been elected to office of surveyor. Ref: Mrs. Edith Frazier Hudson No 77474. Fur infor Cincinnati Chap.

HOSKINS, ASHBEL, (Portage Co.)

Pvt in Conn Continental Line. Placed on Pens Roll Sept 24, 1833. Bur Garrettsville, O. Fur infor Old Northwest Chap.

HOSKINSON, JOSIAH, (Scioto Co.)

Sgt. Maj in Capt Beal's Company, Col Rolwings' Regt. Mar Margaret ——— Bur Calvert Cem, west side. Lived on farm. Fur infor Joseph Spencer Chap.

HOSMER, WILLIAM, (Medina Co.)

Pvt Mass. Br 1741. D 1847. Bur Seville. GM by Western Reserve Chap. Fur infor Western Reserve Chap.

SITE OF FORT LAURENS OFFICIALLY DEDICATED BY D. A. R. OF STATE OF OHIO, SEPTEMBER 21, 1928 THE FIRST AND ONLY AMERICAN FORT OF THE REVOLUTIONARY WAR, ESTABLISHED WITHIN THE LIMITS OF WHAT IS NOW OHIO, WAS BUILT HERE IN DECEMBER 1778, BY GEN. LACHLAN McINTOSH AS A DEFENSE AGAINST THE BRITISH AND INDIANS AND HELD UNTIL EARLY IN AUGUST 1779, WHEN IT WAS RELIEVED AND ABANDONED.

HOSMER, ZACHARIAH, (Geauga Co.)

Br 1762. Children: Alonzo, Hosmer, Andrew, Sylvester. D Aug 6, 1866, Parkman, O. Bur South Cem, Parkman village. MI: "Z. Hosmer died Aug 6, 1856, aged 94 yrs." GM White marble monument. Settled in Parkman in 1819. Ref: Hist Geauga & Lake Cos, p 157. Fur infor Taylor Chap.

HOUSER, MARTIN, (Stark Co.)

Patriot; prisoner by Indians. Br 1756 Bedford Co, Pa. Mar Anna ——— D 1840, Harrisburg, O. Natl No 70985, Vol 71, p 353. D. A. R. Lin. Ref: Mrs. J. H. Hartzell, Stark Co, O.

HOUSTON, WILLIAM, (County not stated.)

Pvt in Capt John Beatty's Company, 5th Pa Bn and was taken prisoner at the capture of Ft Washington, 1776. Br 1757. Mar June Watson. D 1834, Ohio. Natl No 62548, p 183, Vol 63, D. A. R. Lin. Ref: Fur infor Mrs S. D. L. Jackson, Greenfield, Pa.

HOVER, EMANUEL, (Trumbull Co.)

Capt. Member of the Committee of Safety, 1775, and commanded a company in 2nd Regt 3d Bn, Sussex Co, NJ Mil. Br 1748 in Sussex Co, N. J. Mar Mary Schoonover. D 1824 Newton Falls, O. Ref: 27541, Vol 28, p 202 and Vol 37, p 70, Natl No 36193 D. A. R. Lin.

HOVEY, WILLIAM, (Washington Co.)

Br 1748. D Oct 20, 1834. Bur Mt Ephraim Church Yard, 3 miles beyond Lower Salem, Washington Co, O. MI: "A Revolutionary Soldier." GM by Marietta Chap with Revolutionary marker, 1923. Fur infor Marietta Chap.

HOWARD, PETER, (Logan Co.)

Served 3 yrs Pvt in Col Gaskin's Va Regt. In battles of Monmouth and Stony Point, taken prisoner at surrender of Charleston, S. C. Escaped after some mos. Br Mch, 1745. Enl in May or June 1777 at Richmond, Va. Later moved to Philadelphia, thence to Eresboro, Burlington Co, N. J., living there over 30 yrs. Then moved to Logan Co, O. Allowed pens on application executed Oct 23, 1832, while resident of Logan Co. Fur infor Bellefontaine Chap.

HOWARD, PETER, (Logan Co.)

Commissioner of Pensions states he received pens for Revolutionary serv while residing in Logan Co, O. Perry Twp, in 1840, aged 95. Fur infor Bellefontaine Chap.

HOWARD, SOLOMON, (Hamilton Co.)

Br 1761, Conn. D 1834. Ref: S. A. R. Fur infor Cincinnati Chap.

HOWARD, THOMAS, (Wood Co.)

Br 1758. D 1825. Bur Howard Laskey Pratt cem at Grand Rapids, O. Early pioneer of Grand Rapids. See p 100, Vol 50, D. A. R. Lin. D. A. R. descendant, a great-granddaughter, Mrs. Agnes Howard McClaren, Delta, O. Fur infor Ursula Wolcott Chap.

HOWARD, WILLIAM, Capt. (Belmont Co.)

Capt Company Mil, 1776. Capt of 6th Company, 1777. Br 1749, Windham Co, Conn. D Morristown, Belmont Co, O, 1822. Natl No. 12,381, p 147, Vol 13, D. A. R. Lin.

HOWE, AMASI, (Gallia Co.)

Pvt in Revolution, Mass Line under Capt Haskell, 1781. Br 1765, Granville, Mass. Mar a widow, Mrs. Blagg (Maiden name, Polly Steele) D 1853, Gallia Co, O. Bur Glen, a little south of Vinton, O. Farmer. Natl No 84925, Vol 85, p 355, D. A. R. Lin. Ref: Ned McMillan, Cheshire, O. Fur infor Return Jonathan Meigs Chap.

HOWE, PETER, (Washington Co.)

Enl May 1775, as Pvt. Served 8 mos under Capt Isaac Baldwin, John Hale, Col John Stark. Re-enlisted Jan 1, 1776; served under Capt John Hale, Col John Stark, New Hampshire State Tr. In battles of Bunker Hill, Trenton, Bennington. Br Aug 1, 1756. New Marlborough, Mass. Parents: Nehemiah Howe and Bulah Wheeler Howe. Mar Orinda Fuller in 1780. (Br 1762, died 1835). Children: Dianthy, Delinda, Vilaty, Minerva, Lorilla, Sophronia, Cyrenius, Sylvanua, Orinda, Lucinda. D Dec 19, 1842, Ames Twp, Athens Co. Bur Demming cem, Washington Co. MI: "In memory of Peter Howe, who died Dec. 19, 1842, in the 87th year of his age." GM by Marietta Chap with Revolutionary marker in 1920. Came to Ohio in 1801, lived in the old blockhouse in the stockade. Lived in Washington Co 25 yrs, then moved to Athens Co. Ref: Natl No. 56,465, Vol 57, p 160, D. A. R. Lin. Fur infor Marietta Chap.

HOWELL, SAMUEL, (Clermont Co.)

Resided in Village of Williamsburg, 1826, Clermont Co, O. Ref: A. S. Abbott, Bethel, O. Fur infor Cincinnati Chap.

HOWELL, WILLIAM, (Meigs Co.)

Enl 1776, 1 mo. Capt Okey Johnson, Hampshire Co, Va. Enl 1777, 1 mo. Capt Okey Johnson, Hampshire, Va. Enl Aug 1778, 7 mos. Capt Okey Johnson, Van Swearingen Company, Light Inf, April 1781, 2 mo Okey Johnson. Br 1748, N. J. Mar "Elizabeth ———. (d May 2, 1839, in 86th yr of age." On stone by his side. Children: One dau, Rachel (mar Solomon Townsend.) MI: "William Howell, died Mch 28, 1842, in 94th year of age." Oct 13, 1832, pension allowed for 11 mos. service as Pvt Va. Line, while residing in Lee Twp. Athens Co, O, age 84 yrs. Ref: O. D. Dailey, Albany. O. W. Hopkins, Athens. Fur infor Jane Daily, State Chairman.

HOWELLS, DANIEL VEACH, (Trumbull Co.)

Bur Churchyard, South Hubbard. Could not locate grave. Many markers destroyed, many inscriptions could not be read. S. A. R. Yr Bk. Fur infor Mary Chesney Chap.

HOWLAND, JOHN (Brown Co.)

Bur Liberty, Brown Co. Fur infor Lieut Byrd Chap.

HOYT, AGUR, (Huron Co.)

On payroll of those who rode horses. Member James Clarke's Company, 16th Regt. Col Nehemiah Beardsley, July 16, 1779. Br Jan 20, 1761, Danbury, Conn. Parents: Comfort and Anna Beach Hoyt. Mar Dec 11, 1783 to Lois Boughton. Children: Betsy, Amelia, Polly, Philo, Agur Beach, Eli Boughton. D Nov 30, 1836, Norwalk, O. Bur St. Pauls Episcopal Cem, Norwalk, O. MI: Name, dates of birth and death. GM Stone marker by family. Ref: Revolutionary Roll and History, Vol 8, Conn.; Hist Society's Collection, p 194. Natl No. D. A. R. roll No. 71,746 (?) Fur infor Sally De Forest Chap.

HUBBARD, ISAAC, (Ashtabula Co.)

First assistant to Paymaster General, his brother, Nehemiah Hubbard. Br Sept 24, 1749, Middletown, Conn. Parents: Nehemiah and Sarah Sill Hubbard.

Mar Ruth Coleman, Jan 24, 1782, Middletown, Conn. Children: Matthew, Isaac, William, Mary, Ruth, Amos, Daniel, Nehemiah and Henry. D Mch 10, 1848, Ashtabula, O. Bur Chestnut Grove, Ashtabula. MI: Names and dates only, monument. GM D. A. R. marker. In 1800, came from Conn to Oneida, N. Y. In 1834 came to Ashtabula Co, O. Ref: Hubbard Genealogy; Lineage Book, Vol 12, Natl No. 11718 S. A. R. No. 23394. Fur infor Mary Stanley Chap.

HUBBARD, ISRAEL, (Putnam Co.)

Pvt. Br Feb 6, 1752, Vt. One child, Bildad Hubbard. D Mch 20, 1840. Bur Hubbard, O, Sec. 6, Riley Twp. Marble slab, MI: "Israel Hubbard born Feb. 6, 1752, died Mch 20, 1840, aged 88 yrs, 1 mo, 4 das He was a soldier in the Revolutionary War." Descendants, Mrs. H. Bowman, Haskins, O, who verified above data sent by John Mallahan, P. M. at Pandora, who visited stone. Fur infor Jane Dailey, State Chairman.

HUBBELL, ABIJAH, (Meigs Co.)

D Rutland. Bur Miles Cem, Rutland, O, southeast corner of Old Cem. MI: "Abijah Hubbell, died July 18, 1841, 78 years of age. 'Blessed are they that do his commandments, that they may have right to the tree of life and may enter through the gate into the city." Ref: Mrs Bertha Rathburn, Rutland, O. Fur infor Return Jonathan Meigs Chap.

HUBBELL, GERSHOM, (Hamilton Co.)

Br 1766, New York. Ref: S. A. R. Fur infor Cincinnati Chap.

HUBER, ANDREW, (County not stated.)

Pvt. in Capt John Stone's Company, 2nd Bn, Lancaster Co, Pa. Mil. Br 1762, Lebanon, Pa. Mar ———— Kline. Natl No. 74,001, Vol 75, D. A. R. Lin. Ref: Eva Welker Wentz, Massillon, O.

HUDSON, JOHN, (Hamilton Co.)

Br 1768, New York. D 1847. Ref: S. A. R. Fur infor Cincinnati Chap.

HUDSON, JOSHUA, (Cuyahoga Co.)

Pvt. Conn. Br 1760, D 1842. Bur Strongville. Fur infor Western Reserve Chapter.

HUEY, ROBERT, (Montgomery Co.)

Pvt. 1777, in 7th Bn, Lancaster Co, Pa Mil. Br 1757, Lancaster Co, Pa. D 1839, Dayton, O. Ref: Vol 81, p 25, Natl No 90,070 and Natl No 101200, Vol 103, p 61, D. A. R. Lin.

HUFF, (HOFF) JOHN, (Delaware Co.)

2nd Sergt under Cols Seeley and Hankinson, N. J. Tr. D 1848, age 85. Bur Trenton Twp, Sunbury, O. Pensioned. Fur infor Delaware Chap.

HUFF, JOHN, (Franklin Co.)

Served in Revolutionary War. Br about 1750. Bur on Amos Culp farm, Hamilton Twp. GM Revolutionary Grave Committee with bronze marker, May 30, 1912. Came to Ohio in 1807 and settled in Hamilton Twp and lived on the Amos Culp farm. Fur infor Columbus Chap.

HUFFSTETTER, JAMES, (Trumbull Co.)

Bedford Co. Ranger 1778-1783. Bur Pricetown, Newton Twp, Trumbull Co. No stone at Pricetown for James Huffstetter; but one for "Mary Huffstetter" with dates of Revolutionary period was found. Ref: Pa. Archives, Series 3, Vol 23, p 232, 239. Fur infor Mahoning and Mary Chesney Chaps.

HUGHES, ELIAS, (Licking Co.)

Enl at Clarksburg to serve against Indians. In 1774 was with Gen Lewis in battle of Pt Pleasant on Big Kanawha river. Built Ft Nutter, Va. In 1802 was elected Capt of the 1st Company of Mil raised in the county. He served also in war of 1812. Government scout along the Ohio River 21 yrs. Capt of rangers under Col Benj Wilson and Louther. Br 1757, Handy Co, Va. Parents: Thomas Hughes, killed by Indians, Hackers Creek, Va. Mar and had 12 children, Jonathan, David. D Dec 22, 1844, Utica. Bur old cem Utica with military honors. MI: "Revolutionary War." GM Hetuck Chap, 1909. Was a pensioner. Ref: Hist of Licking Co by E. M. P. Brister. Fur infor Hetuck Chap.

HUGHES, HENRY, (Jackson Co.)

Mar Emily Cloar Nov 13, 1852. Children: Henry. Bur near the home of William Johnson, Jefferson Twp. Fur infor Capt John James Chap.

HUGHES, JOSEPH, (Brown Co.)

Pvt in Capt John Walls Company, 2d Bn, Washington Co, Pa. Mil. Br Pa. Mar Catherine Dear, 1796. D 1837, Brown or Adams Co. Supposed to be buried in Decatur Cem. Stone mason. Ref: Belle Stephenson, Ripley, O. Fur infor Lieut Byrd Chap.

HUIET, PHILIP, (Montgomery Co.)

Enl in 1780 in Guilford Co, N. C. and served for 6 mos as a Pvt under Capt Tobias Whitsel. Br Mch 8, 1754, in Berks Co, Pa. Mar Elizabeth Lutz. Children: Fannie, Elizabeth, Catherine, Sarah, Mary, Philip Jr., Henry, Michael, George, Simon P. D June 14, 1846, Miamisburg, O. Bur Hill Grove Cem, Miamisburg, O. Lot No 281, near main entrance. MI "Born March 8, 1754; Died June 14, 1846. Aged 92 years, 6 months, and 6 days." GM Richard Montgomery Chap, S. A. R. May 1919. Removed to N. C. and finally to Montgomery Co, O. Built a flour mill (the first on th Miami River) in the north part of Miamisburg, in 1812. Had a contract for 500 barrels of flour for the army in 1812. Date furnished by Miss Drusella Shepherd, Miamisburg, O. Natl No 60539, 77821 D. A. R. Fur infor Richard Montgomery Chap, S. A. R.

HULBERT, EPHRAIM, (Hancock Co.)

Bur in Hancock Co, unable to locate grave. Fur infor Ft Findlay Chap.

HULET, JOHN, (Medina Co.)

Served in Mass State. Pvt and Sgt, Berkshire Co, Mil. Pensioner when died at Brunswick, O. Br 1755. D 1841. Bur Brunswick Center. GM by Western Reserve Chap. Ref: Natl No 79798, Vol 80, DAR Lin. Fur infor Western Reserve Chap.

HULICK, JOHN, (Clermont Co.)

Was with Washington at Valley Forge; severely wounded at Cowpens by gunshot in side; at surrender of Yorktown; served more than 2 yrs. Br 1754, Sussex Co, NJ. Mar Mary Lott. Children: James, John, Catherine, Cornelius, Mary, Jane, Sarah, Martha. D 1842, Clermont Co, O. Bur private cem (Moore's) near Batavia, O. Moved to Batavia Twp, 1816. At age of 88, resided in Batavia twp where he was receiving a pens in 1840. Carpenter and millwright. Natl No 236005 on this record (Cin. Chap) Ref: A. S. Abbott, Bethel, O. Fur infor Blanchester Chap.

HULING, WILLIAM, (Clermont Co.)

Came to Monroe Twp, Clermont Co, O. in 1807, settled on Ulrey's Run. Br NJ. Children: Samuel, William, Abraham, Jacob, Isaac. D 1826. Ref: A. S. Abbott, Bethel, O. Fur infor Cincinnati Chap.

HULL, ISAAC, (Butler Co.)

D Oct 6, 1833, age 75 yrs, 1 mo and 21 days. Bur Greenwood Cem Hamilton, O. Name appears on Soldiers and Sailors Monument on Ft Hamilton Site, High St. and Monument Ave, under Heading, Revolutionary Soldier. Fur infor John Reily Chap.

HULL, JOHN, (Pike Co.)

Pensioner of 1840, for military service at age of 92, while living in Seal Twp, Pike Co, O. Br 1748. Fur infor Census of Pensions 1840, Copied by Jane Dailey, State Chairman.

HULL, SOLOMON, (Mahoning Co.)

Pvt in Continental Tr. N. J. Men of Revolutionary, p 217. Children: Andrew was only one recorded. Michael is a descendant. Bur Mahoning Co. Came to Mahoning Co from N. J. early in 1800. Fur infor Mahoning Chap.

HULSE, JAMES, (Jackson Co.)

Spoken of in Co historical research. Fur infor Capt John James Chap.

HULSE, WILLIAM, (Belmont Co.)

Sgt of Cav, paid Oct 24, 1783 139£, 19s, 3d, for services Va Line. Br Oct 19, 1753. D Sept 6, 1830. Bur St. Clairsville, O, Methodist Cem. Ref: Laura M. Thompson, St Clairsville, O. "Revolutionary Soldiers" Vol 4, p 212, Va State Library. Fur infor Grace Allen McFarland, St Clairsville, O. D. A. R., Wheeling Chap, W. Va.

HUMASON, JOEL, (Trumbull Co.)

Bur Vienna Center. Name is all that remains on marker. Administrator of estate ordered Aug 11, 1832. Fur infor Mary Chesney Chap.

HUMPHREY, DAVID. (Trumbull Co.)

Bur near Braceville, east of Phalanx Mills. Ref: Baldwin Library, Youngstown, O. Kindness of Miss Kyle. Fur infor Mary Chesney Chap.

HUMPHREY, EVANS (or RICHARD) (Licking Co.)

Name is found as assignor on land bounty papers in Col Yate's Regt, May 20, 1782. Was with Gen Wayne at Stony Point. Br Albany, N. Y. Parents: Hugh and Nancy (Peacock) Humphrey. Mar. Children: A dau mar Chriswold May. D St Louisville, O. Bur north of Newark. Street cuts through old family cem. Ref: Hist of Licking Co by E. M. P. Brister. Fur infor Hetuck Chap.

HUMPHREY, SIMON, (Summit Co.)

Br Conn. Mar Lois Cornelia. (Name on headstone). Bur Western Star. MI: "Sacred to the memory of Simeon Humphrey, who was born Nov 8, 1762. Died at Norton, Ohio, Aug 19, 1835." GM White marble slab. Fur infor Cuyahoga-Portage Chap.

HUNGERFORD, JOSIAH, (Lake Co.)

Responded Danbury Alarm, 1777. Br East Haddam, Conn, 1763. Mar Hannah Bigelow. D Leroy Twp, 1841. Natl No 55,408, p 188, Vol 56, D. A. R. Lin.

HUNT, JONATHON, (Erie Co.)

Served in Bradstreet's command. B 1820, Venice, O. Bur Erie Co. Fur infor Martha Pitkin Chap.

HUNT, THOMAS, (Butler Co.)

Minute Man. Served seven yrs. Br Nova Scotia, 1745. Mar Anie Fitch, (br 1748, d 1832). D June 25, 1814. Bur in old burying ground at Huntsville, O. (That is, the Hunt burying ground, private). Invented the first steamboat in 1732, which was afterward perfected by Robert Fulton. Fur infor John Reily Chap.

HUNTER, GEORGE, (Columbiana Co.)

Bur Bethel Synod Cem, 5 miles south of Lisbon, O. Fur infor S. A. R. Yr Bk, 1917. Copied by Jane Dailey, State Chairman.

HUNTER, JOHN, (Highland Co.)

Pvt in Capt Robert Byers Company, Lancaster Mil. Entered service Jan 13, 1777. Pa Archives, Series 5, Vol 7, p 461. Br 1751, Pa. Mar Margaret Watt, 1770. Children: Elizabeth, Morrow, Robert, Mary, Nesbit, Thomas, Margaret, Robinson. D July 2, 1829, Highland Co, O. Bur Presbyterian Twp. at New Market, O. MI: "John Hunter died July 2, 1829 in the 87th year of his age." Farmer. Came to Ohio about 1807. Was Justice of Peace for many yrs. One of first members of Presbyterian church in Highland Co. Ref: Viola Eyler Iliff, Natl No. 228,415, London, O. Fur infor William Horney Chap.

HUNTINGTON, JOHN, (Muskingum Co.)

Br 1745. D 1815, Norwich, O. Natl No. 22,608, p 213, Vol 23, D. A. R. Lin.

HUNTOON, THOMAS, (Lake Co.)

Enl in Capt Tilton's Company June 12, 1775, under Col Enoch Poor's Regt; later in Col T. Bartlett's Regt of N. H. Tr. Br 1753, Sunapee, N. H. Mar Elizabeth ———. Children: One son was Corbin. D Jan 2, 1831. Bur in Huntoon Cem. Concord Lake, O. GM by New Connecticut Chap. Ref: Natl No 102649, Vol 103, p 199, D. A. R. Lin. Fur infor New Connecticut Chap.

HURLBURT, JEHIEL, SR., (Trumbull Co.)

Pvt. in Capt Holcomb's Company, 18th Regt. Was disch at N. Y. 1776. Also served in line from Middletown, Conn. Mar Eunice Bacon Hurlburt (br July 13, 1755, died 1838.) Children: Jehiel Jr., Eunice, Meloda. D 1813. Bur Hartford Center, southeast part of cem. D. A. R. descendant, Mrs. J. J. Kiepura, 4510 Manor Circle, Sioux City, Ia. Ref: Matilda Baldwin, Tyrrell, O, who fur infor to Mary Chesney Chap.

HUSTED, SHADREN, (Huron Co.)

Bur Sutton's cem. Hunt's Corners. Fur infor Sally De Forest Chap.

HUSTON, ROBERT, (Knox Co.)

Pvt. He rendered material aid during Revolutionary War. At one time he rallied the neighbors and furnished rations to Washington's army which was in camp near Trenton, N. J., where he was living at that time. Br 1756, Trenton, N. J. Parents: James Huston and Isabella Nelson (d May 27, 1805) Mar Deborah Smith Robinson, (br 1760, d Mch 13, 1826.) Children: James, Thomas, Robert, John, Joseph, Polly, Isabella and Jane. D Apr 5, 1838, Martinsburg, O. Bur Presbyterian cem, Martinsburg, east side about the center of cem. Lot No. 79. MI: "In memory of Robert Huston who died April 5, 1838, aged 82 yrs." A verse of Scripture which is illegible. GM Kokosing Chap D. A. R. Dec 1927. Ref: Military record "Officers and Men of the Revolutionary War." Strykers, p 641. Also Natl No. 80,104, Vol 81, D. A. R. Lin. Fur infor Kokosing Chap.

HUTCHENS, HOLLIS, (Noble Co.)

Bur South Olive Cem. MI: "Hollis Hutchens, a native of state of Maine and a Soldier of the Revolution." Settled Olive twp, 1806, south part. Fur infor Mrs. L. B. Frazier, Caldwell, O.

HUTCHINS, MOSES, (Geauga Co.)

Pvt. and Dragoon Conn. Continental Line. Pensioned 1832. Br 1756. Children: Nancy, Sarah, Diana, Jacob, Caleb. D 1837, Burton, O. Came to Geauga Co, 1816. Estate administered Oct 22, 1834. Ref: Pioneer Hist Geauga Co, p 725. Probate records. Fur infor Taylor Chap.

HUTCHINS, WILLIAM, (Lake Co.)

Served in Company of Capt William Hutchins (his father) in an independent Co in Vt, Nov 20, 1781 to May 1, 1782. Br 1762. Parents: William Hutchins. D 1852. Bur Perry, O. GM by stone at grave. Fur infor New Connecticut Chap.

HUTCHINSON, AMAZIAH, (Franklin Co.)

5 Conn. Regt. 1781. Br Dec 14, 1762. D Oct 3, 1823. Mar Betsey Mack, Mch 30, 1791. Bur Dublin, O. Service, P 161, Vol 8, Conn Historical Society Records. Ohio State Library. Fur infor Columbus Chap.

HUTCHINSON, WILLIAM, (Brown Co.)

Was present at surrender at Yorktown. Came to Huntington Twp, Brown Co, O., in 1803. Br Loudoun Co, Va, 1757. Mar Rebecca Cooper, 1783. (br 1767, d 1853.) Eleven children. D Jan 7, 1841. Ref: A. S. Abbott, Bethel, O. Fur infor Cincinnati Chap.

HUTT, JOHN, (Ross Co.)

Artillery, 3 yrs under Capt John Mazarett; present at surrender of Cornwallis. Br 1763, Westmoreland Co., Va. Mar Elizabeth Crockwell. D 1833, Chillicothe, Ross Co, O. Pensioner from Chillicothe, O, where he died. DAR descendant 42362. Vol 43, D. A. R. Lin, p 136. Fur infor Nathaniel Massie Chap.

HUXLEY, DAN—, (Mahoning Co.)

Pvt. in Capt Zenos Wheeler's Company, Col Hopkins Regt, Mass Line. Br 1743, Suffield (or Sheffield) Conn. D 1822, Ellsworth, O. Ref: 31808 Vol 32, and 9173, Vol 92, D. A. R. Lin.

HYDE, ANDREW, JR., (Marion Co.)

Pvt in Capt Charles Dibble's Company, Col Rossiter's 3rd Berkshire Company. Enl Oct 14, 1780, disch Oct 17, 1780. Br 1757. D 1845. Bur Claridon Graveyard. MI "Andrew Hyde—1757—1845, A Soldier of 1776.'" Ref: Mass Soldiers in the Rev. Fur infor Capt William Hendricks Chap.

IDEN, JOHN, (Morrow Co.)

Pvt. Va Mil. Br Nov 5, 1755, Richland, Berks Co, Pa. Parents: Samuel Iden, mar in 1754. Mar twice, 2nd wife, Hannah Russell, 1793. Children: 1st wife: Samuel, James, Margaret, Abigail, Mary, Isaac. 2nd wife: Alfred, Jacob, Thomas, Lot, John, Catherine. D Knox Co, O, June 6, 1847. Bur Mt Tabor Cem, Morrow Co. MI: Name, date of birth and death. GM Government marker, Soldiers Grave. John Iden moved to Loudoun Co, Va, with his parents and his children were all born there. Later he moved to Knox Co, O. Farmer. Placed on pens roll May 28, 1833, as pvt of Va Mil. Ref: Miss Agnes McAnall, Mt Gilead, O. Fur infor Mt Gilead Chap.

INGALLS, JOSEPH, (Franklin Co.)

Served in 6th Regt, NY Inf. Pensioned Mch 15, 1834. Br Dutchess Co, NY, 1752. D Aug 13, 1834, Blendon Twp. Bur Jamison Cem, Blendon Twp. MI: "Joseph Ingalls died August 13, 1834, aged 82 years." GM Revolutionary Grave Committee. Bronze marker, May 30, 1912. Came to Ohio in 1818 and settled in Blendon Twp. Fur infor Columbus Chap.

IREY, JOHN, (Marion Co.)

Pvt. Br Jan 29, 1757, Loudoun Co, Va. Children: Mary, Samuel, John Enos, Stephen. D Dec 20, 1837. Bur Old Caledonia Cem, Caledonia, O. MI: "In memory of John Irey who died December 20, 1837, aged 80 years, 10 months, 22 days." GM D. A. R. marker, Oct 30, 1922. Farmer. Ref: Marion Co History. Fur infor Muskingum Chap.

IRVIN, ANDREW, (Clinton Co.)

Bur New Antioch. Fur infor George Clinton Chap.

IRWIN, JOHN, (Greene Co.)

D July 14, 1854. Bur Hussey Graveyard, now New Burlington Cem. Sugarcreek, 1804. Soldier of 1812. Ref: Robinson's History of Greene Co. Fur infor Catherine Greene Chap.

IRWIN, SAMUEL, (Montgomery Co.)

Lt Col 3rd Bn, Cumberland Co, Pa, Mil. Pa Archives 2nd series, Vol 14, p 367, 388, 399, 425, 456. Br 1745. Mar Mary Potts, Dec 30, 1783. Children: Matilda, Jane, Amos, Moses, William, Isaac, Elam. D Jan 1, 1826, Washington Twp, Montgomery Co, O. Bur Baptist Cem, Centerville, O, on ridge in center of cem, near other Revolutionary soldiers. MI: "In memory of Samuel Irwin, who departed this life Jan 21, 1826, aged 81 yrs." GM Richard Montgomery Chap, S. A. R. bronze marker, June 28, 1922. After the war he went to Iredell Co, N. C. and in 1799 came to what is now Lebanon, O. Two things worked to induce his removal from NC. First, his dislike of slavery and second, the good opinion formed of the Miami Valley, after an interview with Daniel Boone. Late in 1801 or early the next yr he moved with his family to the farm near Centerville. S.A.R. descendant Harvey I. Allen, Y. M. C. A., Dayton. Ref: Natl No 52905, and Natl No 79400, D. A. R. Fur infor Richard Montgomery Chap, S. A. R.

IRWIN, THOMAS, (Butler Co.)

Name appears on the Tablet in the Soldiers and Sailors Monument at Hamilton, as a Revolutionary Soldier buried in that Co. D Oct 3, 1847. Bur Mt Pleasant Cem, St Clair Twp, north of Monroe. Fur infor John Reily Chap.

ISRAEL, BASIL, (Coshocton Co.)

Ensign 1777 Capt John Dorsey's Company, Md Mil. Br 1757 Anne Arundel Co, Md. D New Milford, O, 1829. Mar Eleanor Mansel. Ref: 70870, p 313, Vol 71, D.A.R. Lin.

JACK, ANDREW, (Clinton Co.)

Bur Springfield Cem. Fur infor George Clinton Chap.

JACK, JAMES, CAPT, (Guernsey Co.)

Bur Old Cem, Cambridge, O. Ref: S. A. R. Fur infor Anna Asbury Stone Chap.

JACKSON, BENJAMIN, (Richland Co.)

Pvt and Sgt in Capt Josiah Hall's Company, Col Jacob Ford's Regt, NJ Line. Br Mch 5, 1752, Rockaway, NJ. 10th child of Joseph Jackson. Mar Abigail Mitchell. Children: Ziba, Isaac, Betsey, Phoebe, David, Daniel, Benjamin. D June 6, 1842, Belleville, O, Richland Co, where he is probably bur. Settled in Morris Twp, Knox Co, and received a pens. Ref: Vol 95, p 175, 94570 D.A.R. Lin. Fur infor Kokosing Chap.

JACKSON, DANIEL, (Knox Co.)

Revolutionary soldier and received a pens. Was the 11th child of Joseph Jackson. Br Dec 26, 1753. D Apr 9, 1836. He removed from Northumberland Co, Pa, to Ohio and is bur near Fredericktown, O. Ref: Mrs C K Conrad, Mt Vernon, O. Fur infor Kokosing Chap.

JACKSON, GEORGE, (Muskingum Co.)

Col. Served in Indian and Revolutionary Wars. Was in many engagements and skirmishes with George Rogers Clark, upon the Ohio River. Br Jan 9, 1757, Va. Parents: John Jackson. Mar Elizabeth Von Brake (first wife). D May 17, 1831, Zanesville, O. Bur in family plat, on homestead farm near Zanesville. Was a member of Va Convention adopting the Constitution. Elected fr that state to 4th, 6th and 7th Congresses. Moved to Ohio in 1807 where he was elected State Representative and Senator. Ref: 39929, Vol 40, p 341. Fur infor Muskingum Chap.

JACKSON, MATTHEW, (Hamilton Co.)

Br 1764, Mass. D 1823. Ref: S.A.R. Fur infor Cincinnati Chap.

JACKSON, PETER, (Ross Co.)

D July 31, 1841, aged 84 yrs, 9 mos. Bur Baptist Cem, Deerfield Twp. Mary, his wife, d Sept 24, 1844, aged 84 yrs, 7 mos. His name given in the list of pensioners who died in Ross Co. P 331, History Ross & Highland Cos, says: "Colonel Peter Jackson was one of the very first settlers in Deerfield Twp. He came in the year 1801 or 1802 to Deer Creek." (Called Col as a title of respect in later yrs.) Fur infor Nathaniel Massie Chap.

JACKSON, ROBERT, (Greene Co.)

Pvt. Br 1758, County Derry, Ireland. Parents: David and Elizabeth (Reed-Jackson). (A Revolutionary Soldier also; see p 13 of Genealogy of Jackson family). Mar Elizabeth McCorkle, 1786. Children: Margaret, Jane, Elizabeth, Mary, David, Rachael, Robert, Eleanor, Martha, Nancy. D Sept 26, 1828, Cedarville, O. Bur Massie's Creek Graveyard (Stevenson's) near Xenia. Xenia, 1814. Ref: Pa Archives. Robinson's Hist of Greene Co; Jackson Genealogy. Fur infor Catherine Greene Chap.

JACKSON, STEPHEN, (Madison Co.)

Pensioned 1818 for serv as Pvt and Sgt Mass, NH and Vt lines. Br Rochester, NH. D Madison Co, O. Mar Hannah Jackson. Ref: Natl No 73641, Vol 74, D.A.R. Lin.

JACOBS, JOHN, (Richland Co.)

Pa Continental Army, Pvt. Bur Mansfield Catholic Cem, Mansfield, O. MI: Name and Army. GM Mary Washington D. A. R. bronze marker, 1911. Fur infor Mary Washington Chap.

JACOBS, JONATHAN, (Trumbull Co.)

Bur Newton Falls. Ref: Name from S.A.R. Yr Bk. Fur infor Mary Chesney Chap.

JAMESON, ROBERT, (Delaware Co.)

Bur Old Cem in Delaware, O. Fur infor Delaware Chap.

JANES, ELIJAH, (Co. not stated)

Minute man and also Lt, Col Sheldon's Regt. Br 1744, Coventry, Conn. Mar Anna Hawkins. Children: one was John. D 1826, Ohio. Ref: Natl No 48431, p 201, Vol 49, D. A. R. Lin.

JEFFERIES, GEORGE, (Warren Co.)

Bur Morrow, Salem Twp, Warren Co, O. Fur infor S.A.R. Yr Bk 1917. Copied by Jane Dailey, State Chairman.

JEFFREY, DAVID, (Huron Co.)

Bur M. E. Cem, Ripley Twp, near Greenwich. Fur infor Sally De Forest Chap.

JENKINS, AZARIAH, (Jackson Co.)

Bur Rock Hill Cem, Bloomfield Twp. Fur infor Capt John James Chap.

JEWELL, EPHRAIM, (Lake Co.)

Pvt Capt Morse's Company, Col Reade's Regt, Oct 2, 1777 to Nov 8, 1777. Capt Granston's Company, Col Denny's Regt, Nov 3, 1779, to Nov 23, 1779. Br Aug 19, 1760, Stow, Mass. Parents: Silas and Mary (Whitney) Jewell. Mar Rebecca Brigham, 1781, Marlboro, Mass. Children: Lydia, Ball, Martha, Samuel, Ira, Ephriam. D July 13, 1845, Kirtland Lake Co, O. Pens Census 1840, living in Newbury, O, age 80. Ref: Mass Soldiers and Sailors, p 785. Fur infor Taylor Chap.

JEWETT, ABEL, (Licking Co.)

Pvt in Capt Joseph Parker's Company, Col Enoch Halis' Regt, NH Mil. 1760, mar Sarah Dwinnell in Rindge, NH. D 1821 Johnstown, O. Ref: 58302. Vol 59, p. 106. D.A.R. Lin.

JEWETT, JOSEPH M., (Ashtabula Co.)

Br 1760. Mar Phoebe —— (d 1843). Children: Elsie (Huntly), Nathan, Lavisa (Waters), Holland, Willard. D 1847 at Wayne. Ref: Military records, Columbus, O. Fur infor Eunice Grant Chap.

JOHNS, THOMAS, (Harrison Co.)

Served in Revolutionary War as a member of the 6th (Col John Gibson) and 7th (Col Daniel Morgan) Va Line Regts, 1778-80. Revolutionary pensioner living in Harrison Co in 1819, aged 92. U. S. Pens Rolls 1835. Ref: Eckenrode's Va. Rev. Lists II, 166. Fur infor Moravian Trail Chap.

JOHNSON, ABNER, (Hamilton Co.)

Br 1759, NJ. D 1832. Ref: S. A. R. Fur infor Cincinnati Chap.

JOHNSON, ARCHIBALD, (Mahoning Co.)

Seggett State Tr No 1 and 468. Mar Rebecca ———. Children: Newton, Samuel and Charles and maybe more. D 1806, Canfield. Bur Mahoning Co, Canfield. Ref: History of W Maryland War of Independence, list of soldiers. Old Will. Fur infor Mahoning Chap.

JOHNSON, ASHLEY, (Highland Co.)

Bur Graveyard at Fairfield Quaker Meeting-House, south of Leesburgh, O. Fur infor Waw-Wil-a-Way Chap.

JOHNSON, AZEL, JR., (Athens Co.)

Pvt in Gen Lafayette's Div. Enl at 17. Pvt, Capt Seth Goodwin's Company. Br Nov 27, 1762, Woburn, Mass. Parents: Azel (1732) and Rebecca (Wilson) Johnson. Mar Rebecca Brown, Aug 24, 1788, Leicester, Mass. Children: Azel, Pheba, Samuel, Eliza, Sallie, John, Rebecca, Benjamin. D May 4, 1838, Athens Co, O. Bur Nye's Cem, Chauncey, O. MI: "In memory of Azel Johnson." GM Family. Ref: Natl Records, Bureau of Pensions. Fur infor Nabby Lee Ames Chap.

JOHNSON, BENJAMIN, (Geauga Co.)

Pvt and Corp, Conn Continental Line, 7th Regt. Mch 10, 1777, Corp 1780. Br Edinburg, Scotland, July 22, 1761. Mar Susanna, 1791. Children: Oroon, Datas J., Esther, Dennison J., Billious H., Polly. D Sept 19, 1825, aged 67 yrs. Bur Fox Cem, Burton, O. MI: "Benjamin Johnson died Sept 19, 1828, age 67. Susanna, his wife, the late wife of Amos Foote, died March 26, 1843, age 73." GM Family stone, D. A. R. marker. Was at battles of Stony Point, and Monmouth. Pensioned 1818. Justice of the Peace. Farmer. Was a man buried with military and masonic honors. Came to Burton, O, 1802. Ref: p 441, 442, Geauga Co, Pioneers History, Cheshire History, p 197; Conn Men Rev p 151, 203, 303, 383, 379. Fur infor Taylor Chap.

JOHNSON, RICHARD, (Jefferson Co.)

Lt in Rangers on Frontier 1778-83 Pa serv. Br 1746, Amsterdam, Holland. Mar Elizabeth Nash, 2nd wife. D 1828, Steubenville, O, where he moved 1820. Ref: Natl No 42521, Vol 43, and No 52215 D. A. R. Lin.

JOHNSON, SILAS (Champaign Co.)

Br 1758 in Va. D 1819. Bur Adams Twp in the churchyard along Indian Creek. Fur infor Urbana Chap.

JOHNSON, THOMAS, (Lawrence Co.)

Pvt. In Capt James Read's Company NC Mil. Ill at Valley Forge. D Burlington, O. D. A. R. descendants. Natl No 26542, Vol 27, p 200. Ref: Mrs. Sarah L. Rannels (Wm. H.)

JOHNSTON, SILAS, (Shelby Co.)

Officer in Revolutionary War and Maj in War of 1812. Children: Charles Johnston, (br near Lexington, Ky, 1790, mar Nancy McCaw), was the first white boy living on banks of Mosquito Creek. D Shelby Co. Came from Lexington, Ky. in 1799 to Shelby Co, locating at the head waters of Mosquito Creek, Green Twp. Ref: Sutton's Hist Shelby Co, O. Fur infor Lewis Boyer Chap.

JOHNSTON, WILLIAM, (Huron Co.)

D Apr 7, 1838, aged 85. Bur New Haven. MI "Revolutionary Soldier." Fur infor Sally De Forest Chap.

JOHNSTON, NICHOLAS, (Hamilton Co.)

Came to America as a British soldier; deserted in winter 1778, floated down river to join Washington's Tr below N. Y. Served as a Pvt in Amer Army. Br Sept 23, 1764, Dumfries, Scotland. Mar (1st) Sarah Ferries, May 9, 1796, (2nd) Mary ————. Children: Mary, Elizabeth, Sarah, Hannah, Phebe, William, Susannah, John F., Cathren. D Dec 24, 1821. Bur Plainfield Cem, Hamilton Co. GM Slab; good condition. At Cincinnati, O, in 1789. See "Jones Hist of Cincinnati, p 49. Ref: Mrs. W. B. Johnston, Cincinnati, O. Pa. Archives, Vol 8, Series 6, p 1608; index to same, p 66. Fur infor Cincinnati Chap.

JOHNSTONE, WILLIAM, (Knox Co.)

Pvt in NJ Mil. Br 1756, N. J. D 1813, Knox Co, O. Ref: Vol 90, p 309, Natl No 89950 D. A. R. Lin.

JOLLY, DAVID, (Ross Co.)

Pvt in Capt Adam Clindmen's Company, 3rd Bn, Northampton Co, Pa Mil, 1782. Br 1739, Pa. D 1799, Chillicothe, O. Natl No 74011, Vol 75, D. A. R. Lin.

JOLLY, HENRY, (Licking Co.)

Enl at Washington Co, Pa, Aug 9, 1776, as Pvt in Capt Van Swearingen's Company, 8th Pa Regt. Served under Col Daniel Morgan, Col Mackay, Lt Col Stephen Bayard. Br July 26, 1757, N.J. Mar ————. D July 29, 1842, Jersey Twp. Bur Universalist Cem. GM Hetuck Chap, 1909. He often occupied the pulpits of the early churches, especially those of his own faith. Pension granted while living in Jolly Twp, Washington. Ref: Brister's History. Fur infor Hetuck Chap.

JONES, BENAIAH, JR., (Lake Co.)

Served on Washington's body guard during the war. Br Aug 12, 1755, Hebron, Conn. Parents: Benaiah Jones. Mar Jemina Skinner, Feb 7, 1781, who also did heroic work during the war. D Aug 19, 1839. Bur Mentor Ave Cem, Painesville, O. MI: "Jemima Skinner Jones, Benaiah Jones, Elkanah Jones, Soldiers of the Revolution." GM New Conn Chap. Came to Ohio in Sept 1808. Fur infor New Connecticut Chap.

JONES, BENJAMIN, (Clark Co.)

Pvt in 8th Pa Tr. Br June 9, 1763. Parents: Benjamin Jones. Mar Miriam Russ, June 21, 1786. Children: Hulda, Abraham R., Rubold, Sarah, Miriam, Benjamin, Simon. D Aug 10, 1835. Bur Garlough, near Pitchen, O, old part, not platted. After close of war joined Capt John Clark's Company, Feb to Apr 1778. Oct 7, 1786 took oath of allegiance to Pa before Joseph Whartan. Farmer and stock raiser in Champaign Co, O. Was placed on pension roll Feb 2, 1833. Annual allowance $56.66. Ref: Vol 3, Pa Archives, Series 5, p 367. Fur infor Lagonda Chap.

JONES, CATLETT, SR., (Columbiana Co.)

Lived in Butler Twp, Columbiana Co, O. Fur infor Bethia Southwick Chap.

JONES, ELKANAH, (Lake Co.)

Enl in 1776, for 3 mos under Capt Elijah Wright and Col Roger Enos; in 1777 with Col Robert Lattimore; in 1779 with Lt Noah Day; in 1781 Col William Ledyard's Regt. All services from Conn. Br Apr 28, 1761, Hebron, Conn. D 1849, Painesville, O. Bur Blish or Nye Cem, Painesville, O. Received a pension. Fur infor New Conn Chap.

JONES, FREDERICK, (Medina, O.)

Br 1751. D 1811. MI: "Revolutionary Soldier." Fur infor Western Reserve Chap.

JONES, GEORGE, (Madison Co.)

Enl in Capt Thomas Warman's Company, commanded by Col Thomas Cashkins, Mch 5, 1781. Disch Feb 5, 1782. Was at siege of Yorktown. Granted pens 1832. Br Fauquier Co, Va, Nov 17, 1762. Mar Foster, 1791 in Orange or Culpeper Co, Va. Children: Elizabeth, William, Mason, Phebe, Allen, Nancy, and Charles. D Mch 1844, Pike Twp, Madison Co, O. Bur Old Cem on Upper Barron Run, Pike Twp, Madison Co. MI: Dates and Name, tho broken. Came to Ohio about 1806, settled Pike Twp, Madison Co. Farmer and Twp Justice of Peace. Ref: Pension Dept, Washington D. C. Mrs. William Morgridge, Plain City, O. Fur infor London Chap.

JONES, JOHN, (Hamilton Co.)

Br 1764, Maryland. D 1821 Fur infor Cincinnati Chap.

JONES, JOSEPH, (Ashland Co.)

Enl Jan 1, 1776. Serv as a Pvt in Capt Coles' Co, Col Vermaries Continental Regt. Disch Jan 9, 1777. Reenlisted Nov 10. Serv as a Pvt in Col T Bigelow's Mass Regt. Disch Nov 10, 1780. Br Mass. D Oct 28, 1841, Richland Co, (now Ashland). Bur Old Cem, Green Twp, Perrysville, O. GM Sarah Copus Chap. Farmer and Pioneer. Pensioned June 13, 1818, residing in Richland Co. Fur infor Sarah Copus Chap.

JONES, SETH, (Meigs Co.)

Enl spring to Nov 1775 in Capt Peter Pitt's Company, Col Timothy Walker's Regt, 3 mos, Sept 1777 1 mo; Mch to Jan 1778-1782. Engaged in battle Bunker Hill, Bennington, White Plains. Residence at time of enlmt Dighton, Bristol Co, Conn. Br 1757, Mass. Mar 1st: Sarah Pitts, Sept 27, 1778. 2nd; Esther Ford, Aug 26, 1810. Children: Hetta, Seth, Esther, Sally. D 1826, at Graham, O. (Monroe Co) Natl No 87052, Vol 88 D. A. R. Lin reads. Bur Letart Falls, O. MI: "Seth Jones departed this life 1826. 69 yrs. 4 mos. 15 days. He was a member of Methodist Church." Application for widow's pens Feb 2, 1861. Ref: Mrs. Helen Laughead Elberfeld, Pomeroy, O. and Natl No 102688, Vol 103, D. A. R. Lin. Fur infor Return Jonathan Meigs Chap.

JONES, SILAS, (Trumbull Co.)

Bur Center Fowler Twp Cem. Given a pens Aug 1832. Copied fr S. A. R. Yr. Bk. His will was probated in Trumbull Co, June 1841. Fur infor Mary Chesney Chap.

JONES, SOLOMON, (Delaware Co.)

Ensign under Col Thos Nixon, Capt Elija Danforth, Mass Tr. Bur Burkshire Twp. Pensioned. Fur infor Delaware Chap.

JONES, THOMAS, (Jackson Co.)

Mar Betsey Ann Alexander Mch 9, 1832. Fur infor Capt John James Chap.

JONES, THOMAS, (Clermont Co.)

Enl Hagerstown, Md, 1778 in "Flying Camp" under Capt Dan'l Clapsaddle, Col Otto Williams, Lt Col Henry Schenck, 1st Lt Frederick Nicodemus; 2nd Lt David Harry, Ensign Mathias Hickman, Orderly Sgt Benj Prince under Gen Bell or Beall. Br Washington Co, Md, Jan 26, 1756. Mar. Children: George, Henry, Anthony, David, John, Mary (who mar Elijah Fee, a minister). D 1830, Clermont Co, O. Bur Calvary Cem. Was living in Washington Co, Md until 2 yr after Rev, thence came to Westmoreland Co, Pa and after 16 yrs went to Mason Co, Ky. After 3 yrs to Washington Twp, Clermont Co, O. Wounded at White Plains. Disch at Philadelphia. Pens 1831. $28.33 annually for Md State Tr. Ref: Pens S 2655; A. S. Abbott, Bethel, O. Fur infor Cincinnati Chap.

JONES, WILLIAM, (Clermont Co.)

Br Va. D Union Twp, 2 miles northeast Mt Carmel, aged 102, where he settled in 1807. Ref: A. S. Abbott, Bethel, O. Fur infor Cincinnati Chap.

JONES, WILLIAM, (Perry Co.)

Br 1758, Fauquier Co, Pa. D 1834, Somerset, Perry Co, O. Ref: Natl No 185013. Fur infor Mrs. Lowell Hobart, Washington D. C.

JONES, WILLIAM CLARKE, (Trumbull Co.)

Pvt Conn State Tr. Br June 1760, Conn. Mar Lorany, (d Feb 26, 1819, age 47 yrs). D Nov 25, 1841, age 81 yrs, 6 mos, 16 days. Bur Burghill, Hartford Twp. GM Good Condition. Placed on Pens roll of Trumbull Co, O Inventory estate 1842. Ref; Natl No 27551, Vol 28, p 205 and Natl No 132610 D. A. R. Lin. Fur infor Mary Chesney Chap

JORDAN, JACOB, (Noble Co.)

Saw service with Pa Tr. Settled in Brookfield Twp in 1810, left in 1818. Many descendants. Fur infor Mrs. L. B. Frazier, Caldwell.

JORDAN, (or JORDON), THOMAS, (Belmont Co.)

Served 1776 and 1778 as Pvt and Ensign in Capt Reed's Company, Col Thomas Strawbridge's and I. Taylor's Regt. Engaged in Brandywine and Germantown. Wife pensioned in 1860. Br 1747, Wilmington, Del. Mar Rebecca Starbuck in 1818. D 1850, Belmont Co. Ref: Natl No 73857, Vol 74, p 310, and Natl No 78069, Vol 79, D. A. R. Lin.

JORDEN, JOHN, (Mahoning Co.)

Pvt. Br Ireland. D 1824. Bur Old Brunstetter, Austintown. Came from Chester Co, Pa. Lived in Poland, moved to Austintown in 1813. Farmer. Ref: Pa Archives, Series 2, Vol 13, p 115; Trumbull and Mahoning Co Hist, Vol 2, p 59. Fur Infor Mahoning Chap.

JOSLYN, DARIUS, (Mahoning Co.)

Pvt Capt Langton's Company, Col Mark Hopkins 1st Berkshire Regt. Enl July 15, 1776. Battle of Ticonderoga 1777. Served most of time until 1781. Mar Sybil Herrick (1760-1874). Bur Canfield, O. GM D. A. R. 1915-17. Ref: Mass Soldiers & Sailors D. A. R. No 9295. Fur infor Mahoning Chap.

JOY, EBENEZER, (Lake Co.)

Enl Dec 1778; length of serv 22 mos, under Cols McClelland, Bartlett, Nichols and Wait of Conn. Br 1764, Killingly, Conn. D 1837. Bur Perry, O. He was one of the early settlers of Perry Twp. His name appears among the town officers as early as 1819. Was among the charter members of the Church of Christ. Received a pens. Fur infor New Connecticut Chap.

JUDD, DANIEL S., (Cuyahoga Co.)

Sgt. Conn, also fought in Old French and Indian War. D 1810. Bur Wilson Mills Cem, Mayfield. Fur infor Western Reserve Chap.

JUNKIN, LANCELOT SR., (Greene Co.)

D 1833. Bur Massie Creek graveyard (Stevenson's). Ross 1810. Ref: Robinson's History of Greene Co. Fur infor Catherine Greene Chap.

JUSTICE, JESSE, (Clermont Co.)

Revolutionary soldier who died west of Bethel, Clermont Co, O. Fur infor Cincinnati Chap.

KACKLEY, JOHN, (Also COCKLEY), (Guernsey Co.)

Pvt, Cumberland Co Mil, 3rd Bn, 1781. Br July 10, 1741. D April 7, 1823. Ref: S. A. R. Fur infor Western Reserve Chap.

KARR, MATTHEW, (Co. not stated)

Pvt 1778, in Capt Robert Wilkin's Company, Col Josiah Harmar's Regt. Br about 1734 in Ireland. D 1791 in Ohio. Ref: Natl No 67383, Vol 68, p 137, D. A. R. Lin. Ref: Mrs Emma A. K. Carrhicks, Salisbury, O.

KATZENBERGER, JOHN, (Hancock Co.)

Bur south of Benton Ridge. Fur infor Ft Findlay Chap.

KEATON, ——, (Jackson Co.)

Bur in a country graveyard near Keystone. Fur infor Capt James Chap.

KECKLER, JACOB, (Fairfield Co.)

D Fairfield Co about 1830. Bur on home farm, 3 miles southwest of Bremen. Came to Ohio fr Pa about 1800. Ref: S. B. Keckler, Sealston, King George Co, Va. Fur infor Elizabeth Sherman Reese Chap.

KEELOR, THOMAS, (Hamilton Co.)

Enl 1779 Capt Richard Cox's Company, 3rd Regt NJ Continental Establishment. Br 1764, N. J. D 1851, Cincinnati. Ref: S. A. R. Natl No 55128, Vol 56, p 61, D. A. R. Lin. Fur infor Cincinnati Chap.

KELL, SAMUEL, (Warren Co.)

Pvt in Capt Through's Company. Col Patterson Bell's Regt. Pa Line. D after 1820, Warren Co, O. Ref: Vol 94, p 288, Natl No 93937 D. A. R. Lin.

KELLER, HENRY, (Fairfield Co.)

Pvt in Capt Geo Hudson's Company, Pa line. Br 1755 York, Pa. Mar Catherine Seitz. D 1838, Fairfield Co. Ref: Vol 96, p 46, Natl No 95132 D. A. R. Lin.

KELLER, JOHN, (or KELLAR), (Clark Co.)

Enl from Lancaster, Pa, 1776 as Pvt in Capt George Gantz's Company, Pa Tr. Br 1758 Lancaster Co, Pa. Mar Garber—Annie Ball. Children: Salome, Mary, Christine, Mrs. Reprogle. D 1837, near New Carlisle, Bethel Twp, O. Bur Old Frantz Cem, 4 miles west of Springfield, O. on National Road. MI: "John Kellar Died 1837 Age 79". GM: S. A. R. Metal marker, about 1906. Farmer. Was placed on pens roll 1832 fr Clark Co, O. Ref: Pens Department. D. A. R. Natl No 42046. Fur infor Lagonda Chap.

KELLOG, ELDAD, (Ashtabula Co.)

Enl 1776 under Capt John Stenens, Col Chas Burrall's Continental Regt. Was at the battle of the Cedars, where he was taken prisoner. He reenlisted 1780 and was at West Point when Arnold deserted. Br 1752. Mar Elizabeth Waterhouse, 1783. Children: Sophia, Henry, Ulysses, Erastus, Walter. D 1838, Newton Falls, Trumbull Co. Bur Harpersfield, Ashtabula Co, O. Ref: "Conn Men in the Rev"; Lin Bk Vol. XXXVI. Hist Western Reserve. Fur infor Mary Stanley Chap.

KELLOGG, JOSIAH, (Cuyahoga Co.)

Fifer, Conn Line age 9½ yrs. Br 1770. D 1847. Bur Fair View Cem, Rockport. Fur infor Western Reserve Chap.

KELLOGG, MARTIN, (Huron Co.)

In Capt John Granger's Company. Was at Ticonderoga, and served under different commands. Br 1757, Springfield, Mass. Mar Lucy Dunham. Had a dau named Philena. D 1850, Norwalk, O. Bur Bronson Cem (abandoned). Ref: Vol 44, p 115, D. A. R. Lin. Fur infor Sally De Forest Chap.

KELLOGG, PLINNEY, (Lorain Co.)

In 1777 served as Pvt under Washington, at battle of Monmouth, and under Gates and Arnold at battle of Saratoga, when Burgoyne surrendered. Br 1752, Westfield, Mass. D 1842, LaGrange, (there is also LaGrange in Lawrence Co) O. Mar 1782. Ref: Natl No 56926, Vol 57, p 320, D. A. R. Lin.

KELLOGG, SETH, (Montgomery Co.)

Pvt soldier in Gen Waterbury's Brig, Conn Tr. See p 565 "Conn Men in Rev." Br Feb 8, 1740, Norwalk, Conn. Parents: Deacon John Kellogg, and Ann Coley of Norwalk and Fairfield Conn. Mar Eunice Judd, Sept 6, 1761. Children: Sarah Kellogg Hoyt, Esther, Eunice Kellogg Munger, Jemima Kellogg Tibbalk, Mary Kellogg Ives, Olive Kellogg Porter, Anne, Seth, Ethel, Elihu and Ezra. D on farm near Centerville, Montgomery Co, June 26, 1819. GM by son-in-law, Gen Munger (1812 War). Came to Ohio very early (1797) from Middleburg, Va with wife and children, Jonathan and Edmund Munger (his son-in-law) and Benjamin Maltbie. Traveled in two three-horse wagons, the wheel horses driven by lines and the leader driven by a boy. Came through Pa to Marietta where they remained for a while in the stockade. Thence to Belpre in 1799. To Cincinnati in 1800 by water, thence to Washington Twp, Montgomery Co. Ref: Miss Jean Rowland, London, O. Kelloggs Genealogy, p 154. History of Montgomery Co; Ohio Family records. Fur infor London Chap.

KELLY, JAMES, (Clark Co.)

Pvt Col Gibson's Va Tr. Capt Scott's Company. Br 1752, Scotland. Mar Catherine Stewart, 1783, in Monongalia Co, W Va. Children: Rachel, Joseph, John, Samuel, Thomas, Nathan, Mary, James, Catherine, Stewart, Francis, Leah. D Apr 30, 1837. Five miles south of Springfield, O. Bur Columbia Street Cem, Springfield, O., southeast portion about 25 ft from street. MI: "James Kelly April 30, 1837. Aged 85 years." GM Family and S. A. R. metal marker, 1906. Was with

Washington at Valley Forge 1777 and 1778 and had face and ears so badly frozen fleshy parts dropped off. Later a bullet took the end of his nose. Farmer. Came to Ohio in 1808. During War of 1812 an Englishman hurrahed for King George, Kelly struck at him, missed him and broke a walnut panel in a door. Ref: A printed book of the Kelly Family. Fur infor Lagonda Chap.

KELLY, JOHN, (Lorain Co.)

Bur Huntington Center, O, south of Wellington. MI: "John Kelly died Apr 22, 1842, age 79. Yorktown, 1781." GM Tombstone, seen by Mrs. E. Little, Oberlin, O 1913 S. A. R. list gives "John Keeley" Huntington Cem and no doubt same man. Fur infor Oberlin Chap.

KELLY, JOHN, (Muskingum Co.)

Revolutionary Soldier. D Jan 11, 1853 in Union Twp, Muskingum Co, aged 98 yrs. Bur Rich Hill Cem, Rich Hill twp, Muskingum Co. Fur infor Muskingum Chap.

KELLY, OLIVER, (Hamilton Co.)

Br 1757, N. J. D 1827. Ref: S. A. R. Fur infor Cincinnati Chap.

KELSIMERE, FRANCIS, (Hamilton Co.)

Br 1744, Maryland. D 1826. Ref: S. A. R. Fur infor Cincinnati Chap.

KEMP, JOHN W., (Seneca Co.)

Pvt. 1776 Capt Dame's Company, Queen Annes Co, Md. Br 1745, Md. Mar Mary Miller, 1778. D 1844, Bascom, O. Ref: Natl No 75826, Vol 76, D. A. R. Lin.

KEMPER, PETER, (Co not stated.)

Pvt and Ensign in Va Line. Br 1743, Fauquier Co, Va. D 1829, Ohio. Ref: Vol 95, p 122, Natl No 94377, D.A.R. Lin.

KENDALL, ROBERT SR., (Greene Co.)

Soldier of the Rev. D 1842, aged 91 yrs. Bur Associated Reformed Churchyard, E 3rd St, Xenia. Living in Xenia, 1808. Ref: Robinson's History of Greene Co. Fur infor Catherine Greene Chap.

KENNEDY, DAVID, (Portage Co.)

Lived at Aurora, where pensioned in 1840. Fur infor Old Northwest Chap.

KENNEDY, FRANCIS, (Hamilton Co.)

Pvt. Bedford Co, Pa Rangers on Frontier, 1778-1783. See: Pa Archives, Series 3, Vol 23, p 239; Vol 4, p 242 of 5 Series. Received depreciation pay for services. Br Bedford Co, Pa. Parents came to Pa; Scotch-Irish ancestry. Mar Rebecca, dau of Welch Quaker family about 1775 or 1776. Children: Margaret (1777), David, Francis Jr, Elizabeth, and Rebecca (1788) (mar Reuben Reeder). D 1796, drowned in Ohio river, while ferrying supplies for army, at this post. Body recovered by firing of cannon and bur in First Presbyterian churchyard. Never removed when church enlarged. Wife bur at Pleasant Ridge. He came in a flatboat, and landed Feb 8, 1789, 41 days after landing of first pioneers. Commissioned Lt of 1st Regt Hamilton Co Mil by Gen St Clair, 1790, on day of naming Hamilton Co. He and brother Thomas ran first ferry from Covington to Cincinnati. Ref: Natl No 34924, Margaret Kitchell Whallon, Cincinnati. Certified copy from Pa State Library, 1908. Fur infor Cincinnati Chap.

KENNEDY, HUGH—, (Brown Co.)

Served in Revolutionary War under Washington. Br Lancaster, Butler Co, Pa. Mar Sarah Canada (br Lancaster, Pa). Children: Robert, William, Thomas, James, Hugh, Catherine, Jane, Sally, Jonta. D 1837. Hamersville, O. Bur Hamersville. GM Tombstone. Came fr Pa. Butler Co to Brown Co and lived at Hamersville or where the town now stands. His dau Jane, mar George Flick and lived there also. Ref: Hist of Brown Co. and George Lucas, Hamersville. Fur infor Taliaferro Chap.

KENNISTON, JAMES, (Hamilton Co.)

Br 1756. D 1837. Ref: S. A. R. Fur infor Cincinnati Chap.

KENT, ABSALOM, (Harrison Co.)

Revolutionary Pensioner living in Harrison Co, in 1834, aged 82. Served in Westmoreland Co. Mil. Br 1752. D 1839. Came to Harrison Co about 1805 from Fayette Co, Pa. Ref: Pa Archives, 5th Series, Vol IV, p 443. U. S. Pens Rolls, 1835. Fur infor Moravian Trail Chap.

KENT, JOHN, (Seneca Co.)

Br Feb 7, 1745. D Nov 16, 1844, Bascom, O. Bur Bascom Cem. GM Bronze marker, 1927. Fur infor Dolly Todd Madison Chap.

KENT, JONAS, (Portage Co.)

Pvt in Col Jonathan Humphrey's Regt, Conn Line, in 1776, and served in Capt John Harmon's Company at Germantown and Valley Forge. Br 1757. Mar Ann Plum, 1785. D Oct 23, 1822, at Mantua, O. Ref: Natl No 43261, Vol 44, p 100 D. A. R. Lin. Fur infor Old Northwest Chap.

KENT, THOMAS, (Columbiana Co.)

In 1840 was living in Middleton Twp, Columbiana Co. A pensioner. Fur infor Bethia Southwick Chap.

KENT, WILLIAM, (Ross Co.)

Pensioned for service as Pvt in Capt Bruce's Company, Col Geo Rogers Clark, Md Line. Br 1763, Oldtown, Md. Mar "Sarah, consort of William Kent, d 1839." D Mch 24, 1848, Bainbridge, O, where buried. Ref: Vol 93, p 15, Natl No 92049, D. A. R. Lin. Fur infor Nathaniel Massie Chap.

KENT, ZENAS, (Portage Co.)

Pvt in Conn Line, Capt John Harmon's Company at Germantown and Valley Forge. Br 1741. D 1817, Mantau, O. Ref: Vol 87, p 274, Natl No 86855, D. A. R. Lin.

KENTFIELD, EBENEZER, (Geauga Co.)

Mass Continentals, Capt Warner's Company, 10th Mass Regt. Br 1759. Parents: Salmon and Bertha (Stearns). D Hambden, O, Mch 7, 1834. Bur Hambden Center, Lot 48. MI: "Ebenezer Kentfield died March 7, 1834, aged 75, a veteran of 76."Entered serv July 14, 1779, disch Apr 14, 1780. Pens allowed 1818. Came to Hambden, O, 1817. Ref: Mass Soldiers and Sailors, Vol 9, p 139. Fur infor Taylor Chap.

KERNS, JOHN 1ST, (Highland Co.)

Br Cumberland Co, Pa, 1760. Mar Isabelle Burch, 1790. D Highland Co, 1838. John Kerns 1st, migrated soon after 1815 fr Westmoreland Co, Pa, to Highland Co, O. Fur infor Waw-Wil-A-Way Chap.

KERR, JOHN, (Hamilton Co.)

D 1840. Ref: S. A. R. Fur infor Cincinnati Chap.

KERR, MATTHEW, (Washington Co.)

Pvt in Capt John Buchanan's Company, 7th Bn, Cumberland Co Mil, in Mch, 1778. Of Scotch descent, from northern Ireland. Children: Hamilton, br in Philadelphia). Killed by Indians, during Indian War, when he lived in garrison at the Point. In his memory, in Mound Cem at "unknown graves" by Marietta D.A.R. Emigrated to America before the war and lived in Philadelphia. Soon after the close of the war moved his family west of the mountains near Pittsburgh; then, near Wheeling. In 1787 he transferred his residence to the Island in the Ohio just above the mouth of the Muskingum. Ref: Hildredths Pioneer Hist. Fur infor Marietta Chap.

KERSTETLER, LEONARD, (Stark Co.)

Br 1747, Mackinaw Valley, Northumberland Co, Pa. Children: 8 sons all br in Pa. All grew to manhood. 3 bur in Pa., 5 in Ohio. D 1822, Youngstown Hill, at Newman. Bur Lawrence Twp. Stark Co, northwest of Massillon on Newman Rd. near road, at easterly end of cem. MI: "Leonard Kerstetler, died 1822. A soldier of the Revolution." GM David Kerstetler, a grandson; a small marble slab about 1890. Came to Ohio 1814; purchased a section in Lawrence Twp. Established a saw and grist mill; operated until his death; "donated 1½ acres for school, church, and burying purpose" to Lutheran Church; land dedicated in 1820, and he was first person bur in it. Descendants in Massillon furnished above for Massillon Chap, D. A. R. Fur infor Massillon Chap.

KESTER, JOSEPH, (Morrow Co.)

Bur Shawtown, near Cardimon. Ref: Mrs. Addie Slack, Delaware, O. Fur infor Mt Gilead Chap.

KETCH, THOMAS, (Mahoning Co.)

Ranger, Northampton Co, Pa. Br 1760. D 18—. Bur Cem north of Canfield, O. Ref: Pa Archives, Series 3, Vol. 23, p 246. Fur infor Mahoning Chap.

KETCHAM, SAMUEL, (Coshocton Co.)

MI: "Died Sept 24, 1845, aged 88 yrs, 2 mos, 11 das. A Revolutionary Soldier of 1776." Fur infor Coshocton Chap.

KEYES, ELIAS, (Cuyahoga Co.)

Pvt. Mass Line. Serv 3 yrs; with Washington at Valley Forge; went from home, Genessee Co, N. Y. Br 1763. D 1849. Bur North Royalton. With family came to Royalton, spring of 1811. He said Washington never went into battle without engaging in prayer; he suffered the same privations as his soldiers. Ref: Mrs. Ellen Keyes Mattingly, R. F. D. 2, Brunswick, O. aged 72, (1926) and last of the Keyes family. Fur infor Western Reserve Chap.

KEYES, SALMA, (Scioto Co.)

He served as Pvt, Capt Adam Baily, 2nd Mass Regt, Col Sproat Jan 23, 1781. Enl to serve 2 yrs. D Scioto Co. His name appears on roll at West Point, 1782. Fur infor Joseph Spencer Chap.

KEYS, RICHARD, (Hamilton Co)

Enl in Flying Camp of Lancaster Co, Company 7, under Col James Cunningham, 1776. Disabled, recovered, re-entered army in Col Alex Lowry's 3rd Bn at Brandywine, 1777. Br 1756, Pa. Lancaster Co. D 1830, Cincinnati, O. Bur Spring Grove, Sec 77, lot 7. Ref: Natl No 13501, Vol 14, D. A. R. Lin and Heitman's Reg. of Revolutionary War. (1893 Ed.) p 249. Fur infor Cincinnati Chap.

KIBBEY, EPHRAIM, (Warren Co.)

Enl 1777 at Essex, for the war; transferred 1779, to Capt Seth Johnson's Company, 3rd New Jersey Regt, under Col Elias Dayton. Br New Jersey 1754. D 1809 Warren Co, O. Ref: Natl No. 36,185, Vol 37, p 67, D. A. R. Lin.

KIDD, NATHANIEL, (Washington Co.)

Pvt. The name of Nathaniel Kidd appears on the muster rolls of the war of the Revolution as a Pvt in Capt John Guthery's company, Big Whitely District, Westmoreland Co, Mil 1782. John Pomeroy a Lt Col. Br 1743. Children: John, William, Joseph, Thomas, Amos, Isaac, Nathaniel, Mary. D 1824. Bur Stanleyville, O. GM Marietta Chap D. A. R. in May 1923. Nathaniel Kidd came from Greensboro, Pa. to Washington Co, O. in 1805, settling on a farm below Beverly. Moved to Fearing Twp. near Whipple. Ref: N. E. Kidd, 103 Knox St., Marietta, O. Fur infor Marietta Chap.

KIDD, ROBERT, (Mahoning Co.)

Pvt. Enl Men, Ulster Co, N. Y. 2nd Regt, Mil. Br 1757. D 1837. Ref: p 193, NY Men in the Revolution. Fur infor Mahoning Chap.

KIDDER, REUBEN, (Geauga Co.)

Pvt. N. H. Continentals. Pension allowed 1818; Capt Aukens Company, Col Kelley's Regt. Enl Feb 27, 1781 for 3 yrs. Br Jan 20, 1760, New Ipswich, N. H. Parents: Reuben Kidder and Susannah Burge, Mar Phebe Johnson. Children: Eli, Noah, Lucina, Deborah. D Jan 14, 1840. East Claridon. Bur East Claridon, O. lot 65. MI: "Reuben Kidder died Jan 4, 1840, aged 80 years, Phebe his wife, died Oct 28, 1856, aged 84." GM by family. Stone. Marched from New Ipswich Apr 20, 1775. Ref: Pension Records Vol. 3, p 615, New Hampshire Rolls, Vol. 1, p 34, Vol 2, p 556. Hammonds State Papers N. H. Vol 3, p 235, 507 and 665, Fur infor Taylor Chap.

KIESTER, PETER, (Montgomery Co.)

Served as a scout; and his application for pension was rejected because it was held that he did not serve under competent authority. About Sept 1, 1775 enl in Capt Peter Grove's company at Sunbury, Pa. could not state what authority whether Pa or Confederation of U. S. His pens application recites a long list of Indian engagements until his disch in fall of 1776. Had disch, but lost it coming to Ohio. Br Mch 1751, though this is questionable, probably in 1758, as he claimed he was 15 yrs old when enl. Bur German Twp. Montgomery Co. Grave unknown. He was probably br in Northumberland Co, Pa. settled in Adams Co, O. 9 miles from West Union. Moved in 1811 to the Big Twin Creek sec of German Twp. Was a member of the Lutheran Church, but all trace of his family has been lost. He had a perilous career in the army, was often taken prisoner. Fur infor Richard Montgomery Chap, S. A. R.

KIEVER, (or KEIVER), HENRY, (Butler Co.)

Name appears on the tablet in the Soldiers and Sailors Monument at Hamilton as a Revolutionary Soldier bur in that Co. Grave not located. Fur infor John Reily Chap.

KILBOURN, ———, (Ross Co.)

Pvt. in Shelton's Dragoon. Br 1763, Nova Scotia. D 1829, Chillicothe. Natl No 32,753, Vol 33, p 255, D. A. R. Lin.

KILLIN, JOHN, (Adams Co.)

Musician. Br 1755, Carlisle, Pa. Mar Rachel Harper, Nov 19, 1797. Children: William and George Killen, sons, and Mary, daughter. D Sept 10, 1844, West Union, O. Bur West Union Cem. Enl in Feb 1776, for 14 mos in Capt Robert Adams Company, Col Irwin's Regt. In fall of 1777, in Capt Powers Company, Col Watts Regt. In 1778, served 2 mos in Capt Grimes' Company, Col Dunlap's Regt. Was a pensioner. Ref: Evans and Stivers Hist of Adams Co. Fur infor Sycamore Chap.

KIMBALL, ABEL, (Lake Co.)

Enl from Rindge, N. H. in Col Mooney's Regt, also in Col Enoch Hale's Regt. He was also Ensign; afterwards a Capt in the Mil. Br Oct 10, 1762. Bonford, Mass. Mar Mary Parker (first wife), Abigail Cunningham, (second wife). No children. D Mch 4, 1841. Bur Madison, O. GM New Connecticut Chap. He and his brother, Lemuel, came to Ohio in 1811. Fur infor New Connecticut Chap.

KIMBALL, JARED, (Trumbull Co.)

Wife allowed a pens from U. S. Army. D Jan 23, 1832, Bloomfield. Bur Bloomfield Village Cem, Lot 60. MI: Has a Government marker, 7th Company, 3rd Conn. Mil, Revolutionary War. Fur infor Mary Chesney Chap.

KIMBALL, MOSES, (Huron Co.)

Pvt 1781-82 Capt Hungerford, Col McClellan; fr Oct to Nov 1782. Capt Prent—oss Company, same Regt. Br May 6, 1741, Preston, Conn. Parents: Jacob and Mary Oarke Kimball. D Dec 21, 1835, Norwalk, O. Bur St Paul's Episcopal Cem, Norwalk, O. MI: Name, date birth and death. GM Stone marker, by family. He was visiting his grandson, Moses Kimball, Norwalk, when he was taken ill and died. Ref: Conn Men of the Rev, p 580-7; Kimball Genealogy, p 135, D. A. R. Natl No 4207-4208-4209. Fur infor Sally DeForest Chap.

KIMBALL, MOSES, (Jefferson Co.)

Sgt in Capt Belden's Company at the Lexington alarm. Was at Bunker Hill and in Burgoyne Campaign. Br 1747, Haverhill, Mass. D 1828, Warrenton, O. Ref: Natl No 84216, Vol 85, p 86, D. A. R. Lin.

KIMBALL, NATHAN, (Guernsey Co.)

Bur Milnerville. Ref: S.A.R. Fur infor Anna Asbury Stone Chap.

KIMMEL, DAVID, (Montgomery Co.)

Bur Hillgrove Cem on Eaton Pike, formerly Old Baptist. GM May, 1926. Fur infor Jonathan Dayton Chap.

KINCAID, JOHN, (Mahoning Co.)

Military store keeper. Br Ireland. Mar Martha Hall. Children: Three sons and four dau. Came fr Ireland to Chambersburg, Pa. Came to Mahoning Co. early in 1800. Farmer. Ref: Pa Archives Series 2, p 122, Vol 14; Trumbull and Mahoning Co Hist, p 332. Fur infor Mahoning Chap.

KINCAID, THOMAS, (Adams Co.)

Sgt in Capt William Henderson's Company, Col in Daniel Morgan's rifle Regt in July, 1777, and till after Nov, 1777. Br Dec 13, 1755, near Richmond, Va. Mar Mary Patterson. D Adams Co, O, July 3, 1819. Bur Winchester Cem, Winchester, O. Fur infor Sycamore Chap.

KINDALE, JOSEPH, (Mahoning Co.)

Pvt, 3rd Bn Gloucester, and Somers Bn State Tr, N. J. Men of the Rev, p 654. Bur Goshen Twp. Came to Ohio in 1806 with his brother-in-law Stacy Shreve. Was Constable in Goshen Twp in 1802. Sanderson's Hist of Mahoning Co, p 203, Columbiana Co Hist, p 293-295. Fur infor Mahoning Chap.

KING, BENJAMIN, (Geauga Co.)

Enl Enfield, Conn, Aug, 1776. Served 5 mos as Pvt, Capt Robinson's Company, Col Mott's Conn Regt. Enl 1778, served one mo Capt Ammidon's Conn Company, Gen Sullivan's R. I. Expedition. Br Nov 6, 1742, Enfield, Conn. Parents: Benjamin King and Sarah Pease. Mar Hulda Hill Mch 1, 1764. Hepzibah Pease June 14, 1793, Mindwell Terry Feb 5, 1800. Children: Benjamin, Samuel, Moses, Hulda, Nathaniel, Rhoda, Hosea, Isaiah, Mary, Joseph, Cynthia, Rhoda Mindwell. D Hambden, O, Mch 26, 1837. Bur Hambden Center, Lot 41. MI: "In memory of Deacon Benjamin King who departed this life Mch 26, 1837, in the 95th year of his life." GM by Family, stone monument. Moved to Hambden, O, 1810. Pensioned 1832. Ref: King Gen Pioneer Hist Geauga Co. Pens Bureau. Fur infor Taylor Chap.

KING, PETER, (Ashtabula Co.)

Pvt. Bur Center Cem, Conneaut Twp. Fur infor Mary Redmond Chap.

KING, ZEBULON, CAPT, (Washington Co.)

Enl fr Taunton, Mass. Lt in Col Gamaliel Bradford's Regt; Capt James Cooper's Company; Capt Joseph Wadsworth's 5th Company. Capt Lt in two different Regts. Capt of 8th Company. Br R. I. D 1789, Belpre, O. Ref: Mass Soldiers and Sailors. Fur infor Marietta Chap.

KINGMAN, ALEXANDER, (Morrow Co.)

Mass Line. Capt Abraham William's Tr, (Delaware Ch) Col Ebenezer Sprout. Bur Rivercliff, Mt Gilead. MI: "Alexander Kingman, Mass Lin." No other inscription. GM usual government marker, Soldiers grave. Ref: Miss Hortense Kingman, Mt Gilead Chap.

KINGSBURY, SAMUEL, (Co. not stated.)

Pvt in Capt Heman Smith's Company, Col Coller's Berkshire Co Regt which marched 1781 from Sandisfield to Stillwater. Br 1750, Mass. D 1844, Ohio. On pension roll 1840. Ref: Natl No 49535, Vol 50, 235, D. A. R. Lin.

KINGSLEY, ENOS, (Geauga Co.)

Pvt Capt Peter Porter's Company, Col Benj Sunnod's (Berkshire Co) Regt, Apr 26, 1777, to May 20, 1777. Br 1757, Beckett, Mass. Parents: Isaiah and Abigail. Mar 1st Rachel Crane, Nov 26, 1778, 2nd Sarah Wadsworth, Mch 24, 1787. Children 1st wife: Rachel, Sarah, John; by 2nd wife: Rachel, Lydia, Enos, Dodridge, Abigail, Isaac W, Jonathan W, Rebecca and David B. D Oct 21, 1836, Bainbridge, O. Bur Restland Cem, Bainbridge, Geauga Co, O. MI: "E.K. 1757, 1836." Company marched by order of Maj-Gen Gates, Apr 26, 1777, and marched to Saratoga. Ref: Mass Soldiers and Sailors, Vol 9, p 298. Fur infor Taylor Chap.

KINGSLEY, NATHAN, (Co. not stated.)

Lt in Capt John Franklin's Wyoming Company, Regt Mil. Br Scotland, 1743. D 1822, O. Ref: Natl No 70498, p 180-181, Vol 71, D. A. R. Lin. Mrs. Arline Handrick, Springville, Pa. Berlinghof.

KINNEY, AARON, (Summit Co.)

Though no record of enrollment, his brave and devoted conduct at Fort Griswold, on the fatal 6th of Sept, 1781, in rendering aid to the wounded and dying during the defense and after the massacre, justifies adding his name to the roll of honor. Br 1744. D July 14, 1824, Tallmadge. Bur Tallmadge, O. Fur infor Cuyahoga Portage Chap.

KINNEY, JOHN, (Morrow Co.)

Enl from N. J. Bur Chester Cem, Chester Twp. Ref: Mrs. Etta Kinney Porter, Marengo, O. Fur infor Mt Gilead Chap.

KINSMAN, JOHN, (Trumbull Co.)

Bur Old Cem, Kinsman. Ref: Miss Mary Kinsman, Kinsman, O. Fur infor Mary Chesney Chap.

KIRKPATRICK, WILLIAM, (later changed to Kirk) (Mahoning Co.)

Pvt in different companies. Br 1757. Children: William, James, Isaac. D 1835. Bur Cem in Berlin Twp. Ref: Pa Archives Series 3, Vol 13, p 254-266-283-315-700-705-753-791. Fur infor Mahoning Chap.

KIRKUM, PHILEMON, (Medina Co.)

Served fr Conn, Pvt. Served 4 yrs. Br 1764, Guilford, Conn. Mar —— Mills. Children: George, Eliza. D 1855. Bur Woodlawn, Wadsworth. MI: "Philemon Kirkum. Died July 15, 1854, aged 91 yrs." GM by Western Reserve on headstone and on lot by tall shaft with inscription "Revolutionary Soldier". Lawyer. Came to Ohio in 1814, with wife and son in covered wagon drawn by oxen. Ref: Mrs. Bessie Coris Sawyer, York St., Akron, O. Fur infor Western Reserve and Cuyahoga-Portage Chaps.

KIRKWOOD, ROBERT, (Mercer Co.)

Lt at the Battle of Long Island, White Plains, Capt at Brandywine, Germantown, Monmouth and Camden. Br 1756. D 1791, Fort Recovery, O. Natl No 39396. p 145, Vol 40, D.A.R. Lin.

KIRTLAND, TURHAND, (Mahoning Co.)

Capt Conn State Tr, also in Provisional serv of N.Y. at the time of the defeat of the Amer Army. Was engaged on the boat that convoyed the army over to the mainland. Br 1753. Mar Mary Potter (1772-1850). Children: Dr. Jared P, Henry, Billius, George, Mary P, Nancy. D 1844. Bur Church Cem, Poland, O. GM D. A. R. in 1915-17. Ref: History Trumbull & Mahoning Co, p 73-74, Vol 1, Hist Trumbull & Mahoning Co; p 50, 140 Conn. Men in the Rev; 15901 D. A. R. and others. Natl Nos 19463, 31647, 19462. Fur infor Mahoning Chap.

KISER, JOHN, (Montgomery Co.)

Br 1719 in Germany. Mar Christina Fox. Children: Benjamin Kiser (b 1779), Daniel Kiser (br Feb 14, 1782). D 1821, in Dayton, O, aged 102 yrs. Bur Willow View Cem, Beardshear Rd. MI: "Born 1719—aged 102 years." GM by Richard Montgomery Chap S. A. R., July 1, 1923. Fur infor Jonathan Dayton Chap.

KITCHELL, ASA, (Hamilton, O.)

Pvt in Eastern Bn under Capt Obadiah Kitchell, Morris Co Mil, p 656, "Stryker's Men from NJ." Br Oct 28, 1748, Hanover, Morris Co, N.J. Parents: Joseph and Rachel Bates Kitchell (b N. J.). Mar possibly Nancy. Children: Anna, Grace, Abigail, Benajah, Joseph, Timothy (d young), Tryphina, Wickliff. D and bur Cincinnati, Hamilton Co. after 1799, before 1814. Bur no doubt in Presbyterian Cem as he was in First Presbyterian Church; others of family are known to have been bur there. No stone or marker found. Records of burials lost. Name found on list of town officers in 1799, in Hist of Hamilton Co by Henry A. Ford and Mrs. Kate Ford, published by L. A. Williams & Co., 1881, p 239. His family moved to Ill in 1814. He was one of 14 of name Kitchell who served in Revolutionary War from N. J. Fur infor Cincinnati Chap.

KITCHELL, DANIEL, (Hamilton Co.)

Pvt Minute Man Morris Co, NJ., Mil. Certified copy of Adj Gen office, Trenton, N.J. Br 1747, Morris Co, N.J., near Hanover. Parents: John (1714-1777) and Keziah Ball (dau of Caleb and Elizabeth). Mar (1) Esther and perhaps (2) Rachel. Both d in NJ. Children: Phoebe and Samuel. D about 1800, Cincinnati, O. Bur 1st Presbyterian Churchyard, now covered by enlarged church. MI: On inner wall of church giving its charter members, his name is first. Was first Elder, 1790 Wheelwright-carpenter, a furniture maker; made first gable roof in Cincinnati. Natl No 34924, Mrs. E. P. Whallon, Cincinnati, O. Ref: Strykers' Men in Revolutionary War, p 654, 656. Fur infor Cincinnati Chap.

KITCHELL, JOHN, (Butler Co.)

Served in Company of Obadiah Kitchell (his cousin), 1st Bn Morris Co, N. J., Br Hanover, N. J. Parents: Joseph, (br Jan 6, 1751); mother, Rachel Bates. Mar Abigail—so his will says. Children: Ashbell, Mildau (or may have been Milton), Rosalindah, Polly, Allurah, Johannah, Matilda and Abigail. D on farm, Lemon Twp, 1805. Bur Presbyterian Cem at Monroe, Butler Co, of which church he was founder and elder. MI: Name is on bronze tablet in Soldiers Memorial, Hamilton. Came to Ky, to Cincinnati, then to Hamilton, Butler Co; was atty, Member of first Bar of Hamilton; Commissioner of Constitutional Convention which met at Chillicothe. Will is recorded Book 0, No 1, Butler Co Court House. Fur infor Mrs. Whallon, Cincinnati, D. A. R.

KITCHELL, MOSES, (Hamilton Co.)

Lt in Capt Obadiah Kitchell's Company; Eastern Bn, Morris Co Mil, N.J. Also Forage Master and purchasing Forage Master in Eastern Bn, Obadiah Kitchell Capt. Br 1740, Hanover Neck, N. J. Parents: Joseph Kitchell, (1710-1779) and wife, Rachel Bates Kitchell (d Dec 24, 1789). Mar Phoebe Hedges, dau of Elias Hedges, wagoner (Stryker, p 856). Sister of Samuel Hedges, mar before 1761, N. J. Children: Lydia, mar John Hosbrook, 1780, a Rev soldier in N. J. Rachel, mar Flack; Percy, Luther; Mary mar Daniel Bates, 1787, a Revolutionary soldier in Ohio, Jemima mar Allen, in Ohio 1806. Moses Kitchell is known to have been at dau marriage in 1806, no later record, except that he had lived at Cncinnati until death. Bur likely in First Presbyterian Churchyard. Family scattered; none in Cincinnati at time of removal of graves, marked by only flagstones. New building erected over unmoved graves. In 1786 he emigrated to Ky with his family, thence to Cincinnati in 1787. Ref: Natl No 74474, Vol 78, D. A. R. Lin. (p 656 and 844 Stryker's Men of N.) Fur infor Cincinnati Chap.

KLEVER, JOHN, (Fayette Co.)

Pvt in Capt John Stone's 6th Company, 2nd Bn Lancaster Co Mil, 1780. Br 1755, Germany. Mar Elizabeth Schriver, 1795. Children: Anna Maria, Kathrina, Michael, Jacob, William, John, Elizabeth, Henry. D July 5, 1865, near Bloomingburg, O. Bur Bloomingburg Cem, old part, unplatted. MI: "John Klever died July 5, 1865. aged 110 years. Iron Star, 1776." GM Family and Cem Trustees 1866. Farmer. Ref: Pa Archives, 5 Series, Vol 7, p 122-158, Natl No 172622. Fur infor Washington C. H. Chap.

KLINGER, PHILIP, (Preble Co.)

On pens roll 1832 of Preble Co, O. Service 1775 in Capt Griffin's Company, also 1776 in Capt Jacob Hetterling's Company. Was in battle of Princeton. Was wounded. Br 1754 in Chester Co, Pa. Mar Barbara (br 1759) 1779. D in Ohio. Ref: Natl No 73377, Vol 74, p 142, D. A. R. Lin.

KLIPPINGER, ANTONY, or (ANTHONY CLIPPINGER) (Columbiana Co.)

Pvt in Capt Paul Knauses' Company, Northampton Co Mil, for Spring of 1782. Br about 1765. Parents: Anthony Clippinger, Sr. Mar Margaret A. Miller about 1800. Children: Catherine, Mary, Daniel, Christina, Hannah, Emanuel, John, Susan. D North Georgetown, O, Nov 1846. Bur North Georgetown, Knox Twp, Columbiana Co, O. MI "Anthony Clippinger, 1765, 1846." GM by Committee Jane Bain Chap, Aug 30, 1924. Ref: Misses Mary C Fording, and Susan S. Fording, 825 S. Arch Ave., Alliance, O; Mrs. Mildred Fording Holeson, Niles, O. Fur infor Jane Bain Chap.

KNAPP, JEREMIAH, (Fulton Co.)

Bur Ottokee Cem, Dover Twp. Ref: The Military Record of Fulton Co, O, 1885, p 305. Fur infor Wauseon Chap.

KNOWLES, JAMES, (Washington Co.)

Enl at Haddam, Middlesex Co, Conn, as Pvt. Length of serv 6 mos. Br 1752. D 1830. Bur at Newbury, O, near Little Hocking, Washington Co, O. GM Marietta Chap with Revolutionary marker, 1921. Compare Natl No 39418, Vol 40, p 153, D. A. R. Lin. Ref: Rev War Records Dept of Interior, Washington, D. C. Fur infor Marietta Chap.

KNOWLTON, STEPHEN, JR., (Ashtabula Co.)

Turned out at the Lexington Alarm, and enl at the first call for tr in Capt Thomas Knowlton's Company of Conn Tr. Stationed at Cambridge during the siege. Was a prisoner fr Morgan, Ashtabula Co. Br 1753, Ashford, Conn. Mar Diodema Chubb. Children: Laura, Calvin. D 1830, Morgan, Ashtabula Co, O, Bur Rock Creek. Ref: Ashtabula Co Hist; Lin Bk, Vol LXI, Conn in the Rev, Natl No 29553, Vol 30, D. A. R. Lin. Fur infor Mary Stanley Chap.

KOCH, ADAM, (Stark Co.)

Enl 1781. Capt Jacob Bower's Company. Col Craig's Regt at Yorktown. Br 1756, Germany. D Dec 31, 1844, age 88 yrs, 2 mos, 10 das. Bur Old Lutheran Cem, Navarre, O. MI: "A Revolutionary Soldier died Dec 31, 1844, age 88 yrs, 2 mos, 10 days." Natl No 53537, Vol 54, p 239, D. A. R. Lin. "They say" He came from Pa. Ref: Massillon Chap D. A. R. secured above from Wm. L. Bennett, Navarre, O, a Historian. Fur infor Massillon Chap.

KOHL, GEORGE, (Mahoning Co.)

Ranger, Northampton Co, Pa. also Sgt, Capt Deter's Company Northampton Mil, 1783. Br 1751. Mar Maria (1753-1843). D 1820. Bur near church, in Springfield Twp. Ref: Pa. Archives, Series 3, Vol 23, p 288; Series 5, Vol 8, p 292. Fur infor Mahoning Chap.

KOOKEN, JAMES, or (KOCHEN), (Delaware Co.)

Bur Stratford, O. Founder of Bellepoint, O. Fur infor Delaware Chap.

KOON, FREDERICK, (Highland Co.)

Bur family graveyard 4 miles west of Hillsboro. Grave unmarked. Fur infor Waw-Wil-A-Way Chap.

KREAGER, JACOB, (Muskingum Co.)

Pvt. and Sgt under Capt Thomas Jones. Br Nov 17, 1753. D 1843. Bur family plat near Gratiot, O. MI: "Revolutionary Soldier." GM County marker. Fur infor Muskingum Chap.

KROUSE, JOHN, (Clinton Co.)

Bur Lieurance Graveyard, near Brown School House. Fur infor George Clinton Chap.

KUHN, JOHN, (Stark Co.)

Pvt. in Capt Geo. Hubley's Company, and Capt Bernard Hubley's Company German Regt Continental Tr, commanded successively by Lt. Col Geo Stricker, Col Baron Arendt, and Lt Col Ludwig Weltner, Revolutionary War. Enl Aug 7, 1776, to serve during the war; name appears last on a pay roll of company covering the period from Aug to Dec 1780. This organization disbanded Oct 3, 1780. Br 1757. D July 3, 1845. Bur Uniontown, Stark Co. over the Summit Co line. Native of Pa. and a weaver by trade; removed from Center Co, Pa. to Green Twp. O. in 1832. Fur infor Cuyahoga Portage Chap.

KUR, ROBERT, (Mahoning Co.)

James Bryson's company. Ranger in Westmoreland Co, 1778 to 1783. Br 1749. D 1816. Bur Mahoning Co. Came in early 19th century to Mahoning Co. He was a householder in 1826 in the seventh district of Mahoning Co. Farmer. Pa. Archives, Series 3, Vol 23, p 323; Old deeds. Farmer. Fur infor Mahoning Chap.

KYLE, JOSEPH, SR., (Greene Co.)

Pvt. Capt Matthew Boyd's Company, Chester, Pa. Mil. commanded by Col James Moore, 1776. Br 1749, near Harrisburg, Pa. Mar Katherine Chambers. Children: Joseph, Samuel and four others. D Feb 2, 1821, Xenia, O. Bur Massie's Creek graveyard, (Stevensons). Moved to Xenia, 1803, from Ky. Ref: Robinson's Hist of Greene Co. Natl No 57707, Vol 58, p 242, D. A. R. Lin. Fur infor Catherine Greene Chap.

LACEY, THADDEUS, (Summit Co.)

Bur Springfield. Fur infor Cuyahoga-Portage Chap.

LACY, THOMAS, (Hamilton Co.)

D 1835. Ref: S. A. R. Fur infor Cincinnati Chap.

LADD, JESSE DEA. (Lake Co.)

Served 11 das fr East Windsor, Conn. Br April 10, 1732, Tolland, Conn. Mar Ruby Rachel Taylor. D Dec 14, 1816. Bur West Madison, O. GM New Conn Chap. Fur infor New Conn Chap.

LAFFERTY, EDWARD, (Harrison Co.)

Came from Washington Co, Pa to Moorefield Twp before 1810. Bur at Nottingham Church. An Edward Lafferty served as a member of Maj Thomas Church's Company, 4th Pa. Line Regt 1778 to 1781. Pa. Archives, Series 5, No. II, No. 1069, 1082. Infor fur by Moravian Trail Chap.

LAFLER, JOHN, (Hamilton Co.)

Br 1750 NY. D 1822. Compare Natl No 12958, Vol 13, p 363, D. A. R. Lin. S. A. R. Fur infor by Cincinnati Chap.

LAIRD, JAMES SR., (Trumbull Co.)

Br 1764. Mar Eliza L. ———. (d Aug 23, 1826). D Aug 11, 1826. Twp. Cem at center of Mespotamia, O, good condition. Fur infor Mary Chesney Chap..

LAKE, ASA, (Hancock Co.)

Bur Mt Blanchard. Infor fur by Ft Findlay Chap.

LAKE, REUBEN, (Geauga Co.)

Conn Continental Army. Pensioned 1818. Age 68. Date of death and where, unknown. Ref: No. 35,515 Pensions Dept. Fur infor Taylor Chap.

LAMB, PETER, (Fairfield Co.)

Pvt. in Capt Nehemiah Stokeley's Company, 8th Pa. Regt of foot. Br 1747, Pa. D 1804, Fairfield Co. Bur Pleasant Run Cem, Walnut Twp. Ref: Vol 85, p 89, Natl No 84,223, D. A. R. Lin. Fur infor Elizabeth Sherman Reese Chap.

LAMBERT, JOSEPH, (Greene Co.)

Bur Mercer graveyard. Living at Caesar's Creek, 1803. Ref: Robinson's History of Greene Co. Fur infor Catherine Greene Chap.

LAMME, (or LAMB), JAMES, (Clark Co.)

Sgt in Capt Davis Stephenson's Company, 8th Va. Regt of foot. Col Abraham Bowman Commander. Br Staunton, Va. Parents: William (Lamb). Mar Elizabeth Givens, Staunton, Va, 1775. Children: William, John, James and five daughters. One mar Wm. McNeil; one mar John Boswell; Ann mar Rueben Wallace. D near New Carlisle, O. Private burial. Lot on Lamme farm near New Carlisle, O. MI: Cannot decipher. GM Family. He enlisted Mch 21, 1776 to serve 2 yrs. His name is on rolls fr Mch 1777 to Feb 1778. Farmer. Came to Clarke Co, O, fr Staunton, Va. in 1807. Letters from Pension Office, Washington, D. C. signed by Sec of War, Natl No 13,678, Vol 14, D. A. R. Lin. Fur infor Lagonda Chap.

LAMME, NATHAN, (Greene Co.)

Capt 13th Regt Pa. Line. Pensioned 1826. Br 1745. D Jan 15, 1834. Bur Bellbrook, Sugar Creek Twp, pioneer graveyard. Living at Sugar Creek, 1803. Ref: Robinson's History of Greene Co. Fur infor Catherine Greene Chap.

LAMONT, JOHN, (Ashtabula Co.)

Cem abandoned, but was in Harpersfield Twp. At Harper's field, O. Apr 10, 1843. Age 84 yrs 'Ashtabula Sentinel". Fur infor Eunice Grant Chap.

LAMSON, (or LAMPSON), EBENEZER, (Ashtabula Co.)

Pvt 1775, 6 mos; Capt Elihu Humphrey 1777, 3 mos; Capt Joseph Fuller 1781 3 mos; or Gen at New Haven. Br May 19, 1754, New Haven. Mar 1st wife Dec 1776; 2nd wife; Martha Holbrook July 9, 1818. Children by 2nd wife: Emilus, Chester. D Mch 14, 1835, Windsor, O. Bur north of Windsor village on Sampson lot. GM Family, sandstone slab; also an iron marker fur by county. He was exempt fr payment of certain taxes in state. Name on Soldiers Monument at Windsor, O. Farmer. On the first grand jury called in Ashtabula Co in 1811. Ref: Lillian D. Anthony, Cora D. Hann, both at Jefferson, O. Fur infor Eunice Grant Chap.

LAMPSON, WILLIAM, (Summit Co.)

Pvt. Br Conn 1761. Children: Caroline, Elizabeth, Jemima, Mary Ann, Laura Ann. D Sept 27, 1827. Bur Western Star. MI: "William Lampson died Sept 27, 1827. Aged 66 years." GM White marble slab. Came from Onondaga Co, N J. 1825. Served in War of 1812. Fur infor Cuyahoga Portage Chap.

LANDON, EBENEZER, (Delaware Co.)

Pvt under Cols Bradley, Mead, Arnold, Capt Bebee, Taylor, Osburn, Stone and Cattin. Bur Berkshire Twp. Pensioned. Fur infor Delaware Chap.

LANDON, EDWARD, (Knox Co)

Pvt 1777-81 under different commands, N J. Line; Rec'd pens for such serv 1832, from Knox Co, O. Br 1762, Hackettstown, N J. D 1834, Ohio, Vol 96, p 219, Natl No;95670 D. A. R. Lin.

LANE HENRY, SR., (Trumbull Co.)

Br 1735. D May 24, 1806. Bur Old Cem Mahoning Ave, Warren, O. MI: "In memory of Henry Lane, a native of state of New Jersey who departed this life 24 May, A. D. 1806, aged 71 yrs." GM Name on bronze tablet, 1927 by D. A. R. Für infor Mary Chesney Chap.

LANE, ISAAC, SR., (Trumbull Co.)

Br 1755. Mar Saber Lane, (d Jan 27, 1813). D Oct 17, 1819. Bur Braceville, Braceville Twp. MI: "Isaac Lane Sr. Died Oct 17, 1819 aged 64 yrs." GM Relatives; in excellent condition. Will probated 1819. Fur infor Mary Chesney Chap.

LANE, JOHN, (Portage Co.)

Pvt in New Hampshire State Tr. Placed on Pens Roll May 27, 1833. Drew pens at Ravenna, O. Fur infor Old Northwest Chap.

LANE, JOSEPH, (Geauga Co.)

N. Y. Mil. Pensioned 1833. Age 73. Resided at Thompson, Geauga Co, O. Fur infor Taylor Chap.

LANE, RICHARD, (Muskingum Co.)

Enl by Lt Nathaniel Kinnard Jr. Received and passed by Wm Henry, July 22, 1776 of Md. Vol 18, p 65. Also Pvt 3rd Company of 3rd Regt Md Twp Aug 28, 1781. Br 1740 Yorkshire, England. Mar Catherine Groom. D 1811, home near Zanesville. Bur in field, 300 yds from where he had settled on Frazeysburg Road near the John M. Lane farm known then as Butler farm. Farmer. Ref: Mrs. Ora Delpha Lane, 1723 Terrace Point, Zanesville, O. Vol 79, Natl No 78537 D. A. R. Lin. Fur infor Muskingum Chap.

LANE, ROBERT, (Clark Co.)

D Green Twp, south of Springfield. Bur Ferncliff, Springfield, O. Lot 367. Sec L. MI: McCulloch. Robert Lane a soldier of the Revolution. GM Society Ohio S. A. R. 1906. Farmer. Body moved from McCulloch farm. Fur infor Lagonda Chap.

LANEY, JOHN, (Brown Co.)

Bur Hickory Ridge, Huntington Twp. Fur infor Ripley and Lt. Byrd Chaps.

LANGDEN, L., (Lorain Co.)

Mar Submit. Scanty infor gives: Submit Langden, wife of L. Langden, on stone in LaGrange Cem. On one stone is—died May 6, 1812, age 80 years. Since S. A. R. Yr Bk, 1913, records that Submit Langden was drawing a pens in LaGrange, Lorain Co, at the age of 90, it appears that the stone with no name may be that of L. Langden. Fur infor Elyria Chap.

LANGDON, JOHN W., (Hamilton Co.)

At siege of Boston, under his father. Had charge of powder works in Springfield. Pensioner when he died. Br 1759, Mass. Mar Elizabeth Lucy Ashley. D 1842, Hamilton Co. Ref: S. A. R. and Natl No 13312 Vol 14, D. A. R. Lin. Fur infor Cincinnati Chap.

LANGLEY, JOHN, REV., (Trumbull Co.)

Bur Old Cem, Hubbard. Could not locate grave; markers and inscriptions gone in this cem. Ref: Name fr the S. A. R. Yr Bk. Fur infor Mary Chesney Chap.

LANHAM, ELIAS COL., (Madison Co.)

A Revolutionary Soldier. Bur Madison Co by the side of Samuel Baskerville, (a Revolutionary Soldier) on the latter's farm. Fur infor Mt. Sterling Chap.

LANKTON, LEVI, (Washington Co.)

D Nov 28, 1843. Bur Mound cem. Fur infor Marietta Chap.

LARABEE, JOHN, SR., (Licking Co.)

Enl as a matross in Col Cuane's Regt (artillery). He was at Trenton, N. J. Served fr Jan 1, 1777 to Feb 10, 1780. Br 1760, Lynn, Mass. D Feb 6, 1846, Madison Twp. Bur Lutheran Cem, Linville Road. MI: "Rev. War." GM by Hetuck Chap in 1910. Emigrated to this county in 1801. Was a pensioner. Ref: Brister's History of Licking Co. Fur infor Hetuck Chap.

LARCUM, PAUL, (Portage Co.)

Pvt in Mass. Continental line. Placed on pens roll Mch 1, 1833. Bur Drakesburg. Drew pens at Ravenna, O. in 1840. Fur infor Old Northwest Chap.

LAREW, (LARUE), ABRAHAM, (Hamilton Co.)

Br 1775, Va. D Apr 1, 1858 near Cincinnati, O. About 1834 moved to Logansport, Ind; some yrs before death resided with son-in-law, Stephen Reeder, formerly of Xenia. Was also a soldier of 1812 fr Greene Co. Data: Lived in Xenia, O. 1806. Ref: Geo. F. Robinson's History of Greene Co. Fur infor Cincinnati and Catherine Greene Chaps.

LARKINS, JAMES, (Harrison Co.)

A Revolutionary pensioner living in Harrison Co in 1819, aged 70; served as Sgt in Moylan's Cavalry and in the 4th Pa Line Regt. Pa Archives 5th 11-1083; III 839. U S Pension Rolls 1835. Fur infor Moravian Trail Chap.

LAROSE, JOHN JACOB, (Montgomery Co.)

Bur Miamisburg, O. Ref: Mrs. Homer Ireland, Dayton, O. Fur infor Jonathan Dayton Chap.

LARRABEE, SETH, (Jackson Co.)

Enl for 3 yrs at Windham, Conn. on or about Jan 1777 under Capt Nono Elderkin and Col Herman Swift, until Jan 1780; again for 3 yrs from 1781. Was in battles of Germantown and Monmouth. Bur County graveyard at Liberty, probably near the McCune graveyard. Ref: From Pens filer at Court House dated —— 29, 1821, Jackson, O. Fur infor Capt John James Chap.

LAUNTERMAN, WILLIAM, (Mahoning Co.)

Ranger, Wyoming Co, Pa. 1776-1782 Capt John Franklin 5th Regt, 1st Company, Pensioned. Br 1762. Children: Peter, William, Letitia, (Mar 1st McGregor, 2nd Porter; 3rd Jas. Reed). D 1832. Bur Launterman Cem on farm which he settled. Came from Pa to Mahoning Co 1899. Ref: Biog. Eastern Ohio pp643-4 Summers; Pa Archives, Series 3, Vol 23, p 461; Mrs. Bakody, Canfield Rd., Youngstown, O. Fur infor Mahoning Chap.

LAW, WILLIAM, (Mahoning Co.)

2nd Lt. 2nd Bn. Benjamin Richard. Capt. Bur Mahoning Co. Settled in Jackson Twp. Ref: Conn. Men of the Rev. p 424, Old deeds, Vol A. p 17. Fur infor Mahoning Chap.

LAWRENCE, JOHN, (Lorain Co.)

Served Matrosses in Gen Hospital (?). Br 1758. D Dec 4, 1836. Bur Pioneer Cem, Wellington. GM by Western Reserve Chap in 1920. Ref: Conn Men in the Rev. Fur infor Western Reserve Chap.

LAWRENCE, THOMAS, (Guernsey Co.)

Bur Old Cem, Cambridge, O. Ref: S.A.R. Fur infor Anna Asbury Stone Chap.

LEACH, ABNER, (Mahoning Co.)

N J Tr. Pensioned. Children: Benjamin Leach (came to Mahoning Co 1802 fr Poland); Abram (settled in Trumbull Co 1802, bought a farm and brought his family in 1816); John, Mary, Nancy, Hannah (mar Alexander Truesdale of Morristown, N. J.). Bur Mahoning Co, Four Mile Run Cem. Ref: Trumbull and Mahoning Co History, Vol 2, p 59. Biographical History, Sanderson, p 170-443, N. J. Men of the Rev. Census of Pensions, Vol 111. Fur infor Mahoning Chap.

LEACH, ABRAHAM, (Trumbull Co.)

Bur Champion, O. Old stone on Leach lot, not able to decipher name. Descendant told us he was bur there. Ref: Baldwin Library, Youngstown, O. Fur infor Mary Chesney Chap.

LEACH, GEORGE, (Jackson Co.)

An officer of Rev. When his company disbanded the soldiers presented him a sword, now in possession of A. B. Leach, Wellston, O. On it is inscribed, "Don't Tread on Me." Parents: James Leach. Mar Nancy Bigby. Children: Willis, Lewis, Thomas, George. D 1838 near McArthur, O. Bur Bundy Cem, near Wellston, O. MI: "George Leach died 1838—a Patriot of the Revolution." Fur infor State Chairman, who secured data at Wellston, O. Name filed by Capt John James Chap.

LEACH, VALENTINE, SGT, (Pickaway Co.)

Br 1755, Va. Mar Mary Furrow, June 23, 1785. Children: Schallottee, LeRoy, Peter, Thornton, Elizabeth, Dorothy, Nancy, Benjamin, Robert, Leticia. D Sept 20, 1831, Pickaway Co, O. Bur old country burying ground in Pickaway Co. Ref: Mrs. E. A. Downs, Mt Sterling, O. Fur infor Mt Sterling Chap.

LEASOR, HENRY, (Mercer Co.)

Moved to Hardin Co, Ky, near Nolin; his dau, Elizabeth, mar Abram Murlin in 1832, and moved to Union Twp, Mercer Co, O. Henry came to visit this dau and was killed by a falling tree; bur on Murlin farm in Union Twp, Mercer Co. His father, William Leasor, came from Scotland and settled in Va near Richmond. D in Va. The son Henry and father William both served in Revolutionary War and received land grants for service. (This information received in answer to an item in the Celina paper, by State Chairman, who files it as a Revolutionary soldier buried in Ohio—not verified. A grandson of Henry, living at age of 80, and grandmother told data to the great-granddaughter of Henry, Mrs. Lillian Thomas, 226 W. Livingston St., Celina, O, who sends it in. Fur infor Jane Dailey, State Chairman.

LEAVENS, JOHN, (Washington Co.)

Pvt at time of Lexington Alarm. Capt in the French and Indian War. Br Sept 25, 1734, Killingly, Conn. Mar Esther Williams, 1762. D July, 1799. Bur on the Ohio River bank near Newbury, now Belpre, Washington Co, O. GM Marietta Chap with Revolutionary marker, 1921. Emigrated to Northwest Territory in 1788. Ref: Vol 26, p 118, Natl No 25338, D. A. R. Lin. Fur infor Marietta Chap.

LEAVERTON, JOHN FOSTER, (Highland Co.)

A Pvt in 4th Company of Md Regt Tr, from Talbot Co, Sept, 1776. Enl in Capt James Hindman's Company Jan 28, 1776. Br London, England, 1755. Mar Hannah Wilson (br July 11, 1757, d April 17, 1835). Children: Foster, Nancy, Sarah, Solomon, John, Noah, Wilson, Rachael, Daniel, Anderson, George, Elizabeth, Hannah, Rebecca, James, Thomas. D Highland Co, O, Mch 1, 1838, Leesburg. Ref: Compare Natl No 81250, Vol 82, D. A. R. Lin. Fur infor Nathaniel Massie and Waw-Wil-a-Way Chaps.

LEAVITT, JOHN, (Trumbull Co.)

D Leavittsburg, Warren Twp, where he was drawing a pens in 1840. Ref: Cleveland Hist Library. Fur infor Mary Chesney Chap.

LEAVITT, SAMUEL, (Trumbull Co.)

Br Feb 26, 1756. Mar Abigail (d Sept 4, 1816, aged 66 yrs). D Aug 4, 1830, in 75th yr of age. Bur Leavittsburg Road, back of residence of Samuel Siddal. GM Old stones in good condition. Fur infor Mary Chesney Chap.

LEDMAN, JOHN, (Guernsey Co.)

Br Aug 17, 1770. Children: Henry and Catherine. D Aug 4, 1844, on farm. Bur family cem, Richland Twp, near Senecaville. MI: A unique verse. GM Marble slab. Pioneer farmer, whose deed for farm was signed by Thomas Jefferson. Ref: R. B. Stiers, present owner (1927), Salesville, O. Fur infor Anna Asbury Stone Chap.

LEE, PETER PERRINE, (Hamilton Co.)

Pvt N J. Br 1756, Woodbridge, N J. D 1848 North Bend, O. Natl No 75856, Vol 76.

LEE, ZEBULON, (Hancock Co.)

Conn. Pvt. Enl Sept 17, 1777, Wyoming, Pa. Forest— Capt Joseph Solomen, William Crawford. Nathan Denison. Zeblon Butler. Br May 16, 1758. D Aug 9, 1848. Bur Amanna Twp, Hancock Co, O (located by Mrs. F. G. Pendleton). MI: Dates of birth and death. GM by Ft Findlay Chap, in 1915. Ref: Miss Rose Lee, Findlay, O. Fur infor Ft Findlay Chap.

LEEPER, ARCHIBALD, (Harrison Co.)

Br 1756. D 1826. Bur at Ridge Church; served as a member of Capt George Sharp's Company, 3rd Bn Washington Co, Pa Mil, 1781-2. Pa Archives, 6th Series, 11, 92, 111, 112. Fur infor Moravian Trail Chap.

LEFEVER, MINARD, (Knox Co.)

Served as Pvt under Capt Peter Vorhies Col Mathias Ogdon's 1st Regt. N J Line. He was wounded in battle of Monmouth, 1778; later served under commands. Br 1753 in France. Mar Chartie Teets. D 1832, Fredericktown, O. Natl No 73200, Vol 74, p 75, D.A.R. Lin.

LEGG, ELIJAH, (Franklin Co.)

Served in Mil fr Prince William Co, Va. Br Prince William Co, Va, in 1765 D Sept 24, 1852, in Perry Twp. Bur old Walcutt farm, Olentangy Road. GM by Revolutionary Grave Committee with bronze marker May 30, 1912. Came to Ohio in 1815 fr Va and settled in Perry Twp. Fur infor Columbus Chap.

LEIBY, GEORGE, (Hamilton Co.)

Br 1753, Pa. D 1834. Ref: S.A.R. Fur infor Cincinnati Chap.

LEIGH, BENJAMIN, (Meigs Co.)

York, Fifer, Capt Moulton's (York) Company of Minute Men, which probably marched to 1775 Alarm; enl Apr 21, 1775, serv 4 das. From "Mass Soldiers and Sailors of Rev. V IX, p 662. B June 13, 1754, Halifax, Nova Scotia. Parents: Benjamin and Maersje (Bant) Leigh. Mar Abigail Peirce (b Mch 16, 1754, Newburyport, Mass. d Herman, Ill, Aug 11, 1837). 1775 at Hampton, N. H. Children: Marcia (mar 1st Capt Woodbridge; 2nd Moses Adams); Mary (mar Jacob Swett); Abigail (mar Capt Charles Knight); Sally (mar Samuel Swazey); Anna; Benjamin Jr (mar Sarah Jackson Pearson); Hannah (mar Michael Little); Robert (mar Mary Booth). D on farm of son-in-law Dr. Jacob Swett (one of first doctors in Ohio) in Meigs Co, now near Dexter, O. Lived in Newburyport, Mass, till 1816, when moved to Marietta, O. Wife the dau of Moses and Abigail (Brown) Pierce. Ref: Mrs. Fred Carpenter (Gladys Swett), on this record. Fur infor Governor Worthington Chap.

LEIST, ANDREW, (Pickaway Co.)

Pvt, (c) Mil Northumberland Co, Pa; also Sgt 8 das with Jacob Bard's party (c), May, 1780, Northumberland Co, Pa. Br Berks Co, Pa, Nov 30, 1755. Mar Elizabeth ———, about 1773. Children: David, Catherine, Mary, Andrew, John, Jacob, George, Peter, Phillip, Samuel, Elizabeth. D Nov 30, 1821, Pickaway Co, O. Bur Zion Cem, Washington Twp, Pickaway Co, O, near main entrance. MI: "Andrew Leist, born 1755—Died 1821," with other inscription in German. Farmer. Ref: Mrs. Hervey J. Sweyer. Fur infor Pickaway Plains Chap.

LEIST, SAMUEL, (Fairfield Co.)

Bur Dutch Hollow Cem, Amanda. Fur infor Elizabeth Sherman Reese Chap.

LELAND, THOMAS, (Medina Co.)

Pvt and Corp Thomas Leland of Sutton (also given Grafton, his father's residence), served as a Pvt in Capt John Putnam's Company, Col Larned's Regt. and marched in response to the Alarm of Apr 19, 1775. On June 1, 1775 he enl in Capt Drury's Company, Col Ward's Regt. and served during the Siege of Boston. In July, 1780, he joined the company of Capt Sibley, Col Davis' Regt. as a Corp. and served in the expedition to Rhode Island. Br 1757 Sutton, Mass. Parents: Thomas and Margaret (Wood) Leland of Grafton, Mass. Mar Anna Bass Rawson of Braintree and Grafton, 1778. Children: Anna (br 1779); Margaret (1780); Silence (1782); Lydia (1784); Polly (1786); Thomas (1788) Aaron (1789); Otis (1791); Hollis (1793); Ansel (1796); John T. (1798); Lois (1800); Albert (1803); Sophia (1805). D Guilford Twp, Medina Co, O. 1849. Bur Seville, Medina Co, O, near main entrance, to the right of central walk. MI: Simple stone monuments with names of Thomas and Anna Leland, with dates of births and deaths. GM No permanent marker. Is decorated each Memorial Day as grave of Revolutionary Soldier by Seville Memorial Day Committee. Also Western Reserve. After the Revolution Thomas Leland and his wife Anna went to Schroon, N. Y., lived there several yrs and later in other localities in western New York State. The later yrs of thir lives were spent with their children and grandchildren in Guilford and Seville, Medina Co., O. Ref: Natl No. 20,277, Vol 21, p 99, D. A. R. Lin. and Natl. No. 169,356; Leland Magazine, p 42 and 122. N. E. Gen and Chron. Reg. Vol 111, p 306 Rawson Genealogy); Mass Soldiers and Sailors of Revolution, Vol. 9, p 669. Fur infor Fort Industry Chap; also Western Reserve Chap.

LEMON, ALEX, (Hamilton Co.)

Br 1749, New York. D 1824. Ref: S. A. R. Fur infor Cincinnati Chap.

LEMMON, ALEXIS, (Morrow Co.)

Capt of Mil Company in Baltimore Co, Md, as cited on p 114, Vol 16, of the Md. Archives. Br Mch 12, 1746, in England. Mar Rachel Stausberry. Children: Sarah, Ruth, Elizabeth, Mary, Rebecca, Rachel, Jane, and Temperance. D June 21, 1826, at Johnsville. Bur Schauck Cem, Johnsville, Morrow Co. on southwest corner of Cem. MI: "Alexis Lemmon died June 21, 1826, aged 80 yrs, 3mos, 9 das." Was member of Maryland legislature. Came from wealthy and aristocratic family. Ref: Mrs. Vida Schauck Clements, 2491 La Salle Gardens, North Detroit, Mich. Fur infor Jacobus Westervelt.

LEMOND, WILLIAM, (Hamilton Co.)

Br 1754, Pa. D 1827. Ref: S. A. R. Fur infor Cincinnati Chap.

LEONARD, ABIJAH, (Ashtabula Co.)

In Beaver Twp, Pa. Age 83 yrs, 10 mos. Native of Conn. but moved to NH. Came to Ohio in 1820; resided in Conneaut and 8 yrs in Pa. (Paper dated June 20, 1844). Ref: Ashtabula Sentinel, Ashtabula, O. given by Mrs. Dana Jones, Erie, Pa.

LEONARD, MOSES, (Brown Co.)

Wagoner in Revolutionary War. Br Mch 15, 1759, Pa. Mar Elizabeth Anderson, (br 1773, d 1834). Children: John (mar 1st, Margaret Smith, 2nd, Sarah Smallwood); Elizabeth (mar Andrew Smith); Hannah, (mar Jacob Mason); Casey (mar Frances Homan); Aaron (mar Eliz Perrine); Levi (mar Mary A. Hickey); George (mar Mary Amos); Ellen (mar John Shotwell). D Jan 9, 1844. Ref: A. S. Abbott, Bethel, O. Fur infor Cincinnati Chap.

LEONARD, SILAS, (Columbiana Co.)

D Nov, 1851, aged 96 yrs. Bur East Palestine, O. cem. Fur infor Bethia Southwick Chap.

LESLIE, SAMUEL, (Trumbull Co.)

Br 1760. D April 23, 1832. Bur Seceeders Corners, Liberty Twp. MI: Name, date of birth and death. Fur infor Mary Chesney Chap.

LESTER, THOMAS, (Morrow Co.)

Bur Chester Cem, Chester Twp. Fur infor Mt Gilead Chap.

LETTS, NEHEMIAH, (Co. not stated.)

Served as minute man in NJ Mil. Br 1763 N. J. Mar 1787, Rhoda Ann Reed (br 1771, d 1835). D 1822 in Ohio. Ref: Natl No. 102,243, Vol 103, p 197, D. A. R. Lin.

LEWIS, ANDREW, (Butler Co.)

Name appears on the tablet in the Soldiers and Sailors monument at Hamilton, as a Revolutionary Soldier bur in that Co. D Mch 26, 1847. Bur Bethel cem. Hanover Twp. Fur infor John Reily Chap.

LEWIS, ISAAC, (Hamilton Co.)

Br 1775, Mass. D 1837. Ref: S. A. R. Fur infor Cincinnati Chap.

LEWIS, JOHN, (Guernsey Co.)

Bur Liberty Twp. Ref: S. A. R. Fur infor Anna Asbury Stone Chap.

LEWIS, OLIVER, (Lorain Co.)

18th Regt. Conn Mil 1776 in NY campaign. Br 1758. Farmington, Conn. D 1839, North Ridgeville, O. Natl No. 43,260, Vol 44, p 99, D. A. R. Lin. Fur infor Western Reserve Chap.

LEWIS, PHILIP, (Adams Co.)

Pvt Capt John Heister's Company, Chester Co, Pa, Mil. Br N. J. D 1840, Adams Co. O. Ref: Vol 91, p 421, Natl No. 90,751, D. A. R. Lin.

LIEUZADDER, ABRAHAM (LUZADDER), (Guernsey Co.)

Served under Gen Rogers Clark in the battle of Kaskaskia. Br 1757, Pa. Mar Leah Hogue, 1786. One son Isaac. D 1826, Old Washington, Guernsey Co., O. Bur on his farm about a mile northeast of Old Washington. GM family. Farmer. Ref: D. A. R. Lin By Vol 45, and Mrs. Hellen Gregory Lucas, Brooklyn, Ind. and Natl No. 90,844, Vol 91. Fur infor Anna Asbury Stone Chap.

LIGHT, DANIEL, (Clermont Co.)

Lived on 12 Mile Creek, Ohio Twp, Clermont Co, O. Br Pa. Parents: John Light, a Revolutionary Soldier. Mar Susanna ————. Ref: A. S. Abbott, Bethel, O. Fur infor Cincinnati Chap.

LIGHT, GEORGE, (Warren Co.)

Served from Orange Co. "P 165, N. Y. in Revolutionary War." One of the founders of Lebanon, Warren Co. in 1794. Settled southwest of Bedell's Station in 1794. Fur infor Mrs. Whallon, of Cincinnati Chap.

LIGHT, JACOB, (Clermont Co.)

Came to Ohio Twp, Clermont Co, O. 1797. Founded village New Richmond. Br Pa. Parents: John Light, a Revolutionary Soldier. Mar Catherine. Children: John (br 1786, d 1872); Daniel (d 1873); Jacob (d about 1870); David, Peter, Benjamin (d 1875); one other son, and 4 daughters. Was in Columbia. P 48, Hist of Cincinnati by F. Gors, Vol 15, Pa. Archives and A. S. Abbott, Bethel, O. Fur infor Cincinnati Chap.

LIGHT, JOHN, (Clermont Co.)

Pa. Came to Clermont Co, O. about 1805, residing in Williamsburg. Children: Jacob (a Revolutionary Soldier); Daniel (a Revolutionary Soldier); Peter and Barbara. Ref: See Vol 15, 6 Series, Pa. Archives, A. S. Abbott, Bethel, O. Fur infor Cincinnati Chap.

LILLIE, DAVID, (Warren Co.)

Ensign. Col Charles Webb's Continental Regt, 1775. Br Windham Conn, 1736. Mar Azubah Bissell. D Franklin, O, 1821. Natl No. 63,490, p 161, Vol 64, D. A. R. Lin.

LIMMING, SAMUEL, (Hamilton Co.)

D 1834. Fur infor Cincinnati Chap.

LINCOLN, JOSEPH, Maj., (Washington Co.)

Br 1760, Mass. D Sept 21, 1823, Marietta. Bur Mound cem, Marietta, O. MI: "Maj. Joseph Lincoln, 1760-1823." GM Marietta Chap with Revolutionary marker. Replaced in 1920. Fur infor Marietta Chap.

LINDESMITH, JOSEPH, (Columbiana Co.)

Br Mch 19, 1751. D June 10, 1817. Bur Trinity Churchyard. Lived in Hanover Twp, Columbiana Co, O. Fur infor Bethia Southwick Chap.

LINDLEY, ZIBA, (Athens Co.)

A Pvt. minute man in the Morris Co, NJ Mil. during the Revolutionary War. He was a Col in the war 1812. Br Nov 4, 1762, Sussex Co, NJ. Parents: Levi Lindley, Polly (Stilwell) Lindley. Mar Abigail Lindley Oct 4, 1787. Children: Anna, Phoebe, Jane, Wm D., Ziba Jr., Almus, Isaac N., Sabina, Hilas, Emily. D June 20, 1849, Hebbardsville, Athens Co, O. Bur Union Cem near Hebbardsville, directly back of church in middle of old cem. MI: "In memory of Ziba Lindley. Died June 20, 1849, aged 87 yrs, 8 mos, 16 das. 'My loving Savior shall my life restore, and raise me from my dark abode.'" etc on large marble slab. Marked presumably by his son, Ziba Jr., with whom he made his home at the last, soon after death, 1849, scarcely remember. Moved from N. J. to Washington Co, Pa. in early manhood, near Lindley's Fort and Lindley's Mill, thence to Hebbardsville, Athens Co, O. in 1815 or 1816. Presumably a farmer as he paid cash for 2 mile tract of land from present Fisher Station to beyond town of Hebbardsville settling thereon. Ziba Lindley's wife, Abigail, was sister of first President of Ohio University, Athens, O, oldest University west of the Alleghenies. Ref: Morristown N J. or Washington Co, Pa. records. Emma Caroline McVay, Athens, O, No. 116,384. Fur infor Nabby Lee Ames Chap.

LINDSAY, WILLIAM, (Clermont Co.)

Capt of 2nd Tr, Col Bland's Regt, Lee's Legion. Br 1757, in Va. Mar Nancy Ferguson. Children: One son was John. D 1838, New Richmond, O. Ref: Natl No. 101,229, Vol 103, p 69, D. A. R. Lin.

LINDSEY, HEZEKIAH, (Clermont Co.)

Revolutionary soldier fr Pa. Bur in Ohio Twp, Clermont Co, O. Fur infor Cincinnati Chap.

LINDSEY, JOHN, (Marion Co.)

Br 1760, Richmond, Va. Mar Sarah Rea. Children: One son named Jas Heaton. D 1837, near Marion, O. Ref: Natl No. 44,062, Vol 45, p 25, D. A. R. Lin. by Jane Dowd Dailey.

LINDSLEY, STEPHEN, (or LINGSLEY or LINSLEY), (Trumbull Co.)

Pvt Conn State Tr. Br 1761. Bur old cem Center Gustavus, near Braceville, east Phalanx Mills. Pensioned Aug 1832. Ref: Baldwin Library, Youngstown, O. by Miss Kyle. Fur infor Mary Chesney Chap.

LINE, (LYON), JOHN, (Shelby Co.)

Enl Dec 18, 1777 near Tenmile Creek, Washington Co, Pa, served 6 mo as Pvt in Capt William Harrod's Company, in Col George Rogers Clark's Virginia Regt. In July 1778 served 12 mo as Pvt in Capt John Williams' Company in Col Clark's Regt. He was in the battles Kaskaskia, Vincennes, Old Chillicothe. In 1779, 1780 he served 3 mo as Capt of Virginia Mil. In 1782 he served 1 mo 14 da in Capt Ross Company, in Col Cranford's Virginia Regt and was in battle of Sandusky. Br New Jersey 1758. Father came over from England with Gen Braddock and army. Mar Miss Mary Baltzell (d 1835). Children: 6, Henry C. Line, only one mentioned. D 1834, Shelby Co. Bur private cem on Eli Neaderris' farm in Perry Twp, 2½ miles northeast of Sidney. Drew pens from Oct 18, 1832. Came to Ohio in 1800 to Brown Co, moving to Shelby Co in 1830, on a farm in Perry Twp. Ref: Mrs. Ollie Culbertson, Sidney, O. Fur infor Lewis Boyer Chap.

LINE, JOSEPH, (Shelby Co.)

Br 1756, N. J. Father came over fr England 1755 with Gen Braddock. Mar Magdalena Hoost. Children: Abraham (who mar Sarah Line, a dau of John Line, an uncle, in 1820. Abraham was br in Lexington, Ky in 1800). D 1841, Shelby Co, O. Bur probably in a pvt burying ground on Eli Neadarris' farm, 2½ miles northeast of Sidney, on south side of main road. His brother, John Line, is bur in same cem. Came fr New Jersey to Kentucky thence to Ohio in 1812, locating in Brown Co and in 1835 came to Sheby Co. Ref: Sutton's Hist Shelby Co. Fur infor Lewis Boyer Chap.

LINGO, HENRY, (Mahoning Co.)

Pvt in Continental Line, 8th Pa Regt 1783. Pa Archives Series 5, Vol III, p 370, Vol III, p 103. Pensioned 1834, age 85, Vol IV, p 163, received depreciation pay, Continental line. Br 1749. Children: Allen, Joseph, Robert, Samuel, John, Henry, Hamilton, Susan (mar Robert McKensie). Bur Princetown, Milton Twp. GM by S. A. R. Settled in Milton Twp, 1813. Trumbull and Mahoning Co Hist Vol II, p 181. Fur infor Mahoning Chap.

LINK, ADAM, (Crawford Co.)

Pvt under Capts Williamson, Mason, Noble, Cols Williamson and Shepherd, Pa Line. Pensioned 1833. Br 1760 Washington Co, Pa. D Aug 15, 1864, Sulphur Springs, O. Age 103 yrs. Bur Union cem northeast of Sulphur Springs, O. Ref: Vol 91, p 125, Natl No 90382 D. A. R. Lin. Fur infor Hannah Crawford Chap.

LINKHART, BARNEY, (Clinton Co.)

Bur Miller Cem, near Lumberton. Fur infor George Clinton Chap.

LINN, ADAM, (Guernsey Co.)

A soldier by this name also lived in Liberty Twp, Butler Co, O and name appears on memorial tablet at Hamilton, O. Data states 1810 as date of death, but burial place not stated, hence may have been bur in Guernsey Co, O. at Winterset, Guernsey Co, O. Ref: S. A. R. Fur infor Anna Asbury Stone Chap.

LINN, JOHN, (Guernsey Co.)

Bur old Cem, Cambridge, O. Ref: S. A. R. Fur infor Anna Asbury Stone Chap.

LINN, SAMUEL, (Clinton Co.)

Bur New Antioch. Fur infor George Clinton Chap.

LINNELL, JOSEPH, (Licking Co.)

Enl Apr 2, 1778 at Cambridge, Mass. Corp in Capt Simon Fowler's Company, Col Jonathan Reed's Regt guards. Served 6 mos. Muster roll dated Cambridge, May 8, 1778. Fur infor Hetuck Chap.

LINTON, SAMUEL, (Mahoning Co.)

Pvt. Enl Feb 4, 1781. Pa Archives, Series 6, Vol I, p 256, on p 409 return of 6th Bn. Children: Samuel, Adam and three daus. Bur in Milton Twp. Fur infor Mahoning Chap.

LIPPENCOTT, SAMUEL, (Allen Co.)

Enl at age of 20. (1779?) Br Aug 29, 1759, Shrewsbury Twp, Monmouth Co, NJ. D Sept 16, 1836, Rockport, O. GM by Marker. Ref: Mrs. J. E. Sullivan, Lima, O. (D. A. R. descendant.)

LIPPENCOTT, SAMUEL, (Clark Co.)

Pvt Col Daniel Hendrickson's 3rd Regt, Monmouth Co, NJ Mil. Enl Apr 1779. Br Aug 20, 1759, Shrewsberry, Monmouth Co, NJ. Parents: Samuel Lippencott and Elizabeth Rice Lane. Mar Amy Maxson. Children: Ephraim, Obediah, Eliza, Rebecca, Robert, Simon, John, Constant, William Sarah, Katherine, Samuel, Remembrance. D Feb 24, 1853, North Hampton, O. Cem not platted. MI: "Samuel Lippencott, a soldier of the American Revolution. Born August 20, 1759. Died Feb. 24, 1853." GM by S. A. R. about 1904. Moved fr New Jersey to Harrison Co, Va and in 1828 came to Clark Co, and located in North Hampton. Minister. Was taken prisoner by refugees and confined in Sugar House New York 7 mos 7 das. Owned a large tract of land on Kattylick Creek, Harrison Co, Va. Ref: Affidavit for Pens (Invalid 4599) Bureau of Pensions, Washington, D. C. Fur infor Lagonda Chap.

LITTLE, CORNELIUS, (Hamilton Co.)

Br 1755, New Jersey. D 1834. Fur infor Cincinnati Chap.

LITTLE, NATHANIEL CAPT., (Washington Co.)

Ensign in Col John Bailey's Regt. Br 1759? Mar Pamela Bradford, Feb 16, 1792. Children: Welthea, Charles, Henry, Lewis, Nathaniel, George. D Nov 20, 1808, Newport, O. Bur Methodist Churchyard, Newport Cem, Newport, O. MI: "Nathaniel Little—died Nov 20, 1808, in the 49th year." GM by Marietta Chap with Revolutionary marker in 1922. Farmer. Came to Belpre, O. in 1792. During Indian War was a member of garrison at "Farmers Castle" at Belpre. Ref: Hildreth's Hist Early Pioneers; New England Hist. Fur infor Marietta Chap.

LIVINGSTON, DAVID, (Hamilton Co.)

Br 1737, Pa. D 1831. Ref: S. A. R. Fur infor Cincinnati Chap.

LLOYD, E. GEORGE, SR., (Licking Co.)

Enl in Frederick Co, Va Feb 1776, as Pvt in Capt Berry's Company, Col Peter Muhlenberg's Regt. Br 1758. Va. Children: A dau mar John Shank. D Union Twp. Living in 1840. Pens allowed in Fauquier Co, Va. Ref: Brister's History. Fur infor Hetuck Chap.

LOAR, HENRY, (Hamilton Co.)

Br 1758, Md. D 1823. Ref: S. A. R. Fur infor Cincinnati Chap.

LOCKHART, WILLIAM, (Morrow Co.)

Came fr Pa. Bur Perry Twp. Fur infor Mt Gilead Chap.

LOCKWOOD, DAVID, (Belmont Co.)

Pvt and mariner N. Y. State 1778 and 1780 on Capt Nicholson's ship "Trumbull". Lost 42 men battling British ship "Watt". Br 1762 Westchester Co, N. Y. Mar Rebecca Thomas in 1792. D 1840, Belmont Co. Pensioned 1832; widow also pensioned. Ref: Natl No 79369, Vol 80, D. A. R. Lin and Natl No 31397 Vol 32.

LOGAN, JOHN, SR., (Athens Co.)

Class 6 in Capt Elizer Williamson's Company, 3rd Bn Associate and Mil of Washington Company formed fr Westmoreland Co. Br 1753 Dublin, Ireland. Mar Mary, 1796. Children: James (b Apr 1798), Samuel (br Feb 1800), John Jr. (br Oct 1802 and Rebecca (br 1805). D 1821 Alexander Twp, Athens, Co, O. Bur on a farm at Center Stake, Alexander Twp, Athens Co, O. The ground has been plowed over. Ref: Pa Archives 6 Series, Vol II, p 105, Pa Archives 5 Series, Vol 4, p 408. Fur infor Nabby Lee Ames Chap.

LOGAN, WILLIAM, (Mahoning Co.)

Pvt. Children: Eunice, Elizabeth, Mary, and maybe more. Bur cem at Poland, O. Settled in Poland. Ref: Conn Men of the Rev pp 19, 218 and 564. Biographical History of Mahoning Co, Sanderson's pp 199, 200. Fur infor Mahoning Chap.

LONG, MICHAEL, (Co not stated)

Pvt 1782, Cumberland Co Mil. Br 1756 Pa. D 1822, Ohio. Ref: Vol 92, p 236, Natl No 91743.

LONGWELL, JAMES, (Delaware Co.)

Bur probably near Berkshire. Fur infor Delaware Chap.

LOOMIS, HORACE, (Ashtabula Co.)

Bur in Jefferson, O. cem. GM by stone slab, and June 14, 1925, metal marker by Eunice Grant Chap. MI: "In memory of Lt Horace Loomis, who departed this life" (no more can be made out). Fur infor Eunice Grant Chap.

LOOMIS, URIAH, SR., (Ashtabula Co.)

Rowley's Co, Mass Mil, Revolutionary War. Br 1756. D Mch 28, 1884. Bur Hickock Cem, Jefferson, O. MI: "Uriah Loomis, Died Mar 28, 1844, Aged 88 yrs." Rowley's Company, Mass Mil, Revolutionary War. GM Marble slab. Fur infor Eunice Grant Chap.

LORD, ICHABOD, (Portage Co.)

Pvt in NJ State Tr. Placed on Pens Roll Nov 1, 1833. Bur at Shalersville. Drew pens at Ravenna in 1840. Fur infor Old Northwest Chap.

LORING, DANIEL, (Washington Co.)

Sgt in Capt David Moore's Company, Col John Nixon's 5th Regt. Br 1740, Sudbury, Mass. Mar Bathsheba Howe. Children: Israel, Charlotte, Ezekiel, Bathsheba,

Daniel, Polly, Oliver Rice, Jesse. D 1822, Belpre, O. Bur Belpre Cem, Washington Co, O. GM Marietta Chap with Revolutionary marker, 1921. Farmer, Justice of Peace. Ref: Mass War Records, Andrews History. Fur infor Marietta Chap.

LOSEE, WILLIAM, (or LOSEY) (Lawrence Co.)

Pvt served 8 mos as teamster gathering forage for army NJ Line. Br 1761 Mar Rosanna Cole. D 1852. Pensioned in 1840 while residing in Lawrence Co in Rome Twp, aged 70 yrs. Ref: Natl Nos 58033, 33528, Vol 59, p 13, D.A.R. Lin.

LOSSEE (LOFFEE), PETER, (Trumbull Co.)

Br 1750. D Kinsman, O, Dec 27, 1815, age 65 yrs. Bur Old Cem, Kinsman Twp. Grave in good condition. Fur infor Mary Chesney Chap.

LOTT, EBENEZER, (Delaware Co.)

Bur Stark Cem, near Olive Green. Fur infor Delaware Chap.

LOTT, ZEPPHENIAH, (Delaware Co.)

Br Mch 14, 1747. D Feb 26, 1829. Bur Stark Cem, Porter Twp. GM. Fur infor Delaware Chap.

LOVEBERRY, JOHN WADE, (LOOFBOURROW) (Pickaway Co.)

Served in Capt James Young's Company, 8th Bn, Col Abraham Smith, 1778, 5th Class Cumberland Co, Pa. Br Apr 28, 1748, Amboy, N. J. Parents: Wade Loofbourrow, Amboy, N.J. Mar Mary Haff Sept 10, 1767. Children: Abagail, Jacob, Sarah, Rebecca, Mary, David, John, Benjamin, Wade, Ebenezer, Thomas (br July 21, 1792) Nathan (br Dec 22, 1794). D 1714, near Waterloo, Fayette Co, O. Bur Mesmore Cem, Monroe Twp, Pickaway Co, near line of Fayette Co. Went fr New Jersey into Pennsylvania, where he mar and served in Revolutionary War. Then into Virginia. Came to Ohio 1803. Was Baptist minister. Organized Baptist Church at Waterloo, Fayette Co, O. July 17, 1813. Ref: Mrs. Alida E. Loofbourrow, Cook, O. Fur infor Mt Sterling Chap.

LOUX, WILLIAM, (now spelled LOUCKS), (Gallia Co.)

Teamster in Washington's Army. Br Germany. Children: Jacob, John, William, Henry, Margaret, Sally, Nancy, Kate. D Greene Twp, Gallia Co, O. Bur near Centenary Church. Farmer and teamster. Ref: Mrs. Docia Calhoun, Gallipolis, O. Fur infor Return Johnathan Meigs Chap.

LOVE, THOMAS, (Mahoning Co.)

Pvt Chester Co, Pa, 1780-1783 (Pa Archives, Series 6, Vol V, pp 809, 817, 838, 839, 181, 198; Vol VII, p 650, 48, 93, 97). Seems to have had but one son, William (1793-1885). D Poland, O. Bur Poland Presbyterian Cem. Came to Poland in 1802. Was one of the founders of the Presbyterian Church. Ref: Trumbull and Mahoning Co Hist, Vol II, pp 59 and 69. Sandersons Biography, p 757. Fur infor Mahoning Chap.

LOVEJOY, JOSEPH, (Adams Co.)

Br 1745, Queen Ann Co, Md. Mar (1st) Sarah David; (2nd) Priscilla Anderson. Children: Elizabeth, David. Bur Gift Ridge. Fur infor Sycamore Chap.

LOVELAND, ABNER, (Lorain Co.)

Pvt Conn Continental Line. Bur Greenwood Cem. Fur infor Western Reserve Chap.

LOVELAND, AMOS, (Mahoning Co.)

Pvt. Enl May 1, 1777, served 3 yrs, Continental Line, July 1, 1780, Dec 9, 1780, 7th Regt Col Enderkin. Br 1762, Gastonburg, Conn. Mar Jennie (Jemima) Dickson (1763-1855), mar 1785. Children: David, Mrs. Riddle, Mrs. Joshua Kyle, Clarissa Holland. D 1851, Poland, O. Bur at Poland, O. GM D.A.R. in 1915-17. Came to Ohio in 1798 fr Chelsea, Orange Co, Vt. Ref: History Trumbull and Mahoning Co, p 166-244. Conn Men in the Rev. Natl No 42497, D.A.R., et al. For infor Mahoning Chap.

LOVELAND, FREDERICK, (Geauga Co.)

Pvt Mass Continental Army. Pens allowed 1818. Br Adams, Mass, 1748. Mar Rhoda Combs. Children: Diantha, Lucy, Rhoda, Betsy, Clarissa, Polly, Harvey, Edson, Gilbert. Bur North Newbury Cem, Pleasant Hill. Ref: Loveland Genealogy, Vol 3, p 123. Pens records, Vol 3, p 514. Natl No of Revolutionary Soldier in D.A.R. Honor Roll, 52382, 50568. Fur infor Taylor Chap.

LOVELAND, ISAAC, (Portage Co.)

Pvt in Conn Continental Line. Br 1761 in Glastonbury, Conn. D 1832 in Freedom, O. Natl No 31190, D.A.R. Placed on Pens Roll of Portage Co in 1818. Vol 32, p 70, D.A.R. Lin.

LOWE, BARTON, (Clermont Co.)

In 1840, while residing in Monroe Twp, Clermont Co, O, at age of 78, was drawing pens for Revolutionary services. Br 1762. Fur infor Census of Pensions, 1840. Copied by State Chairman.

LOWE, DERRICK, JUDGE, (Hamilton Co.)

He was Judge of the Court of Common Pleas of Somerset Co, N.J. On Dec 15, 1774, he was on a committee of inspection of Hillsborough Twp, Somerset Co, N. J., a patriotic organization "to resist the arbitrary measures of Great Britain." and in 1775, about two mos after the battle of Lexington, helped to raise money "to furnish arms and ammunition to the Mil of Hillsborough Twp." Br, baptized, Oct 13, 1717. Parents: Cornelius Lowe and Judith Middagh. Mar Rebecca Emmons, June 1, 1747. Children: Jacob Derrick Lowe, the youngest, was later a judge in Ohio, Maria, Derrick, John, Eunice, Catherine, Cornelius, Rebecca, Gysbert, Ann, Judith, Abraham. D 1802, probably Hamilton Co, O. Came to Cincinnati in 1791, and several yrs later removed to the Symmes tract in the Little Miami Valley, where he lived in a little town made of log huts. Here he lived, and at his house in 1794, the first Masonic lodge in Ohio was organized. Ref: John Gilbert Lowe; Richard Montgomery Chap S. A. R.

LOWE, JAMES, (Noble Co.)

Pvt 1st Regt Col John H. Stone, 1778, for 3 yrs. Br 1755. Mar Rosanna Hawback. D 1835, Sharon, O. Fur infor Natl No 42537, Vol 43, p 206, D.A.R. Lin.

LOWES, JAMES, (Hamilton Co.)

Ensign in the 3rd Pa Regt, Continental Line. Br Ballyclare Ireland, 1752. Mar Jane Andrew. D Hamilton Co, O, 1810. Natl No 72537, p 188, Vol 73, D.A.R. Lin.

LOWREY, ROBERT, (Mahoning Co.)

Pvt. Capt Walter McKineey's Company, 8th Company, 4th Bn, Cumberland Co Mil. 1781 (4th class). Br 1749, Ireland. Mar Mary Johnson (1749-1714). D 1833. Bur Cem at center of Poland, O. Ref: History Trumbull and Mahoning Co. Williams; Pa Archives, Series 3, Vol 23, p 763 and 777. Fur infor Mahoning Chap.

LOWRY, DAVID, (Clark Co.)

Was a member of Provisional Train Supplying Gen Anthony Wayne's Army. Br 1767, Pa. Parents: David and Lettice Lowry. Mar 1st: Sarah Hammer; 2nd Jane Wright. Children: 1st wife: Sarah, Susan, Nancy, Elizabeth. 2nd wife: Martha, David W. Robert M, Sarah. D Sept 9, 1859. Bur Minnicks, between Enon and Springfield, County Cem not platted. MI: Name, dates of birth and death. GM Small stone. Settled in Bethel Twp 1799 and was one of the first settlers of Clark Co. House is still standing (1925). Farmer. Ref: Beers Clark Co History. Family Records. Fur infor Lagonda Chap.

LOWRY, JEREMIAH, (Gallia Co.)

Pvt. Served 7 yrs. D on farm in Addison Twp. Bur Guthrie Cem, Kanauga, O. House of William Meigs built over the grave. Stone lost. Took part in the battle of Mt Pleasant. Ref: J. C. Maddy, Bulaville, O. Fur infor Return Johnathan Meigs Chap.

LOWTHER, JOEL, (Meigs Co.)

Pvt. Br Loudoun Co, Va, Aug 4, 1741. Unmarried. D Home of John Stevens, Rutland, Nov 7, 1853. Bur Rutland, Meigs Co, O. Farm hand. Fur infor Return Jonathan Meigs Chap.

LUCAS, WILLIAM, CAPT, (Pike Co.)

Served as a Pvt, Lt, and Capt. Br Jan 18, 1742, Jefferson Co, Va, near Shepherdstown. Mar Susannah Barnes. Children: Elizabeth, Mary, Joseph, Susannah and William, Gen—twins, Samuel, Rebecca, Robert (Gov of Ohio), Levisa, Edward, John (Col in War of 1812). D July 2, 1814, Lucasville. Bur Lucas Cem. MI: "Capt William Lucas died July 1814 in 72nd year of his life. A Revolutionary soldier. Susannah Lucas his wife departed this life May 1809 age 64." Ref: Natl No 52570, Vol 53, p 269. Fur infor Nathaniel Massie and Joseph Spencer Chaps.

LUMMIS, JOSEPH, (Butler Co.)

Name appears on the tablet in the Soldiers and Sailors Monument at Hamilton, as a Revolutionary soldier bur in that Co. D at Middletown, O. Fur infor John Reily Chap.

LUTZ, JACOB, (Pickaway Co.)

Enl 1776 in 1st Regt Pa Continentals commanded by Col Edward Hand in Capt Ross's Company. Br 1760, near Reading, Pa, Berks Co. Mar Elizabeth Demuth in 1787 (br 1756, d 1842). D Sept 4, 1823, Pickaway Co, O. Bur Stumpf Church Cem near Laurelville, Pickaway Co, O. Ref: Natl No 79029, Vol 80, and Natl No 102647, Vol 103, p 199, D.A.R. Lin. Fur infor Mt Sterling and Western Reserve Chaps.

LYNCH, PETER, (Hamilton Co.)

Br 1754, Pa. D 1829. Ref: S.A.R. Fur infor Cincinnati Chap.

LYON, JAMES, (Hamilton Co.)

Artificer under Col Jeduthan Baldwin. Pensioned for 3 yrs actual service. Br 1775, Essex Co, N. J. D 1841, Cincinnati, O. Ref: S. A. R. and D. A. R. Lin., Vol 32, p 154, Natl No 31396. Fur infor Cincinnati Chap.

LYON, NATHANIEL, (Montgomery Co.)

A Pvt in Capt Daniel Wood's Company, Essex Co, NJ Mil; also Continental Tr. Enl when the British landed on Staten Island. His application for pens Sept

11, 1832, shows an extensive string of serv and many engagements. Br July 3, 1758, Essex Co, N. J Mar Massy Wilcox (br Nov, 1777, d Oct 10, 1838), Marion Ind. Children: Sally, Mary, Jotham. D Marion, Ind, 1833 (but another states Montgomery Co). Came to Germantown, Montgomery Co, at an early date and was a school teacher in that German settlement. It is reported that the family removed to Marion, Ind. Ref: Natl No 39540, Vol 40, p 194, D.A.R. Lin. Fur infor Richard Montgomery Chap S.A.R.

LYONS, JOSEPH, (Athens Co.)

Enl as a Pvt fr Halifax, Vt, Jan, 1776, for 5 mos. Capt Hall, Col Seth Warner, Green Mountain Boys, and again in June, 1777, 4 mos, Capt Allen; 4 mos, Goodenough's Rangers of Vt. Br 1755, New England. Mar Mary Cary, 1776 (d July 25, 1820). Children: Mary, Anna, Jane, John, Amity. D June 27, 1836, Amesville, O (Natl No 89714, Vol 90, p 230, D.A.R. Lin.). Bur West State St, Athens, O, east of main driveway. MI: "Joseph Lyons—Died June 27, A. D. 1836—Aged 81 years. GM doubtless by descendants. He applied for pens Oct 13, 1832, fr Athens Twp, Athens Co, O. At the age of 77 his claim was allowed. Ref: Department of Interior, Bureau of Pensions, Revolutionary War records Sec. Fur infor Nabby Lee Ames Chap.

LYONS, SAMUEL, (Columbiana Co.)

In 1840 was living in Liverpool Twp, Columbiana Co, age 78 yrs. A pensioner. Fur infor Bethia Southwick Chap.

LYONS, WILLIAM, (Morgan Co.)

Served in Capt Fishbbourne's Company, 4th Pa Line Regt 1777. Br 1756. D Morgan Co. A Revolutionary pensioner living in Harrison Co 1833. Age 77 yrs. Settled in Washington Twp about 1820. Ref: Pa Archives 5th, 11, 1060, 1083. Fur infor Moravian Trail Chap.

MacLACHLAN, JAMES, (Columbiana Co.)

Pvt, Capt Saml Holliday's Pa Tr. Br 1743, Scotland. D 1834. Ref: Natl No 90121, Vol 91, p 40, D.A.R. Lin.

McALLISTER, ANDREW, (Washington Co.)

Pvt in Capt John Parker's Company; Samuel Young's Company; Col Timothy Bedell's Regt. Br 1745. D 1816. Bur Mound Cem, Marietta, O. GM Marietta Chap with marker on gateway, Nov 30, 1906; marker stolen; replaced 1920. Ref: Adj Gen office, State of N. H. Fur infor Marietta Chap.

McBRIDE, STEPHEN, (Columbiana Co.)

Served 1776 as Pvt and Drummer Boy; with Washington at Yorktown. Br 1761. D 1837, Hanoverton, O. Ref: Vol 92, p 162, Natl No 91500, D.A.R. Lin.

McBURNEY, WILLIAM, (Sandusky Co.)

Served to close of war. Br Ireland. Not mar. D Bradner, O, thought to be 1837 (A. J. Brooks). Bur Bradner, O. Cem is situated in Wood and Sandusky Cos. Grave on Sandusky side. No mark. Came fr Ireland in 1775 to aid Revolutionists. Left no relatives. Fur infor Jane Washington Chap.

McCADDEN, JOHN, (Licking Co.)

Enl July, 1780, in Col George Roger Clark's Regt. He assisted in erecting blockhouse, first bldg on present site of Cincinnati. Served Va. D Licking Twp. Bur Cedar Hill Cem, Newark. GM Hetuck Chap in 1910. Settled in this Co 1826. Ref: Brister's Hist. Fur infor Hetuck Chap.

McCASKEY, WILLIAM, (Columbiana Co.)

Reported by Bethia Southwick Chap as a Revolutionary soldier, but no record yet found. D Columbiana Co, O. Fur infor Bethia Southwick Chap.

McCAUGHEY, WILLIAM, (Wayne Co.)

Pvt 1776. Capt Thomas Church's Company, Col Anthony Wayne's Pa Regt. Br 1745. Mar Margaret Jackson, 1769. D 1826, near Smithville, O. Ref: Natl No 44668, Vol 45, p 267, D.A.R. Lin.

McCLEAN, MOSES, (Ross Co.)

Capt 6th Pa Bn. Br 1737, York Co, Pa. Mar Sarah Watkins, 2nd wife. D 1810 Chillicothe, O. Natl No 76925, Vol 77, D.A.R. Lin.

McCLEAN, WILLIAM, (Adams Co.)

Commanded a Company under Col Thos Hartley, Pa Line, 1777. Br 1733. Mar Jane Witherow. Children: One was Mary. D 1807, Adams Co. Natl No 48899, p 408, Vol 49, D.A.R. Lin.

McCLEAVE, GEORGE, (Clark Co.)

The published family genealogy states he participated in one of the important battles of the Amer Revolution. Br Md. Mar Elizabeth Smith, dau of Peter Smith. Children: John, Elizabeth, Benjamin, Mary, who mar Nathan Reddish at whose home he died. D 1824, near Harmony. Bur Columbia St cem, northwest part. MI: "George McCleave a soldier of Revolution." GM S. A. R. metal marker 1906. Moved from Md to Colerain, O. 1790, then to Ill. In 1819 came alone to Clark Co on horseback. Shoe maker, learned trade in Philadelphia. Ref: Family hist. Fur infor Lagonda Chap.

McCLELLAND, CARY, (Knox Co.)

Pvt. Enl 1776 in Regt of Col Walter Stewart in the battles of Germantown, Brandywine, Trenton, Princeton. Pensioned as Pvt Pa Line. Br Mch 13, 1750, (or 1753 ?) in Ireland. Mar —— McVey and Henrietta Meyers (d 1829). One dau Elizabeth. D Mch 8, 1846 Ross Co tho pensioned in Knox Co. Bur Bell Church Cem southern Knox Co. first row on the west side of cem. MI: "Cary McClelland, born 13th of March 1750, died the 8th of March, 1846." Also a verse on the stone partially illegible. Ref: (Bk 3, Vol 8, pp 2 and 3. J. J. Sprague Clerk: We have the original pens paper granted the 12th day of July 1834 signed by Louis Caso. Also paper fr Bureau of Pensions, Washington, D. C. giving the infor on pensions and also of his services and granting of pens.) Mary Bell Benton, Delaware, O. Compare Natl No 63247, Vol 64, and 82463, Vol 83, D. A. R. Lin. Fur infor Kokosing Chap.

McCLELLAND, JAMES, (Columbiana Co.)

Living in 1840, aged 80 yrs. Centre Twp, Columbiana Co, O. Pensioned. Fur infor Bethia Southwick Chap.

McCLELLAND, SAMUEL, (Harrison Co.)

Lt in Flying Bn of Montgomery Co, Pa. Prisoner at Ft Washington, 1778; exchanged 1780. Br Ireland. Mar Elizabeth Oliver (1753-1853) D 1829, Harrison Co, O. Ref: Natl No 77222, Vol 78.

McCLELLAND, WILLIAM, (Butler Co.)

Name appears on tablet in the Soldiers and Sailors monument at Hamilton, as a Revolutionary Soldier, bur in that co. D Oct 2, 1827. Bur Greenwood Cem. Hamilton, O. Lived in St Clair Twp. Fur infor John Reily Chap.

McCLIMANS, JOHN, (Madison Co.)

Served as substitute in Chester Co, Mil, for the sum of £25 for a term of two mos. Br Apr 29, 1756, Westmoreland Co, Pa. Mar Mary Creviston, 1782. Children: Margaret, William, George, Sarah, John, James, Joseph, Samuel, Isaac, David. D Aug 8, 1829, Madison Co, O. Location of cem James H. McCliman's farm in Madison Co, O. Fur infor Mt Sterling Chap.

McCLINTOCK, WILLIAM, (Pickaway Co.)

Pvt in Capt William Blane's Company 7th Bn Cumberland Co, Mil. 1777. Bn commander not stated. (See p 457, Vol and series as above Pa Archives). Br 1734, in Scotland. Mar a cousin, —— McClintock, in 1755. Children: One son, Joseph. D 1804, near Clarksburg, O. Bur Cedar Grove, Perry Twp, Pickaway Co, O. at southwest corner. GM by stake. He had a brother James. Ref: Natl No 80480 and Miss Frances McClintock, Cook, O. Fur infor Mt Sterling Chap.

McCLURE, WILLIAM, (Perry Co.)

Commanded a Company in Pa Tr. Br 1759, Cumberland Co, Pa. Mar 1st wife Agnes McKeehan in 1786. D 1823, Perry Co (?). Ref: Natl No 45547, Vol 46, p 232, D. A. R. Lin.

McCLURKIN, MATHEW, (Preble Co.)

Location of cem Israel Twp. Fur infor Mary P. Mitchell, Eaton, O. and Mrs. Miller.

McCOMB, WILLIAM, (Franklin Co.)

Enl Capt Jas McConnel's Company, Cols Walle and Morgan, from Cumberland Co, Pa. July 20, 1776 at Ft Washington siege. Served as volunteer with Col Crawford on his expedition to Sandusky in 1782; also on the pension rolls of 1819, on the muster roll from Washington Co, Pa. Taken prisoner Nov 16, 1776; confined on prison ship "Jersey." Paroled; re-enl 1787. 6th Bn Cumberland Co, Pa. Br Washington Co, Pa, 1757. D Feb 10, 1835, Truro Twp. Location of cem near Winchester pike. MI: "William McComb. Died Feb 10, 1835, aged 78 years." GM Rev Grave Committee with bronze marker. Sept 1927. D. A. R. Came to Ohio fr Washington Co, Pa. 1820; located on Walnut Creek about 1½ miles fr National Road. Fur infor Columbus Chap.

McCOMBS, JOHN, (Mahoning Co.)

Pvt Capt Luce's Company. 2nd Bn 2nd Establishment. Pvt 2nd Regt. Transferred to Nichols Regt Continental Army. N. J. Men of the Revolution, p 130. Bur Poland Presbyterian Church Cem. Came to Poland in 1801, Trumbull and Mahoning Co History, p 48, Vol 1. Fur infor Mahoning Chap.

McCOMBS, WILLIAM, (Mahoning Co.)

Pvt Washington Co Regt. Capt Robert Ramseys' Company, 7th Class. Washington Co. Regt. 1782 returned. Pa Archives, Series 6, Vol 11, p 184, 4 Class, 1784 same Vol, p 212. Br native of Washington Co, Pa. When he died left wife and nine children. D in Poland, 1854. Bur Poland Cem. Native of Washington, Pa. Came to Poland, O. 1802. Fur infor Mahoning Chap.

McCONNELL, ALEXANDER, (Montgomery Co.)

Pvt of Capt McClure's Company, Col Lynn's Company 1780, also Col Robert Patterson's Company Ky. Br Jan 26, 1758, Scotland Children: William, Robert, James Lindsay, Alexander, Thomas Jefferson. D Nov 12, 1821, O. Bur Woodland Cem. Ref: Fannie McConnell Lynch, Dayton, O. Fur infor Jonathan Dayton Chap.

McCONNELL, THOMAS, (Brown Co.)

Served in the Revolutionary War from Washington Co, Pa. Br Washington Co, Pa. D Union Twp, Brown Co, O. Bur Redoak, Old Cem. Ref: Mrs. J. W. McTamany, Georgetown, O. Fur infor Taliaferro Chap.

McCORKEL, JOSEPH, Maj., (Miami Co.)

He entered Northwest Traction Quarter of Sec 20, Washington Twp. Br N. C. 1753. D Piqua, O. July 25, 1828. Bur first in lower graveyard, later to Forest Hill. Fur infor Piqua Chap.

McCORKEL, ROBERT, (Lawrence Co.)

Pvt 1776-78 in Capt Michael Bowyer's Company. Col Jas Woods' Regt of Va. Applied for pension 1832. Br 1760, Augusta Co, Va. Mar Elizabeth Forrest. D 1833, Lawrence Co, O. Natl No 68863, Vol 69, p 309, D. A. R. Lin.

McCORMICK, FRANCIS, (Columbiana Co.)

Pension Rolls 1832 of Hamilton Co, Va Line. Br 1764, Va. Mar Rebecca —— (1767-1840). D 1836, Salem, O. Ref: Natl No 79411, Vol 80, D. A. R. Lin. Fur infor Cincinnati Chap.

McCOY, ALEXANDER, (Brown Co.)

Bur old cem, Ripley. Fur infor Ripley Chap.

McCOY, EPHRIAM, (Delaware Co.)

Pvt under Cols Wyllis and Zebulon, Capt Judd. Location of cem Trenton Twp. Pensioned. Fur infor Delaware Chap.

McCOY, GEORGE, (Champaign Co.)

D 1820 in Urbana. Bur Old Ward St Cem. Fur infor Urbana Chap.

McCRACKEN, CYRUS, (Hamilton Co.)

D 1782. Fur infor Cincinnati Chap.

McCRACKEN, WM., Col, (Hamilton Co.)

Pa. 2nd Lt 13th Regt, 1777. He was first Revolutionary soldier bur in Hamilton Co. Ref: Grieve's History, p 128. D Nov 4, 1782. Wounded at Piqua; d after several days' journey on now Mt Auburn. Bur by little blockhouse opposite mouth of Licking River. 50 years later, at his request, 3 of his companions—Simon Kenton, Maj Jas Galloway and John McCadden returned to his grave. Fur infor Cincinnati Chap.

McCREA, GILBERT, (Hamilton Co.)

Br 1758, Pa. D 1824. Fur infor Cincinnati Chap.

McCREARY, GEORGE, (Morrow Co.)

Enl as Pvt in Pa Mil York Co, May 1, 1776. Promoted to End Sgt, served under Capt Gilliland and Col Reed; joined the "Flying Camp" under Col Magaw at Elizabeth N. J. Took part in battle of Ft Washington, was captured and held prisoner on British Man-of-war 2 mos. Br 1752 in County Armagh, Province of

Ulster, Ireland. Mar Mary ——, 1781 or 1782. Children: Thomas, Nancy, James, Mary, Benjamin, Rebecca, Elizabeth, William, Sarah. D Feb 26, 1842, Chester Twp in old part, first row behind church, near road, no monument; marker in preparation; will have Revolutionary record. GM by great-great-granddaughter, with granite marker. He lived a short time in York Co, Pa after Revolution then moved to Loudon Co, Va. from there to Licking Co, O. finally to Knox Co. Farmer, carpenter. Granted a pens Apr 3, 1834. Pension certificate No 26201. Ref: Miss Eva Gardner, Mt Gilead, O. Fur infor Mt Gilead Chap.

McCULLOUGH, ROBERT, (Hamilton Co.)

D 1820. Ref: S. A. R. Fur infor Cincinnati Chap.

McCULLOUGH, WILLIAM, (Harrison Co.)

Br 1751. D 1832. Bur at Crabapple Church. Served in Capt Henry Graham's Company 4th Bn Washington Co Pa, Mil. 1781. Pa Archives 6 Series, 11, p 133. Fur infor Moravian Trail Chap.

McCULLUM, JOHN, (Mahoning Co.)

Ranger on the Frontier 1778 to 1783. Cem Mahoning Co. Owned land in Mahoning Co in early 18th century. Farmer. Ref: Old Deeds Bk G, p 435. Pa Archives, Series 3, Vol 23, p 206. Fur infor Mahoning Chap.

McCUNE, JOHN, (Coshocton Co.)

Location of cem Linton Twp. Ref: Co History, Mrs. A Ripple, West LaFayette, O. member. Fur infor Coshocton Chap.

McCUNE, THOMAS, COL., (Jefferson Co.)

A part of 1776-1778-1780. Col McCune was one of the volunteers of Delaware in the Revolution who took £12,500 in booty fr the British, and as the army under Washington was in extreme distress, it was voted as a supply for the use of the army, and immediately conveyed to it. Br July 12, 1756, Huntington Co, Delaware. Parents: James and Elizabeth McCune. Mar Mary Brady, dau of Gen Joseph Brady, Apr 5, 1785. Children: Mary, Elizabeth, James, Sarah, Mary, Jane, Margaret, Joseph, William. (Mary occurs twice—typist.) D April 12, 1842 in Warren Twp, Jefferson Co. Oak Grove Graveyard, one mile east of Mt Pleasant O. MI: "Col Thomas McCune, 1756-1842." Steubenville D. A. R. with official marker. July 4, 1922. Forty-five years of age Col McCune moved to Ohio, and he was one of those early pioneers who opened the wilderness, and made a home and "local habitation" for generations to come. He was one of Nature's nobility; ever kindhearted as a parent, the friend of man, and an uncompromising Democrat. He represented the people of Jefferson Co for some yrs in the legislature of the state, he was a leading member of the Presbyterian church and fulfilled his duties in life as a Christian and patriot. He died full of yrs, and was bur with the honors of war. Peace to the ashes of the veteran citizen, and patriotic soldier of the Revolution. A large circle of relatives and friends mourn his loss; let them cherish his manifold virtues, and may we all, when overtaken by death, be found as innocent and free fr faults, as the honest old warrior who fought for human rights and the blessings of liberty. Fur infor Steubenville Chap.

McDANIEL, HENRY, (Gallia Co.)

Enl in spring of 1779 as Pvt at Bedford Co, Pa. Served in Capt Thomas Arthur's Company, Regt of Col Lynch of Va. Wounded in battle of King's Mountain. Disch at Camden Oct 1781. Came to Ohio 1810 fr Lewisburg, W. Va. Br Nov 1763 in Pittsylvania Co, Va. Mar Hannah Bryan, May 15, 1788, in Greenbriar Co, Va. Children: Caleb, John, Alexander, Benjamin, Ephraim, Jehu, Sarah, Hannah. D Sept 28, 1838, in Gallia Co, O. Bur on farm of W. L. Eakins, Walnut Twp, Gallia Co, O.

MI: Names, dates, etc. Ref: Mrs. Jesta Richards, Washington, D. C., Ethel F. Clark, Gallipolis, O., et al. Fur infor French Colony Chap.

McDANIEL, JAMES, (Jackson Co.)

Body guard of Gen Washington at Monmouth. Sgt and Pvt in Va. Tr, Capt Thos Arthur, Col Jas Calloway, 1778. Served to close of Rev. Br Dec 26, 1755, Halifax Co, Va. Mar Rebecca Lewis, 1789. Children: Levi McDaniel who mar Frances Massie was a son, though in some references we have, he Levi, is given as the Rev soldier, having been confused with the father. Enoch another; perhaps others, D 1847, at Oak Hill, aged 98 yrs 8 mos. Bur in cem in East Oak Hill, O. MI: legible. GM tombstone. Came to Ohio fr Va where he served as Indian spy, 1790 to 1792, in 1819, settled in Jackson Co where he became one of the first Justices of the peace, until he was very old, he taught country school north of Gallia and Washington stations. He is pictured in old accounts as a very old man with long white hair. Mention is also made of Levi McDaniel baptizing persons at the creek bottoms in country church gatherings. Applied for pens, Jackson Co, 1845. Ref: (Davis Mackley's Random Notes in the History of Jackson Co by D. W. Williams) Rec ver by D. A. R. (1928). Fur infor Capt John James Chap; and Elizabeth Zane Dew Chap.

McDANIEL, VALENTINE, (Brown Co.)

Pvt. Br Jan 11, 1760, South Bank Potomac, Va. Mar Sarah Jones, 1798. D Brown Co, Jan 13, 1846. Location of cem somewhere in Huntington Twp, Brown Co, O. Ref: Pension Dept, Washington. Fur infor Lt Byrd Chap.

McDANIEL, WALTER, (Brown Co.)

Pvt. Served fr Prince George Co, Md. Br Anne Arundel Co, Md 1747. Location of cem Huntington Twp Brown Co. Ref: Record in Pension Dept Washington D. C. I. S. C. File 25691. Fur infor Lt Byrd Chap.

McDERMUT, JAMES, (Putnam Co.)

Sgt Northampton Co, Pa under Capt Johnson and Col Craig. Br 1758, Pa. D Ottawa, O, 1856. Natl No 32860. Miss Jennie Brooks. Fur infor D. A. R. Lin Bk Vol 33, p 292.

McDERMOTT, JAMES, (Richland Co.)

Pvt in Pa Mil. Br 1759. D June 25, 1859. Bur Koogle cem 1½ miles north of M L Koogle farm on Wooster Rd. MI: Rev Soldier. GM 1911. Fur infor Mary Washington Chap.

McDILL, DAVID, (Preble Co.)

Location of cem Israel Twp. Ref: Mary P Mitchell, Eaton, O.

McDONALD, ARCHIBALD, (Logan Co.)

Pvt Pa Mil 1776. Br Scotland, 1759. D Ohio, 1840. Natl No 31810, Vol 32, p 298, D. A. R. Lin.

McDONALD, JOHN, (Warren Co.)

Maj 3rd Bn Cumberland Co, Pa 1780 during Rev. Br 1748. D 1831, Warren Co, O. Ref: Vol 93, p 241, Natl No 92775, D. A. R. Lin.

McDONALD, ———, (Greene Co.)

With Gen Gates. Br 1745. D Mch 26, 1823. Bur McDonald graveyard southeast of Xenia. Xenia, 1800. Ref: Robinson's History of Greene Co. Fur infor Catherine Greene Chap.

McDONOUGH, HUGH, (Harrison Co.)

Br 1752. D 1833. Settled in Harrison Co about 1812 where he died. Served in the Pa Flying Camp. US Pension Rolls 1835. Fur infor Moravian Trail Chap.

McDONNELL, JOHN, (Jefferson Co.)

Surgeon's mate and surgeon. Br 1748. Mar Martha Johnstone. D 1825 Steubenville. Ref: Natl No 18641, p 235, Vol 19, D. A. R. Lin.

McFADDEN, CONLEY, (Co not stated)

Enl 1775 Capt Steven Bayard's Company, Col St Clair's 3rd Pa Regt. Served 1778 Capt Peter Voorhes' Company, Col Ogden's NY Regt. Br Ireland, 1753. Mar Jennie Dillaplain. D 1840. Ohio Natl No 60855, Vol 61, p 287, D. A. R. Lin.

McFADDEN, JOHN, (Harrison Co.)

Br 1746. D 1835. Bur in Cadiz Old Graveyard; removed fr Hopewell Twp, Washington Co, Pa to Cadiz Twp about 1800; served in Capt George Sharp's 3rd Bn Washington Co, Mil 1781. Pa Arch 6 Series, 11, p 92. Fur infor Moravian Trail Chap.

McFARLAND, DANIEL, (Geauga Co.)

Revolutionary Soldier. Capt Jedediah Hurd's Company, Col Jobe Stafford's Regt Mass, Mil. Br 1760 probably Uxbridge, Mass. Parents: Daniel McFarland (McFarling) and Elizabeth Dun. Mar Avis Reynolds. Children: Betsy, Polly, Johnathan, John, Peggy, Abel, Clara, Shadrick, Daniel, Lovisa and Theresa. D Feb 5, 1844. Bur McFarland Cem, Bainbridge. MI: "Daniel McFarland died Feb 5, 1844, age 82 yrs. Avis his wife died Dec 5, 1824, age 64." GM Family stone. Came to Geauga Co in 1818. Ref: Records of office Sec Rev War Service Commonwealth Mass. Fur infor Taylor Chap.

McFARLAND, WILLIAM, CAPT, (Fairfield Co.)

Pvt Sec 35529, D. A. R. Lin. Br Dauphin Co, Pa, 1758. Mar Rebecca Poster, d 1836. Children: One named Walter. D 1838. Bur Hooker Cem. GM D.A.R. Chap. Ref: Natl No 49662, Vol 50, D.A.R. Lin. Fur infor Elizabeth Sherman Reese Chap.

McGARRY, WILLIAM, (Adams Co.)

Enl 1777 Pvt Capt Wood Jones' Company. Later served in Capt Benjamin Hoomes' Company, Christian Febingers' Regt. Enl for 3 yrs. Was in battles around N.J. and Philadelphia. Much time spent hauling supplies to army. Br County Down, Ireland, 1757. Mar 1st Elizabeth Walker, in Washington Co, Pa; 2nd Mary McKee. Children: 5 by 1 mar, 3 by 2 mar. D 1845 Adams Co. Bur near Wrightsville on farm. Early in 1777 emigrated to Va; thence to W Pa; and in 1795 to Ohio. Bought 225 acres, Tiffin Twp; cleared, planted peach trees. Ref: History of Adams Co. Natl No 42116 S.A.R. and Vol 97, 96435 D.A.R. Lin. Fur infor Sycamore Chap.

McGILL, JOHN, (Mahoning Co.)

Pvt 11th Regt NY. Enl in Cumberland Co, Pa, 1776, and served 3 tours of 2 mos each under Capts John Carothers and John Lamb. Br 1747. Children: James, Joseph, Fenton, Robert, John, William, dau not mentioned. D Apr 21, 1834. Location of cem Presbyterian Church, Poland. GM Mahoning Chap, bronze, 1916. Came to Mahoning Co 1800 and settled on farm, where he lived until he died. Ref: N. Y. Men of the Rev, p 118, under enlisted men "the Levies", p 90, Trumbull and Mahoning Co Histories, Vol 2, p 39. Fur infor Mahoning Chap.

McGREW, ANDREW, (Clermont Co.)

Rev soldier, Pvt Pa Mil. Br Baltimore, Md, 1760 (or Scotland). Mar Hannah Rust. Children: Charles, Jonathan (mar Ruth Crawford), William, Paul, Joseph, Andrew (mar Ann McClelland), Isaac (d 1823), Margaret (mar Conduce Gatch 1807) and ——— (mar Jacob Gest). D near Milford , O, Union Twp, 1823. Justice of Peace 6 yrs in Union Twp. Natl No 77544, 19426, D.A.R. descendants. History of Clermont and Brown Co, p 244. By Hobart Pub Co and A. S. Abbott, Bethel, O.

McGUIRE, JOHN, (Jefferson Co.)

Served Va Tr expedition to Canada. Taken prisoner at Quebec 1775. Capt Grayson's Regt 1777, wounded at Germantown. Br Winchester, Va, 1750. Mar Mary Tipton. D Steubenville, 1800. Natl No 60427, p 131, Vol 61, D.A.R. Lin.

McHATTEN, ALEXANDER, (Greene Co.)

Lt Col and Maj Pa Mil. Pens 1833. Br 1744. D Apr 23, 1837. Bur Massie's Creek graveyard. Lived in Miami, 1820. Ref: Robinson's History of Greene Co. Fur infor Catherine Greene Chap.

McHENRY, RICHARD, (Muskingum Co.)

Pvt under Capt Price, Col Proctor, Capt Kennedy, Col Butler. Br Londonderry, Ireland. D June 27, 1835. Bur Sugar Grove Graveyard, 3-5 mile south of Duncan Falls. Pensioned in 1818. Fur infor Muskingum Chap.

McILRATH, ANDREW, (Cuyahoga Co.)

Pvt Conn State Tr. Br 1759. D 1836. Bur First Presbyterian Churchyard, Euclid Ave. Fur infor Western Reserve Chap.

McINTIRE, ANDREW, (Adams Co.)

Pvt in Capt Wm Lowe's Company, Col Chas Campbell's Regt, Pa Line. Br 1746, West Nottingham, Pa. D 1835, Adams Co. Bur Mt Leigh Cem. GM Marked by Sycamore Chap. Ref: Hist of Adams Co. Natl No 95167, Vol 96, D.A.R. Lin. Fur infor Sycamore Chap.

McINTIRE, WILLIAM, (Clark Co.)

Pvt in Capt Samuel Montgomery's Company, 17th Pa Regt, Col Wm Irwin commanding. Enl Aug 1, 1777. Br 1760 in Scotland. Mar Elizabeth Tanner. Children: Samuel. D 1798, Springfield, O. Bur Columbia St Cem, between Center and Wittenburg Aves, northwest corner. Cem not platted. GM S.A.R. metal marker. Name plate removed 1906. Farmer. Was a personal friend of William Henry Harrison. Family hist and W. T. R. Sattrell's records of Revolutionary soldiers and pens papers. Fur infor Lagonda Chap.

McKAY, DANIEL, (Cuyahoga Co.)

Location of cem, Independence, on very high hill. Fur infor Western Reserve Chap.

McKELVEY, WILLIAM, (Richland Co.)

Capt Gilbert Gibbs' Chester Co Regt, 6 yrs serv. Br Chester Co, Pa, 1760. D Richland Co, 1840. Ref: Natl No 16948, p 344, Vol 17, D.A.R. Lin.

McKENNON, JOSEPH, (Columbiana Co.)

Lived in Liverpool Twp, Columbiana Co. Fur infor Bethia Southwick Chap.

McKENZIE, JOHN, (Mahoning Co.)

Pvt Capt William Butler's Company. Pension May 22, 1833. Br 1765. D 1832. Bur Vaughen Cem, Milton Twp. Ref: Pa Archives Series 5, Vol 2, p 98, Series 3, Vol 23, p 539. Fur infor Mahoning Chap.

McKENZIE, JOSHUA, (Ross Co.)

Was a drummer in Lt Col Weltner's Company, German Bn. Enl Apr 20, 1778, again Feb 27, 1779. Br Md, Mch 20, 1764. Mar Mary Jones (br 1768 and mar 1785). D Ross Co, O, 1835. Location of cem Twin Twp, Ross Co, O, Moores' Cem. GM Stone. Bronze marker placed by Nathaniel Massie Chap D.A.R. 1924. His name appears on payroll for period ending Dec, 1780. His brother, Moses McKenzie, was a fifer and served in battles of White Plains, Monmouth and the siege of Yorktown. His brother, Jesse McKenzie, also served in the Revolution, and his widow spent her last days with relatives in Ross Co and received pens there. Ref: Natl No 42021, Vol 43, D.A.R. Lin. Fur infor Nathaniel Massie Chap.

McKINLEY, DAVID, (Columbiana Co.)

Br 1757. Living in 1832 Centre Twp, Columbiana Co, age 75. Pensioner. Fur infor Bethia Southwick Chap.

McKINLEY, DAVID, (Crawford Co.)

Pvt Pa Line. His Company detailed at Ft Washington, and he was the only one not captured. Br 1755, York Co, Pa. Mar Sarah Gray. Children: One was Martha. D 1840. Bur German Lutheran Cem, near Chatfield, on Scioto Trail. Great-grandfather of William McKinley, ex-Pres of U.S., who marked the grave. Pensioned 1832 for 21 mos actual serv, Pvt Va Line. Came to Ohio 1814. Natl No 42542, Vol 43, D.A.R. Lin. Fur infor Hannah Crawford Chap.

McKINLEY, JOHN, (Hancock Co.)

D Jan 14, 1861, aged 107 yrs. Location of cem, Cannonsburg, Hancock Co, O. GM Family marker. Ref: Chas or Samuel Marshall, Findlay, O. Fur infor Ft Findlay Chap.

McKINNIE, JOHN, (Delaware Co.)

Pvt under Col John Scott, Capt Walter McKinnie, 4th Bn Cumberland Co, Pa Mil. Location of cem Liberty Church, Liberty Twp. Pensioned. Fur infor Delaware Chap.

McKINSEY, SAMUEL, (Mahoning Co.)

Pvt, Dec 28, 1780, Association and Mil Cumberland Co, Pa, 7th Company, Capt Patrick Zack. Pa Archives, Vol VI, Series 5, p 95 and 96. Mar Mary ——, who is bur in Springfield Twp, cem not located. Came fr Pa to Springfield early in 1800. Ref: The Late Mr Henry Baldwin. Fur infor Mahoning Chap.

McKNIGHT, ADAM, (Delaware Co.)

Pvt under Cols Maxwell and Tupper, Capts Abbot and Sparks, Mass Tr. D 1848, age 85. Location of cem Sunbury. Pensioned. Fur infor Delaware Chap.

McKNIGHT, DAVID, (Hamilton Co.)

Br 1760, Pa. D 1821. Ref: S.A.R. Fur infor Cincinnati Chap.

McKNIGHT, JOHN, (Clermont Co.)

Fifer in Revolutionary Army. Pensioned 1819, for serv in Md Continental Line; dropped from pension rolls 1920, restored 1823. Br probably in Amherst Co, Va. (Abbott). Lived in Williamsburg, Clermont Co, O. Ref: A. S. Abbott, Bethel, O. Fur infor Cincinnati Chap.

McKNIGHT, WILLIAM, (Clermont Co.)

Br probably Amherst Co, Va. Lived Williamsburg, Clermont Co, O. Tailor by trade, unmarried. Ref: A. S. Abbott, Bethel, O. Fur infor Cincinnati Chap.

McKOWN, JAMES, (Knox Co.)

Pvt, Revolutionary War, wounded at Brandywine. Mar Phebe Casto (d 1852 aged 103) mar at Winchester, Frederick Co, Va, 1782. Children: Gilbert, moved to Va, James to Ill, Phoebe to Mo, Samuel to O. D 1850, age 98. In 1820, with part of family came from Va to Milford Twp, Knox Co, O. Ref: Norton's Hist of Knox Co, p 358; family records. Fur infor Kokosing Chap.

McLANE, JOHN, (or McLEAN) (Greene Co.)

Popularly known as Judge, is bur on his farm about 3 miles north of Bellbrook, Sugar Creek Twp on what is now known as the Huston farm. He is said to have patriotically refused a pension, hence his name is not on the pension roll. Fur infor Catherine Greene Chap.

McLAUGHLIN, JAMES, (Columbiana Co.)

Br 1744. D about 1834. Lived in Hanover Twp, Columbiana Co, O. Fur infor Bethia Southwick Chap.

McLAUGHLIN, JOHN, (Brown Co.)

Pvt in Pa Mil. Capt Joseph Potts Company 5th Regt, Pa Continental Line, Col Francis Johnson 1778. Br Pa, 1756. Mar Frances Calhoun, 1786. Children: David, Rebecca, Frances, Rosa, Mary, Robert, Joseph, Jennette, William. D 1830, near Decatur, Brown Co, O. Bur old part of cem. MI: "Revolutionary Soldier." GM Lt Byrd Chap. Govt. marker, May 30, 1922. Farmer. Ref: Mrs. A. D. Hughes, Decatur, O. Fur infor Lt Byrd Chap.

McLEAN, MOSES, (Ross Co.)

Capt in 6th Pa Bn. Br 1737, York Co, Pa. D 1810, Chillicothe, O. Ref: No 100219, Vol 101, p 67, D. A. R. Lin.

McMAHON, JOHN, (Mahoning Co.)

Pvt. Received appreciation, Continental Line. Children: three. Bur Mahoning Co. Resided N Oberlin Co, Pa in 1790. Ref: Pa Archives, Series 6, Vol 7, p 271, Series 5, Vol 4, p 111. Trumbull and Mahoning Co, Hist. Vol 11, p 149. Fur infor Mahoning Chap.

McMAHON, (or McMECHEN), WILLIAM, (Mercer Co.)

Surgeon 4th Va. Oct 14, 1776, 3rd Va. June 1779 to Oct 1774. At Stony Point N. Y. July 18, 1779 under Gen Wayne. Mar Ann Cox, Mch 21, 1774, Wellsburg, W. Va. Children: Friend, Richard, mar Rachel Cox, John, mar Nancy Cox, Joseph, mar Elizabeth Tomlinson, James, Polly, Susan, mar Joseph Tomlinson. D June 1794, Fort Recovery, Mercer Co, O. Bur in village graveyard. McMahon and companion bur in one grave, which is marked. Served in early wars, then in Revolutionary. Owned land in Montgomery Co, Va. and also what is now Wellsburg, W. Va. Farmer, lawyer, physician. Natl No 76548, Vol 77, D. A. R. Lin says he was killed by Indians. Ref: Heitman Register, p 374. Howe's History of Ohio, Vol 2, p 233-234. He Hass Border Hist. Fur infor Hetuck Chap.

McMAKEN, JOSEPH, (Butler Co.)

Name appears on the tablet in the Soldiers and Sailors monument at Hamilton, as a Revolutionary Soldier in that Co. He is bur in Greenwood Cem. Fur infor John Reily Chap.

McMANIS, CHARLES, (Adams Co.)

Pvt. Br 1754, some place in Pa. D near Cherry Fork, O. 1840. Bur Cherry Fork Cem, Cherry Fork, O. Was a Pvt in a Pack Company not designated. His name appears among the official pensioners of Pa Archives, 3 series, p 583 or 585. Ref: Evans and Stivers Hist of Adams Co, O. Fur infor Sycamore Chap.

McMANNERS, JOHN, (Loraine Co.)

Enl 1778 in Lt P Jackson's Company, Col Chandlers Regt. Pensioned 1818; widow pensioned 1835. Br 1758 Amboy, N. J. D 1845, Sheffield, O. Ref: Vol 97, Natl No 96519, D. A. R. Lin.

McMILLAN, JOHN, (Summit Co.)

Enl at Greensburg, Mch 1, 1776; re-enlisted 3rd Company, Pa. (from Pa state records). Name appears on roll of Capt William Butler's Company. Second Bn, Col Arthur St Clair. Br Mch 18, 1761, Nottingham Twp near the celebrated Log College. Mar Rebecca Wood, who died on their farm, Nov 15, 1821, and bur at Tallmadge beside her husband. They had a large family. D May 8, 1850. Location of cem Tallmadge, O. A resident of Chester Co, Pa, came to Tallmadge 1816. Parents were Scotch-Irish, and Presbyterians. Fur infor Cuyahoga-Portage Chap.

McMILLEN (or McMILLAN), JOHN, (Erie Co.)

Pvt in NJ Continental Line, 1777 Capt Jacob Martin's Inf, 4th NJ Regt. Enl from Norway, N. J. Pensioned in Steuben Co, 1820 for 6 yrs service; transferred to Erie Co, O. Br 1761. D Huron, O, 1841. Bur McMillen Cem, Huron, O. Ref: Vol 34, p 159, Natl No 33445 D. A. R. Lin. Fur infor Martha Pitkin Chap.

McMILLAN, ROBT. (Co. not stated)

Br 1758 Pa. D 1835 in O. Enl 1776 in Capt Ephraim Blackburn's Company, Chester Co, Pa Mil. Served in battles of Germantown and Trenton. In 1832 he was pensioner. Mar Christiana Hater. Ref: Miss Elizabeth Embrose Thomson, Miami Co, Ind. Natl No 67245, Vol 68, p 88, D. A. R. Lin.

McMULLEN, NEIL, (Trumbull Co.)

Pvt Pa Continental Line. Capt Wm Peebles' Company, Col Miles' Regt. Br 1752, Ireland. Mar Susanna —— (d Nov 26, 1781, aged 63 yrs.) D July 21, 1824, aged 72 yrs. Bur Seceeders Corners, Liberty Twp. MI: Name, date of birth and death. Ref: Natl No 78861, D. A. R., Vol 79. Fur infor Chesney Chap.

McMURRAY, WILLIAM, (Morgan Co.)

Pvt Pa Rifle Regt, Wayne's Brig. Br 1753 near Carlisle, Pa. D 1839, Morgan Co, O. Ref: Vol 93, p 229, Natl No 92733, D. A. R. Lin.

McNEIL, THOMAS, (Summit Co.)

Served over 6 yrs. Enl at Whitney, Addison Co, Vt as Sgt under Capts William Scott, Asa Curtis, and Col Jos Cilley, N. H. Br 1757, Vt. D 18—. Bur cem Norton, by side of wife. About 1820, he and his wife came from Vt to Norton Twp, Summit Co, O to live with daughter, Sallie Irish. A grandson has tin box carried by him all through service.

McPHERSON, JAMES, (Logan Co.)

Col. Enlisted Westmoreland Co, Pa in Capt Samuel Miller's, Col McCry's and Wilson's Regts Dec 1776, under Gen Geo Washington; at Trenton, Germantown, wounded at Brandywine. Br Mch 10, 1761, Cumberland Co, Pa. Mar twice; 1st time a fellow prisoner. Children: Mrs. Martha McPherson Miller by second wife. Real daughter of Revolution, d Apr 1, 1837, Logan Co. Location of cem 3 miles northwest of Bellefontaine. GM by family many yrs ago, in 1915 by bronze tablet by Bellefontaine D. A. R. Was taken prisoner by Indians at Lochey's defeat, kept 7 yrs. Ref: Natl No 13825. Howe's Historical Coll, Vol 2, p 104. Fur infor Bellefontaine Chap.

McPHERSON, JOHN, (Coshocton Co.)

D 1821 or 1834. Was with Anthony Wayne's Army. Bur cem White Eyes Twp. Ref: Co Hist. Fur infor Coshocton Chap.

McQUISTON, DAVID, (Preble Co.)

Bur cem Israel Twp. Fur infor George Conger Miller, Org Reg.

McROBERTS, ALEXANDER, (Ross Co.)

Pvt. Served from Battle of Bunker Hill to Yorktown. Br Va. Children; Samuel, John, Alexander H, and four daughters; Jane mar George Wheeland, died Oct 10, 1865, aged 79 yrs, 6 mos. D 1800, Springfield Twp, Ross Co, O. Grave not found. Went to Ky thence to Chillicothe in 1796, built a cabin on northwest corner of Second and Mulberry Sts and returned for his family. Entered three hundred acres in south part section 7 Springfield Twp and in 1798 or 99 built frame house (said to be first in Co.) Ref: p 231, Hist of Ross and Highland Co. Fur infor Nathaniel Massie Chap.

McTEER, ROBERT, (Fairfield Co.)

Commanded a Company 1778 in 4th Bn, Cumberland Co, Pa, Mil. under Col Samuel Lyon. Br 1741, Scotland. Mar Elizabeth Martin, 3rd wife. D 1811, Fairfield Co, O. Natl No 79222, Vol 80, Robert Hutson, Martinsburg, O.

McWILLIAMS, WILLIAM, (Knox Co.)

Various enlmt fr 1777 to 1779 under Capts Ogle Williamson and Maron, Col Brodhead, Pa Line. Br 1759, County of Down, Ireland. First wife —— Boggs. Two children, Jane and David B, second wife Mary Merritt, mar Mch 5, 1793, Washington Co, Pa. Children: John, William, George, Phoebe, Moses, Wallace and Eliza. D April 21, 1840, Martinsburg, Knox Co, O. Bur Presbyterian Cem, Martinsburg, Lot 46, south half, Grave 1. MI: Sandstone marker and is scaling off and the lettering is illegible. Name, date, etc., are given on the plat of the cem. GM Kokosing Chap, Dec, 1927. Helped lay out the town of Martinsburg, Knox Co, O, and gave land on which northern part of town is located. Farmer. Soldier, resided at Washington Co, Pa, at time of enlmt. His wife, Mary Merritt McWilliams, was allowed pens on an application of July 15, 1843, while living in Clay Twp, Knox Co, O. Fur infor Kokosing Chap.

MADDOCK, MOSES, (Hamilton Co.)

Br 1752, Pa. D 1826. S.A.R. Ref. Fur infor Cincinnati Chap.

MAGAW, (or MEGAW), JOHN, (Harrison Co.)

Br 1754. D 1818. Bur Ridge Church. Came fr Westmoreland Co, Pa, to Archer Twp about 1815. Served in 6th Pa Line Regt 1778. Pa Archives 5, 111-182. Fur infor Moravian Trail Chap.

MAGAM, WM., CAPT, (Preble Co.)

Pvt and Capt in S.C. Tr. Br 1750, Ireland. D 1836, Preble Co. Location of cem, Israel Twp. Ref: Natl No 96227, Vol 97, p 72, D.A.R. Lin. Fur infor Grace Conger Miller, Org Regt.

MAHOLM, SAMUEL, (Harrison Co.)

Br 1758. D 1838. A Revolutionary pensioner, living in Harrison Co in 1833, aged 75; possibly same as Samuel McHallon (McCullom), who served as Sgt in Capt Joseph Walker's Company 6th Bn, Lancaster Co, Pa Mil, in 1781. U.S. Pens Rolls 1835; Pa Archives 5, VII, 590. Fur infor Moravian Trail Chap.

MAIN, PERRES, (Delaware Co.)

Pvt under Col Samuel Taylor, Capts William Prentice and Billings, Conn Mil. Bur Troy Twp. Pensioned. Fur infor Delaware Chap.

MALOTT, DORY, (Clermont Co.)

Pvt Md Mil. Pens 1883, received $80, aged 79. Br Md. Came to Clermont Co, O, about 1800; resided at Williamsburg; brother of William Malott, also Revolutionary soldier. Ref: A. S. Abbott, Bethel, O. Fur infor Cincinnati Chap.

MALOTT, JOHN, (Brown Co.)

Rev soldier, who died in Brown Co. Fur infor Cincinnati Chap.

MALOTT, THOMAS, (Adams Co.)

Br 1753, Frederick Co, Md. Mar Rebecca ——. D 1846, near Fairview, Adams Co, O. Ref: Natl No 133304, D. A. R. Copied by Mrs. Lowell Hobart. Fur infor Cincinnati Chap.

MALOTT, WILLIAM, (Clermont Co.)

Br Md. Children: Zedekiah, Thomas, Isaac, William (lived and died on old homestead), 2 dau. Came to Union Twp about 1800, locating along the East Fork. Was brother of Dory Malott, also Rev soldier. Ref: A. S. Abbott, Bethel, O. Fur infor Cincinnati Chap.

MALLOW, GEORGE, SR., (Greene Co.)

Ensign, Capt Robt Craven's Company, Col Benj Harrison's Line, Va. Pensioner 1831, age 82. Br Mch 17, 1752, Lancaster Co, Pa. Mar Anna Catherine. Children: Peter, John, George. D April 14, 1837, Greene Co. Boot's Graveyard, near Xenia, O. Xenia Twp 1817. Ref: Hist of Greene Co Bureau of Pens. Natl No 90372 D. A. R. Vol 91. Fur infor Catherine Greene Chap.

MALTBY, BENJAMIN, (Trumbull Co.)

Pvt in two different Conn Regts. In battles of Long Island and Saratoga. Br May 10, 1750 Brantford, Conn (or Northford which seems to be part of Brantford.)

Parents: Deacon Daniel Maltby. Br Oct 29, 1715. Mar Mary Hamin Sept 16, 1736. Mar Abrigail Munger (br Aug 26, 1750; mar July 5, 1771). Children: Simeon, Benjamin, Abrigail, Jacob, Annis, Hannah, Elon, Nathaniel Harrison, Julia, Daniel, Jesse. D Jan 1, 1847 Southington, Trumbull Co, O. Bur Maltby burying ground, on the farm which he settled in 1819 with son, Daniel Maltby. Grave located on a hill northwest of the house, and belongs to the Maltby heirs. GM by his heirs. Granted pens as a Revolutionary soldier under an act of the legislature 1834. Was a member of the church in Southington and left the reputation of a quiet, capable man with public spirit. Ref: Natl No 48390, Vol 49, p 183, D. A. R. Lin. Fur infor Mary Chesney Chap.

MANCHESTER, JOSEPH, (Harrison Co.)

Ensign in Col Joseph Stanton's Regt. Dec 1776, RI Mil. Served as Ensign in same Regt throughout the war, and continuously until 1800. In Coventry Company, 1796, same Regt Senior Class Record, Kent Co. Parents: Isaac Manchester and Hannah Crendall, of Middletown, dau of Joseph, of Portsmouth. Mar Hannah Cranston, dau of Richmond, Jan 27, 1788 at Middletown, R. I. Children: John, Sarah (mar Allen), David Green, Hannah (mar Chase), Ann (mar Barker), Lydia. He died in the home of his eldest dau, Sarah Manchester Allen, northern part of Harrison Co, near Rumley, June 26, 1827, and buried in the graveyard on the Allen farm adjoining the church they built. Grave is marked with a headstone larger than the ordinary. Ref: See Smith J. J. Civil and Military List of Rhode Island 1647-1800, pub at Providence, R. I. 1900, p 341, and Maud Allen Weeks Michael. Descendants: Innumerable.

MANKINS, WILLIAM, (Columbiana Co.)

Br 1760. D Feb 21, 1848. Was living in Centre Twp, Columbiana Co, O in 1840. Age 80 yrs. Pensioner. For infor Bethia Southwick Chap.

MANN, GEORGE, (Greene Co.)

Pvt in Capt Bradley's 9th Bn. Lancaster Co Mil, Pa Archives, p 941, Vol 7, 5th Series. Br 1728. Mar Elizabeth Palmer. D May 4, 1821. Bur New Burlington Cem Greene Co, O. Fur infor George Clinton Chap and Catherine Greene Chap.

MANN, JOHN, (Richland Co.)

Pvt Capt Robert Wilson's Company, 7th Pa Regt, commanded by Col Wm Irvine, 1777. Br 1746, Ireland. Mar Ann Dean. Children: named one Samuel. D 1826, Mansfield, O. Ref: Natl No 49681. Fur infor Vol 50, p 304, D. A. R. Lin.

MANNING, THOMAS, (Clermont Co.)

Pvt Conn Continental Line. Pensioned 1832, age 69. On a stone in the cem at Amelia is the name, and the following inscription: "A native of Mass., a Revolutionary soldier, a member of the M. E. Church. Died Dec 23, 1853, aged 92 years. Ann, wife of Thomas Manning, died Dec 22, 1853, aged 93 years." She was Ann Todd.) This information was sent by Mrs. J. R. Hicks, Natl No. 98812 D. A. R. of the Cincinnati Chap living at Amelia, O. Br 1764, Stafford, Conn. D 1853, Clermont Co, O. Resided near Lindale, Pierce Twp. (A. S. Abbott, Bethel, O.) Pens Dept. Accepting this infor as authentic Jane Dailey, State Chairman.

MANRING, JORDAN MARSHALL, (Gallia Co.)

Capt. Enl 1777 in Rev fr Kent Co. Continued in service until Cornwallis surrendered, 7 yrs. Severely injured at King's Mountain. Br Sussex Co, Delaware, in 1760. Mar Elizabeth Clark. D Gallia Co 1847. Bur Old Cem, Centerville, O. Left hand of main road, near center of north end. Ref: W. S. Manring, Delaware, O. Fur infor Return Jonathan Meigs Chap.

MANSFIELD, SAMUEL, (Athens Co.)

Fifer in the 3rd Md Regt. Col Ramsey and Capt Henry Ridgley. Served 3 yrs. Disch Mch 1779, at Millbrook, N. J. He was in the battles of Germantown, Brandywine, and Monmouth; severely wounded at Brandywine. Pens allowed May 16, 1818. Br 1740. Mar Charity Boyles, Apr 7, 1778. Hardwick, Sussex Co, N. J. Children: Martin, Peter. D Nov 10, 1819, Athens Co, O. Bur private burial on a farm near Circle Hill, O. MI: "Samuel Mansfield, died Nov 10, 1819. Charity, wife of Samuel Mansfield, died." (Tombstone inscriptions almost obliterated.) Unmarked by patriotic society. Ref: Natl No 57019 and 140393. Fur infor Elizabeth Zane Dew Chap.

MANSFIELD, THOMAS, (Athens Co.)

Pvt under Capt Blake and Col Gist; also a marine under Robt Dashiell on the ship "Chester." Br Sept 14, 1750, Queen Anne Co, Md. Mar Anna Wilkinson (2nd), Oct 11, 1792 or 1793. Children: Louisa. D Jan 19, 1837, Athens Co, O. Bur Nye Cem, Chauncey, Dover Twp, Athens Co, O. GM Family, with a stone; also Jones marker placed by Nabby Lee Ames Chap, D.A.R., 1925. Pens 1834, Athens Co, for service Md Mil. Ref: Bureau of Pens, Washington, D. C., and Natl No 50983, D.A.R. Fur infor Nabby Lee Ames Chap.

MANSON, DAVID, (Miami Co.)

Enl fr York Co, Pa, July, 1776, for two mos as Pvt in Capt Savage's Company, Col Smith's Regt, and Sept, 1776, for 3½ mos as Pvt in Capt W. W. Corby's Company, Col McAllister's Regt, and again in Jan, 1778, for 2 mos as Pvt in Capt John Rippey's Company, Col McAllister's Regt. Br Oct, 1733, County Antrim, Ireland. Mar Jean Johnson, Feb 1, 1780. D Brown Twp, Miami Co, 1836. Bur Brown Twp Schoolhouse, near Fletcher, O. GM Piqua Chap, D.A.R., in Spring of 1906. After close of War resided in Pa and later moved to Ohio, making journey by team; was one of the pioneers of Brown Twp. Purchased land and erected a log cabin, which was used as a fort for protection fr the Indians. Farmer. Participated in the War of 1812, in campaigns in Northwest. Ref: Dept Interior; Bureau of Pens; Ohio Pens Roll; Miami Co, p 146; Genealogical and Biographical Hist Miami Co, p 878 (book published in 1900). Fur infor Piqua Chap.

MARKELL, PETER, (Lake Co.)

Enl in 1781 fr Palatine, N.Y., and was disch in 1782. Was in the battle of Johnstown, N.Y., under Capt Cook and Col Clock. Br Mch 24, 1765. Mar Dec 9, 1792, Elizabeth Koch. Children: John, Benjamin, James, Margarette, Betsy, Peter, Nicholas, Mary, Fanny and Nancy. D May 25, 1837. Bur Kirtland, Lake Co, O. GM New Connecticut Chap. He was a pioneer of Kirtland. Had encounters with Indians. Ref: Vol 71, p 49, Natl No 70135, D.A.R. Lin. Fur infor New Connecticut Chap.

MARKEL, T. ABRAM, (Jefferson Co.)

Capt and Col in Pa Mil. Br Feb 20, 1762, Berks Co, Pa. Parents: Col Caspar Markel and Mary E. Grim. Mar Rachel Blackburn, 1796. Children; Caspar, Joseph, Dr. Abraham, Dr. John, Deborah, Eliza, Maria, Rachel, Hannah Rosanna, Jacob, Sara Jane, Benjamin and Martha. D 1841, Island Creek, Jefferson Co, O. Bur Island Creek Church Graveyard. Family lot. MI: "Abram T. Markel. 1762-1841." GM Steubenville D. A. R. by bronze marker, June, 1923. Served in Westmoreland Co Mil, 1777-1779. Commissioned Major 1800, 1st Bn of 54th Regt, Pa Mil, 13th Div, Cos of Westmoreland, Allegheny and Crawford. Served seven years. Ref: D.A.R. Lin Bk, Vol 26; Jordan Encyclopedia of Biography for Pa, Pa Archives; Markers in Island Creek Cem; Probate Court Records of Berks Co, Pa, and Commission fr Pa Mil in private possession of family. Fur infor Steubenville Chap.

MARSH, JOHN, (Hamilton Co.)

Sgt in Capt Andrew McMeyer's Company, 1st Regt, NJ Tr. Commanded by Lord Sterling. Br Elizabeth, N. J., 1738. Mar Nancy Searing. One son, Searing (br 1769, d 1857). Mar Mary Day (br 1773, d 1828). Removed to Ohio, 1797, and located near Cincinnati. Ref: Natl No 28158, Vol 29, p 58, D.A.R. Lin.

MARSHALL, GEORGE, (Brown Co.)

Bur Sardinia. Fur infor Ripley Chap.

MARSHALL, HENRY, (Miami Co.)

Fr Pa. Br 1752. D July 14, 1837. Came to Piqua about 1807. Fur infor Piqua Chap.

MARSHALL, JAMES, (Mahoning Co.)

Pvt, enl men in the Rev, Westchester Co, 1st Regt, also of 4th Regt. Br 1745. Children: Elizabeth (Calhoun). D 1829. Bur Oak Hill Cem. GM D.A.R. 1915-17. Ref: Mentioned, p 156, Vol 2, Hist Trumbull and Mahoning Cos, Williams, p 52 and 205, N. Y. Men of the Rev. Fur infor Mahoning Chap.

MARSHALL, RICHARD, (Muskingum Co.)

Pvt under Capt Meriwether, Col John Gibson. Capt Jones, Col Washington. Mar Keziah Sherer. D Nov 4, 1841. Bur Blue Rock Graveyard near Gaysport. Pens 1818. Fur infor Muskingum Chap.

MARSHALL, SAMUEL, SR., (Scioto Co.)

Pvt Capt David Marshall's Company, Capt Thomas. Mar Nancy ——. Children: Nancy, Hettie, Jemina, Mary, William, Jessie, Elizabeth, Samuel, Sabina, Fannie. D 1816. Came to Scioto Co, 1796. Fannie, first white child br in Scioto Co, mar Geo Shonkwiler. Ref: Dr. Geo M. Marshall, Dr. Ranchous. Pa. Archives, 3 Series, Vol 23, p 714. Fur infor Joseph Spencer Chap.

MARSHALL, WILLIAM, (Wayne Co.)

Served 1777, Pvt in Capt John Alexander's Company, Col Wm Irvine's 7th Pa Regt. Br Ireland. D Wayne Co, O. Ref: Vol 88, p 37, Natl No. 87,124, D. A. R. Lin.

MARTIN, ALEXANDER, (Brown Co.)

Marched in Mil from Augusta Co, Va. to join Southern army. Br 1760, Va. D 1816, Ripley, O. Bur Pisgah Ridge. Ref: Vol 91, p 275, Natl No. 90,869, D. A. R. Lin. Fur infor Ripley Chap.

MARTIN, ALEX, (Hamilton Co.)

Artificer under Capt Sylvan Seely, Col James Deboise in Flying Camp; was at Springfield and Monmouth. Volunteered as sailor on "Jolly Tar" under Capt Isaac Harrison, as substitute for brother David. Br 1758, N. J. (or 1762 Morristown, N. J.) D 1846 (or 1843) Cincinnati, O. Pleasant Ridge Cem (census 1849). Pensioned in Hamilton Co in 1840 for 22 mos actual service NJ Line. Ref: S. A. R. Natl No. 38,329, Vol 39, D. A. R. Lin. Fur infor Cincinnati Chap.

MARTIN, CHARLES, (Licking Co.)

Served on coasting vessel in 1789; enl fr Warwick, R. I., July, 1777, under Col Barton; 1780 on privateer of State of Conn. Br 1759, Essex, England. Mar Mary Gaylor (or Galer) Aug 22, 1797 (dau of Adrew Galor) at Marietta, O. D Nov 19, 1838. Bur Gaffield Cem Alexandria Rd. MI: "Rev War." Marked by Hetuck Chap 1910. Lived at Marietta, O; in 1781 captured at Ft Griswold and held till 1782, being denied "exchange" as born in England. Pension allowed widow, filed 1878. Ref: Pension Bureau 3—1865. Fur infor Hetuck Chap.

MARTIN, CHARLES HONNEYWOOD, (Licking Co.)

Br Mch 7, 1759, Coggeshall, England. D Nov 19, 1859. Bur Old Colony Burying Ground at Granville. Enl July 17, 1777 in Col Burton's Regt. He was taken at Ft Griswold and held prisoner at Halifax. Fur infor Granville Chap.

MARTIN, HENRY, (Harrison Co.)

A Revolutionary pensioner in Harrison Co, in 1834, aged 77; served in the Pa Mil probably fr Cumberland or Lancaster Co. Pa Archives 5th Series, Vol 6 and 7. U. S. Pens Rolls, 1835. Fur infor Moravian Trail Chap.

MARTIN, ISAAC, (Lake Co.)

Enl in the Conn Tr. Served in the 1st Regt of Gen Wooster in the 9th Company under Capt James Arnold. The Regt marched for the protection of N. Y. and later at Lake George and Lake Champlain. Br 1757. D Nov 6, 1832. Bur Middle Ridge Cem, Madison, O. GM New Conn Chap. He was a pensioner. Fur infor New Conn Chap.

MARTIN, JACOB, (Jefferson Co.)

Capt in Continental Jersey Line. Br 1742, N. J. D 1830, Warrenton, O. Natl No 38869, Vol 39, D A R Lin.

MARTIN, JOHN, (Fairfield Co.)

Enl 1776. Pvt in Capt Peter Mantz's Company, Col Jacob Wiltner's Md Regt. Battle Long Island, White Plains, Ft Washington and Germantown. Br 1756. Md. Mar Margaret Behler. D 1827 Fairfield Co, O. D. A. R. Natl No 57428. P 146, Vol 58, D. A. R. Lin.

MARTIN, JOHN (or JACOB), (Licking Co.)

Enl at Northampton, Mass, Aug 24, 1777, as Pvt in Capt Lyman's Company. He was at capture of Gen Burgoyne. Br 1744, Hanover, Germany. Mar Sept, 1793 to Catherine ——. D May 28, 1845, Johnstown, O. Bur village cem. Pens allowed Oct 30, 1832, at Johnstown. Fur infor Hetuck Chap.

MARTIN, OLIVER, (Hamilton Co.)

Br 1762, N. J. D 1829. Fur infor Cincinnati Chap.

MARTIN, REUBEN, (Morrow Co.)

Pvt under Col Chamberlain, Capt Clung, NJ Tr and in Capt Martin's Company also Harbaugh's Company. Br 1748, Somerset Co, N. J. Mar Mary Van Buren. Children: John, Abner (mar Sarah Hoskinson), Absolom (soldier of War of 1812), Reuben, Alexander, Samuel, Hannah (mar Boggs). D near Mansfield, O (then in Wayne Co, O). Bur Westerfield Twp, which is in Morrow Co, O. Later moved to Martins Ferry, O, where the Martin family established and owned the Ferry named for them. Pensioned. Ref: Records at Washington copied by Mrs. L. Hobart. Fur infor Delaware Chap.

MASON, NATHAN, (Ashtabula Co.)

Served as a Minute Man in Capt Daniel Brown's Company, which marched for Lanesboro at the Bennington Alarm. Br 1757, Swansea, Mass. Mar Elizabeth Cole. Children: Ambrose, D 1847, Andover, Ashtabula Co, O. Bur Andover. MI: "Nathan Mason died June 17, 1847, aged 91 years. He was a soldier of the Revolution." Thought to have been marked by the S. A. R. Ref: D. A. R. Lin Bk, Vol 39, p 84. Fur infor Mary Stanley Chap.

MASON, WILLIAM, (Warren Co.)

Pvt in Pa Continental Line. Br 1760, Bedford Co, Pa. Mar Sarah Murphy, 1811 (br 1790, d 1833). One dau was Cynthia Mason Houseworth. D 1830. Bur Mason, Warren Co, O. Southern part. MI: Dates, and Rev service. Emigrated to Ohio to a town which he laid out and named Palmyra. After his death, name changed to Mason, O. Ref: Mrs. Harry L. Nelson, Chaplain Topeka Chap D. A. R. (1928), Topeka, Kansas, who fur this infor to Jane Dailey, State Chairman, and Natl No 67585, Vol 68, p 208 D. A. R. Lin.

MASSEY, EZEKIEL, (Fairfield Co.)

Marine on ship "United States" Capt Elijah Hand. Br Sussex Co, Del, Jan 15, 1766. Parents: Daniel and Sarah Massey. Mar Esther Oliver May 11, 1789. D Lancaster, O. Dec 19, 1844. Bur Old M. E. Cem in Lancaster, O. GM by Elizabeth Sherman Reese Chap. Revolutionary bronze marker Aug 30, 1927. Ref: Blanch Massey McManany. Fur infor Elizabeth Sherman Reese Chap.

MASSIE, NATHANIEL, (Foss Co.)

Entered the Rev at the age of 17. Br Goochland Co, Va, Dec 28, 1763. Mar Susan Meade, 1800. D Nov 3, 1813. Bur old family burying ground, but in 1870 remains were removed to Grandview Cem, Chillicothe, Ross Co. Received land in Va Military District for his service and made his first journey to this land in 1788. As surveyor of these lands he formed a colony of thirty families and made a settlement in 1790, now Manchester. In 1795-96 he organized a party which settled on his land where Chillicothe now stands. Was Maj Gen of Ohio Mil during War of 1812. Ref: Natl No 90069, Vol 91, p 25, D. A. R. Lin. Fur infor Nathaniel Massie Chap.

MASTICK, BENJAMIN, (Geauga Co.)

Pvt. Enl 1775, Capt Mellen's Company, Col Ward's Mass Regt, 1776; Capt Gardner's Company, Col Brook's Regt. Br 1761, Upton, Mass. Mar Cynthia Wood. Children: Benjamin, Asahel, Elliott, Lavina. D June 5, 1830, Claridon, O. Bur center of Claridon Cem Lot 81, Sec 4. MI: "Benjamin Mastick D June 5, 1830, aged 68 years, 11 months, 16 days." Marked by family with stone. Ref: Mass Soldiers and Sailors, Vol 10, p 340; Mass Soldiers and Sailors Records, Vol 3, p 514. Natl No 73210. Fur infor Taylor Chap.

MATHER, ABNER, (Portage Co.)

Pvt. Enl spring of 1777; served one year under Capts Benjamin Talmadge, Ezekiel Beldin and Col Elish Sheldon. Fought in Battles of Brandywine and Germantown. Children: Harriet, Lucy, Fanny. D Apr 1, 1838, Atwater, O. Bur Atwater, O. Member of Continental Light Dragoons. On pension roll. Lineally descended from Increase and Cotton Mather. Fur infor Old Northwest Chap.

MATHER, ELEAZER, (Summit Co.)

Enl Lyme, New London Co, Conn Apr 1, 1776; served till Dec 31, 1776 in Company of which his brother, Samuel Mather, was captain, under Col Saltonstall and Col Erastus Wolcott. Br Lyme, Conn, 1775. Bur Boston Twp, Summit Co, O. Came to Ohio in 1822. First doctor in Boston Twp and one of early settlers. Fur infor Cuyahoga-Portage Chap.

MATHEWS, JOHN, (Muskingum Co.)

Pvt Worcester Co Mil. Br 1765, Brookfield, Mass. D 1828, Zanesville, O. Ref: Natl No 33519, Vol 34, p 187 D. A. R. Lin.

MATHEWS, WILLIAM, (Trumbull Co.)

Pvt Capt Curry's Company, Col Brohead's 8th Pa Regt. Pens 1818. Br 1754, Ireland. Mar Rachel Gordon. D 1834. Bur Old Cem at Kinsman, O. Center of cem. Ref: Natl No 53928, Vol 54, p 365, D. A. R. Lin. Fur infor Mary Chesney Chap.

MATSON, JOHN, (Hamilton Co.)

1st Regt Pa Line 1776, Col Edward Hand. Br 1740, Hagerstown, Md. Mar Jane ——. D 1804, Hamilton Co, O. Ref: S. A. R. and Natl No 77008, D. A. R. Lin. Fur infor Cincinnati Chap.

MATSON, REUBEN, (Morrow Co.)

Bur unknown, but probably in Westfield Twp. Fur infor Mt Gilead Chap.

MATTHEWS, JAMES, (Mahoning Co.)

Pvt. Ranger, Cumberland Co, Pa. Believed Bur Poland Presbyterian Cem. Bought land of John Young, June 3, 1802. Ref: County Records of Pa Archives, Series 3, Vol 23, p 276, 700, 754. Fur infor Mahoning Chap.

MAURER, JOHN, (Mahoning Co.)

Pvt in Continental Line, from 1777 to 1782. MI: Stone destroyed. Ref: Pa Archives, Series 5, Vol 4, p 263, Vol 5, 277, Vol 7, p 465, Vol 8, p 54. Fur infor Mahoning Chap.

MAURER, JOHN, (Pickaway Co.)

Under Capt Daniel Neill 1780 2 mos; Pvt 1780, 14 mos Capt John Fesig. Engaged in Siege of Yorktown. Br Feb 12, 1763 at Berks Co, Pa. Mar Elizabeth Stimmell. Children: Peter, John, Jacob and Mary (wife of Henry DeLong.) D Feb 24, 1833 in Pickaway Co, O. Bur Tarlton Cem, Tarlton, O. MI: "John Maurer, born Feb 12, 1763. Died Feb 24, 1833." Farmer. His son John changed the spelling to Mowery. Ref: Miss Etta F. Mowery, Laurelville, O. Natl No. 213,546, D. A. R. Lin. Fur infor Mt Sterling Chap.

MAXEY, HORATIO, (Greene Co.)

Pvt. Enl Jan, 1781, served 2 mos under Capt Geo Williamson, Maj Duval and Col John Willis. Re-enlisted Apr 1781, for 6 weeks under Capt Isaac Porter, and Col Goode. Br Apr 28, 1764, Va. Parents: John Maxey, Mary Ann ——. Mar Jane Martin, Sept 2, 1784. Children: Polly, Stephen, Nancy, Jane, Martin, Theodosia, Abner, Enoch, Cynthia, Edna, Malinda, Horatio, George W. D June 6, 1835 in Greene Co, O. Bur old Maxey Cem near Xenia, Greene Co, O. Moved to Xenia Twp, Greene Co in 1804. Serv continued. Servd 2 mos in 2nd Regt, Lawson's Brig. Refused pension because he did not have 6 mos continual service. Battles: Skirmish at Hood's Ferry and Siege of Yorktown. Ref: Jessie M. Martin. Natl No. 126,196. Fur infor London Chap.

MAXWELL, WILLIAM, (Greene Co.)

Pvt McCormick's Rangers. Pensioned Oct 8, 1816, under law of Mch 3, 1817; also commencement of pens on Dec 13, 1826 and Mch 6, 1832. Annual allowance $48. Fur infor Catherine Green Chap.

MAY, GEORGE, (Mahoning Co.)

Pvt. Br 1751. D 1823. Bur Old Forney Cem. Ref: Pa Archives, Series 5, Vol 7, p 35, 64, 90. Fur infor Mahoning Chap.

MAY, JAMES, (Ross Co.)

During the Revolution he manufactured guns and other arms for the patriot army. Br Fredericksburg, Va, 1742. Mar —— (died in Chillicothe, 1816). Children: John, James, Henry (in War 1812), three daughters, one mar Thomas Dick. One Margaret, (1868, aged 83 yrs, 3 mos, 17 days.) D Green Twp, May 12, 1836 in

94th year. Bur Mt Pleasant Cem, near Kingston, Green Twp. By trade a gun and locksmith. Moved to Chillicothe about 1798, where he followed his trade, until about 1822, when he moved near Kingston. Ref: History Ross and Highland, p 236. Fur infor Nathaniel Massie Chap.

MAY, JOHN, I, (Mahoning Co.)

5 days in Conn in battle of Lexington. Mar, Wife was a Boardman. Bur Old Forney Church Yard. Ref: Conn Men of the Revolution. Church Records. Fur infor Mahoning Chap.

MAY, JOHN GEORGE, (Mahoning Co.)

Pvt. Mar Mary Ann Colhan, or Colham or Cobham, Aug 27, 1771. Children: John, 1789, (d 1861); William, (d 1864, age 65 yrs.); Barbara, (wife of John Maurer 2nd br Feb 21, 1781, d Aug 1859); and others. Bur Old Forney Churchyard. MI: Stone gone. Came to Mahoning Co, O. Ref: Pa Archives, Series 5, Vol 7, p 570, 585, 432, 591, Church Records. Fur infor Mahoning Chap.

MAYES, WILLIAM, (Trumbull Co.)

Bur East Center of Kinsman. Name of this soldier given in list of soldiers in Yr Bk compiled by S. A. R. of Ohio. We were unable to locate this soldier of this name, or this cem. Fur infor Mary Chesney Chap.

MEAD, LIBENS, (Trumbull Co.)

Bur East Mecca. Located stone for the wife of Libens Meade. MI: Catherine, D Dec 12, 1851, age 86 yrs. Ref: Historical Library, Cleveland, O. Soldiers Bur in Trumbull Co, and Old Residents of Mecca. Fur infor Mary Chesney Chap.

MEAD, MICHAEL, (Huron Co.)

Bur Day Cem, Clarksfield Twp. Fur infor Sally De Forest Chap.

MEAD, STEPHEN, (Licking Co.)

Enl at Rutland, Vt, June 1778 as Pvt in father's Regt under Capt John Smith. Served with the "Minute Men." Parents: Col James Mead. Mar Dorothy Sachet, Feb 3, 1783. Ten children. D Feb 8, 1844, Granville Twp. GM Granville Chap. Pension allowed Oct 29, 1832. Fur infor Hetuck Chap.

MEEK, ISAAC, (Jefferson Co.)

Lt in Ohio Company, Va Mil, 1778. Br 1746 Anne Arundel Co, Md. Mar Rebecca Thomas, 1792. D 1840, Jefferson Co, O. Ref: Natl No 78350, Vol 79, D. A. R. Lin.

MEEKER, JOHN, (Hamilton Co.)

Br 1759, New Jersey. D 1836. Ref: S. A. R. Fur infor Cincinnati Chap.

MEEKER, NATHANIEL, (Butler Co.)

Name appears on the tablet in the Soldiers and Sailors monument at Hamilton, O, as a Revolutionary Soldier. Bur in that Co. Unidentified. Fur infor John Reily Chap.

MEGRUE, ANDREW, (Clermont Co.)

Only a lad, but served as a soldier. Br 1760, Baltimore. Mar Hannah Rust. D 1823, Milford. Ref: Natl No 15,137, p 56, Vol 16, D. A. R. Lin.

MEHAFFEY, JOHN, (also spelled MAHAFFEY), (Adams Co.)

Pvt, served in 1778, 1779, 1780, also 7 mo in 1784. Enl July 3, 1778 under Capt Jas Moore. Served under Cols Shields and Pomeroy and Maj Jos Wilson. Br Aug 31, 1759, Sussex Co, N. J. Mar Rachel Gordon in 1779, Westmoreland Co, Pa. Children: One was Hannah (br Aug 1848, Adams Co, O.) Bur Liberty Twp Adams Co. Pensioned Oct 25, 1832 while residing in Adams Co. Ref: Jessie M Martin, London, O. Fur infor London Chap.

MELVIN, ISAAC, (Washington Co.)

Br 1753, Ireland. D 1842, Washington Co, O. Ref: Natl No. 23,382, p 135, Vol 24, D. A. R. Lin.

MELVIN, REUBEN, (Geauga Co.)

Pvt. Capt Harwood's Company, Col Dickson's Regt, July 19, 1777 to July 31, 1777, Capt Ward's Company, Col May's Regt, Aug 17, 1777, Aug 22, 1777, Mass Mil. Br Nov 12, 1760, Concord, Mass. Parents: Jacob and Esther (Parlin). Mar Achsah Smith. Children: Keziah, Achsah, Lucia, Reuben. D Aug 28, 1837, Chesterland, O. Bur Chesterland Center Cem. MI: "R. Melvin, died Aug 28, 1837, age 77. Achsah, his wife, died Aug 18, 1858, age 91." GM family. Came from Cummington, Mass to Chester, 1828. Ref: Vital Records, Concord and Cummington, Mass. Mass Soldiers and Sailors, Natl No 38234, Vol 39, D. A. R. Lin. Fur infor Taylor Chap.

MENTZER, JAPHAT, (Licking Co.)

Enl in Lancaster Co, Pa, Sept 1776. Pvt in Col Nagel's Regt, Jack's Company. Was at Brandywine and Germantown. Br 1755, Pa. Mar Polly Callenhan, Jan 15, 1829. D Sept 13, 1841, Franklin Twp. Bur Lutheran Cem Linville Rd. MI: "Revolutionary War." GM Hetuck Chap in 1910. Pension allowed Nov 3, 1832. Ref: Bristers Hist. Fur infor Hetuck Chap.

MERCER, JOHN, (Hamilton Co.)

Br New Jersey. D 1806. Fur infor Cincinnati Chap.

MERCHANT, JOSEPH, (Mahoning Co.)

Pvt Conn State Tr, 1776, Brunell's Company of Wallingford. Br Conn. Bur Boardman. Came to Boardman in 1806 from Wallingford, Conn and settled in that town. Name was in the list of early settlers of Boardman. Ref: Conn Men in the Revolution, p 409, Trumbull and Mahoning Co Hist, p 84. Fur infor Mahoning Chap.

MEREDITH, JOHN W., (Miami Co.)

Veteran of '76; at the meeting of July 4, 1876. Toast given "The Army, Navy and Militia of the U. S.; may they always be victorious over the enemy, and may they never in time of war have to experience the privations of the Soldiers of '76." Bur Rose Hill, Troy, O. GM Miami Chapter, with bronze marker, in 1905. Ref: Natl No. 48,827, p 372, Vol 49, D. A. R. Lin. Fur infor Miami Chap.

MERRIMAN, MARSHALL, (Lorain Co.)

MI: On stone in LaGrange Cem, Lorain Co, is the following: "Member of Washington's Army. Served at Dorchester Heights and the Battle of Bunker Hill. D Dec 6, 1839, age 80 yrs, 5 mos, 15 das." Fur infor Elyria Chap.

MESSENGER, DAVID, (Licking Co.)

Was Pvt in Capt Henry's Company, Col David Brewer's Regt. Was at siege of Boston, 1775. Br 1760, Mass. Children: David. D Apr 1, 1811, Granville, O. Bur Old Cem, Granville, O. GM Granville Chap in 1901. Emigrated to this county in 1805. Fur infor Hetuck Chap.

MESSENGER, ISAAC, (Lake Co.)

Served in Capt Amasa Hill's Company, Col Roger Enos' Regt, July 4. 1778. Was at West Point, and assisted in the construction of the first fortifications there under the command of Washington. Br 1746, Conn. Mar Ann Ward. D May 8, 18 9, Concord, O. Bur Concord, O. GM New Connecticut Chap. Ancestors were French and settled in Canada in the 17th century. Fur infor New Conn Chap.

MESSINGER, BILLIE, (Portage Co.)

Pvt in Mass Continental. Placed on pension roll May 14, 1833. Bur Windham. Fur infor Old Northwest Chap.

METCALF, MASSOM, (Wayne Co.)

D Mch 22, 1843. Bur Knupps Cem, near Millbrook. MI: "In memory of Massom Metcalf, who died March 22, 1843, aged 79 years, 11 mos, 22 days." Fur infor Wooster Wayne Chap.

METCALF, THOMAS, (Geauga Co.)

Pvt in Capt Lemuel Kollock's Company which marched from Wrentham to Warwick, R. I. on alarm of 1776. Br Wrentham 1760-4. Parents: Samuel Metcalf and Hannah Kingsbury. Mar Sybil Chaplin. Children: Thomas, Sidney, Sybil, Eben, Orrin, Elizabeth, Harriet. D Center of Chardon, Mch 17, 1828. Bur on farm at center of Chardon known as Austin Hauden farm, Tract 2, Lot 13 and 16. Ref: New England Register, Vol 6, p 171, 177, Pioneer History Geauga Co, p 312. Natl No of Revolutionary Soldier D. A. R. Honor Roll 77,003, 62,556. Fur infor Taylor Chap.

METZGER, JACOB, (Ross Co.)

Pennsylvania. Br Feb 2, 1747. Mar Mary —— (d Oct 3, 1835, aged 36 yrs, 7 mos, 13 days.) D Green Twp, Ross Co, O Aug 8, 1835. Bur White Churches, on Adelphi Pike, about four miles from Kinnikinnick. MI: "Jacob Metzger died Aug 8, 1835, aged 88 years, 5 mos 11 days." GM Small bronze marker, Nathaniel Massie Chapter, D. A. R. in May 21, 1927. Ref: Recorded in D. A. R. Lin by descendants, out of Ohio. Fur infor Nathaniel Massie Chap.

METZLER, GEORGE, (Holmes Co.)

Pvt in Westmoreland Co, Pa Mil. Br Westmoreland Co, 1755. Mar Margaret Weshaun. D 1825 Holmes Co, O. Ref: Natl No. 69843, p 298, Vol 70, D. A. R. Lin.

MEYER, CHRISTIAN, (Wayne Co.)

Lt 1776-77; Capt 1778, in Lt Col Ludwig Weltner's Bucks Co, Pa Regt. Br Bucks Co, Pa. D Wooster, O. Ref: Natl No 59013, Vol 60, p 5, D. A. R. Lin.

MICKEY, DANIEL, (Franklin Co.)

Ensign in 8th Pa Regt. Commissioned Aug 9, 1776. Afterward promoted to Lt of Capt Cornahous' Company, Col Daniel Brodhead's Regt, Oct 14, 1777. D 1807 near Dublin. Bur old cem on Scioto River Road. GM Revolutionary Grave Committee with bronze marker, May 30, 1912. Came to Ohio from Kentucky in 1804, and settled ½ mile below the Dublin bridge. Fur infor Columbus Chap.

MIDDLESWART, HENRY, (Washington Co.)

Pvt, 5th class, 3rd Bn of Washington Continentals under Capt Geo Sharp, commanded by Col Daniel Williamson's Pa Mil. Br May 5, 1755, Reading, Pa. Parents: Abraham Middleswart and Maria Griggs. Mar Sarah Clark (second wife). Children: Abraham, Charity, Hannah, Emily, Jacob, Nellie, Henry, Clark,

Tunis, Susan, Jonathan, Franklin. D Sept 5, 1823, Lower Newport, O. Bur at Lower Newport, in an old cem on the Ohio River. MI: "Henry Middleswart died Sept 5, 1823, aged 68 years." GM Marietta Chap by Revolutionary marker in 1922. Ref: Farmer. Pa Archives. Fur infor Marietta Chap.

MILES, BENJAMIN, Capt. (Washington Co.)

Corp in Capt David Bent's Company, Col Nathan Sparhawk's Regt. Entered service Sept 5, 1777. Disch Nov 29, 1777. Service 3 mos, 9 days. Br Rutland, Mass. 1754. D, bur Belpre, O, 1817. Settled in Belpre, O in 1789 and located on the farm, which he had drawn in the Middle Settlement. Ref: Mass Soldiers and Sailors; Natl No 26725, Vol 27, D. A. R. Lin. Fur infor Marietta Chap.

MILES, JOHN, (Clermont Co.)

Pvt Va Continental Line. Pensioned 1818 at age 95, $96 annually. Br Va. D Jan 8, 1834. Came to Union Twp, Clermont Co, about 1825 residing in Williamsville. Ref: A. S. Abbott, Bethel, O. Pensions Dept. Fur infor Cincinnati Chap.

MILLER, BENJAMIN, (Wayne Co.)

Carried dispatches for Gen Washington. Br 1762 at Romney, Va. D 1841 in Wayne Co, O. Bur Canaan Bend Cem, Canaan Twp, Wayne Co, O, southwest corner of cem. MI: "Benjamin Miller, born 1762 at Romney Va, died in Wayne Co, Ohio, 1841. Soldier of the Revolution. Carried dispatches for General Washington." Fur infor Wooster Wayne Chap.

MILLER, DANIEL, (Fairfield Co.)

Bur Hopewell Cem. Fur infor Elizabeth Sherman Reese Chap.

MILLER, DANIEL, (Hamilton Co.)

Br 1759, N. C. D 1841. Fur infor Cincinnati Chap.

MILLER, DANIEL, (Mahoning Co.)

Ranger 1778, 1783, on frontier North Hampton Co. Pvt in Lancaster Co, 5th class. Children: Henry (br in 1788) also Jacob and John. May have had more children. Bur Old Springfield Cem, Petersburg, Mahoning Co. Farmer. Ref: Pa Archives, Series 3, Vol 23, p 302, Series 5, Vol 5, p 34. Fur infor Mahoning Chap.

MILLER, EDWARD, (Hamilton Co.)

Br. 1756, Conn. D 1823. Ref: S. A. R. Fur infor Cincinnati Chap.

MILLER, ELIAS, (Butler Co.)

When a boy, rode a pack horse in General Wayne's expedition, which met defeat at the hands of the Indians. In those days the supplies of the expedition were carried on pack horses. Miller rode a horse, driving two heavily burdened horses in front of him. It was owing to this that he was able to crouch flat on his horse and escape. During this engagement the company stopped at the home of Ann Gregory, for refreshments, she having frequently entertained Wayne, and on her tombstone near Le Sourdsville is the following inscription: "Here lies the body of one most loved. She has ascended to her home above. Her table was always filled with the best and Anthony Wayne was often her guest." Lot was purchased from Cleves Symmes, by Israel Ludlow and later came into possession of the Flenner family. MI: Old tombstone in Le Sourdsville not readable. Fur infor John Reily Chap.

MONUMENT ERECTED TO MRS. ELIZABETH LANTZ, REAL DAUGHTER OF AMERICAN REVOLUTION, AKRON, OHIO.

MILLER, HENRY, (Coshocton Co.)

Of Keene Twp, a sharp shooter, in Morgan's Army. Ref: Coshocton Co Hist. Fur infor Coshocton Chap.

MILLER, HENRY, (Coshocton Co.)

Bur Jackson Twp. Ref: Co Hist. Fur infor Coshocton Chap.

MILLER, ISAAC, (Ashtabula Co.)

Enl from Hatfield, Mass in Capt Seth Murray's Company, Col Benjamin Ruggles Woodbridge's Regt. Br 1752, Worcester, Mass. Mar Lucretia Knap. Children: Irene. D 1826. Harpersfield, Ashtabula Co. Ref: Lin Book, Vol 48, p 167. Fur infor Mary Stanley Chap.

MILLER, ISAAC, (Montgomery Co.)

Pvt in Revolution from Va; I. P. D. 152, Pitts 29, Saf 269. Br Va. Children: Susan and others, not known. D Jefferson Twp, Montgomery Co. Came to Jefferson Twp in 1805, and entered land on his Revolutionary serv. Nothing further could be learned. Richard Montgomery Chap, S. A. R.

MILLER, JACOB, (Butler Co.)

Br June, 1750. D Jan 7, 1802. Bur Trenton Cem, Trenton, O. GM Old headstone; inscription partly obliterated. Fur infor John Reily Chap.

MILLER, JACOB, (Mahoning Co.)

Pvt Capt Mach's Company Berks Co, Pa Mil. Pensioned 1820. Br 1750. Mar Eva Fix (1759-1825). D 1825. Bur Cornsburg, Canfield Twp. Ref: Pa Archives, 5 Series, Vol 5, p 287; 3 Series, Vol 23, p 513. Fur infor Mahoning Chap.

MILLER, JACOB, (Seneca Co.)

Soldier of Revolution, 1776. Bur Egberts Cem. GM D. A. R. with iron marker (76) May 30, 1923. Ref: Compare, p 189, Vol 15, D. A. R. Lin Natl No. 14,504. Fur infor Dolly Todd Madison Chap.

MILLER, JOHN ADAM, (Crawford Co.)

Pvt in Capt Henry Kregloh's Mil, Lt Col Peter Burkhalter's Bn, Pa Line. Br 1843, Pa. D 1831, Crawford Co, O. Ref: Natl No 94664, Vol 95, D. A. R. Lin.

MILLER, B. JOHN, (Mahoning Co.)

Ranger, Westmoreland Co, Pa. Pensioned 1833. Br 1754. D 1835. Bur Old Dutch, Canfield, O. GM Mahoning Chap, bronze marker, 1917. Ref: Pa Archives, Series 3, Vol 23, p 285. Fur infor Mahoning Chap.

MILLER, MICHIEL, (Miami Co.)

One of Lafayette's Regt. Bur Raper Chapel, two miles north of Troy. GM Miami Chap with bronze marker, 1904. Fur infor Miami Chap.

MILLER, MOSES, (Clark Co.)

Pvt Capt Benjamin Laing's Company, 1st Regt, Essex Co, NJ Mil. Br 1759, N. J. Mar Phoebe Baker. D Clark Co, O, 1814. Ref: Natl No 72,122, p 45, Vol 73, D. A. R. Lin.

MILLIGAN, DAVID, (Harrison Co.)

1749-1833. Bur in Cadiz Old Graveyard; a Revolutionary pensioner living in Harrison Co in 1833, aged 84; served in the Pa line; also possibly the same David Milligan who served as a member of Bedford Co Mil. U. S. Pension Rolls, 1835. Pa Archives, Series 5, Vol 91. Full infor Moravian Trail Chap.

MILLS, CONSTANTINE, (Ashtabula Co.)

Pvt Conn Mil. Pensioned 1833 as residing in Ashtabula Co. Br Norfolk, Conn, 1761. Parents: Joseph Mills (br in Norfolk, 1726.) Mar Philecta Way, 1783. Children: Martin, 1785; Alfred, Dorinda, Cherry, Rachel, Eben. D Austinburg, Ashtabula Co, O, Oct 1748. MI: "Constantine Mills died Oct 21, 1848, aged 87." Ref: Pension records Taylor Chap. Fur infor Taylor and Eunice Grant Chaps.

MILLS, ELIJAH, (Butler Co.)

Name appears on the tablet in the Soldiers and Sailors monument at Hamilton. Supposed to be Revolutionary soldier bur in that Co. Unidentified. Fur infor John Reily Chap.

MILLS, JOHN, Maj., (Darke Co.)

Major of Mass, throughout the war; became Adj Gen in Gen Wayne's army, located at Ft Greenville, O. D July 8, 1796. Bur probably in Soldiers' Burying Ground, W 3rd St, now occupied by residence (from Adj Gen Dept Washington, D. C.) GM State Historical Society, 1926; D. A. R. placed bronze tablet to him "and all brave soldiers and sailors who died during the occupancy of Ft Greenville, 1793-1796." Ft Greenville Chap 1927. Fur infor Ft Greenville Chap.

MINER, ELISHA, (Licking Co.)

Pvt in Capt Stanton's Company Light Dragoons, Conn Continental Tr. Br 1764, Conn. Mar Amy Wright. D 1864, Johnstown, O. Ref: Natl No. 61,987, p 335 Vol 62, D. A. R. Lin.

MINER, JOHN, (Cuyahoga Co.)

Clerk Conn Regt. Br 1762. D 1849. Bur North Royalton. Fur infor Western Reserve Chap.

MINER, JUSTUS, (Geauga Co.)

Pvt. Served from Conn in Col Canfield's Regt at West Point, 1781. Br Norfolk, Conn, 1762. Mar Mabel Plumb, 1779; Hannah Moss, Jan 1, 1812. Children: Sarah, Anna, Matilda, Betsy, Charlotte, Philo, John, Origen. D 1829, Chester. Bur Old Settlement Cem, Chesterland, O. MI: "Justus Miner, 1762-1829. Settled in Chester in 1802." Ref: Conn Men of Rev, p 508. Fur infor Taylor Chap.

MINGUS, HIERONYMOUS, (Erie Co.)

Pvt 4th Regt, NY in the Revolution. Parents: Angus Mingus. D Berlin Heights, Erie Co. Bur Burbue Cem. Came from Amsterdam Co, NY to Marcellus, NY, then to Berlin Heights, O. Pension granted Sept 6, 1828, when 72 years old. Ref: D. A. R. Magazine Dec 1919 issue. Natl No 136,522. Fur infor Mrs. Effie Whitaker Teemer, Lorain, O.

MITCHEL, DAVID, (Scioto Co.)

Pvt in Capt Erwin's Company, 2nd Bn, Cumberland Co, Pa Mil. Enl Dec 6, 1776, until Dec 24, 1776. Ref: Mrs. Susan Morrison Coe, 1930 Waller St. Fur infor Joseph Spencer Chap.

MITCHELL, DAVID, (Greene Co.)

Enl in Capt James Morrison's Company, Col Thos Porter's Bn of Associators. Mustered in Lancaster Co, Pa. 1776. Br 1737, Scotland. Mar Margaret Mitchell. D 1817, Cedarville, O. Ref: Natl No. 57,707, p 242, Vol 58, D. A. R. Lin.

MITCHELL, ENSIGN, (Madison Co.)

Pvt in Capt Daniel Mill's Company, Col Van Schaik's NY Bn. His name appears on record in Pension Office War Department, Washington, D. C. for the period from Nov 19, 1775, which bears the remarks "Enlisted Jan 26, 1776; Disch Sept. 7." His name also appears on a roll of Daniel Mill's Company same Bn, not dated, which bears the remark "Enlisted Dec 26, 1776." Br 1760, Mass. Mar Lucy Hubbard in 1786. Children: Ensign, Chandler, Roxanna, Experience, Claudius, Polly, Ira, Lydia, Abizer and Newman. D 1839, near Mechanicsburg, O. Bur family cem on the farm of Mrs. Belle Guy Mitchell, in Pike Twp, Madison Co, O. He and wife are bur in a family burial lot located on a small knoll; it was surrounded by a low picket fence. The picket fence is now gone, but the graves are still there. The graves were marked. Br in Mass, lived in Vermont in 1794; a few yrs later in New York, then in Pennsylvania, next in Kentucky, afterwards in Southern Ohio, and in 1815 moved to Madison Co, O. Farmed very extensively during his residence in Madison Co, O. At one time, he owned the farm upon which he is bur. He sold it to his son, Newman, and it has always remained in the possession of his descendants. Ref: Jane Mitchell Marsh, 6244 South Park St, Chicago, Ill., Apt. No. 111. Fur infor London Chap.

MITCHELL, PHILIP, (Hamilton Co.)

Br Pennsylvania. D 1832. Ref: S. A. R. Fur infor Cincinnati Chap.

MITCHELL, SAMUEL, (Miami Co.)

Enl in Va when 16 years of age; served in the Va State Tr. Pensioned 1833 in Miami, Co, O. Br Mch 15, 1759, King George Co, Va. Mar a sister of Daniel Boone, says one report. Mar Malinda Cecil, 1780, say two others. D Apr 25, 1840, Bethel Twp, Miami Co, O. Bur McKendree Chapel. GM D. A. R. with bronze marker. Ref: Pension Bureau U. S. and Vol 56, Natl No. 55,279, D. A. R. Lin. Fur infor Miami Chap.

MITCHELL, SAMUEL, (Union Co.)

Bur Woods Cem, Unionville, O. Fur infor Hannah Emerson Dustin Chap.

MITCHELL, WILLIAM, (Miami Co.)

Pa Mil. Mar Martha Patterson. On Pens Roll, Miami Co, 1831, age 78. Ref: Natl No. 13,697, p 260, Vol 14, D. A. R. Lin.

MITSCO, CONRAD, (Wayne Co.)

1st NJ Inf. Revolutionary Soldier. D Marshallville, O. Bur Marshallville Cem, west and adjacent to the town. North side of Cem. MI: "Conrad Mitsco, 1st N. J. Inf. Revolutionary Soldier." Fur infor Wooster Wayne Chap.

MIX, AMOS, (Muskingum Co.)

Enl 1776, Pvt under Capt Phineas Porter, Col Wooster, Conn Tr. Widow pensioned on his serv. Br 1759, Waterbury, Conn. Mar Clarinda Barnes. D 1844, Muskingum, O. Ref: Vol 92, p 149, Natl No. 91,460, D. A. R. Lin and Natl No. 59,073.

MIX, JOSIAH, (Portage Co.)

Pvt in Conn Mil. Placed on pension roll, May 13, 1833. Bur Rootstown. Drew pension in Ravenna, 1840. Fur infor Old Northwest Chap.

MIXER, PHINEAS, SR., (Lake Co.)

He was in the serv of Mass. Enl Sept 30, 1777 in Capt Benjamin Bonney's Company. Disch Oct 14, 1777. Br 1756. Mar Abigail Fobes. He removed from Mass to Unionville, O, where he kept tavern in a log house. Fur infor New Conn Chap.

MOBERLY, REASON, (Highland Co.)

Bur on Moberly farm 1 mile north of Hillsboro. Grave obliterated. Fur infor Waw-Wil-a-Way Chap.

MOFFAT, ROBERT, (Guernsey Co.)

Bur Old Cem, Cambridge, O. Ref: S. A. R. Fur infor Anna Asbury Stone Chap.

MONETT, ABRAHAM, (Pickaway Co.)

Pvt Capt Ralph Hillary's Company, 2nd Company of 33rd Bn, Md Mil. Col Chas Beatty, from Frederick, Md, Mch 3, 1777, stationed at Bash Ridge, N. J. Associator Frederick, Md, 1775-1776. Br Mch 16, 1748, Calvert Co, Md. Parents: Isaac Monett (1726-1798) mar Elizabeth Osborn (1728) (was Associator). Mar Ann Hillary (1748-1772). Children: Isaac, William, John, Ann, Thomas, Osborn, Margaret, Jeremiah, Elizabeth. D Dec 1, 1810, Salt Creek Twp, Pickaway Co, O. Bur Whistler Cem, Prairie View, moved 1904 from Bald Knob. Grave located left of center of entrance. MI: Dates, name, etc., placed 1810 by family, also by D. A. R. marker, placed by members Columbus Chap. Came to Ohio 1802, original muster roll possessed by Md Hist Society, Baltimore. Ref: Natl No. 94,252, Vol 95. Fur infor Columbus and Nathaniel Massie Chaps.

MONROE, ISAAC, (Delaware Co.)

Bur near Hyattsville, Cole Cem. Fur infor Delaware Chap.

MONTEITH, DANIEL, (Mahoning Co.)

Lt in 1778 in Capt Holmes Stockton's 8th Company, 4th Bn, York Co Mil, Col John Andrews Regt. Br 1750, Chester, Pa. Mar Sarah Leckey. D 1826, Coitsville, O. Ref: Natl No. 53,694, Vol 54, p 311, D. A. R. Lin.

MONTGOMERY, ABRAM, (Butler Co.)

Name appears on the tablet in the Soldiers and Sailors monument at Hamilton, O. as a Revolutionary Soldier, bur in that Co. D Apr 21, 1828, while living in Union Twp. Fur infor John Reily Chap.

MONTGOMERY, MICHAEL, (Guernsey Co.)

Died age 101. Bur West Montgomery, Millwood Twp. Ref: S. A. R. Fur infor Anna Asbury Stone Chap.

MONTGOMERY, SARAH BOONE BROOKS, (Brown Co.)

Carrying water during the siege of Bryan Station, Ky. Parents: Samuel Boone Sr. She was also a niece of Daniel Boone. 1st husband Thomas Brooks; 2nd husband, David Montgomery. Bur Decatur Cem, Brown Co, O. Ref: Mrs. Ora E. Leka, Marion, O. Fur infor Capt William Hendricks.

MOODY, JAMES, (Mahoning Co.)

Ranger. Br 1769. D 1831. Bur Boardman Cem. Farmer. Ref: Pa Archives, Section 3, Vol. 23, p 227; Somers Hist of Mahoning Co. p 82. Fur infor Mahoning Chap.

MOOR, NATHAN, (Mahoning Co.)

Pvt. Enl Aug 4, 1780, served to Dec 6, 1780. "Conn Men in the Revolution," p 166. Was a surveyor, came with Nathanial Church to Canfield, O. Left Sharon, Conn on the 20th day of Aug, 1797, arrived in Canfield, May 24, covered entire distance on foot. Was in same company as Amos Loveland. Ref: Trumbull and Mahoning Co, Hist p 10. Fur infor Mahoning Chap.

MOORE, BENJAMIN, (Franklin Co.)

Served in the 1st Regt, Conn Inf. Br Windsor, Conn, Mch 1, 1756. D 1825. Bur Jamison Cem, Blendon Twp. MI: "Benjamin Moore of Windsor, Hartford Co, Conn. Died Oct 16th, 1825." GM Revolutionary Grave Committee. Bronze marker, May 30, 1912. Came to Ohio with his brother, Simon Moore, in 1807 and settled in Blendon Twp. Fur infor Columbus Chap.

MOORE, EPHRAIM, (Madison Co.)

Br Aug 22, 1743, Delaware. Mar Priscilla Riggin. Children: Isaac. D Mch 12, 1845, Fayette Co, O. Bur Methodist Churchyard, Mt Sterling, O. GM Mt Sterling Chapter with bronze marker in 1911. Ref: Delaware State Library; Vol 71, p 55, Natl No. 70,153, D. A. R. Lin. Fur infor Mt Sterling Chap.

MOORE, JAMES, (Geauga Co.)

Cook. Serv May 29, 1776, paid Nov 15. Mar 2nd Lucy Day Pease. Children: James, William B, Dolly, Polly, Clarrisa, Charlotta, Susa Harriet. D Newbury, 1834. Bur South Newbury, Geauga Co, O. Will dated Sept. 1, 1834, Probated Oct 25, 1834. Fur infor Taylor Chap.

MOORE, JAMES L., (Delaware Co.)

Enl 1776, as a Pvt in Capt John Wood's Company from Goshen, N. Y., and in 1778 in Capt Jones' Company, Col Justin's Regt; at the battles of "White Plains and Wyoming." He was placed on the pension roll, 1822, from Delaware Co, O. Br Palmer, Mass, 1756. D 1837, Delaware Co, O. Ref: Natl No. 50,462, Vol 51, p 210 D. A. R. Lin.

MOORE, JOHN, 3rd, (Geauga Co.)

Enl Schenectady, N. Y., 1777. Pensioned for six years serv, NY Line, 8th Company, 3rd Regt, Capt Leonard Blucher, Col Peter Gansevoort. 2nd Enl June 1, 1782 in 1st Company, Regt, Col Van Schaick. Disch New Eindser, near West Point. Br 1752, Maryland. Mar Leah Grame (Groome). Children: John, Isaac, Rachel, Nancy, Rebecca, Money. D Mch 9, 1842, Fullertown, O. Bur Chester Center. MI: "John Moore, S. A. R. 1775, died 1843.' GM Government marker. Was at Fort Stanwix and Yorktown. Came to Ohio in 1810. Ref: Archives of N. Y., Vol 1, p 208, 185, American Ancestry, Vol 5, p 102, Natl No. 30,762, Vol 31, D. A. R. Lin. Fur infor Taylor Chap.

MOORE, JOSEPH, (Lorain Co.)

Pvt. Mass Continental, body guard to Gen Washington. Br 1764. D 1846. Bur Avon-on-the-Lake. GM Western Reserve, bronze marker. Fur infor Western Reserve Chap.

MOORE, ROBERT, (Trumbull Co.)

Children: Robert Moore, a son, is bur in East Farmington Cem. Bur East Farmington Cem, Farmington Twp. MI: Has no monument or marker, is bur on the same lot as son. Blacksmith and farmer. Ref: A descendant, Bert Steele, lives in vicinity, could give no data about the soldier, Robert Moore. Fur infor Mary Chesney Chap.

MOORE, SIMEON, (Franklin Co.)

Served in the 4th Regt, Conn Inf and fought in the battle of Bunker Hill. Pensioned July 23, 1819. Br Windsor, Conn. Mch 20, 1760. D June 26, 1825. Bur West Pioneer Cem, Blendon Twp. MI: "Died June 26, 1825, aged 64 years and 3 mos. A soldier of 1776." GM Revolutionary Grave Committee. Bronze marker, May 30, 1912. Came with his brother to Ohio in 1807. They lived with their old neighbors, the Phelps, while building their cabin in Blendon Twp. Fur infor Columbus Chap.

MOORE, WILLIAM, (Brown Co.)

Bur Levanna. Fur infor Lieutenant Byrd Chap.

MOREY, SILAS, (Athens Co.)

Sgt in Capt Ichabad Turner's Company, 4th Albany Company, NY Regt. Mar Elizabeth Benson in 1768. D 1825, Athens Co. Ref: Natl No. 74,725, Vol 75, D. A. R. Lin.

MORGAN, DANIEL, (Geauga Co.)

Pvt 3rd Regt Conn Line, 1777-1781, Capt Robert Warner's Company. Enl Apr 30, 1777 from Chatham, Middlesex Co, Conn. Br 1762. D 1855. Bur Hambden Center, O. MI: "Daniel Morgan, 1735-1842, a soldier of the Revolution." Name found in list of pensioners in census of 1840, as living in Hambden, age 78. Ref: Census 1840, Pioneer Hist Geauga Co, p 366. Fur infor Taylor Chap.

MORGAN, JACOB, (Hamilton Co.)

Br 1760, Mass. D 1836. Ref: S. A. R. Fur infor Cincinnati Chap.

MORGAN, JAMES, (Wayne Co.)

Bur on Jacob Bucher farm in Wayne Co, O. Bur in pvt cem, 2 miles south of Moorland. Ref: Mrs. H. W. Stone, R. F. D. No. 1, Wilder, Idaho. Fur infor Wooster Wayne.

MORGAN, PELATIAH, (Delaware Co.)

Pvt under Col Rufus Putnam, Capt Sylvanus Smith, 5th Mass Regt. Bur Kingston Twp, or Cheshire. Pensioned. Fur infor Delaware Chap.

MORGAN, THOMAS, (Harrison Co.)

A Revolutionary pensioner, living in Harrison Co in 1833, aged 81; served in the 2nd Regt Va Line, Col Christian Febiger. U. S. Pension Rolls, 1835; Eckenrod's Lists of Virginia Soldiers in Revolution, Vol 2, p 218. Fur infor Moravian Trail Chap.

MORGAN, THOMAS, (Preble Co.)

Bur Isreal Twp. Ref: Mary P. Mitchell, Eaton, O. Fur infor Grace Conger Miller, Org Regent.

MORIN, RODHAM, (Clermont Co.)

Served in Revolutionary War from Va. Came to Ohio Twp, Clermont Co, O. about 1797, settling 1 mile below present New Richmond. Parents: Edward Morin, also a Revolutionary soldier. One daughter (mar Judson Calhoun) one daughter (mar Wm Calhoun.) Children: John, Benjamin (both served 1812); James, Andrew J, daughter (mar Gordon Applegate); daughter (mar Thomas McClelland). Fell off a boat and drowned. Bur in Ohio Twp, Clermont Co, O. Fur infor Cincinnati Chap.

MORLEY, EZEKIEL, (Lake Co.)

Enl Jan 10, 1777 in Capt Jos Williams' Company, known as the 1st Company 3rd Mass Regt Continental Line. Commanded by Col John Greaton. Disch Jan 10, 1780. Br 1759, Glastonbury, Conn. D Aug 6, 1852, Chester, O. Bur Kirtland, O. GM New Conn Chap. He was one of the original surveyors of the Western Reserve in 1796. Fur infor New Conn Chap.

MORLEY, THOMAS, (Lake Co.)

Served from Conn, Jan 1776, under Capt Wells and Col Cook until Jan 1777. In Aug 1777, same Regt, two mos under Capt Bidwell, again in July, 1779, for two mos. Br 1758. D Sept 1, 1844, Kirtland, O. Bur Kirtland, O. GM New Conn Chap. In 1818 at his home was organized the first religious society; in 1824 this society erected its first building. Ref: Natl No. 71,842, p 297, Vol 27. Fur infor New Conn Chap.

MORRELL, CALVIN, M. D., (Warren Co.)

Revolutionary Soldier from N. J. D near Lebanon, O. Appointed by Masonic Lodge, New Jersey to organize Lodge No. 2 in Cincinnati, Dec 27, 1794. Soon after moved to Union village, (Shakers) near Lebanon, Warren Co. Ref: Mrs. Whallon, Cincinnati, O. Fur infor Cincinnati Chap.

MORRIS, ARCHIBALD, (Noble Co.)

Pvt 5th class, Capt Abner Howell's Company, Washington Co. Mar Elizabeth Enochs. Children: Isaac, Rebecca. Bur Noble Co, O. Ref: Mrs. J. R. Harvey, Athens, O. Fur infor Nabby Lee Ames Chap.

MORRIS, DAVID, (Miami Co.)

Bur Sailors Graveyard, near New Carlisle, O. GM Miami Chap with bronze marker in 1905. At a reunion of Revolution veterans, at Troy, O, July 4, 1827, he gave this toast: "May the precious blood that was spilt between the years '76 and '83 as a sacrifice for our liberty and Independence be ever commemorated." Fur infor Miami Chap.

MORRIS, ISAAC, (Warren Co.)

Wagonmaster, Morris Co, NJ Mil, "Stryker's" p 853. Br 1753, Morristown, N. J. Parents: Daniel Morris and wife Hannah (see records of Morristown, N. J. Presbyterian Church). Mar Rebecca Hathaway May 11, 1768. (p 54, Church Records, Morristown, N. J.) Both received into church Mch 2, 1776. Children: Benjamin, Jacob, John, Robert, Tunis, (died), Child (died 1773). All baptized Morristown, N. J. 3 buried 1772 and 1773. D Lebanon and buried in Presbyterian churchyard. In 1778 Isaac Morris came to Columbia, perhaps, then on to Cincinnati about 1789. One of eight charter members of First Presbyterian Church Cincinnati 1790. He removed to Warren Co before 1800, Sec. 19, northwest of Lebanon. Founder of Turtle Creek Church and when it disbanded a founder of Lebanon Presbyterian Church. Benjamin came with his father to these places and lived near him. His home still standing, 1920, one time known as "Green Tree" tavern. Marriages of other sons secured from Mrs. Whallon. Ref: Church Records, Morristown, N. J. Records copied from family Bible and headstone by Rosamond Fraser, Dayton, O. Filed by Mrs. Whallon, Cincinnati D. A. R. Fur infor Cincinnati Chap.

MORRIS, JACOB, (Hamilton Co.)

Revolutionary serv in "Stryker's Men from New Jersey." A brother of John and Isaac Morris, Revolutionary Soldiers, all were at Columbia, Hamilton Co. He died early, left no family. Bur at Columbia. Fur infor Cincinnati Chap.

MORRIS, JOHN, (Hamilton Co.)

Served as Wagon Master, Stryker's "In Morris Co, N. J." p 853. Parents: Daniel (d 1767) and wife Hannah, whose names are on Roster of Morristown Church, Vol 4, p 54, by Green in 1761. Was brother of Isaac; one daughter, Esther mar William Todd, Cincinnati, O. (A Revolutionary Soldier). Ref: Mrs. Whallon, Cincinnati, O. Fur infor Cincinnati Chap.

MORRISON, FRANCIS, (Co not stated.)

Ranger on Frontier, 1778-83. Br 1752, Scotland. D 1842, Ohio. Ref: Vol 93, p 94, Natl No. 92,289, D. A. R. Lin.

MORRISON, GEORGE, (Guernsey Co.)

D age 47. Bur Wills Twp. Ref: S. A. R. Fur infor Anna Asbury Stone Chap.

MORRISON, JAMES, (Ashtabula Co.)

Volunteered at Endfield, Conn, May 1, 1776. Served as Pvt and carpenter under Capt Harmon, Col Mott, Capt Thaw, Capt Booth, Col Chapman. Was in Sullivan's expedition through the forest country. Br Feb 28, 1757, Easton, Mass. Parents: William and Sarah (Montgomery) Morrison (mar Nov 10, 1748). Mar Hannah Gunn, Pittsfield, Mass in 1783, Children: James Jr., Hannah, Lucretia, William, Strobridge, Sarah, Anna, Riley, twins, Julia and Julius. D Oct 18, 1854, Albion, Pa. Bur Geneva, O, south ridge Ashtabula Co. MI: Name and dates on monument. Was a skilled artisan, learning the work in Boston. After marriage resided in Blanford, Mass till 1793, in Harperfield, N. Y. till 1806, when he moved to Ashtabula Co, O. Ref: Ashtabula Co Hist. Society records, Bureau of Pensions. Fur infor Mary Stanley Chap.

MORSE, BENJAMIN, Maj., (Lake Co.)

Served in the 3rd Regt with Col Israel Putnam on the first call for Tr, was at Bunker Hill, also with the Quebec expedition. Br Nov 7, 1755. Mar a sister of Col Alexander Harper. D Feb 6, 1813. Bur Unionville, O. GM New Conn Chap. He is supposed to be of the party of 1798. Fur infor New Conn Chap.

MORSE, SETH, Capt. (Lcrain Co.)

As a Sgt he was commissioned to build 120 wagons for the army. He delivered them in 6 mos. (record time) and was made 1st Lt for the promptness and excellence of the wagons. He was mustered out at the close of the war as Capt. Br Tyringham, Mass Jan 3, 1752. Parents: Peter Morse (d 1771) and Keziah Clark. Mar Sally Stoddard, Polly Gibson. Children: Abishai, son of first wife. Seth Gibson and Maria by second wife. D Nov 19, 1840 in Brownhelm, O. Bur Brownhelm Cem midway (from north to south) on east side, second line from fence. MI: Names and dates only. GM by Seth G, son, with the usual type of headstones for those days. Marked about 1850. Enl at 19, and was one of the eight men who slept by a strawstack in Somerville the night before the attack on Berks Hill. Owing to high tide they were compelled to go as far as Watertown to find a boat and crossing. All took part in the afternoon defense. He moved from Great Barrington, Mass to Ohio in Autumn of 1823, where he had bought 1,400 acres of heavily timbered land. As Calvanist (Baptist) he declined to pay State tax in Mass to support the Presbyterian work. A young heifer was sold, tax deducted and balance of money returned which he refused, saying it could be applied on subsequent requirements. Fur infor Oberlin Chap.

MORTON, JOHN, (Ross Co.)

Br 1762 at Broughshane, Ballymena Parish, County Antrim, Ireland. Parents: Father a Scotchman, John Morton, his mother, Irish, Jane Peden. Mar Margaret Alexander (died June 9, 1861, in 72nd year) at Fairview, Greenville Co, S. C. 1788. Children: John, Joseph, James, Samuel A, Mary, Jean and Catherine. D Dec 14, 1841, South Salem. Bur South Salem, grave on left side of driveway from central gate of cem and near a large cedar tree about 100 feet from gate. MI: "John Morton died Dec 14th, 1841 in the 79th year." GM Nathaniel Massie Chap, D. A. R. in 1925. Br in Ireland, emigrated to America in 1768, settled S. C. As a boy took part in some of the midnight meetings that culminated in the writing of the Declaration of Independence, later took part in the Revolutionary War. Mar and moved to Ohio. Farmer and schoolteacher and for 35 years an elder in Salem. Did not take an active part in public affairs outside of church work. Fur infor Nathaniel Massie Chap.

MOSES, ROBERT, (Warren Co.)

Served as a Pvt. Claims to have known Gen Washington personally, and related many incidents. Probably in some Maryland outfit, but it cannot be verified. This is merely a newspaper report at the time of his death. Br July 16, 1735, Carlisle, England. Children: John Bradley Moses, (br Mch 2, 1776.) D near Carlisle, Warren Co in 1832. Came to America in 1750 and located at what is now Georgetown, Md. There is also a tradition that he later moved to Virginia before coming to Ohio. He was a tailor and often spoke of making clothing for Gen Washington. No further infor obtainable. Fur infor Richard Montgomery Chap S. A. R.

MOSS, DANIEL, (Hamilton Co.)

Br 1747, Connecticut. D 1843. Ref: S. A. R. Fur infor Cincinnati Chap.

MOTT, JOHN, (Knox Co.)

Pensioned in Rutland Co, Vt, 1818 for serv. Sgt Lt and Capt Vermont Tr. Br 1748, France. Mar Mary Rowley. D 1831, Mt Vernon, O. Ref: Compare Natl No. 22,439, Vol 23, D. A. R. Lin. Natl No. 79,385, Vol 80.

MOURER, JOHN, (Now spelled Mowery), (Pickaway Co.)

Enl twice in 1780, served 2 mos at one time, 14 mos at another. Engaged in the siege of Yorktown. He was a Pvt. His captains were Daniel Wills and John Fesig. Br Feb 12, 1763, Berks Co, Pa. Mar Elizabeth Stimmell in Berks Co, Pa. Children: Peter, John, Jacob, Mary (wife of Henry DeLong), survived their mother, Elizabeth and Catherine deceased before. D Feb 24, 1833, Pickaway Co, O. Grave near southwest part. MI: "In memory of John Mowery, died February 24, 1833, aged 70 years, 12 days." He with his wife and children came to Saltcreek Twp, Pickaway Co, about 1810. Purchased land in sections eleven and fourteen. Farmer. Built his cabin in the dense forest. He received a pension July 21, 1832. Ref: John J. Reichelderfer, Tarlton, Pickaway Co, O. Fur infor Pickaway Plains Chap.

MOWEN, BELZAR, (Mahoning Co.)

Pvt 3rd Company, 1st Bn, Cumberland Co, Pa Mil, Capt Barryhill's Company, 4th class in 1780. Bn 1759. Mar Matelena (1776-1838). D 1845. Bur old cem, North Lima. Ref: Pa Archives, 5th Series, Vol 6, p 101, and p 80. Fur infor Mahoning Chap.

MOWREY, JOHN, (or MOWRA), (Mahoning Co.)

Pvt 4th Company, Capt Brumback, 2nd Bn, Chester Co, Pa Mil. On duty Sept 24, 1781. Br 1765. D 1816. Bur Vaughn Cem, Milton Twp. Ref: Pa Archives, 5th Series, Vol 15, p 539. Fur infor Mahoning Chap.

MULLOY, (or MALLOY), HUGH, (Clermont Co.)

Commissioned as Ensign of the Company, whereof George White is Capt in the Bn, whereof Ebenezer Francis, Esq is Col. Commission dated Nov 6, 1776, at Boston, Mass. by order of John Hancock, president of the Congress. Br 1751 probably Hampshire Co, Va. D 1845. Bur Mt Zion Cem, Clermontville, O. (Clermont Co.) Grave on Parker lot in southern part of cem about 3 miles up stream from New Richmond, O. A slab monument over the grave is well preserved, except for weathering. 20 lines on the slab can be read. Visited by 2 descendants, Nov 1828, Mrs. Saml Wilson, Franklin, Ind, and Bart Parker, Indianapolis, Ind, who gave this infor. MI: "In memory of Hugh Mulloy, a Lieutenant in the Revolution, born in Albany, N. Y. Married one of great worth; joined the army at Cambridge 1775; was personally acquainted with Washington and Lafayette; was in the retreat from Ticonderoga; in both battles of Saratoga; lay at Valley Forge; was at Monmouth and was thrice wounded. Among the bravest he was brave. He came to Ohio 1817, died July 11, 1845, in the 94th year of his age." Taken from printed document of family hist. May be obtained from Bart Parker, Indianapolis, Ind, who holds a copy of the commission and serv from Mass Soldiers and Sailors of the Revolutionary War, Vol 11, p 194. Ref: Mrs. Walter D. Crebs. Fur infor Jonathan Dayton Chap.

MUMMEY, CHRISTOPHER, (Morgan Co.)

Pvt. Br April 2, 1753, Germantown, Pa. Mar Katie Smith. Children: Joshua, John, William, Charles, Thomas, Ellen. D 1832. Bur McKendree, Meigsville Twp, Morgan Co. Ref: Mrs. Vanessa Murray, New Philadelphia, O.; Miss Agnes Pyle, McConnelsville, O. Fur infor Amanda Barker Devin Chap.

MUNGER, JONATHAN, (Warren Co.)

Pensioner of Rev. Corp. Enl July 21, 1775 in 7th Regt of Conn, 7th Company. Sent Sept 15 to Boston. Sullivan's Brig reorganized under Col Charles Weber, 1776. Came to Ohio 1797; served with Edmund, war 1812. Br Nov 30, 1755, Guilford, Conn. Parents: Reuben Munger and Elizabeth Dudley of Guilford, Conn. Mar Elizabeth Lawrence (d June 6, 1830; dau John and Elizabeth Willcockson) Oct 9, 1783. Children: Charlotte, Anetha, Hervey, Polly or Mary, Eliza. D Nov 9, 1837. Bur Washington Church Cem near Holz creek, Warren Co, O. GM by S. A. R. Dayton, O. Farmer. After Rev removed from Conn to Middlebury, Vt. thence to Ohio, 1797. Ref: Mrs. Stanley Cash, Oakland, Coles Co, Ill. Natl No 59206. Accepted by Jane Daily, State Chairman, but not verified.

MUNN, JAMES, Maj., (Scioto Co.)

1778. Adj. 1779, served Adj 2½ mos. Capt. Was wounded and left to die on fields, but escaped with aid of William Brady. Mar Fillissa Oliver. Children: James, William, David, John, Solomon, Margaret, Polly, Nellie, Hannah, Nancy. D Mch 11, 1839, Munns Run. Bur on hill, northeast cor of own farm. GM Old stone disintegrated. Came from Pa to Limestone, Ky, thence to Alexandria, Scioto Co, O. He lived with grandson Ira on Munn land. Coroner 1810; set up hand mill; gave his name to Munn's Run. Fur infor Joseph Spencer Chap.

MUNRO, JOSIAH, Capt., (Washington Co.)

Ensign, Lt 1777 and Capt 1780; served to close of war. Br Feb 12, 1745, Peterboro, N. H. D 1801, Marietta, O. Bur Mound Cem, Marietta, O. MI: "Capt Josiah Munro 1745-1801." GM Marietta Chap with Revolutionary marker and on gateway. Marked Nov 30, 1906; marker stolen and replaced in 1920. Ref: Compare Natl No. 28,753, Vol 29, D. A. R. Lin. Fur infor Marietta Chap.

MUNSELL, LEVI, (Miami Co.)

Pvt in Capt Riley's Company, Col Samuel B. Webb's Conn Regt. Br Norwich, Conn, 1764. Mar Lucretia Oliver. D Miami Co, O, 1849. Fur infor Natl No. 69,467, p 166, Vol 70, D. A. R. Lin.

MUNSON, ISAAC, (Wayne Co.)

Served at White Plains, Elizabethtown and Yorktown as Pvt, Conn Line. Br 1762. D 1830, in Wayne Co. Applied for pension 1818. Ref: Natl No. 43,701, Vol 44, p 268, D. A. R. Lin.

MUNSON, JESSE, (Licking Co.)

Served as 2nd Lt in Capt Ball's Company of Minute Men at the Lexington Alarm. Br 1741, Granville, Mass. Mar Miriam Raleigh in 1767, (Br 1746, d 1830). D 1813, Granville, O. Ref: Natl No 102271, Vol 103 p 84, D. A. R. Lin.

MUNSON, WILMOT, (Morrow Co.)

Bur near Westfield. Fur infor Mt Gilead Chap.

MURDOCK, ASAHEL, (Butler Co.)

Pvt from Jan, 1776 to Jan, 1777. Wounded at second siege of Quebec. Br Apr 17, 1755, Preston, Conn. Mar Elizabeth Starkweather, Feb 28, 1779. Children: John Starkweather Murdock. D Jan 23, 1837, Butler Co, O. Bur Oxford Cem Oxford, O. GM by relatives with standstone slab. Fur infor Oxford Caroline Scott Chap.

MURPHY, EDWARD, (Butler Co.)

Name appears on the tablet in the Soldiers and Sailors monument at Hamilton, O, as a Revolutionary soldier, bur in that Co. Fur infor John Reily Chap.

MURPHY, WILLIAM, (Franklin Co.)

Pvt Gloucester Co, NJ Mil. Br 1742, Gloucester Co, N. J. D 1830, Franklin Co, O. Ref: Natl No. 96,079, Vol 97, p 27, D. A. R. Lin.

MURRAY, JOHN, (Cuyahoga Co.)

Pvt under Col Zebulon Butler's Regt in 1781. Br 1759, Conn. D 1813, Euclid, O. Ref: Natl No. 76,564, Vol 77, D. A. R. Lin.

MURRAY, PATRICK, (Ashland Co.)

Pvt. Enl June 3rd, 1776, Capt Jeremiah Talbot's Company, 1st Regt Pa Line, 3 yrs or during the War. Hon disch 1782. Br Mch 17, 1775; County Donegal, Ireland. Mar Mary Brereton Beatty, Sept 2, 1786. Children: James, Edward, Catherine, Patrick, Susannah, William, John, Mary, Elizabeth, Alice Ann, Sarah, Rebecca, George, Anna Hill, Hugh. D July 23, 1854, on his farm, Orange Twp, Ashland Co, O. Bur Orange Graveyard, just east of village of Nankin, O, east of middle of the graveyard. MI: Worn moss-covered marble slab, name and dates. GM by children. Very energetic, active. Clothier and Fashioner in Harris Ferry, or Harrisburg, Pa. 1783 moved to Greenburg, Westmoreland Co, Pa, then to Stark Co, O, about 1809. After War of 1812 to Orange Twp then Richland, O. He and son James served 2 enlmts War 1812, border defence, Gen Ri-in Beall. Ref: Pa. Archives, Hill's Hist Ashland Co, Genealogical Record by W. H. Egle, M. D. M. A. of the families of Beatty, Egle, Miller, Murray, Orth, Thomas. Fur infor Sarah Copus Chap.

MURRAY, WILLIAM, (Morgan Co.)

Pvt. Br July 19, 1753, Carlisle, Pa. Mar Ann Long. Children: William, George, Mary, Patsey, Beatty, Hannah, Daraniah. D Mch 28, 1839. Bur Stevens Cem, Meigsville Twp, Morgan Co. Ref: Mrs. Elizabeth Dover, McConnelsville, O. Fur infor Amanda Barker Devin Chap.

MUSGRAVE, JOHN, (Greene Co.)

Pvt. Maryland Mil. Pensioned Mch 4, 1831. Age 74 yrs. Annual allowance $36.66. On pens roll July 27, 1833. Fur infor Catherine Greene Chap.

MUSSER, CHRISTIAN, (Coshocton, O.)

Br 1760. Pensioned 1840. Ref: S. A. R. Fur infor Western Reserve Chap.

MUSSER, DANIEL, (Mahoning Co.)

Pvt 2nd class, 1st Company, Capt Adam Stahler's Company, Col Henry Geiger, 6th Bn, Northampton Co Mil. Br 1759. D 1817. Bur Old Church, Petersburg, O. Ref: Pa Archives, Series 5, Vol 8, p 443. Fur infor Mahoning Chap.

MUSSER, PETER, SR. (Mahoning Co.)

Pvt 2nd class, Capt Smyth's Company, Lancaster Co, Pa Mil; also in Capt Joseph Wright's Company Sept 11, 1776. Br 1740. Mar Margaret —— (1743-1821). Children: John, Peter, (founder of Petersburg) Jacob (drum major, war of 1812). There were four sons, and two daughters. D 1808. Bur Old Church Cem, Petersburgh, O. Kept a tavern, built sawmill and gristmill. Came from York Co, in 1801. Was first settler in Springfield Twp, wealthy, bought 4 sections of land. Ref: Pa. Archives, Series 5, Vol 7, p 33, 640; 202, Vol 2, Hist Trumbull and Mahoning Cos, Williams 1877-8. Fur infor Mahoning Chap.

MUZZY, NATHANIEL, (Portage Co.)

Pvt in Mass Mil. Placed on pension roll Sept 21, 1833. Bur Palmyra, O. Drew pension at Ravenna in 1840. Fur infor Old Northwest Chap.

MYER, HEINRICH, (Mahoning Co.)

Pvt Capt John Wright's Company, Lancaster Co, Pa Mil, Sept 1776; also in Capt Weaver's Company, same County in 1777. Br 1752. D 1845. Bur Old Church cem, Petersburg. Ref: Pa Archives, 3rd series, Vol 23, p 428. Fur infor Mahoning Chap.

MYERS, ————, (Delaware Co.)

Bur near Galena. Fur infor Delaware Chap.

MYERS, JACOB, (Fayette Co.)

Served as hammerman, made arms for soldiers and other iron work for use of the Colonies. Served as a Corp in Capt Thomas Church's Company; 5th Pa Regt, also known as Capt Smith's Company. Regt commanded by Col Francis Johnson. Aptd Corp Jan 1, 1777. Br Sept, 1735, Pa. Parents: Jonathan Myers and Lydia Wilson Myers. Mar Christina Schuster, (br Oct 1746.) Children: Samuel Myers (served in war of 1812). D Jan 26, 1829, in Pa. Bur Bloomingburg Cem, Fayette Co, O. Grave back of cem and to the right in Myers lot. MI: "Jacob Myers died Jan 26, 1829, aged 83 years; also iron star 1776." GM Family and Cem trustees in 1830. Patriot, iron worker, Corporal, in Revolutionary War. He made guns for the Colonial army during first of Rev. Ref: War Dept records and family records, Mrs. Margaret Myers Ingram and children. Mrs. J. R. Tanner, London, O. Fur infor London and Washington C. H. Chaps.

MYERS, PETER, (Holmes Co.)

D Jan 2, 1843. Bur in city park in Millersburg, O. MI: "Honor to whom Honor is due." Beneath the stone lies Peter Myers, died January 2, 1843, aged 80 years. "How sleep the brave who've gone to rest, with all their country's wishes blest." GM flat stone covers the grave upon which is inscription. Hero of three wars in the defense of the rights of man, he bore the certificates of his courage in the many scars on his body, received at the battles of Germantown and Monmouth in the Rev. At Fort Greenville and at the glorious termination of that memorable campaign on the Maumee, and in the late war with Great Britain. Fur infor Wooster-Wayne Chap.

MYRICK, JOSEPH, (Cuyahoga Co.)

Pvt NJ Mil. Br 1775. D 1847. Bur Strongville. Fur infor Western Reserve Chap.

NAIL, HENRY, SR., (Richland Co.)

Pa Continental Army, Pvt in the 8th Company, 7th Bn Chester Co Mil, 1782. Br 1775, Pa. Mar Sarah Nail. Children one was Henry Jr. D 1835 in Mansfield, O. Bur Mansfield Protestant Cem. MI: Name and army dates. GM Mary Washington Chap D. A. R. bronze marker in 1911. Ref: Natl No. 48,482, p 222, Vol 49, D. A. R. Lin. Fur infor Mary Washington Chap.

NASH, SAMUEL, (Athens Co.)

Enl Granby, Mass, Capt Dickinson's Company, Col Ruggles Woodbridge's Regt, 1776; also Lt J Chapin's Detachment. Col Elisha Porter's Regt, enl July 9, 1777, disch Aug 12, 1777. Pvt. Br Feb 1, 1760, Granby, Mass. Mar Vashty Pierre. Children: Uriah, Elizabeth, four others. D Sept 5, 1823, Athens Co, O. Bur Nye Cem, Chauncey, Athens Co, O. MI: "Samuel Nash departed this life Sept 5, 1823, aged 63 years. Vashty, wife of Samuel Nash, departed this life July 31, 1820, aged 57 years." GM descendants. Monument in excellent condition. Ref: Mass Soldiers and Sailors in the War of the Revolution, Vol. 11, p. 283. Nash Genealogy. Fur infor Nabby Lee Ames Chap.

NAUMAN, THOMAS, (Clark Co.)

Member of Boston Tea Party. Br 1754, Mass. Mar Catherine Baker in Va. Children: Henry, Samuel, Mary, Amanda. D Jan 1836, German Twp. Bur Vale, New Carlisle Pike, country cem not platted. MI: Name and dates. GM by family. Came to Ohio from Va, and located in German Twp. Farmer. Ref: Family records. Beers' Clark Co Hist. Fur infor Lagonda Chap.

NAYLOR, WILLIAM, (Wayne Co.)

Ensign in Capt Thomas Goald's Company, 3rd Bn York Co, Pa Mil. Br 1760 near Carlisle, Pa. D 1829, Wooster, O. Ref: Vol 86, p 152, Natl No. 85,397, D. A. R. Lin.

NEAL, ROBERT, (Scioto Co.)

Prisoner on a privateer and carried to England. Br 1755. Mar Margaret Lear (1753-1845). Children: One was Mary Neal (1789-1846) mar Wm Tullock. D 1822, Portsmouth, O. Signed the "Test Oath," 1776, and later was a prisoner on a privateer on which he embarked, and was captured by a British man-of-war and carried to England. His home during the Revolution was New Hampshire. Ref: Natl No. 50,638, p 287, Vol 51, D. A. R. Lin. Fur infor Nathaniel Massie Chap.

NEAL, WILLIAM, (Summit Co.)

Enl July 1779, for three mos as substitute for his father; Oct 1779, 3 mos; on Jan 1, 1780, 1 mo; May 1780, 2 mos; in 1781, for 3 mos; served under Cols Mosley, and Mead, Capts Stoddard, Gridley and Orderly Sgt Frazier. Br Sept 15, 1764, Southington, Conn. Parents: New England Puritans. Mar 1st Abigail Denison to whom 4 children were br. 2nd Abigail Lewis, 1812, at Springfield, Portage Co. D Dec 1842. Bur Middlebury Cem. With 1st wife and four children moved from Conn to Paris, Oneida Co, N. Y. in 1799, where purchased a farm; later settled in Boardman, Trumbull Co and in 1808 moved to Tallmadge; from there to Springfield, Portage Co about 1832, living on his farm until his death. Voted for Gen Harrison in Presidential Campaign 1840. Fur infor Cuyahoga-Portage Chap.

NEFF, CONRAD, (Mahoning Co.)

Sgt in Capt Siegfreid's Company, 8th class, Northampton Mil 1778. Series 5, Vol 8, p 238 Pa Archives. Pvt in Capt Albert Diet's Company (p 455). Dismissed for sickness 1781, (p 466). Capt Diet's Company, 1782 (p 516). Children: John, (mar daughter of Abram Kline); Henry, Mary (mar Henry Crum); Margaret (mar Petry); another daughter (mar Henry Brunstetter). Bur Canfield, O. Came from Lynn, Northampton Co, Pa, in 1802. Mahoning and Trumbull Co Hist, p 962. Fur infor Mahoning Chap.

NEGLEY, PHILIP, (NAGEL, NEAGLE) (Montgomery Co.)

Pvt in Capt Robert Gray's Company, Pa State Regt of Foot: Maj Lewis. Farmer. Was a pensioner. Br 1748. Mar Elizabeth Hoffer, Apr 3, 1771. Children: John C. (br 1783, mar Mary Shuey, another pioneer of Ohio). D 1843, German Twp, Montgomery Co, O. Removed from Sunbury and bur in Germantown Cem. About 1795 he removed from Cumberland Co, Pa, to Mercer Co, Ky. Came to Twin Valley in 1808, and entered land. Ref: S. A. R. Natl No. 37,643. Fur infor Richard Montgomery Chap S. A. R.

NEIGHBARGER, CHRISTIAN, (Logan Co.)

Pensioned in 1840, while serving in Rush Creek Twp, Logan Co, O, age 76, which Commissioner of Pensions writes was for Revolutionary service. Fur infor Bellefontaine Chap.

NELSON, DAVID, (Franklin Co.)

1st Lt in 8th Company, 4th Bn Pa Mil. Br Nov 30, 1752 in southeastern Pa, Mifflintown. D Oct 29, 1829 in Columbus. Bur in Greenlawn Cem. MI: "David Nelson, born Nov 30, 1752 and died Oct 29, 1829." GM Revolutionary Committee with bronze marker, May 30, 1912. Came from Pa and located in Marion Twp, near Alum Creek in 1799. Ref: Vol 33, p 148. Natl No 1999, and Natl No 33,522, D. A. R. Lin. Fur infor Columbus Chap.

NELSON, JOHN JR., (Harrison Co.)

A member of Capt John Marshall's Company Independent Regt; also in Samuel Miles' Rifle Regt raised in Hanover Twp, (then Lancaster Co, Pa.) Mch 22, 1776. Later in the 9th Pa. (p 722, Vol 4, series 5, Pa Archives and also p 223, Vol 10, series 11.) Br 1755 in Ireland. Parents: John Nelson, Sr., Margaret Gilliland. Mar Martha Archbold, 1785. Children: John, James, Benjamin, Hugh, Jane, Samuel, Mary. (Benjamin was a soldier of War of 1812, in Regt raised in Harrison Co, d 1846, bur Cambridge, O.) D Oct 1828, Harrison Co, O. Bur Ridge Presbyterian Churchyard, in or near Cadiz, O. Emigrated from Ireland with his parents in 1771, settling in Pa. Ref: Miss Fannie B. Moorehead, 234 N. Tenth St, Cambridge, O, and others. Natl No 187,299. Fur infor Anna Asbury Stone Chap.

NESBITT, JOHN, (Butler Co.)

In Lancaster Co Mil, as Pvt in Capt John Patton's Company. Br 1744. D 1826, Butler Co, O. Fur infor Natl No. 38,456, Vol 39, p 168, D. A. R. Lin.

NESSLE, JOHN, (Preble Co.)

Bur Mound Hill Cem. Ref: Mary P. Mitchell, Eaton, O. Fur infor Grace Conger Miller, Org Regt.

NEVES, WILLIAM, (Hamilton Co.)

Br 1751, Virgina. D 1836. Fur infor Cincinnati Chap.

NEW, JAMES L. (Logan Co.)

Pensioned in 1840, while living in Rushcreek Twp, Logan Co, O. age 77, for serv which Commissioner of Pensions writes was Revolutionary. Fur infor Bellefontaine Chap.

NEWELL, BENJAMIN, (Delaware Co.)

Pvt under Maj James Wilson, Capt Webb, Rhode Island Mil. Bur Delaware Twp. Pensioned. Fur infor Delaware Chap.

NEWELL, JOHN, (Mahoning Co.)

Pvt in Pa. Pensioned. Born 1739. Mar Susan ——. Bur Mahoning Co. Came to Mahoning Co from Pa. Ref: Pa Archives, Series 3, Vol 23, p 646. Mahoning and Trumbull Co Hist Vol 2. Fur infor Mahoning Chap .

NEWELL, NORMAN, (Summit Co.)

Enl 1776 as Pvt under Capts Whitney and Walker, Col Samuel B. Webb's Regt. Br Farmington, Conn, 1760. D New Portage, O, 1850. Fur infor Cuyahoga-Portage Chap.

NEWLAND, JOHN, (Fayette Co.)

Br 1743, Virginia. D near Rock Mills, 184–. Bur on William Sturgeon farm, near Rock Mills. MI: "John Newland died...." Farmer. Ref: Pensioner, Ross Co, 1818. See Vol 65, D. A. R. Lin p 67, Natl No 64193. Fur infor Washington C. H. Chap.

NEWTON, ————, (Clermont Co.)

Came from New Jersey to Ohio Twp, Clermont Co, O, about 1800. Lived near mouth of Boat Run. Ref: A. S. Abbott, Bethel, O. Fur infor Cincinnati Chap.

NEWTON, ELIAS, (Washington Co.)

Fifer in 5th Conn Regt; under Capt Solomon Wills' 2nd Conn Regt, Capt Clark's Company; 3rd Bn Wadsworth's Brig. Br 1755. D 1841, Marietta. Bur Harmar Cem across the Muskingum River. MI: "Elias Newton 1755-1841." GM Marietta Chap by Revolutionary marker Nov 30, 1906. Ref: "Connecticut in the Revolution." Fur infor Marietta Chap.

NICHOLAS, WILLIAM, (Columbiana Co.)

Bur Hanover M. E. Churchyard. Living in Centre Twp, Columbiana Co in 1833, age 75 yrs. Pensioner. Fur infor Bethia Southwich Chap.

NICHOLS, DAVID, (Medina Co.)

Served as drummer boy from Mass. Br 1763. D 1839. GM Western Reserve Chap. Fur infor Western Reserve Chap.

NICHOLS, FRANCIS, (Hamilton Co.)

Br 1765, New Hampshire. D 1808. Fur infor Cincinnati Chap.

NICHOLS, JAMES, (Cuyahoga Co.)

Sgt of Marine for R. I. Br 1756. D 1829. Bur Strongsville. Fur infor Western Reserve Chap.

NICHOLS, JOHN, (Montgomery Co.)

Name secured fr old Dayton newspaper yrs ago but no other data kept; papers lost in 1913 flood. Fur infor Richard Montgomery Chap S. A. R.

NICHOLAS, JONAS, (Lake Co.)

Enl in Col William Malcolm's Regt in the NY Line. Br 1758, Vermont. D 1843, Perry, O. Bur Perry Cem. GM New Connecticut Chap. Fur infor New Connecticut Chap.

NICHOLS, LEVI, (Licking Co.)

Br 1761. Mar Betsey —— (1764-1849). D 1854. Bur Gaffield Cem, Alexandria Rd. MI: "Revolutionary Soldier." GM by Hetuck D. A. R. Fur infor Hetuck Chap.

NILES, DAVID, (Co. not stated.)

In Monroe, O. Nov 18, 1843. Age 85 yrs. Native of Rhode Island and a pensioner in service in Clarendon, Vt. Ref: D. A. R. Magazine.

NISWONGER, JOHN, (Meigs Co.)

Enl Dec 29, 1776, Winchester, Va. Capt Leman's Company, 13th Va Regt, commanded by Col John Gibson Revolutionary War. Served at Ft Pitt, 1779-1780, Ft Henry, one of the heroes of Point Pleasant. Br 1754, in Va, or Md. German extraction. D July 13, 1821, Meigs Co, O. Tombstone found in tearing down old building where it had been used as a hearthstone. MI: "Sacred to the memory of Col John Niswonger who departed this life July 13, 1821, aged 78 years, 4 mos." Companion of Geo Warth on hunting trips from 1811-1814. On lot 182, Ohio Company purchase beside a spring where he made whiskey and peach brandy. Ref: Natl No 85376, Vol 86, D. A. R. Lin. Fur infor Return Jonathan Meigs Chap.

NISWONGER, SAMUEL, (Montgomery Co.)

Bur Hill Grove Cem, Eaton Pike. Grave not located. Name secured from old Dayton newspaper yrs ago, but no other data kept; papers lost in 1913 flood. Ref: Richard Montgomery Chap, S. A. R.

NIXON, JOHN, (Belmont Co.)

Pvt Capt Nathan Reid's Company, 14th also known as the 10th Virginia Regt; commanded successively by Colonels Lewis, Buford and Davies. He enl May 17, 1777, for three years. Br Apr 17, 1750, Virginia. Mar Nancy Potts prior to 1785 birthdate of son John. Children: John, William. There were other children. D Aug 7, 1833, Belmont Co. Ref: Natl No 30744, Vol 31, p 257, D. A. R. Lin. Fur infor Elizabeth Zane Dew Chap.

NIXON, THOMAS, (Butler Co.)

Bur Greenwood Cem, Hamilton, Butler Co, O. MI: "Thomas Nixon, Revolutionary Soldier." Fur infor John Reily Chap.

NOBLE, SETH, Rev., (Franklin Co.)

Pvt in Capt Dyer's Company and Capt West's Company, Mass Mil. Br 1743 in Mass. D 1807 at Franklinton. Bur Old Franklinton Cem. GM Revolutionary Grave Committee with bronze marker, May 1912. Fur infor Columbus Chap.

NOBLE, WILLIAM, (Clinton Co.)

Service in Md. Troops established by Maryland record. Br Sept 25, 1758. D in Clinton Co, July 11, 1834, and probably bur near New Vienna, O. Ref: Mrs. Luella Caldwell, St Marys, O. Accepting this information, Jane Dailey, State Chairman.

NORRIS, ————, (Delaware Co.)

Bur Baptist Cem. Fur infor Delaware Chap.

NORRIS, ANDREW, (Hamilton Co.)

Br 1762. D 1855. Bur New Light Cem near New Burlington. Pensioned in 1840, age 78, residing in Springfield Twp. Ref: S. A. R. Fur infor Cincinnati Chap.

NORRIS, AQUILLA, (Brown Co.)

Capt in Hartford Co, Md Mil. Br Maryland or Virginia. Mar Priscilla Temperance (d 1805). D 1812, Brown Co, O. Fur infor Natl No. 89,402, Vol 90, p 131, D. A. R. Lin.

NORRIS, JOHN, JR., (Ashtabula Co.)

Pvt in Capt Dan Hatch's Company of teamsters, Conn Line. Br 1765, Plymouth, Mass. D 1840, Windsor, O. Ref: Natl No 85305, Vol 86, p 118, D. A. R. Lin.

NORRIS, GERSHOM, (Hamilton Co.)

Br 1745, New Jersey. Children: One daughter mar Oliver Crain (Crane). D 1830. Bur Burlington, Hamilton Co, O. MI: Name and dates. Ref: S. A. R. list by Jones. Fur infor Cincinnati Chap.

NORRIS, WILLIAM, SR., (Coshocton Co.)

Bur Virginia Twp. Ref: County Hist. Fur infor Coshocton Chap.

NORTHUP, STEPHAN, (Geauga Co.)

Pvt in Capt Beardsley's Company 9th Regt. Enl May 16; disch Dec 11 1775. Br Jan 22, 1759, Ridgefield, Conn. Mar Deborah Robinson. Children: Amaziah N., Prudence, Rachel, Margaret, (br 1804), Lewis, Deborah, James. D Oct 17, 1831, Munson Twp, Geauga Co, O. Bur Fowlers Mills, 1 mile west and 1-4 mile north of center of Munson Twp. MI: "Stephan Northrup, died Oct 17, 1831, aged 72 years. Deborah, wife of Stephan Northrup, died Oct 4, 1844, aged 77 years." GM Marble slab, by relatives; Nathan Perry D. A. R. petitioned County Commissioners in 1922 to provide a marker. Ref: Northrup Genealogy, p 111; Conn Men in Revolution, p 70. Fur infor Nathan Perry Chap.

NORTHUP, DANIEL, (Gallia Co.)

Sgt in Col Archibald McCrary's R. I. Regt 1777. Br June 31, 1738, North Kingston, R. I. Mar Ann Hampton Collins. Children: Henry, Thomas J., Vernon, Hampton, Sarah, Elizabeth Jane. D Nov 10, 1811, near Northrup, O. Bur near Gallipolis, O. Family cem. GM by sandstone slab, letters obliterated. Farmer. Ref: "Rhode Island Cowell Spirit of 76." Mary M. Northrup Fellure. Fur infor French Colony Chap.

NORTON, NOAH, (Huron Co.)

Joined Washington's Body Guard at Wolcott, Conn. Was a pensioner. D 1841. Bur Butterfield Cem, New London Twp. Fur infor Sally De Forest Chap.

NORTON, OZIAS, (Portage Co.)

Pvt in Conn Mil. Placed on pension roll Aug 20, 1833. Bur Charlestown, O. Drew pension at Ravenna, O, in 1840. Fur infor Old Northwest Chap.

NORTON, PETER, JR., (Summit Co.)

Pvt. Capt Benjamin Smith's Company. Enl Oct 1775 to Dec 1775, for defense of coast. D 1823. Fur infor Cuyahoga-Portage Chap.

NORWOOD, STEPHEN, (Lake Co.)

Served for eight mos in Boston. Br 1762, Mass. D Aug 1, 1842, Perry, Lake Co, O. Bur South Ridge Cem near the little Church. GM by New Connecticut Chap. Fur infor New Connecticut Chap.

NUTT, AARON, (Montgomery Co.)

Scout and teamster in the Continental Army, Company of Capt Shreve, NJ Mil. Br June 17, 1758, Mount Holly, N. J. Parents: Levi and Anna (Ivins) Nutt. Mar 1st May 4, 1778 Mary Archer, (br Nov 28, 1756, d Sept 22, 1817); mar 2nd wife Martha (Pedrich) Craig, Jan 11, 1818, (d Mch 20, 1856). Children, 1st, Levi, Sarah, Mary, Aaron, Joseph, Abigail, Ann, Bathsheba, Mariah; 2nd wife, Joseph, John. D July 2, 1842, in Centerville, O. Bur Baptist Cem, Centerville, O, in center of cem. MI: "Aaron Nutt, born June 17, 1758, died 2nd of 6 month, 1842, aged 83 years, 10 mos, 16 das." GM Richard Montgomery Chap, S. A. R. July 1, 1919. Prominent surveyor, came from Ky in 1796, and returned for his family, and built a cabin on a farm he selected. This was the nucleus of other frontier homes where the privations and rude pleasures of pioneer life formed a bond of fellowship of sympathy. Benjamin Archer, (probably his brother-in-law) came at same time, but in 1824 removed to Ft Wayne, Ind. He was the founder of Centerville. Ref: S. A. R. descendant Benjamin Weir, Charleston, Ills. Fur infor Richard Montgomery Chap, S. A. R.

NUTT, JOHN, (Fayette Co.)

Served as Pvt in a Regt Tr Va Mil Forces. Br Jan 1737, Loudoun Co, Va. Mar Hannah (?) 1775 in Va. Children: James Nutt, only child. D Jan 1837, Fayette Co, O. Bur Old Burying Ground at Yankeetown, Fayette Co, O. MI: "John Nutt, died Jan, 1837, aged 100 years." Came from Loudoun Co, Va, to Fayette Co, O, 1805. Ref: Natl No 70405, Vol 71, D. A. R. Lin. Fur infor Washington C. H. Chap.

NYE, EBENEZER, (Washington Co.)

Pvt. Served in 3rd Regt Conn Line, formation of 1781-1783, Capt Bulkley's Company; he was paid from Jan 1, 1781, to Dec 31, 1783 (Connecticut Men in the Revolution, p 331). An alphabetical list of the Conn army returned for yr 1781 to 1782 gives Ebenezer Nye in the 3rd Regt (Conn Archives, series 1, Vol 30, p 71). Br Oct 21, 1750, Tolland, Conn. Parents: George and (Mrs) Thankful (Hatch) Nye. Mar Desire Sawyer Mch — 1776. Children: George, Sarah, Lewis, Melzar, Neal, Mathew, Theodorus. D Feb 27, 1823, Rainbow, Washington Co, O. Bur in Rainbow Cem. Pioneer burial ground donated by Ebenezer Nye. MI: "B Oct 21, 1750. D Feb 28, 1823. My Saviour shall my life restore, And raise me from my dark abode, My flesh and soul shall part no more, But dwell forever near my God." Sandstone-tombstone intact. He migrated from Conn to Marietta, O, in 1790, and to Rainbow in 1795. He preached the Gospel, also held civil offices. Member of Baptist Church. Ref: See Nye Genealogy, by G. H. Nye & F. E. Best, 1907, p 211. Natl No 215405. Fur infor Elizabeth Zane Dew Chap.

NYE, GEORGE (NIGH), (Fairfield Co.)

Br 1755, Pennsylvania. D 1830, Fairfield Co, O. Ref: Natl No 238433 D. A. R. Fur infor Mrs. Lowell Hobart, fr Records at Washington.

NYE, ICHABOD, (Washington Co.)

Enl at age of 16 in Revolutionary Army. Br Dec 21, 1763, Tolland, Conn. Mar Minerva Tupper. D Nov 27, 1840, Marietta, O. Bur Mound Cem, Marietta, O. MI: "Ichabod Nye, 1763-1840." GM Marietta Chap by Revolutionary marker and gateway, Nov 30, 1906; marker stolen and replaced in 1920. Ref: Natl No. 28238, Vol 29, p 87, D. A. R. Lin. Fur infor Marietta Chap.

O'BRIEN, DANIEL, (Cuyahoga Co.)

Privateer Maryland Continental. Br 1734. Alive 1818. Bur Rice Cem, Brecksville. Fur infor Western Reserve Chap.

O'DONNELL, WILLIAM, (Columbiana Co.)

Bur Catholic Cem Dungannon. Fur infor Bethia Southwick Chap.

OGILVIE, THOMAS, (Coshocton Co.)

Pvt in Va Tr 1778. Br 1740 in Scotland. Mar 1783, Jane Taylor. D 1842, Coshocton, O. Ref: Natl No 101947, Vol 103, p 288 D. A. R. Lin.

OHLE, HENRY, SR., (Mahoning Co.)

Pvt and Lt in Heidelburg Twp, Northampton Co. Pensioned. Br 1753. Mar Abbie Lark. Children: Michel, David, Henry, John, Jacob, Abraham, Eve Hood, Maria Waggoner, Mary Shotts. D 1849. Bur "Old Dutch" Cem, Canfield. GM: Mahoning Chap, bronze, in 1917. Ref: Pa Archives, Series 3, Vol 23, p 592, Series 2, Vol 13, p 176, Series 5, Vol 8, p 514, Trumbull and Mahoning Co His, Vol 2. Fur infor Mahoning Chap.

OLDFIELD, WILLIAM (Richland Co.)

Enl 1777, serving under Capts William Clark, Rosecrans, DeWitt and Richard Goldsmith, Col Geo Clinton's Regt NY Tr. In 1833 applied for pension and allowed. Br 1750, Orange Co, NY. Mar Elizabeth (Betsy) Taylor (br 1757). D 1834, Bellville, Richland Co. Ref: Natl No. 74046, Vol 75, D. A. R. Line.

OLDRIDGE, HENRY, (Adams Co.)

Bur Ohio Brush Creek, either in Foster or McColm Cem. Fur infor Sycamore Chap.

OLIVER, ALEXANDER, (Clermont Co.)

Lt of Capt Abel Dinsmore's Company, Col David Field's 5th Regt Hampshire Co, Mass Mil 1766. Br 1744, Worcester, Mass. Mar Mary Warner in 1794 (br 1750, d 1808). D 1829, Point Pleasant, O. Ref: Natl No 13680, 100058, Vol 101, p 18, D. A. R. Lin.

OLIVER, ALEXANDER, (Washington Co.)

Corp in Capt Josiah King's Company, Col David Brewer's Regt; also Sgt in Capt Shay's Company, Col Putnam's Regt. Br Brookfield, Mass. D Belpre, O. Bur Belpre, O. Settled at Belpre in 1789 on lot No 16 just below what is now Cedarville. During the Indian War his family found shelter in "Farmers Castle." Ref: Mass Soldiers and Sailors. Fur inform Marietta Chap.

OLIVER, ROBERT, Col., (Washington Co.)

Entered serv as a Lt marching with a Company of Minute Men to Cambridge where he was advanced to a Captaincy in the 3rd Mass Regt. In 1777 he was commissioned Maj and 1779 promoted to Lt Col of the 10th Regt At the close of war made Colonel by brevet. Br 1738, Boston, Mass. D May, 1810, Waterford, O. In company with Maj Hatfield White and Capt John Dodge he erected a sawmill and grist mill on Wolf Creek in Waterford District about a mile from the creek's mouth. In 1790 moved to Marietta. Representative from Washington Co in Territorial Legislature in 1798. Ref: Hildreth's Pioneer Hist. Fur infor Marietta Chap.

OLIVER, THOMAS, (Jackson Co.)

Joined 6th Va Regt under Col Muhlenberg in 1779, served 3 yrs and 7 mos. Br May 10, 1763, Maryland. Mar 3 times; first wife, Sarah Edwards, dau of Joseph Edwards. (d Mason Co, Va.) Children: William, Thomas, Charles, Wesley, Nancy, Rebecca, Elizabeth, Sarah, all lived to maturity. D Feb 23, 1844, aged 80 yrs. Bur Mt. Zion Cem near Jackson, Jackson Co. Monument. Father died when he was 14, lived with Uncle Loffland, Loudoun Co, Va, until enlisting; in 1816 came to Ohio settled at Symee Creek, leasing part of school land. Pensioned 1834, getting $80 a year. Ref: son by second wife, Hiram Oliver, furnished this data to D. W. Williams. Fur infor Capt John James Chap.

OLMSTEAD, FRANCIS, (Franklin Co.)

Served in Col Webb's Regt Continental Line as Ensign in Capt John F. Wyllis' Company from 1778 to 1781. Br Simsburg, Conn, in 1760. D 1828, Blendon Twp. Bur in Central Cem, Blendon Twp, two miles southeast of Central College. MI: "Died Jan 21, 1828, in the 68th yr of his age." GM Revolutionary Grave Committee. Bronze marker May 30, 1912. Emigrated to Ohio with his family of sons in 1810, and settled in Blendon Twp, Franklin Co. Fur infor Columbus Chap.

ORR, JAMES, (Miami Co.)

Enl in Kentucky, 1794, under Wayne. D 1859, aged 85 yrs. Bur Raper Chapel Cem. GM Miami Chap with bronze marker in 1904. Fur infor Miami Chap.

ORR, WILLIAM, (Mahoning Co.)

Ranger in Washington Co, Pa, and Westmoreland Co, Capt Andrew Sweatingen, Cumberland Co, Pa. Pensioned. Br 1755. Mar Mary —— (1759-1849). Children: James, Margaret, Humphrey, William, Thomas, Russell, Anna, Abraham, Isaac, Mary. (Anna, mar John Johnson). D 1815 or 1825 (1815 thus reported). Bur Old Covenanters Cem, Jackson Twp on the brow of the hill. Ref: Pa Archives, 3 series, Vol 23, pp 199, 212, 312, 810, Trumbull and Mahoning Co History Vol 2. Fur infor Mahoning Chap.

ORTON, LEMUEL, (Delaware Co.)

Served 5 yrs as Pvt under Col Elisha Sheldon and Capts Stoddard, Hoagland, Wadsworth, 2nd Regt Continental Light Dragoons, Conn Tr. Battles of Brandywine, Monmouth, Frog's Neck and Young's at Tarrytown. Was shot in the head, but not entirely disabled. Br Mch 5, 1761, Litchfield, Conn. Mar Sibbel Peck in 1785, (br 1762, died 1850). Bur Trenton Twp. MI: "Lemuel Orton, Jr. died Sept 29, 1831, in the 71st year of his age." GM by Revolutionary Grave Committee with bronze marker May 30, 1912. Pensioned Sept 21, 1818. Amount $1,290.66, annual allowance $96.00. Settled in Conn and lived there several yrs. Later moved to Ohio and settled on a farm north of Worthington. Ref: Compare Natl No. 69,100, Vol 70, p 39, and Natl No. 70,281, Vol 71, p 102, D. A. R. Lin. Fur infor Delaware and Columbus Chap.

OSBORN, JOSIAH, (Co not stated.)

Received on claim executed 1833 for serv as Pvt, 1777 Conn Tr, under Capt David Olmstead, and in N. Y. under Capt Thos Hunt 1781. Br 1761, Ridgefield, holdings. Held several Twp Offices and member of M. E. Church. Ref: Mrs. Nellie Osborn Callaway, Lenox, Iowa.

OSBORN, JOSHUA, (Trumbull Co.)

Pvt. Served first in Capt Theopolis Whunson's Company of New Haven, attached to 8th Regt. Participated in battles Germantown and Monmouth, in winter 1778-79. Regt under command Col John Chandler. Granted pension under Act of Congress of 1818. Br Feb 18, 1759, Waterbury, Conn. Parents: Amos Osborn and Elizabeth Hotchbiss. Mar Diana Warner, 1781. Children: Reuben, Chloe, Sheldon, Gilbert, Leonard, Stephen, Sterling, Dorcas, Rosanna, Amanda, Anna, Phebe. D Sept 27, 1837, Southington, O. Bur Center Cem, Southington, about center of cem. MI: Name of Joshua Osborn and wife, date of their births and deaths. GM by his estate. Drew pension under act of legislature of 1812. He wintered in Valley Forge 1777-1778 and quartered in Conn village on the Hudson in 1778-1779. Regt under command of Col John Chandler. Farmer, large land holdings. Held several Twp Offices and member of M. E. Church. Ref: Mrs. Mable Troxal, Glendale, Calif, and Natl No 85,887, Vol 86, D. A. R. Lin. Fur infor Mary Chesney Chap.

OSBORNE, NICHOLAS, (Mahoning Co.)

Served in the Rev in Va. Pensioner. Br 1724, England. Parents: Richard Osborn, Jr. Mar Margaret Conard. Children: Jonathan (mar ——— Russell), Sarah, (mar Jas Russell), Abraham, (mar Rachel Potts), Richard, John, (mar Polly Fig), Betsey (mar Ben Beal), Anthony, Joseph, (mar Marg Wolfcale), Aaron, (mar McSorky), Mary. D June 30, 1818, near Junction of 4 twp corners, (Youngstown, Boardman, Canfield and Austintown.) Bur Cornersburg, near Youngstown, O. On account of his feeling about slavery he sold his fine home in Va and in 1804 moved to Ohio where he purchased 1110 acres of land and settled. P 108 Biog. E. Ohio-Summers. Va Men of the Revolution, p 218 gives Capt Osburne, 1777, but the given name is omitted. Fur infor Mahoning Chap.

OSMAN, CHARLES, (Adams Co.)

Bur on Satterfield farm on Blue Creek. Ref: Hist of Adams Co. Fur infor Sycamore Chap.

OSWALD, JACOB, (Mahoning Co.)

Pvt 6th Continental Line. Enl Apr 3, 1777. Pa Archives, series 5, Vol 111, p 125, 3d class Northampton Co, Capt Stohler's Company, Vol 8, p 227. Mar——— Everett, daughter of Samuel Everett. Children: Charles. Cem not located. Came from Lynn Twp, Northampton Co, Pa in 1802 and located in Canfield, O, later moved to Liberty Twp. Farmer. Ref: "Trusdale's History of Canfield." Fur infor Mahoning Chap.

OTIS, BARNABAS, (Marion Co.)

Enl at Lebanon, Conn in fall of 1775 under Capt Keyer, Col Durkee Continental Establishment, Conn. Disch at Morristown, N. J. Engaged in the battle of Princeton. Pensioner. Br 1756, Mass. Mar Mehitable Turner, 1783, (d 1850). D Jan 15, 1850, Marion Co, O. Bur Paw Paw Cem, Grand Twp, Marion Co, O. Applied for pension in 1818. Ref: Natl No. 102,639, Vol 103, 196 D. A. R. Lin. Fur infor Capt William Hendricks Chap.

OVERLY, FREDERICK, (Ross Co.)

Scout. Br Feb 27, 1766. Parents: Father was Martin Overley. Mar Mary Ann ——— (d Jan 5, 1850, aged 75 yrs 9 mos 4 days). Children: Elizabeth (mar John Hoarp and d Aug 2, 1843), three dau, given names unknown (who mar Mr. Smitley, Mr. Whelan and Mr. Jennings, respectively), and two sons, names unknown, but thought to be Jacob and John. Jacob served in War of 1812. D May 3, 1848, in Springfield Twp, Ross Co. Bur Overly Chapel, Springfield Twp. MI: "In Memory of Frederick Overley, who departed this life May 3, 1848; aged 82 yrs 2 mos 6 days. A Country far from mortal sight, yet, oh, by Faith I see the land of rest, the saints' delight, The Heaven prepared for me." G Meech. Lived in Bourbon Co, Ky. In 1797 came to Ross Co with his father, Martin, and brothers, Boston and Martin. Kept bachelor hall until fall, when they had cleared land and planted crops, they returned to Ky and brought their families back. No road, only an Indian trail. His wife carried 8 wks old babe and spinning wheel on her horse. Ref: Hist of Ross and Highland Co, p 231. Fur infor Nathaniel Massie Chap.

OVERMYER, GEORGE, (Perry Co.)

Capt. Br 1755. Bur village cem, New Reading, O. GM Tombstone. Fur infor Nathaniel Hetuck Chap.

OVERMYER, PETER, (Perry Co.)

Served in Capt George Overmyer's Company Pa. Br 1761. D 1843. Bur village cem, New Reading, O. GM by Tombstone. Fur infor Hetuck Chap.

OVIATT, SAMUEL, (Trumbull Co.)

Br 1741. Mar Sarah ——— (br May 12. 1733, d Sept 7, 1823). D Apr 18, 1818. Bur Braceville. MI: "Samuel Oviatt, born Feb 22, 1741, died Apr 18, 1818." GM by relative and kept in good condition. Fur infor Mary Chesney Chap.

OWEN, JAMES, (Washington Co.)

Pvt 3rd Company Sam'l Phillips, Capt Col Jos Stanton's Regt. 15 mos serv, RI. Return June 6, 1777, Pvt same Regt, received pay from May 10 to Sept 1777. Return dated ——— Nov 10, 1777. Pvt same Company same Regt, under Col Wm Barton, pay for 3 mos serv Sept 1 to Dec 1, 1777. Pvt same Company, same Regt, under Col John Topham from Dec 1, to Mch 16, 1778. Return dated Mch 10, 1778; Enl for town of North Kingston in State Bn June 12, 1778; Pvt Capt Alex Thomas' Company, Col John Topham's Regt. In US serv pay from July 16 to Aug 16, 1778; Nov 16 to Dec 16, 1778; Jan 16 to Mch 16, 1779. Pvt Col John Topham's Regt. On Crary's Balances reported due by a committee Oct, 1785. Br 1750. D 1799. Bur near Lowell, Washington Co. GM by D. A. R. Ref: Military Returns S. A. R. Vol 1, p 48, Vol 2, pp 63, 51, 37, 40, 26, 11, Vol 4, pp 83, 84 85, 66, 65, Vol 3, p 7. Fur infor Marietta Chap.

OWEN, NOAH, (Licking Co.)

In Col Wyllis' Regt of Conn Tr. Br 1756 Hebron, Conn. Mar Elizabeth Gilmore. D 1821, Licking Co, O. Ref: Natl No 56620, Vol 57, p 214 D. A. R. Lin.

OWEN, THOMAS, (Columbiana Co.)

Living in Middleton Twp, Columbiana Co, in 1833 at the age of 80 yrs. Fur infor Bethia Southwick Chap.

OWENS, WILLIAM, (Jackson Co.)

Enl 1775. Pvt in Capt John Stephenson's Company, Col Muhlenberg's Regt, and in 1779 in the 8th Virginia Continental Line, Capt Robert Beall, Col Gibson. Br Frederick Co, Va in 1762. Mar Nancy Creage in (1797). D 1829, Jackson Co. Ref: Natl No 54577, Vol 55, p 249 D. A. R. Lin. Fur infor Captain John James Chap.

OWERY, GEORGE, (Trumbull Co.)

Ensign. Enl Westmoreland Co, Pa. Engaged in battles of Long Island, White Plains, Fort Washington, Trenton. Br Aug 18, 1757. Parents: (He might have been the son "George" of "George Owery" bur in Mahoning Co, O.) D Oct 20, 1844. Bur Marion Cem, Niles, O. MI: no stone but application for stone has been made. War office verified service and notice has been sent that order had been issued to Boston for shipment of stone. Ref: Mrs. Eliza Parker Tibbitts. Fur infor Mary Chestney Chap.

OWRY, GEORGE, (Mahoning Co.)

Ensign. Pensioned. Br 1744. Children: Nancy, Elizabeth, Catherine, Mary, Francis, John, George. D 1844. Bur Old Dutch Cem, Canfield. GM by Mahoning Chap. Bronze, May 30, 1917. Ref: Pa Archives, 3 Series, Vol 23, p 592 and Harriet Comes, Natl No 149180 D. A. R. Lin. Fur infor Mahoning Chap.

PACK, WILLIAM, (Hamilton Co.)

Pvt Maryland Mil. Br 1758, in Frederick Co, Md. D Hamilton Co, O. Mar Phoebe O'Neal. Ref: Natl No. 70,130, p 48, Vol 71, D. A. R. Lin.

PAGE, BENJAMIN, (Stark Co.)

Capt in Rhode Island State Trs, Aug 4, 1775, until Jan 1776. Served in Navy from 1776 to 1780. Was 1st Lt when surrendered to British Navy at Charleston, S. C., May 12, 1780. Paroled and exchanged Sept 13, 1780. Bur West Lawn Cem, Canton Twp. MI: "Revolutionary Soldier." Fur infor Canton Chap.

PAINE, EDWARD, Capt., (PAYNE), (Lake Co.)

1st Lt in June, 1776. Was Lt and Capt in 1777 until the close of the war. Was later Brig Gen in Mil in N. Y. State. Br 1746, Bolton, Conn. Mar Rebecca White. D Aug 28, 1841, Painesville, O. Bur Painesville, O. GM New Connecticut Chap. He came to Painesville from Aurora, N. Y. and purchased a thousand acres of land; pensioned 1831. He lies buried in Painesville under a monument erected to his memory. Ref: Natl No. 30140, Vol 31, D. A. R. Lin. Fur infor New Connecticut Chap.

PAINE, ELEAZER, (Lake Co.)

Enl as drummer boy in Capt Bett's Company, 2nd Conn Regt, commanded by Col Zebulon Butler. Enl July 5, 1780 for six mos. Br 1764, East Windsor, Conn. Parents: Stephen Paine, 5th. Mar Aurel Ellsworth. D Feb 10, 1804. Bur in old cem at Painesville, O. GM New Connecticut Chap. Ref: Natl No 31052. Vol 32, D. A. R. Lin. Fur infor New Connecticut Chap.

PAINE, JOHN, (Delaware Co.)

Bur Baptist Cem, Scioto Twp. Fur infor Delaware Chap.

PALMER, ADAM, (Cuyahoga Co.)

Bur Center Warrensville. GM Western Reserve Chap. Ohio Pension Roll. Fur infor Western Reserve Chap.

PALMER, ALVA, (Huron Co.)

Br 1741; came fr Fairfield Co, Conn. D May 27, 1827. Bur Fitchville, O. Fur infor Sally DeForest Chap.

PALMER, JOHN, (Belmont Co.)

Enl Oct 1780, length of service Oct 29, 1782. Pvt. Serv rendered under Capt Hardage Lane Marshall of Va; Samuel Sheldon, Va; Col Samuel Hawes, 1st Va. Was taken prisoner by the Tories and exchanged. Engaged in battles in Guilford Court House, Camden and Eutaw Springs. Enl at Loudoun Co, Va. Made application for pens Nov 23, 1818. His claim was allowed. Residence at date of application was Belmont Co, Ohio. He was 59 years of age. Ref: Record Division M. B. H. Sur file 8929, Revolutionary War Dept of the Interior Bureau of Pensions, Washington, D. C. Fur infor Kokosing Chap.

PALMER, JOSEPH, JR., (Washington Co.)

Served as Capt of 7th Company or train band in 21st Regt, Mch 1775. This Regt was composed of companies from Plainview, Centerburg and Voluntown and the S. Society of Killingly, Conn. (Ref: "Palmers History." Certified letter of Asst Adj Gen, Hartford, Conn.) Br 1761, Scotland, Windham Co, Conn. Parents: Joseph Palmer, Sr (also a Revolutionary soldier) and Abigail Bassell. Mar Hannah Fox, 1785, Washington Co, O. Bur Palmer Twp. GM Marietta Chap D. A. R. Revolutionary marker, 1825. Joseph Palmer enl at the age of 16 yrs; served his time and disch 10 days before New London was taken by the British. He was rendered a cripple from a sore, after effects of war probably. Ref: Miss Martha Palmer, Williamstown, W. Va; Mrs Julia Reed, Marietta, O. Fur infor Marietta Chap.

PALMITER, JOHN, (Cuyahoga Co.)

Pvt Continental Conn Tr. Br 1751. D 1834. Bur Bedford, in a field. A lot was donated to the twp for burial purposes. Fur infor Western Reserve Chap.

PALMITER, JESHUA, (Cuyahoga Co.)

Pvt RI Mil. Bur Harvard Grove Cem, Lansing Ave and East 57th, Cleveland, O. GM Western Reserve Chap. Fur infor Western Reserve Chap.

PANGBURN, JOSEPH, (Mahoning Co.)

"NJ Men of the Revolution"—Matross. Capt Neil's Company (Eastern) Artillery, State Tr. Disch Mch 1777. "Jersey Men in the Revolution," p 710. Burial place not located. Came to Canfield in 1798. Ref: Trumbull and Mahoning Co Hist, pp 11 and 12. Fur infor Mahoning Chap.

PARK, REUBEN, (Montgomery Co.)

Capt Douglas' Company, 5th Regt Conn Line. Br 1764, Sharon, Conn. D 1856, Miamisburg. Ref: Natl No 87088, Vol 88, p 26, D. A. R. Lin

PARKER, BENJAMIN, (Medina Co.)

Enl 1775 under Capt Isaac Cook; re-enlisted for three years, 1778, and in 1781 served under Capt Lemuel Clift, Conn Line. Br 1755, Wallingford, Conn. D 1823, Brunswick, O. Ref: Natl No 52201, Vol 53, p 94; also Natl No 34580, D. A. R. Lin.

PARKER, HIRAM, (Meigs Co.)

Children: Mrs Wyatt Burgess. Bur Tuppers Plains, upper lot. Fur infor Return Jonathan Meigs Chap.

PARKER, JOHN, (Hamilton Co.)

Br 1761, New Jersey. D 1884. Living in Springfield Twp. Ref S. A. R. Fur infor Cincinnati Chap.

PARKER, JOHN, (Harrison Co.)

A Revolutionary pensioner living in Washington Twp, Harrison Co, 1822, aged 68. Served as Sgt in the 5th, 7th and 8th Pa Line Regts. U. S. Pension Rolls, 1835. Pa Archives 5th Series, Vol III, 43, 57, 86, 225, 372. Fur infor Moravian Trail Chap.

PARKER, LOVELL, (Trumbull Co.)

80 yrs old at time of death. Bur in old cem at Kinsman; location of grave known, but no marker, or monument. Fur infor Mary Chesney Chap.

PARKER, SAMUEL, (Ashtabula Co.)

D 1835. Bur Kelloggsville. Ref: Bert Wiley, Conneaut, O. Fur infor Mary Redmond Chap.

PARKER, STILES, (Delaware Co.)

Pvt under Col John Brooks, Capt Luke Day. 7th Mass Regt. Bur Burkshire Twp. Fur infor Delaware Chap.

PARKISON, DANIEL, or PARKINSON, or PARKESON, (Perry Co.)

Pvt; Served in Capt Samuel McCune's Company; Col Frederick Watts' Bn of the Flying Camp, Pa. Enl Nov 1777. Capt John Geo Overmyer's Company, Col Morrow's Pa Regt served out the yr. Served from Va, for a time; a Pvt in York Co, Pa Mil under Capt Ephriam Pennington in 1781-82; also Ranger on frontiers for Northumberland Co, Pa, 1778-83. Br Mch 2, 1754, York Co, Pa. Parents: Edward Parkison (br in England), (wife of German descent—name unknown). Mar Catherine Overmyer, Feb 16, 1777, dau of John Geo and Eva (Rosenbaum) Overmyer. Children: Mary, George, Margaret, John, Catherine, Elizabeth, Daniel, Jacob, Esther, Samuel. D Jan 7, 1883, Somerset, O. Bur village cem, New Reading, O. MI: Illegible. A witness of Washington's tears at death of his men by Hessians, at capture of Ft. Lee. A scout; 1808 came to Ohio, operated saw mill; farm ½ mile north of Somerset, Glenford Rd, believed his house still stands. Pensioned 1832, No. 18542. Full infor John W. Parkinson, Newark, O. Ref: Anna M. Priest. Pa Archives, Series 5, Vol 4, pp 689-90; Graham's Hist Perry Co. Natl Nos 198884, 98453 and 107555 of D. A. R. Fur infor Hetuck Chap and Mrs. Edith Stanford, Olympia, Washington.

PARKINSON, THOMAS, (Harrison Co.)

Served from Middle District, Frederick Co, in Capt Valentine Creagar's Company, Frederick Co Mil. US Pension Rolls, 1835. Br 1762. D 1838. Bur Greenwood Graveyard, Green Twp. A Revolutionary pensioner living in Harrison Co in 1833, aged 71. Ref: Md Archives XVIII, 411. Fur infor Moravian Trail Chap.

PARKS, AMAZIAH, (Lake Co.)

Served five enlistments in the Conn Tr from 1776 to 1781. Was in the Battle of White Plains. Br 1758, Sterling, Windham Co, Conn. Mar Sabra Barrett, Feb 1798. D Nov 4, 1838. Bur Evergreen Cem, Painesville, O. GM New Connecticut Chap. He was a pensioner. Fur infor New Connecticut Chap.

PARKS, ELIJAH, (Portage Co.)

Lived at Palmyra where pensioned in 1840. Fur infor Old Northwest Chap.

PARKS, MICHAEL, (Huron Co.)

Pensioner. Br Portsmouth, N. H. Bur Episcopal Cem, Norwalk, O. Fur infor Sally De Forest Chap.

PARKS, NATHAN, (Geauga Co.)

Pvt. Enl at Westfield, Mass, 1777, Col Woodbridge's Regt. Disch at White Plains, Dec 1777. Enl June 1778 Col Wm Shepard's Regt. Disch Feb 1781, Gen Patterson. Br Westfield, Conn. May 6, 1758. Mar Mary A. Mally, 2nd widow Bishop. Children: Abigail, Olive, Hiram, Salome, Lewis, Celia, Fanny, Wigram, D Oct 1, 1849, Burton, O. Bur Fox Cem, Burton. MI: "Nathan Parks died Dec 19, 1849 aged 92, Mary his wife died Jan 30, 1831 age 68." GM by Family. Was at battle of Bennington, went to Saratoga after Burgoyne's surrender, spent winter at Valley Forge. Came to Burton, O in 1800. Ref: Ohio Pension Rolls, p 124. Census of Pensions 1843, p 172. Fur infor Taylor Camp.

PARMELEE, JOHN, (Greene Co.)

Drummer in Conn Mil. Br 1755. D 1828, Sullivan, O. (Tho states Greene Co, Sullivan is in Ashland Co, but did not change.) Ref: Natl No 36907, Vol 37, p 316, D. A. R. Lin.

PARRETT, FRED, (Ross Co.)

Called to serv at siege of Yorktown, witnessed the surrender of Cornwallis. Served as Pvt. Br 1764, near Woodstock, Shenandoah Co, Va. Parents: Frederick and Barbara Edwards Parrett. Mar Elizabeth Kellar about 1785. Children: John, Joseph, Sarah P, McArthur, George, Frederick, Rachel Ware, Rebecca, Fernow, Elizabeth, Humphrey, Mary P. Harper, Henry, Barbara P. Harper, Ann P. Harper. D May 8, 1842 near South Salem, O. Bur South Salem. GM Nathaniel Massie Chap D. A. R. Frederick Parrett served in Va Mil as Ensign from 1786. Last commission was dated 1794. Served in war of 1812. Came to Ohio 1814. A farmer near South Salem. Ref: Jessie T. Mains Natl No 172392. Fur infor Nathaniel Massie Chap.

PARROTT, JOSEPH, Capt., (Clinton Co.)

Bur Sugar Grove Cem, Wilmington. Fur infor George Clinton Chap.

PARSHALL, SAMUEL, (Mahoning Co.)

In 1775 Pvt in Capt Phineas Rumsey's Company, later Capt Marvin's Company, Col Drake's Regt. Br 1757, Long Island. D 1817, Ellsworth, O. Mar Elizabeth Goucher. Ref: Natl No 70675, Vol 71, p 244. D. A. R. Lin.

PARSONS, JABEZ, (Erie Co.)

Sgt in Wolcott's Regt of Conn Tr. Minute Man at Lexington. Br 1753, Enfield, Conn. D 1836, Huron, O. Bur in Huron, O. Ref: Natl No 33530, Vol 34, p 190, D. A. R. Lin. Fur infor Martha Pitkin Chap.

PARSONS, JOHN, SR., (Greene Co.)

Bur Union Churchyard, Byron. Living in Bath 1829. Ref: Robinson's Hist of Greene Co. Fur infor Catherine Greene Chap.

PARSONS, OSBORN, (Hamilton Co.)

Br 1763, Conn. D 1827, Cincinnati, O. Ref: S. A. R. Fur infor Cincinnati Chap.

PARSONS, SAMUEL H., (Washington Co.)

Col, Brig Gen and Maj Gen. Br 1737, Lynn, Conn. D Nov 17, 1789. Drowned in Great Beavers Creek, 1789. GM Marietta Chapter, name on gateway, Nov 30. 1906. Harvard Graduate. Lawyer; member of Gen Assembly of Conn. Judge of Supreme Court for Northwest Territory. Ref: Natl No 55256, D. A. R. Fur infor Marietta Chap.

PARTNER, JOHN, (Trumbull Co.)

Enl 1776 in Capt Benjamin Weiser's Company, German Bn Continental Line. Br 1740, Germany. D Trumbull Co, O. Ref: Natl No 58745, Vol 59, pp 255, 56. D. A. R. Lin.

PATEE, EDMOUND, (Morrow Co.)

Fifer under Col John Brooks, Capts Corburn and Thorp 7th Mass Regt. Br 1764, Salem, N. H. D 1824, Westfield, O. Bur Westfield Twp, Morrow Co. Ref: Natl No 27309, Vol 28, D. A. R. Lin. Fur infor Mt. Gilead Chap.

PATTERSON, JAMES, (Mahoning Co.)

Ranger, 1778-1783, Cumberland Co. Bur Mahoning Co. Came to Canfield in 1803. Farmer. Ref: Old Deeds, Pa Archives, Series 3, Vol 23. Fur infor Mahoning Chap.

PATTERSON, JOHN, (Preble Co.)

Bur Isreal Twp. Ref: Mary P. Mitchell, Eaton, O. Fur infor Grace Conger Miller, Org Reg.

PATTERSON, ROBERT, Col., (Montgomery Co.)

He began his military career as a member of a company of rangers in 1774. He accompanied Gen George Rogers Clark in the Illinois Campaign in 1778, and in 1786 Patrick Henry, Gov of Va, commissioned him as Capt. Br 1759, Bedford Co, Pa. Mar Elizabeth Lindsey, 20th of Mch, 1790. Children: Margaret, Elizabeth, Francis, Catherine, Jane, Harriet, Robert, Jefferson. D Aug 5, 1827, Dayton, O. Bur Woodland Cem, Dayton. Lot 2871, Section 13. GM Sons of the American Revolution, Bronze Marker in 1919. In Spring of 1775 he came west to Fort Pitt. In 1779 he laid out the city of Lexington, Ky. 1781 Thomas Jefferson, Gov of Va, commissioned him Capt of Volunteers; and 1783 he was Justice of the Peace in Fayette Co, was chosen delegate to the convention to separate Virginia and Kentucky. Natl No of Revolutionary Soldier in D. A. R. Honor Roll 92345. Pensioned 1812, for serv in Colonial U. S. Inf. Fur infor Jonathan Dayton Chap.

PATTERSON, ROBERT, (Wayne Co.)

Br 1752. D Aug 30, 1834, Congress Village. Bur Congress Cem, Congress Twp, in old cem near Congress Village. MI: "Robert Patterson, Died Aug 30, 1834." He is mentioned many times in the Pa Archives, first as a ship owner or Capt with Mediterranean Registry. Later as a Capt of Inf he commanded a company May 10, 1780. Ref: 5 Series, Vol 5, pp 312, 313, 354, 423, 425, 432, 434, 444. Fur infor Wooster-Wayne Chap.

PATTERSON, WILLIAM, (Mahoning Co.)

Pvt. Washington Co, Pa. Bur Mahoning Co. Farmer. Bought land from Calvin Austin in 1803. Ref: Pa Archives, Series 6, Vol 2, p 134. Fur infor Mahoning Chap.

PATTON, JAMES, (Mahoning Co.)

Pvt in Capt Williams' Company, Cumberland Co, Pa Mil. Br 1755. Children: John. D 1852. Bur Old Four Mile Run, Austintown Twp, about the center of cem. MI: The marker has been renewed by the family. Ref: Pa Archives, 5 Series, Vol 6, p 244. Fur infor Mahoning Chap.

PAULHAMIS, JOHN, (Butler Co.)

Name appears on the tablet in the Soldiers' and Sailors' monument at Hamilton, O. A soldier of the Revolution bur in Butler Co. Unidentified. Fur infor John Reily Chap.

PAXTON, ISAAC, (Butler Co.)

Name appears on the tablet in the Soldiers' and Sailors' monument at Hamilton, O. A Revolutionary soldier, bur in that co. D Oct 7, 1861. Unidentified; probably a Wayne soldier. Fur infor John Reily Chap.

PAXTON, THOMAS, (Clermont Co.)

Officer in Revolutionary War. Name appears on memorial tablet of Hamilton, Butler Co, O, for Soldiers and Sailors. Br 1749, (York Co) Pa. Mar: 1st, Isabella Quate; 2nd, Martha ——. Had 12 children. D 1813, Miami Twp, Clermont

Co. Came to Kentucky in command of advance guard of Gen Anthony Wayne's army. In 1795 to Ohio; settled and died in Miami Twp, Clermont Co. Ref: Natl No 57638, Col 26, D. A. R. Lin. Fur infor Cincinnati Chap.

PAYNE, ABRAHAM, (Columbiana Co.)

Pvt. Br 1758, England. D 1827, Salem, O. Natl 34632, Vol 35, D. A. R. Lin.

PAYNE, SOLOMAN, (Portage Co.)

Pvt and Sgt in Conn Mil. Placed on pension roll Jan 14, 1834. Bur Rootstown. Drew Pens at Ravenna in 1840. Fur infor Old Northwest Chap.

PEACOCK, NEAL, (Harrison Co.)

Served in Capt Jonathan Morris' Company, Col John Gunby's 7th Regt, Md Line. Br 1745, D 1827. Revolutionary pensioner living in Harrison Co in 1819, aged 74. Ref: U. S. Pension Rolls 1835; Scharf's Hist West Md, 1, 157; Md Archives XVIII, p 239, 307. Fur infor Moravian Trail Chap.

PEARCE, THOMAS, (Champaign Co.)

Pvt, Capt Jos Harrison's Company, Col Marinus Willett's Regt NY Tr. Br Jan 1, 1745, New York. D 1826, Urbana, O. Supposed to be bur somewhere on old Pearce, now the Hance farm. Ref: Natl No 87417, Vol 88, p 127, D. A. R. Lin gives birth in Frederick, Md. Fur infor Urbana Chap.

PEASE, ABNER, (Portage Co.)

Lived at Aurora, where pensioned in 1840. Fur infor Old Northwest Chap.

PEASE, ISAAC, (Geauga Co.)

Pvt, Capt David Johnson's Company, 7th Regt Conn Mil. Pensioned 1833. Br June 14, 1753, Enfield, Conn. Parents: Isaac and Rachel (Hall) Pease. Mar Dorcas Pease, Oct 16, 1778. Children: Chandler, Abigail, Dorcas, Anson, Merrick, Tabitha. D Hambden, O. 1842. Bur Chardon Village Cem, lot 411, northwest Section. MI: Monument erected to Peace family lot, Isaac Peace, Enfield Conn, 1754, Hambden, O, 1842. GM Granite Monument by family. Came to Hambden about 1810. Ref: Conn Men of Rev, p 384. Pension Records Vol 3, p 514. Fur infor Taylor Chap.

PEASE, JOEL, (Ashtabula Co.)

Promoted to Capt. In battles at Stony Point and Monmouth. Br Nov 2, 1760, Somers, Conn. Parents: John and Margaret (Adams) Pease. Mar Louisa Mecham (d Jan 4, 1808). Children: Lucy, Sally, Louisa, Samuel, Joel, Abigal. D Oct 3, 1844, age 84. Bur Roberts Cem, Southwest Corner. MI: "Captain Joel Pease a Revolutionary Soldier." GM by Family, Mar 2nd wife Aseneth (?), by whom he had seven children. Local Twp officers; pioneer farmer of Wayne. See Military Roster of Wayne Soldiers p 198, Wayne Hist. Fur infor Eunice Grant Chap.

PEASE, MARTIN, (Clermont Co.)

Enl 1776, aged 11, in an American Privateer; captured by British, taken prisoner to NY. After the war he commanded merchant ships; in Legislature of Mass fr Dukes Co. Br 1765, Island of Marthas Vineyard, Mass. Mar Deborah Butler. Children: Benjamin W, William B, Leavitt T, and 6 daughters. During French Rev he was in France and was an eye witness to the execution of Louis XVI and assisted some of the French nobility to escape to America. Came to Amelia, Clermont Co, O, about 1814. Ref: A. S. Abbott, Bethel, O. Fur infor Cincinnati Chap.

PECK, DAN, (Ashtabula Co.)

In Conn Lines. At Valley Forge in 1777-1778. Br Apr 17, 1762. Parents Silas Peck, Sr. and Elizabeth Caulkins Peck. Mar Lovina Huntley, Apr 19, 1786. Children: Lemuel, Silas, Edward C, Ansel, Polly, Lyman. D Jan 16, 1839, New Lyme, O. Bur Miller family Cem 1½ miles north of Dodgeville, O, outside the cem fence on west side. Fur infor Luther Reeve Chap.

PECK, JESSE, (Trumbull Co.)

Br 1762. Mar Sarah ——. D May 11, 1832. Bur Farmington Cem, Farmington Twp. MI: "Jesse Peck, died May 11, 1832, aged 70 yrs. Sarah, his wife, died Oct 14, 1838, aged 69 years." Ref: A descendant, Leon Peck, lives at West Farmington ,O, RFD. Fur infor Mary Chesney Chap.

PEGG, BENJAMIN, (Miami Co.)

D 1845, Springcreek Twp, Miami Co. Bur Hilliard's cem, Staunton St, Piqua. There is no record of the remains having ever been removed. He was bur in north corner and there is nothing to identify grave, except information from two witnesses. GM Piqua D. A. R. in 1906. Very little known of his actual history. Mr. John Rayner, a local authority, heard description of Mr. Pegg's funeral given by Mr. M. H. Jones and Mr. L. C. Cro—, of Piqua, the latter is still living (Oct. 31, 1923). Mr. Pegg d in an old log cabin out in the country near the Millhouse farm, at the age of nearly 100. Much sought for on July 4th celebrations. Fur infor Piqua Chap.

PEIRCE, ISAAC, (Montgomery Co.)

Served in 1779 as an aide-de-camp on the staff of Gen Horatio Gates. Pvt in Capt Cole's 1st, 7th, 8th companies of 1st and 2nd R. I. Regts. Name first appears on muster roll May 1782; disch Dec 1782. Br Mch 8, 1749, Charlestown, R. I. Parents: Isaac Peirce. Mar Mary Sheffield (dau of Benj and Hannah, Jamestown, R. I.). Children: Samuel, Lucy, Phoebe, Joseph, Elizabeth, Eliza. D Sept 7, 1821 in Dayton, O. Bur Woodland Cem, Dayton, O, lot 16 to 22, section 77. MI: "Isaac Peirce, b March 8, 1749, d Sept 17, 1821." GM S. A. R. Bronze Marker in 1919. Came to Marietta in 1788. Ref: Natl No of Revolutionary Soldier in D. A. R. Honor Roll 13699, Lin Bk Vol 14, p 261. Fur infor Jonathan Dayton Chap and S. A. R.

PEIRCE, LEWIS, (Muskingum Co.)

Ensign of the 4th Bn of Westmoreland Co Mil Apr 2, 1778, John Kyle Capt; Peter Waddell 1st Lt, Jos Peirce 2nd Lt. Br Nov 21, 1748, Bergen Co, N. J. Parents: James and Sarah (Van Horne) Peirce. Mar Mary Howell, May 9, 1773. Children: Sarah, Esther, Lewellen, Jane, Andrew, Mary, Jonathan, Margaret, Elizabeth. D Aug 23, 1825, Muskingum Co. Bur McNaughten family plat on hill above Freeland station. Ref: Pa Archives, 6 series, Vol 2, p 285. Fur infor Muskingum and Waw-Wil-a-Way Chaps.

PELTON, SAMUEL, (Lorain Co.)

Pvt Mass State. Br May 9, 1757, Granville, Mass. Children: Betsy, Allace, Spelman. D Jan 28, 1849. Bur Pioneer Cem, Wellington, O. GM Western Reserve Chap, in 1920. Lived in Otis, Mass. In 1827 moved to Wellington, Lorain Co, O. Fur infor Western Reserve Chap.

PEMBERTON, WILLIAM, (Adams Co.)

Pvt Capt Thos Meriwether's Company, 1st Va State Regt, Col Geo Gibson; name on roll Sept 1, 1777; present at Yorktown surrender. (Fr Hist Adams Co, by Evans Stiers). Br about 1750, Va. Mar Rhoda Luck about 1775 or 76. Children: James, Joyce, William, Anne, Nathaniel, Caty (1790); Fountain, Caty Luck, (1795);

Rhode Jane, Ezekiel. D before 1820, Locust Grove, Adams Co, as he is not listed in census of 1820, tho his widow, Rhoda, is. Bur family cem on Jay Arnold farm (owned 1926 by him). MI: Not marked. Bought land Adams Co 1807; neither he nor widow asked for pens; James, William, Fountain were soldiers in 1812 war. Farmer, hunter, cooper. Enl at one time from Henry Co, Va, 1780. Ref: Va State Library Rec Richmond. H. C. Pemberton, great-grandson, 2038 W. 91st Cleveland, O. Accepting this infor Jane Dailey, state chairman.

PENNELL, ROBERT, (Mahoning Co.)

Pvt 7th Bn Chester Co, Pa Mil. Br 1753. D 1813. Bur Old Cem East of Austintown, O, in the west end near the fence. Ref: Pa Archives, Series 5, Vol 5, p 788. Fur infor Mahoning Chap.

PENNINGTON, EPHRAIM, (Fulton Co.)

Bur Butler Cem, Chesterfield Twp, O. Fur infor Wauseon Chap.

PENNY, HENRY, (Miami Co.)

Pvt. His original pens claim owned by Mrs. Clarke Sullivan. Natl No 117071, D. A. R. Br Jan 11, 1741. N. C. Parents: Penny (br in England.) Mar Hannah Thompson, (died Aug 3, 1829); 2nd Mary; (died Dec 13, 1853). Children: Several; one was John Penny Sr. D Apr 16, 1841, Miami Co, O. Bur Old Ludlow Cem, Laura, Miami Co, O, rear of church. MI: has marble stone, with name, death, age. Father was a soldier in army of King of England; later in Revolutionary war, with his 3 sons, Henry being one. Ref: Mrs. Clarke Sullivan, Jr. Miss Osa Penny and Mrs. W. S. Gunckle all of Dayton, O. Fur infor Jonathan Dayton Chap.

PERIN, LEMUEL (often PERRIN), (Clermont Co.)

Mass Archives gives name as Pvt on Lexington Alarm, Apr 19, 1775, as Capt in John Perry's Company; Sgt on muster roll of Capt Nathan Carpenter's Regt Dec 8, 1776. Br 1749, Rehoboth, Mass. Parents: 1st (——); 2 Amelia Dickinson (br 1760, d 1828) in 1792. Mar 1st Martha Nasel, North Adams, Mass in 1773. Children: 1st wife, John, Rachel, Lucy, Hannah, Samuel, Patty. 2nd wife: Glover and Lemuel (twins), Amelia. D 1822 (or 1814, sent later data) near Connersville, Fayette Co, Ind. Bur near his home in Clermont Co, O. Perintown, with others of family. GM Old slab, with name and dates. The Military Record certified by Secretary of Commonwealth of Mass, 1894. Ref: Natl No 134845 and 12037, and Miss May Perin Hulick, Cincinnati, O. Fur infor Cincinnati Chap.

PERKINS, THOMAS, (Licking Co.)

Enl at Winchester, Va, Oct 1781. Pvt in Col Brown's Regt. Capt Bohaman's Company. Br 1762, Maryland. Mar Mary Trigg, Mch 8, 1783. Eight children. D Aug 18, 1837, Bennington Twp. Ref: Bristers Hist. Fur infor Hetuck Chap.

PERRINE, JOSEPH, (Clermont Co.)

Pvt in NJ Tr and State Mil. Served 7 yrs in army. Br 1748, Cranbury, NJ. Parents: Henry Perrine. Mar Elizabeth Wycoff in 1771 in N J. Children: James, (br 1780 d 1764 mar Polly Kain 1804); Arthur, Ralph, Martha (mar Isaac Dye); Eleanor (mar Jos Holman); Elizabeth (mar John Gill); Ann (mar Andrew Hickey). D 1823, Bethel, O. Bur Bethel, O. Came to Williamsburg Twp, Clermont Co, O. in 1805. Descendants of Dan'l Perrine who came to America in 1665. Ref: Natl No 86110, Vol 87, p 35. D. A. R. Lin.

PERRINE, WILLIAM, (Belmont Co.)

Bur M. E. Cem at St Clairsville, O. MI: "Wm. Perrine, Revolutionary Soldier." Fur infor Mrs. A. L. McFarland, St Clairsville, member of D. A. R.

PERRY, JOHN, (Belmont Co.)

Cornetist in 3rd Continental Dragoons, Baylor's Regt Md Line. Br Pa near Havre de Grace, Md. Mar Jane Blair. D Nov 1825 at Morristown, O. Bur Morristown Cem (old) middle of east tier of lots. MI: "John Perry, a soldier of the Revolution. Died Nov 9, 1825, age 73 yrs. 1 mo, 28 days." GM Family—old sand stone marker. Farming, Fighting and Organizing Presbyterian Churches. Ref: Natl No 90262, Vol 91, p 86, D. A. R. Lin. Fur information Mrs. A. L. McFarland, St Clairsville, O. of Wheeling D. A. R.

PERRY, NATHAN, (Cuyahoga Co.)

Pvt in Capt Isaac Clark's Company of Mil raised for the defense of the frontiers and on Lake Champlain. Serv fr Mch 2, 1778 to May 2, 1778. Also in Col Mead's Regt of Mil and Capt Claghorn's Company in scouting after Tories at sundry times, and also guarding in time of trial such as were taken, supposed to be enemies to America. Served May 22 to May 26, 1777. Br 1760, Waterbury, Conn. Parents: Daniel Perry. Mar Miss Sophia Leonora Root. Children: Horace (br 1781), Larry (br 1783), Philanthropes, Nathan (br 1786), Horatio (br 1790), Sophia (br 1800.) D Oct 25, 1813, Cleveland, O. Bur Lake View Cem, Cleveland, Cuyahoga Co, O. Lot 26, Sec 6. MI: On monument, difficult to decipher; seemed to correspond with that on old tombstone placed flat above the grave. Read: "Sacred to the memory of Nathan Perry Esq, who died Oct 25, 1813, aged 53 years." GM Nathan Perry D. A. R. official marker; by rules of Cem could not be permanently placed, but on certain days, for 3 da would be displayed. Marked June, 1923. Br in Conn; moved to Rutland, Vt, where between 1785-1789 made 8 conveyances of land. Later is said to have purchased a farm and a mill in western N. Y., removing family there after 1790. Family was in Canada for a time. 1806 brought family to Cleveland, O. Invested in land in Lake Co, O. Purchased property in Cleveland, O, and invested in property at Black River, near Lorain, O. In 1796 engaged in trading with the Indians near Buffalo, N. Y. Was with the first party of Surveyors who laid out and named Cleveland, O. Had charge of Commissary part of the outfit and supplied the horses and cattle in the expedition. Engaged in fur trade. Was one of the Court Judges in Cuyahoga Co, O. First bur in old Pioneer Cem, corner of Ontario and Prospect St, Cleveland, O. About 1827 removed to Erie St Cem. Removed to Lake View Cem in 1915. Ref: Pioneer Families of Cleveland, by Mrs. G. V. R. Wickham; Adj Gen office, Vt. Fur infor Nathan Perry Chap.

PERRY, WINSLOW, (County not stated.)

Pvt and drummer Capt Holman's Company, Col Doolittle's Mass Regt. Br 1758, Vermont. Mar Rachel Rice. D 1830 in Ohio. Ref: Natl No 59087, Vol 60, p 31, D. A. R. Lin.

PETERSON, CONRAD, (Wayne Co.)

D Congress Twp, near Congress Village. Bur Congress Cem near Congress Village, in old Cem. MI: "Conrad Peterson. Soldier of 1776." Fur infor Wooster-Wayne Chap.

PETERSON, MATSON, (Seneca Co.)

(The name Watson Peterson on Pens list of 1840, must be the same person) Br 1764, New Jersey. Bur on a hillside on the farm of David Hilsinger in Scipio Twp. Grave not marked. Ref: Langs Hist of Seneca Co. Fur infor Dolly Todd Madison Chap.

PHELPS, ABIJAH, (Hamilton Co.)

Br 1762, Connecticut. D 1833. Bur Sycamore Twp, Pensioned 1840, aged 79, living in 1st Ward, Cincinnati, O. Ref: S. A. R. Fur infor Cincinnati Chap.

PHELPS, EDWARD, (Franklin Co.)

Served in the 8th Co, 1st Regt, Conn Inf. Br Aug 27, 1859, Windsor, Conn. D Aug 10, 1840, Blendon Twp. Bur Central Cem, Blendon Twp. MI: "The son of Timothy Phelps, the son of Cornelius Phelps, the son of Timothy Phelps, the son of William Phelps, who was one of the first settlers of Windsor, Conn. Said Edward Phelps was born Aug 27, 1759, in Windsor, Conn, and emigrated to the State of Ohio in 1800, and died Aug 10, 1840, aged 81 years." GM by D. A. R. Bronze marker, May 30, 1912. Came to Ohio with his family in 1806 and settled in Blendon Twp. Ref: Natl No 87620, Vol 88, D. A. R. Lin. Fur infor Columbus Chap.

PHELPS, IRA, (Geauga Co.)

Pvt in Col Canfield's Mil Regt at West Point, 1781. Br May 3, 1763, Harwinton, Conn. Parents: Samuel and Anna (Barber) Phelps. Children: Fanny, Ruby, Arza, Lois, Richard, Content, Sabra, Ann Arza. D Sept 7, 1848. Bur Welshfield Center, O, lot 258. MI: "Ira Phelps 1763-1848" Removed to Elizabethtown N. Y. about 1795, thence to Geauga Co. Name appears in list of census of pensioners in 1840, living in Geauga Co. Ref: Phelps Genealogy, Vol 1, p 445, Ct Men Rev p 583, Fur infor Taylor Chap.

PHELPS, SETH, (Geauga Co.)

2nd Lt 1777; 1st Lt Jan 1, 1777, Capt May 5, 1778. Br Nov 17, 1751, Windsor, Conn. Mar Lucy Ledyard, Sept 10, 1780; 2nd, Sally Pierce, May, 1797. Children: 1st wife: Lucy, Dr. Seth Phelps, Ann, Alfred, Edwin F, Mary. 2nd wife: Theodore, Nelson, Hamilton, Phyana, Sally. D 1826, Parkman, O. Bur South Cem, Parkman, O. 2nd Lt, 1st Lt Jan 1, 1777, Capt May 25, 1778. Severely wounded at Stony Point, July 15, 1779. 4th Regt. Disch 1782. Presiding Judge, Onondaga Co, N. Y. Member of N. Y. Legislature. Laid out town of Aura, N. Y. Ref: Williams Hist Lake and Geauga Co, Conn Men Rev. Fur infor Taylor Chap.

PHIFER, JACOB, (Knox Co.)

From Strasburg, Germany, located in Brown Twp, Knox Co, O, in 1818. D Oct 9, 1846 aged 89 yrs. He had served ten yrs a soldier in Europe, three yrs in the Revolutionary War, and three mos in the War of 1812. The old soldier was the father of Freeman, John, James and Michael Phifer. Fur infor Kokosing Chap.

PHILBROOK, JOEL, (Licking Co.)

Enl 1777 marines under Capt Hector McNeal, frigate Boston. Br Maine, Aug 14, 1759. Mar Mary Leadbetter, Jan, 1775. D Sept 15, 1820, St Albans, O. Ref: Natl No 55619, p 281, Vol 56, D. A. R. Lin.

PHILIPS, PHILIP, (Lorain Co.)

Enl Feb 15, 1780 and served until Dec 13, 1783, in Capt Strong's Company, Col Herman Swift's Regt Conn Line. He was disch at West Point, N. Y. Pvt. Br Dec 22, 1762, Windham, Conn. Mar Elizabeth Philips, Mch 4, 1789. Children: James, August, Benjamin, John, Jurel. D June 15, 1838, Grafton, Lorain Co. Lived with son August, who owned a small farm in Medina Twp, Medina Co. He died in Grafton, Lorain Co. Ref: Conn Men in Rev, Vol 1, p 328; Vol 2, p 636. Philips Family Bible Leaf; Widow's File No 5532. Fur infor: Copied from D. A. R. Magazine Feb. 1928 issue, Vol 62, No 2 by Mrs. Effie Whitaker Teemer, Lorain, O.

PHILLIPS, JOB, (Athens Co.)

Enl for 2 yrs, was Pvt, then Corp. Capt Samuel Ransom, Simon Spaulding, Cols John Durkee, Jacob Stroud. Enl Wyoming, Pa. Birth date not given. Br in Rhode Island. Grew up in Conn, went to N. Y. when 16 years of age, later to Cooperstown, N. W. Children: Job, Daniel, Spencer, another son, perhaps other children. D Jan 22, 1835, near Amesville, Athens Co, O. Bur Amesville Cem near Amesville. Was in battles of Millstone, Boundbrook, Germantown, Mud Island,

GRAVE OF JOHN PERRY, BELMONT CO. INSCRIPTION ON STONE: "A SOLDIER OF REVOLUTION. D. NOV. 9, 1825—AGE 73 YEARS."

Elizabethtown. Ref: Bureau of Pensions, Dept of the Interior. He applied for a pension at the age of 92. Fur infor Nabby Lee Ames Chap.

PHILLIPS, JOHN, (Butler Co.)

Served in Continental establishment under Capt Daniel Steel and Col John Gibson. Pensioned in Butler Co, O. for 8 yrs actual serv in Va line. Br 1755, Germany. Ref: Natl No 25228, p 81, Vol 26, D. A. R. Lin.

PHILLIPS, SAMUEL, (Ashtabula Co.)

Enl 1776; re-enlisted 1777, serving in Capt Watson's Company, Col Samuel Webb's Regt. In action at Flatbush LI and retreat from NY. Was a pensioner. Was Col (Ref: J. E. Hart, Wick, O.) Br Apr 8, 1760, Milford Conn. Mar Millea Kellog 1781. Children: Halsey; B Frank; Harriet; Cordelia; 2 others mar Canfield and Forman. D 1842, Colebrook, Ashtabula Co, O. Bur northwest corner of Twp of Colebrook. MI: "A Soldier of the Revolution." Aide to Gen Washington. Ref: Conn Men in the Rev; Lin Bk 61. Natl No 60468, D. A. R. and L. H. Phillips, San Jose, Cal. Fur infor Mary Stanley and Eunice Grant Chaps.

PIATT, ABRAHAM, (Co not stated.)

Capt of 2nd Regt Middlesex Co, NJ Mil 1777, Col Neilson's Regt. Br 1741 NJ. Mar Annabelle Andrew (d 1822). D 1791 Watsontown, O. Ref: Natl No 100157, Vol 101, p 49, D. A. R. Lin.

PIATT, BENJAMIN, (Adams Co.)

1st Lt under Gen McCullough. Br 1763 in Virginia. Mar Polly Waddle. Children: Benjamin, Margaret, John, Jacob, Elizabeth, Polly. D near West Union, 1851. Bur near West Union, probably in Trotter Cem. Fur infor Sycamore Chap.

PICKERILL, SAMUEL, (Brown Co.)

Drummer. Enl at Dunfries, Va in fall of 1776 in Capt Gallhuis Company; Col Brent's Regt Va Tr. Served 3 yrs as Pvt and drummer. Br Charles Co, Md, 1757. Parents: Samuel Pickerell, Sr. Mar Mary Lowe (so writing looked) (1767-1844). Children: Jane, Emily, Denis, Clarence, Samuel, Thomas, John, William, Mary, Lucy Ann and Johanna. D May 9, 1850 on his farm 8 miles fr Ripley. Bur Liberty Cem, Brown Co, O. MI: "Samuel Pickerill Died May 9, 1850." GM Lt Byrd Chap May 30, 1916. In battles of White Plains, Monmouth, Stony Point. Applied for pens 1832. Ref: Biography of the Pickerills. Natl No 129252, 102392, Vol 103, p 124. D. A. R. Lin. Fur infor Lt Byrd and Taliaferro Chaps.

PICKETT, JOHN, (Ashtabula Co.)

Was placed on the pens roll of Ashtabula Co, O. 1832 for serv as Pvt in the Mass Mil. Br 1753, Sandsfield, Mass. Mar Ruth Boardman. Children: John, Joseph, Benjamin. D Oct 23, 1840, Andover, Ashtabula Co, O. Bur Andover. MI: "John Pickett Died Oct. 23, 1840 in the 87th year of his age." GM by S. A. R. Moved to Ohio in 1819 with his three sons. Ref: Hist of Ashtabula Co. Lin Bk Vol XXXVIII, p 302. Fur infor Mary Stanley Chap.

PIERCE,MICHAEL, (Butler Co.)

Name appears on the tablet of Sailors and Soldiers monument at Hamilton as a Revolutionary Soldier bur in that Co. D June 4, 1838, Bur Trenton, Madison Twp. Fur infor John Reily Chap.

PIERCE, SAMUEL, (Hamilton Co.)

Br 1759, Connecticut. D 1828. Ref: S. A. R. Fur infor Cincinnati Chap.

PIERSON, ABRAHAM, (Hamilton Co.)

Br Pennsylvania. Ref: S. A. R. Fur infor Cincinnati Chap.

PIERSON, AMOS, (Trumbull Co.)

Children: Lyman Pierson and Hermon Pierson, graves located here and are descendants of the Revolutionary Soldier. Bur Mecca. MI: not marked. Unable to locate grave of Amos Pierson. Revolutionary pens granted Aug 1832. Fur infor Mary Chesney Chap.

PIERSON, DANIEL, (Montgomery Co.)

2nd Lt, Capt Wm E Imlay's Company, 3rd Regt New Jersey Line, Col Elias Dayton, Apr 15 to Nov 1776. 1st Lt 4th Regt NJ Line, Lt Col David Shea, Jan 1, 1777 to Dec 1, 1778. Br Apr 25, 1750, Morristown, Morris Co, NJ. Parents: Benjamin and Patience (Coe) Pierson. Mar Prudence King, dau of Joseph (d Dec 11, 1837). Children: Clarissa, Charles, Edward, John Alfred, William Horace, Elizabeth Ann, Henry Alexander. D Dec 11, 1831, Dayton, O. Bur Woodland Cem, Dayton, O. lot 16 to 22, sec 77. MI: Dates and where born, NJ. GM S. A. R. bronze marker in 1919. In battles of Brandywine and Monmouth. Ill, resigned. While a 2nd Lt was on recruiting serv until company was filled, then served with company. Came to Dayton before 1818. Ref: Wm Neifert, S. A. R. Dayton, O. Fur infor Jonathan Dayton Chap.

PIERSON, DAVID, (Hamilton Co.)

D in 1850. Ref: S. A. R. Fur infor Cincinnati Chap.

PIERSON, JOHN, (Knox Co.)

Pvt in Capt Richardson's Company. Wounded at Germantown. Served all through the Rev. At one time one of the "Minute Men", 1st NJ Regt. Br Orange, Essex Co, NJ, May 24, 1758. Parents: Abraham and Mary Pierson. Mar Sarah Van Dyke Sept 1776. Children: Nicholas, David, Catherine (mar Cook), Arthur, Anna (mar McFarland), Hannah (mar Cook), Sarah (mar Johnson), Philemon, John, Aurumah, Margaret (mar Hurlbert). D 1827, Martinsburg, O. Bur Presbyterian Cem, Martinsburg, O, lot 67, grave 1. MI: "In memory of John Pierson who departed this life Feb 11th, 1827, aged 68 yrs, 8 mos and 17 days." GM Dec 1927 by Kokosing Chap. Farmer and stock raiser. Ref: Natl No 89950, Vol 90, p 309, D. A. R. Lin. Fur infor Kokosing Chap.

PIERSON, JONATHAN, (Darke Co.)

D Jan 11, 1840. Bur Palestine (St John's Cem) north side of cem. MI: "In memory of Jonathan Pierson. A soldier of '76, died Jan 11, 1840, aged 82 years." GM Stone very old but could read it very well. Fur infor Ft Greenville Chap.

PIERSON, MATTHIAS, (Hamilton Co.)

Served in same Regt with his brother Samuel under Col Spencer, NJ 3rd Bn, 4th Company (See p 21, "Strykers" Men from New Jersey") Continental Army 1777, Morris Co. Pvt in Capt Wm Britton's Company. Owned lots in Cincinnati, O, 1790, He and brother owned farm there; a deed shows in court house records. Also a record there shows he bought land in 1812. Known to have been bur in Hamilton Co, O. Fur infor Cincinnati Chap.

PIERSON, SAMUEL, (Hamilton Co.)

Br 1753, NJ. D 1839, Pleasant Ridge Cem, Columbia Twp. (S. A. R.) Fur infor Cincinnati Chap.

PINNEY, ABNER, (Franklin Co.)

Served as Drummer in Capt Roberts Company, 18th Regt Conn tr. He afterward was given the title of Capt. Br 1749 in Connecticut. D Nov 23, 1804. Bur Old Episcopal Cem, Worthington. MI: "Capt Abner Pinney died Nov 23, 1804 in the 55th year of his age." "Here Abner Pinney lies, the kind, the just. His flesh is turning to its kindred dust. Love, friendship dwelt within his faithful heart. Yet from his dearest friend was called to part. And now, we trust, he's landed on that shore, where death ne'er comes and friends shall part no more." GM by Revolutionary grave Committee with bronze marker May 30, 1912. Came to Ohio and settled in Worthington in 1804. Fur infor Columbus Chap.

PITCHER, BENJAMIN, (Lake Co.)

Served in the 3rd Regt, Duchess Co, Mil, 1782, in N. Y. Col John Field's Regt. Br 1767. D 1849, Kirtland, O. Bur Angel Cem, East Kirtland, O. GM New Connecticut Chap. A brother of Benjamin Pitcher served in 1812 as Capt and Col. Fur infor New Connecticut Chap.

PITMAN, JONATHAN, (Hamilton Co.)

R. I. Tr; Commissioned as Capt and Lt in 1775. Br 1747 NJ. Parents: Isaac Pitman, a member of Boston Tea Party. Children: A son, mar Anna; one mar Jerusha. D 1834. Bur near Reading, O on farm. Came to Ohio, settled at Columbus. (Jones' History of Cincinnati, p 18) Later to farm near Reading. On a tax list of Springfield Twp 1808 name of Jonathan and others, which are no doubt his sons, appear: Joshua, Calvin, Ephraim, Pierson, David, Daniel, Simon. Ref: S. A. R. Fur infor Cincinnati Chap.

PLACARD, CHRISTIAN, (Clermont Co.)

Drawing pens 1840 for serv while residing in Ohio Twp, Clermont Co, O, aged 88, at home of Jeremiah Gaskins. Br 1752. Fur infor Census of Pensioners 1840. Copied by State Chairman.

PLATTER, CHRISTIAN, (Ross Co.)

Revolutionary serv in Pa. Division of Public Records. Muster Roll, Vol 4, p 417. Br Nov 15, 1760, Neuweiler, Germany. On stone next to his is "Christena Platter, wife of Christian Platter, d Dec 12, 1842, in 69th yr of her age." D Sept 10, 1837. Bur Platter Cem, near Bainbridge, O. MI: Dates, name, age 76. Fur infor Nathaniel Massie Chap.

PLATTER, PETER, SR., (Ross Co.)

In Capt Robert Ramsey's Pa Company. Was in Battles of Bunker Hill and Brandywine. Br 1758 in Germany. Mar Sarah. D Jan 2, 1832. Bur Grandview Cem, Chillicothe. MI: "Peter Platter, Sr., died Jan 2, 1832, aged 73 years, 3 months. Sarah, his wife, died Feb 23, 1832, aged 60 years, 11 mos." Came with his father to Pa in 1764, when he was only five yrs old. He mar and with his wife and one child, moved, about 1793, to Ky. After six or seven years he moved to Adams Co, O. In 1811 he traded his three hundred acres of land in Adams Co for a like number of acres in Haller's bottom, in Twin Twp, Ross Co, O. He was a consistent member of the Associate Reformed Church (afterwards called the United Presbyterians). Ref: Ross and Hamilton Co, Hist, p 295, Vol 4, p 417, Pa records, original rolls gives record. Natl No 33291, D. A. R. Fur infor Nathaniel Massie Chap.

PLYLEY, CASPER, (Ross Co.)

Served in the war of the Rev. His father had been the owner of considerable real estate in the vicinity of Philadelphia, and had lost much of his property through the worthlessness of the continental money. Mortified by the reverses of his family although then a minor, enl in the army, and subsequently participated in numerous engagements under Gen Greene. He died at an advanced age. D Mch 28, 1849, aged 86 years. Bur Concord Presbyterian Church Cem, Concord Twp. MI: "Casper Plyley died March 28, 1849, aged 86 years." His wife's reads: "Margaret, wife of Casper Plyley, died March 19, 1836, aged 60 yrs." Emigrated from Philadelphia to Ohio about the year 1801. The list of pensioners of the Revolutionary War, who died in Ross Co, gives his name. Ref: Ross and Highland Co. Hist, p 294. Fur infor Nathaniel Massie Chap.

PLUM, CHARLES, (Portage Co.)

Mariner on "Oliver Cromwell," from Middleton, Conn, where he was br in 1749. D 1831, Aurora, O. Ref: Natl No 85616, Vol 86, p 238, D. A. R. Lin.

POAGE, JAMES, (Brown Co.)

Lt in 1782, Va line. Br 1760, Augusta Co, Va. D 1820, Ripley, O. Bur Old Cem, Ripley. Ref: Natl No 95182, Vol 96, p 62, D. A. R. Lin. Fur infor Ripley Chap.

POE, ADAM, (Stark Co.)

Bur Sixteen Cem, 1 mile south of Massillon, O. Authority: Hist of Stark Co, edited by William Henry Perrin. Fur infor Canton Chap.

POE, JOHN (Ross Co.)

Volunteer rifleman, 18 mos under Morgan. Regular dragoon under Cols White and Washington. At battle of the Cowpens; battle of Guilford's Court House; at Bluford's defeat at Hanging Rock. Was taken prisoner, after being wounded by swordcut on head and his horse shot under him. Was exchanged and present at Cornwallis' surrender at Yorktown. During serv rode express for Gen Lafayette from Williamsburg to York. Br Sept 14, 1750, at Winchester, Frederick Co, Va. Parents: German descent. D Oct 7, 1843, Scioto Twp, Ross Co. Moved from Va with his family and settled near Chillicothe, Ross Co, O, in 1806. In Jan, 1833, made a profession of religion in Associate Reformed Church under Rev. J. Claybaugh. Was almost last soldier of Rev to die in Ross Co. Ref: Scioto Gazette of Oct 12, 1843. Register of the Ohio Society of. S A. R., 1912-13, p 69 under list of Revolutionary soldiers in Ohio in 1840. 9th Annual Report Library Board, Va, 1911-12, p 242. War Dept files. Fur infor Nathaniel Massie Chap.

POMEROY, DANIEL, (Geauga Co.)

Lexington Alarm, Apr, 1775, Pvt Conn Continental. Pensioned 1833. Br Apr 8, 1762, South Hampton, Mass. Parents: Noah and Temperance Pomeroy. Mar Mary Loveland, Mch 29, 1789. Children: Eleazer, Polly, Leonard, Dolly, Lydiah, Altha. D Apr 3, 1834. Bur Maple Grove Cem, Thompson, O, Lot 1, sec 148. MI: "Daniel Pomeroy died Apr 3, 1834 aged 82 years." GM Stone by Family. Enl from Coventry, Mass. Came to Thompson, O, from Peru, Berkshire Co, Mass. Ref: Conn Men of Rev, pp 7, 643. Fur infor Taylor Chap.

POMEROY, ICHABOD, (Geauga Co.)

Pvt Capt John Kirkland's Company, Col Ruggles Woodbridge's Regt. Enl Aug 16, 1777, disch Nov 29, 1777. Br Mch 9, 1757, South Hampton, Mass. Parents: Noah and Temperance Pomeroy. Mar Lucy Harris, Feb 14, 1782. Children: Eltweed, Anna, Daniel, Ann, Lucy, Sarah, Josiah, Temperance, Daniel, Tirzah, Ichabod, Althus Noah. D Nov 13, 1843, Hambden, O. Bur Hambden Center, lot 13. Ref: Pension Records, Vol 5, p 514; Mass Soldiers and Sailors, Vol 12, p 522; also p 131, Vol 15, D. A. R. Lin. Natl No 14354. Fur infor Taylor Chap.

POND, ———, (Huron Co)

A Revolutionary Soldier. Father of W. H. Pond, Richmond Twp, who came to Richmond with his father, 1837. Fur infor Sally De Forest Chap.

PONTEOUS, JOHN, (Mahoning Co.)

Pvt in Col Samuel Miles' Regt. A Rifle Regt. Bur Springfield Twp Cem. Ref: Pa Archives, Series 5, Vol 2, p 399. Fur infor Mahoning Chap.

POOLE, JEPTHA, (Geauga Co.)

Placed on pens roll Madison Co, NY 1831 for 26 mos serv as Pvt and Corp, Capt Cobb's, Col Mitchell's Regt 1775, also Gen Thomas' Regt and Col Jacobs' Regt. Br 1756, Abington, Mass. Parents: Deacon Samuel and Rebeckah (Shaw) Poole. Mar Olive Whitmarsh Noves, Apr 16, 1779. Children: Amos, Jeplathah. D Mch 8, 1838, Welchfield. Bur Welchfield Center Cem lot 260. MI: "Jeptha Poole, 1756-1836.' GM by family. Ref: Natl No 32357, Vol 33, D. A. R. Lin; Mass Soldiers and Sailors Vol 12, p 546; Vital Records Abington. Fur infor Taylor Chap.

POOLE, WILLIAM, (Clark Co.)

Pvt in Capt James Clay's Company, Col Bradley's Vermont Regt, 1782. Br Springfield, Mass. Feb 25, 1759. Mar Lois Moore. Putney, Vt Jan 10, 1789. Children: Lucy, only one given. D Clark Co. Bur Fletcher Chapel 8½ miles northeast of Springfield, O. grave not platted. MI: "William Poole borne Feb 25, 1759." GM by family. Farmer. Ref: Vermont State official records, stamped with state seal. Fur infor Lagonda Chap.

POPE, HENRY, (Highland Co.)

Br Aug 8, 1759. D Oct 3, 1815. Bur near Greenfield. GM by Juliana White D. A. R. in 1926. Fur infor Juliana White Chap.

POPPELTON, SAMUEL, (Richland Co.)

Pvt and Sgt in Vermont State Tr. Br 1748, Pownal, Vt. D 1832, Belleville. Bur Poppleton Burial Ground, 1 mile south of Bellville, O. farm now owned by Mr. Bolinger. MI: Name and State Troop. GM Mary Washington D. A. R. Chap bronze marker in 1911. Ref: Natl No 39705, D. A. R. Compare 22379, Vol 23, p 131, D. A. R. Lin. Fur infor Mary Washington Chap.

PORTER, EBENEZER, (Portage Co.)

Lived at Aurora, where pensioned in 1840. Fur infor Old Northwest Chap.

PORTER, ELIJAH, CAPT. (Medina Co.)

Br 1757. D 1823. Bur River Styx, Guilford Twp. GM Western Reserve Chap. Fur infor Western Reserve Chap.

PORTER, JOSEPH, (Cuyahoga Co.)

Corp Conn State Tr. Br 1760. D 1844. Bur Evergreen Cem, Dover. Fur infor Western Reserve Chap.

PORTER, ROBERT, (Harrison Co.)

A Revolutionary pensioner living in Harrison Co in 1834, aged 71 yrs; served as Sgt (with Sgt John Parker, also of Harrison Co) in 8th Regt Pa Line. U. S. Pens Rolls, 1835; Pa Archives 5, III, 372. Fur infor Moravian Trail Chap.

POSEY, ZEPHANIAH, (Hamilton Co.)

Pvt Col Daniel Morgan's 11th Va Regt. Made Sgt and served in 15th Va Regt. Br 1758, Virginia. Mar Mary Jackson (b 1760-1839). D 1826, Hamilton Co, O. Ref: Natl No 75227, Vol 76, D. A. R. Lin. Fur infor Cincinnati Chap.

POST, DAVID, (Richland Co.)

Pvt in the NJ Mil. Br 1751, NJ. May 26, 1746. Bur Millsboro Cem, Millsboro, O. GM Mary Washington Chap, bronze marker in 1911. Ref: Natl No 18077, p 29, Vol 19, D. A. R. Lin. Fur infor Mary Washington Chap.

POTTER, BORDON, (Geauga Co.)

D Oct 25, 1846. Bur Welchfield Cem, lot 269. MI: "Borden Potter, 1764-1846." Ref: Geauga Co, Pioneer Hist, p 659. Fur infor Taylor Chap.

POTTER, JOSEPH, (Delaware Co.)

Entered serv from NJ. Br 1754. D 1855. Bur Old Blue Church Cem, Kingston Twp. Ref: See Vol 46, p 221, D. A. R. Lin, same name bur in same county but dates of birth and death differ a few yrs. They give Jemima Skinner as wife. Fur infor Delaware Chap.

POTTER, MOSES, (Butler Co.)

Pvt Essex Co, NJ Mil. Br 1761, NJ. Mar Rhoda Osborne. D 1802, Middletown, O. Ref: Natl No 99291, Vol 100.

POTTER, RUSSEL, (Butler Co.)

Pvt Minute Man, Essex Co, NJ Mil. Br July 23, 1754, Essex Co, NJ. Mar Rhoda Maxwell. Children: one was Samuel M Potter. D Feb 15, 1814 in Ohio. Bur Old Baptist Church, Trenton, O. MI: "Russel Potter died Feb 15, came to Ohio in 1807." Ref: Natl No 70133, Vol 71, p 49, D. A. R. Lin. Fur infor Col Jonathan Bayard Smith Chap.

POTTERF, JASPER, (Preble Co.)

Br 1759. D 1836. Bur Mound Hill Cem, Eaton. MI: "Revolutionary Soldier, 1759-1836" and name. By his grave, a stone, "His Wife, Susannah Ridenauer, 1768-1831." Ref: Mary P Mitchell, Eaton, O. Fur infor John Reily Chap.

POTTS, DAVID, (Marion Co.)

Enl Dec 5, 1776. Served as a Pvt in Capt Smith's and Wm Slaughter's Companies; Col Dan Morgan's and James Wood's Companies Va Regt. Also served under Col West. Br Nov 1756. Children: Nancy, David. One, name not given, but mar to man named Wolverton. D May 27, 1834. Bur Old Cem in Marion. MI: Date of death and age. Fur infor Capt Wm Hendricks Chap.

POTTS, JOHN, (Carroll Co.)

Pvt. Capt Wm Smith, Col Daniel Morgan 11th Va Regt. Pens Claim W 4767. Br 1751, Loudoun Co, Va. Parents: Jonas and Mary (Heckathorn) Potts. Mar Susan Hibbens, Mch 14, 1782. Children: John (br 1790); there were other children. D Oct 1820 in Carroll Co, O. Bur Country graveyard, near Scroggsfield, Fox Twp. Ref: Potts Family Genealogy, by T M Potts, 1901, pp 314, 316, 321. Natl No 225742. Fur infor Elizabeth Zane Dew Chap.

POTTS, JOHNATHAN, (Jefferson Co.)

Br 1754. D 1831. He was bur in old cem near East Springfield, Jefferson Co, but body was removed and placed in Union Cem, Jefferson Co, on plot dedicated to the soldiers of the Civil War. Permission was granted by the Sons of Veterans for placing the body in this plot. The removing and placing the body was done under the supervision and at the expense of Steubenville Chap of D. A. R. Fur infor Steubenville Chap.

POWELL, ABRAHAM P., (Champaign Co.)

Br 1755. D Jan 3, 1817. Supposed to be bur in a family cem on the Muzzy farm. Fur infor Urbana Chap.

POWELL, WILLIAM, (Logan Co.)

Pvt. Name on alphabetical list of soldiers who received pay for service in Revolutionary War. Br 1757, Lancaster Co, Pa. D 1835, Bellefontaine, O. Ref: Natl No 75454, Vol 76, D. A. R. Lin. For infor Bellefontaine Chap.

POWERS, GREGORY, (Summit Co.)

Boatswain on brig Minerva, which was fitted out on Act of Colony of Conn by order of his Honor, the Governor, and Committee of Safety for the defense of said colony in 1775. Vessel commanded by Capt Giles Hall; carried 16 guns and was in the list of privateers. Was of Italian ancestry, brave, eccentric and independent; erected own monument before death, which still stands in old Maple Grove Cem near Darrowville, in Stow Twp. A descendant tells he planted the beautiful trees now on the streets of Darrowville. His wife's death 1807, the first in the Twp; the first marriage in Twp was of his dau to Mr. Singletary. Gregory Powers, spoken of in our country's early history, a brilliant lawyer, was his son. D Cuyahoga Falls reports "Died June 12, 1833, aged 95 yrs." as on the monument, makes birth 1738. Has S. A. R. Marker. Ref: (Cuyahoga-Portage) and (Cuyahoga Falls) Chaps.

PRATT, EPHRAIM, (Vinton Co.)

Enl Feb 1780 or 1781 as a Pvt, Capt Fox, Col Henry Jackson, Mass. Battles engaged in, Kings Bridge and Morrisania. Birthplace not known. Enl from Middlesex. In 1820 he referred to his wife as 59 and son 18, but gave no names. D Vinton Co formerly part of Athens. Bur Prattsville, O. Mi:"Ephraim Pratt, A Revolutionary Soldier died Mch 23, 1855, aged 92 yrs, 9 mo, 27 da." Pensioned in Bradford Co, Pa. His name was transferred to the Ohio pension agency, Sept 6, 1823. Ref: Bureau of Pensions, Dept of the Interior; Jane Dailey, State chairman. Fur infor Nabby Lee Ames Chap.

PRATT, NATHAN, (JONATHAN,) (Warren Co.)

Pvt. Col Tupper's Regt Mass Line. Enl for 3 yrs. Br Needham, Mass. 1763. Living in Geauga Co 1833. Pens records show letter asking transfer from Pittsburg agency to that of Cincinnati, letter dated Lebanon, Warren Co, O. 1835. Ref: Pension Records 40270. Fur infor Taylor Chap.

PRATT, OLIVER, (Ashtabula Co.)

Served with the six mos men raised by the town of Lunenburg, for serv in the Continental army during 1780. Br 1761 Boston, Mass. Mar Jedidah Luce. D 1844, East Windsor, O. Ref: Natl No. 62156, p 52, Vol 63, D. A. R. Lin.

PRATT, WORTHY, (Licking Co.)

Verified by war record. Fur infor Hetuck Chap.

PRENTISS, JAMES, (Cuyahoga Co.)

Pvt. N. H. and Maine. Bur Warrensville, Highland Park Cem. GM Western Reserve Chap. Fur infor Western Reserve Chap.

PRENTISS, STANTON, CAPT., (Washington Co.)

Capt. Br Nov 17, 1750, Lancaster, Mass. Parents Dr. Stanton Prentiss and Mary Jennison. Mar Mary Fowler. D July 21, 1836, Marietta, O. Bur Mound Cem, Marietta, O. MI: "Stanton Prentiss, 1750-1836". GM Marietta Chap with Revolutionary marker and on gateway, Nov. 30, 1906; marker stolen and replaced in 1920. Served as Wagon master in Lafayette's army. Fur infor Marietta Chap.

PRESKETT, WILLIAM, (Highland Co.)

Bur Barr's Cem near Danville. Applied for pension but was refused because he had not served 6 mos. Fur infor Waw-Wil-a-Way Chap.

PRESTON, DAVID, (Summit Co.)

Enl Feb 15, 1776, Capt John Stevens' Company at Camp Mount Independence, Ticonderoga, Nov 25, 1776. Also member Col Chas Burratt's Regt, which served in Northern Dept under Gen Schuyler; taken prisoner at "The Cedars," Canada, May 19, 1776. Disch May 20, 1780, from army, having served for 3 yrs previous as Pvt in Capt Jesse Kimball's Company, Col John Chandler's Regt, 8th Conn Line. Br Feb 25, 1758, Ashford, Windham Co, Conn. Mar Miss Cynthia Sprague of Sharon, Conn, Oct 28, 1781. (She died Mch 26, 1817, age 61 yrs; bur Middlebury, Conn.) He then married Violet Fellows of Canaan, Conn. D July 11, 1827, on his farm. Bur Tallmadge. Accompanied with John S. Preston and wife and 2 children, left Conn for Western Reserve about 1810. Religion, Congregational. Fur infor Cuyahoga-Portage Chap.

PRICE, STEPHEN R. (Franklin Co.)

Was a Sgt in 2nd Regt, Md Line. Received a medal for bravery at Stony Point. Was pensioned Sept 1, 1825. Br Radmanshire, Wales, in 1757. D May 22, 1832. Bur on Enieg's Hill, one mile from Gahanna. MI: "Stephen R. Price died May 22, 1832, in the 76th year of his age." GM Revolutionary Grave Committee with bronze marker, May 30, 1912. He was educated in London, England, for the ministry. When 19 he ran away to America, enl in the army and fought throughout the war. Came to Ohio from Virginia in 1815 and settled in Mifflin Twp. Fur infor Columbus Chap.

PRICE, WILLIAM, (Pike Co.)

At age of 96, was receiving a pens in 1840, while residing in Seal Twp, Pike Co, O, according to Census of 1840. At that extreme old age the State Chairman is filing his record as Revolutionary serv, as unable to secure a more authentic record, there being no D. A. R. chap and no response to appeals for data. Br 1744. Fur infor Jane Dailey.

PRICHARD, BENJAMIN, (Portage Co.)

Pvt in Conn Continental. Placed on pens roll May 21, 1819. Bur Nelson, O. Fur infor Old Northwest Chap.

PRICHARD, JARED, (Logan Co.)

Pvt in Capt Samuel Brunson's Company, Col Baldwin's Conn Regt. Br 1750, Waterbury, Conn. Mar 2nd: Elizabeth Allen in 1820 (br 1784, 1871). D 1836, Logan Co, O. Pensioned. Ref: Natl No 100711, Vol 101, p 221, D. A. R. Lin.

PRICKETT, JOSIAH, (Clermont Co.)

Enl at Garrett's Fort, Washington Co, Pa, May 1778. Pvt and Scout, Capt Samuel Swnigler, Pa, Apr 1781, 1 mo. John Holton Capt Aug 1781, 20 da, John Huston Mch or Apr 1782, 6 mo, Indian Spy. Theophilus Phillips, Spring 1783, 1 mo. Br 1764 at Forks of Gunpowder Creek, 20 miles from Baltimore, Md. Parents: John and Elizabeth Robinson Prickett. Mar Sarah Van Camp, dau Lawrence Van Camp, July 4, 1783, Washington Co, Pa. Children: John, Nancy, Joseph, George, Isaac, Elizabeth, Hiram, Tolbert, Josiah, Sarah, William. D Dec 3, 1845, Stonelick Twp, Clermont Co, O. Bur Prickett family burying ground in Stonelick Twp.

near Newtonville, O. Pensioned 1883 for Pvt Pa Line. Came to Clermont Co, 1801. Was a farmer and great hunter. Was wounded in war and used cane. Rode horse through woods to hunt. A grandson has his cane with deer horn for handle. He killed the deer. Ref: Matella Prickett Doughman, Blanchester, O. Natl No 210453. Fur infor Blanchester Chap.

PRIDDY, JOHN, (Fayette Co.)

Pvt. Served 2 mos under each Capt, Massie, Tillman and Hade in Col Campbell's Regt, Va. Br Apr 8, 1758, in Grandville, N. C. Mar Martha Rowe, Va. Children: William, Elias, Andrew, George and Lucy. D Apr 8, 1847, on farm in Green Twp. Bur Cochran Cem. on New Martinsburg Pike, old part, unplatted (near church. MI: "John Priddy died April 8, 1847, aged 89 years." GM Family in 1848. Lived in North Carolina, in Virginia, in Goochland and Fluvanna Cos, Va. Ohio, 1816. Farmer. Pensioner. Fur infor Washington Court House Chap.

PRIEST, JAMES LOUDEN, (Ashland Co.)

Pvt at siege of Boston in 1776, and in the Battle of Bunker Hill. Br 1736, near Boston. Children: James Louden Priest, Jr. D Aug 10, 1821. Bur Loudonville Cem, Loudonville, O. GM Sarah Copus Chap in 1927. He came to Ohio in 1808 with his son. He laid out and founded the town Loudonville. Fur infor Sarah Copus Chap.

PRIEST, JEREMIAH, (Clark Co.)

Pvt. Enl from Culpeper, Va, 1779, and served 2 yrs under Col Francis Taylor, Capt John Roberts and John Purvis. Br 1755, Shenandoah Co, Va. Mar Millie Gardner, 1781. Children: Anna (1783), Obediah (1784), Mary (1785), Agnes (1787), Basheba (1789), Casandra (1790), Elijah (1792), Nancy (1793), Elizabeth (1795), Phoebe (1797), William (1800), Jermiah (1802), Millie (1804), John M. (1807). D Mch 4, 1804, Clark Co. Bur private cem, destroyed 1913, near Honey Creek, New Carlisle, O. MI: "Jeremiah Priest, born 1755, died Mar 4, 1804." GM Photo of grave and marker before cem was destroyed in possession of Dr. F. A. Priest, Indianapolis, Ind. War records show he came to Clark Co from Va. Entered a piece of land upon which he lived, died and was bur. Farmer. The land he entered was a grant for Revolutionary serv. Ref: War Dept and Dept of Interior. Fur infor Lagonda Chap.

PRINTY, WILLIAM (Brown Co.)

1775, enl for one yr under Capt Brearly's and Col Maxwell, of the 2nd N. J. Regt. Was at battle of Three Rivers. Re-enlisted for three yrs, in same Company and Regt under Capt Yard who resigned. He was then commanded by Capt Phillips and Col Shreve. At battle of Short Hills and Brandywine. Br 1749, Ireland. Mar Rhoda. Children: Jesse (perhaps others). D Brown Co, O, 1826. Bur Shinkles Ridge, Lewis Twp, Brown Co, O, a few miles from Higginsport. Ref: Mrs. Ruth Lyons Ross, Georgetown, O. Natl No 96899, Vol 97, D. A. R. Lin. Fur infor Taliaferro Chap.

PRIOR, SIMEON, (Summit Co.)

Pvt in Capt Jedediah Waterman's Company, Col John Durkee's Conn Regt. Pensioned in Portage Co. Br Norwich, Conn, May 16, 1754. D Northampton, O. June 29, 1837. Bur Northampton, O, Summit Co. GM S. A. R. First settler in the town. Ref: Natl No 36696, D. A. R. A member of this chapter has complete services. Fur infor Cuyahoga Falls Chap.

PRITCHARD, JAMES, (Ross Co.)

Pvt. Maryland Line. Br Frederick Co, Md. Mar Tabitha White. D Chillicothe, 1813. Came to Northwest Territory 1799; Judge of Supreme Court. Ref: Natl No 69015, p 7, Vol 70, D. A. R. Lin. Fur infor Nathaniel Massie Chap.

PROCTOR, FRANCIS, SR.., (Trumbull Co.)

Served 1776 as Pvt in Capt Robert Dodge's Company, Col Ebenezer Francis' Mass Regt. Br 1758, Ipswich, Mass. Mar Abigial Edwards. D 1832, New Bloomfield, O. Bur Center Bloomfield. MI: Name, "B. 1758—Died 1832." Ref: Historical Library, Cleveland Revolutionary Soldiers bur in Trumbull Co and Natl No 100194, Vol 101, p 60, D. A. R. Lin. Fur infor Mary Chesney Chap.

PRUDEN, JOSEPH, Trumbull Co.)

Baptized 1760, Morristown, N. J. Will dated June 7, 1821, probated Dec. 11, 1827. Bur Casterline Cem, Bazetta Twp. MI: "Joseph Pruden." Ref: Revolutionary Soldiers bur in Trumbull Co. Cleveland Historical Library. Fur infor Mary Chesney Chap.

PUCKET, WILLIAM, (Highland Co.)

Served from Prince Co, Va as a Pvt in Capt Thomas Moore's Company. Engaged in battle at Guilford C. H., when he was wounded in the thigh by a musket ball. Br Virginia, 1747. Children: Allen, Susannah, Greene, Martin, Nathanial, Jonathon, Sallie, James, Andrew. D 1833 in Highland Co, O, near Buford. Bur Barr Graveyard. Migrated to Highland Co, O, soon after Revolution. He was crippled in his hip fr engagements for life. Fur infor Waw-Wil-a-Way Chap.

PUTNAM, ALLEN, (Washington Co.)

Enl at Danvers, Mass when 18 yrs old for 6 mos term and served as Pvt fr July 25 to Dec 7, 1780. Br Denvers, Mass Oct 25, 1762. Mar Anna Porter Apr 26, 1785. Killed by a fall in Marietta, O, in 1807. He was the first of Gen Rufus Putnam's party to leap ashore in Marietta. Ref: Dec of Commonwealth of Mass. Natl No 21328, Vol 32, D. A. R. Lin.

PUTNAM, EZRA, (Washington Co.)

Maj in Col John Mansfield 19th Regt. Served 3 mo 3 da. Br 1728, Middletown, Mass. D 1811. Bur Mound Cem, Marietta, O. MI: "Maj. Ezra Putnam 1725-1811." GM Marietta Chap by Revolutionary marker and gateway, Nov 30, 1906; marker stolen, replaced in 1920. Fur infor Marietta Chap.

PUTNAM, ISRAEL, JR. (Washington Co.)

Served as aide to his father, Gen Israel Putnam. Raised a company of volunteers at time of Lexington Alarm. Attained rank of Col. Br 1739, Salem, Mass. Parents: Gen Israel and Hannah Pope Putnam. Mar Sarah Waldo, 1764. Children: Aaron, Waldo, Israel, William Pitt, David, Sarah, Mary, Elizabeth, George W. D 1812, Belpre, O. Bur Belpre, Washington Co, O. on Putnam lot in Belpre Cem. MI: "Israel Putnam 1740-1812." GM Marietta Chap with Revolutionary marker in 1921. After Revolutionary War came with family to Ohio and settled in Belpre in 1789. Was a prosperous and progressive agriculturalist. Ref: Pioneer Hist by Dr Hildreth and Williams Hist of Washington Co. Natl No 12286, p 111, Vol 13, D. A. R. Lin. Fur infor Marietta Chap.

PUTNAM, RUFUS, GEN., (Washington Co.)

Lt Col in May, 1775. Employed as engineer in the defenses of New York in 1776. Col Aug 6, 1776. Commissioned Brig Gen in Jan 1783. Br Apr 9, 1738, Boston, Mass. D May 4, 1824 Marietta, O. Bur Mound Cem, Marietta, O. MI: "Gen Rufus Putnam 1738-1824." GM Marietta Chap with Revolutionary marker and on gateway Nov 30, 1906; marker stolen and replaced in 1920. Appointed judge of northwest territory in 1789. U. S. Surveyor Gen in 1793. Member of Ohio Constitutional Convention in 1803. Ref: Natl No 31403, D. A. R. and many others. Fur infor Marietta Chap.

QUIGGLE, PETER, (Geauga Co.)

Served as Pvt in Capt Alexander Parker's Company 7th Regt Pa Mil. Br 1732, Lancaster, Pa. Parents: Christian Quickel (Quiggle). Mar Ann Sophia Nehemia. Children: George, Peter Jr, John, Philip, Michael, Fanny. D 1828, Geauga Co, O. Bur Hambden, Geauga Co, O. on lot 35. MI: "Peter Quiggle, Parker Co, 7 Pa Regt Rev War." GM Government Marker. He removed to Geauga Co where he died. Ref: D. A. R. Honor Roll 63258. Fur infor Taylor Chap.

QUIGLEY, ROBERT, (Trumbull Co.)

Bur Oak Grove, Warren. Unable to locate grave. Ref: Baldwin Library, Youngstown, O. Kindness of Miss Kyle. Fur infor Mary Chesney Chap.

QUINN, JOHN, (Columbiana Co.)

Living in 1833 in Liverpool Twp, Columbiana Co. Age 74 yrs. A pensioner. Fur infor Bethia Southwick Chap.

QUINN, ROBERT, (Preble Co.)

Br Feb 24, 1761. D Apr 10, 1844. Bur Mound Hill Cem, Lanier Twp. Fur infor Grace Miller, Org Regt, Eaton, O.

RADABACH, PETER, (Co not stated.)

Br 1764, Pa. D 1834. Fur infor Natl No 49923, Vol 50, p 413, D. A. R. Lin.

RADER, ADAM, (Champaign Co.)

Br 1764, in Virginia. D Apr 14, 1847. Bur in cem adjoining church at Kingscreek. Fur infor Urbana Chap.

RALSTON, ANDREW, (Muskingum Co.)

Enl 1776 in Capt Wetzell's Company, Col Samuel Miles Pa Rifle Regt as a Pvt. Br 1753 Scotland. D 1827. Bur Bloomfield, O. Ref: D. A. R. Lin Bk. Natl No 99552, also Natl No 78871, Vol 100, p 175. Fur infor Nathaniel Massie Chap.

RALSTON, ARCHIBALD, (Trumbull Co.)

Br 1742. D 1810. Bur Seceeders Corners, Liberty Twp. MI: Name (date of death and birth). Fur infor Mary Chesney Chap.

RAMEY, LAWRENCE, (Brown Co.)

Pvt. Br Berkley Co, Va, in 1758. Mar Anne Nimon in 1784. D Apr 3, 1835, Brown Co, O. Bur Decatur, O. MI:"Sacred to the memory of Lawrence Ramey, who departed this life Apr 3, 1835, aged 81." GM May 30, 1922. Fur infor Lieutenant Byrd Chap.

RAMSEY, JOHN, (Trumbull Co.)

Br 1743. D Jan 6, 1810. Bur Seceeders Corners, Liberty Twp. MI: Name, date of birth and death. Fur infor Mary Chesney Chap.

RAMSEY, NATHAN, (Preble Co.)

Bur Israel Twp. Ref: Mary P. Mitchell, Eaton, O.

RAMSEY, WM., (Preble Co.)

Bur Israel Twp. Ref: Mary P. Mitchell, Eaton, O. Fur infor Grace C. Miller Org Regent.

RAMSEY, WILLIAM (RAMSAY), (Belmont Co.)

Ensign in Pa Tr in 1776, 2 mos in Capt Samuel Patton's Company, Col Culbertson's Regt. In the winter of 1776-77, 2 mos in Capt George Matthews Co. Next yr 2 mos in Capt Patrick Jack's Company, Col Culbertson's Regt. In 1778 or 1779, 2 mos in same command. He was allowed pens executed Jan 29, 1834, while a resident of Morristown, Belmont Co, O. Br Jan 1, 1756, Bucks Co, Pa. Parents: Capt William Ramsey and Margaret Allen. Mar Martha Allen Aug 26, 1780. D Jan 1, 1841 Morristown, O. Pioneer families of Western Pa. Came to Ohio in 1815. Ref: S. A. R. Natl No 42668. Fur infor or S. A. R. Richard Montgomery.

RANDALL, REUBEN, (Portage Co.)

Lived at Streetsboro, age 73, where he drew a pens in 1840. Fur infor Old Northwest Chap.

RANKIN, DANIEL, (Brown Co.)

Br 1752. D 1833. Ref: Natl No 48430, Vol 49, p 201.

RANKIN, HENRY, (Harrison Co.)

A Revolutionary pensioner living in Harrison Co, in 1819, aged 72; a Henry Rankin served in Capt Alexander Martin's Company, Col Peter Grubb's Bn, Lancaster Co Mil, in 1776. U S Pens Rolls 1835; Pa Archives 5, VII, 801. Fur infor Moravian Trail Chap.

RANKIN, JAMES, (Harrison Co.)

Served as a member of Washington Co, Pa Mil, in Crawford's Expedition against the Sandusky Indians in 1782. Br 1747. D 1823. Br in Cadiz Old Graveyard. Ref: Pa Archives 6, II, 402. Fur infor Moravian Trail Chap.

RANKIN, THOMAS, (Harrison Co.)

Served with his brothers, Lt John, Jesse and Zachariah, in Capt David Reed's 4th Company, Col John Marshal's 4th Bn, Washington Co Mil, 1781-82. Br 1760. D 1832. Bur in Rankin Graveyard. Son of William; grandson of David. Ref: Pa Archives 6, II, 133, 144. Fur infor Moravian Trail Chap.

RANKINS, JONATHAN, (Trumbull Co.)

Br 1739. Bur Old Cem, Mahoning Ave, Warren. MI: Died Sept 20, 1812, aged 73 years. GM Name on bronze tablet, 1827, by D. A. R. Fur infor Mary Chesney Chap.

RANNEY, NATHANIEL, (Summit Co.)

Enl for 3 yrs Capt Edward Eel's Company Conn Line. Br 1735, Upper House, Conn. D 1800, Hudson, O. Ref: Natl No 90374, Vol 91, p 123, D. A. R. Lin.

RANSOM, JOSEPH, (Erie Co.

Pvt in Conn State Tr. Pensioner. Bur in Erie Co. Fur infor Martha Pitkin Chap.

RANSOM, ROBERT, (Erie Co.)

Bur Erie Co. Fur infor Martha Pitkin Chap.

RATHBONE, JOSEPH, (Ashtabula Co.)

Was placed on the pens roll of Ashtabula Co, O, 1831, for services as a Pvt, Mass Continental Line. Enl Tyringham, Mass. Br 1763, Rhode Island. Mar Olivia Pearson. D 1854, Conneaut, Ashtabula Co, O. Ref: Natl No 49765, Vol 50, Lin Bk, Vol XLIII. Fur infor Mary Stanley Chap.

RATHBURN, SEN EDWARD, (Cuyahoga Co.)

Pvt Mass Tr. Br 1754. D 1849. Bur Harvard Grove Cem, Lansing Ave and E 57th St. GM Western Reserve Chap. Fur infor Western Reserve Chap.

RAVENSCROFT, WILLIAM, (Coshocton Co.)

D 1854. Bur White Eyes Twp. Ref: Co Hist. Fur infor Coshocton Chap.

RAWDON, EZRA, (Trumbull Co.)

Br 1760. D Sept 16, 1824. Bur Old Cem, Mahoning Ave, Warren. MI: Formerly fr Conn. Died Sept 16, 1824, in 64 years of his age. "He was killed by a kick from a horse. God who first gave him breath afterwards called him back by sudden death." GM Name on bronze tablet, 1927, by D. A. R. Fur infor Mary Chesney Chap.

RAYMOND, LEMUEL, (Huron Co.)

Pvt Mass Mil in John Brown's Regt, Berkshire Co, Mass. Br 1759 at Richmond, Mass. D 1829, Huron Co, O. Norwalk, O. Ref: Natl No 25379, 30247, p 86, D. A. R. Lin, Vol 31.

RAYMOND, THADDEUS, (Huron Co.)

Bur Hunt's Corners, Suttons' Cem. Fur infor Sally De Forest Chap.

READ, NATHANIEL, (Ashtabula Co.)

Served as Pvt in many battles. Capt Parker's Company, 3rd Bn, Wardsworth's Brig, Col Sage Conn Line. Br 1758, Tyringham, Mass. Parents: Amasa Read and Fannie Sprig, his wife. Mar Rhoda Sedgwick, in Conn, June, 1785. Children, Sally, Acheah, Ira, Polly, Grace, Melinda, Irema, Grave. D 1831, Williamsfield, Ashtabula Co, O. Bur Roberts Cem, Wayne Twp, near Williamsfield. MI: "In memory of Nathaniel Read, who departed this life Apr 10, 1831, in the 73 year of his age." GM Family stone that is fast crumbling. The 3rd Bn was raised June, 1776, to reinforce Washington at N. Y. Time expired Dec 25, 1776. Ref: Lin Bks XXXVI and XLI. Family Bible record written by Nathaniel Read. Mrs. Bert Presley, Chardon, O. Natl No 62556, D. A. R. Fur infor Mary Stanley Chap.

REASONER, PETER, (Guernsey Co.)

Served as a ranger on the frontier. Br 1735, probably Beaver Co, Pa. Parents: Nicholas Reasoner, wife's name not known. Mar Mary Sheers in 1763. Children: Nicholas, Benjamin, John, Sarah, Jacob, Solomon, Henry, Regina, Susan, Mary. D about 1810, Guernsey Co, on Reasoner homestead near New Concord, O. Burial ground given by John Reasoner living near Cem. MI: Sandstone marker, partly crumbled, inscription obliterated. May 16, 1791, given 136 acres of land as depreciation claim. Fur infor Anna Asbury Stone Chap.

REAVES, ASHER, (Greene Co.)

Pvt Va Mil. Pensioned 1833. Br 1758. D July 1, 1845. Bur Baptist Graveyard, Jamestown. Silver Creek, 1813. Ref: Robinson's Hist of Greene Co. Fur infor Catherine Greene Chap.

RECHER, PETER, (Montgomery Co.)

A Pvt in a command from Montgomery Co, possibly from Frederick Co, but the identical command could not be ascertained from Md and U. S. Authorities. He was not a pensioner. Pa Archives, 5 series, Vol 4, p 662, show that one Peter Recher was a Pvt in the Continental Line. "Rangers on the Frontiers 1778-1783." One "Peter Rickes" took oath of Fidelity to Md in Frederick Co, Md. Br Aug 14, 1763, Frederick Co, Md. Parents: Peter Recher, came from Switzerland about 1735, and settled near Wolfsville, Md. Mar Elizabeth Protsman, d Feb 1, 1836, age 67 yrs, 3 mos, 5 das. Children: Jacob, Peter, Joseph, John, Daniel, Frederick, Elias, Lewis, Lica, Mary and Susan. D June 3, 1833, Jefferson Twp, Montgomery Co. Bur Ellerton. GM Richard Montgomery Chap, S. A. R., 1919. Official bronze marker. Peter Recher purchased in the fall of 1804, 389 acres of land and settled here the following yr. One of the pioneer families. Ref: "Dr. Brumbaughs." Rev Records of Md, p 23. Many men are preparing blanks for membership in S. A. R. Fur infor Richard Montgomery Chap, S. A. R. Infor furnished by J. C. Recher, R. F. D. 3, Miamsburg, O.

REECE, DAVID, (Butler Co.)

See Pa Archives, p 189, a Revolutionary Soldier. MI: For Pioneers in Butler Co, O, his name appears. Ref: Mrs. E. P. Whallon, Wyoming, O. Fur infor Cincinnati Chap.

REED, ALEXANDER, (Wyandot Co.)

Enl 1776 Sgt, Capt Andrew Wallace's Company, Col Jas Woods 8th Va Regt. Br 1760, Va. Mar Elizabeth Crosby 2nd wife. D 1847, Wyandotte Co, O. Ref: 75675, Vol 76, Natl No 64577 D. A. R. Lin.

REED, DAVID, JR., (Meigs Co.)

Pvt. Penobscot Expedition. Br 1767, Topsham, Me. D 1858, Pomeroy, O. Mar Nancy Phillips. Ref: Natl No 39910, p 334, Vol 40, D. A. R. Lin.

REED, GEORGE, (Butler Co.)

Br Jan 1757. Mar Sarah? (br Dec 28, 1761, d Aug 1829.) D July 1834. Bur on Mary Eva Marshall farm near Sevenmile, O. MI: "Rev Soldier." GM Headstone restored by D. A. R. Fur infor John Reily Chap.

REED, JACOB, JR., (Stark Co.)

Bur Justus, Sugar Creek Twp, Starke Co. Fur infor Canton Chap.

REED, JAMES, SR., (Mahoning Co.)

Pvt. May to Oct 1775 "Conn Men of the Rev," p 67, disch Sept 9, 1776, p 458, Enl in Oct 1776. Br 1736 in Conn. Name of one son was James who mar Elizabeth Calloway. D 1806, Canfield. Lived in Conn until his wife d when he came to Canfield with his son James. Trumbull and Mahoning Co Hist, Vol II, pp 14 and 96. Also Pioneer Women of Western Reserve. Fur infor Mahoning Chap.

REED, JAMES, JR., (Mahoning Co.)

Pvt. Pensioned 1833. Br 1760. Mar Mary (1748-1831). Children: James William, Samuel, and others not mentioned. D 1834, Poland Twp. Bur Presbyterian church, Poland. GM Mahoning Chap, bronze, in 1916. Ref: Pa Archives, Series 3, Vol 23, p 590. Trumbull and Mahoning Co Hist, Vol 2, p 61. Fur infor Mahoning Chap.

REED, JAMES, COL., (Mahoning Co.)

Lt in NC Brig 1776; Capt 1779; (Rev Army accts of NC, Vol VIII, pp 24 to 40, folio 3); Disch 1782; Heitman Hist Rec. Land Grant No 522 State of NC to James Reed for 130 acres in 1783. Br Rowan Co, NC. Mar Margaret Baley,

Sept 21, 1766; (2nd Mary McMahan, Dec 6, 1774). Children: Susannah Elizabeth, Isaac. D Butler Twp 1812. Bur Reed graveyard on Springfield road 2 miles east of New Troy Pike, and 2 miles from Vandalia. Location of grave in center of this small burying ground beside wife, and next to son Isaac and wife. MI: Head stones not marked. Came to Ohio in 1805, settling on grant of land mentioned above. Farmer. Ref: George S. Dial, Dial Building, Springfield, O. Fur infor Richard Montgomery Chap, S. A. R.

REED, JOHN, (Darke Co.)

Placed on Ohio Pens Roll 1832 for serv as Pvt in Maryland Tr. Br 1758, Maryland. Mar Martha. D Aug 27, 1844, Darke Co, O. Bur Hollinsburg, southeast cor of old cem. MI: "John Reed Soldier of the Rev a member of the Baptist church. Died Aug 27, 1884, aged 96 years 3 mos 27 days." Grave stone very old and marking almost obliterated. Ref: Natl No 52529, Vol 53, p 252, D. A. R. Lin. Fur infor Ft Greenville Chap.

REED, PHINEAS, (Mahoning Co.)

Pvt from Dutchess Co, NY 6th Regt "NY Men of the Rev," p 250. He also had land bounty rights. Bur Canfield, O. Came to Ohio in 1799 and located in Canfield. Turnbull and Mahoning Co Hist Vol II, p 12. Fur infor Mahoning Chap.

REED, THOMAS, (Mahoning Co.)

Ranger in Washington Co, Pa. Pa Archives Series III, Vol 23, p 232. Pvt in Cumberland Co Mil. Capt John Young. Series V, Vol VI, pp 17, 82, 558, 576 same in 1782. Children: Benj, John, Catherine, mar Thomas Fenton, Mary mar James Chalfant. Bur Milton Twp. Came to Milton Twp in 1798. Fur infor Mahoning Chap.

REED, WILLIAM, (Mahoning Co.)

Ranger Washington Co Mil. Pa in record of 1778-1783. Br 1746. Mar Mary (br 1748 d 1823). Children: James, William, Samuel. D 1831. Bur Presbyterian Cem, Poland. GM by Mahoning Chap, bronze marker in 1916. Ref: Pa Archives, Vol 23, Series 3, Trumbull and Mahoning Co Hist Vol W, p 90. Fur infor Mahoning Chap.

REEDER, JACOB, (Trumbull Co.)

Master of ceremonies at Fort Constitution 1776. Br 1742. D 1826, Trumbull Co. Ref: Vol 91, p 196, D. A. R. Lin.

REEDER, JACOB, (Hamilton Co.)

Master Armorer Continental Army. Rank of Capt June 1776. A. D. 16-426 NY line also p 250 "NY in Rev." Br Nov 1760, NJ. Parents: Joseph Reeder III (1716) and Susan Gano (1722). D 1860, and bur at Hamilton Co after 1803 (later data sent in). Charter member Elder and Trustee 1st Presbyterian Church Cincinnati, 1789. Descendent of William of Orange. Ref: Natl No 34924 D. A. R. Lin. Fur infor Cincinnati Chap.

REEDER, JOSEPH, 4th, (Hamilton Co.)

5th Regt Col Du Boys, Albany Co, NY Line. Br 1745. Parents: Joseph Reeder III (br 1716) and Susan Gano (br 1722). Mar Annie Huff (br 1743). Children: George br 1764, Elijah 1770, John 1773, Jonathan 1775, Micaiah 1779, Reuben, Mar Rebecca Kennedy (dau Francis a Rev Soldier) Ralph 1788, Elizabeth 1765, Sarah 1763, Jessie 1776, Anna 1782, Mary 1791, a supposed son, Joseph A. D 1829. Bur Pleasant Ridge, Hamilton Co, O. GM by stone marker. Ancestral Hist to William of Orange; name appears on tax list Columbia Twp; 1st Presbyterian Church Cincinnati, O. 1790. Ref: p 58, NY Men in Rev War by Roberts. Fur infor Cincinnati Chap.

REEDER, STEPHEN, (Hamilton Co.)

4th Regt Orange Co, NY. Br 1762. Parents: Joseph Reeder III and Sarah Gano Reeder. Bur Hamilton Co, O. Owned lot 20 in 1st plat of Cincinnati. Ref: Natl No 34924 D. R. R. Lin. Fur infor Cincinnati Chap.

REEDER, WILLIAM, (Hamilton Co.)

See p 166 NY in Rev War 4th Regt Orange Co. Br 1735. Parents: Joseph (III) (br Apr 24, 1716) and Susan Gano Reeder. D Hamilton Co, O. Age 100 yrs. Ref: Natl No 34924, D. A. R Lin. Fur infor Cincinnati Chap.

REEVE, EBENEZER, Lt., (Trumbull Co.)

Lt. Br 1751. D July 26, 1825 in 74th yr. Bur Old Cem at Kinsmore, O. in northwest cor. MI: "In memory of Ebenezer Reeve a soldier in Rev and first that came with his family fr Conn, to this place in 1802. To end of his life set an example of industry and economy, served his generation by will of God and fell asleep July 25, 1825 in 74th year of his life." Marker needs fixing, nearly gone to pieces. Fur infor Mary Chesney Chap.

REEVE, LUTHER, (Ashtabula Co.)

In the Conn Lines. Sgt. Enl from Lynne, Conn. Served in Conn Line as Sgt under Capt Ely, Col Huntington 1777-1781. Also under Capt Brigham 5th Regt, 1781-1783. Was pensioner Act of 1818 Conn. Br 1760, Southold, L. I. Parents: Israel Reeve and Theodosia Case Reeve. Mar Ann Pearson, Jan. 31, 1785. Children: Benjamin, Rumsey, Sarepta, Mary, Hannibal, Anne. D Dec 13, 1843, New Lyme, Ohio. Bur Dodgeville Cem, New Lyme, O, a few rods west of gate in eastern part of Cem. MI: Mr. Luther Reeve, Died Dec 13, 1843, aged 83 years. GM by the family, brown slate stone slab. Ref: Natl No 61422, D. A. R. Conn Men in the Rev; Lin Bk. Vol LXIV p 247. Further infor Luther Reeve Chap.

REEVES, JOSEPH, (Trumbull Co.)

Pvt and Sgt NJ Mil. Received Pens. Supreme Court Records p 247. D Warren, O. Bur Old Cem, Mahoning Ave. in family lot near Isaac Fithian, another Revolutionary soldier. MI: Stone has been broken. Name on Memorial Monument erected for Revolutionary soldiers. Ref: Court Records Family Hist. and Historical Library. Cleveland, O. Fur infor Mary Chesney Chap.

REEVES, NATHANIEL, (Clermont Co.)

In 1840, while residing with Nathaniel Reeves, Clermont Co, O. Batavia Twp. received a pens at age 84, for Revolutionary services. Br 1756. Fur infor Census of 1840. Copied by State Chairman.

REICHELSDOEFER, JOHN, (now Reichelderfer), (Pickaway Co.)

Pvt in Capt Ferdinand Ritter's Company, 3rd Bn Lt Jacob Morgan's Sr. Berk Co, Pa Mil 1777 and 1778. Pa Archives, Vol 6, pp 284, 308; also Mounett Family Genealogy p 434. Br Dec 26, 1741, Berks Co, Pa. Parents: Frederick Reichelsderfer. Mother's name in Mounett's Genealogy. Mar Ann Elizabeth Hagenbuch (see Mounett's Genealogy) Aug 24, 1825 Children: Maria Catherine (br 1775) Barbara, John, Christian, Henry, Maria (or Mary), Jacob, Andrew, Elizabeth, Susannah and Magdalena. D Aug 30, 1810, Pickaway Co, O. Bur Stump's or Slump Cem, Salt Creek Twp, Pickaway Co, O, near extreme northeast part of cem. MI: Johannes Reichelderfer, Geboren Dec 26, 1741, Gestothen Aug 30, 1810, after 68 yrs, 8 mos, 4 Tag. GM by sons and daughters. Settled in Salt Creek Twp., Pickaway Co, O, about 1805. Parents were pioneer residents of Albany Twp, Berks Co, Pa. Farmer. He died suddenly after building a cabin and planting an orchard for each child. Ref: John J. Reichelderfer, Tarlton, Ohio, and Natl No 76053, D. A. R. Lin. Fur infor Pickaway Plains Chap.

REILY, JAMES, (Butler Co.)

Br June 15, 1755, Chester Co, Pa. D 1840. Bur in Sutherland Cem, since converted into a park. Remains never transferred. Ref: Mrs. William Mikler (Adda Strant). Fur infor John Reily Chap.

REILY, JOHN, (Butler Co.)

Pvt in Revolutionary War. Joined Army 1870 and served 18 mos under Gen Nathaniel Greene. Br Apr 10, 1763, Chester Co, Pa. D June 8, 1850, Hamilton, O. Bur Greenwood Cem. MI: Name dates of birth and death. Was first postmaster in Hamilton, 1804-1832. Also served as Clerk of Courts, Clerk of Legislature in 1800-1801. Trustee of Maimi University. After serv in Revolutionary War returned to Hamilton, served wtih Gen. Anthony Wayne and Alexander Hamilton. John Reily Chap, D. A. R. named for him. Ref: Mrs. E. G. Rathbone, granddaughter, Friendship, N. Y. Fur infor John Reily Chap.

REMAY, JOHN, (Muskingum Co.)

Pvt. Enl in Culpeper Co, Va, Mch, 1776, under Officers Green and Muhlenberg, James Pendleton. Engaged in battle of White Plains. Br 1754. D July 27, 1834. Fur infor Muskingum Chap.

REMINGTON, JOSEPH, (Erie Co.)

Br Groton Twp. Bur in Erie Co. Fur infor Martha Pitkin Chap.

RENICK, JOHN, (Pickaway Co.)

Ensign in Va Tr. Br Hampshire Co, Va, 1750. Mar Mary Heath, 1771. Children: Thomas, Mathen, Rachel, Seymour, Margaret, James, Abel, Asabel, Ann, Catherine, Mary. D Jan 13, 1814, Pickaway Co, Jackson Twp. Bur family graveyard in Jackson Twp. Bur at the foot of an Indian mound, near the home of Elias Florence. MI: "John Renick, born 1759 died 1814." GM Plain marble stone. Farmer. His commission signed by Thomas Jefferson is in the hands of H. C. Renick, Circleville, O. Ref: Natl No. 82697, Vol 83, D. A. R. Lin. Fur infor Mt. Sterling Chap.

REPPART, DANIEL, (Harrison Co.)

Pa Mil 1785. Bur West Grove Cem. Fur infor Moravian Trail Chap.

REUBEN, JOHN, (Trumbull Co.)

Unable to locate grave. Name given in list compiled by S. A. R. of Ohio. Fur infor Mary Chesney Chap.

REYNOLDS, ELY, (Athens Co.)

Enl as a Pvt Soldier in the 4th Regt of NY Line under Cols Henry Livingston and James Holmes. Over 80 years of age when he died probably Barnstable, Mass. Name of wife not known to descendants living here. Mar about 1747 or earlier. Children: Justus, Mary, Electa, Sarah, Orpha, Ruth, Hannah, Samuel, Isaac, Eli. D Nov 28, 1827, Athens Twp, Athens Co, O. A very strenuous effort to locate his grave failed, even his descendants can not tell. He is known to have died at the home of his son Eli on a farm four miles south of Athens. MI: If a monument was ever placed, it has crumbled. He brought his family, excepting Mary and one other child who remained in New York, to Athens Co, O, in 1805. Farmer, served on the Grand Jury of the Co in 1809 and 1810. He outlived his wife. Ref: New York in the Rev, pp 47, 53. Fur infor Nabby Lee Ames Chap.

REYNOLDS, JOHN, (Lake Co.)

Was in the Lexington Alarm, also in Bigelow's Company of artillery; Mch 7, 1777, was in the 4th Regt Conn Line as a musician. Was also a Sgt in Capt Horton's Company. Br Mch 16, 1760, Norwich, Conn. D Mch 3, 1840, Mentor, Lake Co, O. Bur Mentor at Little Mountain. GM New Connecticut Chap. He received a pens with rank of Sgt under the Act of 1818. Fur infor New Connecticut Chap.

RHOADS, FREDERICK, (Co not stated.)

Served 1778 to 1781. Br Germany. D 1841, Ohio. Fur infor Vol 74, D. A. R. Lin.

RHODES, NICHOLAS, (Green Co.)

Served as a farrier in Light Horse Harry Lee's Legion, Continental Tr. Pensioned in Ohio 1829, for serv as Dragoon, Va Line. Br 1761. D 1830. Mar Elizabeth Taylor. Ref: Natl No. 45408, p 168, Vol 46, D. A. R. Lin.

RIBLET, CHRISTIAN, (Richland Co.)

Pvt in the Pa Mil. Br 1762. D Apr 6, 1844. Bur Riblet Cem, several miles west of Ontario, O. MI: Large marker, name and troop. GM Mary Washington D. A. R. bronze marker in 1911. Fur infor Mary Washington Chap.

RICE, AARON, (Trumbull Co.)

Br 1749. D 1832. Bur Old Harrington Cem, northeast of Greene. MI: Name and above dates. Fur infor Mary Chesney Chap.

RICE, ENOCH, (Trumbull Co.)

Br Old Salem, Mass. Mar, wife (d Nov 6, 1837, aged 87). D July 12, 1843, aged 96 yrs. Bur Greene, O. Was associated with Israel Putnam throughout the war. Polly Rice, sister of Enoch Rice, was the wife of Israel Putnam, a Revolutionary Soldier. Ref: C. B. Rice, Greene, O. Fur infor Mary Chesney Chap.

RICE, EPHRAIM, SR., (Trumbull Co.)

Bur Harrington Cem, Greene Twp. MI: No monument, but bur beside wife who has stone. Ref: Descendants Ephraim Rice Sr and Revolutionary Soldier bur in Trumbull Co, Cleveland Historical Library. Fur infor Mary Chesney Chap.

RICE, FREDERICK, (Wayne Co.)

Pvt. Volunteered under Capt John Berry; marched to Morristown, N J., joined under Col Potter; several skirmishes on Staten Island. Br 1753. Mar Catherine Laufer in 1783. D Jan 23, 1848. Bur Wooster Cem, south of Wooster. MI: Frederick Rice. A soldier of the Revolution. Died Jan. 23, 1848, aged 94 yrs. 3 mos. 23 da." Applied for pens 1834 fr Wayne Co, O. Ref: Mrs. J. C. Talbot, 317 N. Bever St., Wooster, O., and Natl No. 99019, Vol 100, D. A. R. Lin. Fur infor Wooster Wayne Chap.

RICE, ISAAC, (Trumbull Co.)

Br 1762. D Apr 5, 1842, in his 80th yr. Bur Old Cem south of center of Vernon. MI: Marker is all right; grave needs cleaning off. Fur infor Mary Chesney Chap.

RICE, JASON, (Athens Co.)

Br 1757, Vt. Mar Sarah Hibbard (d 1824). Children: Reuben, Ambrose, Jonas, Sabinus, Sally, Jason, Melona. D Dec 31, 1843. Ames Twp. Bur Carter, north of Amesville, O. MI: "Jason Rice died Dec 31, 1843 in his 87th year." GM by family. Monument of sandstone now crumbling. Came to Ohio from New England in 1800. Farmer. He received a pens for Revolutionary serv. Ref:

Bureau of Pensions, Dept of Interior, Walker's Hist 6 413. Fur infor Nabby Lee Ames Chap.

RICE, MICHAEL, (Fairfield Co.)

Bur Greenfield Cem. Fur infor Elizabeth Sherman Reese Chap.

RICE, NATHAN, (Washington Co.)

Enl as Pvt in Capt John Nixon's Company of Minute Men; also in Capt Davis Mon's Company, Col John Nixon's Regt. Br 1763, Vermont. Mar Jemima McClure. D 1841. Bur Rainbow Cem on Muskingum River in Washington Co. GM Marietta Chap with Revolutionary marker, in 1921. Ref: Natl No 65663, Vol 66, p 224, D. A. R. Lin. Fur infor Marietta Chap.

RICE, OLIVER, MAJ., (Washington Co.)

Pvt in Capt John Nixon's Company of Minute Men; Corp in Capt David Moor's Company; Sgt Maj in Col James Morris' Regt; Ensign in same Regt; Lt in Col John Brooks' Regt. Br 1752, Mass. D 1836, and bur Belpre, Washington Co, O. MI: "Maj. Oliver Rice born 1752 died 1836.' GM Marietta Chap, with Revolutionary marker in 1921. Fur infor Marietta Chap.

RICHARDS, JEDEDIAH, (Summit Co.)

Br May 4, 1759, Norfolk, Conn. Children: Jedediah Jr., Robert Usher, Julius, Geo. W. D Jan 30, 1831. Bur Western Star. MI: "Jedediah Richards, a Soldier of the Revolution. Born Norfolk, Conn., May 4, 1759. Died Jan. 30, 1831." GM White marble slab. Fur infor Cuyahoga Portage Chap.

RICHARDSON, JACOB, (Hamilton Co.)

Pens 1821 for serv as Pvt, Pa Line. Br 1750, Pa. Mar Mary Hutchinson. D 1825, near Harrison, Hamilton Co. Ref: Natl No. 13691 D. A. R. Natl No. 86019, Vol 87, p 7, D. A. R. Lin.

RICHARDSON, JESSE, (Muskingum Co.)

Enl Somers, Conn, 1775. Pens in Ohio 1832 for 2 yrs actual serv as Pvt, Conn Line. Br 1758. D 1840, Muskingum Co. Ref: Natl No. 44313, Vol 45, p 127, D. A. R. Lin.

RICHARDSON, JOHN, (Hamilton Co.)

Br 1756, Pennsylvania. D 1823. Ref: S. A. R. Fur infor Cincinnati Chap.

RICHARDSON, JOHN, (Highland Co.)

Bur in Co graveyard near Dunn's Chapel. Grave obliterated. Fur infor Waw-Wil-a-Way Chap.

RICHARDSON, WILLIAM, (Auglaize Co.)

At 17, a scout in Indian border wars of Western Va and Pa. Two yrs on skirmish line in Rev. Br 1765, Montgomery Co, Va. Mar 1 Mary Adney (1784 d 1811); 2nd Catherine Willhouse, said to have been mar seven times. Children: David L; another a dau. D Hamer, Paulding Co, at age 109, at home of a dau, from injuries received in breaking a colt. Was a cousin to Gen Anthony Wayne, their mothers having been Mattie and Nancy Hiddens; was also in 1812 War. Of powerful physique and great endurance. Shot the 3 Indians who murdered his sister's family. Served as public flogger so effectively that converted the punished. Ref: W. T. McMurray, Wapakoneta, O. Fur infor Jane Daily, State Chairman.

RICHCREEK, PHILIP, (Muskingum Co.)

Received pens 1840 for serv. Br 1761. D Aug 27, 1842, aged 81 yrs. Bur on his farm, 2 miles southeast of Bridgeville, O. Location of grave Perry Twp. MI: Dates. Fur infor Muskingum Chap.

RICHEY, JOHN, (Muskingum Co.)

Enl under Capt Walker Pa Regt. Pa Archives Series 5, Vol 1, p 160, Bucks Co. Pvt. Br in York Co, Pa. July 8, 1755. Mar Mary Welch wife was br York Co, Pa, May 23, 1760, d Jan 6, 1835, both dying in Muskingum Co, O. Resided in Hopewell Twp. Ref: Muskingum Co Hist of 1892, p 544.

RIDDLE, JOHN, COL., (Hamilton Co.)

Fr Apr 1776 (other data gives 1778) as a Pvt in Capt McCoy's Company, Col Freylinghuysen's Regt for 6 weeks; fr June 1778 in Capt Wm Logan's Company, Col Freylinghuysen's Regt for 3 weeks, and was at a skirmish at the Drawbridge below Trenton and at the Battle of Monmouth. Other serv indicated by Pension Claim R-8799. Br Dec 4, 1761, Somerset Co, N. J. Mar had five wives: 1st Phebe Schmocke; 2nd Mary James; 3rd Nancy Nutt Riddle in 1801; 4th Jane Marshall; 5th Jane Ross. Reported to have had 22 children: John Jr, Jacab A, Adam, James, Mary, Nancy, William, Anna, James, Joseph Ross, Hon Adam Nutt, Isaac Bates; Henry, George W, Thos Jeff, Alfred Columbus, David Wade, Eliza Jane, Andrew Jackson and Samuel Marshall Riddle. D June 17, 1847, Hamilton Co, O. Bur Spring Grove Cem, Cincinnati, O. GM by monument. Came to Hamilton Co, O., about 1790 and was commissioned Ensign by Gen St. Clair, promoted to Lt, Capt, Maj, and Col of Mil and held said offices for about 25 yrs. Commander at Greenville during first and last treaty with Indians. Ref: D. A. R. Lin. Vol 11, p 276; Grieves Centennial Hist. Cincinnati p 354; Judge Lester L. Cecil, Dayton, O. Fur infor Cincinnati and Richard Montgomery Chap S. A. R.

RIDDLE, JOHN, (Hamilton Co.)

Br 1761, New Jersey. D 1847. Ref: S. A. R. Fur infor Cincinnati Chap.

RIDDLE, SAMUEL, (Mahoning Co.)

Pvt Capt John Taylor's Company 1777; Capt John Hamilton's Company 1780. Br 1759. Mar Martha Johnson (br 1766 d 1830). D 1825. Bur Canfield, O., Mahoning Co. GM by Mahoning Chap D. A. R. in 1917. Came fr Washington Co, Pa, to Canfield. Ref: Pa Archives Series 3, Vol 23, pp 446, 672, 729. Fur infor Mahoning Chap.

RIDER, BENJAMIN, (Geauga Co.)

Pvt Enl June 13, 1781 for 3 yrs, age 19. Capt Pray's Company, Col Vose's Mass Regt, 1881. Br 1763. Mar Sarah? Children: Benjamin Jr, Rufus, Isaiah, Samuel, Crosby, Polly, Nancy, Hannah, Lucy. D Mch 1854, Painesville, O. Bur Rider Cem, North St., Chardon, O. MI: "Dea. Benjamin Rider died Mch 20, 1854, aged 91 years 3 months and 17 days." GM Family, stone marker. Benjamin Rider, boy on Brigatine "Treedon" Aug and Sept 1776. Deacon. Came to Chardon 1816 fr Hampshire Co, Mass. Ref: Mass Soldiers and Sailors Vol 12, p 308. Fur infor Taylor Chap.

RIDENOUR, PETER, (Preble Co.)

Bur Israel Twp. Ref: Mary P. Mitchell, Eaton, O.

RIDGELY, JR., (Clermont Co.)

Enl Aug 26, 1776. D 1834, Batavia, Clermont Co, O. Fur infor Cincinnati Chap.

RIDLEY, JOHN, (Auglaize Co.)

He with elder brother enl 1776; participated at Bunker Hill, Princeton, Brandywine, Germantown. Also wintered at Valley Forge. At Yorktown after being in 1778-9. Br Nov 11, 1760, Saco, Maine. Parents: Mathias Ridley. Mar Abagail Holmes Dec 15, 1779, Scarborough. Children: John Jr. D May 12, 1867, 106 yrs 3 mos old. Bur Waynesfield, one mile north, but 2 yrs later removed to Fairmont Cem, Union Twp. MI: Dates, name, etc. A descendant is Mrs. Samuel Winegardner, Harrod, O. After marriage returned to Saco. Then to his brother's, Hollis, York Co, where cleared a farm. Thence to Vermont, where wife died, he mar again then but no children to this union. Back to Miami Co, O, then to Auglaize Co, near Waynesfield, lived with son till death. Carried the scars of frozen feet and legs from Valley Forge all his life. Never known to be sick; at 100 carried his chair to the orchard and shot birds that came for cherries. Though quiet, he at times spent hours relating his adventures in woods of Maine and hardships in army. Fur infor W. J. Murray, Wapakoneta, O.

RIED, JOAB, (Brown Co.)

Pvt. Capt Wm Mason, Col Phillips Va. Sept 1, 1780, to Jan 24, 1781, 1 mo 10 da Sgt Elisha Warden. Br Fairfax Co, Va, July 26, 1762. Mar Sarah West, Fairfax Co, Va. Children: Travis, D 1853, Brown Co. O. Bur Decatur. Brown Co, O. in old part of Cem. MI: "Jacob Ried, Rev Soldier 1762-1853." GM Lt Byrd, D. A. R. May 30, 1922. Served in Adams and Brown Co, O. Was a pensioner V. L. M. SF 4057 Revolutionary War, Washington D C. Ref: Mrs. Anne Hughes, Decatur, O. Fur infor Lt Byrd Chap.

RIGBY, WILLIAM, (Fairfield Co.)

In Md in battles Brandywine and Monmouth. Disch 1780 Christian Creek, Pa. Br 1753 Calvert Co, Md. Mar 2nd wife Ara Lemon, Mch 1817. D 1830, Fairfield Co, O. Bur Mt Zion Cem. Widow pens 1853. Ref: Natl No. 79468, Vol 80, D. A. R. Lin. Natl No 36446 Vol 37, p 158, D. A. R Lin Fur infor Elizabeth Sherman Reese Chap.

RIGGS, BETHUEL, (Hamilton Co.)

Pvt and Capt NJ Mil. Pens Hamilton Co, 1832. Br 1757, N J. Mar Nancy Riggs. D 1835 or 1832, Hamilton Co. Ref: S. A. R. and Natl No. 63635, Vol 64, p 209, D. A. R. Lin. Fur infor Cincinnati Chap.

RIGGS, WILLIAM, (Clinton Co.)

2nd Lt in Capt David Platt's Company of Cumberland Co N J. Mil. D 1828, in Cuba, Ohio (which is in Clinton Co). Ref: Natl No 26747, Vol 27, p 276.

RILEY, DANIEL, (Summit Co.)

New Jersey Tr Capt Allen's Company. Bur Stimpson Cem. Copely Twp. Early settler of Copley, coming fr Pa. with several sons about 1815. No dates given. Fur infor Cuyahoga Portage Chap.

RILEY, JULIUS, (Portage Co.)

Lived at Aurora where pensioned in 1840. Fur infor Old Northwest Chap.

RILEY, WILLIAM, (Muskingum Co.)

Enl as Pvt in Berkeley Co, Va, in 1778, under Capt John Lyle, Col John Morrow. Re-enlisted under Capt Jackson, Col Merriweather. Was at surrender of Cornwallis. Br New Castle, Pa. D Feb 14, 1837. Bur Cody Cem, near Frazeysburg. Fur infor Muskingum Chap.

RILLY, JAMES, (Mahoning Co.)

Pvt. 1st Bn, 2nd Establishment, 1st Regt N J. Pensioned. Br 1765. D Poland. 18—. Bur Presbyterian Church, Poland. Ref: New Jersey Men of the Revolution, p 274. Fur infor Mahoning Chap.

RIPPITH, WILLIAM, (Carroll Co.)

Pvt in Capt James Wilson's Company, 9th Bn, Lancaster Co, Pa Mil. Br 1749, Prussia. Mar Sarah Ross (1748-1836). D 1845, Carroll Co, O. Natl No. 78131, Vol 19, D. A. R. Lin.

RISLEY, SAMUEL, (Athens Co.)

Br 1761. Mar Stacey (d Oct 11, 1855, aged 72 yrs, 9 mos 2 da.) D Apr 3, 1838. Bur West State St Cem, Athens, O, west of main driveway. MI: "Samuel Risley Died Apr 3, 1838, aged 76 years 9 months 22 days." GM Family. Granite monument in fine condition. Ref: Bureau of Pensions, Dept of the Interior. Fur infor Nabby Lee Ames Chap.

RITCHEY, JACOB, (Harrison Co.)

Served in the Pa Line, and possibly in the Bucks Co Mil. Br 1755. D 1836. Bur Ridge Church. A Revolutionary pensioner living in Harrison Co in 1833, aged 78. Ref: U. S. Pension Rolls, 1835. Pa Archives, Vol 5, pp 394, 427, 432. Fur Infor Moravian Trail Chap.

RITCHEY, JAMES, (Perry Co.)

Pvt in Pa Rifle Regt under Lt Col Daniel Brodhead. Br July 9, 1757, Baltimore, Md. Parents: James and Rebecca (Woods) Ritchey. Mar Elizabeth Wilson, June 1, 1801. Children: Mary, Thomas, Elizabeth, Jane, Gideon, James, Rebecca Woods, Wilson, William, John, George. D Nov 11, 1838, Perry Co, O. Bur Zion M. E. Cem two miles east of Somerset, O. beside Gen Thomas Ritchey. Original marker crumbled and destroyed No marker standing. GM by family. He lived in Bedford Co, Pa. until 1815 when he came to Perry Co. Farmer. Lt in War of 1912. (Pa Archives, Series 6, Vol 10, p 164.) He was the father of General and Congressman Thomas Ritchey who appointed Phil Sheridan to West Point. Ref: Pa Archives, Series V, Vol 2, pp 343, 346, 349, 351, 354. Mrs. James R. Marker No 156227, (papers pending). Accepting this infor Jane Dailey, State Chairman.

RITTER, JOHN, (Mahoning Co.)

Pvt. City of Philadelphia, 5th Bn. Pa Archives series 3, Vol 23, p 260; also series 3, Vol 24, p 359, Land Grant. Bur Mahoning Co. Came from Lynn Twp, Northampton Co, Pa, in 1802 with Samuel Everett. Farmer. Ref: Pa Archives, Series 5, Vol 5, p 17. Dr. Truesdales History of Canfield. Fur infor Mahoning Chap.

ROBBINS, JASON, (Cuyahoga Co.)

Pvt. Mass Mil, Capt Wm Ford's Company, Col John Brown's Regt of Berkshire Co, 1777-1780. Br 1762 Pittsfield, Mass. D 1852 in Solon, O. Ref: Natl No 30639, p 225, Vol 31, D. A. R. Lin.

ROBBINS, JOHN, LT., (Ross Co.)

1st Lt in Pa Regt of Cav commanded by Col Stephan Moylan. This reference found in the Pa Achives 2 series, Vol II, p 134, and on the roster of Invalid Regt commanded by Col Lewis Nicola. Disch Apr 1783. Br Apr 10, 1760, Sussex Co, N. J. Parents: John Robbins. Mar Sarah Dailey, dau of Philip and Mercy Dailey, Feb 20, 1781, Wash Co, Pa. Children: Rachel mar Col John Jones of War

1812; Charles, John and Oliphant. D 1840, on farm in Ross Co, O. Bur farm, family burying ground. One of first on entering lot. MI: Name, date of birth and death and service. GM Juliana White Chap. Official marker with name plate, June 1923. Lt Robbins acquired the right of one half pay commutation and bounty land and was one of the officers who afterwards received warrants. Came to Ohio in 1796, floated down Monogahela river on flat boats and on to Ohio river to the mouth of the Scioto river, and settled, first at High Banks near Chillicothe. Later he and family moved to farm in Ross near Highland Co boundary on Buckskin Creek, where buried. Ref: Natl No 89114, Vol 90, D. A. R. Lin. Fur infor Juliana White Chap.

ROBERTS, EDWARD, (Clinton Co.)

Bur New Antioch. Fur infor George Clinton Chap.

ROBERTS, JOHN, (Montgomery Co.)

Pvt 2nd Regt Essex Co Mil, NJ. Capt Abraham Lyon's Company, also drummer in Capt J Forman's Company, Col Martin's Regt. Served at the battle of Monmouth, Springfield, and seige of Yorktown. Br May 5, 1767, in Atlantic City, N. J. Parents: John Roberts and Elizabeth Haines. He was also a Revolutionary Soldier. Mar Esther Somers, (dau of John Somers, a Revolutionary Soldier.) Children: John, Sarah, Elizabeth, Josiah, Tamison; and 5 others, unknown. D Oct 18, 1850, Centerville, O. Bur Rehobeth Cem (abandoned), 3 miles south of Centerville, O. MI: "John Roberts, 5-5-1767; 10-18-1850." GM Richard Montgomery Chap, S. A. R., May 28, 1922. Ref: Natl No. 52741 Fur infor Richard Montgomery Chap, S. A. R.

ROBERTS, JOHN, SR., (Trumbull Co.)

Br 1749. D Aug 2, 1823. Bur Braceville. MI: "John Roberts, Sr. Died August 2, 1823, aged 73 years 3 mo." GM by relatives; kept in good condition. Fur infor Mary Chesney Chap.

ROBERTS, WILLIAM, (Trumbull Co.)

Pvt Conn State Tr. Br 1762, Canton, Conn. D 1833, Gustavus, O. Natl No 78619, Vol 79, D. A. R. Lin.

ROBINSON, JAMES, (Union Co.)

Bur Woods Cem, Unionville. GM Robinson family. Ref: Ethel Robinson Helser, Unionville, O. Fur infor Hannah Emerson Dustin Chap.

ROBINSON, JOHN, (Hamilton Co.)

Br 1756, Virginia. D 1842. Fur infor Cincinnati Chap.

ROBINSON, LEWIS, (Highland Co.)

Bur Baptist Cem, New Market, O. Fur infor Waw-Wil-a-aWay Chap.

ROBINSON, OLIVER, (Seneca Co.)

Pvt in Capt Luther Bailey's Company, Col E. Sprout's Regt, Mass Mil. Br Mass. Bur Rock Creek Cem, Eden Twp, Fleet Rd. GM by relatives, with stone marker, in 1927, bronze D. A. R. marker. Ref: Mrs. Jessie Davis. Fur infor Dolly Todd Madison Chap.

ROBINSON, THOMAS, (Highland Co.)

Pvt in Capt John Wall's 2nd Bn, Westmoreland Co Mil. Ordered to Rendezvous 14th of June 1782 Washington Co, later Westmoreland. Br 1754, Ireland. Mar

Nancy McMillan. Children: Susan, George, Elizabeth, Jane, William, Sidney, Adams, Robert, Nancy, Sallie Polly. D 1852, Highland Co, O. Bur Presbyterian Twp at New Market O,. Farmer, later in war of 1812 as Capt. Ref: Fannie H. Nevin, Connersville, Ind. Natl No. 92650. Fur infor William Horney Chap.

ROBINSON, WILLIAM, MAJ., (Coshocton Co.)

Served as Adjt of 5th and 9th Va Regt under Col O Towles. Br 1743, Clarksburg, Va. Mar Margaret See Roach. D 1815. Bur Franklin Twp. Was granted a tract of land by President for his services. Returned to Va. Ref: Co History. Natl No. 62188, Vol 63, D. A. R. Lin. Fur infor Coshocton Chap.

ROCKWELL, JOB, (Meigs Co.)

Drummer in Capt David Pardee's Company, Col Thaddeus Crane Regt of Westchester Co, N Y Mil. Mar Hannah Burt. One child was Rebecca. D 1834, Harrisonville, O. Though Meigs Co was not stated in the record, the only Harrisonville, O, is in Meigs Co. Ref: Natl No 48823, p 376, Vol 49, D. A. R. Lin.

RODDY, EZEKIEL, (Brown Co.)

Bur Arnheim. Fur infor Ripley Chap.

RODGERS, BIXBY, (Delaware Co.)

Bur Burnside Graveyard, Genoa Twp. Fur infor Delaware Chap.

RODGERS, JOSIAH, (Cuyahoga Co.)

Bur Chagrin Falls. Fur infor Western Reserve Chap.

RODGERS, WILLIAM, (Clark Co.)

D Moorefield Twp. Bur Farm, grave has been destroyed, but marker has been found with name on it. Ref: Col W. L. Curry has name on pensions granted in 1840. State Library. Fur infor Lagonda Chap.

RODGERS, WILLIAM, (Ross Co.)

Served in 4th Va. Made 2nd Lt Mch 19, 1776, 1 Lt Sept 28, 1776, Capt Apr, 1778. Was transferred to 5th Va Feb 12, 1781. Br June 8, 1750. Mar Phoebe Swartz, 1772. Children: John, Hamilton, Elizabeth, Thomas, Jane Hannah, Phoebe, Ann, James, Isabelle. D 1824, Ross Co, O. Bur Union Cem, South Union Twp, near entrance. MI: William Rodgers. Went to Kentucky from Loudoun Co, Va, in 1787, fr there to Ross Co, O, 1798. Tavern keeper. Disch June 18, 1783. Received Military Land Grant 4000 A-859, also one half pay for life as officer. Ref: Yr Bk 1913, Society of Sons of Revolution Catalogue of Va Military land warrants in Kentucky. Fur infor Mt. Sterling Chap, Mrs. Martha Harrison Baker, Cook, O.

ROGERS, HENRY, (Hamilton Co.)

1775 in Lord Sterling's Company, and Col William Winds, 1 yr, N J Continental Line. Br 1752, N. J. Mar Phobe Burnett. D 1840, Cincinnati, O. Bur Roll Cem, Cummingsville (S. A. R. Bk.) 1826 on Hamilton Co Pens Roll. Ref: S. A. R. and Natl No. 39483, D. A. R. Fur infor Cincinnati Chap.

ROGERS, HENRY, (Portage Co.)

Lived at Deerfield, where pensioned 1840. Fur infor Old Northwest Chap.

ROGERS, JOSEPH, CAPT., (Washington Co.)

Officer in Gen Morgan's Rifle Company at the taking of Burgoyne. Bur Mound Cem, Marietta, O. MI: Capt Joseph Rogers. GM by Marietta Chap Nov 30, 1906. Fur infor Marietta Chap.

ROGERS, JOSIAH, (Geauga Co.)

Pvt Col Cook's 2nd Regt. 1780-1781, 6 mos. Pensioner residing in Geauga Co in 1840. Transferred from NY. Enl fr Wallinton, Conn. Br Aug 3, 1766. Mar Alice Brokway Mch 22, 1804. Children: George B. and Henry A. D July 8, 1852, Russell, Geauga Co, O. Ref; Pension Dept. Fur infor Taylor Chap.

ROGERS, RICHARD, (Portage Co.)

Pvt in Conn Mil. Placed on pens roll May 9, 1833. Bur Randolph. Fur infor Old Northwest Chap.

ROGERS, SAMUEL, COL., (Lake Co.)

Served fr NH in Capt Samuel Richard's Company, Col Stark's Regt. Br Nov 13, 1766, in Wendall, NH. Mar Sally Pike (first wife) Rhoda Harvey (second wife). D Sept 9, 1850, Concord, O. Bur Concord Cem, near Fay's Mills. GM by New Connecticut Chap. He was also in the war of 1812, in which he received a Lt commission, but was also known as Col Rogers. Was Justice of the Peace in NH, coming to Ohio in 1831. Ref: Natl No. 74308, Vol 75, D. A. R. Lin. Fur infor New Connecticut Chap.

ROICE, ISAAC, (Fulton Co.)

Ref: The Military Record of Fulton Co, O, 1885, p 305. Fur infor Wauseon Chap.

ROLL, MATHIAS, (Butler Co.)

Name appears on the tablet of Sailors and Soldiers Monument at Hamilton. A Revolutionary Soldier bur in that Co. Unable to identify. Fur infor John Reily Chap.

ROLLER, JOHN, SR., (Mahoning Co.)

Pvt Bedford Co, Pa Mil. Br 1757. D 1819. Bur Lutheran Cem, Washingtonville. Ref: Pa Achives, Series 5. Vol 4, p 612. Fur infor Mahoning Chap.

ROLLINS, JOSIAH, (Miami Co.)

Bur Raper Chapel. Fur infor Miami Chap.

ROOD, ROGER, (Ashtabula Co.)

Br 1752. Mar Betsy Lawrence. Children: Isaac Rood, Asel Rood. D May 21, 1849, Jefferson, O. Bur Jefferson Cem. MI: "Roger Rood, Died May 21, 1849, aged 97. A Soldier of the Revolution." GM by Isaac Rood with marble slab June 14, 1925, by Eunice Grant Chap D. A. R. Metal Revolutionary Soldier marker. Came to Ohio fr Canaan, Litchfield Co, Conn, in 1832. Ref: Mrs. H. H. Webster, Jefferson, O. Fur infor Eunice Grant Chap.

ROOSA, JACOB, (or JACOBUS), (Hamilton Co.)

See "N Y In Rev War," Ulster Co, N Y, also 3rd Regt Col Gansevort and Col John Clinton, p 45 "N Y in Rev War" by Roberts. Came to Hamilton Co in 1794 with five or six families fr New York. Wife's name was Felter. Bur in Hopewell Cem, Hamilton Co, O. Fur infor Cincinnati Chap.

ROOT, AZARIAH, (Delaware Co.)

Pvt under Col Joseph Vose, Capt Moses Ashby Mass Tr. Br 1762. Pensioned. Fur infor Delaware Chap.

ROSA, ISAAC, (Lake Co.)

Served in the Mil of N Y under Col Abraham Culyer. Br Aug 27, 1767. Mar Agnes Storm. Children: Dr. Storm Rosa. D Feb 27, 1841, Painesville, O. Bur Evergreen Cem, Painesville, O. GM by New Connecticut Chap. Fur infor New Connecticut Chap.

ROSE, EZEKIEL, (Muskingum Co.)

Capt in Rangers on Frontier. One son William br 1794, Washington Co, Pa. D 1813 or 1814 at Roseville, O. Bur Roseville. Also served as Capt in the expedition against Sandusky. Surveyor and founded town of Roseville, which he called New Milford. Lived in Milford, Cumberland Co, Pa, prior to and during war, then in Washington Co Pa, before moving to Muskingum Co. Ref: Miss Winters, 5 Northwood Ave, Columbus, O. Fur infor Jane Dailey, State Chairman.

ROSE, JESSE, (Mahoning Co.)

Br 1760. D 1852. Bur Mahoning Co. Came fr Va. Ref: Vol R 3 War Dept 65, 5 p 74, 2 p 296, 1. Virginia Regt 2, 7, War Dept pp 306, 1. Fur infor Mahoning Chap.

ROSE, JOHN, (Hamilton Co.)

Br 1760, New Jersey. D 1837. Ref: S. A. R. Fur infor Cincinnati Chap.

ROSE, LEMUEL, (Licking Co.)

First substituted for brother, then enl Mch 14, 1781. Served 2 yrs 9 mos as Pvt in Col Shephard's Regt. Br 1764, Granville, Mass. Mar Achsah Hale Oct 28, 1784. D Sept 13, 1835, Granville, O. Bur Old Cem, Granville, O. GM by Granville Chap in 1901. Emigrated to this colony at Granville, O, in 1805. Pens allowed. Fur infor Hetuck Chap.

ROSE, MICHAEL, (Belmont Co.)

One of Lafayette's Soldiers. Mar Catherine Patterson, 1802. D 1825 on farm 2½ miles southeast of Barnesville, O. Bur private grounds on farm where he died. Grave not marked, as wife and her people were members of the Friends' church and do not mark graves. Clockmaker. No definite records can be obtained. Ref: B. C. Patterson, H. E. Frost, Fairview, O., and Wm. Boswell, Barnesville, O. Accepted by Jane Dailey, State Chairman.

ROSE, TIMOTHY, (Licking Co.)

Enl July 27, 1779, at Granville, Mass, in Col Timothy Bigelow's Regt. Was Sgt at siege of Yorktown, captured a British officer, took his sword. B 1762, Granville, Mass. Mar Lydia Munson (br 1768, d 1855). D Nov 27, 1813, Granville, O. Bur Old Cem, Granville, O. GM by Granville Chap in 1901. Was agent to this Co for the Licking Land Company; was an influential citizen. Pens allowed. Ref: Natl No 102271, Vol 103, p 84, D. A. R. Lin. Fur infor Hetuck Chap.

ROSEBROOM, HENRY, (Ross Co.)

Minute Man 1776 battle of Long Island. Br Reddington, N J, 1757. Mar Rachel Smawley. D Frankfort, O. Ref: Natl No. 61550, p 188, Vol 62, D. A. R. Lin. Fur infor Nathaniel Massie Chap.

ROSS, ALEXANDER, (Warren Co.)

Enl fr Philadelphia in the Mil. Br 1754, Pennsylvania. D Warren Co, O, 1809, where he moved in 1800. Mar Anna Philips. Ref: Natl No. 36190, p 69, Vol 37, D. A. R. Lin.

ROSS, BENJAMIN, (Mahoning Co.)

Pvt in N Y State Tr. Pensioned. Bur Mahoning Co. Resident of Youngstown in 1801. Taxed in Youngstown in 1803. Supervisor of Highway. Ref: N Y Men of the Revolution, p 124. Trumbull and Mahoning Co Hist, Vol 2, p 373. Fur infor Mahoning Chap.

ROSS, JAMES, (Mahoning Co.)

Pvt in Pa. Pensioned. Br 1754. Bur Mahoning Co. Supervisor of Twp. Lived in Youngstown, Seventh District, 1803. Ref: Pa Archives, Series 2, Vol 13 or 14, p 196. Pension Roll Senate Document 23 Congress 1833-1834. Trumbull and Mahoning Co Hist, Vol 2. Fur infor Mahoning Chap.

ROSS, JOHN, (Harrison Co.)

Served as Ensign in Capt Walker's Company, Col James Taylor's 6th Bn, Lancaster Co, Pa Mil. Br 1750, in Ireland. Mar Charlotta Nacher in 1779. Bur Cadiz, Old Cem. A Revolutionary Soldier living in Harrison Co in 1833 aged 82 yrs. U S Pens Rolls 1835. Ref: Pa Archives, Series 5, Vol 7, p 567, and Compare Natl No 100637, Vol 101, p 199, D. A. R. Lin. Fur infor Moravian Trail Chap.

ROSS, JOHN, (Noble Co.)

Soldier, who settled for a time in Beaver Twp. Was a miller at House's Mill, built in 1816. No data of death or burial found. Fur infor Mrs. L. B. Frazier, Caldwell, O.

ROSS, JOSEPH, (Hamilton Co.)

Pensioned as Pvt in N J Mil, Continental Line. Br 1750, Westfield, N. J. D 1834 or 1838, Cincinnati, O. Bur M E Cem, Madisonville (S. A. R.). Ref: S. A. R. and Natl No. 80122, Vol 81, D. A. R. Lin. Fur infor Cincinnati Chap.

ROUCH-ROUSH, PHILIP, (Gallia, O.)

Pvt in Capt John Vanetten's Company, 7 mo Volunteers, Northampton Co, Pa, Mil. Was at the battle of Nescopeck, Sept 10, 1780. See p 342, Vol IV, and p 574, Vol VIII, Pa Archives, 5 series. Br Mch 18, 1741, Northampton Co, Pa. Parents: John Roush Johannes Rausch)and Susannah. Mar Catharine Kalchner-Kelchner. 1764. Children: John, Michael, Philip Jr, Henry, George, Jonas, Elizabeth Bowman, Susannah Pense, Catharine Circle, Sarah Wills, Molly Knopp, Eva Pence, Hannah Roush and Magdaline. D Mch 1, 1820, Cheshire, Gallia Co, O. Bur Old Roush Cem, about a mile back of Cheshire, O. MI: "In Memory of Philip Roush who was born March 18, 1741, and Died March 1, 1820." GM Headstone shows age, but still in good condition, and inscription quite legible. Resided a few years near Forestville, Shenandoah Co, Va, where some of his children were born as evidenced by the parish records of Old Pine Church (St Mary's Lutheran), of which church he was a trustee. His father is buried in this churchyard. Philip removed to Gallia Co, O, about 1798. Tanner in Shenandoah Co. Ref: Lyman Plummer Roush, Pennsylvania S. A. R. Natl No. 2171, and 45892. Fur infor French Colony Chap.

ROUNDS, CHARLES, (Lorain Co.)

Enl in spring of 1777 in state of Mass. He was a Pvt under Capt Cooper and Col Bradford; prisoner 2 yrs; captured at Monmouth; in several battles. Br 1759, Scotland. Mar Lydia Pierce, about 1785. Children: Lydia, Nathaniel, Almira,

Roba. D Mch 25, 1843, La Grange, Lorain Co. Bur near there in an old Cem in Pittsfield Twp, right of center path. MI: "Revolutionary Soldier 1775-1783" placed by Elyria Chap D. A. R. July 4, 1928. Ref: Mrs. J. A. Reublin, Elyria, O. Fur infor Elyria Chap.

ROUSH, GEORGE, (Meigs Co.)

Pvt. Br 1761, Holman Fort, Shenandoah Co, Va. Parents: John and Susannah Roush. Mar Catherine Zerke, 1781; 2nd Mrs. Cath. Wolfe (Ref: S. A. R. Dayton). Children: Michael, Magdalene, John, Daniel, George, Lewis, Katharyn, Samuel, Susannah, Jacob, Mary, Jonas, Hannah. D May 31, 1845 Racine, O. Bur Weldon Cem within the corporation of Racine near the East side of Cem. MI: "George Roush, a Soldier in the Revolution, died May 31, 1845. Aged 84 yrs." GM by the family soon after death, a well preserved granite slab set in sandstone, but recently reset in concrete. He received pens for serv which commenced Mch 4, 1831. He was in the battle of Yorktown with Washington. He served as a Pvt in the Company of his brother Capt John Roush, a Shenandoah Company. He was one of nine brothers who had serv in this war. His pension claim is S. 8579. For detail of this family and serv of other brothers see list of "The Roush Family of America" by Rev Lester L. Roush, published 1928 by the Shenandoah Publishing House, Strasburg, Va. and "History of the Great Kanawha Valley." These brothers were all ardent supporters of the Lutheran Faith. Fur infor Rev L. L. Roush, 5725 Gallia Ave., Portsmouth, O. Name filed by Jonathan Meigs Chap.

ROUSH, HENRY, (Meigs Co.)

Pvt. Capt John Tipton's Company 88 days in early part of Revolutionary War—later in 1781 Va Tr. Br 1752 near Woodstock, Shenandoah Co, Va. Parents: John Adam Roush and Susannah his wife. Mar Dorothy ? before 1778. Children: Michael, Christina, Henry Jr. Elizabeth, Susannah, Adam, Eva, Anthony, Dorothy, Balser, D Oct 26, 1831. Just below Letart Falls, O. Bur: Plants (formerly Wolfe) Cem. Roush section toward road and river. MI: "In memory of Henry Roush who died 10-26-31 aged 79 yrs." Expect to mark grave as Revolutionary soldier. Farmer. He is known as the church builder, having given the land and endowment for Solomon's Church. Owned considerable land in Meigs Co, O. Ref: Hist of Great Kanawha Valley, Pension Record Va State Library, U. S. Census, Shenandoah Co, Va. Deeds, Pomeroy, Ohio, Minutes of Solomon's church. Natl No 42837 S. A. R. Fur infor H. A. Roush, Pittsburgh, Pa. Accepted by Jane Dailey, State Chairman.

ROUSH, JACOB, (Gallia Co.)

Pvt under Capt John Tipton. See Romney and Winchester Pay Roll, pp 29 and 30. Br about 1756, in Shenandoah Co, Va. Parents: John and Susannah Roush. Mar Catherine Fox, 1776. Children: Rosina, Dorothea, Catherine, John, Adam, Susannah, Paul, Cornelius. D 1830 in Cheshire, Gallia Co, O. Bur Roush or Lucky Cem, 1 mile back of Cheshire, O. Gallia Co. Grave not marked but supposed to be near that of Adam and Paul, his sons. He was in the battle of Point Pleasant against the Indians in 1774, under the command of Gen Lewis. He owned land in Shenandoah Co, Va. where his children were born. A stock holder in Ohio Land Co. He was a farmer, owning the tract of land just above Cheshire where Horton H. Roush now lives. This was for years known as the Roush Landing. He settled in Gallia Co, 1803. Ref: For full particulars see Hist of the Roush Family in America, by Rev. L. L. Roush, published by Shenandoah Publishing Company and also Miss Jessie Palmer, Gallopolis, O. Fur infor French Colony Chap.

ROUSH, JONAS, (Meigs Co.)

Br Shenandoah Valley. D New Haven, W Va. Bur Gilmore Cem, Nease Settlement, Meigs Co, O. GM by slab erected by family. Ref: Roush Genealogy. Fur infor Return Jonathan Meigs Chap.

ROWE, JESSE, (Fayette Co.)

A Company of Artificiers under Gen Knox Brigade. Enl Sept 5, 1776, Dec 16, 1776, in 1778 40 days under Capt Chas Dabney. Children: John, Jesse,

James, Susanna, Mary, Jane, William, Elizabeth, Sarah. D Nov 18, 1843, Fayette Co., near Staunton. Bur Rowe Cem, Henry Cripps Farm, Anderson Pike. (one of four graves). MI: "Jesse Rowe". GM by family in 1846. Farmer, Justice of Peace and Twp Trustee. Pensioner. Ref: Adjutant Gen Office War Department Dept 1279715, Survivors File, 4122 and Natl No 118851. Fur infor Washington C. H. Chap.

ROWLAND, JOHN, (Harrison Co.)

Served in the Revolutionary War in Capt James Edgar's Company, York Co Mil, and as an Indian scout. Br 1758. D 1855. Bur Rankin Church. Settled in Moorefield Twp in 1815. Ref: Pa Archives 6 11, 789. Fur infor Moravian Trail Chap.

ROWLAND, JOHN, (Pickaway Co.)

Served with Pa Tr as Pvt Soldier. Enl 1777; prisoner 1777; Reenlisted 1778; Retired 1783. Br 1745 State of Delaware. Mar Mary Osborne before 1792. Children: Samuel, Elon, Naamah, An Mary, Wooldsey Robinson, Henry, Elizabeth, John M. D Mch 18, 1850, in Pickaway Co. Bur on his farm, Pickaway Co. between Mt Sterling and Five Points on Clark's Run Road. MI: John Rowland, died March 18, 1850, aged 105 years. GM by stone slab. Restored and marked also by bronze Revolutionary marker by descendant, Jean Rowland. Moved with family fr State of Delaware in 1811. Farmer. In this cem which has been fully restored are buried 3 generations the same family. The father John a soldier of the Rev, the son Samuel a soldier of 1812 and his son Samuel, a soldier who died in the Civil War. Ref: Will on file at Circleville, O. Pens Department Bible records, and Natl No 51499 D. A. R. Lin. Fur infor London and Mt Sterling Chap.

ROWLAND, JOSEPH, (Wyandot Co.)

Pvt. Corp and Sgt in Capt William Anderson's Company, 7th Pa Regt by Col William Irvine; enl for War; commenced pay, May 27, 1777. Served with Pa Tr in Gen Washington's army; served in commissary department part of time army was encamped at Valley Forge. Br Hanover, Germany, Oct 20, 1760. Mar Christina dau of a German immigrant, after close of Revolutionary War, date unknown. Children: Isaac, Jonathan, Susan, Samuel, Nancy, John, Christina, and Peter. D Sept 21, 1856, Mifflin Twp, Wyandot Co. Bur 2 1-2 miles southeast of Kirby, O. east central row of graves. MI: Date of birth and death and "Patriot of 1776". GM by small tombstone, placed by grandson, M. C. Rowland about 1880. Came to America with parents 1764, when 4 yrs of age. Landed at Hagerstown, Md. After few yrs he moved to Lancaster, Pa. where father set up flour mill which he operated during the Revolutionary War. After death of wife lived with son John, Mifflin Twp to which place he had moved in 1855 fr Orange Twp Ashland Co where he settled 1825. Was tailor and farmer. Ref: Leefe E. Rowland and Margaret A. Rowland, Upper Sandusky, O. D. A. R. members. Fur infor Colonel William Crawford Chap.

ROWLAND, LUKE, (Huron Co.)

D Mch 9, 1839, aged 81 yrs. Bur Day Cem Clarksfield Twp. Fur infor Sally De Forest Chap.

ROWLAND, WILLIAM, (Mahoning Co.)

Pvt in Chester Co Mil, Capt Rowland's Regt 1780. Mar Elizabeth ———. D 1805. Came to Mahoning Co early 1800. Ref: Pa Archives, Series 5, Vol 5, p 616, Trumbull Co Records and vital records. Fur infor Mahoning Chap.

ROWLER, BELZAR, (ROLLER), (Mahoning Co.)

Pvt in Bedford Co, Pa Mil. Br 1758. Mar Alse (1764-1819). D 1841. Bur Lutheran Cem, Washingtonville. Ref: Pa Archives Series 5, Vol 4, p 612. Fur infor Mahoning Chap.

RUBLE, JOHN, (Highland Co.)

From Rockingham Co, Va. Served as Indian Spy in Capt Anthony Rader's Company, 1777. July 1778 served as Drummer in Capt Lukhorn's Company. Was in expedition against Indians. Pvt 1781 Capt Bagg's Company. Br 1761 in Shenandoah Co, Va. D Dec 29 in Highland Co. Fur infor Waw-Wil-a-Way Chap.

RUCKER, LEMUEL, (Monroe Co.)

8th Va Regt for 2 yrs. Br Apr 15, 1752 Va. Mar Anna Booten (br Dec 11, 1763). Eight children. D 1844, Monroe Co. Bur Rucker Mechem Cem, Monroe Co. Pensioner. Fur infor Marietta Chap.

RUDE, ZELAH, (Hamilton Co.)

Rank not stated. Served in Ens Wm Colvin's command of Va Mil, Revolutionary War, dated at Redstone Jan 1778, showing that he entered Dec 23, year not stated. Nothing further found. (Record given by Record and Pension Office). Br Holland or Wales. Mar Rachel ——— (br in England). Mar before 1770 in Pa or Va. Children: Polly Rude Whetstone, Margaret Rude Yost, Rachel Rude Pollack, Hannah Rude Thompson, Cynthia Rude Crist (br 1785-1832), Zelah Jr, Felix, James. D on farm and bur in farm burial lot, farm 100 acres, Sec 33, Symmes Twp near present site of Remington, location of grave on farm. MI: Unmarked now. The creek or flagstone marker obliterated. When the son's family were removed to a cem in 1867, dust of parents left undisturbed. At close of war came with his family and sons-in-law to Columbia, near Cincinnati, in 1796. After serving under Gen Wayne and Indians were subdued, purchased land near present site of Remington, Sec 33, Twp 5 (Symmes) of 100 acres, in range 1. Ref: Mrs. Margaret E. Kitchell Whallon, Natl No 34924, D. A. R. Cincinnati Chap.

RUDISILL, JOHN, (Mahoning Co.)

Pvt York Co, Pa Mil. Br 1767. Mar Katharine (1767-1807). D 1809. Bur Old Church, Petersburg. Ref: Pa Archives, Series 5, Vol 4, p 477. Fur infor Mahoning Chap.

RUDISILLY, HENRY, (Logan Co.)

Pensioned in 1840 while living in Perry Twp, Logan Co, O. at age of 85, which the Commissioner of Pensions states was for Revolutionary service. Fur infor Bellefontaine Chap.

RUE, BENJAMIN, (Warren Co.)

Served as Capt in Col Wingate Newman's Regt, Pa Line. Br 1755, Bucks Co. Pa. Mar 1777, Mary Taylor (1757). D 1820, Lebanon, O. Ref: Natl No 100649, Vol 101, p 202, D. A. R. Lin.

RUGG, MOSES, (Franklin Co.)

Served in the 10th and 3rd Mass Regt until 1783. Br 1759 in Mass. D Apr 21, 1832 in Blendon Twp. Bur Riverside Cem, Parks Mills. MI: "Moses Rugg. Born 1759. Died April 21, 1832. He was a Revolutionary soldier, whose memory is honorable." GM Revolutionary Grave Committee. Bronze marker, May 30, 1912. Fur infor Columbus Chap.

RUPERT, ADAM, (Columbiana Co.)

Br 1756. D 1840. Bur Forney Cem in Columbiana Co, O. GM by stone. Fur infor Bethia Southwick Chap.

RUPERT, GEORGE, (Fayette Co.)

Br 1750. D Sept 2, 1846, Fayette Co. Bur Sugar Creek Baptist Cem, Fayette Co, in old part behind the church, unplatted. MI: "George Rupert died Sept 2, 1846 aged 96 years. A revolutionary soldier who fought (and there the marker is broken off). GM by family in 1846. Farmer. Pensioner. Fur infor Washington C. H. Chap.

RUPERT, JACOB, (Columbiana Co.)

No data found except he was a Rev soldier. Bur Forney Cem, Columbiana Co. O. Fur infor Bethia Southwick Chap.

RUSE, AARON, (Highland Co.)

Bur Laurel Hill, near Lynchburg. Fur infor Waw-Wil-a-Way Chap.

RUSH, JOHN, (Mahoning Co.)

Ranger, Washington Co, Pa. Northumberland Co, Pa. Bedford Co, Pa. Br 1757. Mar Amy Lacock. D 1832. Bur—grave desecrated, Youngstown, O. Ref: Pa Archives Series 3, Vol 23, pp 16, 132. Fur infor Mahoning Chap.

RUSK, JAMES, (Montgomery Co.)

Enl 1777 York Co, Pa. under Capt James Greer. Disch honorably 1781. Br 1754, Ireland. D Clayton, O. 1839. Ref: Natl No 25635. p 233, Vol 26, D. A. R. Lin.

RUSSELL, ENOCH, (Jackson Co.)

D Aug 29, 1848. Bur Keystone Cem at top of hill. GM by monument. Fur infor Capt John James Chap.

RUSSELL, GIDEON, (Geauga Co.)

Pvt Conn Line, 3rd Regt. Pens allowed 1834. Br Dec 25, 1759, South Hadley, Mass. Parents: Gideon of Middlefield, Mass. Mar Jemenice Alvord, Feb 1786. Children: Justin, Silvester, Silvertus, Alpheus, Sarah, William, Gideon, Jemenice, Ebenezer. Bur Morton Cem, Newbury, O. MI "Gideon Russell died age 78. Jeminia wife of Gideon Russell died Nov 20, 1837 age 75." GM Monument of sandstone, by R. Hubbard 1837 at Little Mountain. S Hadley Middlefield, Mass. p 91, 132 Conn Rolls Vol 8, pp 127, 128. Fur infor Taylor Chap.

RUSSELL, JACOB, (Cuyahoga Co.)

Pvt, Continental Regt, Conn. Br 1746. D 1821. Bur Shaker Heights on South Park Boulevard near Lee Rd. GM Western Reserve Chap. Fur infor Western Reserve Chap.

RUSSELL, JAMES, (Mahoning Co.)

Pvt. Pensioned in Pa. Br 1736. Children: Robert, John, Joseph, two daughters. D 1826, Poland, O. Bur Presbyterian Cem, Poland, O. GM Mahoning Chap, bronze marker in 1916. Came to Poland about 1803. Ref: Pa Archives series 2, Vol 13, p 197; Series 3, Vol 23, p 294; Series 7, Vol 13, p 197, Trumbull and Mahoning Co Hist, p 69, Vol 2. Fur infor Mahoning Chap.

RUSSELL, JAMES, (Harrison Co.)

Served in Westmoreland Co, Pa Mil. Br 1745. D 1836. Bur at Moorefield. A Revolutionary pensioner living in Harrison Co in 1831, aged 90. Ref: Pa Archives 5, IV, 454, U.S. Pension Rolls 1835. Fur infor Moravian Trail Chap.

RUSSELL, JAMES, (Washington Co.)

Lt 1775, Capt 1775 in Col William Prescott. Br 1746, Litchfield, N H 1821, Belpre, O. Ref: Natl No 32633, p 213, Vol 33, D.A.R. Lin.

RUSSELL, ROBERT, (Mahoning Co.)

Ensign 1780. Bur Mahoning Co. (Possibility of grave being in Trumbull Co.) Ref: Gleanings of Va Hist in Revolution, p 218. Fur infor Mahoning Chap.

RUSSELL, SAMUEL, (Geauga Co.)

Pvt Mass St Tr Capt Lyman's Company, Col Porter's Regt Hunsphere Co. Pens allowed 1832. Br 1749, Franklin Co, Mass. Mar 2nd Mary Rice. Children: Otis, Jerusha, Spencer, Diana, Eliakin, Samuel, Senus, Mrs. White. D Jan 25, 1838, Middlefield, O. Bur Middlefield Village Cem. MI: Samuel Russell died Jan 25, 1828, age 87. GM by family. Came to Middlefield, in 1815. Ref: p 724 Pioneer Hist Geauga Co Mass SS 13, p 700. Natl No 149186, D. A. R. Lin. Fur infor Taylor Chap.

RUSSELL, WILLIAM, (Mahoning Co.)

Pvt Continental Line Pa. Received depreciation pay. Br 1746. GM by Mahoning Chap, with bronze marker in 1916. Ref: Pa Archives, Series 5, Vol 4 p 221. Fur infor Mahoning Chap.

RUSSELL, WILLIAM, (Geauga Co.)

Served through war in Somerset Co, NJ Mil Capt Jacob Mathias' Company. Br 1756 NJ. Mar Jane Sewell, 1790. One child, Amanda. D 1832, Lebanon, O. Ref: Natl No 42877, Vol 43, p 326, D. A. R. Lin.

RUST, ALONEY, (Trumbull Co.)

Pvt Capt Daniel Canfield's Company. Br 1766, near Hartford, Conn. D 1857, Fowler, O. Fur infor Natl No 36662, Vol 37, D.A.R. Lin.

RUTAU (or N), JOHN, (Trumbull Co.)

Br 1744. D Sept 19, 1833. Bur Old Cem, Mahoning Ave., Warren. MI: d Sept 19, 1833, aged 89." GM Name on bronze tablet, 1927, by D. A. R. Fur infor Mary Chesney Chap.

RUTLEDGE, MICHAEL, (Trumbull Co.)

D Vernon Twp. Bur East Center, where he was living and drawing pens in 1840. Ref: Cleveland Historical Library. Fur infor Mary Chesney Chap.

RYNIERSON, JOHN, (or RYNEARSON), (Hamilton Co.)

Served with Somerset Co Mil. "Strkyers Men from New Jersey in Rev," p 743. Mar dau of Abraham Voorhes (Revolutionary soldier). Bur Reading, O, Hamilton Co. Came to Ohio with family of father-in-law; settled Sycamore Twp, 1794. Fur infor Cincinnati Chap.

SABIN, ELIJAH, (Clinton Co.)

Pensioned 1833 as Pvt in NY Mil. Br 1755, Scotland. Mar Mary Salmon, 1773. D 1845, Wilmington, O. Bur Oakland. Ref: Natl No 80694, Vol 81, D.A.R. Lin. Fur infor George Clinton Chap.

SACKETT, SKENE DOUGLAS, (Ashtabula Co.)

Pvt Conn Line. Pensioned as residing in Ohio. In 1840 list of Revolutionary Soldiers residing in Windsor, Ashtabula Co. Br 1764, Milford, New Haven Co, Conn. Mar Hannah Saxton of Waterbury, Conn. Children: Polly (1st Mrs. A.

Crandall) (2nd Mrs. Luman Fisher), Garry, Chauncy, Horace. D Windsor. Bur probably Old Sackett Cem, Windsor. Pensioner, 1840, at age 76, while residing in Windsor Twp. Moved to Whitestown, Oneida Co, N. Y., 1798 or 1799; came to Ohio in 1803, lived in Painesville, Lake Co, 2 or 3 yrs. Ref: Pioneer Hist of Geauga Co, p 795. Hist Ashtabula Co, p 250; Conn Men Rev 646. Fur infor Taylor Chap.

SADLER, WILLIAM, (Cuyahoga Co.)

Pvt N.Y. Mil. Bur Lake Shore Cem, Bay Village. Fur infor Western Reserve Chap.

SAGE, HARLEIGH, (Pickaway Co.)

Pvt, Capt David Strong's Company. Br 1764, Berlin, Conn. Mar Lucinda Page. D 1828, Pickaway Co. Ref: Natl No 59424, p 144, Vol 60, D.A.R. Lin. Compare p 205, Vol 72, D.A.R. Lin.

SAGE, SAMUEL, (Vinton Co.)

Placed on Pension Roll 1818, Athens Co, for serv as Sgt in Pa Continental Line. Br 1755, England. Mar Judith Callivan in 1785. D 1820, McArthur, O. Ref: Natl No 83027, Vol 84, D.A.R. Lin. Fur infor Jane Dailey, State Chairman.

SALTONSTALL, NATHANIEL, (Washington Co.)

Commandant and Capt in Artillery Company, New London, Conn. Br 1727, New London, Conn. Mar Rebecca Young. D 1807, Marietta. Bur Mound Cem, Marietta, O. MI: "Capt Nathaniel Saltonstall 1727-1807." GM Marietta Chap by Revolutionary marker and gateway Nov 30, 1906; marker stolen and replaced 1920. Ref: Vol 62, p 4, D.A.R. Lin. Fur infor Marietta Chap.

SAMPSON, ISAAC, (Huron Co.)

Rev: S. A. R. Yr Bk 1917. Firelands Pioneer Vol 5, p 56. Hist of Ruggles Twp. Fur infor Sally De Forest Chap.

SAMPSON, SPAULDING, (Co. not stated).

Sgt Capt John Frull's Company, Col Ebenezer Bright's Regt, Lexington Alarm. Br Tewksbury, Mass. 1745. Mar Experience Merrill. D 1832, Ohio. Ref: Natl No 55817 p 364, Vol 56, D. A. R. Lin.

SAMS, JONAS, (Brown Co.)

Bur Ripley. Fur infor Ripley Chap.

SANDERS, JOHN, (Greene Co.)

Pvt NJ Continental Line. Pensioned 1831. Bur Mount Holly. Living in Xenia, 1812. Fur infor Catherine Greene Chap.

SANDERS, WILLIAM, (Columbiana Co.)

In 1832 was living in Center Twp, Columbiana Co. Age 88 yrs. A pensioner. Fur infor Bethia Southwick Chap.

SANDERSON, JOHN, (Trumbull Co.)

Bur Mesopotamia, Where he was living and drawing a pens in 1840. Ref: Cleveland Hist Library. Fur infor Mary Chesney Chap.

SANFORD, SAMUEL, (Lorain Co.)

Pensioned 1832, service 1776. Pvt in Capt Jonathan Dimon's Company, Col Chandler's Conn Regt, 1776-82; served several other enlistments—different commands. Br 1760, Fairfield. Mar Ruhannah Wheeler. D 1834, Ridgefield. (Probably North Ridgefield, Lorain Co.) Ref; Natl No 74482, Vol 75, D. A. R. Lin.

SANFORD, SAMUEL, (Portage Co.)

Enl in serv as waiter for his father, who was Capt. Pvt. Br Apr 15, 1766. D Oct 1858, Mantua, O. Bur Mantua, O. Was buried with Military honors. Fur infor Old Northwest Chap.

SANFORD, ZACHEUS, (Mahoning Co.)

Enl fr Litchfield Twp, Conn, in 1778. Pvt to the end of the war. Children: Samuel (br 1789, mar Dorcas Alderman), there may have been more children. Bur somewhere in Mahoning Co. Was one of the early settlers of Mahoning Co. Ref: Conn Men of the Revolution pp 294, 637. Biog Hist of Ashtabula, Trumbull and Mahoning Co. Fur infor Mahoning Chap.

SANOR, MICHAEL, (Columbiana Co.)

Pensioned as Pvt in Pa Line. Br Alsace-Lorraine, Germany, 1745. Mar Mary Shrader. Children: Julia, Catherine, Mary, Jacob, Michael, Susan, Elizabeth, George, William, Sarah, John. D Columbiana Co, O. Nov 18, 1829. Bur private burying ground on Sanor farm. MI: "Michael Sanor, Revolutionary Soldier, 1745-1829." GM Committee Jane Bain Chap Oct 1924. Ref: Mrs. Elizabeth (H. V.) Knowles, Mrs. Ella Newcomer, Alliance, O. Fur infor Jane Bain Chap.

SARGENT, JAMES, (Pike Co.)

A resident of Frederick Co, Md. he served on the Committee of Observation and on a List of Associators. Br Snow Hill, London, England, 1717 or 18. Mar Eleanor Taylor, Dec 9, 1735. Children: Snowden, Richard, Anna, James, Eleanor, William, John, Elijah, Mary, Sarah and Nancy. D ,1825, Pike Co, O. Fur infor Nathaniel Massie Chap.

SARGENT, JAMES, (Logan Co.)

Pensioned in 1840, while living in Harrison Twp, Logan Co, O, age 85, which the Commissioner of Pensions writes was for Revolutionary services. He also notes "In 1832, James Sargent, aged 77 years, was living in Harrison Twp, Champaign Co, O." We believe it is the same man, State Chairman. Fur infor Bellefontaine Chap.

SARGENT, SNOWDEN, (Pike Co.)

Served the colonies as a patriot as shown on the list of Associators and on the Committee of Observation of Frederick Co, Md. Br Anne Arundel Co, Md., Feb 27, 1742. Mar Mary Heathman in 1763. Children: Eli, James, George, John, Samuel, William, Snowden, Mary, Elizabeth, Ellen. D Sargent's Station, Pike Co, O. in 1814. Fur infor Nathaniel Massie Chap.

SAUNDERS, ABRAHAM, (Washington Co.)

Sgt 1777, Capt Edw Scull's Company, Lt Col Wm Butler's Regt, Pa Line. Received pension 1818 for 3 yrs serv. Pvt Pennsylvania Line. (27373 D. A. R.) Br 1748, London, England. D 1824, Washington Co, O. Ref: Natl No 68411, p 153, Vol 69, D. A. R. Lin.

SAWTELL, BENJAMIN, (Lake Co.)

Fur infor New Connecticut Chap.

SAWVEL, ADAM, (Harrison Co.)

Settled in Rumley Twp, 1815; said by family to have served in Revolution from York Co, Pa. Fur infor Moravian Trail Chap.

SAWYER, JACOB, (Cuyahoga Co.)

Pvt Mass Regt. Br 1765. D 1857. Bur North Solon. Fur infor Western Reserve Chap.

SAWYER, NATHANIEL, (Athens Co.)

Br Mch 12, 1757. D Mch 11, 1813. Bur Pioneer Cem, Rome Twp, Athens Co, near mouth of Federal Creek. MI: "In memory of Nathaniel Sawyer, born March 12, 1757, and departed on March 11, 1813, age 56 years. He was a man of undaunted courage and was a soldier in the Revolution. He was one of the pioneers in the wilds of Ohio, and shared the dangers of a frontier settlement through a long and bloody Indian War. He was a kind, affectionate and industrious parent. 'Blessed are the peacemakers, for they shall see God'." A horizontal slab marks the grave. Nothing is known of this man, excepting what the inscription gives. Fur infor Nabby Lee Ames Chap.

SAYLOR, JOHN, (Montgomery Co.)

Soldier from Va. Nothing further known. Br Va. Children: Elizabeth (who mar John Vance). Bur Jackson Twp, Montgomery Co, O. He was an early settler in Jackson Twp. A true pioneer of the county and bore his share of the hardships and deprivations of the early days. Deserves great credit but no trace has been left of them, so it is impossible to give them the credit these pioneers so richly deserve. Fur infor Richard Montgomery Chap. S. A. R.

SAYRE, PIERSON, (Butler Co.)

Said to have been the last Revolutionary soldier in Butler Co. D Apr 4, 1852. Bur Greenwood Cem. MI: Name, Revolutionary Soldier. Name appears on Soldiers and Sailors Monument, High and Monument Aves., Hamilton, O. Fur infor John Reily Chap.

SCHAEFER, LAMBERT, (Erie Co.)

Pvt in NJ Continental Line. Bur about 2 miles south of Birmingham, O, on bank of Vermilion River. Fur infor Martha Pitkin Chap.

SCHENCK, GARRET G., (Warren Co.)

Br Monmouth Co. N. J. 1776 served several enlistments, different commands. Br 1758. Mar Jane Vankins. Children: one dau was named Jane. D 1839. 1832 pensioned in Warren Co for Pvt, N. J. Mil. Ref: Natl No 44658, Vol 45, p 264, D. A. R. Lin.

SCHENCK, REV. WILLIAM, (Warren Co.)

Chaplain. Br 1740, Marlboro, N. J. Mar Ann Cumming. D 1826, Franklin, O. Ref: Natl No 44657, Vol 45, p 264, D. A. R. Lin.

SCHOOLY, JOHN, (Hamilton Co.)

Pvt N. J. Mil. Br 1761, Middlebrook, N. J. D 1834, Hamilton. Ref: S. A. R. and Natl No 39003, Vol 40, D. A. R. Lin. Fur infor Cincinnati Chap.

SCHRONEFELD, VON JOHN, (Mahoning Co.)

Pvt, 4th Class, 4th Bn, Cumberland Co Pa Mil. Br 1766. Mar Rosian Gatten (1772-1835). D 1837, North Lima. Bur "Old Cemetery," North Lima. Ref: Pa Archives, Series 5, Vol 6, p 430. Fur infor Mahoning Chap.

SCHULTZ, GEORGE, (Harrison Co.)

Settled in German Twp 1804: Said by family to have served in the Revolution. A George Schultz was a member of Capt Peter Nagle's Company, 4th Bn, Berks Co Pa Mil. Br Mch 16, 1752, Germany. Mar Elizabeth Shoemaker, to which union 11 children were born. D Oct 16, 1827, age 75 yrs, 6 mos, 20 days. Bur in Zion Cem. On Monument are names and dates. Infor fr grandson, Samuel Hoobler, of Annapolis and W. L. Schultz (5th Gen) Hopedale. Ref: Pa Archives, 5 Vol, p 249. Fur infor Moravian Trail Chap.

SCHURR, JACOB, (Morrow Co.)

Bur Chester, (country). Fur infor Mt Gilead Chap.

SCOTT, EBENEZER, (Delaware Co.)

Bur Stark Cem, near Olive Green, O. Fur infor Delaware Chap.

SCOTT, HUGH, JR. or J., (Licking Co.)

Served in Capt Wall's Company, Washington Co, Pa Mil, 2nd Bn, 1782. Br Chester Co, Pa. 1763. Mar Jean Latta, 1786. D Newark, O. 1849. Ref: Natl No 60596, p 199, Vol 61, D. A. R. Lin.

SCOTT, JOEL, (Lucas Co.)

Pvt and Corp in Capt Chapin's Company, Hampshire Co, Mass Mill. Br Oct 29, 1751, Hatfield, Mass. D Nov 8, 1836. Bur East Swanton Cem, Swanton, O. GM Government. Ref: Vol 43, p 139, D. A .R. Lin. Fur infor Fort Industry Chap.

SCOTT, JOHN, (Greene Co.)

Matross. Crane's Mass Regt. Pensioned 1829. Br Va. D 1840. Bur M. E. Graveyard, east Third St., Xenia. Living in Xenia 1827. Ref: Robinsons Hist of Greene Co. Fur infor Catherine Green Chap.

SCOTT, MARK, (County not stated.)

Pvt Capt John Scott's Company, Col Benjamin Foster's Regt, 1779. Br Scarboro, Me. 1763. Mar Mehitable 1786. Ref: Natl No 63373, 22218, p 123, Vol 64, D. A. R. Lin.

SCOTT, MATTHEW, (Marion Co.)

Br 1760, Culpeper Co, Va. D 1848, Knox Co, O. Ashes were removed to Marion Co in the winter of 1925 and interred in Brush Ridge Cem, Grand Prairie Twp. GM Capt Wm Hendricks D. A. R. Marion in 1926. Fur infor Capt Wm Hendricks Chap.

SCOTT, OLIVER, (County not stated.)

Pvt Conn Continental Line. Br 1763. D 1845 in Ohio. Fur infor Natl No 49403, Vol 50, p 177, D. A. R. Lin.

SCOTT, SAMUEL, (Logan Co.)

7th Bn Pa Tr Lancaster Co under Capt Andrew Boggs. Br 1740 near Gettysburg, Pa. Mar Rachel Tidball. D 1823, Logan Co, O. (Cherokee). Ref: Natl No 84858, Vol 85, p 331, D. A. R. Lin.

SCOTT, WILLIAM, (Miami Co.)

Bur Salem Cem near Carlisle. GM Miami Chap. Fur infor Miami Chap

SCOVILLE, AMASA, (Brown Co.)

Br Connecticut. D in Trumbull Co. Bur in Brown Co, O. Fur infor Cincinnati Chap.

SCOVELL, MOSES, (Licking Co.)

Enl June 1, 1870 as Pvt in Col Isaac Sherman's 8th Regt for 8 mos. Drove Artillery Wagon under Capt Carty. Was at Yorktown. Br Dec 6, 1762, Conn. Mar May 5, 1785, Rachel Baker. D July 24, 1836. Monroe Twp. Pens allowed. Ref: Bristers Hist; Edith Leach, Akron, O. Fur infor Hetuck Chap.

SCOVIL, (SCHOFIELD) JONAS, (JONAH), (Mahoning Co.)

Pvt, Conn Men of the Rev, pp 500 and 513. Children: Pamela (mar Ed Wadsworth); Frances (mar John Reid); Susan (mar Chauncy Hickox); Jonah (br 1772 mar Mabel Bailey). Bur at Canfield. Came from Wallingford, Conn. Built first sawmill in 1802. Truesdales Hist of Canfield, Hist of Mahoning Co, Sanford, p 183, Trumbull and Mahoning Co Hist, p 255. Lumberman and Farmer. Fur infor Mahoning Chap.

SCRIBNER, ESTHER, (Ashtabula Co.)

Messenger in 1780. Br 1763. Norwalk, Conn. D 1840, Ashtabula Co, O. Mar Hezekiah Dikeman. Ref: Natl No 70712, p 256, Vol 71, D. A. R. Lin.

SCRIBNER, SAMUEL, (Delaware Co.)

Pvt in the N H Line under the commands of Capts James Shephard and Ebenezer Webster, Cols Wyman and Nichols. Br Kingston, N. H. 1743. D 1810, Delaware Co, O. Natl No 76053, Vol 77, D. A. R. Lin.

SCUDDER, MATHIAS, (Miami Co.)

He entered all of Tractional sec 33 Spring Creek Twp prior to 1808. D Oct 1, 1837. Bur in graveyard off his own farm, later called McKinley Cem. Fur infor Piqua Chap.

SEAMAN, HENRY, (Greene Co.)

Pvt Va Mil Pensioned 1831. Br 1758, Virginia. D 1838. Bur Middle Run Churchyard, near Bellbrook. Living in Sugar Creek, 1813. Ref: Robinson's Hist of Green Co. Fur infor Catherine Green Chap.

SEARL, ABRAHAM, (Mahoning Co.)

Pvt and pensioned. Br 1748. D 1840. Bur Austintown. Ref: "New York Men of the Revolution" p 124, United States Census of Pension, 1841. Fur infor Mahoning Chap.

SEARL, REUBEN, (Highland Co.)

Name taken fr S. A. R. 1917 Yr Bk as authority, but located correctly in Highland Co, O. Bur Fairfield Quaker Meeting House. South of Leesburg, Highland Co, O. Accepting this infor Jane Dailey, State Chairman.

SEBRING, FULKARD, (Delaware Co.)

Pvt in Bucks Co, Pa Mil. Bur Redbanks Graveyard, Genoa Twp. Fur infor Delaware Chap.

SEDAM, CORNELIUS, (Hamilton Co.)

Ensign. Br 1759, New Jersey. D 1823, Sedamsville, O. Ref: S. A. R. Natl No 34744, Vol 35, D. A. R. Lin. Fur infor Cincinnati Chap.

SEELY, JOHN, (Portage Co.)

Served as Pvt 7 yrs, 6 mos, in Mass Line. Bur Windham, O. Placed on Pension Roll Aug 8, 1828. Fur infor Old Northwest Chap.

SELLERS, NATHAN, (Preble Co.)

Pvt in Capt William Kirk's Company, Chester Co, Pa. Br 1762, Chester Co, Pa. Mar Sarah Finley. D 1826, Preble Co. Bur Mound Hill Cem. Ref: Natl No 72496, Vol 73, p 175, D. A. R. Lin. Fur infor Grace Miller, Org Regent, Eaton.

SELLS, LUDWICK, (Franklin Co.)

Capt Martin Bowman's Company. See Pa Archives, 1777. 1780 in Assembly. Br Huntington Co, Pa. in 1743. Parents: John Sells and Sarah Haak. Mar Catherine Deardorf, 1770. Children: Samuel B, John, Benjamin, Peter, Mary, Sophia, Margaret, William H., and George. D at Dublin, Franklin Co, O. Oct 13, 1823. Bur Odd Fellows Cem, Dublin, O. First large marker entering Cem. MI: "In memory of Ludwick Sells B, Huntington, Pa, 1743. Settled Franklin Co, 1798. Died 1823. Erected by his descendants Sept 10, 1915." By large monument and bronze tablet. Sept 10, 1915. Farmer. Came to Franklin Co. 1798. Came over mountains to Pittsburgh. Bought flat boat and poled up Scioto River. Moved to Dublin. First Court held in his home. Member of Pennsylvania Assembly in 1780. One of Pioneer settlers of county. Name on Memorial Tablet in Memorial Hall as Revolutionary Soldier and Pioneer of county. Ref: Natl No 87668, Vol 88, p 203, D. A. R. Lin. Historic Huntington, p 17. Eagles Hist, Martins Hist. Fur infor Columbus Chap.

SELMAN, JOHN, M. D., (Hamilton Co.)

Surgeon's Mate in Revolutionary War. Came to Cincinnati with Gen Wayne; later gave serv at Arsenal and Barracks as Citizen Surgeon. Br Annapolis, Md 1764. D 1827, Hamilton Co, O. Practised at Cincinnati (Sycamore and Broadway). Ref: Greves Cent Hist of Cincinnati, p 366. Fur infor Cincinnati Chap.

SERING, SAMUEL, (Warren Co.)

Enl near Hannastown, Pa at Cortanian; served 3 yrs; disch; served Autumn 1775 to 1778; in one battle under Washington (fr records written 1800). Not officially recorded). Br 1758, Morris Co, N. J. Parents: Samuel and Ann Pearsall Sering (near Oct 1757). Mar Sarah Mann (1764-1842), 1778 near Greensburgh, Pa. Children: Sarah, Eunice, Samuel Jr, Margaret, John, Elizabeth, Theodocia, Daniel, Nancy, Mary, Jane. The 5 older children bur in Westmoreland Co. D 1823. Bur Shakers Cem near Union town, Warren Co, O. GM Family stone. He and wife charter members 1st Presbyterian Church, Cincinnati, 1790. Went to Lebanon 1800, and later drawn to Shakers. Was cooper and farmer. Ref: Dr E. R. Booth, S. A. R. Cincinnati, O. and Family Bible Fur infor Cincinnati Chap.

SESSIONS, ANSON, (Lake Co.)

He had much serv in the frontier and was with Gen Wayne at Maumee. He received 160 acres of land as bounty. Br Apr 16, 1770, Windham, Conn. Mar Asenath A. Fobes, Dec 16, 1804. Children: Norman, Aurel, Mariner, Horace. D Aug 1827, Painesville, O. Bur on his own farm, but his name is inscribed on a monument in Evergeen Cem. GM by New Connecticut Chap. Fur infor New Connecticut Chap.

SEVEMS, EDWARD, (Miami Co.)

Enl while resident of N. J. and served at various times amounting to 12 mos in all. Served as Pvt under Capt Ely Twigly, was in the battles of Milestone and Monmouth. Ref: Bureau of Pensions Washington DC. Br Nov, 1758, near Trenton, N. J. Mar Hannah Burns, Jan 13, 1787, near Trenton, N. J. They had 11 children, the only ones given are: Mary (br 1789 mar John Barnett Sept 10, 1812); John (b 1799) and Hannah, the youngest, (mar Joshua Worley). D Feb 11, 1814, in Miami Co, O. Place of burial not yet located, tho he and widow both died in Miami Co. Was a Revolutionary pensioner; War Claims Records 9394. After his death, his widow was a resident of Piqua, Miami Co, O. in 1849. D Mch 15, 1850 at 83 yrs. Fur infor Lewis Boyer Chap.

SEVERANCE, BENJAMIN, (Morgan Co.)

Pensioned 1832, for serv 1778-79 in Capt Spurr's Company, Col Nixon's Mass, Regt. Br 1761. Mar Rebecca (Sweet) Holcomb, in 1784. D 1845, Brookfield Twp, Morgan Co, O. Ref: Natl No 74551, Vol 75, D. A. R. Lin.

SEVERN, JESSE, (Clermont Co.)

Revolutionary Soldier who died in Ohio Twp, Clermont Co, O. Fur infor Cincinnati Chap.

SEWARD, DANIEL, (Hamilton Co.)

N J Mil. Br 1758. D 1794 in Hamilton Co. Ref: S. A. R. and Natl No 101584. Vol 103 D. A. R. Lin. Fur infor Cincinnati Chap.

SEWARD, JOHN, (Portage Co.)

Pvt in Mass Continental Line. Placed on Pension Roll, Nov 30, 1819. Bur Aurora, O. Drew pens at Ravenna, O. in 1840. Fur infor Old Northwest Chap.

SEWARD, SAMUEL, (Butler Co.)

Name appears on the tablet of the Sailors and Soldiers Monument, at Hamilton, O. as a Revolutionary Soldier living in Butler Co. D Apr 22, 1828, while living in Union Twp. Fur infor John Reily Chap.

SEXTON, CHARLES, (Fayette Co.)

Br 1762, Virginia. Mar Mrs Blakemore. D Feb 1, 1842, Washington C. H. Bur Old Cem, Washington C. H. MI: "Charles Sexton died Feb 1, 1842, aged 79 years and 9 months." GM Family in 1842. Farmer, near Jasper. Pensioner. Fur infor Washington C H. Chap.

SEXTON, EZRA, (Lorain Co.)

Enl as Corp under Capt Robinson, Col Enos Regt. Br 1758. D Jan 10, 1843, aged 85 yrs. Bur Pioneer Cem, Wellington. GM Western Reserve Chap, in 1920. Ref: Conn Men in the Rev. Fur infor Western Reserve Chap.

SEXTON, STEPHEN, (Mahoning Co.)

Ensign Somers Provincial Regt of Conn, 1781. Br 1764. Mar Elizabeth. Children: Joseph, Nancy. D 1856, Poland, O. Bur Presbyterian Church, Poland, O. GM Mahoning Chapter, bronze marker May 30, 1916. Ref: Conn Men of the Rev p 586; Trumbull and Mahoning Co Hist. Vol 2. Fur infor Mahoning Chap.

SEYMOUR, THOMAS, (Licking Co.)

Enl in Hardy Co, Va. served under Gen McIntosh. Was in war 1792. Br Jan 25, 175-, Harding Co, Va. Parents: Felix Seymour. Mar Catherine Hider, Oct 15, 1782. Children: Adam, D Apr 16, 1831, Madison Twp. Bur on Son Adam's farm, Madison Twp. Removed to Cedar Hill, Adam Seymour's lot. GM Hetuck Chap. in 1910. Ref: Bristers Hist and Natl No 744439, Vol 75, D. A. R. Lin. Fur infor Hetuck Chap.

SHAFER, ANDREW, (Highland Co.)

Served from Maryland. A Stone by his reads: "Martha, wife of Andrew Shafer died Oct 19, 1846, aged 83 years." Bur Old Dutch graveyard, six miles west of Hillsboro. MI: "Andrew Shafer, died Dec 2, 1853, aged 93 yrs, 1 mo, 2 da. A Revolutionary Soldier." Fur infor Waw-Wil-a-Way Chap.

SHAFER, WILLIAM, (Butler Co.)

Pvt, Capt Vorheis' Company, 1st Bn, 2nd Continental Establishment of N J. Mar Katherine Koolbaugh. Children: One dau was Rachel. D Butler Co. Ref: Natl No 45968, Vol 46, p 406, D. A. R. Lin. Fur infor Jane Dowd Dailey.

SHAFFER, JACOB, (Mahoning Co.)

Pvt in Berks Co, Pa, Continental Line. Br 1739. Mar Katherine (1767-1828). D 1826. Bur "Old Cem" North Lima. Came to Ohio in 1802. Ref: Pa Archives, 5 Series, Vol 4, p 266. Trumbull and Mahoning Co Hist. Vol 2, p 202. Fur infor Mahoning Chap.

SHAFER, PETER, (Butler Co.)

Pvt in Somerset Co, N. J. Mil. See p 749 "Officers and Men in the Rev from N. J." Br 1781, N. J. Mar Katherine Kohlbach. Children: William (br 1783, N. J., mar Jane Ryerson). D 1818, Amanda, Lemon Twp, Butler Co, O. Bur Amanda. Grave not marked. Went to Lexington, Ky with his family in 1793, and thence to Ohio in 1803, where he lived until his death. Ref: Natl No 60007, and S. A. R. No 36486. Fur infor Richard Montgomery Chap S. A. R.

SHANKLAND, ALEXANDER, (Wayne Co.)

Pvt under Capt Whitacre and Wall (or Hall.) State of N. Y. Br May 3, 1756, Cherry Valley, N. Y. Parents: Robert and Sarah Beatty Shankland. Mar Vintintia Wilson. Children: Jesse, Beatty, Robert, Vincent, Alexander, Mary Margaret, Vintintia, Elizabeth, Sarah. D Feb 20, 1833, Canaan, Wayne Co, O. Bur Canaan Cem, Canaan Twp, Wayne Co, O. on east central part, fourth row of graves. MI: "Alexander Shankland, born May 3, 1756, died Feb 20, 1833." GM Small white marble stone. Dates of enlmt May 1, 1777, Spring 1778 to July 1781. Farmer. Ref: Mrs. J. W. Irvin, 231 N. Market St., Wooster, O. Fur infor Wooster Wayne Chap.

SHANNON, GEORGE, (Belmont Co.)

Pvt Capt James Young's Company, 8th Bn Cumberland Co, Pa Mil. Col Abraham Smith. Br 1759, Ireland. D 1803, Belmont Co, O. Ref: Natl No 50080, D. A. R. Lin.

SHARON, WM., (Jefferson Co.)

Pvt Cumberland Co, Pa. Mil, 1777. Br 1753 in Pa. D 1809 Jefferson Co, O. Ref: Natl No 65012, Vol 66, p 5.

SHARP, GEORGE, (Wayne Co.)

Br 1757. D Oct 17, 1840. Bur Tracy Cem, two miles east of Apple Creek. Fur infor Wooster Wayne Chap.

SHARP, JOB, (Logan Co.)

Bur Country Churchyard between East Liberty and West Middleburgh. Fur infor Bellefontaine Chap.

SHAW, BENJAMIN, (Washington Co.)

Sgt Maj in Ebenezer Francis' 11th Mass Bay Regt. Oct 3 he was promoted to Ens of Brig Gen John Patterson's Brig. Mch 18, 1780 he received his commission as Lt of 10th Mass Regt. Br 1753, Beverly, Mass. Parents: Peter Shaw and Elizabeth Meacham. Mar Elizabeth Cushing. Children: Sally, Cushing, Benjamin, Peter, Boylston, Betsey. D 1838, Round Bottom. Bur Round Bottom Cem on the Muskingum River. MI: "Benjamin Shaw born 1753, died 1838." GM Marietta Chap with Revolutionary marker in 1921. He was one of the original settlers arriving at Marietta Apr 7, 1788. Fur infor Marietta Chap.

SHAW, EBENEZER, (Medina Co.)

Served fr Mass and Conn. Br 1752. D 1834, Bur Chatham Center. GM Western Reserve Chap. Fur infor Western Reserve Chap.

SHAW, KNOWLES, (County not stated.)

Br 1758, Wilbraham, Mass. Mar Margaret Hungerford. D 1832, Venice, O. (Erie or Butler Co.) Ref: Natl No 23738 and 58700, Vol 59, p 240, D. A. R. Lin.

SHAW, NATHAN, (Jefferson Co.)

Ens and Lt in Capt Jonathan Smith's Company, 1st Bn. Cumberland Co, N. J. Mil, 1776. Br 1740. Mar Julia Myers. D Jefferson Co, 1820. Ref: Natl No 60012, p 5, Vol 61, D. A. R. Lin.

SHAW, PETER, (Washington Co.)

Ist Lt of Capt Woodbury's 4th Beverly Company, Col Henry Herrick's 8th Essex Company Mass Mil. Br 1730, Beverly, Mass. Mar Elizabeth Meacham. Children: Benjamin. D Sept 24, 1823, Beverly, O. Bur Round Bottom Cem Washington Co, O. Peter Shaw bought one share in the stock of the Ohio Company. He was the original proprietor of one full section in Ames Twp. Fur infor Marietta Chap.

SHAW, THOMAS, (Shelby Co.)

Pvt. Br 1753, Ireland. Children: Alexander (br in Kentucky 1792, mar Martha Culbertson, their son Samuel br in Green Twp). D 1835. Bur Graceland in the south line (Dixie Highway) of city of Sidney. Had been moved from old Presbyterian Cem Jan 13, 1911 to present lot No 83, Sec 4; has a metal G. A. R. marker. MI: "Thomas Shaw died 1835, aged 82 years, 2 months, 11 days." GM by Shaw family, old tombstone or marker moved from Presbyterian Cem, which is now used for city High School lot. Came to America in 1765, located in Kentucky, was a neighbor and intimate acquaintance of Daniel Boone, noted hunter and Indian scout. Ref: Suttons Hist of Shelby Co. Fur infor Lewis Boyer Chap.

SHAWHAN, FREDERICK, (Seneca Co.)

Served under Gens Wayne, Green, Lafayette and Washington. Br Aug 12, 1760, Kent Co, Md. D Aug 26, 1840. Bur Greenlawn Cem Tiffin, O. MI: "Frederick Shawhan a soldier of the Revolution of 1776." GM Dolly Todd Madison Chap with small iron marker May 30, 1922. Fur infor Dolly Todd Madison Chap.

SHAYLOR, JOSEPH, (Clermont Co.)

Enl 1776, serving to close of war. Served in regular army as a Capt. Turned out at Lexington Alarm. Ensign at Long Island and White Plains battles; Lt in Meigs Light Inf at Stony Point. "Thrice thanked by Washington." (Ref: 5359 D. A. R.) Br 1737, Conn. D 1816, Union Twp, Clermont Co, O. Came early to Union Twp, settled on Shaylors Run, at branch of East Fork. In 1792 helped funds to build Presbyterian Church at Fort Washington (Cincinnati) he being there with the regulars. Ref: Natl No 6988 and 5359, and A. S. Abbott, Bethel, O. Fur infor Cincinnati Chap.

SHAYLOR, MAJ., (Clermont Co.)

He entered serv Apr 24, 1775; was in Col Jonathan Meigs' Regt Leather Cap 5th and 6th Conn. Ens and Maj. Name Jacob. I have no record of his name as Joseph. He entered farm which he called a "Plantation," 16 miles fr Cincinnati and designated as Sixteen Mile Stand. Afterwards co line ran through plantation and the Clermont Co Hist claims his grave is on Clermont side. County line is 3 or 4 miles from present town of Sixteen Mile Stand in Hamilton Co. Drabout 1810, Union Twp, Clermont Co, O. (This might be "Joseph Shaylor," which see for Ref.) Ref: Mrs. E. P. Whallton, Cincinnati, O. Fur infor Cincinnati Chap.

SHEELY, LUDWIG, (Wyandot Co.)

Mar Mary M. Stone too defaced to read when died. Bur Lutheran Cem McCutchenville, O. GM Sandstone slab G. A. R. marker. Fur infor Col Wm Crawford.

SHEETS, CHRISTIAN, (Columbiana Co.)

No record has been found. Bur Forney Cem, Columbiana Co. Fur infor Bethia Southwick Chap.

SHEHY, DANIEL, (Mahoning Co.)

Pvt in Capt Laurance Keen's Company, Lt Col John Park, 11th Pa Continental Line. Br 1749, Ireland. Mar Jane McLain. Children: Catherine, mar Neal Campbell, Robert, mar Char Bennet, Mary, mar Wm Woods, John mar Anna Kimmell, Daniel mar Charl Pearson, Margaret mar Daniel McAlister, James mar Maria McArter, Jane mar John Lett, Lucius mar Julia Bedell. D 1831, Youngstown, O. Bur Oak Hill Cem. Youngstown, O. GM Mahoning Chap D. A. R. bronze marker in 1915. Ref: Pay roll for Aug 1778, Mass Men of the Rev. Trumbull and Mahoning Co Hist, Vol 2, and Natl No 55902 D. A. R. Lin. Fur infor Mahoning Chap.

SHELDON, EBENEZER, (Portage Co.)

Responded to the Lexington Alarm, Apr 19, 1775, fr Suffield, Conn. Br Feb 20, 1754, Suffield, Conn. Mar Huldah Hanchett. Children: Mary. D July 24, 1825, Aurora, O. Bur Aurora, O. He was a Minute Man in Col Wolcot's Regt. His commission of Capt is in possession of a descendant in Aurora. Ref: Record of service of Connecticut men. Natl No 34920. Fur infor Old Northwest Chap.

SHELHOUSE, MARTIN (SCHELHOUSE), (Lorain Co.)

Pvt. Conn Mil; also Corp in War of 1812. Br 1759. D 1813, GM Western Reserve Chap. bronze marker. Fur infor Western Reserve Chap.

SHEPARD, BENJAMIN, (Morgan Co.)

Pvt. 8 mos serv in NJ Continental Army, in Capt Hedley's Company, Col Aaron Hankinsons Regt, Sept 1776 to Sept 1777 in Capt Staat's Company. He was in battle Germantown. Data secured from Revolutionary War pension claim S. 4826. Br Feb 27, 1760, in Somerset Co, N J. Children: John and Isaiah. Undoubtedly there were other children. D after Mch 23, 1837 in Morgan Co, Date of last payment of Pension. He enl when residing near Newton, N J at the age of 16 yrs and came to Belmont Co, O. in the early pioneer days of that county. He was allowed pension on his application executed Aug 1, 1832, in Belmont Co. At that time he was a resident of Morgan Co. Ref: Natl No 230402, Miss Myrtle Moore, Nelsonville, O. Fur infor Elizabeth Zane Dew Chap.

SHEPARD, JOHN, (Cuyahoga Co.)

Member of Col Washington's Command, Pa. Served in French and Indian War. Br 1729. D 1847. Bur North Royalton. Fur infor Western Reserve Chap.

SHEPARD, PHINEAS, (Cuyahoga Co.)

Pvt Conn Continental Line. Br 1754. D 1842. Bur Riverside Cem 25th St. Junction Scranton Rd. GM Western Reserve Chap. Fur infor Western Reserve Chap.

SHEPHERD, ELISHA, (Hamilton Co.)

Sgt N J Mil, Capt Thos Hunn. Taken prisoner and confined in New York. Br 1750, N. J. D 1834 in Ohio. Ref: Compare Natl No 48507, Vol 49, p 233, D. A. R. Lin and S. A. R. for Ref. Fur infor Cincinnati Chap.

SHEPHERD, JACOB, (Wyandot Co.)

Enl fr Monmouth, N. J. in Capt John Smock's Company. Col Asher Holmes N. J. Regt, 1776. Applied for pens in 1833, his claim allowed. Br 1757. D in Carey, Wyandot Co.? Ref: Natl No 71493, p 177 Vol 72, D. A. R. Lin.

SHEPHERD, ENOCH, CAPT., (Washington Co.)

Capt Pay Roll of Officers of a detachment fr 3rd Hampshire Company, commanded by Lt Col Timothy Robinson. Marched to Ticonderoga Oct 21, 1776, to reinforce army by order of Gen Schuyler. Br 1743 or 1742, Westfield. D Sept 17, 1821, Marietta, O. Bur Mound Cem, Marietta. O. Location of grave "in front of Ward vault," says an aged lady of Marietta. MI: "Capt Enoch Shepherd, 1743-1821." GM Marietta Chap by marker and gateway Nov 30, 1906; marker stolen, replaced 1920. Fur infor Marietta Chap.

SHEPHERD, PHINEAS, (Van Wert Co.)

Pvt Conn Continental Line. Br 1757, Hartford, Conn. Mar Deliverance Smith in 1783. br 1766; d 1831). D 1842, Ohio City, O. Placed on Pension Roll of Cuyahoga Co 1832, for serv as Pvt Conn Continental Line. Ref: Natl No 100471, Vol 101, p 144, D. A. R. Lin.

SHERER, JOHN, (Mahoning Co.)

Sgt Nov 5, 1777, of Capt Martin Weaver's Company, Lancaster Co Mil Commanded by John Rogers. Bur Mahoning Co. Bought land in 1803. Ref: Old Deeds, Vol A, p 62, Pa Archives, Series 3, Vol 23, p 814. Fur infor Mahoning Chap.

SHERMAN, ABEL, (Washington Co.)

Enl July 22, 1779, as Pvt in Capt Joshua Shaw's Company, Col Elisha Porter's Regt. Disch Aug 27, 1779. Br 1744 Massachusetts. Children: Ezra, Josiah, Amy. D Aug 14, 1794. Bur Round Bottom Cem near Beverly, O. MI: Abel Sherman, born 1744, Died 1794. GM Marietta Chap with Revolutionary marker in 1922. Presumably killed by "Silver Heels," a noted Indian of that region. Farmer. Ref: Mass Soldiers and Sailors in Revolution. Fur infor Marietta Chap.

SHERMAN, EZRA, (Hamilton Co.)

Br 1765, Connecticut. Ref: S. A. R. Fur infor Cincinnati Chap.

SHERRARD, JOHN, (Jefferson Co.)

Pvt Flying Camp of Pa. Br 1750, Ireland. Mar Mary Cathcart. D 1809, Smithfield, O. Ref: Natl No 55433, p 200, Vol 56, D. A. R. Lin.

SHERWIN, AHINAAZ, (Cuyahoga Co.)

Fifer, Mass Tr, 3 yrs. Br 1759, Rutland, Mass. D 1840, Cleveland, O. Bur Lake View, Euclid Ave. GM Western Reserve Chap. On Vermont Pension Roll 1820. Ref: Natl No 31792, Vol 32, D. A. R. Lin. Fur infor Western Reserve. Chap.

SEWARD, WILLIAM, (Might be STEWARD), (County not stated.)

1st Lt, under Col Knowlton's Conn Regt. Bur Fargo Cem, Bennington Twp, Morrow Co. Fur infor Delaware Chap. S. A. R. 1917.

SHIELDS, DAVID, (Clinton Co.)

Pvt 1779-81 under Capts McCutchin and Cunningham, Cols Boyer and Matthews' Va Line. Br 1752, Virginia. D 1841, Clinton Co, O. Bur Old Baptist Cem, Port William. Ref: Natl No 86417, Vol 87, p 133, D. A. R. Lin. Fur infor George Clinton Chap.

SHINKLE, CHRISTIAN, (Brown Co.)

Pvt in the Heidelburg Twp, Lancaster Co, Pa, 1775, Capt Geo Hudson. Took oath of allegiance to the State of Pa in Heidelburg Twp, June 22, 1778. Ref: Pa Archives, 5 Series, Vol V, VII, p 10. Br July 10, 1756, Heidelburg, Lancaster Co, Pa. Parents: Philip Carl Shinkel (son of Nicholas and grandson of Bartholomew Schenkel), Maria Elizabeth Shinkle. Mar 1st Maria Magdalena; 2nd Elizabeth Stayton (1817). Children: Maria, Elizabeth, Maria Katharina, Magdalena, Barbara, John B, Christian L., George, Christina, Margaret, Susannah; By 2nd marriage: Joseph, Henry,Jesse. D 1833, Shinkle Ridge, Lewis Twp. Bur Shinkle Ridge, 3½ miles northwest Higginsport, O. South central part of Cem (donated by him). Farmer; 1000 acres in Jacob's survey. Ref: County Hist, Beers, p 462, C. A. Shinkle, Higginsport, O. Family Bible, Family genealogy while he was living. Fur infor Taliaferro Chap.

SHINKLE, HAN PHILIP, (Brown Co.)

Pvt in the Heidelberg Company, Lancaster Co, Pa. Mil, under Capt George Hudson, 1775. See p 10, Vol VII, Pa Archives, 5 Series. Br Oct 25, 1753, Heidelberg Twp, Lancaster Co, Pa. Parents: Philip Carl Schenckel, br June 8, 1717. D after June 22, 1778, mother was Maria Elisabetha Zimpel, (br Feb 28, 1717.) Mar Barbara Walderin. Moved to Ohio in 1796. Children: John Lienenger, Christian, Elizabeth, Henry, Catherine, John, Jacob, Peter, Barbara and Eve. D May 29, 1829. Bur near Feesburg, Brown Co, O. Ref: Natl No 34924, Cincinnati, Hamilton Co, O.

SHINKLE, PHILIP JACOB, (Brown Co.)

Pvt Lancaster Co, Pa. Mil, Heidelberg Company, under Capt George Hudson, 1775 in the war of the Rev. See p 10, Vol VII Pa Archives, 5 Series. Br Mch 5, 1747, Edenkoben, Rhenish Palatinate, Bavaria. Parents: Philip Carl Schenckel, (br June 8, 1717,) and Maria Elisabetha Zimpel, (br Feb 28, 1717.) They are both bur in Lancaster Co, Pa. Mar Julia Ann Bolender, a sister of Stephen Bolender. Children: Philip, Jacob, Peter, Johannas H, Maria Barbara, Elizabeth, Christian W, Henry, David, Catherine. D after 1805-3, in Brown Co, O. and is bur near Feesburg, O. Ref: Fr Family Bible and fr Genealogical Hist written by a grandson while soldier still lived. Natl No 34924, for data. Fur infor Cincinnati Chap.

SHIPMAN, JOHN, (Hamilton Co.)

Br 1760, N J. D 1834. Ref: S. A. R. Fur infor Cincinnati Chap.

SHIRTLIFF, NOAH, (Portage Co.)

Pvt in New York Mil. Placed on Pens Roll July 30, 1834. Bur Shalersville. Drew pens in Ravenna in 1840. Fur infor Old Northwest Chap.

SHIRTS, MATTHIAS SR., (Columbiana Co.)

He served in the Revolutionary War, 2 yrs, 5 mos and 8 das. Quoted from grave stone. Served as soldier in 1st Regt and old 3rd of N J, under Col Albert Ogden. Br Feb 13, 1747. D Jan 14, 1845, Clarkson, O. On farm. Bur Clarkson, O. Presbyterian Churchyard. MI: "Matthias Shirts. Jan 14, 1845, aged 97 years, 11 mos and 1 day. He served in the Revolutionary War 2 years, 5 mos and 8 days." GM by his children with a head stone of white marble. Fur infor Bethia Southwick Chap.

SHOEMAKER, ABRAHAM, (Mahoning Co.)

Pvt 2nd Class, Capt Klunhang's Company, Northampton Co, Pa Mil. Pensioned Nov 11, 1833. Br 1767. Mar Mary—1774-1850. D Springfield Twp, 1856. Bur Old Church, Petersburg. Pvt 2nd Class, Capt Klung's Company. Ref: Pa Archives, 5 Series, Vol 8, p 89, 3 Series, Vol 23, 527. Fur infor Mahoning Chap.

SHOEMAKER, JOHN, (Mahoning Co.)

Pvt 6th Class, Lancaster Co, Pa Mil, 1782. Br 1739. D 1814, Springfield Twp. Bur Old Church, Petersburg, Springfield Twp. Came to Ohio from Pa in 1804. Ref: Pa Archives, Series 5, Vol 7, p 1025. Is mentioned in Trumbull and Mahoning Co History, Vol 2, p 203. Fur infor Mahoning Chap.

SHOTTS, DAVID, (Ross Co.)

Pvt. Entered Huntington (Twp) in 1809. He was a native of Va, and was in the Revolutionary War He also assisted General Washington in the suppression of the whiskey rebellion. Br Va. Children: Catherine, Jacob, Elizabeth, Margaret, (married Jacob Bishop), Hannah, Mary, Daniel, Sophia, Jonas and Susan. Struck by lightning, under large oak tree, 1825. Location of grave not found. Farmer. Ref: Hist of Ross and Highland counties pp 288, 97. Fur infor Nathaniel Massie Chap.

SHOVER, HENRY, (Union Twp.)

Bur Woods Cem, Union Twp. Ref: Hist of Union Co. Fur infor Hannah Emerson Dustin Chap.

SHREVE, JOHN, (Stark Co.)

At the age of 14 he accompanied his father to the war. He was made Ensign and was with Washington when he crossed the Delaware. Br Apr 6, 1762, Burlington Co, N J Parents: Col Israel Shreve and Grace Curles Mar Abigail Ridgway in 1786. Children: Joseph, John, Mary, Israel, George, Thomas, Benjamin, Solomon, Elijah. D Sept 8, 1854, at Mt Union. Bur Mt Union Cem, near entrance. MI: "John Shreve died April 8, 1854, aged 92 years 5 months." GM by Canton Chap. Fur infor Jane Bain Chap.

SHUEY, J. MARTIN, (Montgomery Co.)

Pvt in Capt Casper Stover's 3rd Company, 2nd Bn, Lancaster Co Mil in 1780 and 1782, Pa Archives, Vol 7, p 124 and 170, 5th series. Br June 20, 1750, Bethel Twp, Lancaster Co, Pa. Grandfather, Daniel Shuey, a Palatine came to Philadelphia in 1732. His father, Lewis Henry Shuey, was a member of the Committee of Inspection of Lancaster Co but d before the Declaration was signed. Mar Margaret Elizabeth Conrad (d 1838). Children: John, Catherine, Christina, Martin (br Sept 28, 1785 in Dauphin Co, Pa, was in the war of 1812, and a Gen in 1818), Barbara, Margaret, Henry, Mary (br 1795, mar Capt John C Negley, son of Philip Negley), Eve, Adam. D Feb, 1829, German Twp. Bur Greencastle Cem. In

1805 he came with his family, in flat boats down the Ohio River to Cincinnati, thence to the Miami Valley, settling near Germantown where both he and wife died. Ref: Col George I Gunckel, U. S. Army 527 West 2nd St., Dayton. Edward T. Weakley. 335 West First St., Dayton, O. Fur infor Richard Montgomery Chap, S. A. R.

SHUMAKER, WILLIAM, (Fairfield Co.)

Bur Mt Carmel Cem, Clearport, O. Fur infor Elizabeth Sherman Reese Chap.

SIFRITT, ANDREW, OR CYPRUS OR CYPRESS, (Madison, O.)

Served 8 yrs; Pvt in Capt Waggoner's Company, Col James Woods 12th Regt of Va; in many battles; taken prisoner at Charleston Br Mch 16, 1750, near Harper's Ferry, Va Mar Susan Schrock about 1786 (1st wife), Hannah Morrilis or Marrle (2nd wife). Nine children by each wife, 1st wife: Mary, Catherine, John, Elizabeth, James; by 2nd wife: Rebecca, Julian, George, Jacob, Maria, Lawrence and Michael—so listed. D Oct 16, 1847, Madison Co, O. Bur Paint Twp, Madison Co, O, where he was the first pioneer settled. Bur on Jacob Sifrit Lot. MI: "The grave of Andrew Sifrit a Soldier of the Revolutionary War. Virginia Troops.' GM by Mt Sterling Chap with bronze marker in 1911. Came with his family to Ross Co, O, in 1803, and in 1804 moved to Madison Co. Applied for pens Mch 29, 1818. Received 200 acres land. Ref: Grace Sifrit Thompson, London, O. Fur infor Mt. Sterling Chap.

SILVESTER, JOSEPH, (Meigs Co.)

Served 1 yr under Capt Clapp, Col Wood's Regt, and 3 yrs as Pvt in Capt Geo Dunham's Company. In battles of Long Island, Saratoga and Monmouth. Br July 15, 1755, Plymouth, Mass D July 1828, Rutland, O Bur Miles Cem, Rutland, O. MI: "Joseph Silvester, Br 1755—Died 1828." GM by D. A. R. with Government marker in 1913. Applied for pens June 23, 1818. Fur infor Return Jonathan Meigs Chap.

SIMERAL, ALEXANDER, Lt., (Jefferson Co.)

Served as Lt of 18th Regt of Pa Line, commanded by Col Encas Mackey, Aug 6, 1776. He was wounded in the Battle of Brandywine and received a pens in Jefferson Co, O. at the age of 77. Br Chester Co, Pa. 1747. Parents: Alexander Simeral, mar Jennet Lindsay, Apr 1737, Chester Co, Pa. Mar Martha McGrew, 1779, West Newton, Westmoreland Co, Pa. Children: Andrew, Margaret, William, Isabell, Jane, James, Archibald, Priscilla, Joseph, John. D 1834, in Jefferson Co, O. Bur Center Cem, Jefferson Co, O. MI: "Lieutenant Alexander Simeral 1747-1834." GM Steubenville D. A. R. Removed to Westmoreland Co, Pa. in 1773. Alexander Simeral and brother James for 300£ (about $1500) bought two tracts of land on banks of Youghiogheny and operated a ferry known for many years as Simeral Ferry. Ref: Pa Archives, Second Series, Vol 10, p 667; Chas. Hannah "Ohio Valley Genealogies." Chester Co Wills, Westmoreland Co Wills. Fur infor Steubenville Chap.

SIMMONS, PELEG, (Lake Co.)

Served fr Conn on a war vessel, which was used to protect the coast. Br June 3, 1761, Middletown, Hartford Co, Conn. Mar May 22, 1788. D Oct 1, 1854. Bur Willoughby Plains, Lake Co, O. GM New Connecticut Chap. Fur infor New Connecticut Chap.

SIMMONS, THOMAS, (Butler Co.)

Fought in Battle of Yorktown and present when Cornwallis surrendered his sword. Bur Collinsville Cem, Collinsville, Butler Co, O. Fur infor Oxford, Caroine Scott Chap.

SIMMONS, WILLIAM, (Coshocton Co.)

Entered Continental Army at age 18, in which serv he rose to the rank of Col and commanded a brig at the battle of Trenton, N. J. Br 1757, Newburg, N. Y. Mar Josephine Bertrand Lapoint, Nov 18, 1799, Philadelphia. Children: William Henry Simmons, Charles William Simmons, Mrs Elizabeth Simmons Carrhart. (All deceased). D Apr 15, 1825, Coshocton Co, O. Bur private burying ground, one mile west of Warsaw, O. Grave unmarked (1924). Entered Continental Army at age 18, became Col. Commanded brig at battle of Trenton, N. J. Trusted friend of George Washington, Gen Greene and other Revolutionary generals. Commissioned by President Washington as accountant to the Dept of War on Apr 17, 1795. Received second commission fr the President, and another from President Adams. Resigned this office in 1815, having served the government in civil and military capacity for nearly 40 years. President Madison offered him any office within his gift if he would remain in the service. Govt gave him a grant of 4297 acres, at the head waters of the Muskingum river in Coshocton Co for his services. To this land he removed his family in 1820, taking into Ohio the first family carriage, his colored servants, and solid silver to set a table for twenty. Fur Ref: Mrs. Augustus Ripple, West Lafayette, O. Fur infor Coshocton Chap.

SIMON, JACOB, (Mahoning Co.)

Pvt in Washington Co Pa Mil. Lt Harnard's Company. Br 1750. D 1818. Bur Pleasant Grove, Youngstown. In the western part of Cem. Ref: Pa Archives, Series 2, Vol 14, p 218. Fur infor Mahoning Chap.

SIMON, MICHAEL, (Mahoning Co.)

Pvt Capt Graham's Company, New York Line. Br 1741. Mar Gertrude—(1750-1837). Children: Adam, Peter, Jacob, Abraham, Henry. D 1834. Bur Pleasant Grove Cem Youngstown in the western part. Ref: NY in the Rev State Archives, p 188, Trumbull and Mahoning Co Hist, Vol 2, p 85. Fur infor Mahoning Chap.

SIMONS, JOSEPH, (Washington Co.)

Served as Pvt in Capt John Harmon's Company in 4th Regt, Col John Durker commanding. Enl Oct 7, 1778. Disch Jan 1, 1779. Br Sept 1, 1776, in Conn. Mar Abigail Neal, Feb 1, 1788. Children: Meigs, Hosea, Edmund, Reuben, Mary, Jane, Patience, Elizabeth, Hugh, Alfred, Orrin. D June 12, 1828, Washington Co, O. Bur Lowell, Washington Co, O, near center of cem. MI: "Died June 12, 1828, 61 years of age. This is the place that I love to take my rest, till Christ my God, shall call me from the dust." GM Marietta Chap with Revolutionary marker in 1923. Joseph Simons was bound out to a tanner and thinking his master cruel, ran away and joined the Continental Army. Came to Ohio about 1788. Ref: Hist of Washington Co. Fur infor Marietta Chap.

SIMPKINS, EPHRAIM, (Clermont Co.)

Pensioned 1833, aged 78 yrs for NJ Continental serv. Under Gen Washington at Monmouth, Brandywine and several small engagements. Br Mch 10, 1754, Orange Co, NY. Mar 1st (pension papers say) Rebecca Chandler (Br 1756); 2nd Mary Chandler, 1804 (br 1781). (A. S. Abbott, Bethel, O, says) Children: David, John, Archibald. D 1855, Clermont Co. Bur Stonelick Twp, Clermont Co, where he settled in 1805 at Belfast. Came to Clermont Co, 1805. Ref: Natl Nos 134, 845 and 113, 758. Fur infor Cincinnati Chap.

SIMPSON, ALEXANDER, (Montgomery Co.)

At age of thirteen enl as a drummer boy in Maxwell's Jersey Brig of Continental Tr. Was at Elizabethtown and Springfield. Br May 2, 1763, Elizabethtown, N. J. Parents: John Simpson and Sarah Carle. Mar Elizabeth Caldwell (D Feb 3, 1829). Children: Aaron (Br 1792), Moses (Sept, 1793), Dolly (1795), Electra (1800),

Betsy (1803). D 1833, Dayton, O. Bur Woodland Cem, Lots 682-683, Sec 99. GM Bronze marker in 1919. Natl No of Revolutionary Soldier in D. A. R. Honor Roll 19456. Fur infor Jonathan Dayton Chap.

SIMPSON, ALEXANDER, (Erie Co.)

Served under several commands Rhode Island. Br 1756 Windham, N. H. Mar Mary Rogers. D 1834 Sandusky, O. Ref: Natl No 74361, Vol 75, D. A. R. Lin.

SIMPSON, JOSIAH, (Meigs Co.)

Pvt. N. H. Continental Line. Br Penobscot, Maine 1760. (Reports differ.) Mar " Bethia Simpson, wife of Josiah Simpson, died July 5, 1840 aged 64 years" on stone by his. D Feb 18, 1837 Rutland, O. Bur Miles Cem West of Rutland. MI: "J. S." stone broken. Ref: Natl No 22344, Vol 23, p 119, D. A. R. Lin. Fur infor Return Jonathan Meigs Chap.

SINCLAIR, JOSHUA, (Co not stated.)

Enl July 23, 1776 in 10th N. H. Regt with brother Richard, Aug 29, 1776; enl as fifer. Enl in Continental Army in his uncle's, Col Culley's Regt, served fr June 20, 1777, to June 20, 1780 Hon disch at West Point. Fourth in the battle of Burgoyne in Oct 1777. Battle of Monmouth, June 28, 1778 and against the Indians of five nations. Br Apr 16, 1760 Nottingham, N. H. Parents Capt Richard Sinclair Sr, and Polly Cilley Sinclair. Mar Abigail Potter of Vassalboro Dec 22, 1794 Children: George Washington, Abigail, William, Thomas Jefferson, Mary, Joshua, Jane, Elizabeth Lovejoy, Dorcas Burnham. D Maumee City Nov 1849. "He was buried in Western Soil." Do not know what this quotation means. By trade a carpenter. At one time operated saw mill with his brothers Samuel and John Sinclair. Ref: Hist of the Sinclair Family by Leonard Allirin Morrison.

SINCLAIR, RICHARD JR., (Co not stated.)

Enl July 23, 1776 under Col Joshua Wingate to reenforce Amer Army at Crown Point Aug 29. Enl in the same company for serv in Canada; marched to Ticonderoga as drummer boy; Enl Apr 23, 1777 in Col Alexander Seammell's Company in 3rd Bn of N. H. forces; Enl Apr 23, 1779, for 1 yr in same Company; Enl in the Regt of Col Thomas Bartlett as Ensign in the Company of which his father, Capt Richard Sinclair was Capt and went to West Point. In last yr returned to private life. Br Oct 1756, New Market, N. H. Parents Capt Richard Sinclair Sr and Polly Cilley Sinclair. Mar Elizabeth Hadgon of Barnstead Oct 27/1784. Children Nancy Sinclair, Polly Cilley Sinclair, Charlie Grandison Sinclair, Eliza S. Sinclair. D enroute to Cincinnati, O. 1820. Selectman 1781-82. Collection of Taxes 1783-85. Surveyor of Highways 1785-91. Justice of the Peace Dec 23, 1788. Moderator of Special Town Meetings Feb 2, 1791 Jan 13, 1807 Fur infor "Hist of Sinclair Family' by Morrison.

SKEEL, NATHAN, (Hamilton Co.)

Br 1748. D 1829, Cincinnati, O. Ref: Natl No. 99554, also 62351, Vol 100, p 176 D. A. R. Lin.

SKILLMAN, JACOB, (Hamilton Co.)

Wagonmaster (perhaps in Capt Wm Davidson's Company) p 854, "Strykers Men of N. J." Mar dau of Gen Luke Foster. Jacob Skillman was bur on his farm and many of family lie near his grave. Stones still standing. Name of tax list in Springfield Twp in 1809, he having bought the farm fr Symmes in 1805. A descendent of the 5th generation, Mr. Foster Skillman, is a son of the Sons of the Rev. Fur infor Cincinnati Chap.

SKINNER, ABRAHAM, (Lake Co.)

He served fr Windsor, Conn, for the relief of Boston in the Lexington Alarm, and was in the 4th Regt, Conn Line. Br 1757, Glastonbury, Conn. Parents: Abraham Skinner and Phoebe Strong. Mar Mary Ayres in 1788. D Jan 14, 1826. Bur Evergreen Cem, Painesville, O. He came to Painesville with Edward Paine in 1798 and settled at "Skinner's Landing." He was bur with Masonic honors. Fur infor New Connecticut Chap.

SKINNER, ELI, (Mahoning Co.)

Enl as Pvt in Continental Line Sept 1, disch Dec 16, 1780. Was with Amos Loveland and Nathan Moor. Came to Canfield in 1802 fr Salisbury, Conn. Ref: Trumbull and Mahoning Co Hist. Fur infor Mahoning Chap.

SLACK, JOHN, (Muskingum Co.)

Enl in Pa, 1776, under Capt Jacob McConkey and Maj James McMasters. Re-enlisted in Va under Capt Adam Vinsells, Col Meriwether and Maj Bisbee. Br June 27, 1754, in Bucks Co, Pa. D Apr 17, 1838. Bur Sonora Cem. Came to Ohio in 1806. Applied for pens Apr 29, 1833, Washington Twp. Ref: See Natl No 18907, p 326, Vol 19, D. A. R. Lin. Fur infor Muskingum Chap.

SLAUGHTER, FREDERICK, (Belmont Co.)

Revolutionary War as independent rifler. Br 1743, Saxony, Germany. Mar Katherin Stigler. Children: One son was Philip. D 1856, Belmont Co. Ref: Natl No 48647, p 294, Vol 49, D. A. R. Lin.

SLAUTER, EPHRAIM, (Lorain Co.)

Pvt Conn Line. Served under Capt Theo Woodbridge. Br 1755, Sharon, Conn. D 1843, Lorain Co. Ref: Natl No 31834, p 308, Vol 32, D. A. R. Lin.

SLAYBACK, WILLIAM, (Hamilton Co.)

Br 1759, New Jersey. D 1836. Ref: S. A. R. Fur infor Cincinnati Chap.

SLEMMONS, WILLIAM, (Harrison Co.)

Served fr Salisbury Twp, Lancaster Co, Pa, in Capt William Brisben's Company, 1781. 1st Bn, Lancaster Co Mil. Pa Archives 5, VII, 45, 75. Br 1761. D 1827. Bur Ridge Church. Fur infor Moravian Trail Chap.

SLITOR, (SLUYTER), JAMES, (Geauga Co.)

Pvt 3rd Regt, Col Levi Pawling, Ulster Co, N. Y. Mil. Br. 1760. Mar Fanny. Children: Richard Van Alstyne, Enoch. D Jan 3, 1840, Burton. Bur Slitor Cem, Burton, near Steel's Crossing. MI: "James Slitor, died Jan 3, 1840, age 80. Fanny, his wife, born Columbia Co, N. Y., Oct 20, 1766, died at Burton, O., Apr 27, 1851." GM Family. Family tradition; Dutch family name Sluyter, wife of James of French Huguenot parentage. Ref: Pioneer Hist Geauga Co, p 462. New York in Rev, p 198. Fur infor Taylor Chap.

SLOANE, WILLIAM, (Clermont Co.)

Served as Pvt under Capt John Ramsey Londonderry Company, Chester Co, Pa. After serving in Rev was bugler under Gen Anthony Wayne in Indian War. 1794. Came to Wayne Twp, 1802, settled 1 mile north of Edenton, O. Br Pennsylvania. Mar Elizabeth Prickett. Children: One son was William. D Jan 16, 1843, near Edenton, O. Bur Old Cem near Edenton. GM by his descendants and the Blanchester Chap, D. A. R. Sept 5, 1927, with bronze tablet. Emigrated to Ohio. Ref: Pa Archives, Series 5, Vol 5, p 707. Fur infor Blanchester Chap.

SLY, WILLIAM, (Clermont Co.)

Lost a leg in Rev. Came to Clermont Co, O, 1800, settled on Bear Creek, Franklin Twp, thence to Monroe Twp, 1802. Br Hampshire Co, Va. Children:

Samuel, Jonathan, William, Joseph, and dau mar George Harvey. Ref: A. S. Abbott, Bethel, O. Fur infor Cincinnati Chap.

SMALL, ANDREW, (Miami Co.)

Enl under Gen Richard Montgomery in the year 1774. Br Scotland, 1756. Children: Mary, Daniel, Catherine, Agnes, Andrew, Susannah, James, John, Elizabeth. D Mch 1, 1840, Piqua, O. Bur Forest Hill Cem, Piqua, O. MI: "Andrew Small, a soldier of the Revolution. Died Mch 1, 1840, aged 84 years." Schoolmaster. Fur infor Piqua Chap.

SMALL, JAMES, (Greene Co)

Br 1758. D Apr 23, 1842. Bur Massie's Creek Graveyard (Stevenson's), Xenia, 1803. Drew pension in 1840. Ref: Robinson's Hist of Greene Co. Fur infor Catherine Greene Chap.

SMALLEY, DAVID, (Highland Co.)

Pvt, 1777, in Capt James Ratican's Company. Pvt, 1781, Maj Rucker, Col George Must, Va. Br Dec 20, 1755, in Hunterden Co, NJ. D on farm near Greenfield, O. Bur in family graveyard on farm. Fur infor Waw-Wil-a-Way Chap.

SMALLEY, JOHN, (Butler Co.)

Served 1779. Pvt NJ Mil. Br 1749, Somerset Co, NJ. Mar 1st Amy Sutton; 2nd Rachel Clawson. D 1838, Hamilton, Butler Co, O. Bur on his farm. Ref: Natl No 75248, Vol 76, D. A. R. Lin and Natl No 33054 and 60007, D. A. R.

SMALLEY, JONATHAN, (Butler Co.)

(This may be "John Smalley" of Butler Co, but nothing to decide definitely.) MI: Distinguishable on stone: "Revol——Wa——Soldi——"; situated on creek on property now owned by the Country Club. Ref: Mr C W Fenner, 135 Main St, Hamilton, is to the effect that he recalls that 50 years ago this grave was often visited, and at that time they were able to read inscriptions, etc. Fur infor John Reily Chap.

SMEAD, SAMUEL, (Lake Co.)

Enl fr Deerfield, Mass, Apr, 1775, under Capt Jos Lock. In Dec, 1775, under Capt Leonard and Col Woodbridge. In Aug, 1776, with Capt Samuel Taylor. In 1777 was Sgt under Capt Sheldon. Br Jan 18, 1748, Deerfield, Mass. D Oct 26, 1842, Madison, O. Bur Madison, O. GM New Connecticut Chap. He received a pens. Fur infor New Connecticut Chap.

SMITH, ABNER, (Cuyahoga Co.)

Corp Detachment fr Mil Horse, Mass Continental Line. Bur Evergreen Cem, Dover. Fur infor Western Reserve Chap.

SMITH, ABRAHAM, (Hamilton Co.)

Br 1761, New Jersey. D 1824. Ref: S. A. R. Fur infor Cincinnati Chap.

SMITH, ABRAHAM, (Ross Co.)

Pvt in Capt Samuel Reading's Company, Col Elias Dayton's 2nd NJ Regt. Br Cumberland Co, NJ. D Chillicothe, O. Ref: Natl No 90492, Vol 91, p 159, D. A. R. Lin.

SMITH, ABSOLOM, (Clermont Co.)

Pensioned 1833, aged 78, for serv New Jersey Mil. Br Orange Co, Va. (Lived in Williamsburg Twp, Clermont Co, O.) Ref: A. S. Abbot, Bethel, O. Fur infor Cincinnati Chap.

SMITH, BALLARD, (Hamilton Co.)

D 1794. Fur infor Cincinnati Chap.

SMITH, BENJAMIN, (Geauga Co.)

Ensign. Br 1748, Haddam, Conn. D 1831, Parkman, O. Ref: 49897, Vol 50, p 403. Fur infor Taylor Chap.

SMITH, BENJAMIN H., (Fairfield Co.)

Bur Old Methodist Cem, Lancaster, O. Fur infor Elizabeth Sherman Reese Chap.

SMITH, CHARLES, (Montgomery Co.)

Enl as Pvt in Morris Co, NJ Mil, as Minute Man in Regt of Col Jacob Ford, Capt Obadiah Kitchell's Company. Another term in Regulars Jan 1, 1777 to Apr 1, same yr. In Capt Jonas Ward's Company, Col Matthias Ogden's Regt. Served at various points in New Jersey, an efficient soldier, serv of the most active kind, always ready and generally solicited service requiring peculiar activity and confidence. Pens application Sept 11, 1832, cites a long list of engagements, etc. Br Dec 24, 1760. Hanover Twp, Morris Co, NJ. (Another report makes it Hunterdon Co, NJ.) D Sept 22, 1838 at West Carrollton, Montgomery Co. Fur infor Richard Montgomery Chap S. A. R.

SMITH, DANIEL, (Delaware Co)

Bur Marlboro Twp. Fur infor Delaware Chap.

SMITH, DAVID, (Geauga Co.)

Pvt 1778-81, Conn Tr Mil. Pensioned 1833. Br Conn, 1763. Mar Lucy Prindle, 1785. Hannah Orton, 1814, Children: Lucy, Anna, Charry, Irena, David. D 1852, Auburn. Bur Auburn Corners on Lot 3. MI: "David Smith Jr. 1762-1852. Hannah Smith, 1772-1854." GM Family. First Postmaster in Auburn, 1823, served 15 yrs. Came to Auburn, O, in 1816. Widow was pensioned. Ref: Pension Records, Vol 3, p 514; Natl No 101804, Vol 103. D. A. R. Lin. Fur infor Taylor Chap.

SMITH, DENNIS, (Clermont Co.)

Ranger on Pa Frontier, 1778-85. Mar Elizabeth Sook. One son was named Christopher. D Ohio, age 93; record proven by Mrs Kate Smith Jackman, Bethel, O. Name appears in "Hist of Clermont Co." by Byron Williams, p 378, as Capt. Ref: 43972, Vol 44, p 366, D. A. R. Lin.

SMITH, DRUMMOND, (Highland Co.)

Bur Country graveyard near Fairfax. Fur infor Waw-Wil-aWay Chap.

SMITH, GAGER, (Trumbull Co.)

Br 1765. Mar Aslnath, (d Feb 12, 1854, aged 87 years). Bur Center of Mesopotamia. GM A new stone has been placed on the lot by relatives. Fur infor Mary Chesney Chap.

SMITH, HENRY, (Adams Co.)

Pvt. Br 1760 Conn. Children: Oliver. D Adams Co in 1802. Bur in a field near his home on Beasley Fork. His grave is marked by a stone. Ref: Hist of Adams Co. Fur infor Sycamore Chap.

SMITH, JACOB, (Greene Co.)

Bur Middle Run Baptist Cem, Sugar Creek Twp. Fur infor Catherine Greene Chap.

SMITH, JAMES, (Columbiana Co.)

Pensioner.

SMITH, JESSE, (Muskingum Co.)

Br 1759, probably in Mass. "An alteration in a road beginning at Moxahala Mill, thence to intersect the state road at a point between Andrew McBride's and Araham Deevers." Committee on the alteration viewers; John Goshen, Daniel Stickney, Jesse Smith and William Craig were appointed surveyors to meet at the house of John Mathews Oct 15th. "Census of Pensioners of 1840 of Revolutionary War Soldiers then living." (In State House p 176). Lived with son Ezra. Fur infor Muskingum Chap with Mrs F. B. Backus and Alice Boardman.

SMITH, JOHN, (Butler Co.)

Enl Hunterdon Co, NJ 1779 as Minute Man, Capt Jos Clunn's Company, Col John Taylor's Regt 1781 volunteered in "Jersey Blues," Capt David Smalley. Br 1762. Mar Rebecca Griffin, 2nd wife. Children: One son John H. D 1851. Was team driver at close of war. Pensioned 1832, Reily Twp in Butler Co for 18 mos serv New Jersey Line. Name of Capt John Smith enrolled on memorial at Hamilton, O. as Revolutionary Soldier. Possibly Capt though D. A. R. Lin did not give it. Ref: Natl No 44066, Vol 45, p 26, D. A. R. Lin by Jane Dowd Dailey.

SMITH, DR. JOHN C., (Clermont Co.)

"Enl in Revolutionary War 1776, 1st Mass Regt, Col Jos Vorce; served during Rev." copied fr granite stone, with dates. Br Apr 25, 1757, Westfield, Mass. (on stone). Mar 1st Sarah Merrill, of Hollis. They had three children br between 1778 and 1786; Margaret, Sarah, Benjamin, Jerusha and Daniel. Ref: (Worcesters Hist of Hollis). 2nd wife, Sarah Jane Abercrombie, (1772-1856) bur by husband. Their Children: Nancy Eunice, Margaret (Peggy). D May 25, 1834 (on stone). Bur Christian Chapel Cem near Amelia, O. Was a captive among Indians 4 yrs. Indians pried him highly, for he was a gunsmith, as well as doctor. They allowed him to accompany them on a fur trading expedition to Great Lakes, where he gave the Masonic distress signal and was bought for a large heap of beads and trinkets. Fur infor Cincinnati Chap (Mrs. Whallon).

SMITH, JOHN, (Franklin Co.)

He was a member of the 1st Regt, Continental Line of New Jersey. First enrolled in Morris Co Mill under Col Jacob Drake; then served in a Bn of State Tr commanded by Col Jacob Ford, Jr, and then in the 1st Regt, Continental Line. Br 1742. Passaic Co, NJ. Mar Sarah Snider. D May 24, 1813 in Plain Twp. Bur in Smith Cem, 2 miles fr New Albany. GM by D. A. R. bronze marker May 30, 1912. Came to Ohio fr New Jersey in 1813 and located in the southeastern part of Plain Twp. Ref: Natl No 60867 D. A. R. Lin. Fur infor Columbus Chap.

SMITH, JOHN, REV., (Hancock Co.)

Bur near Mt Blanchard, grave not marked. Fur infor Ft Findlay Chap.

SMITH, JOHN, (Lake Co.)

Served in the Mass Continentals, receiving a pens in 1818 at the age of 66. Br 1752. D 1836. He held town offices. His name appears on the roll books until 1836, when he would have been 84 yrs of age. Fur infor New Connecticut Chap.

SMITH, JOHN, (Morrow Co.)

Bur Chester Cem, Chester Twp. Fur infor Mt Gilead Chap.

SMITH, JONATHAN, (Cuyahoga Co.)

Pvt NH Continental Line. Br 1762. D 1824, Bur Evergreen Cem, Dover. Fur infor Western Reserve Chap.

SMITH, JONATHAN, (Fairfield Co.)

Pensioned 1819 in Fairfield Co, O. for serv as Pvt in 1775, Capt Jas Hubbell's Company, 3rd NH Regt. Was at Trenton and Princeton. Br 1755, Kennebunk Port, Me. Mar Jemima Merrill in 1784. D 1830, Fairfield Co, O. Ref: Natl No 79464, Vol 80, D. A. R. Lin.

SMITH, JONATHAN, SR., (Mahoning Co.)

Lt and Corp in Lexington Alarm, Enl May 9, 1777, disch Dec 10, Enl May 3, for 3 yrs. Br 1758. Mar Anna ? (1767-1841). D 1747. Bur Oak Hill Cem, Youngstown. GM Mahoning Chap, 1915, bronze marker. Ref: Conn Men of Revolution, pp 20, 54, 201, 227, 453, 588, 599. Trumbull and Mahoning Co Hist. Trumbull Co pension list, p 179 ,for 1840. Fur infor Mahoning Chap.

SMITH, JONATHAN, SGT., (Trumbull Co.)

Served as Sgt fr Stonington, Conn. Br Jan 24, 1746. Mar Hannah Witter, Nov 23, 1769 (d May 29, 1823, aged 73 yrs). D Aug 10, 1840, Mecca, O. Bur West Mecca, Smith burying ground. MI: "Jonathan Smith, died Aug 10, 1840, aged 94 yrs," GM by family on family lot in Cem, but Jonathan Smith was bur with two others of Smith family on Smith farm, 2 miles north of Mecca on east side of road under large tree upon a bluff. Ref: Family records, C. V. Chase, Ashtabula, O. Hist of Pioneers, Women of the Western Reserve, Descendant S. T. Smith, Cortland, O. Fur infor Mary Chesney and Taylor Chaps.

SMITH, JOSEPH, (Morrow Co.)

Pvt under Col William Douglas and Meigs, Capt Elijah Humphrey's Conn Tr. Was pensioned. Bur Bennington Twp, now Morrow Co. Fur infor Delaware Chap.

SMITH, JOSIAH, (Geauga Co.)

Pvt 7th Company, 5th Bn, 3rd call, 6 mos. Mar Thankful Hitchcock, Jan 21, 1779. Children: Merva Cook. Bur Claridon Center, O. lot 45, Sec 4. Ref: Conn Men Rev Hist, Cheshire, Conn. Fur infor Taylor Chap.

SMITH, LEVI, (Butler Co.)

Fifer 1775, Fife Maj 1777. Served 7 enlmts under different commands. D Hamilton, 1826, aged 67. Ref: Natl No 12175, p 66, Vol 13, D. A. R. Lin.

SMITH, MARTIN GEN., (Trumbull Co.)

Gen; Conn State Tr. Br June 25, 1762. Mar Sarah Kellogg, (D July 22, 1831, age 72 yrs). Children: Havilah, (br 1801). D Mch 20, 1853, age 91 yrs., Vernon, O. Bur Old Cem south of center of Vernon. Came here from Hartland, Conn with Thos Giddings and Aaron Brockway, arriving June 18, 1798. He made a clearing, built a log cabin and in the fall went back to his family. In the spring of 1799 he returned to the Western Reserve, bringing with him his wife, Sarah Kellogg, and six children. Ref: Natl No 29428, Vol 30, D. A. R. Lin. Fur infor Mary Chesney Chap.

SMITH, NATHAN, (Hamilton Co.)

Served in last six mos of war. 3rd Bn Gloucester Co, N. J. Br 1765 Connecticut. Mar Catherine Porter. D 1839, Cincinnati, O. Ref: Natl No 66832, Vol 67 p 305 D. A. R. Lin.

SMITH, NOAH, (Portage Co.)

Lived at Palmyra, where pensioned 1840. Fur infor Old Northwest Chap.

SMITH, PHILIP D., (Hamilton Co.)

Br 1759, Maryland. D 1837. Ref: S. A. R. Fur infor Cincinnati Chap.

SMITH ROBERT, (Mahoning Co.)

Pvt, 4th Bn, Cumberland Co Mil, Pa, 5th Company, 6th Class, Capt Wm Huston, May 1, 1781. Br 1763. Mar Kaziah Stewart, (1779-1847). Children: James, Robert, John, Stewart, Joseph, Samuel, and four dau. (names not given). D Poland, 1833. Bur Presbyterian Cem, Poland, O. GM by Mahoning Chap, D. A. R. bronze marker May 30, 1916. Ref: Pa Archives, 3 Series, Vol 23 p 757, Trumbull and Mahoning Co Hist, Vol 2, p 57. Fur infor Mahoning Chap.

SMITH, SAMUEL, (Madison Co.)

Pvt, Enl Nov 13, 1777 at Newbury, Mass. in Mil, Capt Caleb Kimball's Company, Col Jacob Gerrish's Regt. Served 5 mos. In Aug 1778 enl Capt Wm Rogers' Company, Col Peleg Wadsworth's Regt, served 3 mos. Br July 22, 1757. Mar Sept 16, 1784 to Sarah Bailey, a native of Newbury, Mass. D June 6, 1844. After 12 yrs at Newbury, Mass moved to Vermont. In 1827 to Madison Co where lived till death. Applied for pens June 23, 1834. Granted. Fur infor Hannah Emerson Dustin Chap.

SMITH, SIMEON, (Co not stated.)

In 1778 was a Pvt in Col Peter Yates' Regt. Albany Co, N. Y. Br 1760. D 1855 in Ohio. Ref: Natl No 92361, Vol 93, p 116, D. A. R. Lin. (Might be same as Morrow Co. Simeon Smith).

SMITH, SIMEON, (Morrow Co.)

Called out with the Berkshire Company, Mass Mil in 1780; served 2 1-2 years as Pvt; in one battle. Br Feb 29, 1756, at Bradford, Conn. D at advanced age; bur in old Baptist Cem, north of Westfield, Morrow Co. Resided at time of enl in Washington, Berkshire Co, Mass. Moved to Ohio; was Baptist preacher. Pensioned Nov 20, 1832. Ref: Dr. Florence S. Goodhue, Cardington, O. Fur infor Mt Gilead Chap.

SMITH, SOLOMON, (Delaware Co.)

Bur Old Cem, Delaware, O. Fur infor Delaware Chap.

SMITH, SYLVANUS, (Cuyahoga Co.)

Minute Man, Lexington, First Lt, Mass. Br 1745. D 1830. Bur Evergreen Cem, Dover. Fur infor Western Reserve Chap.

SMITH, WILLIAM, (Hamilton Co.)

Enl 1777, Capt Uriah Springer's Company, Col John Gibson's Regt. On Hamilton Co pens roll, 1819, for 6 yrs serv Continental Line. Br 1760. D 1841. Ref: Natl No 25874, Vol 26, D. A. R. Lin. Fur infor Cincinnati Chap.

SMITH, WILLIAM, (Highland Co.)

Bur Old Presbyterian Graveyard near Greenfield. GM by Juliana White D. A. R., 1924. Fur infor Juliana White and Waw-Wil-a-Way Chaps.

SMITH, WILLIAM, (Licking Co.)

Pvt, Delaware Regt. Br 1754, Ireland. D Granville, O., 1825. Mar Elizabeth Campbell. Ref: Natl No 70142, p 52, Vol 71, D. A. R. Lin.

SNIDER, ADAM, (Clermont Co.)

Came to Williamsburg, 1795, with William Lytle, Deputy Surveyor. Never married. In winter 1804 or '05, in company with Adam Bricker, spent over 2 mos traveling over 500 miles among Indians in Northern Ohio searching for Lydia Osborne, lost child since previous summer. Ref: A. S. Abbott, Bethel, O. Fur infor Cincinnati Chap.

SNODGRASS, JAMES, (Greene Co.)

Fur infor Catherine Greene Chap.

SNODGRASS, ROBERT, (Union Twp.)

Bur Woods Cem, Unionville. Ref: Col W. L. Curry Hist of Ohio. Fur infor Hannah Emerson Dustin Chap.

SNODGRASS, SAMUEL, (Greene Co.)

Pvt Pa Mil. Pensioned 1831. Br 1754. D May 6, 1844. Bur Jamestown, O Living in Ross, 1821. Fur infor Catherine Greene Chap.

SNOW, OLIVER, (Geauga Co.)

Pvt. Capt Porter's Company, Col Simond's Berkshire Co, Mass Regt. Br 1742, Ashford, Conn. Parents: Oliver and Elizabeth Snow. Mar (1st) Rebecca Wadsworth 1774; (2nd) Roxana Franklin 1784. Children: (1st wife) Oliver Jr, Roxana, Franklin, Charlotte, Hastings, Rebecca. (2nd wife) Electa, Loren, Lury, Alvirus, Lucina. D Auburn, O. Aug 5, 1841. Bur Auburn Corners Cem. MI: "Oliver Snow died Aug 5, 1841 aged 93 years 4 mo 10 da. Roxelane, wife of Oliver Snow, died Dec 24, 1836, aged 85 yrs 6 mo 13 days." GM Stone by family. In Burgoyne Campaign 1777. Removed to Becket, Mass., 1772, Auburn, O., 1822. Ref: Natl No 35782, D. A. R. Roll. Fur infor Taylor Chap.

SNYDER, CORNELIUS, SR. (Hamilton Co)

Pvt in Col Hathorn's Regt in New York Mil. The period of his serv is not shown, but his name appears on a receipt roll. Certificate No 692 for £2, s 18, d 7¾ WD. Br before 1750, in Orange Co, NY. Mar Katryna Felter, in Orange Co, NY. Children: Cornelius Jr., Katrina Snyder mar Terwilleger; David Snyder. Brought 4 sons and two daughters to Ohio. D Mch 6, 1793, at Montgomery, Hamilton Co, O. Bur Hopewell, near Montgomery, O., family lot. Came to Ohio in 1796. Bought farm adjoining present town of Montgomery, O. 640 acres; $1,440, fr Thos Espy. Was one of the four men who founded town of Montgomery, O. in honor of Fort Montgomery, NY, the former home of this Colony in Ohio. Ref: Mrs. Nellie S. Kitchell Fouts (Mrs. Earl). Fur infor Cincinnati Chap.

SNYDER, CORNELIUS, JR., (Hamilton Co.)

Records of Adj Gen's Office, War Dept show that one "Cornelius Snyder served in Capt John Burnet's Company, Col Lewis Duboy's Regt of NY. Levies in year 1780. Two certificates of £8 and £0-12-5 were received by Justus Banks on Jan 8, 1785, fr Beintow Paine." Br Apr 21, 1762, Orange Co, NY. Parents: Cornelius and wife, Katryna (Felter) Snyder. Mar 1st, Hannah Moore, 2nd, Amy Auten, dau of Ralph Auten about 179—. Children: 1st wife; Cindora, Rosina, Ethalinda, Mary, Martha, and Cornelius III. 2nd wife: Ralph, Asbury, N. S. (so called), William, Eliza Jane. D 1823, Montgomery, O. Bur Hopewell, near Montgomery, O. on Snyder lot. Came to Montgomery with his father and family in 1796. (See Hist of Cornelius Snyder, who was br before 1750. Farmer. Land of 640 acres, Sec 4, Twp 4, R. I. Bought from Thomas Espy. Ref: Natl No 134625 D. A. R. (but not on this data) Fur infor Cincinnati Chap

SNYDER, GEORGE, (Montgomery Co)

Served 2 mos as Pvt in the spring of 1777, in a Company of Mil commanded by Capt Duderow; guarding prisoners taken at Burgoyne's surrender. Next in an artillery Company with his two brothers under Capt Abram White; Pvt in Col Moses Hazen's Regt of Continental Tr. Enl Oct 10, 1782, to serve for the remainder of the war, disch by Commander in Chief June 17, 1783. Br Mch 19, 1754, in Maryland. Mar Christiana. Children: John (1784-1864) mar Rebecca Davis; George and Kate. D Feb 23, 1841, Dayton, O. Bur in the old Presbyterian burying ground in Dayton, but the remains were never removed when it was abandoned. MI: Family tradition states that the original stone contained a long inscription, and mentioned 13 battles in which he participated. He lost his disch. After leaving the serv he lived for 22 yrs in Baltimore. Came to Dayton about 1788. Granted a pens May 14, 1833, and after his death it was granted to his widow. Ref: Mrs William W. Whittier, 2010 Country Club, Prodo, Coral Gables, Florida. Fur infor Richard Montgomery Chap S. A. R.

SNYDER, MARTIN, (Harrison Co.)

Mil 1776. Br 1728. D 1810. Bur Greenwood Cem, Green Twp. Served in Capt George Hoover's Company, York Co, Pa. and in Capt Henry Kessler's Company in 1782; settled in Green Twp about 1802. Pa Archives 611—609. Fur infor Moravian Trail Chap.

SONNER, ANTHONY T., (Highland Co.)

Bur Sonner's Graveyard, Whiteoak Twp, near Taylorsville. Fur infor Waw-Wil-a-Way Chap.

SOUTH, PETER, MAJ., (Clermont Co.)

Maj of Minute Men; was in battle Brandywine. D in Perintown, Clermont Co, O. Fur infor Cincinnati Chap.

SOWERS, JOHN, III, (Huron Co.)

Enl as soldier at the outbreak of the Revolutionary War. Served a little more than 4 yrs. Present at the battles of White Plains, Trenton, Brandywine, Germantown, and Monmouth. Enl fr Little York, Pa. Br Little York, Pa., about 1757. Parents: John Sowers, II, mother unknown. Mar Mary Anna Kramer after the close of the Revolutionary War. Children: Mary Ann (Sowers) Davis: John Sowers IV: Moses Sowers; Daniel Sowers; James Sowers. D July 23, 1820, Monroeville, O. Bur Riverside Cem, Ridgefield Twp, Monroeville, O., in Sowers family lot; he donated the land for this cem. MI: "John Sowers. Died July 23, 1820, aged 63 yrs." GM Marble headstone erected by the family. Also bronze marker and flag holder by G. A. R. and bronze D. A. R. marker by chapter there through Amanda Skilton. After the close of the Revolutionary War he settled near Gwinn's Mills, 18 miles fr Baltimore, Md. About 1814 he moved to Lancaster, Fairfield Co, O., and in 1815 to Monroeville, Huron Co. Farmer and land owner. Ref: Firelands Pioneer, June, 1864, p 30; Hist of the Firelands, W. W. Williams; Hist of Huron Co., A. J. Baughman; Dr. Henry Skilton and descendants, p 171. Fur infor Sally De Forest Chap.

SPAID, GEORGE, (Guernsey Co.)

Bur 1 mile north of Pleasant City. Ref: S. A. R. Fur infor Anna Asbury Stone Chap.

SPANGLER, PETER, (Pickaway Co.)

Mch 1777, to Mch 1780, in 3rd Bn of Pennsylvania, Capt Ritter's Company fr Berks Co, Pa, as recorded in Pa Archives, 3 Series, Vol 6, pp 284, 308. Br Berks

Co, Pa. Date unknown. Children: Jacob, Henry, George, Christina, and a daughter that died young. D 1815 at Tarlton, O. Bur Tarlton Cem, Tarlton, O. Mrs. Zehring and Mrs. John Reichelderfer, of Tarlton, O, can locate the grave. Farmer. Came fr Pennsylvania to Ohio in 1813 or 1814. Ref: Noah Spangler, Circleville, O. Fur infor Pickaway Plains Chap.

SPARHAWK, NOAH, (Washington Co.)

QM in Col J. W. Cushing's Regt, Gen Warren's Brig. Disch Aug 29, 1777. Br 1730 in New Hampshire. Mar Miriam Green. Children: Nathan. D 1807, Belpre. Bur Belpre Cem, Belpre, O. GM Marietta Chap with Revolutionary marker in 1921. Settled in Belpre shortly after the Indian War, securing land fr Capt Geo Ingersoll, the original proprietor, below Cedarville. Ref: Williams' Hist of Washington Co. Fur infor Marietta Chap.

SPARR, RICHARD, (Hamilton Co.)

Br 1757, Virginia. D 1836. Fur infor Cincinnati Chap.

SPAULDING, ABEL, (Delaware Co.)

Pvt under Col Benjamin Wait, Capt Chas Nelson, New Hampshire Tr. Pensioned. Fur infor Delaware Chap.

SPEAKS, WILLIAM, (Coshocton Co.)

Bur Bethlehem Twp. Ref: Hist of County. Fur infor Coshocton Chap.

SPELMAN, TIMOTHY, (Licking Co.)

Enl May 4, 1777. Br Massachusetts. GM Granville Chap. Fur infor Hetuck Chap.

SPENCER, JAMES, (Clinton Co.)

Pvt in Ohio Co, Va, Capt Laurence L Buskirk, Col Abraham Shepherd. Pensioned 1832. Br 1762, Ohio Co, Va. Mar Mary McClieve, 1793. D 1843, aged 80, Clinton Co, O. Bur near Reeseville, on Three C's Highway, near Sabina. Ref: Natl No 33416, Vol 34, D. A. R. Lin. Fur infor George Clinton Chap.

SPENCER, JAMES, (Perry Co.)

Pvt in Capt John Man's Company, 1st Bn, Philadelphia Co, Pa Mil. Br 1730, England. Mar Mary Abrams. D 1825, Somerset, Perry Co, O. Ref: Natl No 76971, Vol 77, D. A. R. Lin and Natl No 32350, D. A. R.

SPENCER, JOHN, (Portage Co.)

Pvt in Conn Continental Line. Placed on pens roll Sept 6, 1819. Bur Mantua, O. Fur infor Old Northwest Chap.

SPENCER, OLIVER, (Hamilton Co.)

Commanded a Continental Regt fr 1777-1781; at Brandywine, Germantown, Monmouth, member of Cincinnati. Br 1736, New Jersey. D 1811, age 75 yrs. Ref: S. A. R. Natl No 10013, p 7, Vol 11, D. A. R. Lin. Fur infor Cincinnati Chap.

SPERRY, ELIAS, (Trumbull Co.)

Bur Old Cem south of center of Vernon, location of grave unknown. Name in S. A. R. Bk. Fur infor Mary Chesney Chap.

SPERRY, GEORGE, (Trumbull Co.)

Bur East Mecca, Mecca Twp, where he was living and drawing a pens in 1840. Ref: Cleveland Historical Library.

SPERRY, MARAUCHIE VAN ORDEN, (Lake Co.)

She was a protege of Gen and Mrs Washington; was present at the capture of Burgoyne, and "assisted the suffering Americans on that memorable day." Br 1754, Holland. Parents: Pieter Van Orden. Mar Lieut Elijah Sperry in Apr, 1779. D May 13, 1845, Kirtland, O. Bur Angle Cem, Kirtland, O. GM New Connecticut Chap. Fur infor New Connecticut Chap.

SPERRY, PETER, (Ross Co.)

Pvt. D Nov 24, 1836, Ross Co. Bur 1 mile east of Frankfort on Chillicothe pike. MI: "Peter Sperry, died Nov 24, 1836, aged 76 yrs. 10 mos." Fur infor Nathaniel Massie Chap.

SPICER, JOHN, (Muskingum Co.)

Enl as Pvt in 1777. Served for NJ 6 yrs and was disch in June, 1783. In battles of Short Hill, Brandywine, Monmouth and Siege of Yorktown. D Aug 6, 1838. Bur Baptist Cem, Adamsville. GM County soldiers marker. Tradition says that he was an English soldier, who assisted in burning the residences of a certain section of Pa. Later he espoused the cause of the Colonists. Fur infor Muskingum Chap.

SPICKARD, GEORGE, (Highland Co.)

Bur Family graveyard, 1 mile west of Fairview. Fur infor Waw-Wil-a-Way Chap.

SPILLER, JOHN, (Jefferson Co.)

Pa Archives Vol 4, 5 Series, p 421, states that John Spiller belonged to the Continental, Washington Co, Pa Mil, as a Pvt. The list called Rangers on the Frontier 1778 to 1783, gives the name John Spiller. Br about 1741, Va. Parents: John Spiller. Mar 1st: Rachel Jackson; 2nd: Catherine Marquis, Sept 24, 1810. 7 children by first wife. 2nd wife: Matilda Boyd, Warrington, Mary Cline, Susannah Pickering, Catherine Martin, Eliz Livingston, Rosannah Wilson, Sarah Hale, John Spiller Jr. D 1829, Jefferson Co, O. Bur Port Homer on Ohio River. Port Homer is above Steubenville in Jefferson Co. Not sure but think Port Homer is called Empire now. Ref: Natl No 177458, D. A. R. Census of 1790-1800-1810-1820, Knox Twp, Tefferson Co, O. Pa Archives ,5 Series, Vol 4- 421-729. Fur infor Nabby Lee Ames Chap.

SPINNING, ISAAC, (Montgomery Co.)

Served in Essex Co, N. J. Mil; also his two brothers, Mathias and Ichabod. Br Elizabeth, NJ, Oct 3, 1759. Mar Catherine Pierson of Morristown, NJ. (1767-1818). Children: Pierson, George and Charles (br Elizabethtown, Feb 7, 1793.) Three dau, Harriet, Charlotte ,Phebe D, one mar Dr. Job Haines; one mar Dr. Monfort. D Dayton, O., Dec 24, 1825; 6 Revolutionary Soldiers carried body. Bur Woodland Cem, Dayton, O. Lot 444, Sec 89. GM S. A. R. Bronze Marker in 1919. In 1803 was appointed one of the first two associate Judges of Ohio. Isaac to Dayton, O. 1801; Mathias near Lebanon; Ichabod went to Cincinnati 1805. Ref: Edgar's Pioneer Life in Dayton, Mary Steele's Early Dayton. Fur infor Jonathan Dayton Chap and Richard Montgomery S. A. R.

SPIRES, RICHARD, (Brown Co.)

Soldier under Gen Washington three yrs, during which time he was severely wounded. Br native of Maryland. English descent. Mar Rebecca Gentle. Children: Sallie, Nancy, Jane, John. Bur Young's Cem, near New Hope, Brown Co,,

O. MI: "Richard Spires, Md Line. Revolutionary War." GM D. A. R. Marker. Fur infor Taliaferro Chap.

SPOONER, ———, (Ashtabula Co.)

Pvt. Br 1739, Dartmouth, Mass. D 1815, Conneaut, O. Fur infor Natl No 34864, Vol 35, p 302, D. A. R. Lin.

SPRAGUE, FREDERICK, (Franklin Co.)

Enl in Conn as Pvt, Mch 1779 to Dec 1779, under Col Meigs; re-enl 1781; at Stony Point and Johnstown; also 3 mos under Capt Clark, Col Willet. Br 1752, Vermont or Nova Scotia. Parents: Maj Joshua Sprague (Rev Off), Abigail Wilbur. Mar Rebecca Nichols, 1782, Conn. Had 15 children: David, Nancy, Ellis, Rebecca, Joshua, John, Catherine, Abagail, infant, infant, Jacob, infant, Austin E, Mary Maria, Frederick N. D 1837, Jan 4, Truro Twp, Franklin Co. Bur Truro. MI: name, birth, age. GM Dau Mary; and D. A. R., Columbus, O., pensioned 1818. Ref: Jessie Barr, Columbus, O. Fur infor Columbus Chap.

SPRAGUE, JAMES, (Muskingum Co.)

Served fr Mass. County Hist, p 573. Bur Otsego. No grave, or record found. Pensioner 1840. Ref: S. A. R . Fur infor Muskingum Chap.

SPRAGUE, JONATHAN, (Mahoning Co.)

Pvt. Enl for serv in Capt Branch's Company, Jan 8, 1778. Conn Men in the Rev, p 527 and on p 566, Twp of Killingsley Co. Served 11 days. Said to have had 11 children. No names recorded. Came to Canfield fr Conn 1802. Ref: Truesdales Hist of Canfield. Fur infor Mahoning Chap.

SPRAGUE, JOSHUA, MAJ., (Washington Co.)

Pvt and Maj. Br July 3, 1729, Smithfield, R. I. Parents: William Sprague and Ellis Brown. Mar Amy Darling (first wife); Abigail Wilbur (second wife). Children. Amy, Elijah, Nancy, William, James, Frederick, Jonathan, Nehemiah, Samuel, Wilbur. D Oct 1, 1816, Adams Twp, Washington Co, O. Bur Sprague family cem, Adams Twp, Washington Co, O. MI: "Major Joshua Sprague born July 3, 1729. D Oct 1, 1816." GM Marietta Chap with Revolutionary marker in 1920. Br in R. I. Emigrated to Nova Scotia. Driven out by the English. Came to Ohio with two sons in July, 1788; built one of the Block Houses, receiving therefor $100. Settled on the Muskingum, where he died. Lived in Waterford Garrison during the Indian Wars. Ref: Mass Soldiers and Sailors; Sprague Family Hist; Washington Co Hist. Fur infor Marietta Chap.

SPROAT, EBENEZER, COL., (Washington Co.)

Maj and Lt Col. Br 1752, Middleborough, Mass. D 1805, Marietta, O. Bur Mound Cem, Marietta, O. MI: Col Ebenezer Sproat, 1752-1805. GM Marietta Chap with Revolutionary marker in Nov 30, 1906; marker stolen and replaced in 1920. Emigrated to Ohio in 1788 and called by the Indians "The Big Buckeye." Fur infor Marietta Chap.

SPRINGER, JACOB, LT., (Hamilton Co.)

In Capt Robert Beall's Company, 13th Va Regt, afterwards 9th Regt, commanded by Col William Russell, also John Gibson. Enl for 3 yrs. On command at Pit, Oct 10, 1777, and various services, acting in capacity of Pvt and Lt. Br 1759, Augusta Co, Va. Mar Barbara Welch in 1792. Children: Catherine, Susan, John, Emanuel, David, Jacob. D 1818 at Hamilton Co, O. Bur near Mt Washington, O. Ref: Natl No 225816, D. A. R. 8R, Revolutionary War Department. Family Bible in possession of Miss Marie Silver, Lamar, Colo. Fur infor Ann Simpson Davis Chap.

SPRONG, DAVID, (Hamilton Co.)

Br 1763, New York. D 1842. Ref: S. A. R. Fur infor Cincinnati Chap

SPRY, WILLIAM, (Knox Co.)

Pvt 1 yr actual serv in Md Tr. Br 1756, Queen Anne Co, Md. D 1836. Knox Co, O. Ref: Natl No 24325, p 116, Vol 25, D. A. R. Lin.

SQUIER, MEEKER, (Butler Co.)

Pvt Essex Co, NJ Mil. Br 1750 in New Jersey. Mar Rachel. D 1818, Butler Co. Ref: Natl No 59109, pp 37, 38, Vol 60, D. A. R. Lin.

SQUIRE, EZRA, (Lorain Co.)

Pvt in Capt Zadok Everest's Company, Col John Strongs Vt Mil. Widow received pens on claim 1839. Br 1761, Canaan, Conn. D 1836, Elyria, O. Ref: Natl No 89648, Vol 90, p 210, D. A. R. Lin.

STACY, THOMAS, (Hamilton Co.)

Br Pennsylvania. D 1837. Ref: S. A. R. Fur infor Cincinnati Chap.

STACY, WILLIAM, JR., (Washington Co.)

Pvt Capt Wm Hooper's Company. Company receipt for advance pay for 1 mo, given to Daniel Hopkins, dated Salem, Sept 26, 1775. (Soldiers and Sailors of Mass, Vol 14, p 805). Br July 21, 1755. (Gloucester Vital Records (Mass) Vol 1, p 672). Parents: Col William and Sarah Day Stacy. Mar Mehitable Wheeler in 1776. Children: Samuel (br 1782). There were other children. Wm Stacy, son of Col Stacy, wife and two or three children settled in Rainbow or Union Twp on the Muskingum after the war. (Pioneer Hist of Ohio Valley and Early Settlement Northwest Territory, by S. P. Hildreth, 1848, p 333). D Rainbow, Washington Co in 1824. Dec 21, 1821, Bible record. Bur old pioneer Cem. Tombstone reported intact and legible. Grave not marked by patriotic society as yet. Resided in Mass, came to Ohio with his father in the pioneer days of Marietta. Ref: Natl No 224639. Fur infor Eliabeth Zane Dew Chap.

STACY, WILLIAM, SR., Lt. COL., (Washington Co.)

Made Capt of company formed at time of Lexington Alarm. Rose to rank of Lt Col. He was taken prisoner Nov 11, 1778 and held for 4 yrs. Br 1730, Capetown, Mass. Parents: Benjamin Stacy. Mar Sarah Day, Dec 9, 1750. Children: Benjamin, Sarah, William Jr, Joseph, Elizabeth, John, Philemon, Gideon. D 1804, Marietta, O. Bur Mound Cem, Marietta, O. in northwest corner. GM Marietta Chap with Revolutionary marker and on gateway, Nov 30, 1906. In early life was a sea-faring man of Salem, Mass. Later moved with his family to New Salem and took up farming. After the war he removed to Marietta, O. Overseer of construction of garrison at Point Marietta, O. Foreman of first grand jury in Ohio. Ref: Vol 14, p 805 Soldiers and Sailors of Mass. Natl No 53312, Vol 54, D. A. R. Lin. Fur infor Marietta Chap.

STADDEN, ISAAC, (Licking Co.)

Verified by war records. Bur Bowling Green Twp, Licking Co, O. Fur infor Hetuck Chap.

STALTER, HENRY, (Perry Co.)

Served fr Md. Pvt in Lt Col Weltmer's German Regt, 1779-1783. Br 1764 while parents were crossing Atlantic. Parents: Nicholas Stalter. Mar Rachel Mohler, or Molar, 1790. Children: Harrison, Joseph, Jerome, Hiram, John, Nicholas,

Rachel, Ann, Samuel, William, Julia A. D. 1840, Somerset. Bur Lutheran Cem, or Somerset Cem, Perry Co, O. in a field on the Glenford side of the Dunkard Church, southwest of Glenford. Emigrated to Ohio 1818 fr Fredericktown, Md. Henry served in the Montgomery Co, Pa Mil fr 1783 to 1790. Rachel Mohler was br in Maryland. Ref: Mrs. B. E. Winters, Columbus, O. Securing this infor Jane Dailey, State Chairman.

STAMBACH, PHILLIP, (Mahoning Co.)

Pvt 4th Class, Wm Strain's Company, Cumberland Co, Pa Mil, 1782. Br 1763. Mar Anna Catherine (1766-1821). D 1836. Bur Pleasant Grove, Youngstown in the western part. Ref: Pa Archives, 5th Series, Vol 6, p 430. Trumbull and Mahoning Co Hist, Vol 2, p 85. Fur infor Mahoning Co.

STANAGE, THOMAS, (Logan Co.)

This record on the stone was reported to, but not verified, by the Chap there. MI: "Thomas Stanage, died July 9, 1835, in his 77th year. A soldier of the Revolution of 1776——". erected by W H Stanage, a grandson. Fur infor Bellefontaine Chap.

STANARD, CLAUDIUS, (Cuyahoga Co.)

Pvt. Conn Mil. Br 1761. Alive 1831. Bur Wilcox Corners. Fur infor Western Reserve Chap.

STANLEY, THOMAS, (Washington Co.)

Enl July 21, 1778, as Pvt under Capt Jos Walker, Col Samuel B Webb's Regt. Pvt in 1st Company under Capt Edw Buckley, Col Samuel B Webb's Regt. Corp in 3rd Company under Capt Ezra Selden. Br Sept 27, 1762, Wethersfield, Conn. Parents: Thomas and Mary (Francis) Stanley. Mar Anna Ford, Nov 27, 1783 (first wife), Mixand Nott (second wife). Children: Daniel G, Thomas Ford, Francis R, James, Nancy, Lucy, Cynthia, Joseph, Mary, Elizabeth, Clarissa, Sarah, Mixanda, George W. D Mch 14, 1816, Stanleyville, Fearing Twp, Washington Co, O. Bur Stanleyville Cem, Fearing Twp, Washington Co, O. MI: "Thomas Stanley, Sept 27, 1762, March 14, 1816." GM Marietta Chap with Revolutionary marker in 1923. Lived in garrison at the "Point", Marietta in 1792. Was one of the first settlers of Fearing Twp. Ref: Hist of Marietta by Summers. Fur infor Marietta Chap.

STARR, JOHN, (Franklin Co.)

Volunteered serv in the fight at Ft Griswold, 1781; was wounded. Br 1743, Groton, Conn. Mar Mary Sharp. D 1824, Columbus, O. Ref: Natl No 66967, Vol 67, p 351, D. A. R. Lin.

STARR, RICHARD, (Hamilton Co.)

This record has same dates as Richard Sparr, (which see) but since confusion as to name, and names often in error, we publish both. In S. A. R. Yr Bk, 1898, signed "C" (indicating name reported by Col Curry) is "Richard Starr. 1757-1836, Va Serv 1776, 13th Va Regt. Thence to 7th under Col Gibson to end of war. D at Fulton. Fur infor Cincinnati Chap.

STARR, SAMUEL MOORE, (Geauga Co.)

Enl Jan 1, 1779 or 1781, as Pvt; served under his father, Capt David Starr, and under Col Meigs and Col Butler, in Conn Tr, until end of war. Pensioned in 1819. Br Nov 1, 1765, Middleton, Conn. Parents: Capt David Starr and Ruth Moore Starr. Mar Abigail Rockwell, Aug 3, 1790, in Middleton, Conn. Children Fanny Starr Allen ,Diana Starr Watros, Submit Starr Beebe, Samuel Starr Jr. D June 21, 1844, Hambden, O. Bur Hambden Cem, Hambden Center, O, lot 14.

MI: "Samuel M. Starr died June 21, 1841, age 78, Abigail." Br Middleton, Conn. After war serv moved with his parents to Steuben, NY. Left NY state about 1822 and settled in Hambden, Geauga Co, O. Farmer. Ref: Conn Men of Rev pp 341, 644. Fur infor Taylor Chap.

STARRETT, JOHN, (Franklin Co.)

He served in Pa Mil and was pensioned Apr 15, 1833. Br Chester Co, Pa, Mch 14, 1757. D Mifflin Twp Jan 25, 1840. Bur in cem at Gahanna. MI: "In Memory of John Starrett, who was born in Chester Co., Pa., on the 14th day of March, 1757, A. D. and after spending a long life as a pilgrim, traveller and sojourner in this world, he calmly resigned his life and bid adieu to this world and its pleasures on the morning of the 25th of January, 1840, in the hope of a blessed immortality beyond the grave at the advanced age of 82 years, 10 months and 1 day." GM by D. A. R. 1912. Came to Ohio from Westmoreland Co, Pa, in 1818 and settled in Mifflin Twp. Fur infor Columbus Chap.

STAUDT (OR STOUT), GEORGE WILHELM, (Fairfield Co.)

Commissioned Ensign 1777 in the 7th Company, Col Henry Spycker, 6th Bn, Berks Co Mil. Br 1748, Berks Co, Pa. Mar Christine Weidenhammer. D 1820, Fairfield Co. Natl No 83635, Vol 84, D. A. R. Lin.

STEARNS, JOHN, CAPT., (Medina Co.)

Br 1749. D 1841. Bur Brunswick Center. GM Western Reserve Chap. Ref: Natl No 49435, Vol 50, D. A. R. Lin. Fur infor Western Reserve Chap.

STEELE, ELDAD, (Licking Co.)

Enl Apr, 1783, as Pvt in Col Fletcher's Regt at Pawlet, Vt. Br Feb 25, 1763, Vermont. Parents: Solomon Steele and Mary Guernsey. Mar Sybal Bates. Children: Ada, Polly, Ester, Sarah, Daniel, David. D Oct 20, 1841, Newark. Bur Old Cem. Sixth St. Newark. GM Hetuck Chap in 1910. Pens allowed at Auburn, N. Y., 1832. Ref: Brister's Hist. Fur infor Hetuck Chap.

STEELE, ISAAC, (Summit Co.)

Pvt, Mil, York Co, Pa, and received depreciation pay. Br 1765. Parents: Adam Steele (Br 1744 in Northern Ireland, of Scotch Irish descent.) Mar Betsy Galloway. Had six children. D Sept 16, 1850, aged 76. Bur O'Brien Cem, Hudson, O, by side of his wife. GM S. A. R. Ref: Pa Archives, Vol IV, p 479. Fur infor Cuyahoga-Portage and Cuyahoga Falls Chaps.

STEEL, MATTHEW, (Mahoning Co.)

Pvt. Enl Apr 11, 1781, for 3 yrs in Conn 2nd Regt. Br 1762, Cornwall, Conn. Mar Lydia Pratt. D 1805, Canfield, O. Bur Canfield, O. GM Mahoning Chap. Bronze marker 1917. A daughter gives the following: "He served as a waiter in the Military family of Gen Washington for three years; at the age of seventeen the general gave him a commission as Orderly Sargent. He continued in service until end of the war." Ref: Conn Men of the Rev, pp 361, 369. Fur infor Mahoning Chap.

STEEL, SAMUEL, (Preble Co.)

Bur Isreal Twp. Fur infor Organizing Regt Mrs. Miller.

STEPHENS, GEORGE, (Darke Co.)

Bur Palestine (St. John's Cem), north side of cem. GM A boulder set at the head and also a smaller one at the foot of the grave. Initials G. S. cut in the head stone—perhaps by some of the family. This meager infor given by a great grandson, Mr. Lee Woods, Palestine, O. Mrs. L. C. Ankerman, also a descendant, is a D. A. R. Fur infor Fort Greenville Chap.

STEPHENS, JABEZ, (Co. not stated.)

Enl 1775 Capt Josiah Stevens Company, Col Ephraim Doolittle's Regt, Mass Tr. Br New Bedford, Mass, 1758. Mar Esther Bemis, 1784. D 1850, Ohio. Ref: Natl No 55953, p 427, Vol 56, D. A. R. Lin.

STEPHENS, JOSHUA, (Shelby Co.)

Served 1781, Pvt, Capt Robert Cochran's Company, Chester Co Mil. Br 1733, Berks Co, Pa. Mar Priscilla Humphreys in 1771. D 1823, Hardin, O. Natl No 79492, Vol 80.

STEPHENSON, JOHN, (Jackson Co.)

Va Tr under Col Geo Gibson, Sept 14, 1777 to Oct 1779 as Pvt. Br South Carolina. Children: James, John. D Dec 20, 1827. Bur Markam farm east of Rocky Hill. MI: "John Stephenson, A Revolutionary Soldier, dates, etc." GM D. A. R. 1927. Native of S. C.; after marriage moved to Cabell Co, Va. In 1814 took up land in Bloomfield Twp. Appointed by legislatures as one of first commissioners to lay out Jackson Co. Ref: Mrs Ada Michael, Mrs Millie Gahm, Mrs Mabel Kinnison etal D. A. R. Fur inform Capt John James Chap.

STEPHENSON, WILLIAM, (Brown Co.)

Bur Ripley. Fur inform Ripley Chap.

STEPP, GEORGE, (This may be STIPP), (Greene Co.)

Pvt Virginia Mil. Pensioned May 4, 1831. Age 77 yrs. Annual allowance $21.56. On pension roll Aug 8, 1833. Fur infor Catherine Greene Chap.

STEVENS, EPHRAIM, (Warren Co.)

Br 1759, Billerica, Mass. Mar Sybil Foster. Children: 1 son was Ephraim Jr. D 1839, Maineville, Warren Co, O. Pensioned as Pvt N. H. Mil. Ref: Natl No 45967, Vol 46, p 405 D. A. R. Lin. Fur infor Jane Dowd Dailey.

STEVENS, JOHN, (Lucas Co.)

Pvt in Col Nathaniel Gist's Va Regt. Br 1763, Lancaster Co, Pa. D Waterville, O. Ref: Natl No 27887, Vol 28, p 320. D. A. R. Lin.

STEVENS, NICHOLAS, (or STEPHENS) (Hamilton Co.)

Br 1761, New Jersey. D 1838. Ref: S. A. R. Fur infor Cincinnati Chap. 1898, S. A. R. Yr Bk.

STEVENS, PHINEHAS, (Sandusky Co.)

May 1775, 8 mos Pvt, Capt Samuel Patch, Mch, 1776, 11 mos. Pvt. Capt Asabel Wheeler. Battles engaged in: Lexington, Bunker Hill, Lake Champlain. D Aug 8, 1840, Sandusky, O., aged 67. Date of application for pens, May 8, 1818. Allowed. Residence at date of application, Ontario Co, N. Y. GM by L. M. Kelley, Commissioner. Fur infor Col George Croghan Chap.

STEVENSON, CHARLES, (Adams Co.)

Pvt. Br Jan. 1, 1759, Glasgow, Scotland. Mar Sept 24, 1791, Margaret Kain. Children: William, Elizabeth, George, Charles. D Apr 13, 1841. Bur Ralstin Graveyard on Beasleys Fork. Enl for short terms fr May, 1776, captured Nov 1776, prisoner until Nov 1777. Weaver. Ref: Evans and Stivers Hist of Adams Co. Fur infor Sycamore Chap.

STEVENSON, JAMES, (Mahoning Co.)

Pvt and Sgt. Enl July 1, 1776 fr Chaster Co, Pa. Capt Barker, Col Evans' Regt. Sgt under Capt Scott. Pensioned 1833, received depreciation pay. Br 1755, Ireland. Mar (1st) Hannah Bull, (2nd) Catherine Moore. Children: 1st wife: Margaret, Lucy, Nancy, Sarah, Hannah, Mary, Thomas, Elijah, Andrew; 2nd wife: Robert, James, William, Rebecca (mar Elisha McCurdy, Silas, Sampson, Samuel, and an infant child. D 1836, Poland. Bur Presbyterian Cem, Poland. Grave never marked. Emigrated fr Donegal, Ireland, in 1773. Taken prisoner Nov 17, 1776 at Derby by a detachment under Cornwallis, detained nine mos, exchanged. Was Auditor for depreciation pay. Ref: Natl No 57520, D. A. R. Pa Archives, Third series, Vol 23, p 500. Series 5, p 479, Vol 4. Letters and papers in the possession of the family. Fur infor Mahoning Chap.

STEVENSON, JOHN, (Franklin Co.)

Capt; Lt. Baltimore Co, Md. Mine Run Hundred, Md. Archives, Vol II, p 428. Br Mch 17, 1757, Baltimore Co, Md. Parents: John and Susanna Stevenson. Mar Mary Havenor; twice mar. Children: John, Richard, Zachariah, Edward, Susannah, Elizabeth, Rebecca, Basil, Sarah, Rachel, George K, Mary, Anna, Hannah, William, Joshua and Matilda. D Sept 11, 1831, Madison Twp, Franklin Co, Bur near Canal Winchester, on his farm. MI: "In memory of John Stephenson, who departed this life Sept 11, 1831, aged 74 yrs 5 mo, 25 da." GM Columbus D. A. R. marker. Brave, courteous, commanding; a Christian gent. Came to Ohio, 1799. Farmer; live-stock shipper, gave ground and helped build church. Fur infor Columbus Chap.

STEVENSON, OBADIAH, (Portage Co.)

Pvt in Mass Mil. Placed on Pens Roll, Feb 28, 1833. Drew pens at Ravenna, O, in 1840. Fur infor Old Northwest Chap.

STEVENSON, ROBERT, (Brown Co.)

Enl July 27, 1777 as Pvt fr Cumberland Co, Pa. Br Mch 25, 1759, York Co, Pa. Mar Elizabeth Baird, Sept 7, 1781. Children: Esther, Mary, Hannah, John, Elizabeth, William, Catherine, Robert, Joseph. D July 23, 1835, near Decatur, Brown Co, O. Bur Decatur, O. MI: Robert Stevenson died July 23, 1835, aged 77 years, 3 mo and 28 da. GM Agnes Stevenson with government marker in May, 1916. Came to Brown Co, O. about 1816 with his family. Ref: Natl No 85318, Vol 86, p 122, D. A. R. Lin. Fur infor Lieutenant Byrd Chap.

STEWART, CHARLES, (Trumbull Co.)

Pvt in Capt Wm Guthrie's Company, Westmoreland Co Mil, 1780. Br 1759, Cumberland, Pa. Mar Francis Stockton, 1783. D 1840 Hubbard, O. Ref: Natl No 78861, Vol 79, D. A. R. Lin.

STEWART, DANIEL, (Athens Co.)

1775, 5 mos Col Enos, Conn; Apr 1778, 6 mos Col Meigs. July, 1778, 3 mos, Col Hinman, Conn. May, 1779, 4 mo, Col Beebe, Conn; Apr, 1780, 9 mo, Col Welb; Apr, 1781, 12 mo, Pvt. Br Nov 18, 1762, Litchfield, Conn. Mar Ruth Fueford. Children: Andrew, William, Charles, John, Ezra, George, Lois, Sarah, Mary, Lucinda, Harriet, Alexander, Daniel B., Hiram. D Feb 20, 1858, Rome Twp, Athens Co. Bur Old Cem, West State St, Athens, O, east of main driveway. MI: "To the memory of Daniel Stewart, who died Feb 20, 1858, aged 95 yrs, 3 mos and 2 das." GM Descendants—a marble monument. When 15 yrs old he enl in the Revolutionary Army. At the close of the war he removed to Sussex Co, N. J., thence in 1802 to the Ohio country. Farming, justice of the peace, county commissioner, and was one of the early appraisers of the college lands. He was a native of Conn; served in the Revolutionary War 5 yrs. Came to Ohio in 1802. Ref: Walker's Hist of Athens Co; Bureau of Pensions. Natl No 21926, Vol 22. D. A. R. Lin. Fur infor Nabby Lee Ames Chap.

STEWART, DAVID, (Miami Co.)

Br Apr 3, 1775, Bahwaz, N. J. Bur Raper Chapel, two miles north of Troy. GM Miami Chap with bronze marker in 1904. Fur infor Miami Chap.

STEWART, HUGH, (Ross Co.)

Pvt City Guards. Br 1756, Philadelphia. D Frankfort, O. Ref: Natl No 25873, p 317, Vol 26, D. A. R. Lin.

STEWART, JOSEPH, CAPT., (Union Co.)

Bur Raymond Cem, Liberty Twp. Fur infor Hannah Emerson Dustin Chap.

STEWART, SAMUEL, (Cuyahoga Co.)

Minute Man, Sgt, Capt, Mass and Vt. Br 1749. D 1827. Bur North Royalton. Fur infor Western Reserve Chap.

STEWART, WILLIAM, SR., (Greene Co.)

Pvt, Capt Feliz Warley's Company, 3rd Regt Scouts, S. C. Line, 1779. Br 1739, Ireland. Mar Sarah Calhoun. D Aug 4, 1830, Xenia, O. Bur Woodland, Xenia, O. Caesars Creek, 1820. Ref: Natl No 29227, Vol 30, D. A. R. Lin. Record and Pension Office; Pa Archives; Robinson's Hist of Greene Co. Fur infor Catherine Greene Chap.

STEWART, WILLIAM M., (Clinton Co.)

Br 1757. D 1837. Bur Smithson Graveyard, near New Vienna. Fur infor George Clinton Chap.

STILES, ASA, (Cuyahoga Co.)

Bur Shaker Heights on South Park Boulevard near Lee Rd. GM Western Reserve Chap. Fur infor Western Reserve Chap.

STIMSON, JAMES, (Ross Co.)

Pensioned in Ross Co, 1831, for serv in N. J. Line. Br 1761, Essex Co, N. J. D 1851, Ross Co, O. Ref: Natl No 94220, Vol 95, p 71, D. A. R. Lin.

STIPP, JOSEPH, (Greene Co.)

Bur Middle Run Churchyard. Came to Xenia, 1823. Fur infor Catherine Greene Chap.

STITES, BENJAMIN CAPT., (Hamilton Co.)

Capt in Mil in Greene Co, Pa in Frontier and Revolutionary struggles "Hist of Cincinnati," by Greves. Br Scotch Plain, Essex Co, N. J. Children: Phoebe, Rachel mar Maj Eph Kibby, Ann W., Benjamin Jr and Jonathan (either his sons or those of his brother Hezekiah). D 1804. Bur in Columbia, Hamilton Co, O. Fr New Jersey went to Ten Mile Creek, Pa; fr Redstone, Pa came to Kentucky, thence to Ohio, landing below mouth of Miami 1788; besides 20000 acres where Columbia was, bought 7 sec on Mill Creek and 4 near Covalt Station paying 158 £ 8 s 8 d. First sermon preached in first blockhouse built him. Ref: S. A. R. Yr Bk. Fur infor Cincinnati Chap.

STITES, ELIJAH, (Warren Co.)

Br 1758, Essex Co, N. J. One son was named Henry. D 1844, Warren Co, O. On Pens Roll for 2 yrs actual serv as Pvt, N. J. Line. Ref: Natl No 43428, Vol 44, p 163, D. A. R. Lin.

STITES, HEZEKIAH, (Hamilton Co.)

Minute Man 1778. Capt Moss' Company, Col Jacques' Regt, to guard lines and watch moves of Tories and British. See "Strykers" p 471. Br 1761, Essex Co, NJ. Mar 1st Deborah Ferris, dau of Jeduthan Ferris; 2nd Elizabeth Ferris, dau of John Ferris. Children 1st wife:Mary, (br 1792); 2nd wife: children not found. D 1842 or 3, Hamilton Co, O. Bur Columbia, Hamilton Co, O. First one to set foot on the land, at Columbia, and kneeling with two others sought God's blessing on their new enterprise. Benj and Elijah Stites were his brothers. Ref: Son of Rev proven record. Fur infor Cincinnati Chap.

STITT, WILLIAM, (Fayette Co.)

Br 1763. Children: Luke. D Mch 18, 1819. Bloomingsburg, O. Bur Bloomingsburg, in old part, unplatted. MI: "William Stitt died March 18, 1819, aged 56 years. Iron Star 1776." GM Family and Cem Trustees in 1819. Fur infor Washington C. H. Chap.

STIVERS, DANIEL, (Meigs Co.)

Enl at Oxford, Sussex Co, N. J. Served six mos in the NJ State Tr, Capt Geo Bibbs, and other short terms; in Mil also. Br 1763. Parents; Randle Stivers and Janet Skinner Stivers. Mar Margaret Rupert, about 1786. Children: (not in order of age). Randal, John, Peter, Benjamin, Jacob, Robt, Daniel, (James, Catherine and Jas died young.), Polly, Sally Carr and Margaret Wade. D about 1844. Bur Flatwoods, near Pomeroy, O. MI: "Daniel Stivers br 1760-Died." GM by D. A. R. with government marker. Blacksmith. Applied for pens Sept 24, 1832. Pens continued to his widow. Ref: Mrs Nellie Stivers Pattison (W Rea) Woodside, Md. Fur infor Return Jonathan Meigs Chap.

STIVERS, JOHN (Brown Co.)

Served in Capt Robert Daniel's Company, Col Spencer. Enl under Capt Harris. Br 1764, Virginia. D 1828, Decatur, O. Bur Decatur. Fur infor Ripley and Cincinnati Chaps.

ST. JOHN, JOHN, (Warren Co.)

Bur Churchyard, top of Ft Ancient Hill west of Little Miami river, Turtle Creek Twp. Ref: S. A. R. Yr Bk 1917.

STOCKING, REUBEN, (Geauga Co.)

Lt on the privateer "Sampson." Br Haddam, Conn, 1744. Parents: George Stocking. Mar Sarah Hulburt, 1765. Children: George, Reuben, Samuel, Steven, Hezekiah. D Chardon, O. Oct 20, 1825. Bur lot 10. MI: "Our grandparents Reuben Stocking died October 20, 1825, age 81 years. Sarah Hulburt his wife February 24, 1840, aged 93 years." Was taken prisoner and suffered great hardship on prison ship in New York. Ref: Pens Records for Ohio, Vol 3, p 415, Honor Roll 44256, 58224. Fur infor Taylor Chap.

STOCKWELL, JESSE, (Licking Co.)

Enl at Athol, Mass, Sept, 1776. Pvt in Col Dana's Regt, Col Cushing's Regt, Mil. Was at the taking of Burgoyne. Br Jan 5, 1759, Petersham, Mass. D St. Albans Twp. GM Granville Chap. In 1832 lived at Essex, Vt.; came to this co in 1836; was still living in 1840. Pens allowed. Fur infor Hetuck Chap.

STODDARD, AMOS, MAJ., (Wood Co.)

Pvt and Sgt Massachusetts Infantry. Was at surrender at Yorktown and witnessed the execution of Andre. Capt 2nd Artillerists and Engineers, June 4, 1798; Maj, June 30, 1807, Deputy Quartermaster Gen, July 16 to Dec, 1812. Br. Oct 26, 1762 Woodbury, Conn. Parents: Anthony and Phebe (Read) Stoddard. D May 11, 1813, Camp Meigs, O. Burial place unknown, among the ruins of Camp Meigs.

After the Revolution became a clerk in the Supreme Court at Boston. Aptd an Ensign and served in Shay's Rebellion. Practiced law at Hallowell, Me. Made trip to London. In 1798 aptd Capt of Artillery in what is now the regular army. He evidently stood high in the army, and although his rank was only a Capt, he was selected to receive the cession of Upper Louisiana under the direct authority of Gov Clairborne at New Orleans. Joined with Stoddard were the later famous explorers, Lewis and Clarke. On Mch 9, 1804, the American flag was first hoisted over what is now Missouri, Capt Stoddard receiving possession of the province, which he next day transferred to the United States and he became the first Civil Commandant (or Governor), of what is now Missouri. After his residence and rule at St Louis, he served at eastern posts, during which time he wrote his great work, "Sketches, Historical and Descriptive, of Louisiana," published by Matthew Carey, Philadelphia, in 1812. During this year he was at Fort Columbus, N. Y. and received promotion to the grade of Maj. The next year found him on duty at Fort Meigs, where he died. Ref: S. A. R. Fur infor Richard Montgomery Chap, S. A. R.

STONE, BENJAMIN, REV., (Harrison Co.)

Sgt. Minute Man, Culpeper, Va. Col Roebuck's Regt, South Carolina. Later in 2nd S. C. Regt, 1779-1780. In 4th, 6th and 9th Companies, at Valley Forge, 1777. Br. 1743, Westmoreland Co, Va. Parents: Thomas Stone and Mary Ritler Stone. Mar at Culpepper, Va., 1773, Anna Asbury, dau of George Asbury and Hannah Hardage. Children: Rhoda, Elizah, William, Hannah, Mary, Anna, Jeremiah, Benjamin, Thomas, Nellie, Rebecca. D near Beech Spring, Cadiz, Harrison Co, O., 1833. Bur Green Twp, near Cadiz. During Rev lived Fauquier Co, Va. Organized North River Church, Hampshire Co, Va, 1787; Crooked Run Church, 1790; called to Bethel Church, Uniontown, Pa, 1794. Was minister in Hampshire Co, Va, and at Uniontown until about 1818, when he came to Harrison Co, O, and lived with a son until death. Minister (Baptist). Wife rode fr Va to Valley Forge and carried a message to Washington fr York, Pa. Ref: Mary A. Stone, Cambridge, Ohio Natl No 62586. Fur infor Anna Asbury Stone Chap.

STONE, CHARLES, (Hamilton Co.)

Br 1757. D 1848. Fur infor Cincinnati Chap.

STONE, ISAAC, (Muskingum Co.)

Answered Rhode Island Alarm as a substitute for Nathan Perry, under Capt Moses Wilmot, 1778; 1779, volunteered under Capt Jos Franklin. At West Point, 1780, under Capt Abner Howard. Br 1764. Mar Chloe Morey (br 1764), mar 1792. D 1844, at Muskingum. In 1832 placed on Pens Roll of Chatauqua Co, N. Y., for 15 mos actual serv as Pvt, Mass Line. 1844, his widow applied for pens in Ohio, where he died in Muskingum Co. Ref: Natl No 38232, Vol 39, p 87, D. A. R Lin.

STONE, ISRAEL, (Washington Co.)

Pvt and Corp. Pvt in Capt Thomas Eustic's Company, which marched on the alarm of Apr 19, 1775. Pvt in Capt David Bent's Company. Corp in Capt Samuel Hubbard's Company. Disch Nov 29, 1777. Br Apr 15, 1749, Rutland, Mass. Parents: John Stone and Elizabeth. Mar July 12, 1768, Lydia Barrett. Children: Sardine, Elizabeth, Matilda, Jasper, Lydia, Israel, Augustus, Benjamin Franklin, Christopher Columbus, Polly, Harriet, John. D July 13, 1808, Rainbow settlement, Union Twp. Bur Rainbow Cem, on Muskingum River in Washington Co. MI: "Israel Stone, born April 15, 1749. Died July 13, 1808." GM by Marietta Chap with Revolutionary marker in 1921. Farmer. Ref: Mass Archives and Revolutionary War Rolls, Natl No 95615, Vol 96, p 201, D. A. R. Lin. Fur infor Marietta Chap.

STONE, JOEL, (Cuyahoga Co.)

Sgt Capt James Burt's Company, Col Asa Whitcomb's Regt, which marched to Lexington Alarm. Born Groton, Mass. D Cleveland, O. Ref: Natl No 84093, Vol 85, p 39, D. A. R. Lin.

STONE, JONATHAN, CAPT., (Washington Co.)

Enl as Pvt in the Lexington Alarm. Served throughout the war. Commissioned Capt on June 22, 1781. Br Mch 4, 1752, Leicester, Mass. (or Braintree, Mass.) (Natl No 26458, D. A. R.). Parents: Jonathan Stone and Elizabeth Lamb. Mar Susannah Matthews, 1776. Children: Grace, Benjamin, Franklin, Samuel, Rufus Putnam, John, Melissa, Wilson. D Mch 24, 1801, Belpre, O. Bur Belpre, Washington Co, O. MI: "Jonathan Stone, who departed this life on March 24, 1801, in his 50th year. A Capt and an active officer in the American Revolutionary War. One of the first settlers of this town." GM by Marietta Chap with Revolutionary marker in 1921. Shortly after the death of his father in the battle at Crown Point, he was apprenticed to his brother, a tanner. He ran away and joined a whaler for two years. Farmer. 1792 appointed Treasurer of Washington Co. Employed by Ohio Company after the Indian War to complete surveys of their land. Ref: Mass Records of Soldiers and Sailors. Hildreth's Hist, Washington Co. Fur infor Marietta Chap.

STONE, JOSEPH, (Clermont Co.)

Revolutionary soldier. Lived in Union Twp, Clermont Co, O. On July 4, 1829, he was one of speakers at a celebration there. Ref: A. S. Abbott, Bethel, O. Fur infor Cincinnati Chap.

STONER, JOHN, (Richland Co.)

Pvt in Pa State Tr. Bur 1 mile west of the village of Rome, O. MI: U S Soldier of Rev War. GM Mary Washington D. A. R. Chap, bronze marker in 1911. Fur infor Mary Washington Chap.

STONER, PHILIP, (Clermont Co.)

Br Virginia. Mar Sarah, who received a pens in 1840, aged 74, living with Ann Smith in Jackson Twp, Clermont Co, O. (Fr Pensioners of Census of 1840, of Revolutionary Soldiers.) Children: Philip, possibly others. D Jackson Twp. Ref: A. S. Abbott, Bethel, O. Fur infor Blanchester Chap.

STORTZ, JOHN JACOB, (Perry Co.)

Enl to take his father's place in the Continental Army at the age of 11, Red Hill, Pa. Was among the troops at Valley Forge; was in 30 engagements, including Yorktown. Br Red Hill, Pa. in 1766. Mar Mary Allen Barket, Perry Co, O. Children: Maria Stortz Allen (br Oct. 1841), who is the only living real Daughter of the American Revolution in Ohio, a member of Elizabeth Sherman Reese Chap, Lancaster, O. (Feb 2, 1929). D in 1850 and is buried 5 miles east of New Lexington, O. The D. A. R. have erected a stone to his memory. Fur this infor Jane Dailey, State Chairman.

STOUT, ANDREW, (Hamilton Co.)

Revolutionary serv fr Hunterdon Co, N. J., 1st Regt (see "Strykers," p 471), also in Capt Henry Phillip's Company, 1st Regt (see "Strykers," p 771). Bought land fr Ichabod B. and Sarah W. Halsey. 1805, sold land (see Courthouse bk L, p 76). Bur in Colerain Twp, Hamilton Co, O. Fur infor Cincinnati Chap.

STOW, COMFORT, (Trumbull Co.)

Br 1762. Mar Rachel (died May 12, 1842, 79 yrs.). D July 31, 1853. Bur Braceville, O. MI: Comfort Stow. Died July 31, 1853, aged 91 yrs. GM by relatives; kept in good condition. Fur infor Mary Chesney Chap.

STRAIN, SAMUEL, (might be "s" on name Strains), (Highland Co.)

Bur Rocky Spring Cem near New Petersburg. GM by Juliana White D. A. R. in 1924. Fur infor Waw-Wil-a-Way and Juliana White Chaps.

STRAIN, THOMAS, (Highland Co.)

Pensioned in 1776 as Pvt in Capt Green's Company, Col Cunningham's Regt, Pa Line. Br 1756, Lancaster Co, Pa. D 1833, Highland Co. Ref: Natl No 78056, Vol 79, D. A. R. Lin.

STRAIN, WILLIAM, (Mahoning Co.)

2nd Lt Capt Campbell's Company, Cumberland Co, Pa. Mil Br 1756. D 1845, Poland Twp. Bur Poland Center, Poland, about the center of the Cem. Ref: Pa Archives, Fifth series, Vol 6, p 142. Fur infor Mahoning Chap.

STRAIT, JOHN, (or STRAIGHT), (Gallia Co.)

Br about 1758, England; native of West Greenich, R. I. Mar twice. Taken from stone: "Died Jan 7, 1860, age 101-4-7. Revolutionary Soldier." Bur McCall Cem, Harrison Twp, Gallia Co. Settled in Pa. U. S. A. Later moved to Clay Lick, Gallia Co, O. Spelled "Straight" also. Ref: Natl No. 31624, Vol 32, p 235, D. A. R. Lin. Fur infor French Colony Chap.

STREVE, PAUL, (STREEVEY), (Ross Co.)

Pvt in Northampton Co, Pa Mil. Enl 6 weeks prior to Battle of Long Island, served 3 yrs under Captains Graydon and Lennox, and Col John Shee. Was at Long Island, Kingsbridge, and Fort Washington, and in a number of skirmishes not specified. Br Germany in 1755. Mar Mary (?) 1780 (br 1760 and d 1823.) Children: Daniel, Joseph, Peter (all in 1812 war) and 2 girls. D 1829, Ross Co, O. Bur Bishops Hill, Huntington Twp. GM D. A. R. 1923 and slab. Came from Pennsylvania to Ohio in 1800. Received a pens. Ref: Mrs. C. U. Ebenhack; p 287 Ross and Highland Co Hist. Fur infor Nathaniel Massie Chap.

STRONG, BARNABAS, (Hamilton Co.)

Br 1759, Connecticut. D 1821. Ref: S. A. R. Fur infor Cincinnati Chap.

STRONG, DAVID, (Hamilton Co.)

Taken prisoner at battle of the Cedars. In many battles; retired as a Capt. Br 1744, Litchfield Co, Conn. Mar Chloe Richmond. D 1801, Cincinnati, O. Ref: Natl No 43698, Vol 44, p 269, D. A. R. Lin.

STRONG, JOSEPH, (Erie Co.)

Corp 1st Company, 3rd Mass Regt. Br 1765, Lenox, Mass. D 1835, Lyme, O. Ref: Natl No 94225, Vol 95, p 73, D. A. R. Lin.

STRONG, NATHAN, (Ashtabula Co.)

Responded to the Lexington Alarm fr the town of Bolton, Conn, and served as clerk 6 da, Apr, 1775. He enl Aug 5 in the Mil Regt, 1778, Col Chapman's Regt, Capt Olcott's Company. Disch Sept 21, '78. Br 1749. Mar Lucy Cornell. Children: Polly, Nathan, Lucy, Samuel, Jabez, Nathaniel, Timothy, Elihu, Sarah. D 1826. Ashtabula. Bur Chestnut Grove, Ashtabula. Regt Chaplain. Ref: Conn Men in the Rev. Fur infor Mary Stanley Chap.

STROTHER, ROBERT, (Lawrence Co.)

Served as Pvt Va Lines at Cowpens and Stony Point. Br Culpeper Co, Va. Mar Martha Radcliff. D Lawrence Co, O. Ref: Natl No 101779, Vol 103, p 234, D. A. R. Lin.

STRUTHERS, JOHN, (Mahoning Co.)

Served in War of Rev. Commander of a Company of Rangers in Washington, Pa. Br 1759. Mar Mary Foster (1758-1841, in 1798). Children: Drusilla, Emma

Ebenezer, Lt Alexander, Thomas. D 1845. Bur Village Cem, Poland. GM D. A. R. bronze marker in 1916. Built first iron mill in Mahoning Valley, 1802, came in 1798. Took up 400 acres of land. Was sheriff, owned a flour mill. Came from Washington Co, Pa. Ref: Hist Trumbull and Mahoning Co. Hist of Struthers Family; S. A. R. List by Thomas Struthers. Fur infor Mahoning Chap.

STRYKER, PETER, (Co. not stated.)

Served in N J Mil. Br 1760, New Jersey. D 1810, Ohio. Ref: Natl No 39573, D. A. R. Lin and Natl No 25766, Vol 26, p 281, D. A. R. Lin.

STULL, JAMES, (Mahoning Co.)

Pvt in Continental Line, Pa. Br 1761. Mar Catherine McGhee. D 1856, Poland. Bur Presbyterian Church Cem. GM Mahoning Chap, D. A. R. May 30, 1916. Settled in Boardman in 1801. Ref: Pa Archives, Series 5, Vol 4, p 727, 420, and also Trumbull and Mahoning Co Hist, p 48. Fur infor Mahoning Chap.

STULTZ, JOHN, (Highland Co.)

1776, fr Pennsylvania in Capt Henry Fisher's Company, Col Nicholas Hansseg-ger's Regt, Conn Tr. Appointed Corp 1778 till 1779. Br 1754, Germany. D 1865, Highland Co, O. Ref: Natl No 48443, p 206, Vol 49, D. A. R. Lin.

STUMP, DANIEL, (Greene Co.)

Bur Mount Holly, Greene Co, O. Sugar Creek, 1840. Ref: Robinson's Hist of Greene Co. Fur infor Catherine Greene Chap.

STUMP, DANIEL, (Warren Co.)

Br Frederick Co, Va. D Warren Co, O. (Might be same as Greene Co. soldier). Ref: Natl No 24294, Vol 25, p 106, D. A. R.

STUMP, GEORGE, SR., (Mahoning Co.)

Pvt Rifle Regt, Capt Lewis Farmer's Company, Pa. Pensioned in 1833. Br 1750. Mar Elizabeth (1752-1826). Children: George, Abraham, Henry, John. D 1839, Milton Twp. Bur Rickert farm, Milton Twp, at the crest of the hill. GM Marker is broken down. Ref: Pa Archives, 5 Series, Vol 23, p 593. Trumbull and Mahoning Co Hist, Vol 2, p 202. Fur infor Mahoning Chap.

STURGEON, JEREMIAH, (Mahoning Co.)

Pvt. Bur Mahoning Co. Bought land of John Young, Youngstown. Farmer. Ref: Pa Archives, Series 5, Vol 7, pp 342, 1004. Fur infor Mahoning Chap.

STURGIS, JEDEDIAH, (Hamilton Co.)

Br 1758, New Jersey. D 1838. Ref: S. A. R. Fur infor Cincinnati Chap.

SUDDUTH, ISAAC, (Harrison Co.)

A Revolutionary pensioner living in Nottingham Twp in 1840, aged 80. U. S. Pension Rolls, 1835. Fur infor Moravian Trail Chap.

SULLIVAN, PATRICK, (Hamilton Co.)

Br 1747, Pennsylvania. D 1821. Ref: S. A. R. Fur infor Cincinnati Chap.

SULTZER, FREDERICK, (Ashland Co.)

Br July 25, 1762, Green Co, Pa. D Mch 30, 1857, Ashland Co, O. Bur private burying lot, Milton Twp, Ashland Co, O. MI: Stone monument with name, date of birth, date of death, and words, "A Soldier of the Revolution." GM Sarah Copus Chap Sept 11, 1923. Drew a pens of $96.00 per annum for many yrs prior to his death, as a compensation for his services on the border in Western Pa in his youth. Was a cousin of Louis Wetsel, famous Indian fighter. Ref: History of Ashland Co (Hills). Fur infor Sarah Copus Chap.

SUMMER, VON JOHN, (Mahoning Co.)

Land bounty rights, Albany Co, N. Y. New York Men in the Rev, p 225. Br 1752. Children: Samuel, Jacob, John, David, Joseph, Solomon, a dau (mar Geo Elder). D 1838. Bur Kurtz, Springfield Twp. Said to have had 16 children to whom each one was given 100 acres of land at marriage, except the youngest, who received 300. Farmer. Ref: Trumbull and Mahoning Co Hist, pp 178, 203; Columbiana Co Hist, p 316; Biographical Hist of Mahoning Co, Sanderson, p 490. Fur infor Mahoning Chap.

SUMMERLAND, DAVID (or DANIEL), (Seneca Co.)

Bur Swamp Cem, Venice Twp. GM D. A. R. bronze marker, 1927. Fur infor Dolly Todd Madison Chap.

SUMNER, THOMAS, (Summit Co.)

Pvt in Company of Volunteers under command of Capt Asa Danforth who marched fr Brookfield, Mass, 1777, to join Revolutionary Army under command of Gen Gates. Took part in the Battle of Saratoga, Oct 7. Total amount of serv credited 4 3-4 mos. Br Edgarton, Mass, 1757. D Middlebury, O, in 1825. Bur Old Middlebury Cem. MI: "Thomas Sumner, died April 19, 1825, aged 68 years. Elizabeth Holland, his wife, 1760-1842." Fur infor Cuyahoga Portage Chap.

SUNDERLAND, PETER, (Auglaize Co.)

Enl 1775. Was at Bunker Hill; his Regt intrenched themselves on Breed's Hill; after 3rd attack by British, only 3 rounds of powder left, firing his last charge, he picked up 3 guns (empty), in succession. Picking a 4th gun, he discharged it in face of an enemy (who attacked him with a saber), and thrust his bayonet through his body. Peter after 3 days in a swamp was rescued. Br Philadelphia, Pa, 1737. Children: One son, Dye; Isabell. D Aug 1, 1827, aged 90 yrs. Bur Military Cem at Ft Amanda. MI: "Peter Sunderland, a soldier of Revolution, fought at Battle Bunker Hill, died Aug 21, 1827, aged 90." Came to Ohio, 1817; entered land near Dayton, but in 1822 he and wife went to Logan Twp, Auglaize Co; his grand dau, Suzane Russell (dau of Isabell), was first white child br at Ft Amanda. Was a descendant of fourth Earl of Sunderland. Fur infor W. J. McMurray, Wapakoneta, O., and Lima Chap.

SUNDERLAND, WILLIAM (or SUNDERLIN), (Montgomery Co.)

D 1823 (?). Bur Baptist Cem, Centerville, O, on crest of hill in center of the cem. Red sand stone gravestone, and is so badly "weather beaten" that inscription is almost illegible. GM Richard Montgomery Chap, S. A. R. Montgomery Co, bronze marker July 3, 1919. Fur infor Richard Montgomery Chap.

SUTTON, BENJAMIN, (Brown Co.)

Pvt. Br Sept 20, 1759, Somerset Co, N. J. Children, Sarah, Otha and Tingley. Bur Decatur, O. MI: Benjamin Sutton, Rev Soldier. GM Lieutenant Byrd Chap, May 30, 1916. Came to Brown Co, O, in pioneer days; owned quite a lot of land around where Decatur is located. Justice of the Peace. Fur infor Lieutenant Byrd Chap.

SUTTON, MOSES, (Huron Co.)

Served 7 yrs Washington's Life Guard. Br 1745, Fairfax Co. D Dec 2, 1833. Bur Sutton's Graveyard, Hunt's Corners. Fur infor Sally De Forest Chap.

SWAGER, HENRY, (Trumbull Co.)

Bur Church Hill, Liberty Twp. MI: Marker broken off and reset, so that only the name appears above the ground. Fur infor Mary Chesney Chap.

SWAN, TIMOTHY, (Mahoning Co.)

Pvt. Pensioned. Br 1745. Bur Mahoning Co. Mentioned in Co Hist. Ref: Mahoning and Trumbull Co Hist. Pa Archives, Series 3, Vol 23, p 653. Fur infor Mahoning Chap.

SWARTZ, JOHN, (Delaware Co.)

Bur Thompson Twp. (Probably.) Ref: S. A. R. Fur infor Delaware Chap.

SWAYZE, DAVID, (Fairfield Co.)

Pvt in Capt Abraham McKinney's Company, NJ Tr. Enl 1776, for 5 mos; in battles of Long Island and Fort Washington; also under Capts Wm Hazlett, Geo Ribbles, and Jas Bonnel. Disch 1781. Br Hunterdon Co, NJ, Mch 11, 1762. Mar Alice Mulligan (or Milligan) Swayze, 1792 or 1788 (?) Children: Edith, Elizabeth, Jennie, Polly, William, Sarah. D Mch 2, 1838, Fairfield Co, O. Bur New Salem, O. M. E. Cem. MI: "David Swayze, New Jersey, 1762-1838." GM Elizabeth Sherman Reese, D. A. R. 1927. Ref: Curtiss Beery S. A. R. Lancaster, O., certified copy fr Adj Gen New Jersey and Natl No 122212, D. A. R. Lin. Fur infor Elizabeth Sherman Reese Chap.

SWEET, CALEB, (Lake Co.)

While in New York he served in the 4th Regt, Albany Co Mil. D Mch 3, 1828, Perry, O. Bur on his farm in Perry, O. In 1817 he was an officer in Perry Twp, and was Justice of the Peace until his death. Fur infor New Connecticut Chap.

SWEET, JOSHUA, (Lake Co.)

Served in Capt Smart's Company, 3rd Regt, in July, 1781. Br 1764. D 1840, Painesville, O. Bur Madison, O. MI: "Memorial of Joshua Sweet, a Revolutionary soldier, who died 2nd May, 1840, age 76 years." GM New Connecticut Chap. He received a bounty for enlisting in the Conn army for a term of three yrs. Fur infor New Connecticut Chap.

SWEM, JESSE, (Clermont Co.)

Enl 1778 for 9 mos. Capt Thos Patterson's Company, 3rd Regt, New Jersey Line. Col Elias Dayton; at Monmouth. Pensioned 1819, file No R 10358. Br Pennsylvania. Mar 1st Polly. 2nd, Catherine Vail 1789, Bourbon Co, Ky Children: 1st wife, Catherine, Elizabeth, Polly, Jesse, (mar Lindsey), Daniel, Ephraim; 2nd wife, Andrew, John, Jane (Anderson), Thomas, and 5 others. (All residents of Clermont Co.) D Oct 1837. After second marriage moved to Middlesex Co, NJ, till 1810; Came to Ohio Twp (Clermont Co) locating near Locust Corner. Ref: Pens Records by Mrs Hobart and A. S. Abbott, Bethel, O. Fur infor Cincinnati Chap.

SWERINGEN, JOSEPH, (Butler Co.)

Name appears on the tablet of the Sailors' and Soldiers' Monument at Hamilton, O, as Revolutionary Soldier. Fur infor John Reily Chap.

SWETT, JONATHAN, (Athens Co.)

Br 1759. Never mar. D May 11, 1847, Athens Co, O. Bur Concord Churchyard in Ames Twp, near Trimble line, Athens Co, O. MI: "Jonathan Sweet, Died May 11, 1847 in the 88th year of his age." GM by relatives. Stone in good condition. Ref: Bureau of Pensions, Washington, DC. Fur infor Nabby Lee Ames Chap.

SWICKHART, MARTIN, (Co. not stated.)

Pvt in Washington Co, Pa Tr. Br 1745, France. D 1840, Ohio. Ref: Natl No 91504, Vol 92, p 164, D. A. R. Lin.

SWINNERTON, JAMES, (Marion Co)

Pvt in Capt John Putnam's Company. Enl May 1, 1775. Br Aug 13, 1757, Salem, Mass. D Dec 6, 1824, Grand Prairie Twp. Bur Grand Prairie Graveyard. He came to Delaware, O, in 1808 and to Marion Co about 1819. He was among the first settlers in Grand Prairie Twp. Ref: Revolutionary War Records, Department of Interior, Washington, DC. Fur infor Capt William Hendricks Chap.

SYMMES, CLEVES JOHN, (Hamilton Co.)

Chairman of Commission of Safety, Sussex Co, N. J., 1774; Col, 1775; (appointed Supreme Court Judge of Northwest Territory. Br 1742, New Jersey. D 1814, Cincinnati, O. Ref: S. A. R. and Natl No 28436, Vol 29, p 159. Fur infor Cincinnati Chap.

SYMMES, TIMOTHY, (Hamilton Co.)

Quartermaster of Sussex Co. NJ Mil. Br 1744, New Jersey. Mar Abigail Tuthill, 1st wife. D 1797, Cincinnati, O. 1783, Judge of Common Pleas in Sussex Co, N. J. 1790, joined his brother, John Cleves Symmes, in Cincinnati, O, where he died. Ref: S. A. R. and Natl No 39298, Vol 40, D. A. R. Lin. Fur infor Cincinnati Chap.

TAIT, THOMAS, (Trumbull Co.)

Bur Oak Grove Cem, Warren, O. Unable to locate grave. Ref: Baldwin Library, Youngstown, O. Kindness of Miss Kyle. Fur infor Mary Chesney Chap.

TALBOT, RICHARD, (Washington Co.)

Ensign, Lt and Adjutant. Served as 2nd Lt and 1st Lt in the 4th Maryland Regt. Resigned Nov 6, 1777. Fought in the battles of White Plains, Brandywine and Germantown. Br Dec, 1753. D Dec 22, 1821, Grandview Twp, Washington Co, O. Bur Grandview Twp, in Carson's Cem. Ref: Maryland Archives; Adjutant General's Office, Washington, D. C. Fur infor Marietta Chap.

TALCOTT, ELIZAR (or ELEAZOR), (Trumbull Co.)

Pensioned in 1833 for serv as Pvt in Conn Tr. Br 1759, Enfield, Conn. Mar Sarah Baxter in 1791 (br 1767). One dau was Betsy. D 1835, Mesopotamia, O. According to records in Baldwin Library soldier bur here, several old monuments here with inscriptions totally obliterated. Ref: Records taken fr Baldwin Library, Youngstown, O. and Natl No 45863, Vol 46, p 363, D. A. R. Lin. Fur infor Mary Chesney Chap.

TALIAFERRO, RICHARD, (Clermont Co.)

Served under Gen Roger Clark in expedition against Vincennes and Kaskaskia, in 1778, of Carolina Co, Va. D 1835, Clermont Co. Ref: Natl No 242251 and Natl No 82971, national number of soldier. Fur infor Cincinnati Chap and by Mrs. Whallon.

TANNER, TYRAL, (Mahoning Co.)

Lt in Col Elmer's Regt, 1776, Dec 16, 1777, Jan 1, 1777. Br 1751. Mar, 1st, Hulda Jackson, 2nd, Lydia Doud. Children: Archabald, Edmond, Julia, Nancy, Peggy, Laura, Bridget, Panthia, dau died young. D 1833, Canfield, O. Bur Canfield. GM by Mahoning Chap, D A. R. Bronze marker on May 30, 1918. At the breaking out of the Rev, he was a Sgt on Gen Arnold's disastrous campaign in Canada. At the close of this campaign he enl in the Conn Continental Regt as Lt. Promoted to Adjutant. Was in Battle of Monmouth, in 1780, resigned to work for family. Farming, tavern, store. Came to Conn 1802 as farmer. Was sheriff 2 terms. The type of man is shown in the statement which he made when Eleazar Gilson applied for pension: "I declare on the honor of an old Revolutionary officer, that I know Eleazar to have been an officer in the 5th Continental Regt, 2nd Brig, fr 1777 to 1780, and know him to be a man of truth." Ref: Conn Men of the Rev, pp 113, 218, Trumbull and Mahoning Co Hist, Vol 2, p 37. Fur infor Mahoning Chap.

TANNER, W. M. (Trumbull Co.)

Pvt, Rhode Island State Mil. Bur Fowler Twp, center of Fowler. Name given in S. A. R. Yr Bk of Ohio. We did not look up his grave. Fur infor Mary Chesney Chap.

TAPSCOTT, JAMES, (Warren Co.)

Pvt in Capt John Walton's Tr of Light Dragoons, N J Mil. Br 1750, New Jersey. Mar Sarah Baird. D 1815, Carlisle. Ref: Natl No 72211, p 77, Vol 73, D. A. R. Lin.

TAULMAN, HERMANUS, (Hamilton Co.)

Br 1731, New York. D 1796. Fur infor Cincinnati Chap.

TAYLOR, BENJAMIN, (Champagin Co.)

Pensioned 1818. Pvt, 1776-77, in Capt Amos Emmerson's Company, Col Joseph Cilley's Regt. Br 1759, Stratton, N. H. Mar Anna Lowe in 1782. D 1839, Mechanicsburg, O. Ref: Natl No 74719, Vol 75, D. A. R. Lin.

TAYLOR, DANIEL, (Delaware Co.)

D 1853, aged 93. Bur Sunbury. Fur infor Delaware Chap.

TAYLOR, ELISHA, (Portage Co.)

Enl June 29, 1777. Disch July 26, 1777. Enl Sept 19, 1777. Disch Oct 11, 1777. He was a Corp and Pvt. Br Aug 7, 1760, in Mass. Mar Anna Kimball. D June 9, 1836, Nelson O. Bur Nelson, O. Ref: Mass Archives. Fur infor Old Northwest Chap.

TAYLOR, FREEGIFT, (Medina Co.)

Bur Spencer. Fur infor Western Reserve Chap.

TAYLOR, HENRY, (Butler Co.)

Br Nov 5, 1752. Mar (two wives). D July 18, 1832. Bur on Miss Eva Marshall's Farm, near Sevenmile, Butler Co. MI: Stone bears Revolutionary Soldier. GM Headstone was restored to upright position by John Reily Chap summer of 1925. Fur infor John Reily Chap.

TAYLOR, JAMES, CAPT., (Muskingum Co.)

Served under Gen Wayne. Wounded at Fort Recovery. Resigned 1802. Cavalry. D 1843, aged 73 yrs. Bur Woodlawn Cem, Zanesville, O. Lot 7, Sec 1. Pensioned as an invalid, 1832. Fur infor Muskingum Chap.

TAYLOR, JAMES, (Licking Co.)

Served in 5th Pa Regt under Col Anthony Wayne. Commissioned Capt Jan 5, 1776, Maj Sept 23, 1777. Was with Wayne in Williamson expedition, being one of the 17 who voted against the murder of the captives. Br 1753, Lancaster, Pa. Mar 1780, Mary Ann Cully. Children: William, Mary, Thomas. D May 24, 1844, Newark, Union Twp. Bur Old Cem. Re-interred Maholm lot, Cedar Hill. MI: "Rev. War." GM by Hetuck Chap in 1910. Associate Judge, this county in 1808-1809. One of first elders First Presbyterian Church. Pens allowed. Ref: Pa Archives, Vol 10, p 156, and Vol 15, p 445. Fur infor Hetuck Chap.

TAYLOR, JAMES, (Mahoning Co.)

Pvt. Br 1732. Mar Martha, age 78 when died. D 1854. Bur Old Springfield Cem. Lived in Northumberland Co, Pa. in 1790. Ref: Pa Archives, Series 3, Vol 23, p 672. Fur infor Mahoning Chap.

TAYLOR, JASHER, (Co. not stated.)

Br 1753 in Ashfield. Mar Dolly Carr. D Dover, O. Ref: Natl No 99706, Vol 100, p 218, D. A. R. Lin.

TAYLOR, ROBERT, (Butler Co.)

Cumberland Co, Pa, Mil. Br 1720, Ireland. D Butler Co, 1790, aged 70. Ref: Natl No 11988, p 369, Vol 21, D. A. R. Lin.

TAYLOR, ROBERT, Col., (Washington Co.)

Br 1748. D 1801. Bur Mound Cem, Marietta, O. MI: "Colonel Robert Taylor, 1746-1801." GM Marietta Chap by Revolutionary marker and on gateway, Nov 30, 1906; marker stolen and replaced in 1920. Fur infor Marietta Chap.

TAYLOR, SAMUEL, (Miami Co.)

Bur Sodom Graveyard on Casstown pike. GM Miami Chap with bronze marker in 1904. Fur infor Miami Chap.

TAYLOR, SAMUEL, (Portage Co.)

Enl as Pvt in 1780 or 1781 in the Massachusetts Regt Continental Line, Ralph H. Bowles, Adjt. Was disch for disability. Br June 4, 1768, Springfield, Mass. Mar Sarah Jagger, May 28, 1789. Children: Sally, Rebecca, Elmina, Malinda, Samuel, Worthy, Royal, Marcus. D Apr 10, 1813, Aurora, O. Bur Aurora, O. He was a drummer boy in the band at Washington's headquarters. Ref: Bureau of Pensions. Natl No 80481, and 143966. Fur infor Old Northwest Chap.

TAYLOR, SIMON, (Trumbull Co.)

D Warren, O, 1828. Bur Old Cem, Mahoning Ave, Warren, O, in family lot. MI: Marker placed by American Legion; also name on monument erected for Revolutionary Soldiers. Ref: Mrs. Laura Harsh, Warren, O. Fur infor Mary Chesney Chap.

TAYLOR, TIMOTHY, (Huron Co.)

Pvt. Volunteer fr Hillsboro Co, N. H. Br Sept, 1754, Merrimac, N. H. Parents: Timothy Taylor and Rachel Converse. Mar Esther French. Children: Gilman, Benjamin, Fannie and Esther. D Feb 21, 1851, Norwalk. Bur Episcopal Cem, Norwalk, grave second tier lots south of Episcopal Church, 2nd lot east of center path. MI: Name, dates and "soldier of the Revolution." GM by great-grandchildren, at request of grand dau, Lucy Preston Wickham, in 1915. Justice of Peace, etc. Ref: Natl No 58042, Vol 59, D. A. R. Lin. Fur infor Sally De Forest Chap.

TAYLOR, TOM, (THOMAS), (Perry Co.)

Pvt. Br 1750. D 1882, south part of the Joe Wigton farm, near Roseville, O. This lies in the neighboring part of Perry Co. Ref: Natl No 27053, Vol 28, p 18 D. A. R. Lin. Fur infor Muskingum Chap.

TAYLOR, THOMAS, (Richland Co.)

1789 was Pvt in Capt Curtis Lowne's Company, Chester Co, Pa Mil, under Col Caleb Davis. Br 1760, Chester, Pa. D 1832, Mansfield, O. Ref: Natl No 86604, Vol 87, p 193, D. A. R. Lin.

TAYLOR, WILLIAM, (Auglaize Co.)

Enl 1776, served to close of war. At Brandywine, Stony Point and Yorktown. Br July 4, 1754, New Jersey. Mar 4 times in Pennsylvania. Children: Margaret, Susan, Robert and Harriett. D July 4, 1868, aged 114 yrs. Bur Fort Amanda, but no marker. Veteran of 3 wars. After Rev was on sea till 1793. Under Wayne at battle of Fallen Timbers, and many others of Indian Wars. After war ended, returned to Pa and mar. Was authority on wars. At age 104 divided up his farm and effects. Last ten yrs of life lived with dau, Mrs. Harriet Dehart, near Spencerville. Fur infor W. J. McMurray, Wapakoneta, O. On request of Jane Dailey, State Chairman.

TAYLOR, WILLIAM, (Jefferson Co.)

Br 1753, County Down, Ireland. D 1845. Bur Bergholz, Jefferson Co. GM by D. A. R. Fur infor Steubenville Chap.

TAYLOR, WILLIAM, (Mahoning Co.)

Pvt in Weland's Pa Company. Pensioned in 1824, aged 84 yrs at time. Br 1740. Bur Mahoning Co. Ref: Pa Archives, Series 3, Vol 23, D. A. R. Lin. Fur infor Mahoning Chap.

TAYLOR, WILLIAM, (Miami Co.)

Bur Northeast of Casstown Cem. Fur infor Miami Chap.

TAYLOR, WILLIAM, (Ross Co.)

Pvt in Capt Bateman Lloyd's Company, 2d Regt NJ Continental Line. Br Dec 27, 1744, Monmouth Co. N. J. Parents: Joseph Taylor and Elizabeth Taylor. Mar Lucy Imlay, Dec 3, 1768. Children: Joseph, William, Edward, David, John, George, Elisha, Isaac, Jonathan, Mary, Sarah, Eleanor, Lucy, Elizabeth. D Apr 24, 1830, Bainbridge, Ross Co. Bur Bainbridge, O. GM by family with monument. Came to Ross Co about 1798, fr Mason Co, Ky. Farmer. Ancestor of Mrs. Lowell Hobart, State Regt, D. A. R. 1923-1926. Ref: Natl No. 12061, D. A. R. Lin. Fur infor Nathaniel Massie Chap.

TEATSORTH, ISAAC, (Hancock Co.)

Br 1744. D Dec 25, 1834. Bur at Findlay, Maple Grove Cem in north-east section. MI: "Isaac Teatsorth. Died December 25, 1834. A Volunteer of the Revolution of 76." GM G. A. R. Ref: R. P. Teatsworth, 214 S. Cory St., Findlay, O. Fur infor Fort Findlay Chap.

TELFORD, ALEXANDER, (Miami Co.)

Enl and fought under Gen Washington; was at the siege of Yorktown and witnessed the surrender of Lord Cornwallis. Br on shipboard on the Atlantic Ocean. Bur Rose Hill Cem at Troy, O. GM Miami Chap with bronze marker in 1904. He was a farmer. Fur infor Miami Chap.

TEMPLETON, WILLIAM, (Mahoning Co.)

Pvt and Ranger. The former in Bedford Co, Pa. The latter in Berks Co, D Cornersburg. Bur Cornersburg southwest of Youngstown. Ref: Pa Archives, 5th Series, p 53, Third Series, p 238, Vol 23, pp 450 and 760. Fur infor Mahoning Chap.

TERFLINGER, CHRISTOPHER, (Wyandot Co.)

Br Nov 28, 1766. Mar Elizabeth. D Mch 28, 1866. Bur Lutheran Cem, McCutchenville, O. MI: "Christopher Terflinger, Died aged 100 years." GM by limestone monument by family G. A. R. marker. Fur infor Colonel William Crawford Chap.

TERRELL, ELIHU, (Lorain Co.)

Pvt Massachusetts Continental Army. Br 1758. D 1844. Bur Butternut Ridge Cem, Field's Corners. GM by Western Reserve, bronze marker. Ref: Think the one filed S. A. R. 1917 Bk bur Ridgeville, Henry Co, is the same as this, as North Ridgeville is in Lorain Co. Fur infor Western Reserve Chap.

TERRELL, OLIVER, (Lorain Co.)

Pvt fr North Milford Co, Conn. Bur Columbia Station. GM by Western Reserve, bronze marker. Fur infor Western Reserve Chap.

TERRY, JULIUS, (Huron Co.)

Pvt. Drafted at Enfield, Conn, Oct 1778, Company Capt Hezekiah Parsons, Guard over prisoners fr Gen Burgoyne's army. In 1779 enl with Capt Jonathan Bush at New London, Conn. Served 3 mos. Br Oct 21, 1761. Parents: Jacob Terry, Grace North. Mar Sarah King, Dec 4, 1788. Children: Edith, Sally, Polly, Julius, Isaiah, Jerry. D July 17, 1843. Bur Townsend. Descendant of Samuel Terry. Ref: A bk of Samuel Terry, Public Library, Hartford, Conn and Congressional Library; Washington Allen's Hist of Enfield, Conn. Fur infor Sally De Forest Chap.

TERWILLIGER, NATHANIEL, (Hamilton Co.)

Rank not stated. Served in Capt Tarpening's Company, Col Hashbrouck's Regt, N Y Mil, Revolutionary War, fr Ulster Co. Librarian of Albany, N. Y. gives following: "Nathaniel Terwilliger on roll of 4th Regt, Orange Co Mil, Col Hathorn. Br Orange Co, N. Y., near Ft Montgomery, to which locality his ancestors had come fr Holland. Founders of Dutch Reformed Church in Montgomery, O. Mar Katrina, dau of Cornelius Snyder, (Revolutionary Soldier), and wife, Katrina Felter Snyder. Children: Cornelius, John, Nathaniel Jr. (br 1785), Mathias, Elizabeth, Catharine, Mary, James (br 1808), son by 3rd wife, Mrs. McGee, nee Whiteside. (No children by second wife, Mrs. Taulman). D 1785 at Montgomery. Bur Hopewell, Montgomery, O. Bur Terwilliger lot, next south of Nathaniel Jr's. grave, his son. Grave not marked. 25 men, names spelled variously. Terwilliger and gar; Terwileger, Teewilla from Ulster and Orange Counties in Revolutionary War. Above Nathaniel is only Nathaniel in NY records, and only Nathaniel in Ohio Hist. Came to Ohio, bought the entire section of land 3, Twp 4, fr Symes in 1796. Was one of the founders of Montgomery, named for the N Y home town, Fort Montgomery. Fur infor Cincinnati Chap.

THARP, JOHN, (Warren Co.)

Serv copied fr Official Records of Adj Gen of N J, signed by Notary Public May 7, 1917. Printed Records pp 443, 98, 124, Continental Line and Mil, Somerset Co, N. J. Enl Feb 16, 1776. Disch 1785, paid Feb 24. Lt. Br 1751, Somerset Co, N J. First name of father not found. Mother, Margaret Eliz. Frezier. Mar Hannah Hurin (1754-1846), (bur Lebanon). Children: Three died in infancy: Hurin, Mary and a son. Elizabeth (mar Samuel Sering) and Jane (mar Robert Porter). D 1819, Lebanon. Purchased lots 134, 217 in 1789 and '90 in Cincinnati. Later owned lot now facting Fountain Square, Vine and 5th Sts. Removed to Warren Co. One of founders of Lebanon and the Presbyterian Church. Ref: Records fr family Bible and tombstone, those of serv given above; Dr. E. R. Booth, Cincinnati (S. A. R.). Fur infor Cincinnati Chap.

THATCHER, AMOS, (Greene Co.)

Pvt, New Jersey Mil. Pensioned 1831. D Ross Twp. Fur infor Catherine Greene Chap.

THAYER, JOEL, (Summit Co.)

Entered Continental Army Apr 21, 1777. Served for 3 yrs as Pvt and Sgt in 6th Mass Regt under Capts Japhet Daniel and John Holden and Col Thomas Nixon. Also did Pvt duty in Capt Peter Clayes' (Light Inf) Company, Lt Col Calvin Smith's Regt, Mass Tr, in 1782. A native of Mendon, Mass; early settler of Copley and buried in Montrose Cem, Copley, O. Fur infor Cuyahoga Portage Chap.

THOMAS, ABRAM, (Miami Co.)

He fought in Pa and Va and afterward was a scout with Boone with army of Gen Roger Clark in 1782, when the army of Clark destroyed the Indian village of Piqua, near the mouth of the Loramie River. Bur Thomas Cem, one mile fr Troy. GM by Miami Chap with bronze marker in 1904. Fur infor Miami Chap.

THOMAS, MICHAEL, (Ross Co.)

Spy under Gen Wayne in his expedition to the Maumee Valley. Once pursued by Indians, hid in a hollow tree until after dark. Br Pa, date unknown. Had two wives, names not known. Three children by first wife; nine by second. Tabitha, oldest dau, mar Peter Streevey. D Ross Co (Huntington Twp.). Grave not found. Came to Huntington Twp, Ross Co, soon after it was formed, fr Chillicothe, whence he had come on horseback fr Pa in 1796. Bought 100 acres of land in Chillicothe; traded for 500 in Huntington Twp. Ref: Hist of Ross and Highland Cos. Fur infor Nathaniel Massie Chap.

THOMPSON, ALEXANDER, (Clermont Co.)

Pvt, Capt Wm Lithgow's Company, marched Mch 11, 1776; Company stationed at Falmouth, Cumberland Co, for defense of sea coast. Also served in same Company, Col Mitchell's Regt, fr Aug 31 to Nov 23, 1776, stationed at same place, for defense of sea coast. See p 326 in Mass Soldiers and Sailors, Vol XV, Maine. Br May 7, 1758, Georgetown, Maine, now Bath, Maine. Parents: Benjamin (3), Thompson and wife, Abigail (5), Philbrook, (mar Oct 17, 1744.) Mar Hannah Baker in 1777 or 1778. She was his first wife and mother of all his children (d at Amelia May, 1821), bur same lot. Children: Olive, Rev David, Jeremiah, Charlotte, Alexander P, Rachel, Sophia and Elisha Baker. D 1830. Bur in family cem on farm owned by his son-in-law, Josiah Fairfield. Up to twenty years ago cared for by descendants. Went to Amelia, O, in 1815. When about 70 yrs old, built a church there and dedicated it with these words: "Here stands a fine frame and it shall have a fine name. It shall be called Republican—free for all denominations to worship God in." And many denominations worshipped there. Ref: Natl No 228905, D. A. R., also Natl No 112267, D. A. R. Lin. Fur infor Mrs. Herbert Allen Black, 2201 Greenwood St, Pueblo, Col., State Regt of Col (1927).

THOMPSON, ISAAC, Lt., (Geauga Co.)

Enl Carlisle, Pa, in 1775. Lt 6th Pa Regt. In battles Brandywine, Germantown. One of Washington's body guards. Br 1751, Thompsontown, Pa. Parents: John Thompson and Mary Greenlee. Mar, 1st, Martha Larimore, about 1778; 2nd, Jane Evans Well, about 1783. Children: James, John, Eliza, Polly, William, Robert,

John, Lydia. D 1823, Middlefield, O. Bur Middlefield Village Cem. MI: "Lieut. Isaac Thompson. Born Thompsontown, Pa., 1752, died Middlefield, Ohio, 1823. Soldier of Revolution." GM by his grandson, P. T. Thompson. Monument, marker, name in 1880. Was with his son, James, the first settler of Middlefield, in Mch, 1799. Farmer, first Justice of Peace of Middlefield. Family Bible Descendants John Thompson. Pioneer Hist Geauga Co. Pension Record. Roster Pa Officers. Fur infor Taylor Chap.

THOMPSON, JAMES, (Union Co.)

Served under Lafayette. Bur Watkins Cem, Jerome Twp. Ref: Col W. D. Curry's History of Union Co. Fur infor Hannah Emerson Dustin Chap.

THOMPSON, JOB, (Portage Co.)

Pvt in N H Continental Line. Placed on Pens Roll Feb 28, 1833. Bur Shalersville. Drew pens at Ravenna in 1840. Fur infor Old Northwest Chap.

THOMPSON, JOHN, (Brown Co.)

Enl fall 1780. Served 2 mos Capt McCollister, 25 mos Lt Johnson's Company Rangers. Disch spring of 1783. Pvt. Br Feb 28, 1761, Foggs Mana, Pa. Parents: William Thompson. Mar Margaret Mitchell, 1790. Children: William, Jean, James, Sally, David, William, John, Robert, Jessie. D Nov 24, 1840, Brown Co, O. Bur Mt Zion, Lewis Twp, Brown Co, O. MI: "John Thompson, 1761-1840. Revolutionary Soldier." GM Government marker by his descendants, July 4, 1915. Pioneer Methodist Minister, emigrated fr Pa to Adams Co, thence to Brown Co. Pens allowed Oct 26, 1832. Ref: Bureau of Pensions, Series File No 3792; Natl No 93331, Vol 94, D. A. R. Lin. Fur infor Taliaferro Chap.

THOMPSON, JOHN, (Medina Co.)

Bur Seville. GM Western Reserve Chap. Fur infor Western Reserve Chap.

THOMPSON, JOSEPH, (Coshocton, Co.)

Drummer. At Lexington Alarm commanded a Company of Minute Men, 1779. Made Lt Col 10th Mass Regt. Br 1733. D 1795, in Ohio. Bur Virginia Twp. Ref: Natl No 86525, Vol 87, p 168, D. A. R. Lin and also Co Hist. Fur infor Coshocton Chap.

THOMPSON, PETER, (Geauga Co.)

Pvt Capt Parker's Company, Col Weymon's Regt N H Mil, 1776; disch by Col Peabody Dec 1776. Pensioned in 1832. Br 1752. Mar 2nd Susannah Jan 15, 1793. Children by 2nd wife: Peter, Esther, (Easter), Charlotte, Joseph, and Elizabeth. D Dec 19, 1845, Munson, O. Bur Fowlers Mills, Munson, in lot of Ramson Wright. Enl fr Rindge, N. H. Marched to Skinesbough N. Y., thence to Ticonderoga, labored on Fort Independence. Fr 1814 to 1824, resided in Boome, Schohare Co, N. Y. Mar in Washington Co, NY. Fur infor Taylor Chap.

THOMPSON, PRICE, (Hamilton Co.)

Br 1756, N. J. D 1842. At 84 yrs receiving pens (in 1840 census). Ref: S. A. R. Fur infor Cincinnati Chap.

THOMPSON, R., (Belmont Co.)

Capt. D Sept 5, 1848, age 88 yrs. Bur Union Cem, St Clairsville, O. MI: "Soldier of Revolution." Ref: Mrs. A. L. McFarland, St Clairsville, O. Wheeling, W. Va. D. A. R.

THOMPSON, RICHARD, (Delaware Co.)

Bur Fancher Graveyard, Harlem Twp. Fur infor Delaware Chap.

THOMPSON, STEPHEN, JR. (Summit Co.)

At age of only fourteen yrs he enl in the First Regt Conn Line, serving until the consolidation of the 5th with the 1st Regt in 1781. Br May 6, 1764, Goshen, Conn. Parents: Deacon Stephen Thompson Sr, Mary Walter Thompson. Mar Abigail Hutchinson. D Hudson, O. Bur Old Cem on College St, Hudson, O. MI: "Stephen Thompson Jr." GM by D. A. R. Was sent home by his father at the consolidation of the 1st and 5th Regts. Fur infor Cuyahoga Portage Chap.

THOMPSON, DEACON STEPHEN, SR., (Summit Co.)

Fr June 1776, to close of war, he served his country nobly. Took active part in battle of Long Island, and retreat to New York. Battles of White Plains, Germantown, Monmouth, Stony Point, Siege of Yorktown. Pvt. Br Apr 1734, New Haven, Conn. (See 55908.) Mar Mary Walter (br May 27, 1742, d Feb 27, 1821.) Children: Stephen Thompson Jr. D Feb 25, 1823, Hudson, O. Bur Old Cem, College St. MI: "Stephenson Thompson Sr." GM D. A. R. He served in Capt Brackett's Company, Col Wm Douglas' Regt, Wadsworth Brig, Conn; Munson's Company, 8th Conn Regt, Capt Douglas' Company, 5th Conn Line fr formation until its consolidation with the 1st Regt of Conn Line in Autumn of 1781. Was at Valley Forge when Cornwallis surrendered. Also with Gen Washington in and about New York and Philadelphia. Ref: Natl No 59459, Vol 60, D. A. R. Lin. Fur infor Cuyahoga Portage Chap.

THOMPSON, WILLIAM, (Geauga Co.)

Pvt 5th Regt, Col Waterbury's 1775 Conn Line. Br 1757, Suffield. Mar Ann Rhodes. D Oct 2, 1843, Thompson, O. Bur Maple Grove Cem. Grave 4, Lot 3, Section 61. MI: "William Thompson, 1757-1843." Grave marked. Enl May 8, 1777, re-entered Nov 17. List of Pensions Census 1840, Thompson, O, age 95. Ref: Conn Men Rev, p 65. Fur infor Taylor Chap.

THOMAS, THORLA, (Noble Co.)

Pvt. Br New England, 1748. D Olive, Dec, 1835. Bur Olive Cem, Caldwell. Came to Noble Co, 1828. Fur infor Mrs. L. B. Frazier, Caldwell, O.

THRALL, SAMUEL, JR., (Licking Co.)

Enl May 6, 1777, as Pvt in Capt Cannon's Company in 1780. Br Aug 3, 1760, Mass. Natl No 71607 D. A. R. says br in Conn, Vol 72. Mar Triphosa Cooley. Twelve children. D May 10, 1815, Granville, O. Bur Old Cem, Granville, O. Emigrated to this County with Granville Colony in 1805. Fur infor Hetuck Chap.

THRIFT, WILLIAM, SR., (Knox Co.)

Pvt. He was 16 yrs old when he enl in Rev and served in Capt Andrew Russell's Company, 5th Va Regt fr Sept 28th to Nov 28, 1776. Br 1760, Loudoun Co, Va. Parents: Charles (br 1753, d 1794) and Rebecca (Hamilton) Thrift. Mar Hannah Moffet June 16, 1791. Children: Elizabeth (br 1792); Martha (1793); William (1797); Rachel (1799); Absolom (1801); Hamilton (1803); Hanna (1805); Sarah (1808); Jane (1811); Josiah (1815). D 1821 Mount Vernon, Knox Co, O. Bur the Old Frederick Cem located between the upper Fredericktown Road and the B & O Railroad. Baptist Minister. Ref: Jane Fresno Pittinger, 346 W. 7th Ave., Columbus, O; Natl No 117070, D. A. R. Fur infor Kokosing Chap.

THURBER, AMOS, (Portage Co.)

Pvt in Rhode Island Continental. Placed on Pens Roll Sept 21, 1833. Bur Palmyra, O. Drew pens at Ravenna, 1840. Fur infor Old Northwest Chap.

THWING, JOHN, (Geauga Co.)

Pvt in Capt Joseph Browning's Company, Col Seth Murry's 1st Mass Regt for 3 mos, June 22, 1780. Stationed at or near West Point at the time Arnold turned traitor and sold West Point. Br Jan 27, 1761, Wilbraham, Mass. Parents: James Thwing and Prisca Meecham. Mar Ruth Beebe, Dec 15, 1875, in Wilbraham, Mass. Children: Polly, Hannah, Luther, Calvin, Ruth, John, Margaret, James, David, Prisca, Silas, Rufus, Sophia, Lovina, William. D June 19, 1844, Chardon, O. Bur Thwing Cem, west of Chardon. MI: "John Thwing died June 19, 1844, aged 83 yrs, 4 months and 22 days. His wife, Ruth, died July 1, 1853, aged 87 years." GM David Thwing. Moved fr Wilbraham, Mass to Willington Conn and to Wilbraham, Mar 26, 1793. Moved to Ohio, 1832. Mass Soldiers and Sailors Vol 16, p 215. Ref: Thwing Family Genealogy. Fur infor Taylor Chap.

TIBBETTS, ISAAC, (Hamilton Co.)

Br 1759, Massachusetts. D 1825. Ref: S. A. R. Fur infor Cincinnati Chap.

TICHINOR, JONATHAN, (Hamilton Co.)

Served fr Morris and Essex Co, N. J., p 785, "Strykers Men fr New Jersey." Came early to Cincinnati. Was one of founders of 1st Presbyterian Church. Settled on farm near Pleasant Ridge. Bur Hamilton Co. A grandson found his name misspelled on his commission in Civil War, so his branch has since spelled "Teachinor." Fur infor Cincinnati Chap.

TIDD, ———, (Trumbull Co.)

Location of grave known but has no marker or monument. One of the first settlers of Kinsman. Fur infor Mary Chesney Chap.

TILDEN, DANIEL, Col., (Portage Co.)

Col under Washington. Br 1743, Lebanon, Conn. D Dec 8, 1833, Hiram, O. Bur Hiram, O. MI: "To perpetuate to Posterity the Memory of the Philanthropist Philomath, Patriot and Statesman, Col Daniel Tilden, an Officer of the Revolution under General Washington, who died Dec 8, 1833, aged 90 years." Fur infor Old Northwest Chap.

TILTON, JOHN, (Ashland Co.)

Battle of Princeton, Monmouth, Yorktown and others, including Germantown and Jamestown. Pvt and Sgt N J Line. Br 1760, Princeton, N. J. (?) Mar Maria Sutphen. D Aug 12, 1849, Orange Twp, O. Bur Nankin Cem, Orange Twp. GM Sarah Copus Chap. Farmer. Ref: Natl No 42898, Vol 43, and Natl No 75872, Vol 76, D. A. R. Lin. Fur infor Sarah Copus Chap.

TINEY, RICHARD, (Fulton Co.)

At age of 77, received pens in 1840, while residing in Royalton Twp, then a part of Lucas Co. S. A. R. 1913, and Census 1840. Bur Edgar Cem. Ref: Military Record of Fulton Co, O, 1885, p 305. Fur infor Wauseon Chap.

TINGLEY, JEREMIAH, (Jefferson Co.)

Served in Rev as a member of the Somerset Co Mil, N J. B 1755, Somerset Co, N. J. Mar Ester Liddell. D 1803, Jefferson Co, O. Bur at Hopewell Church, Jefferson Co. Ref: Strykers New Jersey in the Rev, 786, and Natl No 25690, Vol 26, D. A. R. Lin. Fur infor Moravian Trail Chap.

TINGLEY, LEVI, (Clermont Co.)

Revolutionary Soldier, came to Tate Twp, 1804, settled one mile south of Bethel, where had a tannery till he died. Children: Jacob, Benjamin (was in War 1812), and Jonathan. D 1832, Clermont Co, O. Ref: A. S. Abbott, Bethel, O. Fur infor Cincinnati Chap.

TIPPEY, URIAH (TIPPIE), (Athens Co.)

Br in Pa. Age at time of death 102 yr, 11mos, 9 da. Mar 3 times, names of wives not known here. Children: Susan, (br about 1790). Three small children drowned in Pa. D about Jan 3, 1847, at the home of his grandson, Uriah Tippie, in Dover or Ames Twp, Athens Co, O. At age of 82, received a pens in 1840, while residing in Alexander Twp. Shoemaker. Fur infor Nabby Lee Ames Chap.

TIPTON, SOLOMON, (Coshocton Co.)

Bur Baptist Cem, Perry Twp. Fur infor Coshocton Chap.

TIPTON, THOMAS, (Champaign Co.)

Br Mch 1, 1748, in Virginia. D Sept 20, 1862. Bur Johnson Cem, near Heathtown. Fur infor Urbana Chap.

TODD, WILLIAM, (Hamilton Co.)

Pvt in Somerset Co, N J. Was at Cincinnati in his earliest yrs, where he is bur at Spring Grove, Cem. Mar Esther Morris, dau of John Morris. One dau was Esther Todd. Ref: Vol 18, p 173, D. A. R. Lin; "Strykers Men fr New Jersey." Fur infor Cincinnati Chap.

TODD, WILLIAM, (Harrison Co.)

A Revolutionary pensioner living in Notingham Twp in 1840, aged 84; came fr Washington Co, Pa, about 1818. A William Todd was a member of Bedford Co, Pa, Mil; also a member of Capt Samuel Benezet's Company, Col Robt Magaw's 5th Pa Bn; taken prisoner Nov 16; paroled Dec 26, 1776. Pa Archives, 5th Series, II, 175, 187; IV, 252, 615, U. S. Pension Rolls 1835. Fur infor Moravian Trail Chap.

TOLLEN, CORNELIUS, (TOLAND) (Clark Co.)

Pvt in Capt Caleb North and Christy's 4th Company, Col Anthony Wayne's 4th Pa Regt. Enl Feb 1776. Served to Apr 1777. Granted pens July 10, 1818. Br County Derry, Ireland. Parents: Owen Toland. Mar 1st, Rosana, 2nd, Katharine Duffy. Children: John, Cornelius, Jerry, Morgan, David, Neal, Sarah, Owen, Hugh, Michael, Nancy. D Aug 1, 1835. Bur Columbia St, Springfield, O. about 60 ft fr south line, close to center of ground, not platted. GM Official marker, S. A. R. about 1906. Came to America with British Army. Deserted them and joined Amer Forces. Farmer. Funeral was first Military one held in Co. Ref: Family records. Pens 5-40584 War Dept Washington, DC. Fur infor Lagonda Chap.

TOMPSON, ALEXANDER, (Mahoning Co.)

Pvt in 1st Regt. The Line, N. Y. Men of the Revolution, p 27, Albany Co, 8th Regt, p 115, Ulster Co Rangers, p 203. Grave not located. Came to Austintown in 1802. Ref: Trumbull and Mahoning Co Hist, p 59, Vol II. Fur infor Mahoning Chap.

TORRENCE, JOHN, (Greene Co.)

Pvt and Sgt 1777 in Capt Eskew's Company, Col Dunlop's Regt, and was in Battle of Brandywine. 1832, pensioned in Greene Co. Br 1758, Ireland. Mar Jane Jolly. Children: Susan, William, Jane, Betsy, May, Aaron, Ann, John, David, Clarissa. D 1840, Greene Co. Bur Woodland Cem, Xenia. Ref: Pa Archives; Bureau of Pensions, Washington DC. Natl No 89339, D. A. R. Lin. Fur infor Catherine Greene Chap.

TOWNSEND, JAMES, (Meigs Co.)

Enl Aug, 1776, 3 mo Pvt, Capt Andrew Lovick; Apr, 1778, 3 mo. Capt Robt McCleorg, at Clarksburg, Va. 1778 3 mo Pvt, Capt Thos Hecklin. Br 1754, Va.

Mar Catherine Allen, (d Oct 25, 1836, 75 yrs.) On stone. Children: Solomon, Allen, James, Elizabeth, Rebecca, and Catherine. D Jan 15, 1840. Bur The Temple, Mt Blanco, which land his son Solomon gave. Bur Northeast corner. MI: "James Townsend, d Jan 15, 1840, 86th year of age." Grave old style, in good condition. Pens applied for Oct 13, 1832; granted; Ohio Pens Rolls, p 103. Natl No 92930, D. A. R. and O. D. Dailey, Albany. Fur infor Jane Dailey, State Chairman.

TOWNSEND, ROBERT, (Meigs Co.)

In addition to the time stated in the Bureau of Pensions, he served four yrs under the immediate command of Gen Washington. Br Belgrade, Me, 1756. Mar 1st wife, Ruth Santeel. D Apr 10, 1846. Bur Harrisonville, O, by his first wife. Fur infor Return Jonathan Meigs Chap.

TOWNSLEY, JOHN, (Greene Co.)

Pvt in Capt Talbot's Company, 6th Pa Bn, Col Wm Ervine. Br May 1, 1753, Cumberland Co, Pa. Mar Hester Martin. D 1822, Cedarville, Greene Co, O. Bur Stevenson's Cem or Massie's Creek Graveyard. Ref: Certified statement in Pa State Library, Harrisburg, Pa. Fur infor Catharine Greene Chap.

TOWNSLEY, THOMAS, (Greene Co.)

Pvt. Br 1756. Mar Sarah Patterson. D 1841. Bur Clifton Cem. Fur infor Catherine Greene Chap.

TRACY, SETH, (Trumbull Co.)

Br 1759. Mar Sylphina. (D Oct 26, 1845, aged 85 yrs.) D July 31, 1829. Bur Mesopotamia, O. MI: Names obliterated. Bought land Sept 27, 1800. Ref: Baldwin Library, Youngstown, O. Fur infor Mary Chesney Chap.

TRASK, RETIRE, (Geauga Co.)

Pvt Pa Mil. Pens granted 1832, at age of 75. Br 1757. Children: Retire Jr, Benjamin, Isaac. Bur on Oat Bartlet's farm, in the west part of Thompson, O. Farmer. Come to Thompson, 1809. Ref: Pens Records, Vol 3, p 514, Pa Archives, Vol 23, p 586, Section 3. Fur infor Taylor Chap.

TRAVIS, JOHN, Capt., (Columbiana Co.)

May be Elk Run Twp, Columbiana Co. Lived in Madison Twp, Columbiana Co. Fur infor Bethia Southwick Chap.

TRAXIER, EMANUEL, (Jackson Co.)

Indicated in Co Hist, but yet to be secured. Children: Samuel and six others. One of first Jackson Co Commissioners appointed by the Legislature in Mch, 1816. Was also on first Grand Jury, court was held under a tree. Built a watermill on Fourmile in 1816 . Fur infor Capt John James Chap.

TREBER, JOHN, (Adams Co.)

Children: Jacob Treber. D on Treber farm on Dunkinsville and West Union Pike. Bur in cem on the farm. Located there in 1796. Fur infor Sycamore Chap.

TREES, JOHN, (Clermont Co.)

Revolutionary Soldier. Came to Washington Twp, Clermont Co, 1801, locating 2 miles west of Point Isabel. Br Westermoreland Co, Pa. Children: John (br 1784, d 1866, mar Nancy). He served in War 1812; Adam, Jacob, Peter, and 6 dau. Ref: A. S. Abbott, Bethel, O. and Natl No 166297, D. A. R., who reports he died in Pa. Fur infor Cincinnati Chap.

TREMAIN, PHILIP, (Co. not stated.)

Turned out on the Lexington Alarm as Corp in Capt John Holmes' Company fr Egremont, Mass. Br 1744, New London, Conn. Mar 1766, Althea Warren. D 1805 in Ohio. Ref: Natl No 99870, Vol 100, p 270, D. A. R. Lin.

TREVITT, HENRY, (Licking Co.)

Enl at Amherst, N. H., 1775 as Pvt in Capt Taylor's Company. In 1775 in Col Stickney's Regt. Was at Bennington and Burgoyne. Br 1760, Marblehead, Mass. Mar in 1840. D St Albans Twp, near Luray, on farm. GM by Granville D. A. R. Pens allowed Oct 15, 1832. Fur infor Hetuck Chap.

TREW, EPHRAIM, (Washington Co.)

Pvt in Capt Samuel Noyes' Company, Col Phiney's Regt, Mass Line. Br Dec 21, 1756, Salisbury, Mass. D Aug 17, 1835, near Mt Ephraim, Washington Co, O. Bur Mt Ephraim, 3 miles fr Lower Salem, O. MI: "Ephraim Trew, Born Dec 21, 1756, D Aug 17, 1835." GM Marietta Chap with Revolutionary marker, in 1923. Ref: Mass Soldiers and Sailors; Natl No 86418, Vol 87, p 134, D. A. R. Lin. Fur infor Marietta Chap.

TRIMBLE, JOHN, (Holmes Co.)

Br 1748. D Aug 9, 1838. Bur Hopewell Cem, Holmes Co, in old part of cem. MI: "In memory of John Trimble who departed this life Aug 9, 1838, in the 90th year of his life." Fur infor Wooster-Wayne Chap.

TROBRIDGE, LEVI, (TROWBRIDGE), (Gallia Co.)

Capt Nathaniel Johnson's Company at Lexington Alarm. Br 1753, Oxford, Conn. Mar Hannah Smith. D Dec 14, 1843, in Ohio Twp, Gallia Co, O. Bur on farm of Thomas Waughm, Ohio Twp, Gallia Co, O, (Swan Creek). MI: Marker has only recently been knocked down and broken. Ref: Natl No 60252, p 84, Vol 61, D. A. R. Lin. and Miss Mary F. Waugh, Bladen, O. Fur infor French Colony Chap.

TROVILLO, JONATHAN, (Warren Co.)

Bur South Lebanon, Hamilton Twp, O. Ref: S. A. R. Yr Bk 1917.

TROWBRIDGE, EBENEZER, (Portage Co.)

Enl as Pvt in Conn Continental Line; fought in battles of Germantown and Monmouth. Br June 4, 1757, Wilton, Conn. D June 2, 1836, Palmyra, O. Bur Palmyra, O. Placed on Pens Roll May 2, 1816. Fur infor Old Northwest Chap.

TROXEL, JOHN (TROXELL), (Madison Co.)

Pvt. Enl July 19, 1776, and served 7 yrs. Enl in Capt Henry Hardman's Company in Frederick Co, Md. Br 1748 in Virginia. Mar Margaret Harpole in 1782. Children: Eva, Fanny, Jacob, Isaac, Adam, 10 in all. D 1835, Paint Twp, Madison Co, O. Bur on a little knoll on the farm under two walnut trees. No marker. Moved to Paint Twp, Madison Co, O, in 1810. Received land grant for serv. Farmer, dying on the farm given him by the government. Ref: Md Archives, Vol 18, p 51. Mrs. Jessie Martin, London, O. Fur infor London and Mt. Sterling Chaps.

TRUAX, DAVID, (Preble Co.)

Bur Friendship Church Cem, Dixon Twp. Three times aide-de-camp to Gen Washington; mentioned also in the new Hist, America, as a remarkable brave soldier and one of the prime movers. Ref: Mary P. Mitchell, Eaton, O.

TRUMAN, PETER, (Medina Co.)

Bur Hinckley, O. GM by West Reserve Chap. Fur infor Western Reserve Chap.

TRUE, SURGEON JABEZ, (Washington Co.)

Engaged as a surgeon on board a privateer ship. Br 1760, Hampstead, N. H. D 1823. Bur Mound Cem, Marietta, O. MI: Surgeon Jabez True, 1760-1823. GM by Marietta Chap by Revolutionary marker, Nov 30, 1906; marker stolen and replaced in 1920. Ref: Mass Soldiers and Sailors. Fur infor Marietta Chap.

TRUSDALE, JOHN, (Mahoning Co.)

Pvt in Capt Wm Black's Company, 5th Bn, Cumberland Co Pa Mil. Pensioned Br 1745, Ireland. Mar Hannah Robinson. Children: John, James, Jane, Nancy, Hugh, William, Mary, Abraham, Samuel, Margaret, Robinson, Joseph. Mrs. Sheldon Jacobs. D. A. R. Natl No 48107 is a descendant of John Trusdale. D 1819, Austintown. Bur Presbyterian Cem, Poland. GM Mahoning Chap, D. A. R. Bronze marker, May 30, 1916. Ref: Natl No 48107, Vol 49, D. A. R. Lin. Ref: Trumbull and Mahoning Co Hist, Vol 2, p 61, Pa Archives, 3rd Series, Vol 23, p 90, 785. Fur infor Mahoning Chap.

TRYON, EZRA, (Wayne Co.)

Enl 1777. Capt Ed Bulkley's Company, S. B. Webb's Regt. Served till 1783. Br 1760. Mar Anne Tryon. D 1847. 1818 pensioned in Wayne Co, services Conn Line. Ref: Natl No 42916, Vol 43, p 340, D. A. R. Lin.

TUCKER, HENRY, (Hamilton Co.)

Br 1760, New Jersey. D 1844. Ref: S. A. R. Fur infor Cincinnati Chap.

TUCKER, JAMES, (Trumbull Co.)

Pens—shows to be for Revolutionary serv in Vt Continentals. Bur center of Fowler,—but no stone. Ref: Cleveland Hist Society, gives as a Soldier pensioned in Trumbull Co, O. in 1818. Fur infor Chesney Chap.

TUCKER, JOHN, (Hamilton Co.)

Served in 4th Regt in Col Holmes' Regt, New York (see page 54, "New York in Rev War".) Br Passaic Valley, NJ. He with Henry Tucker (not of same family) established Aucker's Station, now Springfield Twp, where he lived and was bur (no dates found.) See Jones and Teetor's Hist of Cincinnati, p 42, and other local Histories. Fur infor Cincinnati Chap.

TUFTS, FRANCIS, (Warren Co.)

1775-77. 3 enlmts under different commands, Mass Mil; Enl Lincoln Co, Maine. Br 1744, Medford, Mass. Mar Lydia Blunt. One child Francis Jr. D Mainville, 1833, age 89. He was a pensioner 1832. Ref: Natl No 10536, and 25737, Vol 11, and Vol 26, D. A. R. Lin.

TULLIS, AARON, (Miami Co.)

Bur Rose Hill Cem, Troy, O. GM Miami Chap with bronze marker. Fur infor Miami Chap.

TULLIS, JOHN, (Logan Co.)

Enl in Company Capt Lee, 3rd Va Regt, in Gen Woodford Brig; also served under Col Marshall in War of Amer Rev; served in battle of Brandywine, also under Washington at Valley Forge. Br 1750, Prince William Co, Va. D Bellefontaine, O. Bur Powell Park Cem. GM by D. A. R. with bronze tablet in 1923. One of founders of Bellefontaine; given large tract of land there for Revolutionary serv. Ref: Compare Natl No 61183, Vol 62. Fur infor Bellefontaine Chap.

TULLIS, JOHN, (Warren Co.)

Pvt in Capt Philip Lee's Company, 3rd Va Regt. Br Va. Mar Nancy Dark. D Warren Co, O. Compared with John Tullis, of Logan Co, O, and altho the same serv, the Chap there was sure its record was authentic as bur there. Pioneer residents located grave and remembered man. Fur infor Natl No 61183, Vol 62, D. A. R. Lin.

TUPPER, ANSELM, (Washington Co.)

Lt in Benj Tupper's 11th Regt. Appointed Adj in Col Sprout's Regt in 1779, at the age of 16, and was at Trenton, Princeton and Monmouth. Br Oct 11, 1763, Easton, Mass. Parents: Benjamin Tupper. D Dec 25, 1808. Bur Mound Cem, Marietta, O. MI: "Maj Anselm Tupper—1763—1808." GM Marietta Chap by Revolutionary marker and gateway, Nov 30, 1906; marker stolen, replaced 1920. Ref: Chaffin's Hist of Easton, Mass. Fur infor Marietta Chap.

TUPPER, BENJAMIN, GEN., (Washington Co.)

Maj; Lt Col; Col; Brevetted Brig Gen. Br 1738, Stoughton, Mass (or Sharon?) D June 7, 1792, Marietta, O. Bur Mound Cem, Marietta, O. MI: "Gen Benjamin Tupper, 1738-1792." GM Marietta Chap by Rev marker and on gateway, Nov 30, 1906; marker stolen and replaced in 1920. Settled in Ohio in 1788; one of founders of Marietta in 1788. Member of Mass Legislature fr Chesterfield. Ref: Natl No 33082, Vol 34, D. A. R. Lin. Mass Archives. Continental Officers, Vol for 1777-79, p 138. Fur infor Marietta Chap.

TUPPER, SIMEON, (Summit Co.)

Musician, 1781-83, under Cols Benj Tupper and Joseph Vose; Capts Turner and Remich of Mass. Bur Fairview Cem, Boston Twp, Summit Co. MI: "S Tupper, Revolutionary War, Jan 5, 1771, Dec 2, 1845. Phoebe, his wife, Mch 10, 1774, July 17, 1842." In 1818 was living at Parishville, St. Lawrence Co, N. Y. but 1837 moved to Boston, Summit Co, O. where all his children lived. Fur infor Cuyahoga-Portage Chap.

TURNER, ADAM, (Mahoning Chap.)

Corp, Capt John Francis' Company, 1775, Muster in Pembroke, Plymouth Co. Br 1763. Mar Margaret Mizner (1766-1837). Children: John, Eliza, Conrad, Mary, James (mar Rachel Reed); Geo Robert, Charity (mar Henry Edsell; lived in Canfield.) D 1837. Bur Canfield. Ref. Trumbull and Mahoning Co Hist. Vol 2, p 15 and 96, Mass Sailors and Soldiers of the Rev. Fur infor Mahoning Chap.

TURNER, ALLYN, (Portage Co.)

Served 4 years. A portion of the time he was a prisoner in England, sent there with other prisoners because of lack of stockades. Released at the close of the war. Br Oct 1, 1761, Rehoboth, N. Y. D June 26, 1852, Hiram, O. Bur Hiram, O. A pensioner in 1840. Fur infor Old Northwest Chap.

TURNER, BENJAMIN, (Licking Co.)

Bur on Holler, now Lensing farm. Ref: Brister's Hist. Fur infor Hetuck Chap.

TURNER, JOHN B., (Hamilton Co.)

Br 1760, New Jersey. D 1832. Ref: S. A. R. Fur infor Cincinnati Chap.

TURNEY, ASA, (Lake Co.)

Enl when 18 yrs old, served throughout the war. Served under Gen Arnold and was in the battle of Danbury, Conn, when that town was burned by the British. Br 1759, Fairfield, Conn. Mar Polly Downs. D Sept 5, 1833, Madison, O. Bur Middle Ridge Cem, Madison, O. GM New Connecticut Chap. He purchased 100 acres of land in Madison, which is still in the family. Ref: Natl No 39305, Vol 40, D. A. R. Lin. Fur infor New Connecticut Chap.

TURRELL, JOHN, (Portage Co.)

Lived at Windham, where pensioned 1840. Fur infor Old Northwest Chap.

TURRILL, JARED, (Hamilton Co.)

Br 1757, Connecticut. D 1833. Fur infor Cincinnati Chap.

TUTTLE, CLEMENT, (Ashtabula Co.)

Enl July 24, 1780. Disch Dec 9, 1780, 5th Regt of the Line (p 204 Adp Gen report of War of Revolution for Conn.). Br June 29, 1776, North Haven, Conn. Parents: Jehiel and Elizabeth Dayton Tuttle. Mar Abigal Dutton, 1785. Children: Clarissa, Ara, Iva, Charity, Levi, Harvey, Rhoda Philecta, Abigal. D June 26, 1840, Morgan, Ashtabula Co, O. Bur Old Pioneer Cem, Austinburg, Ashtabula Co, O. MI: "Deacon Clement Tuttle, died June 18, 1840, aged 84, Abigail, wife of Clement Tuttle, died Sept 11, 1833, in the 70th year of her age." GM Family, marble slab. Agriculture. Ref: See Bureau of Pensions, claim Survivors File No. 16276, Dept of Interior. Mrs. Chas Wayne Ray, North Platte, Nebraska. (S. A. R.) Mr. H. E. Painer, Scranton, Pa. Fur infor Eunice Grant Chap.

TUTTLE, JOHN, (Portage Co.)

Enl as Pvt in June or July, 1779 to Apr, 1780. Capt Smith, Col Sprout, Sgt Artillery Companies. Placed on Pension Roll Mch 24, 1819. Br Apr 8, 1763, Sunderland, Mass. Mar Sarah Broad, July 20, 1790. (Second wife.) Children: James, Sarah, Joseph, Abigail, Lafayette, Betsey, Nelson, Hector. D in 1829 at Palmyra, O. Bur Palmyra, O. Ref: Bureau of Pensions Ref: Natl No 97191, D. A. R. Fur infor Old Northwest Chap.

TUTTLE, SOLOMON, (Athens Co.)

Entered service May 1775, was at taking of Ticonderoga by Ethan Allen, and of Ft St Johns by Gen Montgomery. Served as Minute Man 3 yrs. Was prisoner 1 yr 9 mo 3 da. Br Sept 3, 1757, Salisbury, Conn. Parents: Capt Thomas Tuttle. Mar Deborah Strong, about 1777; and 3rd wife Sarah (Lows) Seamons. Children: Almora; one dau by 3rd wife was Cyrena, see Natl No 48113, Vol 49, D. A. R. Lin. D Nov 30, 1830, Trimble Twp, Athens Co. Bur Boudinot farm, Dover Twp, 1 mile north of Millfield. Location of grave unknown to descendants who live near. No monument. Farmer. He built one of the first houses in Athens. Ref: Walkers Hist of Athens Co. Natl No 162130, D. A. R. Fur infor Nabby Lee Ames Chap.

TUTTLE, SYLVANUS, (Clark Co.)

Pvt and Minute Man in Morris Co, N J; also in Capt Keen's Company; Morris Co Mil, Eastern Bn. Br 1760, Littletown Co, N J. Parents: Thomas and Mehitable Tuttle. Mar Mary Brown 1784. Children: Eunice, Thaddeus, Mehitable, Thomas, John, Dorcas, Caleb, Zebedee, David. D Jan 1, 1843, or 1846 (?) on farm near Sinking Creek. Bur Family burial place on farm. Grave not platted.

MI: "Tuttle." GM Family about 1910. Came to Ohio fr Va. 1806, settling near Catawba, O. Moved to Moorefield Twp, 1808. Farmer. Ref: Certified copy fr Adj Gen, Trenton, NJ. also Natl No 61927, Vol 62, p 318, D. A. R. Lin. Fur infor Lagonda Chap.

TYLER, DAVID or DANIEL, (often confused as "Daniel Taylor"), (Highland Co.)

Br Feb 18, 1758. D Mch 10, 1843. Bur on S. Q. Duncan's farm near Greenfield. GM by Juliana White Chap in 1924. Fur infor Juliana White Chap.

TYLER, JACOB, (Lake Co.)

Enl fr New Haven, Conn, 1779 for 3 mos under Capt Mix, and Col Sabin. He made several enlmts and served as Sgt. Br 1762, Branford, Conn. Mar Abi Wheeler, Sept 11, 1789. D Feb 19, 1847. Bur Mentor Cem, Mentor, O. GM New Connecticut Chap. He applied for a pens fr New York. Fur infor New Connecticut Chap.

TYLER, JOHN, (Lake Co.)

Bur Fairfield Twp. Fur infor Waw-Wil-a-Way Chap.

ULPH, JARED, (or ULP), (Trumbull Co.)

Bur Ulph farm, located on the border of Sharon, Pa. No grave or marker is to be found on this farm. Ref: S. A. R. Yr Bk; Baldwin Library, Youngstown, O. Fur infor Mary Chesney Chap.

UNDERHILL, DAVID, (Huron Co.)

Bur Episcopal Cem, Norwalk, O. Fur infor Sally De Forest Chap.

UNDERWOOD, JAMES, (Highland Co.)

Pvt in New Connecticut Continental Line. Br 1752, Pa. Mar Margaret Campbell. D 1834, Highland Co, O. Ref: Natl No 78616, Vol 79, D. A. R. Lin.

UTTER, JOSEPH, (Clermont Co.)

Br 1773, Pa. Mar Margaret (br. 1742, d July 4, 1822). Children: Joseph, br in Pa, 1776, d 1839. D Nov 6, 1818. Bur Johnson Cem, near Mt Olive, Franklin Twp with his wife. Came to Franklin Twp, 1798. Ref: A. S. Abbott, Bethel, O. Fur infor Cincinnati Chap.

——————, (Coshocton Co.)

Two Soldiers. Unknown. Graves unmarked. One located near Franklin Church, Virginia Twp, one bur near Warner Church, Virginia Twp. Ref: Mrs. A. Ripple, West Lafayette, member. Fur infor Columbus Chap.

VALENTINE, GEORGE, (Seneca Co.)

Bur Woodland Cem at Bloomfield. GM Bronze marker, 1927. Fur infor Dolly Todd Madison Chap.

VAN BACHMAN, LAWRENCE OR LORENTZ, (Mahoning Co.)

Pvt 2nd class Capt Adam Stettler's Company, North Hampton, Conn. Bur Mahoning Co. Ref: Pa Archives, Series 5, Vol 8, pp 503, 547, 553. Fur infor Mahoning Chap.

VAN BENSCHOTEN, AARON, (Erie Co.)

Pvt in Capt Coulter's New York Company. At one time hostler for Gen Washington. Br 1746. Parents: Isaac Van Benschoten and Nellie Van Vliet. Mar Margaret Hoffman in 1773. D 1836. Bur Peaks' Burying Ground, near Ceylon, O. Fur infor Martha Pitkin Chap.

VANCE, C. JOSEPH, (Champaign Co.)

Pvt in Va Line, Col Daniel Morgan. Br Oct, 1759, in Va. Mar Sarah Wilson in 1781. Children: Joseph Vance. D May 16, 1809. Bur Oak Dale Cem, Urbana. Ref: Natl No 58041, Vol 59, p 16, D. A. R. Lin. Fur infor Urbana Chap.

VAN, CLEVE JOHN, (Hamilton Co.)

Pvt in Monmouth Co, N J Mil. Br May 16, 1749, New Brunswick, N. J. Parents: Benjamin (a Rev Soldier), and Rachel Van Cleve (she mar, 2nd, Samuel Thompson). Mar Catherine Bonham, 1772. Children: Benj, Ann, William, Margaret, Mary, Amy. D June 1, 1791. Ambushed and murdered by Indians. Ancestors came to Flatbush, N. Y. fr Amsterdam in 17th century. Thence to Staten Island to N. J.; to Washington Co, Pa.; to Losantiville, O., Jan 3, 1790, the day name changed to Cincinnati, O. Prominent citizen in Dayton to his death. Ref: S. A. R. Richard Montgomery Chap., Dayton. Fur infor Cincinnati Chap.

VANDEMAN, JOHN, (Ross Co.)

Pvt Pa Mil. Br 1754-5. Mar Mary? D Jan 17, 1840, aged 85 yrs. Bur Concord Presbyterian Cem, Concord Twp, Ross Co, O. MI: "John Vandeman died January 17, 1840 aged 85 years; Mary, wife of John Vandeman, d Dec 17, 1854, aged 91 yrs, 11 mos." GM by County Commissioners marker, bronze star marker, 1776. 1913 S. A. R. list. Ref: Pens list as recorded in offices of Commissioner of Pensions and War Dept, Washington, DC. Fur infor Nathaniel Massie Chap.

VANDERHOOF, CORNELIUS, (Athens Co.)

Enl Jan 1, 1781 for 1 yr, Capt Moses Sheppard, Col Jonathan Forman, Burrowes Morgan, N. J. Pvt. Br May 7, 1752, Monmouth Co, N. J. Mar 1st, Henderson (?), 2nd, Mary Paterson, Apr 6, 1791. Children: Maria, the only child, and by first wife, married Mordecai Jackaway. D Apr 22, 1844, Vanderhoof, Carthage Twp, Athens Co, O. Bur near Baptist Church. MI: "In memory of Cornelius Vanderhoof, A Soldier of the Revolution, Died Apr 22, 1844 in the 92nd years of his age." GM No doubt by descendants; beginning to crumble. Applied for a pens fr Uniontown, Pa, Fayette Co, Jan 16, 1824. His claim was allowed. First came to Ohio in 1804 fr Pa, but returned and lived in Pa a number of years. Came back to Ohio where he d 1844. Ref: Bureau of Pensions, Dept of Interior. Fur infor Nabby Lee Ames Chap.

VANDERVEER, JOSEPH, (Warren Co.)

Matross in New Jersey Mil, Capt Barnes Smock's Company of Artillery in Monmouth Co, N. J. Strykers List, p 796. Br 1759, NJ. D 1842, in Warren Co, O. Bur New Jersey Presbyterian Church, near Carlisle, Warren Co, in the south corner. MI: "Joseph Van Derveer, a Native of New Jersey, died 1842, aged 82 years." He was a pensioner and in his application made in this sec June 26, 1833, he gave his age as 74. Fur infor Richard Montgomery S. A. R.

VANDINE, MATHEW, (Butler Co.)

Br 1752. D Dec 15, 1837. Bur Seward Burial ground (private) in Butler Co. Location of grave on C. H. Shepherd farm at Westchester, O. (Formerly Sewards). MI: Date of birth and death. GM Old Headstone. Fur infor John Reiley Chap.

VANDORN, GILBERT, (Delaware Co.)

Bur Vans Valley (probably). Fur infor Delaware Chap.

VAN DORN, HEZEKIAH, (Pickaway Co.)

Served 1780-82 as a Pvt in Capt Jonathan Holmes' Company, Col Israel Shreve's 2nd Regt, N J Continental Line. Br in Monmouth Co, N. J. 1757. Mar Lydia Balser at close of Rev. Children: Catherine (b 1785); William; Hannah, Hezekiah, Jacob, Tyla, Isaac (b 1797). D in or near Circleville, O. 1800. Burial place not located, but probably on his homestead in Pickaway Co, whither he, his family, and mother came fr Green Co, Pa whence they had come from NJ. Ref: D. A. R. Lin Vol 70, p 179, Natl No 69504. and Vol 77, p 212. Natl No 76562. Also "The Van Doorn Family in America" p 619-20. Fur this infor Mrs. M. B. Goodwin, 426 E Park Place, Oklahoma City. Accepted by Jane Dailey, State Chairman.

VAN FLEET, JOSHUA, (Marion Co.)

Pvt in "The Levies Col Weisenfel's Regt. Entered the army at the age of 14. Br July 22, 1764. D Jan 8, 1849. Bur Pleasant Hill Cem. MI: "Sacred to the memory of Joshua Van Fleet Esq. aged 85 yrs. 5 months and 17 days." "Early in youth he espoused his Country's cause and officially devoted his life to her laws". Came to Marion Co, in 1832 and settled in Big Island Twp. Member of the New York Legislature and helped draft a law forbidding slavery in that state. Fur infor Capt William Hendricks Chap.

VAN FOSSEN, JACOB, (Columbiana Co.)

Said to be bur in Van Fossen Cem. Lived in Madison Twp, Columbiana Co. Fur infor Bethia Southwick Chap.

VAN GORDEN, ALEXANDER, (Butler Co.)

Pvt, Ensign and Lt in Capt John Vannatta's Company, Col Jacob Stroud's Regt, Pa Line. Widow pensioned. Br 1752, New York State or Del. D 1820, Butler Co. Name on memorial tablet at Hamilton, O. Ref: Natl No 86107, Vol 87, p 35, D. A. R. Lin. Fur infor John Reily Chap.

VANHORNE, ISAAC, (Muskingum Co.)

Enl as Ensign under Capt John Beatty, Col McGaw, in 5th Pa Regt in Jan, 1776. Taken prisoner at Fort Washington in Nov, 1776. Exchanged Apr 10, 1778. Commissioned Lt in 6th Pa Regt. Promoted to Capt June 10, 1781. Br Jan 13, 1754, Bucks Co, Pa. D Feb 2, 1834, Zanesville, O. Bur Woodlawn Cem, in Summit Sec, Lot 5. GM Marble monument. Removed to Zanesville in 1805. Congressman. Aptd by President Jefferson as receiver of the Land Office. Resigned in 1826. Fur infor Muskingum Chap.

VAN HYNING, HENRY, (Summit Co.)

Member Col Van Veghton's Albany Co Regt, N Y. Served 2 yrs in Continental Army. Br 1738, native of Saratoga, N. Y. Mar Hannah, 2nd wife. D Sept 14, 1823, aged 62 yrs. D Dec 25, 1840, aged 102 yrs. Bur Norton Cem. GM by S. A. R. Settled in Norton Twp, 1815, of Dutch origin; came fr New York in 1805 with 2 yoke of oxen and wagon; wife followed with him, on horseback, taking 2 mos time on journey to Buffalo, Erie, Pittsburgh, Canfield, thence to Summit Co. Fur infor Cuyahoga Portage Chap.

VAN NOTE, JOSEPH, (Warren Co.)

Pvt in New Jersey Mil, Co not given. See Stryker's lists, p 802. Br about 1746 in N. J. Mar Deborah (br and raised in N. J.). Children: Eleanor, br Jan 13, 1773, d July 19, 1841, wife of Lewis Bastedo. Is bur beside the mother. D Mch 28, 1838, in Warren Co, O. Bur Presbyterian Cem, near Carlisle, O, in northeast corner. MI: "Joseph Van Note, died Mch 28, 1836, in his 91st year. Born and raised in New Jersey. He was an old Revolutionar." (sic). Nothing more is known, as this date was taken fr the head stones while visiting the cem last fall. His wife is bur at his side. She was br June 9, 1755, and d May 28, 1820. Application for pens Mch 19, 1833, stated his age as 82 yrs. Fur infor Wm W. Neifert, Gen of S. A. R., Dayton, O.

VAN OSDOL (or VANNOSDOL, OAKEY), (Clermont Co.)

Br Dec 22, 1757, in N J. Children: Oakey, Robert, James, Isaac, Wright. D July 7, 1849. First bur in family cem on farm 1 1-2 miles southeast of Bethel; later removed to New Cem, Bethel. Was residing in Tate Twp at the age of 83, when receiving a pens in 1840. (Fr Pensioners Census in 1840). Farmer and lived on same farm on which he settled in Clermont Co in 1804. Fur infor Blanchester Chap. by A. S. Abbott, Bethel, O.

VAN SICKLE, PETER, (Delaware Co.)

Pvt under Col Rawlings, Capts Roberson and John Graines, NY Mil. Br Hunterdon Co, NJ. D Delaware Co. Bur Porter Twp. Ref: Natl No 91602, Vol 92, p 196, D. A. R. Lin. Fur infor Delaware Chap.

VAN SWEARINGEN, (or ger) JOHN, (Butler Co.)

Name on memorial at Hamilton, as a Revolutionary soldier bur in that Co. D 1852, while living in Union Twp. Fur infor John Reily Chap.

VAN VOORHEES, ABRAHAM, (afterwards the "Van" omitted), (Hamilton Co.)

Drummer. Pvt in Capt Ten Eyk's Company, 1st Bn of Somerset Co Mil, (p 482, Stryker's N. J. Men in Rev War.) Also Sgt, (p 473), in Capt John Sebring's Company, and in Capt Ten Eyck's Company, Sgt also. Br Somerset Co, NJ, first ancestor, Coert Alberts, in Netherlands ancestors, br 1600; d 1684. Son was Steven Coerts Van Voorhees, to LI Nov 29, 1660. Was magistrate in 1664-67. First wife unknown. 2nd wife Willempia Senbering. Children: Abraham Jr, Minah, Garrett, John, Jacob, two daus who mar Thos Higgins and John Rynerson. All the sons-in-law Revolutionary soldiers. Bur on farm 1812. Grave lost. Town of Lockland now covers site of farm. Farm was Sec 33, Symmes Twp, bought in Spring of 1794. Tax list bears his name in 1809 in Springfield Twp. The most outstanding record of family is that of Daniel Voorhees who served as US Senator fr Indiana during several terms. With his sons and sons-in-law built a double cabin which served as a block-house, as Indians were still troublesome. Was founder of town called Voorheestown 1798, changed to Reading in 1804. Ref: Natl No 11731, Vol 12, D. A. R. Lin. Vance Phillips Edwards, Berkely, Calif, Natl No 19434, great grandson. (See Yr Bk 1808, p 258.) Fur infor Cincinnati Chap.

VAN WINKLE, MICHAEL, (Preble Co.)

1776 Corp in Capt Isaac Halsey's Company, Col Jacob Ford's Regt, Morris Co, NJ Mil. Br 1736, NJ. D 1808, Preble Co, O. Ref: Natl No 77078, Vol 78, D. A. R. Lin.

VAN WINKLE, WILLIAM, (Highland Co.)

Bur two miles southeast of New Market. Grave marked. Fur infor Waw-Wil-a-Way Chap.

VARNUN, JAMES M. GEN., (Washington Co.)

After battle of Lexington, aptd Col of one of the three Regts raised by RI in 1776, in Gen Nixon's Brig. In 1778 commanded an expedition in Sullivan's expedition on Rhode Island. Br 1749, Dracut, Mass. D Jan 10, 1789, Marietta, O. Bur Oak Grove Cem, Marietta, O. MI: "General James Mitchell Varnun 1749-1789." GM by Marietta Chap by marker and gateway Nov 30, 1906. Fur infor Marietta Chap.

VAUGHN, GARNER, (Butler Co.)

Name appears on the tablet on the Sailors' and Soldiers' Monument at Hamilton, O, as a Revolutionary soldier. Bur Butler Co, not identified. Fur infor John Reily Chap.

VICORY, MERRIFIELD, (Clark Co.)

Sgt and drummer boy, Col Moses Hazen's Regt, Capt Hern's Company, Continental Tr. Regt known as 2nd Canadian and also as Congress' Own. Enl Sept 30, 1779. Disch June 30, 1783. Br 1762, Bennington, Vt. Mar Anna Nye (or Nie), Petersham, Vt. Sept 22, 1788. Children: Merrifield, Freeman, Elizabeth. D Mch, 1840, Springfield, O. Bur Greenmount, E High, Main Florence Greenmount. Location of grave, south half of lot 114. MI: "Victory." GM Metal marker. S. A. R. about 1904. Was in battle of White Plains. Ref. Pens 1818, Pens Bureau, Washington, D. C. Natl No 91990, Vol 92, D. A. R. Lin. Fur infor Lagonda Chap.

VINNEDGE, JOHN, (Butler Co.)

Name appears on the tablet of the Sailors' and Soldiers' Monument at Hamilton, O, as a Revolutionary Soldier, bur in that Co. D Aug, 1868; lived in Union Twp, may have been only a Wayne soldier, unable to verify. Fur infor John Reily Chap.

VIOLET, JOHN, (Pike Co.)

Br 1752. D Pike Co. O. 1847. Originally bur at Ferree Chap, but moved to Mt Gilead Cem nearby. MI: "John Violet, Born 1752, Died 1847, aged 95 Years. A man that fought for liberty, but now his soul rests in eternity." GM Stone. Fur infor Nathaniel Massie Chap.

VON ETTON, JOHN, (Mahoning Co.)

Capt of Rangers, 1778-1783. Came to Mahoning Co fr Pa about 1800 to Milton Twp. Ref: Pa Archives, Series 3, Vol 23, p 297, Trumbull and Mahoning Co Hist, p 185, Vol 2. Fur infor Mahoning Chap.

VOORHEES, ABRAHAM, JR., (Hamilton Co.)

Br New Jersey, 1760. D Reading, O, 1830. Ref: S. A. R. Fur infor Cincinnati Chap.

VOORHEES, GARRET, (Hamilton Co.)

Pvt in NJ Mil, Somerset Co. Sgt in Sussex Co; also Pvt in Continental Army. In Capt Kinner's Team Brigade (p 869, Strykers Men fr NJ in Revolutionary War). Br NJ. Parents: Abraham Voorhees and wife. Children: Ann, mar Mindert Wilson; Garret Jr, mar Jerusha Rugg, 3rd wife, perhaps, Jacob, mar Sarah Tucker, Richard, Harvey, Joseph, 2 unmarried; Katy, Hetty, Mary (mar Henry Brewer). One mar John Tucker. D and bur Reading, O. Farmer. Name on list of taxpayers in Springfield Twp, 1809. Ref: Vance Phillips Edwards, Berkeley, Calif, No 19434, S. A. R. Fur infor Cincinnati Chap.

VOORHEES, JACOB, (Jefferson Co.)

Pvt, Minute Man, in Somerset Co, NJ Mil. Pvt. Capt Peter D Vroon's Company, 2nd Bn, Somerset Co, N J. Pvt, Capt Conrad Len Eycs (?) Company, 2nd Bn, Somerset Co, N. J. Br 1742. Parents: Albert Van Voorhees and Adrianna Vanderroort. Mar Hannah Sickles; 2nd, Sarah Sickels. Children: John, James, Samuel, Stephen, Jacob, Richard, Mary, Catherine, Isaac, a dau mar Samuel Baxter. D Feb 2, 1838, near Smithfield, Jefferson Co, O. Ref: Miss Isabel Whitney, Circleville, O. Fur infor accepted by State Chairman.

Courtesy: Columbus Citizen.

MRS. MARIE STORTS ALLEN, LEXINGTON, OHIO, DAUGHTER OF JOHN JACOB STORTS, REVOLUTIONARY SOLDIER, AT THE AGE OF 87

VROOMAN, BARTHOLOMEW, (Lake Co.)

Enl fr Schoharn, N. Y. in Aug, 1776, in Capt Ephraim Vrooman's Company, Col Peter Brooman's Regt. Br 1761, Holland. Mar Hannah Mattice, Feb 15, 1792. D Dec 8, 1839, Concord, O. Bur Huntoon Cem, Concord, O. GM by New Connecticut Chap. He received a pens. Fur information New Connecticut Chap.

WADDELL, ALEXANDER, (Gallia Co.)

On stone near by: "In memory of Elenor, wife of Alexander Waddell, died Oct 9, 1827, in 75th yr of her age." D Sept 6, 1834. Bur Hilbert Cem, Green Twp, Gallia Co, O. MI: "Alexander Waddell, a native of Scotland, died Sept 6, 1834, aged 102. A member of the church 72 years. A man that fought for liberty but now his soul doth rest in Paradise." Fur infor French Colony Chap.

WADDELL, JAMES, Lt., (Ross Co.)

Lt in 1777 in 6th Pa Regt. Br 1733, Glaslough, Ireland. D 1806, Frankfort, O. Ref: Natl No 94094, Vol 95, p 30, D. A. R. Lin.

WADE, ABNER, (Muskingum Co.)

Bur New Hope Lutheran Cem, near Adamsville, Salem Twp. Fur infor Muskingum Chap.

WADE, E. DAVID, (Hamilton Co.)

Br 1763, NJ. D 1846. Came to Columbia, Hamilton, Co, O, in early yrs. Ref: S. A. R. Fur infor Cincinnati Chap.

WADE, ZEPHANIAH, (Knox Co.)

Commanded a Company of Riflemen fr Loudoun Co, Va. in 1777. He moved to Brown Twp, Knox Co, O, in Oct, 1816, with his son, Thomas. His wife was Irene Longly. Fur infor Kokosing D. A. R. Chap.

WADSWORTH, ELIJAH, (Mahoning Co.)

Pvt, Capt Sheldon's Light Dragoons during the whole war. Was at West Point when Maj Andre was taken prisoner. Br Nov 14, 1747, probably Hartford, Conn. Mar Rhoda Hopkins (1750-1832), 1780. Children: Henry, Rhoda, Frederick, Edward, George, Archibald. D Canfield, Dec 30, 1817. Bur Canfield, southwest of Youngstown. GM Mahoning Chap. Regular D. A. R. marker, May 30, 1917. Came to this state about 1800. Civil Engineer. Maj Gen in the War of 1812. His ancestor, Joseph Wadsworth, hid the charter in the oak tree, Conn. Ref: Mahoning and Trumbull Co Hist, Conn Men of the Rev, pp 271, 376, Natl No 17237, p 92, Vol 18, D. A. R. Lin. Fur infor Mahoning Chap.

WAGGONER, JOHN, (Sandusky Co.)

Pvt, served in Gen Washington's Life Guard till the close of the war. His Capt was VanHorn. Mar Sarah Minnie at Somerset, Perry Co, O, June 20, 1833. D Dec 15, 1842, Washington Twp, Sandusky Co, O. Bur Four Mile House, Sandusky Co, O. GM V. Warner, Commissioner. His wife was allowed a pens, Sept 13, 1853, aged 70. Fur infor Col George Croghan.

WAGNER, MICHAEL, (Fairfield Co.)

Bur Baugher Cem. Fur infor Elizabeth Sherman Reese Chap.

WAGSTAFF, WILLIAM, (Harrison Co.)

Virginia Mil. Br 1751. D 1840. Bur Cadiz Old Graveyard. Living in Harrison Co in 1835, aged 82 yrs. US Pension Rolls 1835. Fur infor Moravian Trail Chap.

WAIT, JENKS, (Franklin Co.)

Pvt in Capt Angell's Company, Col Hitchock's RI Regt. Br 1756, RI. Mar Sarah Brown (see Natl No 70866, D. A. R.) D 1824, Franklinton, O. Pens 1818, Franklin Co for serv as Pvt in Lexington Battle. Ref: Natl No 75341, Vol 76, D. A. R. Lin.

WAITE, BENJAMIN, (Cuyahoga Co.)

Pvt, in Capt Murry's Company and the Burgoyne Campaign. Br 1759, Hatfield, Mass. D 1814, Brecksville, O. Ref: Natl No 39906, p 333, Vol 40, D. A. R. Lin.

WAITE, CHARLES, (Clermont Co.)

Revolutionary Soldier who lived and died at Williamsburg, Clermont Co, O. Fur infor Cincinnati Chap.

WAITE, JAMES, (Clermont Co.)

Revolutionary Soldier who lived and died at Williamsburg, Clermont Co, O. Fur infor Cincinnati Chap.

WAITE, WILLIAM, (Lake Co.)

Served in the Conn Line. Enl May 26, 1780, under Col William Douglas. Br 1765. Mar Spedy Ferry. D Oct 3, 1844, Willoughby, O. Bur Waite Hill Cem, Willoughby, O. GM New Connecticut Chap. Fur infor New Connecticut Chap.

WAKEFIELD, LYMAN, (Trumbull Co.)

Bur South of Kenilworth, as given in the S. A. R. Yr Bk. Unable to locate a cem or grave. Fur infor Mary Chesney Chap.

WAKEFIELD, PETER, (Ashtabula Co.)

Enl 1781 as Pvt in Capt John Mills' Company, Col Runnel's NH Regt. Br 1764, Amherst, N. H. Mar Keziah Burns. Children: George Washington Wakefield. D 1847, Windsor, Ashtabula Co, O. Bur Windsor. Ref: Natl No 55405, Bk LVI, p 187, D. A. R. Lin. Fur infor Mary Stanley Chap.

WAKLEY, JONATHAN, (Trumbull Co.)

Bur Old Cem, Bristolville. Unable to locate grave; a number of headstones removed several yrs ago, and were lost. Ref: S. A. R. Yr Bk, Ohio. Fur infor Mary Chesney Chap.

WALCUTT, WILLIAM, (Franklin Co.)

Enl in 5th Maryland Continental, May 7, 1778. Taken prisoner Feb 10, 1781. Pensioned May 12, 1820, as a Pvt in Md Continental. Br Talbot Co, Md, in 1760. D June 23, 1833, Columbus. Bur Greenlawn Cem, Columbus. MI: "William Walcutt, Soldier of the American Revolutionary, took part in the battles of Stony Point, was at Valley Forge and the surrender of Cornwallis at Yorktown." GM Revolutionary Grave Committee with bronze marker, May 30, 1912. Moved to Ohio with his family in 1815 and settled in Franklin Co. Ref: Natl No 48093, p 45, Vol 49, D. A. R. Lin. Fur infor Columbus Chap.

WALDEN, ELIJAH, (Adams Co.)

Pens 1831, Ohio Roll for serv. Pvt, 2nd Company Light Inf, Lt Col Lee, of Va. Br 1761, Staunton, Va. Mar Mary Phillips. D 1833, Adams Co. Ref: Natl No 77721, Vol 78, D. A. R. Lin.

WALDORF, JOHN, (Trumbull Co.)

Bur Old Cem at Hubbard. Unable to locate grave. Many markers thrown out and many inscriptions obliterated. Ref: Baldwin Library, Youngstown, O. Fur infor Mary Chesney Chap.

WALDRON, JOSEPH, (Huron Co.)

In battles of Lexington and Bunker Hill. Taken prisoner and kept on British Man-of-war. Br near Boston, Mass. Had 3 sons. D June 15, 1822. Moved to Hartland Ridge, fr Bristol, Ontario Co, NY, June 2, 1821. Fur infor Sally De Forest Chap.

WALDRON, (or EN), PHILIP, (Vinton Co.)

Served in Virginia Line. Br in England. Bur in Salt Spring Cem. GM by grandson with inscription "Revolutionary Soldier." For infor write Milton S. Cox, McArthur, O. Accepted by Jane Dailey, State Chairman.

WALES, ELIAL, (Licking Co.)

Pvt, Continental Line. Br 1757, Windham, Conn. D 1821, Licking Co, O. Ref: Natl No 16106. Vol 17, p 42, D. A. R. Lin.

WALES, TIMOTHY, (Shelby Co.)

Joined Continental Army at the age of 17, was with Washington at Valley Forge, and served throughout the entire war. Promoted to Lt for services. Br about 1759. Children: Timothy, Thomas. D 1825 in Summer, about 92 yrs old. Bur in old burial ground, 1-2 mile east of village of Montra, Jackson Twp, on north side of the road. 3rd unmarked grave fr the first tombstone, at the south end of the first row of graves on the east end of graveyard. Had a military funeral conducted by Capt John C. Elliot and Lt Japthy M Davis of the Mil with a full Company of Mil. For services in war the Government gave him a tract of land in Jackson Twp, Shelby Co. Located in Shelby about 1836, moving fr Pa. Was of Welch Quaker descent. Received a pens of $800 fr Government which was envied by many of the old settlers. Fur infor by C. C. Elliott, a son of Capt John C. Elliott, who conducted funeral, who attended funeral when a boy of 10. Fur infor Lewis Boyer Chap.

WALKER, CHRISTOPHER, (Hamilton Co.)

Enl 1776 in Capt Henry Hardman's Company, Md Line. Br 1757, Baltimore, Md. Mar Rachel Wiltsu. D 1841, Cincinnati, O. Ref: Natl No 57023, Vol 58, D. A. R. Lin.

WALKER, DAVID, Lt., (Highland Co.)

While a resident of Salisbury, Iredell Co, N. C. he enl in Capt Erven's Company, Col White's Regt of NC Mil. Was commissioned Ist Lt, Nov 27, 1780. Br Oct 17, 1760, Chester Co, Pa. Mar Lydia Russell, Oct 15, 1785, in Bedford Co, Va. Children: James, Sarah, William, Jesse, David, John, Elias, Catherine. D Apr, 1842, in Lynchburg, O. Grave not located. Farmer. Fur infor Waw-Wil-a-Way Chap.

WALKER, JOHN, (Summit Co.)

Beginning Aug 1, 1780, served 8 mo as Pvt under Col George Rogers Clarke and Capts Wm McClue and Wm Chinneth, of Va. Br Oct 1, 1764, Carlisle, Cumberland Co, Pa. Mar Rachel Cochran, May 29, 1789, at Green Spring Valley, Hampshire Co, Va. D 1841 at Hudson, O, six yrs before the death of his wife, Oct 29, 1847, aged 79 yrs. Bur Stow, O. His family lived in Va many yrs; about 1801 he with his father, Robt. Walker, and 3 brothers came to Hudson, O. It is told that a pig brought with them to Ohio escaped and followed the trail back to Va. Fur infor Cuyahoga Portage Chap.

WALKER, JOSIAH, (Mahoning Co.)

Pvt in Capt Booth's Company 15 days. Conn Historical Society Records, p-181. On p 253, Naval Record "Yoeman," Apr 18-Sept 22, 1777. On p 232 Marine disch Oct 15, 1776, Capt Booth's Company served 15 da. Br in Connecticut. Mar Nancy Poke, who d in 1859. Bur Presbyterian Cem, Poland. Went fr Conn to Westmoreland Co, Pa, and in 1800 to Poland, O. Was a cousin of Mrs. John Struthers and brother of Nathaniel Walker. Ref: Dr. Grace Walker, of Salem, O, is a descendant. Hist of Eastern Ohio, by Sommers, p 110 and 456, Mahoning Co Hist, Butler, Vol III, p 520. Fur infor Mahoning Chap.

WALKER, NATHANIAL, (Mahoning Co.)

Capt Hinckley's Company. Enl June 30, 1777. Disch June 30, 1780. Children. One son, Isaac, maybe more. Bur Mahoning Co. Came and settled in Poland about 1802. Ref: Conn Men of the Rev, p 164. Fur infor Mahoning Chap.

WALKER, NATHANIEL, (Wayne Co.)

Pvt, 1776, in Capt James McDowell's Company, Col Montgomery's 4th Bn, Chester Co, Pa. Br 1751. D 1822, Wayne Co, O. Ref: Natl No 95609, Vol 96, p 199, D. A. R. Lin.

WALKER, PETER, (Hamilton Co.)

Served 1780 as a musician under Col Michael Jackson, 8th Mass Regt. Br 1765, Mass. D 1838, at Whitewater, Hamilton Co, O. Ref: Natl No 92997, Vol 93, p 313, D. A. R. Lin. Also S. A. R. Fur infor Cincinnati Chap.

WALKER, WALTER, (Ashtabula Co.)

Br 1759. Mar Lois (?) (d Aug 21, 1853, aged 85). Children: Josiah, Irwin Walker, possibly others, living in Wayne, O, North Creek Rd. D Apr 13, 1842, aged 83 yrs. Bur Roberts Cem. Ref: Military Roster, Wayne Soldiers ,p 188, Wayne Hist. Fur infor Eunice Grant Chap.

WALLACE, JOHN, (Butler Co.)

Pvt, 1777, Capt Wm. Payne's Company fr Albemarle Co, Va, where he was born. Br 1736, Albemarle Co, Va. D 1814, Butler Co, O. Ref: Natl No 79476, Vol 80, and Natl No 49983, D. A. R. Lin.

WALLACE, JOHN S., (Hamilton Co.)

Disch Mch 29, 1780, Virginia, p 282, Saffels Records. Bur Hamilton Co, O. (Filed by Mrs. Whallon, Cincinnati, O, who states not same as Butler Co record.) In command at Dunlap's Station, Hamilton Co, 1790; White's Station, 1792; was Auditor of Hamilton Co; entered farm sec 21, Sycamore Twp, where in 1795 was Surveyor. A sister, Sarah, mar Thomas Goudy. Ref: Olden's Hist. Saffel's Men in Revolutionary War. Ford's Hist, p 239, date of 1795. Fur infor Cincinnati Chap.

WALLACE, WILLIAM, (Guernsey Co.)

D age 86. Bur Cumberland, Spencer Twp, Guernsey Co, O. Ref: S. A. R. Fur infor Anna Asbury Stone Chap.

WALLACE, WILLIAM, (Hamilton Co.)

From Va. 2nd Lt Grayson's Continental Regt 1777; 1st Lt 1778; transferred to Gist's Continental Regt 1779; 2nd Lt 1st Regt Continental Artillery 1779; taken prisoner at Camden, Aug 6, 1780, then on parole to close of war. Entered farm sec 27, Sycamore Twp, Hamilton Co, O. Was commissioned Col—perhaps in State Mil. Ref: Heitman's p 567, and "Rangers on Frontiers" p 224, Westmoreland Co. Fur infor Cincinnati Chap.

WALLER, JESSE, (Noble Co.)

Pens roll of Morgan Co 1833 for services as Pvt, Virginia Mil. Br 1759, Virginia. Mar Mary Farley. D 1837, Olive Green (One in Noble Co the file says Morgan. Noble Co at one time was part of Morgan). Ref: Natl No 72425, Vol 73, p 149, D. A. R. Lin.

WALTER, CHRISTOPHER, (Guernsey Co.)

Pvt 2nd Pa Continental Line. Br Pennsylvania. Mar Mary (or Stotts) 1804-5. Pennsylvania. Children: Margaret, William, Mary, Katherine, Elizabeth, Rachel, Rebecca, Hannah. D Guernsey Co, O. 1834. Bur on the Hawthorne Farm, Guernsey Co, O. Farmer. Received a pens. Ref: Pa Archives 5 Series, Vol 2, p 892. Mrs Blanche Walter Johnson and Mrs Corda Walter Lofland, Cambridge, O. Fur infor Anna Asbury Stone Chap.

WALTER, JAMES, (Fairfield Co.)

Sgt "Forage Master." Br Maryland, 1759. Mar Margaret Ann Levan, of Maryland, after the Revolutionary war, date not known. Children: Nancy, mar Leevir; Elkanah, mar Rachel Decker; Catherine Ann Dent, mar David Levayzee; Eliz, mar Chas Stockard 1, James Gurley 2; James, mar Polly ——; John, mar Belinda Reese. D May 10, 1838, Lancaster, O. Bur Old Methodist Cem and City Burial Plot Lancaster, O. Cem converted into park, bodies moved to new Cem in Lancaster, marking on head stone obliterated and identification impossible. MI: "James Walter, died May 10, 1838, aged 86 years, 2 mo, 23 da." Jan 4, 1804 received transfer of 400 acres in Ky for serv in Rev War. Deeded in Frederick Co, Va. His name appears on a muster roll of a detachment of artillery commanded by Capt Lt Booker, belonging to the 1st Regt, dated Camp near Bacon Bridge, Apr 2, 1782, covering the months of Jan, Feb and Mch, 1782, which shows that he enlisted for the war. Ref: Natl No 12581 James Lincoln (Capt) Mass. Old Northwest Genealogical Quarterly Vol 3, p 74. Letter fr War Dept signed "Lutz Wahl,, Brigadier Gen, Acting the Adj Gen, by E. W. M." Fur infor War Dept The Adj Gen Office Washington.

WALTER, JOHN, (Guernsey Co.)

Pvt under Capt Parker, Col Wm Butler and Richard Butler, Pa Tr. Br 1758, Pa. D 1829, Guernsey Co. Ref: Natl No 91414, Vol 92, p 160, D. A. R. Lin.

WALTERS, FREDERICK, (Harrison Co.)

A Revolutionary pensioner living in Harrison Co in 1840. A Frederick Walter was Corp in Capt Joseph Gehr's Company, 3rd Bn Lancaster Co, Pa Mil in 1781. Fur infor Moravian Trail Chap.

WALTERS, PETER, (Noble Co.)

Pvt. Served in 3rd Regt of Foot, Pa Tr. Enl Aug 10, 1780. Bur Sailors' graveyard, Sharon Twp, Noble Co, O, a few miles west of Caldwell. Ref: Dr. A. E. Walters, Zanesville, O. Fur infor Muskingum Chap.

WALTZ, MICHAEL, (Wayne Co.)

Served fr Md, 7 yrs and 7 mo in Mil, fr Apr 1775 to Nov 1783. Br Berks Co, Pa. Parents: John Reinhardt Waltz, Hagerstown Md. Mar Elizabeth Gower, (d 1817.) D 1838, Sharon, O. Bur High Church, northeast of Doylestown, O. MI: "Michael Walz, a Revolutionary Soldier, Apr 1775 to Nov 1783, died 1838." Moved West; came to Ohio 1820. Fur infor Cuyahoga-Portage Chap.

WALTZ, PETER, (Wayne Co.)

Served fr Pa under Capt Mantz's Company, 5 yrs 8 mo. Was in 14 hard fought battles; served Apr 1775 to Sept 1780. Br 1749, Berks Co, Pa. Parents: John Reinhardt Waltz;. Mar 1st, Miss Moon; 2nd, Eva Milliron (1790) Westmoreland

Co, Pa. Children: John, Catherine, Christiana, Peter, David. D Apr 26, 1832. Bur High Church, Summit Co, northeast of Doylestown, O, east side. MI: "Peter Waltz, A Revolutionary Soldier, April 1775 to Sept 1780, died April 26, 1832, aged 83 years. Eva, his wife, died Jan 11, 1823, aged 60 years." GM Western Reserve Chap. Elder of Emmanuel's Church. Fur infor Western Reserve and Cuyahoga-Portage Chaps.

WARD, AMOS, (Hamilton Co.)

Br 1761, New Jersey. D 1837. Ref: S. A. R. Fur infor Cincinnati Chap.

WARD, BENJAMIN, (Ashtabula Co.)

Mar Betsey —— (d Mch 4, 1849, age 74 years). Children: Sylvester, Augustus, Benjamin, Matilda Wick. D Apr 14, 1850, age 86, 1 mo 8 days. Bur Hayes Cem, 1 mile northeast of Wayne Center. GM by family, with marble monument. Was one of the 2 Rev soldiers living in Wayne in 1840. Ref: Columbus Military Records. D. A. R. descendant: Mrs. L. O. Turner, Warren, O; Mrs. Flora Sweet, Conneaut, O. Ref: Wayne Hist, p 198, Mil Roster of Wayne Soldiers. Fur infor Eunice Grant Chap.

WARD, DAVID, (Darke Co.)

With Gen Wayne at Stony Point, and was the first man to scale the heights at the taking of this important crossing-place on the Hudson. This was on July 15, 1779. Br Virginia, Hardy Co. D Versailles, O. (at his nephew's home, David Ward). Bur Old Baptist Cem, 1½ miles south of Versailles. Fur infor Fort Greenville Chap.

WARD, EDWARD, (Perry Co.)

Enl 1777. Pvt under Capt Wm Duval and Col Baker Johnson, Maryland Line. Pensioned. Roll of Ohio, 1831. Br 1754, Charles Co, Md. Mar Lucy Wiggins 1776. D 1840, Perry Co, O. Ref: Natl No 76944, Vol 77, D. A. R. Lin.

WARD, JOHN, (Medina Co.)

Served fr Connecticut. Br 1739. D 1831. Bur Brunswick Center. GM Western Reserve Chap. Fur infor Western Reserve Chap.

WARD, NATHAN, (Ross Co.)

Soldier in Mass. D Ross Co. Bur in a field near the old State Dam, near Three Lock. MI: "In memory of Nathan Ward, Patriot of the Revolutionary War, died March 19, 1836, aged 85 years." Allowed a pens. Fur infor Nathaniel Massie Chap.

WARD, NEHEMIAH, (Clermont Co.)

Br New Jersey. Mar Elizabeth (?). Children: Elijah, Lewis, James, one or 2 others, names not known. D 1842 at Locust Corner, Pierce Twp. Was residing in Ohio Twp at the age of 84, when he received a pens in 1840. (Fr Census of Pensioners of Revolutionary Soldiers in 1840). Came to Clermont Co, 1815. Fur infor A. S. Abbott, Bethel, O, to Blanchester Chap, D. A. R.

WARD, RUFUS, (Knox Co.)

Enl (aged 17), in Sutton, Mass, 1776. Was in battle of White Plains, assisted in capture of Burgoyne and entire command at Saratoga, Oct 17, 1777. Corp. Br Jan 6, 1759, Shrewsbury, Mass. Parents: Jonas Ward (br 1720, d 1792), and Abigail Child Ward. Mar Elizabeth Barnes at Southington, Conn, 1787. Children: Mary, Elizabeth, Abigail, Emma, Jonas, Rufus, Truman, Levi Barnes. D Sept 8, 1834, Knox Co, O, Miller Twp. Bur Mount View Cem, Mount Vernon, O. GM by his family, slab monument. Farmer and Cooper. Ref: Genealogical Register of the First Settlers of New England Farmer, p 304. Lenox Library. See Natl No 14769. Fur infor Kokosing Chap.

WARD, WILLIAM, (Champaign Co.)

Col He fought at battle of Point Pleasant. His father, Capt Jas Ward, was killed, and William, Lt, stepped into his father's place and led his father's Company the rest of the battle. Br Dec 14, 1752, Greenbrier Co, Va. D Dec 24, 1822, Urbana, O. Bur Oak Dale Cem, in Urbana. Came to Urbana, O, with Simon Kenton, settling the town. Ref: Judge Middleton's Hist Champaign Co, Vol I, p 1088. Fur infor Urbana Chap.

WARD, WILLIAM, (Pickaway Co.)

Pvt in Capt Francis Taylor's Company of the 2nd Va Regt, commanded by Col Alexander Spotwood, Mch, 1777-Mch, 1778. (Va Archives Saf, p 274). Br Dec 25, 1743, in England. Parents: William Ward, Sr. Mar Nancy (Ann). Children: Charles, Elizabeth, Mary, William, Robert, George and Richard. D Nov 28, 1814, Walnut Twp, near Circleville, O. Bur Reber Hill Cem, near Ashville, O, on Snider J. Ward's lot. MI: "William Ward—Died November 28, 1814." Farmer. Ref: Mary Alice Stein, Worthington, O. Natl No 209204, Columbus Chap No 696. Fur infor Pickaway Plains Chap.

WARDEN, JAMES, (Butler Co.)

Mar Mercy, (d May 19, 1834, age 90 yr 24 da). D June 27, 1830. Bur Trenton, Butler Co. MI: "James Warden, died June 27, 1830, age 91 years, 19 days." Fur infor Col Jonathan Bayard Smith Chap.

WARDLOW, ROBERT, (or WARDLAW), (Brown Co.)

Fought at the battle of Guilford C. H. supposed to have been in the Virginia Mil. Br Augusta Co, Va 1750. Parents: William Wardlaw, Janet Harper his wife. Mar Janet Downing. Children: William, br 1771, Samuel 1773, Martha 1776, John 1779, Janet 1784, James 1788, Joseph and Hugh (twins) 1791. D 1824, Brown Co, O. Bur family Cem on farm near the present home of J. R. Wardlaw, White Oak, near Arnheim. Ref: Foote's Sketches of Va. 2 Series, p 141. C. J. Wardlaw, 196 W. Eighth Ave., Columbus, O. Fur infor Taliaferro Chap.

WARING, JONATHAN, (Hamilton Co.)

Br 1764, Connecticut. D 1836. Ref: S. A. R. Fur infor Cincinnati Chap.

WARNER, NOAH, (Ashtabula Co.)

Mar Mary (?) D May 5, 1831, Ashtabula. Bur Edgewood Cem, Ashtabula. MI: "Revolutionary soldier for seven years." GM by wife. Fur infor Mary Stanley Chap.

WARREN, EDWARD, (Greene Co.)

Pvt. D Aug 5, 1824. Pensioned Nov 5, 1819, under act of Mch 16, 1818; dropped fr Revolutionary roll under act of May 1, 1820 and placed on invalid roll. Annual allowance $96.00, same received $32.49. Fur infor Catherine Greene Chap.

WARREN, MOSES, (Cuyahoga Co.)

Pvt in Capt Seth Newton's Company; Col Abijah Stearn's Mass Regt. Br 1760. D 1851. Warrensville, Cuyahoga Co, O. Pensioned in Ohio. Ref: Natl No 92769, Vol 93, p 240, D. A. R. Lin. Fur infor Western Reserve Chap.

WARREN, THOMAS, 2nd, (Delaware Co.)

Pvt in the Pa Line. Br 1757, York, Pa. D 1838, Delaware Co. Ref: Natl No 28948, Vol 29, p 347. D. A. R. Lin.

WARRINGTON, JOHN, (Delaware Co.)

On Washington's Staff. Bur Baptist Cem. Fur infor Delaware Chap.

WARRINGTON, WILLIAM, (Delaware Co.)

Pvt under Col Matthews, Capt Snead, Washington Life Guards. Enl 1776 fr Va; 1777 was transferred to Conn in Chiefs Guard, under Capt Caleb Gibbs. Br 1751, Accomac Co, Va. D 1850. Bur Scioto Twp. Ref: Natl No 27253, Vol 28, D. A. R. Lin. Fur infor Delaware Chap.

WARTH, GEORGE, (Co. not stated.)

Guarded the Hessian prisoners who were sent to Virginia. Br 1747 near Winchester, Va. D 1812, Ohio. Ref: Natl No 52035, Vol 53, p 15, D. A. R. Lin.

WASHBURN, NATHANIEL, (Adams Co.)

Pvt in 1775 in Capt Abel Thayer's Company, Col John Fellow's Mass Regt. Br 1728, Massachusetts. D 1814, Adams Co. Bur probably Washburn graveyard, Brier Ridge, or near Manchester. Ref: Natl No 57495. Fur infor Capt Wm Hendricks Chap.

WATERMAN, CHARLES, (Butler Co.)

Pension Roll 1832, Butler Co, for serv as Pvt, 1777-81, under Capts Abraham Sheperd, Benj Bacon, Webb and Robbins. Br 1761, Gloucester RI. Mar Sarah Alpin. D 1840, Oxford, O. Fur infor Natl No 61958, Vol 62, p 327, D. A. R. Lin.

WATERMAN, GLADDING, (Wood Co.)

Pvt and Seaman. Sailor on "Oliver Cromwell" in 1778. At Siege of Boston and at Trenton and Princeton in Connecticut Line. Br 1759, Lebanon, Conn. D 1834 in Portage, Wood Co, O. Pensioned 1832. Ref: Natl No 26739, 30286, Vol 3, p 99, D. A. R. Lin.

WATERS, ABNER, (Trumbull Co.)

Enl Mch 1776 and served as a Pvt 11 mos and 23 days, in Capt Libbens Ball's Company, Col Larned's Mass Regt. Allowed pens in application Jan 4, 1833. Br Hebron, Conn, Apr 1758. Parents: Solomon Waters, Mary Anne Brewster. Children: Abner, Solomon, Lester, Hiram, Chene, Aruba, Laura, Lura, Phebe. D Dec 11, 1838, Gustavus Twp, Trumbull Co, O. Bur Gustavus, Trumbull Co, O, on family lot. Ref: See D. A. R. Lin Bk No 74-1909, p 112, 113, Natl No 73297. 20th Century Hist of Trumbull Co, O., H. T. Upton, p 477. Bureau of pensions, Pension claim S 3474. Fur infor Nabby Lee Ames and Mary Chesney Chaps.

WATERS, BENJAMIN, J., (Ashtabula Co.)

Br Otis, Berkshire Co, Conn, 1761. D Lenox, O. Nov 4, 1850. Bur Ray's Corners, Lenox, O. MI: Benjamin J. Waters, Died Nov 4, 1850, aged 89 years. GM Marble Slab. Ref: Mrs C. A. Hitchcock, Jefferson, O. Fur infor Eunice Grant Chap.

WATERS, THOMAS, (Adams Co.)

Bur Monroe Twp. Ref: Evans and Stivers Hist of Adams Co. Fur infor Sycamore Chap.

WATKINS, JONATHAN, (Athens Co.)

Enl Jan, 1778, as Pvt in Capt John Pugh's Pa Company. Was disch Nov, 1778. Enl Apr 1779. Served two mos Capt John Quinn's Pa Company. Enl fall of 1779 or 1780 on the Brig Fox, Capt James Buchanan. Br 1761, near Valley Forge, Chester Co, Pa. Mar twice. Names of wives not known. D in Athens Twp. Bur in the country, east of the city of Athens. Strenuous effort to locate grave has been futile. Farmer. Served on the Grand Jury of Athens Co in 1811. Applied for a pens while a resident of Athens Twp, May 9, 1833. His claim was allowed. Ref: Bureau of Pensions, Washington, D. C. Fur infor Nabby Lee Ames Chap.

WATKINS, WILLIAM, (Montgomery Co.)

Drummer in 3rd Maryland Regt, Lt Nathan Wright, in 1782; also same Regt, Capt Edward Squires, Lt Joseph Rutledge. Br 1740, England. Mar Rachael Mullem in 1768. She was br in 1740 in Scotland, and died 1839, Montgomery Co, Ind. Children: Charles, Joseph, Jonathan, William Jr., David, Caleb, Joshua, Hannah, George, Elizabeth, Amy, Rachael, Daniel. D 1821, Washington Twp, Montgomery Co. Unmarked grave in Hopewell Cem, now abandoned. Was a planter and farmer. Data fur by descendant (Natl No 23240, S. A. R), Winfield Scott Fox, 233 Edgewood Ave. Filed by Richard Montgomery Chap, S. A. R.

WATROUS, ALLEN, (Sandusky Co.)

Pvt 1 mo, Capt Jonathan Kilbourne, June 1, 1780; 8 mo Pvt, Capt Benton. Br in Lyme, Conn, 1708. Residence at enlmt, East Haddon, Conn. Application for pens, July 27, 1833, allowed. Residence at date of application, Ridgefield, Huron Co, O. GM by Commissioners. Fur infor Col. George Croghan Chap.

WATROUS, JOHN, Capt., (Ashtabula Co.)

Capt of a Company in Col Worthington's Conn Mil Regt, which repelled the enemy at New Haven in Tryon's Invasion. Br 1754, Chester, Conn. Parents: Gideon and Rebecca Watrous. Mar Rosannah Buck, 1780, dau of Justus and Rosamond (Parmelee) Buck. Children: William, Mary, Sarah, John Buck, Winthrop, Sylvia, Rosalinda, Nancy, Warren, Parmelee, Martin. D Sept 8, 1810, Ashtabula, O. Bur Chestnut Grove, Ashtabula, O. MI: Name and dates. John Watrous came of a long line of fine American ancestry; his great-great-grandfather, Jacob Waterhouse, coming to America 1630. Farmer and Miller. Came to Ashtabula, O, 1810. Ref: Town Histories, Family Documents, Conn Men in the Rev. Natl No 26622, D. A. R. Lin. Fur infor Mary Stanley Chap.

WATSON, AMORIAH, (Richland Co.)

Pvt in Conn Mil. Br 1750. D Nov 29, 1836. Bur Lexington, O. MI: "Revolutionary Soldier." GM Mary Washington D. A. R. in 1911. Ref: Mrs. Georgiana Fuchs, 69 Marion Ave, Mansfield, O. Fur infor Mary Washington Chap.

WATSON, THOMAS, (Fairfield Co.)

In 1779 in Capt John Gist's Company, Col Nathaniel Gist's 3rd Md Regt. Br 1756, County Down, Ireland. Mar Christiana Clelland. Children: William, James, Clelland, Thomas, Richard, Elizabeth, Jane, Christiana. D June 20, 1822, Fairfield Co, New Salem, O. Bur New Salem Cem, Thornville Rd, entering 1st tier on left. MI: "Thomas Watson, June 20, 1822, aged 66 years." GM by Slab. Family is Scotch, moved to Ireland before his birth. Ref: Natl No 91139, Vol 92, p 48, D. A. R. Lin. Fur infor Columbus Chap.

WATSON, WALTER, (Madison Co.)

Pvt. Served as a substitute 12 mos in Md., Prince George Co. Br 1761, Prince George Co, Md. Mar Rachel Stone, Oct 8, 1779. Children: James, Eleanor, David, Lydia. D 1822, Madison Co, O. Bur Paint Twp Cem, Madison Co, O. GM by family stone. Farmer. Ref: Maryland Archives, Adjutant Gen's Office, and Natl No 140172. Fur infor Mt Sterling Chap.

WATTS, JAMES, (Highland Co.)

Bur Rocky Springs. GM Juliana White D. A. R., 1926.

WAUGH, JOSEPH, (Ross Co.)

Was in Conn Continental Line. Mar Mary? Bur in Concord Twp, Ross Co, O, on Waugh's Hill, west of Austin. MI: "Joseph Waugh, died Jan 14, 1850, aged 86 years. Mary, wife of Jos. Waugh, died Aug 1, 1861, aged 87 yrs, 7 mo, 2 da." GM County Commissioners. Ref: Pens list. Fur infor Nathaniel Massie Chap.

WEAGER, JOHN, (Summit Co.)

Pvt, Col Van Ness' NY Regt. Br Dutchess Co, NY. Mar Elmira Stelle. D Copley, O. Natl No 55399, Vol 56, p 183, D. A. R. Lin.

WEARD, JOHN SEN, (Medina Co.)

Br 1760. D 1860. Bur Fairview Cem, Weymouth. GM Western Reserve Chap. Fur infor Western Reserve Chap.

WEAVER, CHRISTOPHER, (Champaign Co.)

Bur Terre Haute Cem. Fur infor Urbana Chap.

WEAVER, HENRY, (Butler Co.)

Joined a crew of Privateersmen and was among the first that ventured upon the ocean under the American flag. When cruising in the West Indies, after a desperate fight, captured a British vessel. In the act of boarding the vessel had 3 fingers cut off by a stroke of a cutlass aimed at his head. Later captured, made prisoner, carried to England, confined for 18 mos, released after the treaty and returned to NY. Br Apr, 1761, NY. Parents: William Weaver (1730-1777), a Revolutionary Soldier, and Jane Cassart. Mar, 1st, Miss Meeker, 2nd, Susan Ross Crane, of Elizabethtown, NJ. One child by first wife; a dau mar Daniel Keyt; by 2nd wife, Nathaniel, Leonard, Nancy, William, Abraham, John, Polly, Samuel, Eliza, Clark. D Aug 17, 1829, Madison Twp, Butler Co. Bur Trenton, Butler Co Graveyard adjoining Baptist Church. In 1790 came to Columbia, O. In 1792 located on a tract of land on the west branch of Mill Creek. Later settled at Middletown, and then on Elk Creek, in Madison Twp, where he remained until his death. He was Surveyor. He was Justice of the Peace, and in 1805, elected an Associate Judge of the Common Pleas Court. Ref: Natl No 17800, p 292, Vol 16, D. A. R. Lin. Butler County Biographies. Fur infor Richard Montgomery Chap, S. A. R.

WEAVER, WILLIAM, (Champaign Co.)

Bur Terry Haute Cem. Fur infor Urbana Chap.

WEBB, DAVID, (Trumbull Co.)

Br 1756. Mar Sarah ——, (who d Oct 6, 1852, aged 96 years). D Mch 26, 1829, aged 71. Bur Township Cem, Johnson. MI Above date and also "a soldier in the Revolution." Fur infor Mary Chesney Chap.

WEBB, SAMUEL B., (Greene Co.)

Mar Mary Bull, Silver Creek, 1828. Ref: Robinson's Hist of Greene Co. Fur infor Catherine Greene Chap.

WEBBER, BENJAMIN, (Co. not stated.)

Br July 30, 1748, Kittery, Me. Mar Hannah Parker, Nov 26, 1774. D in Ohio, no place stated. Ref: Mrs. Ada (Webber) Angell, Chicago, Ill., D. A. R. Fur infor Mrs. Lowell Hobart, Records at Washington.

WEBSTER, PHILOLOGAS, (Franklin Co.)

Served in Capt Asa Braif's Company, Col Hooker's Regt, Conn Mil, in 1777. Br Hartford, Conn, in 1758. D May 24, 1824, at Clintonville. Bur Cook's Cem, Clintonville. MI: "Philologas Webster, died May 24, 1824, aged 66 yrs." GM Rev Grave Committee with bronze marker, May 30, 1912. Came with his sons to Ohio in 1812 fr Hartford, Conn, by wagon and were 3 mos en route. Settled in Clinton Twp. Fur infor Columbus Chap.

WEESE, GEORGE, (Jackson Co.)

Has descendants in Liberty Twp. Fur infor Capt John James Chap.

WEIR, JOHN, (Co. not stated.)

Horseman, Continental army. Br 1756, Ireland. D in Ohio. Ref: Natl No 48446, p 206, Vol 49, D. A. R. Lin.

WEIST, JACOB, (Fairfield Co.)

Pvt in Capt Martin Bowman's Company, Pa Mil. Br Germany, May 6, 1730. Mar Mary Roshon, 1751. D Lancaster, Pa, Dec 4, 1806. Bur Baugher Cem, north of Lancaster, O. GM Elizabeth Sherman Reese Chap, 1927. Ref: Cora Gundy, Lancaster, O. Fur infor Elizabeth Sherman Reese Chap.

WELCH, DANIEL, JR., (Harrison Co.)

Served in Capt Robert Miller's Company, 4th Bn, Washington Co, Pa Archives, 6th II, 142-155. Served in Mil. Br 1763. D 1819. Bur Beach Spring Church. Fur infor Moravian Trail Chap.

WELCH, FELIX, (Wyandot Co.)

Served under Gen Washington. Br County Derry, Ireland. Mar Margaret Barnes. Children: Hugh, Martin, John, Thomas. D while on a visit to Wyandot Co and bur in Mexico Cem. Ref: Lang's Hist of Seneca Co. Fur infor Dolly Todd Madison Chap.

WELDON, JESSE, (Champaign Co.)

Enl 1777 in Capt Stedman's Company (Del Blues), under Gen Wayne. Was in battles of Brandywine, Poole, Germantown. Br 1759, New Castle, Del. D 1837, Champaign Co, O. Ref: Natl No 48406, Vol 49, p 190.

WELDON, ————, (Clermont Co.)

Revolutionary Soldier. Came to mouth of Boat Run, in Ohio Twp, Clermont Co, O, about 1800. D Clermont Co, O. Ref: A. S. Abbott, Bethel, O. Fur infor Cincinnati Chap.

WELLER, LODOWICK, (Hamilton Co.)

4th Regt of Orange Co Mil, Col Hathorn (p 168, 194, NY in Rev War). Br Orange Co, near Montgomery. N. Y. Parents: Possibly was son of Wm. Weller. One son was John B. Weller, br Feb 22, 1812, who was Representative in US Congress 3 terms. John B was Territorial Gov of Calif. 1852-57. Minister to Mexico, 1875. D 1875. Ref: Greve's Hist of Cincinnati, p 67. Bur Montgomery, Hamilton Co. Came to Montgomery in 1796. Owned land. Record at Court House of deed signed by Lodowick Weller. It is supposed that he removed to Hamilton or Oxford, O, in early years of 1800. Ancestral record same as that of William Weller. Ref: County Court House, Hamilton Co. Fur infor Cincinnati Chap.

WELLER, WILLIAM, (Hamilton Co.)

Name with enl men in Dutchess Co Mil, Cols Humphrey and James Vandeburgh (p 143, "New York in Rev War," by Jas. Roberts, 2nd Edition). His Captain was Wm Clark. Br New York State, Oregon Co, near Ft Montgomery. Parents: Descended fr Anna Catrina Moul, dau of Christoffel, who came to New York, 1710. Anna Catrina, br Nov 3, 1717, mar Henrich Weller. Children: Joseph, Jefferson, Eliza Jane, Amelia (Jesse, Mrs. Wm. Pierson), and perhaps Lodowick—it is supposed. D near Symmes Station in 18--. Came with family and four other men and their families, bought land fr John Cleves Symmes, in Sec--. Platted the town of Montgomery. Farmer. The ancestor of Henrich Weller came fr Holland to NY. His maternal ancestor, Christoffel Moul, mar Anna Juliana Servin. He served in Indian and Colonial Wars. Was Elder in First Reformed Church, Montgomery, N. Y, in 1730. Ref: Mrs. E. P. Whallon, Natl No 34924, D. A. R., Cincinnati, O. (Wyoming). Admitted to D. A. R. on Rev serv of Daniel Kitchell of NJ. Fur infor Cincinnati Chap.

WELLMAN, ABRAHAM, (Lorain Co.)

Pvt, Mass Continental Army. Br 1759. D 1849. Bur South Amherst. Fur infor Western Reserve Chap.

WELLS, BENJAMIN, (Brown Co.)

Mariner, Maryland State Navy. Had a hand shot off in serv. Came to Straight Creek, 1810, Franklin Twp, Brown Co. Br Wales, 1753. (Pens Records). Came with parents to Maryland. Mar 1st, (?) Rice, in Maryland; moved to Va and mar 2nd, Mary Aultz. Children: Nancy, mar 1st, Hezekiah Lindsey; 2nd, William Dye; 3rd, Allen Jones; Jacob mar Jermima Rice, Sarah mar Andrew Newman, Henry mar Elsie Devore; Adam, br 1805, mar Eliz Rice, 2nd Rhoda Stansberry, Catherine mar David Rice, Jane mar Samuel Smith, 2nd David Day. Diadema mar Cecil Shaw, Elizabeth d at age 18 yrs. Mary d young. D 1847, Brown Co, O. Ref: A. S. Abbott, Bethel, O. Fur infor Cincinnati Chap.

WELLS, BENJAMIN, (Co not stated).

(Compare one in Brown Co for reference). Br 1750, Hopkinton, R. I. Mar Rachel Hall. D 1834, Blackleyville, O. Ref: Natl No 171692, D. A. R. Fur infor Mrs. Lowell Hobart fr D. A. R. Records.

WELLS, CHARLES D., (Harrison Co.)

A Revolutionary pensioner living in Cadiz Twp, before 1813; aged 76 in 1833; Served in Md State Regt. U. S. Pension Rolls, 1835. Fur infor by Moravian Trail Chap.

WELLS, JAMES, (Fairfield Co.)

1st Lt, 4th Artillery, Continental Line. Br 1751, Frederick Co. D Fairfield Co, Jan 29, 1814. Bur Hooker Cem, D. A. R. in 1927, bronze marker. Ref: Cornelia Reiger, Lancaster D. A. R. Fur infor Elizabeth Sherman Reese Chap.

WELLS, JOHN, (Darke Co.)

Maj of Mass, served as an officer throughout the Revolution, and who became Adj Gen in Gen Wayne's Army, which located in Fort Greenville, and signed the treaty of Greenville, O. D 1796, Greenville, O. Fur infor Fort Greenville Chap.

WELLS, ROBERT, (Clermont Co.)

Page 213, Hist of Scioto Co, reads: "Robert Wells, a soldier of Revolution fr Va. After war moved to Bracken Co, Ky. In 1806 to Clermont Co, O. where he d about 1827, aged 84, Ancestor of Dr. Wells Teachnor, Columbus, O." Fr A. S. Abbott, Bethel, O, comes this data: Br in NJ; d 1830; came to Tate Twp. 1807. Children: Aaron, Solomon, Isaac, Nathan, Jesse, John, Robert (br 1788, d 1868), Eli, and Anna (mar James Callon). Accepting this infor Jane Dailey, State Chairman.

WELLS, ROBERT, (Erie Co.)

Served as Pvt in Capt Yate's Company', Col Whiting's Regt, Conn Mil. Br 1762, Huntington, Conn. Mar Ann Wheeler, 1786. D 1847, Vermillion, O, Erie Co. Ref: Natl No 102183, Vol 103, p 58, D. A. R. Lin and by Mrs. Lowell Hobart.

WELLS, TIMOTHY, (Geauga Co.)

Sgt. Disch 1778. His pens claim filed 1819 was allowed. Br 1747, West Hartford, Conn. Parents: Thomas Wells. Mar Esther Clark, 1780. Children: Timothy, Ebenezer, Chester. D 1820, Claridon. Bur Center Claridon on lot 96. MI:

"Timothy Wells, died December 29, 1820 in the 74th year of his life. A soldier of the Revolution." GM stone, marked by family. Was at battle of Germantown 1777, at Valley Forge, fought at Monmouth, suffered fr smallpox which injured his sight. Came to Claridon fr Hartland, Conn in 1781. Ref: Pens Records Vol 5, p 514, Natl No of Revolutionary Soldier in D. A. R. Honor Roll 74937. Fur infor Taylor Chap.

WELTON, ELIJAH, (Summit Co.)

Served all through the war, but after about 2 yrs, wounded in one arm by a poisoned ball, which disabled him fr active serv. After that he drove Washington's private baggage wagon. When his Capt and many of his men were killed, served for a time in Capt's place, which title clung to him. Records show served under Col Hooker, Capt Jesse Curtis Company. Br 1740, in Conn. Parents: Direct descendant of John and Mary (Upson) Walton, who came fr England about 1667 and settled in Waterbury Conn, in 1679. Mar Hannah (?) One son, Stephen, mentioned. D 1820. Bur Cem north of West Richfield, a part of his old homestead, and later given to Twp by his son. He and wife charter members of first church of Richfield, 1818, under name "Church of Christ," now the Congregational. When 79 walked to Ravenna one day and back the next, over an Indian trail bringing home 18 lbs of nails a blacksmith had made. Came fr Goshen, Conn to Richfield, O. in ox-cart, arriving Mch 1816 with his wife, son Stephen and his wife. Fur infor Cuyahoga Portage Chap.

WENTWORTH, BENNING, (Ross Co.)

Served 5 yrs as a drummer. Br Oct 2, 1763, Kittery, Me. Parents to be found in History of Kittery, Me. Mar Phebe, last name and date given in above Hist. She d Mch 17, 1851, aged 79 yrs. Children: See Hist of Ross and Highland counties. D Mch 3, 1852, Huntington Twp, Ross Co. Bur Huntington Twp, Ross Co, above Rallston's Run. MI: "Benning Wentworth br in Kittery, Me, Oct 2, 1763, d March 3, 1852. Loved and honored by all who knew him." GM Nathanial Massie Chap, D. A. R. small bronze marker. Movel to Huntington Twp, Ross Co, O. in 1816. Was the second schoolteacher in that locality, and his wife was the first woman school teacher. She organized the first Sabbath School in the Twp. Ref: Natl No. 25679. D. A. R. Descendants in Washington C. H. Chap Hist of Ross and Highland Counties. Fur infor Nathaniel Massie Chap.

WEST, BASIL, (Champaign Co.)

Br 1745 in Virginia. Bur in Honey Creek Cem, Jackson Twp. Fur infor Urbana Chap.

WEST, JOHN, (Brown Co.)

Pvt in Va Serv and paid on Apr 8, 1782, forty-seven pound, full amount for his serv. Br 1758, Fairfax Co, Va. Parents: Thomas West and Sarah Trammel. Mar Eleanor Edwards Children: William, James, John, Edward, Elizabeth, Lettuce, Sarah, Jane, Ellen. D Aberdeen, O. Aug 8, 1808. Bur Aberdeen, O. old Cem. Farmer. Came to Ohio in 1798, lived 4 yrs under Territorial Government. Ref: Natl No. 87678, Vol 88, p 206, D. A. R. Lin. Fur infor Lt Byrd Chap.

WEST, JOHN, (Jackson Co.)

Pvt under Lafayette and Washington. Br Mch 19, 1762, Bedford Co, Va. Mar Elizabeth Loyd (second wife), (br 1783, d 1875). D Feb, 1858. Bur on a hill near Samsonville. GM New stones placed by descendant. Land grant received 1832. Ref: D. W. Williams. Fur infor Capt John James Chap.

WEST, JOSEPH, (Highland Co.)

Enl in Col William Grayson's Regt of Continental Tr, 1777. Was pensioned 1840. Mar Judith Ballinger. Br 1747 in Virginia. D 1845, Highland Co, O. Ref: Natl No 73746, Vol 74, p 271, D. A. R. Lin.

WESTFALL, ABRAHAM, CAPT., (Carroll Co.)

Capt NY State Line. Capt was in Dunmore's Campaign (before Revolutionary War), at the battle of Grand Creek below Wheeling; was engaged in the battles of Bunker Hill, Stony Point, Trenton, Bloody Run and Brandywine, wounded at the battle of Bunker Hill; fought under Lafayette and Washington. Br Orange Co, NY, Nov 18, 1755. Mar Blandian or (Blandina) Van Etten, Feb 2, 1781. Children: Joseph, Hannah, Anne, Unice, Levi, Naomi, Simeon, Catherine, John, Thomas, Abraham, James. D Sept 5, 1829, Carroll Co, O. Bur on private ground near Augusta, Carroll Co. MI: "Captain Abraham Westfall, 1755-1829." GM Jane Bain Chap, D. A. R., Oct, 1924. Ref: Natl No 29209, D. A. R. Also see Natl No 17957, p 349, Vol 18, D. A. R. Lin. Fur infor Jane Bain Chap.

WESTLAKE, GEORGE, (Union Co.)

Bur Amine Cem, Paris Twp. Fur infor Hannah Emerson Dustin Chap.

WESTON, JOHN, (Summit Co.)

Enl at Harrington, Conn, as Pvt, then Sgt, under Capt John Cooke, and Col Samuel Canfield; also Capt Wilson and Col Gay of Conn Tr. Br Litchfield, Conn, Nov 19, 1755. D 1839, and bur by side of wife in East Akron Cem. He is a descendant of the Westons who came here in the 17th century. Mar Margaret Dean, of Litchfield, Conn, and came to Springfield, Summit Co, O, 1813, settled on Weston Road, where lived till his death. Fur infor Cuyahoga Portage Chap.

WESTON, SAMUEL, (Summit Co.)

15th Regt, Lt Col Stanley, Capt Hall's Company. Br 1779. D 1830. Fur infor Cuyahoga Portage Chap.

WHALEY, GEORGE, (Jackson Co.)

D Jan 27, 1821. Bur in Whaley Cem, Liberty Twp. Fur infor Capt John James Chap.

WHALEY, JAMES, (Meigs Co.)

Enl Dec 1776 under Capt Robert Bell, in the 13th Va Regt, commanded by Col William Crawford. In battles of Brandywine and Germantown. Br Dec 13, 1750, in Virginia. Parents: Edward Whalley and Elizabeth Mapy. Mar Mch 6, 1808 to Elizabeth Page Hall. Children: James, Elizabeth, Anne, Rebecca, William H., Harriet, Kitty Ann, Lucretia, Almira and David Charles. D Dec 4, 1840, Salisbury, Meigs Co, O. Bur Beech Grove Cem, Pomeroy, O. MI: "James Whaley Rev soldier br 1750 d 1840." Monument erected by his son and D. A. R. marker Apr 1914, Capt in the War of 1812. Later moved with his family to Wood Co, and afterwards to Meigs Co, O. Ref: Bureau of Pensions and Pennsylvania Archives; Natl No 95144, Vol 96. Fur infor Return Jonathan Meigs Chap.

WHEELER, ASA, SR., (Huron Co.)

Bur Clarksfield Twp. Fur infor Sally De Forest Chap.

WHEELER, JOHN, (Clermont Co.)

In 1840, was residing with William Wheeler, in Ohio Twp, Clermont Co, O. Aged 88 and drawing pens for serv. Br 1752. Fur infor Census of Pensions of 1840, copied by State Chairman.

WHEELER, JOHN, (Ross Co.)

Corp in 1777. Later Sgt in Capt Dorsey's Company 1st Artillery Regt 1777-80. Maryland Continental Tr. Br 1760. Maryland. Mar Tabitha Warrington in 1791. D 1832, Ross Co. Ref: Natl No 80722, Vol 81, D. A. R. Lin.

WHEELER, SAMUEL, (Lucas Co.)

Capt Stephen Bloom's Company Mil. Br 1757, Pa. D 1818, Ohio. Ref: p 300, Vol 32, D. A. R. Lin.

WHEELER, STEPHEN, (Hamilton Co.)

Pvt in Col Elias Dayton's NJ Mil. Br New Jersey 1749. Mar Rhoda Spinning. D Cincinnati, 1806. Natl No 72211, p78, Vol 73, D. A. R. Lin.

WHIPPLE, ABRAHAM COM. (Washington Co.)

Commodore of Rhode Island fleet in June 1775. Commissioned Capt in Navy, Dec 7, 1776. Commodore of fleet of vessels during summer of 1779. Br Sept 27, 1733, Providence, R. I. D May 27, 1819, Marietta, O. Bur Mound Cem. MI: "Comm. Abraham Whipple 1733-1819." GM by Marietta Chap with marker and gateway. Nov 30, 1906; marker stolen and replaced in 1820. First American to fire upon British on sea. Two days before battle of Bunker Hill, he attacked two British vessels on Narragansett Bay, captured one and forced the other to retire. First to fly the American flag on the Thames. Advanced large sums of money for naval supplies and served without pay fr Dec 1776 to Dec 1782. Fur infor Marietta Chap.

WHIPPLE, EIZRA, (Trumbull Co.)

Bur Mesopotamia. Did not find grave, many inscriptions obliterated. Ref: Baldwin Library Youngstown, O. by Miss Kyle. Fur infor Mary Chesney Chap.

WHIPPLE, ZEBULON, (Portage Co.)

Conn Mil. Placed on Pens Roll July 20, 1833. Bur Streetsboro, O. Drew pens at Ravenna, O. in 1840. Fur infor Old Northwest Chap.

WHIPPLE, ZEBULION, (Stark Co.)

Pvt in Capt Dana's Company; Col McClellan's Regt Conn Line. Br 1764 Plainfield, Conn. D 1851. Bur West Lawn Cem. Canton, O. Ref: Authority: Hist of Stark Co by William Henry Perrin, Natl No. 89780, Vol 90, D. A. R. Lin. Fur infor Canton Chap.

WHITCOMB, ANTHONY, (Hamilton Co.)

Br 1766, Vermont. D 1809. Fur infor Cincinnati Chap.

WHITCOMB, JOHN, (Hamilton Co.)

Br 1761, Vermont. D 1822. Fur infor Cincinnati Chap.

WHITE, ADAM, (Brown Co.)

Served in the Rev, substituting himself in his father's stead. Br July 13, 1765. Parents: Peter White and Eva (Fox). Mar Susanna Osburne. Children: Daniel, Solome, Eva, Catherine, Nancy, Adam, Christopher, Anna. D Mch 28, 1854, on the farm (near Hiett's Chapel) in Huntington Twp, Brown Co. Bur Family Cem. Came to Ohio 1795, lived for five yrs near the mouth of Eagle Creek, then moved on to the farm near Hietts Chapel, where he died and where his descendants lived for many years. Ref: Hist Brown Co, Ohio 1883, p 177. Fur infor Taliaferro Chap.

WHITE, CHARLES, (Highland Co.)

Pvt. Served in the Va Tr in Capt Kendall's Company; Col Skinner's Regt. Br Sept 5, 1761, Westmoreland Co., Va. Mar 1st Sarah Monroe, 2nd Charlotte Downs. Children: 1st wife: William, John, Betsy, Daniel, Samuel, George. 2nd wife: Deborah, Kitty, Linda, Charles, Eliza, Henry, Nancy, Polly, Jahana, James,

Garrett. D Oct 19, 1854, Greenfield O. Bur Greenfield Cem northeast of Greenfield O. Sec 2, Lot 138. MI: "Charles White a soldier of the Revolution born in Westmoreland Co Va. Sept 5, 1761 was present at the surrender of Cornwallis at Yorktown Va. Died Oct 19th. 1854, aged 93 years. 6 weeks." GM Juliana White Chap Official marker, with name plate, June 30, 1923. Papers on file in the pens dept show that he participated in the siege and Battle of Yorktown. Farmer. His pens was allowed for 13 months in the Va Tr. Ref: Ohio Pension Roll p 132. Fur infor Juliana White and Waw-Wil-a-Way Chaps.

WHITE, EDWARD, II, (Hamilton Co.)

See p 182 "N Y in Rev" says Pvt. Br England. Children one Jacob, proprietor of White's Station (also Rev Soldier). Bur Whites Station, Hamilton Co., O. MI: "Edward White II.' Br 1746 d 1798.' Later the family removed to Ky, but soon returned to Ohio. Ref: Olden's Hist and HB Teetor, p 30, 34, Natl No 34924, D. A. R. Fur infor Cincinnati Chap.

WHITE, HATFIELD, (Washington Co.)

Maj. At opening of Rev was an officer in a company of Minute Men. Was in the first battle of the war. Br Jan 3, 1739, Wenham, Mass. D Dec 13, 1818, Waterford, O. Bur Cedar Ridge Cem near Waterford, Washington Co. MI: "Major Hartfield White 1739-1818." GM Marietta Chap with Rev marker in 1920. Became a member of Ohio Company in 1787 and was commissary of the first group of settlers to come to Marietta. He located at Waterford, where he was one of the proprietors of the first mill in Ohio. Ref: Natl No. 50797, D. A. R. Fur infor Marietta Chap.

WHITE, HENRY, (Trumbull Co.)

D Feb 21, 1858. Bur Center of Southington. MI: "Henry White Died Feb 21, 1858 aged 93 years." GM by Family. Ref: Cleveland Historical Library Rev Soldiers bur in Trumbull Co and Descendants. Fur infor Mary Chesney Chap.

WHITE, JOHN, Maj., (Meigs Co.)

Maj. Br Pomfret, Conn. Oct 21, 1758. Mar Priscilla Duval. Blockhouse, Marietta 1780. Children: Mrs. Samuel Fair, of Chester. D Chester, O. Apr 17, 1845. Bur Southwest part of yard, near evergreen tree. MI: "He was a soldier of the Revolution, a friend to his country and all mankind, and died in the hope of a glorious resurrection." GM headstone by daughter. One of the body guard of Maj Andre, lived in the block house at Marietta 1789 serving at time as scout. Was substitute for his uncle, Amos Grosvenor; pensioned 1832 for 2 yrs serv as Pvt and Sgt in Conn Line. Natl No 62524, Vol 63, p 175. D. A. R. Lin. Fur infor. Return Jonathan Meigs Chap.

WHITE, SAMUEL, (Franklin Co.)

Served seven yrs in Revolutionary War. Was scalped at Stony Point by Indian, and left for dead. Br Virginia about 1750. D fr injuries received in a runaway. Bur Union Cem near Briggsdale. GM Rev Grave Committee with bronze marker May 30, 1912. Came fr Virginia to Ohio in 1805. Fur infor Columbus Chap.

WHITE, THOMAS, (Hamilton Co.)

Capt of Lancaster Co Pa Mil. Removed fr Lancaster Co Pa to Clermont Co, O and d in Cincinnati, O. Burial place not stated. Ref: Natl No 95806, Vol 96, p 258, D. A. R. Lin.

WHITE, WM., (Montgomery Co.)

Enl 1776 Capt Alex Howard Magruder's Company, Col James Sims Regt, 11th Bn. Br 1736, Prince George's Co Md. Mar Elizabeth Smith 1756. D 1780, Montgomery Co. Ref: Natl No 80303, Vol 81, D. A. R. Lin.

WHITEMAN, BENJAMIN, (Greene Co.)

Br 1759. D July 30, 1852. Bur Clinton. Beaver Creek, 1803. Ref: Robinson's History of Greene Co. Fur infor Catherine Greene Chap.

WHITEMAN, SAMUEL, (Mahoning Co.)

Sgt in Conn. Pvt in Maj Skinner's Army in Conn. Pensioned Bur Austintown, Mahoning Co. Settled in Austintown and developed salt springs. Ref: Sanderson's Hist, p 170. Trumbull and Mahoning Co, Vol 11, p 129, 130. Conn Men of the Rev, p 49, 246, 368, 476, 629. Fur infor Mahoning Chap.

WHITMER, PETER, (Perry Co.)

Pvt Northumberland Co, Pa. Br Jan 11, 1760, Northumberland Co, Pa. Parents: Peter Whitmer Sr. Mar Mary Magdalene Overmyer, Dec 19, 1787. Children: Jacob, George, Sarah, Mary Magdaline, Elizabeth, Lydia, Peter Jr., Solomon, John, Daniel, Susannah. D Nov 19, 1835 near New Reading, Perry Co, O. Bur New Reading Cem, Perry Co, O. MI: Name and dates. Frequently mentioned in Lumis Annals of Buffalo Valley. Farmer. Ref: Josephine C Diefinbach. Akron, O. Pa Archives Series V, Vol IV, p 384 and 697. Fur infor Cuyahoga Portage Chap.

WHITTIER, ANDREW, (Guernsey Co.)

Br 1716 in Germany. Mar Mrs Mary MacKay. D 1840. Jackson Twp, Guernsey Co, O. 124 yrs old). Was first bur in a cem on the creek near Byesville, Guernsey Co. The action of the water washed some of the bodies out. Friends and relatives removed the body of Whittier to Cem at Old Cambridge Church graveyard about 1894, under auspices of Cambridge G. A. R. Post 343, near center of Cem. Came to this country fr Germany, and settled at Baltimore when it was only a village. Lived later in Va and Pa. Coming fr Pa to Guernsey Co, O or that part of it which was a military reservation for Revolutionary soldiers. (Jackson Twp) shortly after the war of 1812. A story that has been handed down through some of the families residing in this rural community concerning this old Revolutionary soldier is as follows: "The year before his death, when 123 years old, during wheat harvest he cut with a sickle and put up unaided, twelve dozen sheaves of wheat a feat rarely equalled by many men in the prime of life. Farmer. Ref: Histories of Guernsey Co and others. Fur infor Anna Asbury Stone Chap.

WHITZELL, MARTIN, (Mahoning Co.)

Ranger in Capt John Whitzell's Company Monongahela Co Regt, 1778, (Pa Archives Series 6, Vol 11, p 860.) Children: Mary, mar Saml Gilbert; Susan, mar-Jacob Wise, Catherine mar Jacob Dustman. Bur Canfield. Came to Canfield about 1802 fr Lynn Twp, Northampton Co., Pa. Ref: Dr. Truesdales Hist of Canfield. Fur infor Mahoning Chap.

WICK, WILLIAM, (Mahoning Co.)

Pvt in N. J. Mil, Pensioned Sept 17, 1833. Br Feb 25, 1759 in either Long Island or N J. Came fr the latter place to Youngstown. Mar Phoebe Wick, dau of Lemuel Wick, L. D. Children: Unknown, except Wm Jr. D Youngstown Bur Old Hill Cem, Youngstown, O, southwest corner among the graves removed fr old burying ground. GM by Mahoning Chap D. A. R. May 30, 1915. Came to Youngstown fr NJ in about 1800 where he settled. Ref: NJ Men of the Rev p 819, N. J. Mil. E. M. M. P., F. J. Louise and S. T. Wick and Mrs W. B. Curtis, Youngstown. Fur infor Mahoning Chap

WICKERSHAM, PETER, (Washington Co.)

Pvt Capt Wright's Company of Pa. Wounded in serv. Br 1756. D 1841. Ref: Natl No 22326, Vol 23, p 113, D. A. R. Lin.

WICKHAM, JOSEPH, (Athens Co.)

Br England, 1759. Mar in Vermont. Children: John (child of 1st wife), Joseph. D in Rome Twp. Athens Co, May 3, 1833. Bur Pioneer Cem at Mouth of Federal Creek, Rome Twp. MI: Illegible because of disintegration of stone. GM. Descendants. Br in England, was serving on an English vessel, when the Revolutionary War broke out. He deserted joined the American army and served until the close of hostilities. Ref: Walker's Hist of Athens Co, p 508. Hist of Hocking Valley p 647. The Continental Atlas p 74. Fur infor Nabby Lee Ames Chap.

WICKHAM, WILLIAM, (Monroe Co.)

Pvt in Capt Isaiah Vail's Company N Y Mil, Col James McClaughey's Ulster Co Regt. Br Ulster Co., N. Y. Children: One dau was Margaret. D Monroe Co., O. Ref: Natl No 102648, Vol 103, p 199, D. A. R. Lin.

WILBER, JOSEPH, (Geauga Co.)

Pvt Capt Jonathan Shaw's Company, Col Daggett's Regt. Entered serv Aug 21, 1778. Disch Apr 15, 1779, serv 24 days in R. I. Br 1759. Mar 1st Hannah (?) 2nd Sally Burnett. Children: Ithil, Hannah, Joseph, Eleazer, Polly, Betsey. D South Newbury, O. Sept 26, 1830. Bur South Newbury No. 1. MI: "Joseph Wilber died September 26, 1830 aged 71 years. "Blessed are the dead that die in the Lord." GM by Family. Came to Newbury 1816 or 1817. Children br in Raynham Mass. Conn Men Rev 452, 504 Vital Records Raynham, Mass. Fur infor Taylor Chap.

WILCOX, ————, (Huron Co.)

D and bur in Ruggles Twp. Ref: "Firelands Pioneer" Vol 5, p 56. Fur infor-Sally De Forest Chap.

WILCOX, HOSEA JR., (Summit Co.)

Enl at Canaan, Capt Jas Watrous Company, Col Buell's Regt, which went north under Gen Montgomery; served in hospital, as services needed there, and not in any engagements. Br 1754, Simsbury, (Salmon Brook) Granby Twp, Conn. Parents Miss (Griffin) Wilcox. Moved to Litchfield, Conn. Mar Abigail Mills, Sept 1774, (age 17). Children, nine. D 1832, Feb 29, age 78 yrs. Bur Middlebury Cem, Ohio by wife. 1802 came to Morgan, O, when 1811 or 12 came to Tallmadge. Fur infor Cuyahoga Portage Chap.

WILCOX, JEHIAL, (Delaware Co.)

Pvt under Col Noah Phelps, Capt Jonathan Humphrey Conn Tr. Bur Norton Cem. Grave marked. Pensioned. Fur infor Delaware Chap.

WILCOX, JEREMIAH, (Trumbull Co.)

M. D. Br Simsbury, Conn, Dec 1760. Mar Amelia G, (br in New Haven, Conn. Jan 14, 1759. D in Vernon, O. Dec 25, 1838, aged 80 yrs.) D Vernon, O. Nov. 7, 1823, aged 64 yrs. Bur Old Cem south of center of Vernon. GM by their son, Dr. J. G. Wilcox, Richfield, O. Moved to Ohio in 1806. Fur infor Mary Chesney Chap.

WILEY, SAMUEL, (Coshocton Co.)

Pvt in Capt Watson's Company. Br Mass. Mar Elizabeth Hull. D Coshocton Co. Ref: Natl No 59457, Vol 60, p 155, D. A. R. Lin.

WILEY, SAMUEL, (Miami Co.)

Served as aide to Gen Washington during the Rev. Also Pvt in Capt Gibson's Company, Col Johnston's Regt, Pa line. Br Cecil Co, Md, 1749. D Miami Co., O Bur Lower Piqua Cem, and body was moved to Forrest Hill. Arrived in Piqua on the day the Dilbone's were killed by the Indians, Aug 18, 1813. Ref: Natl No 86109, Vol 87, p 35. D. A. R. Lin. Fur infor Piqua Chap.

WILEY, WILLIAM, (Noble Co.)

Came fr Pa to Sharon Twp. Bur Old Cem at Sharon, O. Fur infor Mrs. L. B. Frazier Caldwell, O.

WILKINSON, JAMES, Major, (Butler Co.)

Name appears on memorial tablet for Rev soldiers at Hamilton, Butler Co., O. though a non resident. Commandant at Fort Hamilton; later involved in Aaron Burr affair, no further data available. Fur infor John Reily Chap.

WILL, GEORGE, (Ross Co.)

1st Lt 6th Pa Regt. Served 11 yrs in English and Prussian Serv. Br May 3, 1747, in Germany. Parents (Suppose Eng). Mar Susanne Hunsucker. D 1828, Adelphi, Ross Co., O. Bur Old Cem near center. GM Family, early yrs. Ref: Natl No 83925 D. A. R. Lin. Hist of 6th Pa Regt very scant as captured with all its records in disaster at Fort Washington. Fur infor Jane Dailey, State Chairman.

WILLCOX, JOSIAH, (Cuyahoga Co.)

Pvt. Mass. Br 1753. D 1844. Bur Rice Cem, Brecksville. Fur infor Western Reserve Chap.

WILLEY, ALLEN JR., (Cuyahoga Co.)

Pvt. Capt Webber's Company, Col Hobort's Regt. NH Tr Battle of Bennington. Br 1760 Lempster, N. H. D 1835, Cleveland, O. Ref: Natl No 81994, Vol 82, D. A. R. Lin.

WILLIAMS, ABRAM, (Delaware Co.)

Served with Conn Tr. Fought at Battle of Fort Griswold, Conn. Bur Oak Grove Cem, Delaware, O. Fur infor Delaware Chap.

WILLIAMS, BENJAMIN, (Hamilton Co.)

Br 1758, Maryland. D 1839. Ref: S. A. R. Fur infor Cincinnati Chap.

WILLIAMS, CHARLES, (Coshocton Co.)

Bur Oak Ridge Cem, Coshocton, O. Ref: Mrs A. Ripple, West Lafayette, O. member of Coshocton Chap.

WILLIAMS, EBENEZER, (Portage Co.)

Lived at Deerfield, age 82 yrs, where pensioned 1840.

WILLIAMS, ISAAC, (Ashtabula Co.)

Br 1756. Parents: Mathew Williams. Mar 1st wife Mehitabel Whitney, d 1796. Children: Lydia, Mch 20, 1784, at Colebrook, Conn. Levi Sept 3, 1788. Osmond, Apr 20, 1790. Also Sarah and Mehitabel, Children of 2nd wife Almond, Isaac, Lorene, and Janette. D Sept 17, 1853, Lenox, O. Bur Lenox Center. MI: "Isaac Williams. D September 17, 1853 aged 97 yrs. Ref: Mrs. Effie Clark, Jefferson, O. Fur infor Eunice Grant Chap.

WILLIAMS, JAMES, (Adams Co.)

Pvt. Br Feb 22, 1759, Chester Co, Pa. D 1844. Bur Copas Cem, Blue Creek, O. Enl in fall 1777, served 4 mos Oct 1780. Reenlisted served 2 mos, in 1781 enl third time for 4 mos. Fur infor Sycamore Chap.

WILLIAMS, JEREMIAH, (Seneca Co.)

Soldier of Rev of 1776. D 1841. Bur Corfman Cem, Adams Twp. MI: ('76). GM D. A. R. a little iron marker (76) May 30, 1922. Fur infor Dolly Todd Madison Chap.

WILLIAMS, JOHN, (Coshocton Co.)

A brother of Charles, who built first tavern in Coshocton. D 1833. Bur Keene Twp. Ref: County Hist. Fur infor Coshocton Chap.

WILLIAMS, JOHN, (Hamilton Co.)

Bur 1754, Pa. D 1823. Ref: S. A. R. Fur infor Cincinnati Chap.

WILLIAMS, JOHN (or JAMES), (Delaware Co.)

Bur Marlboro Twp. Fur infor Delaware Chap.

WILLIAMS, JOSEPH, (Guernsey Co.)

Served as Wagon master, in Wagon Master Gen Dept. under Wagon Master Gen Gershon Johnson, owner of one wagon, 4 horses, which was in serv 47 days between July 31, and Sept 17, 1778 and 45 days between Sept 17 and Nov 1, 1778. Br 1762. Cheshire Co, Eng. Parents: Judea Williams. Mar Sarah Woodward, (br 1764 d 1849) dau of Geo Woodward, Chesterfield, N. J. June 4, 1786. Children: Woodward (d young); Anthony, mar Sarah Cook, Constantine mar Benj Sherrock, Margaret, mar Isaac Depew, Phoebe mar Samuel King, Nimrod mar Rebecca King, Abner 1st mar Luda Chalfant (no Children) 2nd Jane White of Belmont Co, 9 children. Joseph mar Sarah St Clair, Jacob mar Mary A. Plummer. D Dec 3, 1838. Bur family graveyard, on home farm, Guernsey Co. MI: Dates birth and death. GM sandstone marker. Came with father to in or near Monmouth, Monmouth Co, N. J. After marriage moved to Montgomery Co, Md. Here surrounded by the evil influence of slavery, and on account of his opposition to the system, was looked upon with disfavor; probably 1800 left Md came to southeast Ohio, spending one winter on land of David Newell, (now St Clairsville) 1801 he, wife and family settled Northwest sec 10 twp 1, r 1 Millwood Twp, in Guernsey Co. Brought the first chickens to Leatherwood valley. All were intelligent, industrious progressive people. Ref: Mrs. Orea Thompson, Granville, O. Fur infor Granville Chap.

WILLIAMS, KENT, (Ross Co.)

Pvt in Pa Mil. Br 1764. D Mch 24, 1849. Bur Bainbridge Cem. Receive a pens. Fur infor Nathaniel Massie Chap.

WILLIAMS, MILES, (Hamilton Co.)

Br 1762, New Jersey. D 1837. Ref: S. A. R. Fur infor Cincinnati Chap.

WILLIAMS, NEHEMIAH, (Delaware Co.)

Bur Marlboro Twp. Fur infor Delaware Chap.

WILLIAMS, THOMAS, (Hamilton Co.)

Br 1754, Pa. D 1836. Ref: S. A. R. Fur infor Cincinnati Chap.

WILLIAMS, THOMAS, (Muskingum Co.)

Soldier. D Apr 1810. age 61 yrs. Bur Williams Cem, Falls Twp. Fur infor Muskingum Chap.

WILLIAMS, WILLIAM, (Coshocton Co.)

Bur Linton Twp. Ref: County Hist. Fur infor Coshocton Chap.

WILLIAMS, WILLIAM, (Gallia Co.)

Enl 1780 as Pvt, served 18 mos. Battles of Camden, and Guilford C. H. under Gen Green. Br Fairfax Co, Va. Sept 17, 1757. Mar Mary Walls, May 21, 1795 in West Virginia. Children: James, John, William, Mary Boggs. D Aug 31, 1832 in Gallia Co. Bur Bethesda, Walnut Twp, Gallia Co, O. Ref: Violetta M. Allison, Bidwell, Ohio, a great grand dau. Fur infor Return Jonathan Meigs Chap.

WILLIAMS, WILLIAM, (Preble Co.)

Was placed on the pens roll, 1833 for serv 1777 as fifer in Capt Richard Elliott's Company, Col Dowman's Va Regt; also served 1778-81 several other elmts. Br 1760 Ft Pitt, Pa. D 1841 Preble Co, O. Ref: Natl No 76202, Vol 77, D. A. R. Lin.

WILLIAMSON, ELEAZER, Lt., (Pickaway Co.)

Served under Gen George Washington, command of the 2nd Company 3rd Bn Washington Co Pa. Mil. Shown in Archives of Pa as fr Washington Co, under Col David Williamson, as Lt in Capt Wm Crawford's Company 1782. Br 1747, Chester, Pa. Parents: John Williamson and Mary Davidson. Mar Miss Oriental McConnell, in 1774. Children: David, Joseph, Eleazer, John, William, Mary, Lydia, Martha, Ruhamah and Margaret. D Feb 28, 1838, near Commercial Point, Pickaway Co, O. Bur Presbyterian Cem, 3 miles south Commercial Point in western portion. Br 1747, mar 1774. Served as soldier in Revolutionary War. Lived in Chester and Washington Cos, Pa. Migrated to Chillicothe, O in 1800 and 8 yrs later moved to Scioto Twp. Pickaway Co. Farmer, Trapper, and hunter. Served in campaign against the Indians in 1782. Was in command of the 2nd Company of the 3rd Bn Washington Co Mil. Ref: Natl No 53814, Vol 54, D. A. R. Lin. Fur infor Mt. Sterling Chap.

WILLIAMSON, JOHN, (Montgomery Co.)

Reputed to have been a Revolutionary Soldier, but no evidence could be located. Br Pennsylvania. Children: Joseph. D Clay Twp, Montgomery Co. Came to Cincinnati in 1803, then settled in Warren Co, and finally settled in Clay Twp. Fur infor Richard Montgomery Chap, S. A. R.

WILLIAMSON, JOSEPH, 2nd Lt., (Mahoning Co.)

Pvt. Pa Cumberland Co, 2nd Lt Lancaster Co Mil. Pa. Br 1765. Mar Margaret Fu Slis. D 1827, Youngstown. Bur Oak Hill Cem, Youngstown, in the western part. Ref: Pa Archives, Series 5, Vol 4, p 642, Vol 7, p 467. Trumbull and Mahoning Co Hist. Fur infor Mahoning Chap.

WILLIAMSON, SAMUEL, (Washington Co.)

Ensign 1778 Virginia Mil. Br 1745, Md. Mar Sarah Claypole. D 1808 in Washington Co, O. Ref: Natl No 65458, Vol 66, p 156, D. A. R. Lin.

WILLIAMSON, WILLIAM REV. (Adams Co.)

Served under Gen Gates in the hard campaign in the summer of 1780. Was captured at the battle of Camden, S. C., Aug 10, 1780. Br Sept 23, 1762, near Greenville, N. C. Parents: Thomas Williamson, Anne Newton. Mar Catherine Buford and Jane Smith, Hannah Johnson 3rd wife. (Dates not given). Children: Anne Newton, Mary, Elizabeth and Esther by his 1st wife; Thomas Smith and B. Jane Smith. D at "The Beeches" near Manchester, O. Nov 29, 1830. Bur Manchester Old Cem, at Manchester, O. GM. Was educated at Hampden Sidney College in Virginia, and was installed as pastor of the Fair Forest Presbyterian Church, Apr 1793. Was a devoted worker and looked upon the slavery as a great evil. Ref: Hist of Adams Co. Fur infor Sycamore Chap.

WILLIAMSON, WILLIAM, (Brown Co.)

Pvt Mfl Middlesex Co, N. J. Served at various times 10 mos and 8 days; served under his father Capt Williamson's Company, Col Duyken's Regt. Br April 6, 1759, Middlesex Co, N. J. Parents: William Williamson. Mar Helen Terhune, June 13, 1784. Children: Samuel, John, Mary, William, Albert, Daniel, Abraham, Margaret. D Dec 22, 1835, Brown Co. Bur Red Oak, 5 miles south of Russellville, Brown Co. Lawyer. Ref: Adj Gen Office of NJ Bureau of Pensions, and Natl No 96436, Vol 97, p 138 D. A. R. Lin. Fur infor Taliaferro Chap.

WILLIS, JOSEPH, (Jefferson Co.)

NJ Line under Capts Baker, Craig and Clark, Cols Ogden and Potter. Br 1759 near Elizabethtown, N. J. D 1842 in Jefferson Co, O. Ref: Natl No 101773, Vol 103, D. A. R. Lin.

WILLIS, THOMAS, (Richland Co.)

In Plymouth, O. Dec 6, 1846, age 90 yrs. Formerly fr Livingston Co, N. Y. Ref: "Ashtabula Sentinel."

WILLYARD, HENRY, (Hamilton Co.)

Br 1749, Pennsylvania. D 1830. Ref: S. A. R. Fur infor Cincinnati Chap.

WILMUTH, THOMAS, (Hamilton Co.)

Joined Continental Army at the Brandywine; was in other battles; at age 18, served to end of war. Members of family now quite old still treasure his flint lock musket and recall stories of battles he told. This record was not verified, says Mrs. Whallon, reporting. Br Frederick, Md. 1758. Mar 1st Mary Pender, dau Ralph Pender later spelled Pendery 2nd Jane Evatt dau Wm Evatt. Children: 1st wife Joseph, George W., Eliza mar McCormick, Harriet Symmes, Isabel Dum. 2nd John Warren, Ellen Glenn, Mary Ann Lank, Amanda Hill. D 1860, he and 2 wives bur Reading, Hamilton Co, O. Fr Cincinnati went to farm of 40 acres, which corners on Wilmuth Ave. and Springfield Pike, Wyoming, adjoining Pendery farm. Fur infor Mrs. Whallon, Cincinnati, O.

WILSON, ANDREW, (Butler Co.)

A member of the Committee of Safety of Norfolk Co, Va. Br 1761, in Va. Mar Lilly Porter. D 1832 in Butler Co, O. Ref: Natl No 101716, Vol 102, p 214, D. A. R. Lin.

WILSON, ARCHIBALD, Capt., (Licking Co.)

Made Capt 1777. Served in Virginia. Br Jan 13, 1749, Shenandoah, Va. Parents: William Wilson and Elizabeth Beachburn. Mar Anna Claypool, June 12, 1775, (1st wife), Nancy Newman, Aug 31, 1791, (2nd wife). Children: 28 children, 24 of whom attended his funeral. William B, (mar Margaret Stadden), Enoch, (mar Mary Ann Bishop), Elizabeth, (mar Andrew McMillen). D Nov 27, 1814 near Newark, O. Bur Wilson burying plot; re-interred at Cedar Hill. GM by Hetuck Chap in 1910. In Mch 1896, settled on Wilson sec. "Enterprising man of affairs, leader in public movements." Was magistrate under the crown; took oath of allegiance Jan 12, 1776. Ref: Hist of Licking Co by E. M. Brister; Natl No 28722, D. A. R. Lin. Fur infor Hetuck Chap.

WILSON, BENJAMIN, (Harrison Co.)

In Expedition against Lord Dunmore 1777. Took trail to avenge massacre in Tygarts Valley. Valuable serv in Indian warfare. Br 1747, Shenandoah, Va. D 1827. Harrison Co. His opinion of Cornstalk as an orator often quoted. Ref: Natl No 49220, Vol 50, p 98, D. A. R. Lin. Fur infor Jane Dowd Dailey.

WILSON, DANIEL, (Montgomery Co.)

Drafted in NJ Mil, June 1776. Company of Capt Samuel Stout, Col Dykens; Again Jan 1777 same command; Apr 1777, same company, Col Hyer; Oct 1777, Capt Conover, Col Hyer; stationed at numerous NJ points. In spring 1778, volunteered under Capt Robert Nixon, tr of Horse, furnished self and horse, while engaged as express rider for Col Scudder. Received only a verbal disch. Br Apr 21, 1759, N. J. Parents: Father was John Wilson, a Revolutionary soldier. Mar 1st Sarah Sutton Sept 23, 1784; 2nd Elizabeth Price, Feb 17, 1807, (br Jan 17, 1776.) Children: John Sutton; James, Mary. D Sept 7, 1847, Sugar Creek Twp Greene Co, near Washington Twp Montgomery Co Line. Bur Baptist Cem, Centerville, O, on slight ridge in center of cem. MI: "In memory of Daniel Wilson, departed this life Sept 7, 1847, aged 88 years, 4 mos and 17 days." GM Richard Montgomery Chap, S. A. R. Official Montgomery Co metal marker, July 3, 1919. Moved to Washington Co, Pa thence to Ohio, settling on the west branch of Mill Creek, about 11 miles fr Cincinnati, and in 1796 or 7 removed to Greene Co, settling Sugar Creek Twp. His father lost all his property in the Revolutionary War. He and his son, Daniel (generally known as "Maj") were men of intelligence and integrity. The elder was a member of the first Constitutional Convention of Ohio. Fur infor Richard Montgomery Chap, S. A. R.

WILSON, EBENEZER, (Lake Co.)

Enl Dec 8, 1776 and served in an alarm of R. I. in Capt Robert Crossman's Company, Col George Williams' Regt. Br May 16, 1745, Swansea, Mass. (then R. I.) D Willoughby, O. (Ref: Natl No 26245 D. A. R.) Bur Mentor Cem, Mentor, O. GM New Connecticut Chap. Fur infor New Connecticut Chap.

WILSON, ISAAC, (Clark Co.)

Name on lists of Presbyterian Church, South Charleston, O. Was received into church with his wife 1822. Beers' Clark Co Hist 1881 p 761, 756. Ref: Col Curry fur name from pens list of 1840 State Library. Fur infor Lagonda Chap.

WILSON, ISRAEL, (Geauga Co.)

Sgt Capt Thrall's Company, engaged Aug 21, 1781. Disch Nov 5, 1781 under Col Willet on Mohawk River. Br 1759, Conn. Children: Mary Williams. D July 1, 1842 at Montville, O. aged 83 yrs, 6 mos. Bur Cem, at Montville Center, in rear, northeastern part. MI: Name, date of death, age. Estate administered June 18, 1853. Back pens mentioned in Court records. Fur infor Taylor Chap.

WILSON, JAS., (Adams Co.)

Pvt Va Tr. Br 1715, Augusta Co, Va. Mar Rebekah (1728-1820). D 1809, Adams Co, O. Ref: Natl No 79040, Vol 80, D. A. R. Lin.

WILSON, JAMES, (Muskingum Co.)

Pvt Va Regt Continental Line. Br 1753, Va (?). Mar Catherine Collins. D Aug 8, 1839. Bur Timber Run Cem, Hopewell Twp, Muskingum Co. Ref: Natl No 70413, Vol 71, D. A. R. Lin. Fur infor Muskingum Chap.

WILSON, JAMES, (Ross Co.)

Br Pa. Children: John, Wilson, Eleanor, Sarah, Amanda, Edward, Polly, Betsey, Rebecca, Robert, Sallie. D 1850, near South Salem, O. Bur South Salem, Ross Co, O. GM Nathaniel Massie Chap, D. A. R. Ref: Mary Moomaw Natl No 190345, Greenfield, O. R. F. D. 1. Fur infor Nathaniel Massie Chap.

WILSON, JAMES, (Mahoning Co.)

Ensign in Continental Tr Pa. (Pensioned) Capt John McGowan's Company, Col Wm Butler. Br 1744, Ireland. Mar Martha Willock. Children: Andrew, James, Mary, Eleanor, Martha. D 1835, Youngstown. Bur Oak Hill, Youngstown. Ref: Natl No 36451 D. A. R. Lin. Pa Archives, Series 3, Vol 23, p 514, and 785, Trumbull and Mahoning Co Hist, Vol 2. Fur infor Mahoning Chap.

WILSON, JAMES, (Trumbull Co.)

Pvt. N J State Mil. Br 1749. D June 26, 1833. Bur Wilson cem 2 miles south of Warren. MI: "Died June 26, 1833, aged 84 years." "Farewell my friends, Both far and near. Here I must lie "Till Christ appear." Fur infor Mary Chesney Chap.

WILSON, SAMUEL, Col., (Trumbull Co.)

Br 1736. D Apr 7, 1820. Bur Brookfield Center. MI: Name, date of birth and of death. Fur infor Mary Chesney Chap.

WILSON, WILLIAM, (Hamilton Co.)

Br 1757, Pennsylvania. D 1838. Ref: S. A. R. Fur infor Cincinnati Chap.

WILSON, WILLIAM, (Fairfield Co.)

Natl No 156227, D. A. R. filing supplemental on his record (1926) as follows: Vol V, Series V, p 114, Pa Archives "Pvt. Capt Charles Taggarts Co Mil, Bedford Co Pa. also Ref: p 90 same Vol). Had 8 sons, 5 dau one Thomas, (a bachelor) is bur by Father. Bur Old Tent Cem 2 miles west of Rushville ½ miles south of Marysville pike, Richland Twp on land he owned (200 acres) one time. MI: "In memory of William Wilson, son of Mary and Thos Wilson, br Apr 17, 1755, Frederick Co Md. Moved to state of Pa (Bedford Co) May 29, 1777 fr thence to State of Ohio in yr 1800 (May 16) (Some characteristics follow, then this: "His wife, Esther Fickle is bur beside him. Died May 10, 1840, aged 88-1-10." Capt in War of 1812, Fairfield Co, O. Grandfather of Gen and Congressman Thomas Ritchie who aptd Phil Sheridan to West Point. Ref: Record to be proven (Mrs. Dailey, State Chairman.) Fur infor Mrs. Jas. R. Marker, Columbus, O., member Columbus Chap D. A. R.

WILSON, WILLIAM, (Trumbull Co.)

Bur Bristolville. Ref: S. A. R. Fur infor Western Reserve Chap.

WILTSEE, CORNELIUS, (Hamilton Co.)

Sgt in Capt John Van Benschoten's Company, Col Roswell Hopkins' Regt, Dutchess Co Mil of NY. Br 1761, Columbia Co, N. Y. Mar Bowers. D 1828, Cincinnati, O. Ref: Natl No 57023, Vol 28, p 8, D. A. R. Lin.

WINANS, ISAAC SR., (Trumbull Co.)

Pvt. Enl Orange Co Mil. Br 1764, Mar Eleanor. D 1852. Bur Princetown, Newton Twp. MI: "Isaac Winans Sr, Died Dec. 26th, 1852, Age 88 years." Ref: Cleveland Historical Library Revolutionary Soldiers bur in Trumbull Co. Fur infor Mary Chesney and Mahoning Chaps.

WINANS, JACOB, (Mahoning Co.)

Adj of 6th Bn Northampton Co Mil, under Col Jacob Stroud. Br 1726, Perth Amboy, N J. D 1810, Milton, O. Bur Princeton Cem. Ref: Natl No 74446, Vol 75, D. A. R. Lin.

WINANS, JAMES, (Mahoning Co.)

Land Bounty rights, Dutchess Co, N. Y. N Y Men in the Rev, p 245. Bur Milton Twp. Settled in Milton Twp in 1804. Ref: Trumbull and Mahoning Co Hist p 179, Vol 1 Sandersons Biography p 211. Fur infor Mahoning Chap.

WINANS, SAMUEL, (Miami Co.)

Bur Raper Chapel 2 miles north of Troy, O. GM by Miami Chap with bronze marker in 1904. Toast of July 4, 1827 "The Star Spangled Banner, Long may it wave, O'er the land of the free, and home of the brave," given by him. Fur infor Miami Chap.

WINGATE, JOHN, (Butler Co.)

In Gen Wayne's army, Sgt in Van Reusseler's Cav of Fallen; War of 1812. Br 1774, New York; (at his age, is said to have taken part in last battles of Rev.) Mar 1st Mary Dillon, 2nd Emma Torrence, in Oct 1807, D Apr 14, 1851, Hamilton, O. Bur Greenwood Cem, Hamilton, O. Ref: Name recorded on tablet under heading "Revolutionary Soldiers" in Soldiers and Sailors Monument, High and Monument Ave, Hamilton, O. Fur infor John Reily Chap.

WINSLOW, JOHN, (Coshocton Co.)

Bur Tiverton Center. Ref: Hist of Coshocton Co. Fur infor Coshocton Chap.

WINSLOW, STEPHEN, (Ashtabula Co.)

Pensioned 1832, Ashtabula Co, for one yr actual serv as Pvt Mass Line. Br 1746, Rochester, Mass. D 1839, Windsor, O. Ref: Natl No 38587, Vol 39, p 217, D. A. R. Lin. Fur infor by Jane Dowd Dailey.

WINSLOW, WILLIAM, (Coshocton Co.)

Bur Tiverton Center. Grave not marked. Ref: Mrs. A. Ripple, West Lafayette, member Coshocton Chap.

WINTER, STEPHEN, (Greene Co.)

Br 1752. D Jan 16, 1837, Xenia. Bur Massies Creek graveyard (Stevenson's). Xenia, 1806. Ref: Robinsons Hist of Greene Co. Fur infor Catherine Greene Chap.

WINTERS, JOHN, (Geauga Co.)

Pvt in Capt John Patton's 7th Company, 6th Bn Lancaster Co Mil. Br 1774, England. Mar Martha Jones, 1778. D 1839, Burton, O. (so data read but must be error for Burton, O, is in Geauga Co.) Ref: Mrs. Sadie Dickerson Christman, Hamden, O. and Natl No 78117, Vol 79, D. A. R. Lin.

WINTERS, THOMAS, (Vinton Co.)

Served fr Westmoreland Co, Pa. Pvt in John McClelland's Company. Br London, England. Parents: Henry Winters. Mar Mary Jane. Children: John Winters, and three dau. D McArthur, O. Bur Old Colvin Cem, McArthur, O. Have birth certificate of John Winters br 1781. Name appears on same records, as Winter. Ref: Dr. B. C. Winters, Columbus, O. Fur infor Jane Dailey State Chairman.

WINTERSTEIN, PHILIP E., (Trumbull Co.)

Br 1742. D Oct 4, 1829. Bur Brookfield Center. MI: Name, date of birth and death. Fur infor Mary Chesney Chap.

WINTON, NATHAN, (Butler Co.)

Revolutionary Soldiers fr Pa. See p 245 Pa Archives. Name appears on a tablet of "Pioneers" in Butler Co, O. Fur infor Mrs. Whallon and Cincinnati Chap.

WIRT, CONRAD, (Highland Co.)

Pvt fr Rappo Twp, Lancaster Co, Pa, under Col Alexander Lowry. Grave not located. Farmer. Will of Conrad Wirt on record in Highland Co courts. Fur infor Waw-Wil-a-Way Chap.

WIRT, MARTIN, (Lake Co.)

Enl as a teamster. Was in the battle of Brandywine. Br 1760, Germany. Mar Catherine Homan. D July 1815. Bur in an old burying ground in Willoughby O. He came to this country fr Germany when 7 yrs old. Came to Ohio and purchased a farm and mill on the Chagrin River owned by David Abbott. Fur infor New Connecticut Chap.

WISE, JACOB, (Mahoning Co.)

Pvt fr Cumberland and Lancaster Co in 1781 and 1782, also a substitute. Pa Archives Series 5, Vol IV, p 308, 355, Vol VI, p 397, 430, Vol VIII, p 322, 392, 461. Children: Jacob and John. Settled in Austintown Twp. Ref: Trumbull and Mahoning Cos Hist. Fur infor Mahoning Chap.

WISE, PETER, (Stark Co.)

Bur Cem at Marlboro, O. Ref: Authority: Hist of Stark Co, edited by William Henry Perrin. Fur infor Massillon Chap.

WISEMAN, JOHN, (Fairfield Co.)

Ranger on the frontiers 1778-1783. Was with Washington and Lafayette through the memorable winter at Valley Forge. He served two terms in the Rev. Br Aug 18, 1760, Berks Co, Pa. Parents: Isaac and Elizabeth Wiseman. Mar Sarah Green of Virginia, May 10, 1786. Children: Elizabeth, Mary, Margaret, Ann, James Green, John Ray, Sarah, Joseph Green, Abner, Phillip Smith, Jacob Gruber, Isaac. D Jan 22, 1842, New Salem, O. Bur New Salem Cem, south side of Cem, ground given by the Wisemans. MI: "Rev John Wiseman died Jan 22, 1842, aged 81 yrs. 5 mos and 4 days." Soon after the war he went with his parents to Rockingham Co, Va. In 1818 he moved to Fairfield Co, O. D on farm in Perry Co. Minister of the Gospel, Methodist Episcopal Church. Commissioned 1785 by Bishop Asbury. Settled in New Salem 1819. Ref: Eva Kelsey Crates, great grand dau of John Wiseman, 200 Glendale Ave., Findlay, O. Fur infor Fort Findlay Chap.

WITTER, JOSEPH, (Geauga Co.)

Pvt Capt Black's Company, Col Chapen's Regt. Engaged for town of Merryfield, 1779 and 1780. Mar Hannah Washburn, Mch 5, 1783. Children: William, Hannah, Lucy, Dolly, Joseph, Abraham. D 1831, Bainbridge, O. Bur old southwest burying ground, Bainbridge, O. Was one of the guards of the execution for Maj Andre. Will probated in Courts of Geauga Co, Feb 28, 1831. Ref: Mass Soldiers and Sailors Vol 17, p 698 and 648. Middlefield Mass Vital Records. Fur infor Taylor Chap.

WITTERS, CONRAD, (Montgomery Co.)

Enl at Reading, Pa, Apr 5, 1779, in a command of artillery commanded by Capt James Thompson, Col Anthony Proctor. Brig commanded by Gen Knaus, continued in said company until Dec 6, 1782, when he was disch at Burlington,

N. J. Was in the battle of Springfield, N. J. where he was wounded. Was at Stony Point and at Yorktown. Br 1760, in Berks Co, Pa. Mar Susannah ———. Children: Daniel, David, Conrad, William, and George, (the oldest br in 1790) and perhaps 3 others. D June 11, 1842, Clay Twp, Montgomery Co, O. Bur Pyrmont. MI: "In memory of Conrad Witters, served in the Revolutionary War, Departed this life, June 11, 1842, aged 96 years and 6 mos." Grave not marked. In his application for pens dated Aug 19, 1819, he states that he is 59 years old. Appeared again, July 25, 1820, states that he was poor without property, poor clothing and poor bedding. Granted pens, which went to his widow, at his death. Farmer or laborer. Fur infor Richard Montgomery Chap, S. A. R.

WOLCOTT, DAVID, (Portage Co.)

Lived at Windham, age 75 years, where pensioned 1840. Fur infor Old Northwest Chap.

WOLCOTT, JOSIAH, (Trumbull Co.)

Enl 1776, under Capt Oliver Pomeroy, re-enlisted under Capt Benj Wright. Was at battles of Long Island and Harlem Heights. Obligated to hire a substitute; pensioned, as was his widow, 1853. 3rd wife was Elizabeth Brown. mar 1829. Real dau, Mrs. Nancy Squire, (br 1834). Br Withersfield, Conn, 1755. D Farmington, O. 1838. Ref: Natl No 35980, Vol 36, p 361, D. A. R. Lin.

WOLFE, ADAM, (Richland Co.)

Pvt in Pennsylvania Tr. Bur Newville Cem, village of Newville, O. MI: Bronze marker, name and company. GM Mary Washington D. A. R. Chap, bronze marker in 1911. Fur infor Mary Washington Chap.

WOLFENBARGER, PHILIP, (Pike Co.)

Pensioned for serv and in 1840, residing in Beaver Twp at about age of 96 yrs. Br about 1744. Bur Beaver Cem, verified by C M Emory, Stockdale, O. Fur infor Census of Pensions 1840. Copied by Jane Dailey, State Chairman.

WOOD, BENJAMIN, (Hamilton Co.)

Br 1736, Connecticut. D 1834. Ref: S. A. R. Fur infor Cincinnati Chap.

WOOD, CHARLES, (Mahoning Co.)

Pvt. Enl in 1777, for 3 yrs. Disch 1780, "Conn Men of the Rev" p 154. On p 156, enl 1780 served to Dec 31, 1781; p 144 he was pensioned in 1819. Bur probably in Canfield. Came to Canfield in 1802. Ref: Trumbull and Mahoning Co Hist Vol II. Fur infor Mahoning Chap.

WOOD, DAVID, (Ashtabula Co.)

Corp Conn Mil. Pens Roll Ashtabula Co. Br 1759, Hartford, Conn. Mar Rebecca King. D Kingsville, O. 1835. Ref: Natl No 25637 and 135215, Vol 26, p 234, D. A. R. Lin.

WOOD, DAVID, (Clermont Co.)

Va Continental Line; Moved to Ky 1791, thence to Washington Twp Clermont Co, O, 1795; he and two brothers erected a heavy stockade, "Woods and Manning Station" near Calvary M. E. Church, Daniel Boone and Simon Kenton often stopped there. Br 1764, Va. Children: John S, (mar Eliz. Cameron), George, (mar Sarah Fee), Joseph, (mar Margaret Bennett), Absolom, (mar Phoebe McGohan), David, (mar Mary Day), Bazil C, Alfred, dau mar Wm Barkley, dau mar Robert Badgley, dau mar Joseph Dole, dau mar Jas Buchanan. D 1848. Ref: A. S. Abbott, Bethel, O. Fur infor Cincinnati Chap.

WOOD, EBENEZER, (Hamilton Co.)

Pvt Virginia Tr. Br 1760, Nyack, NY. Mar Charity Miers. D 1840, Cincinnati, O. Ref: Natl No 59741, Vol 60, p 252, D. A. R. Lin.

WOOD, EBENEZER, (Morrow Co.)

Pvt in Mass Regt. Br 1754, Pittsfield, Mass. Mar Mary Hutchins in 1775. D 1831. Said to be bur in Cem near Westfield, O. Ref: Natl No 75611, Vol 76, D. A. R. Lin. Fur infor Mt Gilead Chap.

WOOD, ISRAEL, (Hamilton Co.)

Br 1763, New Jersey. Ref: S. A. R. Fur infor Cincinnati Chap.

WOOD, JOHN, (Pickaway Co.)

Capt. Br Jan 14, 1754, probably Eastern Pa. Parents: Josiah Wood. Mar Abigail (Barnes probably). Children: Naomi, Sarah and Mary. D Nov 21, 1821, near Tarlton. Bur Tarlton, Pickaway Co, O. MI: Name, birth and death. Farmer. Ref: Emily Holderman Baker, Kingston. Fur infor Mt Sterling Chap.

WOOD, LEVI, (Hamilton Co.)

Br 1757, Connecticut. D 1835. Ref: S. A. R. Fur infor Cincinnati Chap.

WOOD, NICHOLAS, (Brown Co.)

Revolutionary Soldier, Brown Co. Br Pa. Children: Nicholas, George, Michael. D Byrd Twp, Brown Co. Bur Wood Cem, Byrd Twp. Came to Ky to live, then moved to Ohio. Farmer. Ref: Brown Co Hist p 196. Fur infor Lieutenant Byrd Chap.

WOODEN, CHARLES, (Summit Co.)

During 1779 and 1780 served 7 mo as Pvt under Col Hubbard and Capt John Riggs. Br Woodbridge, Conn. Nov 17, 1778. Later lived at Oxford, New Haven Co, Conn, and Ovid, Seneca Co, NY. After death of wife, came to Portage Co, O, to live with dau; old residents of Stow Twp and sexton of Cem claim he is bur in cem at that place, but if so, grave is unmarked and unknown. Fur infor Cuyahoga Portage Chap.

WOODMANSEE, JAMES SR., (Butler Co.)

Name appears on the tablet of the Sailors and Soldiers Monument, at Hamilton, O., as a Revolutionary Soldier. Bur in Butler Co. Lived in Liberty Twp. Fur infor John Reily Chap.

WOODRUFF, DAVID, (Mahoning Co.)

Pvt Allen's State Tr, NJ. Br 1740. Mar Joanna, (1751-1841). D 1823, Cornersburg. Bur Cornersburg, southwest of Youngstown. Ref: N. J. Men of the Rev p 822, Mahoning and Trumbull Cos Hist. Fur infor Mahoning Chap.

WOODS, THOMAS, (Clermont Co.)

Came to Pierce Twp, Clermont Co, O 1805, settled 2 miles west of Amelia. Filed by A. S. Abbott, Bethel, O, as a Revolutionary Soldier. Many meetings of Methodists held at his house. Fur infor Cincinnati Chap.

WOODWARD, ASA, (Licking Co.)

Entered as a Pvt when only 17. He served in several places and under several officers, his last enlmt being in Poundwelis Co. Br Feb 15, 1760, Canterbury, Conn. D Aug 3, 1837, Homer, O. Bur at Homer, O. GM Granville Chap Aug 23, 1912. Ref: Compare Natl No 45866, Vol 46, D. A. R. Lin. Fur infor Granville Chap.

WOODWARD, OLIVER, (Washington Co.)

Br Oct 1, 1749, Coventry, Conn. D Oct 2, 1842. Bur Yankeeburg Cem, Washington Co, O. MI: "Soldier of the Revolution." GM Marietta Chap with Revolutionary marker in 1921. He was given a grant of land near where he was bur for Revolutionary serv. Fur infor Marietta Chap.

WOODWARD, SAMUEL, (Shelby Co.)

Pvt. Entered the army when a boy of 16 yrs under Command of Gen Green, was actively engaged in battle of Guilford and several other hard tested battles. Br Jan 11, 1760, Va. Mar Miss Sara Roberts (2nd wife) Children: Rachel, Samuel R, and Eliza, children of second wife. D Sept 25, 1852, Green Twp, Shelby Co. Bur Old Plattsville Cem, Green Twp ¼ mile northeast of Plattsville on creek, about center of the East side of Cem. MI: Samuel Woodward born Jan 11, 1760, died Sept 25, 1852. GM by Woodward family. After Rev took part in several Indian raids, then mover to Green Co, O. where his first wife died, then mar Miss Sarah Roberts. In 1839 he moved his family to Shelby Co., Green Twp. His wife d Sept 1, 1879. Ref: Sutton's Hist of Shelby Co. Fur infor Lewis Boyer Chap.

WOODWORTH, EZEKIEL, (Lake Co.)

Enl fr Hampden Co, Mass in Capt Charles Colton's Company, Col John Greaton's Regt fr 1777 to 1780. Br 1759. D Feb 27, 1839. Bur Unionville, O. MI: "In memory of Ezekiel Woodworth, a Revolutionary soldier who died Feb 27, 1839, aged 80 years." GM by New Connecticut Chap. He was a pensioner. Fur infor New Connecticut Chap.

WOODWORTH, JAMES, (Lake Co.)

Ensign of the 4th Company or train band in the 12th Regt of the State of Conn. Br July 8, 1766, Coventry, Conn. Children: Harvey. D Nov 2, 1859, Painesville, O. Bur Evergreen Cem, Painesville, O. GM New Connecticut Chap. Fur infor New Connecticut Chap.

WOODWORTH, RICHARD, (Adams Co.)

Corp in Capt William Gray's Company, Col Wm Butler's Regt, Pa Line. Enl 1775, served entire war. Br Dublin, Ireland in 1758 or 1755. Mar Sarah Ann Robinson in 1802. Children: Laban Mary Wheeler, Nellie William, James Richard, Sarah Rebecca. D 1843 or 1842, Adams Co, O. Bur Blue Creek. Ref: Natl No 95169, Vol 96, p 57, D. A. R. Lin. Fur infor Sycamore Chap.

WOOLSEY, DANIEL, (Lake Co.)

D Willoughby, O. Ref: Natl No 48617, p 281 Vol 49, D. A. R. Lin.

WORK, SAMUEL, (Fairfield Co.)

Chester Co, Pa Mil, Capt Samuel Evans and Col Evan Evans. Br Ireland. Mar Jean McCune (McEwen). Children one was Aaron. D 1816, Bremen, Fairfield Co., O. Ref: Natl No 75097, Vol 76, D. A. R. Lin.

WORKMAN, DANIEL, (Logan Co.)

Was a resident of Logan Co. Burial place unknown. Was pensioned by the U. S. Government Mch 18, 1818 at $8.00 per mo, as a soldier of the Rev. Notification of pens signed by J. C. Calhoun, Sec of War. Fur infor Bellefontaine Chap.

WORLEY, DAVID, (Union Co.)

Bur New Dover Cem, Dover Twp. Fur infor Hannah Emerson Dustin Chap.

WORT, JOHN, (Delaware Co.)

Pvt under Col Wm Wirtz, 10th Pa Regt. Bur Trenton Twp. Pensioned. Fur infor Delaware Chap.

WRIGHT, ELI, (Seneca Co.)

Bur McCutchenville Cem. GM Bronze marker in 1927. Fur infor Dolly Todd Madison Chap.

WRIGHT, ELIPHAS, (Licking Co.)

Enl Apr 19, 1775 in Capt Jonathan Allen's Company, Gen Pomeroy's Regt. Served as Sgt of Capt Daniel's Company, Gen Danielson's Brig. Served under Gen Stark, Northern Dept and Canadian Expedition, 1776. Br 1740, Northampton Mass. Mar 1779 Anna Mosely (d 1785). Children: Spencer. D Dec 10, 1813, Granville, O. Bur Maple Grove Cem, Granville, O. GM Granville Chap in 1901. Ref: Natl No 70164, Vol 71, p 59, D. A. R. Lin. Fur infor Hetuck Chap.

WRIGHT, GEORGE, (Greene Co.)

Served fr Berkley Co in Cav under Robert Yancy; in battles Camden, Guilford and Yorktown. Br 1756. D Sept 28, 1829. Bur Woodland Cem, Xenia. 1820, pensioned in Frederick Co, Va for 4 yrs actual serv Va Line. Caesars Creek, 1816. Fur infor Catherine Greene Chap.

WRIGHT, JOAL, (or JOAB), (Seneca Co.)

1780, 8 mo. Pvt. Capt Caleb Baldwin. Br at Saybrook, Conn. D Aug 16, 1844. Residence at time of enlmt, Saybrook, Conn. Application for pens, July 27, 1833. Allowed. Residence ,at application Thompson Twp, Seneca Co, O. GM Commissioners. Fur infor Col George Croghan Chap.

WRIGHT, JAMES, (Lake Co.)

Enl 1775 in Col John Patterson's Regt, and served to the close of the war in the Conn Line. Mar Elizabeth Lee, 1768. Children: Tom L., Lucina. D 1813, Painesville, O. One of the very early settlers of Perry, O. Ref: Natl No 39305, Vol 40, D. A. R. Lin. Fur infor New Connecticut Chap.

WRIGHT, JOHN, Capt., (Summit Co.)

Pvt in Capt Edward Shipman's 6th Company, Col Chas Webb's 7th Conn Continental Regt July 15, 1775 to Dec 18, 1775; also in Capt Robt Warner's Company,

Col Saml Wylly's 3rd Regt, Conn Line, Oct 14, 1777 to Nov 4, 1781; and Capt R. Warner's Company, Col Durkee's 1st Regt Conn Line. Served in Conn Mil before and after the Rev; Commissioned Ensign Nov 2, 1785, and Capt Nov 1, 1791. Br Goshen, Conn. Jan 22, 1743. Parents: Lt John Wright, who served in French and Indian war. Mar Lydia Mason, Aug 14, 1770 (who d Nov 11, 1771); he then mar Sarah Case, Mch 24, 1774, who was the mother of his children. Four sons are mentioned as serving in War 1812, with a son-in-law. D July 29, 1825, Tallmadge. Bur Tallmadge, O. Moved to Winchester, (Winsted) Conn; thence to Morgan, O, in 1802, and 1809 to Tallmadge, O, where he lived till death. Wife Sarah, died Feb 14, 1826. Fur infor Cuyahoga-Portage Chap.

WRIGHT, SHADRACH, (Co not stated)

Capt in 1st Georgia Bn. Br 1750, Savannah, Ga. D 1816, Ohio. Ref: Natl No 95112, Vol 96, p 38, D. A. R. Lin.

WRIGHT, SIMEON, Capt., (Licking Co.)

Capt in Revolutionary War. Fought under Stark at Bennington; Ethan Allen at Ticonderoga. Ref: "Hills Hist of Licking Co." Br Oct 18, 1751. Mar Freelove Foot, about 1769. (Foote Gen) D Sept 11, 1847. Bur Croton, O. Lived in Rutland Co Vt fr 1769 (or earlier) to about 1810, then came to Licking Co, O. Fur infor Helen Whigam 2212 N. Keeler Ave., Chicago, Ill in 1924.

WRIGHT, WILLIAM, (Butler Co.)

Name on memorial tablet at Hamilton, O. Was placed on Pens Roll of Ohio 1831, for serv of Pvt in Pa Line. In 1840, at age of 79, was living in Liberty Twp. Br 1762. D 1841, Butler Co, O. Ref: Natl No 25228, Vol 26, p 81, D. A. R. Lin. Fur infor John Reily Chap.

WYATT, JOSHUA, (Athens Co.)

On Lexington Alarm Roll of Capt Asa Prince's Company, which marched on the alarm of Apr 19, 1775, serv 2 da in 1779 in Col Larkin Thorndike's Regt. Br Dec 5, 1756, Danvers, Mass. Mar Elizabeth Shaw. Children: Betsy, Sally, John. D May 13, 1822, Ames Twp, Athens Co, O. Bur Ames Cem. MI: "Joshua Wyatt br in Danvers, Mass, Dec 5, 1756, died May 13, 1822. A soldier of the Revolution and an earnest Christian." GM by family. Sandstone slab, First-Marble Shaft 2nd. See Walker's Hist of Athens Co p 414. Office of the Secretary of the Commonwealth of Mass. Vol 1350. Ref: Natl No 61441, Vol 62, D. A. R. Lin. Fur infor Nabby Lee Ames Chap.

WYATT, NATHANIEL SR., (Marion Co.)

Lt in Orange Co, New York Mil. Br 1761, Albany, N Y. D 1824, Waldo, Marion Co, O. Bur Wyatt Graveyard. Moved to Virginia and subsequently to Pickaway Co, O. Ref: Natl No 28240, Vol 29, D. A. R. Lin. Fur infor Capt William Hendricks Chap.

WYCKOFF, SAMUEL, (Various spellings) (Ross Co.)

Pvt in Capt Bruce's Company, Col Clicket. Pensioned 1832 for serv in Md Tr, (while living in Licking Co, O, Eden Twp). Br June 10, 1760, Hunterdon Co, NJ. Mar Maria Berger. Children: a son Nicholas. D Mch 4, 1842, Ross Co., O. Bur near Chillicothe, O. Lived in Allegheny Co, Md. near Cumberland at time of enlmt in Loudoun Co, Va; thence Hardy Co; thence Licking Co, O. Ref: Natl No 95760, Vol 96, p 246, D. A. R. Lin. Fur infor Hetuck Chap.

WYLIE, ADAM, (Harrison Co.)

Mil. Br 1749. D 1827. Bur Beach Spring Church. Served as a member of Capt Andrew Sweringon's Company, in Col David Williamson's 3rd Bn Washington Co, Pa. Mil 1782, Pa Archives 6 II, 107, 114, 123. Fur infor Moravian Trail Chap.

WYLLYS, JOHN PALSGRAN, (Co not stated)

He was with Gen Harmon in 1790 at the Battle of the Miami where he was killed at the head of his Regt in 1790. Descendant of Gov Wyllys, 3rd Governor of Conn. Bur somewhere in Ohio. Fur infor Office of Adj Gen Ohio.

WYMAN, WILLIAM JR., (Lake Co.)

Enl fr Putney, Vt, in Jan 1781, serving 10 mos as Pvt in the Company commanded by Josiah Fish in Col Samuel Fletcher's Regt. Br June 16, 1765, Northfield, Mass. Parents: William Wyman and Margaret Holmes. Mar Malinda Eaton, May 4, 1799. Children: Marietta, Lavinia, Czarina, Don, Guy, William, Franklin. D Mch 6, 1842, Perry, O. Bur Perry, O. GM New Connecticut. Fr Vermont he removed to Ohio. His father served in the same Company. Fur infor New Connecticut Chap.

WYNN, WILLIAM S., (Pike Co.)

Br 1750. Mar Mildred, who d Feb 13, 1828. D Pike Co, O. Feb 7, 1828, aged 78 yrs." Bur Mound Cem, Pike Co, O. At base of mound. GM now has a stone. Nathaniel Massie Chap will mark. Fur infor Nathaniel Massie Chap.

YATES, BENJAMIN, (Adams Co.)

Enl in Mch 1778 for 1 yr in Capt Pichett's Company. Re-enlisted May 1781 in Capt Murdock's Company. Wounded at Yorktown by piece of shell. Br Meadville, Pa. 1746. Mar Sarah Robinson, July 16, 1835. D Manchester, O. Jan 30, 1849. Bur in old Cem at Manchester, O. Applied for pens May 10, 1834, at which time he was 88 yrs old. His claim was allowed. Fur infor Sycamore Chap.

YEAGER, HENRY, (Mahoning Co.)

Ensign, Berks Co, 7th Company, 4th Bn, Pa Archives Series 6, Vol III, on p 850, 6th Class, Jacob Buss' Company, Northampton Co, 1784, Vol V, Pvt in Pami, 2nd Bn. Children: John, Daniel (mar Elizabeth), Mary (mar Jacob), Sarah (mar Henry Brunsetter), Elizabeth (mar Philip Stittle), Cristine and Saml. Bur Canfield. Grave not located. Came fr Lynn Twp Northampton Co Pa in 1802 with Saml Everett. Ref: Dr. Truesdales Hist of Canfield, Trumbull and Mahoning Co, Hist Vol II, p 57. Fur infor Mahoning Chap.

YOCUM, JOHN, (Wayne Co.)

Br 1755. D July 26, 1844, near Congress Village. The grave was in a small plot in the corner of a field, ½ mile south of Congress Village. MI: "John Yocum Soldier of 1776." A Pvt in Lt James Gleaves detachment of Berks Co Pa guarding convention prisoners. Ref: Series 5, Vol 5, p 293. Fur infor Wooster Wayne Chap.

YOEMAN, STEPHEN, (Fayette Co.

Spy back of the British Lines around New York City. Br 1748, New York. Children: Walter, James. D May 10, 1829, near Good Hope, O. Bur Rock Mills Cem, Fayette Co. Cem unplatted. MI: "In memory of Stephen Yoeman, who died May 10, 1829 in his 82 year." GM by family in 1829. Spy around New York, then a farmer and miller at Rock Mills. Bought 1400 acres in Richard Bibb's Survey (later Fayette Co.) in 1815. He and his sons Walter and James built first mill race and dam at Rocks Mills in 1817. Ref: Dill's Hist of Fayette Co 1881. Fur infor Washington C. H. Chap.

YOUNG, GEORGE, (Wyandot Co.)

Enl in Baltimore Co, Md, 1st Aug 23, 1776, later 1782; disch Nov 15, 1783. Br 1739, as parents enroute fr Ireland. Parents: John Young; the mother died at sea. Mar: 1st Mary Mackenzie; 2nd wife Rachel Allen nee Elsey bur by him. Reared a large family; youngest was David Y (br 1812, d about 1900 at Forest, Hardin Co, O.) D 1839. Bur 1½ mile north of Marseilles, Wyandotte Co, O, (on Enoch Thomas's Burying ground east bank of Tymochtee Creek). Landed at Baltimore, Md, where son was reared by "Polsen" family. Lived in Coshocton and Licking Cos, thence to Franklin, O.; thence about 1828 to Marseilles, O. (then Burlington P. O.) later to farm on west bank of Tymochtee, near Marseilles, O. Fur infor Mrs. Lullah Walker Merriman, Ex-State Chairman, Natl Old Trails Chap.

YOUNG, ISAAC, (Knox Co.)

Served in the Revolutionary War. Br Fairfield Co, Conn, 1760. D 1842 at the age of 82 yrs and 19 days. In 1790 moved to Uniontown, Pa, where he lived for many yrs and fr thence to Ohio in 1830 and to Monroe Twp, Knox Co, in 1836, where he resided until his death. Ref: Nortons Hist Knox Co, p 317. Fur infor Kokosing Chap.

YOUNG, ISAAC, (Knox Co.)

Pvt in the Westmoreland Co (Pa) Mil during the war of the Rev. (This data fr records at State Library, Harrisburg, Pa.) Br Sept 23, 1730. D Oct 18, 1812, aged 82 yrs 26 days. Bur Mound View Cem, Mount Vernon, O, Block 1, Lot 2. MI: "Isaac Young, died Oct 19, 1812, aged 82 years and 26 days." Fur infor Kokosing Chap.

YOUNG, JACOB, (Fayette Co.)

Br 1751. D May 29, 1833, Washington C. H. Bur Washington, C. H. Lot 205, Sec 8. MI: "Jacob Young died May 29, 1833 aged 82 years." GM by family in 1833. Fur infor Washington C. H. Chap.

YOUNG, MORGAN, (Delaware Co.)

Pvt under Cols Munson and Frelinghuyson, Capts Gaston, Carnes, Samuel Morris, and William Young. Bur Berkshire Twp. Pensioned. Fur infor Delaware Chap.

YOUNG, ROBERT, (Meigs Co.)

Pvt. Br about 1756 in Merrimack Co, N. H. Children: one son Abiathar Young. Bur Tupper Plains Cem Meigs Co, O.; GM by family soon after death. Ref: New Hampshire State Papers Vol 33. Fur infor L. L. Roush, 5725 Gallia Ave., Portsmouth, O. Accepted but not verified by Jane Dailey State Chairman.

ZANE, EBENEZER, (Belmont Co.)

Col. Defended Ft Henry, 3 da siege. His home a store house for munitions. Br Berkeley Co, Va. D Nov 19, 1812, (age 66 yrs). Bur Walnut Grove Cem, Martins Ferry, O. MI: "He was the first permanent inhabitant in this part of the Western World. He died as he lived an honest Man." Founder of Zanesville, O. D in Wheeling. Ref: Natl No 48124, p 59, Vol 49, D. A. R. Lin. and Mrs. Etzler, Wheeling Island, Wheeling, W. Va. Mrs Guy Hetzel "Stone Acres" Wheeling W. Va. Fur infor Wheeling W. Va. Chap.

ZANE, ELIZABETH, (Belmont Co.)

(Wife of Ebeneezer Zane, of "Powder fame") she went fr Ft Henry to Col Zane's house, where he tied a table cloth around her wrist, filled it with powder. Fleet of foot, she returned amid volleys, unharmed. "A man will be such great loss. I will not be missed" she had said. Mar Ebenezer Zane. D 1814 at 66 yrs of age. Bur Walnut Grove Cem, Martins Ferry, O. Grave not marked but being marked both in Martins Ferry and monument in Wheeling Park. Ref: Same as "Ebenezer Zanes." Fur infor Mrs A. L. McFarland, St Clairsville, of Wheeling D. A. R. Lin.

ZANE, ISAAC, (Muskingum Co.)

Captured by Indians at age 9, and carried to Lakes; Gave important information to Gen Edwd Hand, 1777; Granted land patent on Mad River Northwest Territory. Br 1753, Berkeley Co, Va. D 1816, Zanesville, O. See Howe's Hist Coll of Ohio Vol 2, p 104, altho a conflict of statements, his record has been accepted by the D. A. R. for services in Rev. (Jane Dailey State Chairman). Fur infor Natl No 36680, p 239, Vol 37, D. A. R. Lin.

ZANE, SILAS, Capt., (Co not Stated)

1st Lt and Capt 13th Virginia, Dec 28, 1776, Capt Feb 9, 1777. Dismissed Jan 25, 1778. (Heitmans Historical Register of the Officers of the Continental Army. p 611). Br between 1747-1753, Berkeley Co, Va. Mar 1st ——, 2nd Mrs. Katherine Ryan, near 1780. Children: Elizabeth by 1st mar; Silas by 2nd mar. Killed by Indians on the Scioto River (Ohio) 1785. The traditions of the family and the suppositions of some historians are, that his body was thrown over board in the Scioto river. He was in command of Ft Henry, when his sister "Betty" ran for the gunpowder. He was an active partisan during the Revolution and the border wars. He participated in the defense of Ft Henry when it was besieged by Indians and British in Sept 1782. (Beach's Indian Miscellany, p 59). He was in the defense of Ft Henry when invaded by Indians, Aug 31 and Sept 1, 1777. (Field Bk of the Rev, Vol 2, p 478). He was a bold, able and gallant co-laborer with his pioneer brothers. The Zane family was a remarkable one. (Pioneers of Fairfield Co (Ohio) p 13, 16). He died young, leaving two small children, Elizabeth Zane Dew Chap, Nelsonville, O, named for his dau, 1926. Fur infor Elizabeth Zane Dew Chap.

ZEHRING, CHRISTOPHER, (or CHRISTIAN), (Warren Co.)

Served as Pvt in Casper Steover's Company, 3rd of 2nd Bn Lancaster Co, Mil, 4th class, in 1781 and 1782. John Gloninger, Lt. Pa Tr, Lancaster Co. Served with brothers Henry and Lewis. Br Oct 5, 1755, Lancaster Co., Pa. Parents: A descendant of Ludwig Zehring, who came fr Baden, Germany, to Pa in 1725. Mar 1 ———— Umberger who d before his removal to Ohio in 1819; mar 2nd Anna Maria Rauch, (br Apr 11, 1762, d June 22, 1839, bur Germantown). Children: Henry, Elizabeth, Catherine; 2nd wife, Christian, John, Philip, William D, Jacob, David, Bernhard, Peter, Anna Maria, Susan, Martha. D June 5, 1832 in Warren Co, O. Bur Springboro, Warren Co, O. Came to Ohio in 1819. Ref: Natl No 38391 and 44661, D. A. R. Lin. Fur infor Richard Montgomery Chap. S. A. R.

ZEIGLAR, DAVID, Maj, (Montgomery Co.)

In 1775 joined the American Forces, and served with honor in the army of the Rev till the treaty of 1783. Br in Heidelberg, Germany, Aug 16, 1748. Parents: Johann Heinrich and Louisa Fredericka Kern Zeiglar. Mar Lucy Anna Sheffield at Marietta, 1789, (d Nov 18, 1820). D Cincinnati, O. Sept 1811. Fur in Presbyterian Church Cem but re-interred in Woodland Cem, Dayton, O. lot 1 to 4, Sec 55 to 65. MI: "Major David Zeigler, to whose memory this stone is erected was born in the city of Heidelberg 1748. Held a commission and served in the army of Russia. Migrated to Pa 1775; joined Army of Revolution, till by the treaty of 1783 the Independence of his adopted country was acknowledged. In the western country he served under Gen Harney and St Clair and died in this city Sept 1811; Universally esteemed and respected." GM by S. A. R. Bronze marker in

1919. 1st Pres (Mayor) of Cincinnati, O. Ref: Howes Hist of Ohio, Vol 1, p 853. Fur infor Jonathan Dayton D. A. R. and S. A. R. of Montgomery Co.

ZIMMERMAN, JOHN, (Mahoning Co.)

Pvt, Col Ludwig Wettner's 2nd German Regt. Continental Line, 1776. Corp Capt Strough's Company. Enl for 3 yrs July 25, 1776; disch Oct 12, 1779. This name also appears in 1782 in Balzar Orth's Company. Br 1747, came from Germany 1757. Mar Christina, Jan 7, 1770. Children: Joseph (in war of 1812) and others. D 1829, Washingtonville, O. Bur Lutheran Cem, Washingtonville, O. Grave not marked as soldier. Farmer. Ref: Pa Archives, 5th series Vol 3, p 801, Vol 5 p 242. Miss Mary Pow, Salem, O, 3 great grand dau. Fur infor Mahoning Chap.

ZUCK, JACOB, (Mahoning Co.)

Pvt Chester Co Mil. Capt Evan Anderson 1780. Same as above in 1781. Br 1746. D 1819. Bur Old Mennonite Cem, east of Byers Corners. Ref: Pa Archives, Series 5, Vol 5, p 596 and 630. Fur infor Mahoning Chap.

ALPHABETICAL LIST OF COUNTIES AND THEIR CHAPTERS

Sycamore Chapter

ADAMS COUNTY

Alfred, Henry
Baldridge, Rev. Wm.
Baldwin, John
Blake, Nicholas
Browser, Hendrick
Campbell, William
Cole, Ephraim
Collings, James
Copple, Daniel
Edgington, Joseph
Falkner, William
Falls, William
Faulkner, William
Fenton, Samuel
Fields, Charles
Finley, Joseph
Floyd, William
Foster, Nathaniel
Graham, John
Gustin, Amos
Killin, John
Kincaid, Thomas
Lewis, Phillip
Lovejoy, Joseph
McClean, William
McGarrah, William
McGarry, William
McIntire, Andrew
McManis, Charles
Malott, Thomas
Mahaffey, John
Mehaffey, John
Oldridge, Henry
Osman, Charles
Pemberton, William
Piatt, Benjamin
Smith, Henry
Stevenson, Charles
Treber, John
Walden, Elijah
Washburn, Nathaniel
Waters, Thomas
Williams, James
Williamson, Rev. William
Wilson, James
Woodworth, Richard
Yates, Benjamin

Lima Chapter, Lima, Ohio

ALLEN COUNTY

Chenoweth, William I.
Cochrun, Simon
Lippencott, Samuel

Sarah Copus Chapter, Ashland, Ohio

ASHLAND COUNTY

Anderson, William
Connie, Jeremiah
Fast, Christian
Heiffner, Jacob
Jones, Joseph
Murray, Patrick
Priest, James Louden
Sultzer, Frederick
Tilton, John

Luther Reeve Chapter, Rome, Ohio
Mary Redmond Chapter, Conneaut, Ohio
Mary Stanley Chapter, Ashtabula, Ohio
Eunice Grant Chapter, Jefferson, Ohio

ASHTABULA COUNTY

Allen, Elihu
Amsden, Abraham
Andrus, David
Arnold, Thomas
Atkins, Josiah
Austin, Eliphalet
Austin, Nathaniel
Barrett, Benjamin
Barrett, Thomas
Belknap, Calvin
Benham, Thomas
Benjamin, Asa
Brakeman, John
Brooks, Hannaniah
Brown, Henry, Jr.
Castle, Amasa
Cheney, William
Coleman, Nathaniel
Cowles, Noah
Crosby, Elijah
Deane, Walter
Dewolph, Abda (Dolph)
Dodge, Jeremiah
Dodge, Shadrach
Dolph Abda
Durkee, Solomon, Sr.
Fobes, Nathan
Fobes, Simon Capt.
Fobes, Simon
Gage, Abner
Goodale, Ebenezer
Hackett, Allen
Haines, Benjamin
Harper, Alexander
Harrington, Jonathan
Heath, Eleazer
Hickok, Durlin
Holman, Thomas
Hubbard, Isaac
Jewett, Joseph M.
Kellog, Eldad
King, Peter

(ASHTABULA COUNTY—Concluded)

Knowlton, Stephen, Jr.
LaMont, John
Lamson (Lampson), Ebenezer
Leonard, Abijah
Loomis, Horace
Loomis, Uriah
Mason, Nathan
Miller, Isaac
Mills, Constantine
Morrison, James
Norris, John, Jr.
Parker, Samuel
Pease, Joel
Peck, Dan
Phillips, Samuel
Pickett, John
Pratt, Oliver
Rathbone, Joseph
Read, Nathaniel
Reeve, Luther
Rood, Roger
Sackett, Skene Douglas
Scribner, Esther
Spooner, ——
Strong, Nathan
Tuttle, Clement
Wakefield, Peter
Walker, Walter
Ward, Benjamin
Warner, Noah
Waters, Benjamin J.
Watrous, John
Williams, Isaac
Winslow, Stephen
Wood, David

Nabby Lee Ames Chapter, Athens, Ohio

ATHENS COUNTY

Beebe, Hopson
Bingham, Alvan
Bingham, Silas Sr.
Brice, James
Brown, Benjamin
Brown, Samuel
Buckingham, Ebenezer
Burrell, Nathaniel

Elizabeth Zane Dew Chapter, Nelsonville, Ohio

Culver, Bezaliel
Dailey, David
Davis, Nehemiah
Dorr, Mathew
Dow Matthew
Fuller, James, Dr.
Gabriel, Abraham
Gates, David
Hatch, Elijah, Sr.
Hill, James
Johnson, Azel, Jr.
Lindley, Ziba
Logan, John, Sr.
Lyons, Joseph
Mansfield, Samuel
Mansfield, Thomas
Morey, Silas
Nash, Samuel
Phillips, Job
Reynolds, Ely
Rice, Jason
Risley, Samuel
Sawyer, Nathaniel
Stewart, Daniel
Sweet, Jonathan
Tippie, Uriah
Tuttle, Solomon
Vanderhoof, Cornelius
Watkins, Jonathan
Wickham, Joseph
Wyatt, Joshua

AUGLAIZE COUNTY

Richardson, William
Ridley, John
Sunderland, Peter
Taylor, William

BELMONT COUNTY

Alexander, James
Alexander, Margaret Clarke (Ross)
Barton, David
Broderick, William
Brokaw, George
Brown, Samuel
Coleman, Leonard
Cooper, Ezekiel
Davies, Marmaduke
Dickson, Robert
Gougan, Alexander M.
Hardesty, Richard
Howard, William
Hulse, William
Jordan, Thomas
Nixon, John
Palmer, John
Perrine, William
Perry, John
Ramsay, William
Ramsey, William
Rose, Michael
Ross, Margaret Clarke Alexander
Shannon, George
Slaughter, Frederick
Thompson, R.
Zane, Ebenezer
Zane, Elizabeth

Lieutenant Byrd Chapter, Decatur, Ohio
Ripley Chapter, Ripley, Ohio
Taliaferro Chapter, Georgetown, Ohio

BROWN COUNTY

Abbott, Joseph
Baird, William (Beard)
Barr (Baer) Adam
Barr, Christian
Barr, Christopher
Bartholomew, Samuel
Beard, William
Beasley, Benjamin
Bratton, Elisha
Brown, Gear
Burgett, Valentine
Cahall, James
Campbell, Matthew
Canary, Charles
Cochran, William

(BROWN COUNTY—Concluded)

Conely, Michael
Cooper, John
Cooper, William
Curry, Robert
Davidson, Joshua
Devore, Nicholas
Dixon, William
Dunlap, Alexander
Dye, John
Edwards, James
Ellis, Jesse
Ellis, Nathan
Ellis, Samuel
Evans, Edward
Feagin, Daniel
Gardner, Benjamin
Glaze, Basil
Harden, Richard
Heaton, Thomas
Heizer, John
Higgins, Robert
Hill, Alexander
Holden, Nehemiah
Hopkins, Archibald
Howland, John
Hughes, Joseph
Kennedy, Hugh
Laney, John
Leonard, Moses
McConnell, Thomas
McCoy, Alexander
McDaniel, Valentine
McDaniel, Walter
McLaughlin, John,
Malott, John
Marshall, George
Martin, Alexander
Montgomery, Sarah Bonne Brooks
Moore, William
Moses, Leonard
Norris, Aquila
Pickerill, Samuel
Poage, James
Printy, William
Ramey, Lawrence
Rankin, Daniel
Ried, Joab
Roddy, Ezekiel
Sams, Jonas
Scoville, Amasa
Shinkle, Christian
Shinkle, Han Philip
Shinkle, Philip Jacob
Spires, Richard
Stephenson, William
Stevenson, Robert
Stivers, John
Sutton, Benjamin
Thompson, John
Wardlow (Wardlaw), Robert
Wells, Benjamin
West, John
White, Adam
Williamson, William
Wood Nicholas

Col. Jonathan Bayard Smith Chapter, Middletown, Ohio
John Reily Chapter, Hamilton, Ohio
Oxford Caroline Scott Chapter, Oxford, Ohio

BUTLER COUNTY

Anderson, Isaac
Anderson, Robert
Armstrong, John
Bain, Jeremiah
Baker, Daniel
Barrett, Jonathan
Bathano, J.
Bathman, J.
Beckett, John C.
Berry, Thomas
Black, David
Blackburn, James
Bonnell, Paul
Butler, Richard
Butler, Thomas
Caldwell, William
Campbell, Enos
Carr, Thomas
Catterlin, James
Compton, Joseph
Cook, Joseph
Craig, John
Cummins, Peter
Darke, William
Dickey, Samuel
Dickson, Christopher
Dorsey, John Hammond, Jr.
Eggers, George
Emerson, Jonathan
Freeman, John
Garner, Henry
Garrigus, David
Gordon, George
Griffis, David
Grimes, James
Hall, John
Hammond, Isaac
Heston, Daniel
Hinsey, Cornelius
Hinsly, Cornelius
Hull, Isaac
Hunt, Thomas
Irwin, Thomas
Keiver, Henry
Kiever, Henry
Kitchell, John
Lewis, Andrew
Lummis, Joseph
McClellan, William
McMaken, Joseph
Meeker, Nathaniel
Miller, Elias
Miller, Jacob
Mills, Elijah
Montgomery, Abram
Murdock, Asahel
Murphy, Edward
Nesbitt, John
Niles, David
Nixon, Thomas
Paulhamis, John
Paxton, Isaac
Phillips, John
Pierce, Michael
Potter, Moses
Potter, Russell
Reece, David
Reed, George
Reily, James
Reily, John
Roll, Mathias
Sayre, Pierson
Seward, Samuel
Shafer, William
Shafor, Peter
Simmons, Thomas
Smalley, John
Smalley, Jonathan
Smith, John
Smith, Levi
Squier, Meeker
Sweringen, Joseph
Taylor, Henry
Taylor, Robert
Vandine, Mathew
Van Gorden, Alexander
Van Swearenger, John
Vaughn, Gardner
Vinnedge, John
Wallace, John
Warden, James
Waterman, Charles
Weaver, Henry (Judge)
Wilkinson, James
Wilson, Andrew
Wingate, John
Winton, Nathan
Woodmansee, James, Sr.
Wright, William

CARROLL COUNTY

Bushong, Joseph
Potts, John
Rippith, William
Westfall, Abraham

Urbana Chapter, Urbana, Ohio

CHAMPAIGN COUNTY

Burgis, John
Cheney, Thomas
Cranston, John
Dorsey, Charles
Fusen, William
Grafton, Thomas
Gump, William
Harnist, John
Johnson, Silas
McCoy, George
Pearce, Thomas
Powell, Abraham P.
Rader, Adam
Taylor, Benjamin
Tipton, Thomas
Vance, Joseph C.
Ward, William
Weaver, Christopher
Weaver, William
Welden, Jesse
West, Basil

Lagonda Chapter, Springfield, Ohio

CLARK COUNTY

Albin, John
Bacon, Richard
Bailey Timothy
Baird, William
Baker, Melyn
Bancroft, John
Bardwell, Simeon
Bayley (Bailey) Timothy
Beardsley, Elijah
Bridge, Benjamin
Brown, Frederick
Christie, Jesse
Craig, John S.
Davisson, Isaac
Dawson, Henry
Ebersole, Jacob
Farnham, John
Galloway, James
Garlough, John II
Gerlach, John Heinrich
Gerlough, John Henry
Harrimon, Stephen
Hempleman, George
Jones, Benjamin
Keller or (Kellar) John
Kelly, James
Lamb, James
Lamme, James
Lane, Robert
Lippencott, Samuel
Lowry, David
McClean, George
McCleave, George
McIntire, William
Miller, Moses
Nauman, Thomas
Poole, William
Priest, Jeremiah
Rodgers, William
Toland, Cornelius
Tollen, Cornelius
Tuttle, Sylvanus
Vicory, Merrifield
Wilson, Isaac

CLERMONT COUNTY

Allison, Richard
Arthur, James
Applegate, Zebulon
Ayers, ——
Baum, Charles
Bolender, Stephen
Bonser, Nathaniel
Branson, Jonathan
Bricker, Adam
Brown, Thomas
Buchanan, Alexander
Bunton, Ramoth
Byrns, Larry (or Lawrence)
Carter, James
Chambers, James
Clark, Perry
Cook, Absolom
Cowen, William, Lt.
Dennis, John
Dickey, Hughey
Dickey, Robert
Donley, James
Dowdney, Samuel
Eldridge, ——
Elstun, Eli
Fennel, Stephen
Ferguson, Isaac
Fisher, Adam
Glancy, Jesse
Hair, John
Harlow, Samuel
Hartman, Christopher
Howell, Samuel
Hulick, John
Huling, William
Jones, Thomas
Jones, William
Justice, Jesse
Light, Daniel
Light, Jacob
Light, John
Lindsay, William
Lindsey, Hezekiah
Lowe, Barton
McGrew, Andrew
McKnight, John
McKnight, William
Malloy, Hugh
Malott, Dory
Malott, William
Manning, Thomas
Megrue, Andrew
Miles, John
Morin, Rodham
Mulloy, Hugh
Newton, ——
Oliver, Alexander
Paxton, Thomas
Pease, Martin
Perin, Lemuel
Perrine, Joseph
Placard, Christian
Prickett, Josiah
Reeves, Nathaniel
Ridgely, ——, Jr.
Severn, Jesse
Shaylor, Joseph
Shaylor, Major
Simpkins, Ephraim
Sloane, William
Sly, William
Smith, Absolom
Smith, Dennis
Smith, Dr. John C.
Snider, Adam
South, Peter
Stone, Joseph
Stoner, Philip
Swem, Jesse
Thompson, Alexander

(CLERMONT COUNTY—Concluded)

Tingley, Levi
Trees, John
Utter, Joseph
Vannosdol, Oakey
Van Osdol, Oakey
Waite, Charles
Waite, James
Ward, Nehemiah
Weldon, ——
Wells, Robert
Wheeler, John
Wood, David
Woods, Thomas

Blanchester Chapter, Blanchester, Ohio
George Clinton Chapter, Wilmington, Ohio

CLINTON COUNTY

Achor, John
Boring, Absalom
Byard, George
Ellis, Abraham
Fuller, Benjamin, Jr.
Gaddis, Thomas
Gaskill, Samuel
Grant, Isaac
Hamrick, David
Hardin, Thomas
Hiney, George
Irvin, Andrew
Jack, Andrew
Krouse, John
Linkhart, Barney
Linn, Samuel
Parrott, Joseph
Riggs, William
Roberts, Edward
Sabin, Elijah
Shields, David
Spencer, James
Stewart, William M.

Bethia Southwick Chapter, Wellsville, Ohio

COLUMBIANA COUNTY

Altman, William
Armstrong, William
Beer, James
Bilgear (Bilger), Frederick
Black, John
Blackburn, Moses, Sr.
Boatman, Barnerd
Boyd, James
Brown, Isaac
Burger, Nicholas
Butler, Benjamin
Cameron, Lewis
Carnaghey, William
Catlett, Jonas
Chamberlain, Stout
Chapman, Nathaniel
Clippinger, Anthony
Coburn, John
Cormody, John
Crowl, George
Crozer, John
Dickey, Moses
Dildine, John
Dill, Thomas
Dixon, Joshua
Farrall, William
Figgins, James
Fisher, Henry
Fisher, Paul
Frederick, Thomas
Flanagan, John
Grant, Noah
Hawke, Jacob
Hight, John
Hoopes, Benjamin
Hunter, George
Huston, Samuel
Jones, Catlett, Sr.
Kent, Thomas
Klippinger, Anthony
Leonard, Silas
Lindesmith, Joseph
Lyons, Samuel
MacLachlan, James
McBride, Stephen
McCalla, Thomas
McCaskey, William
McClelland, James
McCormick, Francis
McKennon, Joseph
McKinley, David
McLaughlin, James
Mankins, William
Meek, Samuel
Moore, John
Nicholas, William
O'Donnell, William
Owen, Thomas
Palmer, Steven
Payne, Abraham
Quigley, Samuel
Quinn, John
Rupert, Adam
Rupert, Jacob
Sanders, William
Sanor, Michael
Sheets, Christian
Shirts, Matthias, Sr.
Smith, James
Travis, John
Van Fossen, Jacob

Coshocton Chapter, Coshocton, Ohio

COSHOCTON COUNTY

Adams, John
Bantum, John
Buel, John
Carpenter, John
Collins, John
Fought, John Morris
Fowler, Richard
Israel, Basil
Ketcham, Samuel
McCune, John
McPherson, John
Miller, Henry
Miller, Henry
Musser, Christian
Norris, William, Sr.
Ogilvie, Thomas
Ravenscroft, William
Robinson, William, Maj.
Simmons, William
Speaks, William
Thompson, Joseph
Tipton, Solomon
Wiley, Samuel
Williams, Charles
Williams, John
Williams, William
Winslow, John
Winslow, William
Two unknown soldiers

Hannah Crawford Chapter, Bucyrus, Ohio
Olentangy Chapter, Galion, Ohio

CRAWFORD COUNTY

Carson, Robert
Couts, Christian
Dowd, Isaac
Link, Adam
McKinley, David
Miller, John Adam

Lakewood Chapter, Lakewood, Ohio
Moses Cleaveland Chapter, Cleveland, Ohio
Western Reserve Chapter, Cleveland, Ohio

CUYAHOGA COUNTY

Adams, Samuel
Adamy, Henry
Baldwin, Seth C.
Bosworth, John
Brainard, Amos
Brainard, Jabez
Burk, Sylvanus
Burke, Joseph
Burke, Sylvanus
Coleman, Jacob
Cooper, Obediah
Crocker, Jedediah
Crozier, John
Currier, Sergeant
Dean, Samuel
Dille, David
Edwards, Adonijah
Emery, John
Farrand, Jared
Fenton, Gamaliel
Foot, David
Ford, Hezekiah
Fuller, William
Hall, John
Hanchett, Jonah
Hudson, Joshua
Judd, Daniel S.
Kellogg, Josiah
Keyes, Elias
McIlarth, Andrew
McKay, Daniel
Miner, John
Murray, John
Myrick, Joseph
Nichols, James
O'Brien, Daniel
Palmer, Adam
Palmiter, John
Palmiter, Jeshua
Perry, Nathan
Porter, Joseph
Prentiss, James
Rathburn, Edward, Sr.
Robbins, Jason
Rodgers, Josiah
Russell, Jacob
Sadler, William
Sawyer, Jacob
Shepard, John
Shepard, Phineas
Sherwin, Ahinaaz
Smith, Abner
Smith, Jonathan
Smith, Sylvanus
Stanard, Claudius
Stewart, Samuel
Stiles, Asa
Stone, Joel
Waite, Benjamin
Warren, Moses
Willcox, Josiah
Willey, Allen, Jr.

Fort Greenville Chapter, Greenville, Ohio

DARKE COUNTY

Adams, George
Ashley, William
Beam, ———
Brown, William
Dugan, James
Grimes, George
Pierson, Jonathan
Reed, John
Stephens, George
Ward, David
Wells, John

Fort Defiance Chapter, Defiance, Ohio

DEFIANCE COUNTY

Delaware City Chapter, Delaware, Ohio

DELAWARE COUNTY

Adams, Abraham
Adams, David
Atherton, James
Beddow, Thomas
Bennett, Oliver
Bidlack (Bidlock), Philemon
Black, Isaac
Black, William
Blain, Alam
Brown, Ezekial
Byxbe, Moses
Carpenter, Judge Benj.
Carpenter, Rev. Gilbert
Carpenter, Hiram
Carpenter, Nathan
Caulkins, Roswell
Clark, James
Conklin, David
Conrad, Cline
Cook, Roswell
Coykendall, Harmon
Dunlap, Joseph
Fisher, Jacob
Gaylord, Justus
Hemrod, Andrew
Hill, Zimri
Hillman, Benj.
Hillman, John
Himrod, Andrew
Huff (Hoff), John
Jameson, Robert
Jones, Solomon
Kooken, James
Landon, Ebenezer
Longwell, James

(DELAWARE COUNTY—Concluded)

Lott, Ebenezer
Lott, Zeppeniah
McCoy, Ephraim
McKinnie, John
McKnight, Adam
Main, Perres
Monroe, Isaac
Moore, James L.,
Morgan, Peletiah
Myers, ———
Newell, Benjamin
Norris, ———
Orton, Lemuel
Paine, John
Parker, Stiles
Potter, Joseph
Potter, Joseph, Jr.
Rodgers, Bixby
Root, Azariah
Scott, Ebenezer
Scribner, Samuel
Sebring, Fulkard
Smith, Daniel
Smith, Solomon
Spaulding, Abel
Swartz, John
Taylor, Daniel
Thompson, Richard.
Vandorn, Gilbert
Van Sickle, Peter
Warren, Thomas 2nd
Warrington, John
Warrington, William
Wilcox, Jehial
Williams, Abram
Williams, John or James
Williams, Nehemiah
Wort, John
Young, Morgan

Martha Pitkin Chapter, Sandusky, Ohio

ERIE COUNTY

Bates, Daniel
Brooks, John
Carpenter, Daniel
Carswell, David
Chapman, Michael
Cherry, Henry
Churcn, John (Jonathan)
Cook, Chauncey
Falley, Frederick
Haliday, Eli
Hunt, Jonathan
McMillan, John
McMillen, John
Mingus, Hieronymus
Parsons, Jabez
Ransom, Joseph
Ranson, Robert
Remington, Joseph
Schaefer, Lambert
Simpson, Alexander
Strong, Joseph
Van Benschoten, Aaron
Wells, Robert

Elizabeth Sherman Reese Chapter, Lancaster, Ohio

FAIRFIELD COUNTY

Allen, Silas
Alspaugh, John
Alspaugh, Michael
Barr, Andrew
Bartoon, John
Beatty, John
Beers, Matthew
Binckley, Christian
Binckley, Henry
Blundon, Elijah
Bobenmier, Gabriel
Buffington, David
Carpenter, Emanuel, Sr.
Carpenter, Emanuel, Jr.
Carpenter, John
Coleman, John
Collins, James S.,
Courtright, Abram Van Campen
Cradleebaugh, John (Kreidelbach)
Critchefield, Joshua
Cross, John
Crowerciler, Henry.
Davis, William
Eruman, Frederick
Eyman, Henry
Guseman, John, Sr.
Heller, Henry
Hensel, Michael
Hill, George
Keckler, Jacob
Keller, Henry
Kreidelbach, John
Lamb, Peter
Leist, Samuel
McFarland, William
McTeer, Robert
Martin, John
Massey, Ezekiel
Miller, Daniel
Nigh, George
Nye, George
Puppingmeyer, Gabriel (see Bobenmier)
Rice, Michael
Rigby, William
Shumaker, William
Smith, Benjamin H.
Smith, Jonathan
Staudt, George William
Stout, George William
Stevenson, John
Swayze, David
Wagner, Michael
Walter, James
Watson, Thomas
Weist, Jacob
Wells, James
Wilson, William
Wiseman, Rev. John
Work, Samuel

Washington Court House Chapter, Washington C. H., Ohio
William Horney Chapter, Jeffersonville, Ohio

FAYETTE COUNTY

Allen, Adam
Blue, Michael
Bryant, Ross
Bush, Leonard
Christy, Robert
Cockerill, Thomas
DeFord, John
Fanshir, Isaac
Fent, Philip
Gregory, Nehemiah
Griffith, Samuel
Hess, Peter
Klever, John
Loufbourrow, John Wade.
Myers, Jacob
Newland, John
Nutt, John
Priddy, John
Rowe, Jesse
Rupert, George
Sexton, Charles
Stitt, William
Yoeman, Stephan
Young, Jacob

Ann Simpson Davis Chapter, Columbus, Ohio
Columbus Chapter, Columbus, Ohio
Jacobus Westervelt Chapter, Westerville, Ohio

FRANKLIN COUNTY

Baughman, George
Beckett, Humphrey
Bull, Thomas, Jr.
Clouse, John
Crawford, James
Culbertson, Robert
Dague, Mathias
Davis, Ann
Davis, John
Davis, Samuel
Deardorf, Abraham
Dierdorf, Abraham (Ger.)
Denmore, John
Denune, John
Foos, John
Hess, Bolser
Hickman, Joseph
Hoover, John
Huff, John
Ingalls, Joseph
Legg, Elijah
McComb, William
Mickey, Daniel
Moore, Benjamin
Moore, Simeon
Murphy, William
Nelson, David
Noble, Seth (Rev.)
Olmstead, Francis
Orton, Lemuel, Jr.
Phelps, Edward
Pinney, Abner
Price, Stephen R.
Rugg, Moses
Sells, Ludwick
Smith, John
Sprague, Frederick
Starr, John
Starrett, John
Wait, Jenks
Walcutt, William
Webster, Philogus
White, Samuel

Wauseon Chapter, Wauseon, Ohio

FULTON COUNTY

Brown, Phineas
Hilton, William
Holland, Dr. William
Knapp, Jeremiah
Pennington, Ephraim
Roice, Isaac
Tiney, Richard

French Colony Chapter, Gallipolis, Ohio

GALLIA COUNTY

Blazer, Jacob
Clark, Thomas
Ewing, William
Hayward, Solomon
Howe, Amasi
Loucks, William
Loux, William
Lowry, Jeremiah
McDaniel, Henry
Manring, Jordan Marshal
Northrup, Daniel
Rouch, Philip
Roush, Jacob
Roush, Philip
Strait (Straight), John
Trobridge, Levi
Waddell, Alexander
Williams, William

Molly Chittenden Chapter, Geauga County
Taylor Chapter, Chardon, Ohio

GEAUGA COUNTY

Alden, David
Alford, Benedict
Barnes, Israel
Barnes, Mark
Barnes, Moses
Beard, Amos
Benton,, Zadock
Bradley, Thaddeus
Bridgman, Elisha
Brooks, David
Carlton, Darius
Carter, Jonas
Church, Philemon
Cleveland, Samuel
Cook, Mariman
Curtis, Reuben
Damon, Abraham
Davenport, Esquire
Dunwell, Stephen
Eggleston, Eliab
Elliott, John
Ellsworth, William
Fellows, Parker
Ford, John
Ford, Nathan
Fowler, Caleb
Ganson, Nathan
Gilmore, James
Goff, James
Hayes, Seth
Heminway, Samuel
Herrick, Libbeus
Hickok, Nathaniel (Hickox) (Various spellings)
Hopkins, Ebenezer
Hosmer, Zachariah
Hutchins, Moses
Johnson, Benjamin
Kentfield, Ebenezer
Kidder, Reuben
King, Benjamin
Kingsley, Enos
Lake, Reuben
Lane, Joseph
Loveland, Frederick
McFarland, Daniel
Mastick, Benjamin
Melvin, Reuben
Metcalf, Thomas
Miner, Justus
Moore, James
Moore, John 3rd
Morgan, Daniel
Northrup, Stephan
Parks, Nathan
Pease, Isaac
Phelps, Ira
Phelps, Seth
Pomeroy, Daniel

(GEAUGA COUNTY—Concluded)

Pomeroy, Ichabod
Poole, Jeptha
Potter, Bordon
Quiggle, Peter
Rider, Benjamin, Sr.
Rogers, Josiah
Russell, Gideon
Russell, Samuel
Slitor, James
Sluyter, James
Smith, Benjamin
Smith, David
Smith, Josiah
Snow, Oliver
Starr, Samuel Moore
Stocking, Reuben
Thompson, Isaac
Thompson, Peter
Thompson, William
Thwing, John
Trask, Retire
Wells, Timothy
Wilber, Joseph
Wilson, Israel
Winters, John
Witter, Joseph

Catherine Greene Chapter, Xenia, Ohio
Cedar Cliff Chapter, Cedarville, Ohio
George Slagle Chapter, Jamestown, Ohio

GREENE COUNTY

Adams, Thomas
Aley, Abraham
Allen, William
Batchelor, George
Berry, Bartholomew
Berryhill, Alexander
Buckles, William, Sr.
Bull, William, Sr.
Campbell, James
Cane, Daniel
Case, Elijah, Sr.
Cunningham, Richard
Cusbott, Robert
Davis, Silas
Davis, Thomas 2nd
Davis, Wm. F. R.
Deeds, George
Dunn, Reuben
Elam, Joshua
Ervin, John
Espy, Josiah
Galloway, James, Sr.
Galloway, Joseph
Gregg, John, Sr.
Greiner, George
Harbison, Robert
Harper, John, Sr.
Haughey, Thomas
Horney, William
Irwin, John
Jackson, Robert
Junkin, Lancelot, Jr.
Kendall, Robert, Sr.
Kyle, Joseph, Sr.
Lambert, Joseph
Lamme, Nathan
McDonald, ——
McHatten, Alexander
McLane, or McLean, John
Mallow, George, Sr.
Mann, George
Maxey, Horatio
Maxwell, William
Mitchell, David
Musgrave, John
Parmelee, John
Parsons, John, Sr.
Reaves, Asher
Rhodes, Nicholas
Sanders, John
Scott, John
Seamon, Henry
Small, James
Smith, Jacob
Snodgrass, James
Snodgrass, Samuel
Stewart, William, Sr.
Stepp, George
Stipp, Joseph
Stump, Daniel
Thatcher, Amos
Torrence, John
Townsley, John
Townsley, Thomas
Warren, Edward
Webb, Samuel B.,
Whiteman, Benjamin
Winter, Stephen
Wright, George

Anna Asbury Stone Chapter, Cambridge, Ohio

GUERNSEY COUNTY

Bailey, Jared
Bay, Robert
Bonnell, Isaac
Bratton, James
Chambers, Robert
Christopher, Walter
Cockley, John
Cook, Thomas B.
Danhaeffer, Christopher, Sr.
Dilley, Ephraim, Sr.
Eaton, Joseph
Jack, James
Kackley, John
Kimball, Nathan
Lawrence, Thomas
Ledman, John
Lewis, John
Lieuzadder, Abraham
Linn, Adam
Linn, John
Moffat, Robert
Montgomery, Michael
Morrison, George
Reasoner, Peter
Spaid, George
Wallace, William
Walter, Christopher
Walter, John
Whittier, Andrew
Williams, Joseph

Cincinnati Chapter, Cincinnati, Ohio

HAMILTON COUNTY

Allen, Jacob
Allison, Richard
Alston (or Allston), Thomas
Andrew, John
Arnold, Richard
Auten, Thomas
Baldwin, Eleazer
Bartle, John
Bates, Isaac
Baxter, Schuyler (?)
Bell, John

(HAMILTON COUNTY—Continued)

Bevis (or Beaves), Issachur
Bickel, Christian
Black, David
Bonham, John
Bonnel, Aaron
Bonnell, James
Boss, Adam
Bowen, Thomas
Brasher, John
Brewster, William
Broadwell, Jacob
Brown, William
Brown, William
Bruen, Jabez
Bryson, James
Buckingham, Levi
Buell, Ephraim
Burrows, Jeremiah
Bushnell, Jason
Caldwell, Robert
Cameron, Alexander
Campbell, John
Carey, Christopher
Carle, John
Cavender, John
Chapin, Lucius
Charlton, John
Cilley, Jonathan
Clark, Daniel
Clark, Dennis
Clark, George
Clark, James
Clark, John
Clark, Nathaniel
Clark, Thomas
Clark, William
Coke, Philip
Coleman, Neniad
Cooper, Spencer
Cortelyou, Henry
Covalt, Abraham
Cox, Andrew
Cox, James
Cox, Tunis
Crane, Caleb
Cranmer, John
Crary, John
Crist, Christian
Cunningham, James
Cutter, John
Cutter, Seth
Davis, Daniel
Davis, Joshua, Sr.
Day, Jehial
Deats, Henry
De Camp, James
Delzell, William
Dodson, John
Douglass, Randall
Downs, Jesse
Drake, Isaac
Drake, Joshua
Dregden, William
Dugan, Henry
Dunn, Abner Martin
Dunn, Duncan
Eaton, Alexander
Ebersole, Solomon
Elliott, Robert
Engart, Benjamin
Enems, John
Ewing, Thomas
Felter, Cronymus
Felter, Isaac
Felter, Jacob
Felter, Matthias
Fenton, Solomon
Ferguson, James
Ferguson, John
Ferguson, William
Ferris, Isaac
Ferris, John
Filson, John
Finch, William
Findlay, Robert W.,
Finney, Ebenezer W.
Finney, Major
Flinn, Benjamin
Flint, Hezekiah
Foster, Asa
Frazee, Jonas
Gage, Reuben
Gard, Gershem
Gloyd, Asa
Goforth, William
Goldtrap, John
Gowdy, James
Grant, William
Green, Joel
Griffin, Daniel
Griffin, Robert
Guest, Moses
Gunsalus, Henry
Gwinnup, George
Hageman, Adrian
Hahn, Michael
Halsey, Joseph, Jr.
Halsey, Luther
Halstead, John
Hankins, Richard
Hardin, John
Harner, James
Harris, Joseph
Harris, William
Hatch, Abner
Hathorn, James
Hawley, Eben Rice
Hays, Oliver
Higgins, John
Hillyer, James
Hipsher, Anderson
Holden, Richard S.
Hopple, Casper
Horn, Frederick
Hosbrook, John
Howard, Solomon
Hubbell, Gershom
Hudson, John
Jackson, Matthews
Johnson, Abner
Johnston, Thomas
Johnston, Nicholas
Jones, John
Keelor, Thomas
Kelly, Oliver
Kelsimere, Francis
Kennedy, Francis
Kenniston, James
Kerr, John
Keys, Richard
Kitchell, Daniel
Kitchell, Moses
Lacy, Thomas
Lafler, John
Langdon, John W.
Larew, Abraham
Lee, Peter Perrine
Leiby, George
Lemon, Alex
Lemond, William
Lewis, Isaac
Limming, Samuel
Little, Cornelius
Livingston, David
Loar, Henry
Lodowick, Weller
Lowe, Judge Derrick
Lynch, Peter
Lyon, James
McCrackin, Cyrus (Cypress? SAR)
McCracken, William
McCrea, Gilbert
McCullough, Robert
McKnight, David
Maddock, Moses
Marsh, John
Martin, Alexander
Martin, Oliver
Matson, John
Meeker, John
Mercer, John
Miller, Daniel
Miller, Edward
Mitchell, Philip
Morgan, Jacob
Morris, Jacob
Morris, John
Moss, Daniel
Neves, William
Nichols, Francis
Norris, Andrew
Norris, Bethnal
Norris, Gershom
Pack, William
Parker, John
Parson, Osborn
Phelps, Abijah
Pierce, Samuel
Pierson, Abraham
Pierson, David
Pierson, Matthias
Pierson, Samuel
Pitman, Jonathan

(HAMILTON COUNTY—Concluded)

Posey, Zephaniah
Price, Thompson
Reeder, Jacob
Reeder, Joseph 4th
Reeder, Stephen
Reeder, William
Richardson, Jacob
Richardson, John
Riddle, John
Riggs, Bethuel
Robinson, John
Rogers, Henry
Roosa, Jacob (Jacobus)
Rose, John
Ross, Joseph
Rude, Zelah
Rynearson, John
Rynierson, John
Schooly, John
Sedam, Cornelius R.
Selman, John
Seward, Daniel
Shepherd, Elisha
Sheppard, Elisha
Sherman, Ezra
Shipman, John
Skeel, Nathan
Skillman, Jacob
Slayback, William
Smith, Abraham
Smith, Ballard
Smith, Nathan
Smith, Phillip D.,
Smith, William
Snyder, Cornelius Sr.
Snyder, Cornelius Jr.
Sparr, Richard
Spencer Oliver
Springer, Jacob
Sprong, David
Stacy, Thomas
Starr, Richard
Stevens, Nicholas
Stites, Benjamin
Stites, Hezekiah
Stone, Charles
Stout, Andrew
Strong, Barnabas
Strong, David
Sturgis, Jedediah
Sullivan, Patrick
Symmes, John
Symmes, Timothy
Taulman, Harmanus
Terwilliger, Nathaniel
Thompson, Prize
Tibbetts, Isaac
Todd, William
Tucker, Henry
Tucker, John
Turner, John B.
Turrill, Jared
Van Cleve, John
Van Voorhees, Abraham
Voorhees, Abraham
Voorhees, Abraham Jr.
Voorhees, Garret
Wade, David E.
Walker, Christopher
Walker, Peter
Wallace, John S.
Wallace, William
Ward, Amos
Waring, Jonathan
Weller, Lodowick
Weller, William
Wheeler, Stephen
Whitcomb, Anthony
Whitcomb, John
White, Edward II
White, Thomas
Williams, Benjamin
Williams, John
Williams, Miles
Williams, Thomas
Willyard, Henry
Wilmuth, Thomas
Wilson, William
Wiltsee, Cornelius
Wood, Benjamin
Wood, Ebenezer
Wood, Israel
Wood, Levi

Fort Findlay Chapter, Findlay, Ohio

HANCOCK COUNTY

Beam, Jacob
Brown, William
Carroll, William
Fight, Jacob
Fisher, John
Fox, Jacob
Helmick, Nicholas
Hulbert, Ephriam
Katzenberger, John
Lake, Asa
Lee, Zebulon
McKinley, John
Smith, Rev John
Teatsorth, Isaac

Moravian Trail Chapter, Cadiz, Ohio

HARRISON COUNTY

Alexander, Joseph
Allen, Josiah
Ames, Mordecai
Archbold, Thomas
Bartow, Zenas
Beman, Moses
Biner, George
Black, James
Boone, Squire
Boyles, Timothy
Brannon, John
Brannon, John
Carle, Ephraim
Clark, James
Conaway, Charles
Conaway, Michael
Dickerson, George
Dickson, George
Ferguson, Henry
Ferguson, William
Finney, John
Forney, Abraham
George, John
Greery, John
Haley, Thomas
Haun, John
Helmick, Nicholas
Hines, Rudolph
Holland, Gabriel
Holmes, Francis
Johns, Thomas
Kent, Absalom
Lafferty, Edward
Larkins, James
Leeper, Archibald
Lyons, William
McClelland, Samuel
McCullough, William
McDonough, Hugh
McFadden, John
Magaw, John
Maholm, Samuel
Manchester, Joseph
Martin, Henry
Megaw, John
Milligan, David
Morgan, Thomas
Nelson, John Jr.
Parker, John
Parkinson, Thomas
Peacock, Neal
Porter, Robert
Rankin, Henry
Rankin, James

(HARRISON COUNTY—Concluded)

Rankin, Thomas
Reppart, Daniel
Ritchey, Jacob
Ross, John
Rowland, John
Russell, James
Sawvel, Adam
Schultz, George
Slemmons, William
Snyder, Martin
Stone, Benjamin
Sudduth, Isaac
Todd, William
Wagstaff, William
Walters, Frederick
Welch, Daniel Jr.
Wells Charles D.
Wilson, Benjamin
Wylie, Adam

Juliana White Chapter, Greenfield, Ohio
Waw-Wil-A-Way Chapter, Hillsboro, Ohio

HIGHLAND COUNTY

Anderson, James
Barnard, Thomas
Barnes, Jacob
Beatty, Andrew
Bell, William Jr.
Bernard, Thomas
Brown, Daniel Jr.
Buntian, William
Byram, Edward
Collier, James
Crawford, John
Creed, Matthew
Douglass, William
Downing, William
Evans, Evan
Evans, Hugh
Ferguson, John Sr.
Gall, George Jr.
Gibson, Samuel
Harper, John W.
Higgins, William
Horn, Joseph
Hunter, John
Johnson, Ashley
Kerns, John 1st
Koon, Frederick
Leaverton, John Foster
Moberly, Reason
Pope, Henry
Preskett, William
Puckett, William
Richardson, John
Robinson, Lewis
Robinson, Thomas
Ruble, John
Ruse, Aaron
Searl, Reuben
Shafer, Andrew
Smalley, David
Smith, Drummond
Smith, William
Sonner, T. Anthony
Spickard, George
Strain, Samuel
Strain, Thomas
Stultz, John
Taylor, Daniel
Tyler, David
Tyler, John
Underwood, James
Van Winkle, William
Walker, David
Watts, James
West, Joseph
White, Charles
Wirt, Conrad

HOLMES COUNTY

Brasbridge, John
Critchfield, John
Gwin, John
Metzler, George
Myers, Peter
Trimble, John

Sally DeForest Chapter, Norwalk, Ohio
Firelands Chapter, Willard, Ohio

HURON COUNTY

Bacon, George
Baker, Abner
Barbee, Amaziah
Barre, Ira S.
Bishop, Daniel
Bishop, Joel
Brooks, James (Or John)
Carney, John
Church, John (or Jonathan)
Cook, Aseph
Cook, Ebenezer
Cook, Joseph
Cooley, Luther Sr.
Curtis, Isaac (or Custis)
Drake, Benjamin
Fay, Aaron
Fish, Ephraim
Foote, Timothy
Furnace, William
Hand, Abraham
Haskell, Prince
Higgins, David
Hoyt, Agur
Husted, Shadren
Jeffrey, David
Johnston, William
Kellogg, Martin
Kimball, Moses
Lampson, Isaac
Mead, Michael
Norton, Noah
Palmer, Alva
Parks, Michael
Pond ——
Raymond, Lemuel
Raymond, Thaddeus
Rowland, Luke
Sampson, Isaac
Sowers, John III
Sutton, Moses
Taylor, Timothy
Terry, Julius
Underhill, David
Waldron, Joseph
Wheeler, Asa Sr.
Wilcox, ——

Capt. John James Chapter, Jackson, Ohio

JACKSON COUNTY

Anthony, George
Arthur, Joel
Calhoon, Samuel
Canter, William
Clark, William
Corn, George
Crow, William
Dailey, William
Davis, John
Davis, Walter
Dawson, James
Exline, John
Graham, James
Hanna, John
Horton, Josephus
Hughes, Henry
Hulse, James
Jenkins, Azariah
Jones, Thomas
Keaton, ——
Larrabee, Seth
Leach, George
McDaniel, James
Oliver, Thomas
Owens, William
Russell, Enoch
Stephenson, John
Traxler, Emanuel
Weese, George
West, John
Whaley, George

Steubenville Chapter, Steubenville, Ohio
Michael Myers Chapter, Toronto, Ohio

JEFFERSON COUNTY

Alban, George
Andrew, John
Cable, Philip
Day, George
Dorhrman, Arnold Henry
Fisher, John C.
Hall, Reuben
Hamilton, Williams
Hill, Robert
Johnson, Richard
Kimball, Moses
Lingley, Gereniah
McCune, Thomas
McDowell, John
McGuire, John
Markle, Abram T.
Martin, Jacob
Meek, Isaac
Potts, Johnathan
Sharon, William
Shaw, Nathan
Sherrard, John
Simeral, Alexander
Spiller, John
Taylor, William
Tingley, Jeremiah
Voorhees, Jacob
William, Joseph

Kokosing Chapter, Mt. Vernon, Ohio

KNOX COUNTY

Ackerman, John
Blair, Abraham
Bouton, Jehiel Jr.
Chapman, Lemuel
Cook, Stephen
Cowden, John
Critchfield, Joseph
Critchfield, Nathaniel
Critchfield, William
Curtis, Zarah
Ewalt, John
Giffin, Stephen (or Giffin)
Harrod, Levi
Huston, Robert
Jackson, Benjamin
Jackson, Daniel
Johnston, William
Landon, Edward
Lefever, Minard
McClelland, Cary
McWilliams, William
Mott, John
Phifer, Jacob
Pierson, John
Spry, William
Thrift, William Sr.
Wade, Zephaniah
Ward, Rufus
Young, Isaac
Young, Isaac Jr.

New Connecticut Chapter, Painesville, Ohio

LAKE COUNTY

Abel, John
Ames, Stephen
Antisel, Silas
Bailey, Silas
Bartram, Daniel
Bates, Benjamin
Beebe, Ezra
Bidwell, William Sr.
Bissell, Benjamin
Blish, Benjamin
Branch, William
Brass, Garritt
Brown, Oliver
Cahoon, William
Call, Joseph
Campbell, John
Card, William
Carpenter, Ezra
Carter, Jabez
Cleveland, Tracy
Cole, Justin
Colson, Christopher
Craine, Roger
Cram, Roger
Crandall, Amariah
Danforth, John
Eddy, William R.
Ellis, Lemuel
Emerson, Jesse
Emerson, Joseph
Emms, Joshua
Ensign, William
Evans, Ora
Ferguson, John
Fobes, Lemual
Ford, Andrew
Forgeson, John
Fox, Israel
French, Nathan
French, Seba
Fuller, Joseph Sr.
Furguson, John
Green, Joseph
Hall, Hezekiah
Halstead, Edward

(LAKE COUNTY—Concluded)

Hanks, Elijah
Harmon, Oliver
Hayden, Samuel
Hill, Amasa
Hidges, Simeon
Holcomb, Joel
Hollister, Ashel
Hungerford, Josiah
Huntoon, Thomas
Hutchins, William
Jewell, Ephraim
Jones, Benaiah Jr.
Jones, Elkanah
Joy, Ebenezer
Kimball, Abel
Ladd, Jesse (Dea)
Markell, Peter
Martin, Isaac
Messenger, Isaac
Mixer, Phineas Sr.
Morley, Ezekiel
Morley, Thomas
Morse, Benjamin (Major)
Nichols, Jones
Norwood, Stephen
Paine, Edward
Paine, Eleazer
Parks, Amaziah
Pitcher, Benjamin
Reynolds, John
Rogers, Samuel
Rosa, Isaac
Sawtell, Benjamin
Sessions, Anson
Simmon, Peleg
Skinner, Abraham
Smead, Samuel
Smith, John
Sperry, Marauchie Van Orden
Sweet, Caleb
Sweet, Joshua
Turney, Asa
Tyler, Jacob
Vrooman, Bartholomew
Waits, William
Wilson, Ebenezer
Wirt, Mertin
Woodworth, Ezekiel
Woodworth, James
Woolsey, Daniel
Wright, James
Wyman, William Jr.

LAWRENCE COUNTY

Losee, William
McCorkle, Robert
Strother, Robert

Granville Chapter, Granville, Ohio
Hetuck Chapter, Newark, Ohio

LICKING COUNTY

Adams, Elujah
Albaugh, Zachariah
Allberry, John
Baker, Daniel
Ball, Samuel
Beard, John
Beem, Michael
Benjamin, Jonathan
Brandt, Adam
Brown, Nicholas
Bryan, Elijah
Callahan, George
Carpenter, Samuel
Channell, John
Colville, James
Coombs, Mahlon
Conklin, David
Coulter, John
Cox, Benjamin
Davis, Azariah
DeWolf, Benjamin
Edman, Samuel
Edwards, John
Elliott, Samuel
Emmitt, John
Everett, Samuel Sr.
Freeman, Solomon
Gavitt, William
Gilbert, Sewell
Green, Benjamin
Harris, William Sr.
Hill, Caleb
Holmes, James Sr.
Horn, George (or Horne)
Hughes, Elias
Humphrey, Evans (or Richard)
Jewett, Abel
Jolly, Henry
Larabee, John Sr.
Linnell, Joseph
Lloyd, George E. Sr.
McCadden, John
Martin, Charles
Martin, Charles Honneywood.
Martin, John
Mead, Stephen
Mentzer, Japhat
Messenger, David
Miner, Elisha
Munson, Jesse
Nichols, Leve
Owen, Noah
Perkins, Thomas
Philbrook, Joel
Pratt, Worthy
Rose, Lemuel
Rose, Timothy
Scott, Hugh (J. or Jr.?)
Scovell, Moses
Seymour, Thomas
Smith, William
Spelman, Timothy
Stadden, Isaac
Steele, Eldad
Stockwell, Jesse
Taylor, James
Thrall, Samuel Jr.
Trevitt, Henry
Turner, Benjamn
Wales, Elial
Wilson, Archbald
Woodward, Asa
Wright, Eliphas
Wright, Simeon

Bellefontaine Chapter, Bellefontaine, Ohio

LOGAN COUNTY

Carrell, William B.
Cowgill, ——
Cox, Michael
Culver, David
Curle, William
Evans, Moses
Howard, Peter
McDonald, Archibald
McPherson, James
Neighbarger, Christian
New, James L.
Powell, William
Prichard, Jared
Rudisilly, Henry
Sargent, James
Scott, Samuel
Sharp, Job
Stanage, Thomas
Tullis, John
Workman, Daniel

Elyria Chapter, Elyria, Ohio
Nancy Squire Chapter, Oberlin, Ohio
Nathan Perry Chapter, Lorain, Ohio

LORAIN COUNTY

Allis, Moses
Bacon, George
Barnum, John
Beebe, David
Bouton, Noah
Brooks, James
Burt, Aaron
Calkins, John Prentiss
Eldred, Samuel
Ferris, John
Foster, Albio
Kelley, John
Kellogg, Plinney
Langden, L.
Lawrence, John
Lewis, Oliver
Loveland, Abner
McManners, John
Merriman, Marshall
Moore, Joseph
Morse, Seth
Pelton, Samuel
Philips, Philip
Rounds, Charles
Sanford, Samuel
Sexton, Ezra
Shelhouse, Martia (Schelhouse)
Slauter, Ephraim
Squire, Ezra
Terrell Elihu
Terrell, Oliver
Wellman, Abraham

Fort Industry Chapter, Toledo, Ohio
Ursula Wolcott Chapter, Toledo, Ohio

LUCAS COUNTY

Bradley, Ariel
Scott, Joel
Stevens, John
Wheeler, Samuel

London Chapter, London, Ohio
Mt. Sterling Chapter, Mt. Sterling, Ohio

MADISON COUNTY

Baldwin, John
Baskerville, Samuel
Beach, Obil
Converse, Jeremiah
Crawford, John
Durham, John
Jackson, Stephen
Jones, George
Lanham, Elias
McClimans, John
Mitchell, Ensign
Moore, Ephraim
Sifrilt, Andrew
Smith, Samuel
Troxel (Troxell), John
Watson, Walter

Mahoning Chapter, Youngstown, Ohio

MAHONING COUNTY

Adair, James Sr.
Allerton, John
Anderson, Thomas
Applegate, Benjamin
Applegate, James
Applegate, Joseph
Armstrong, Daniel
Arner, Henry
Atwater, Kaleg
Atwood, Ichabod
Babbet, Stephen
Baldwin, Amos
Baldwin, Caleb
Beard, John
Beardsley, Philo
Beats, Urban (Betz)
Best, John
Bilgear, Frederick (Bilger)
Bissell, John Partridge
Blackbourne, Moses
Blackburn, John
Bougher, John (Bower, Boher)
Bowman, Philip Casper
Bradley, James
Bryson, Saul
Buchanan, Gilbert
Buck, William Jr.
Butler, Benjamin
Cain, Hugh
Calhoun, Samuel
Callahan, Jeremiah
Campbell, Alexander
Campbell, William
Canada, James
Canfield, Judson Private
Carson, John
Cartwright, John
Cattell, Jonas
Cattell, William
Cherry, John
Childister, William
Combs, John
Cotton, John Sr.
Countryman, Geo.
Countryman, Jacob
Craig, John
Crane, Calvin
Crooks, James
Davidson, James
Davidson, John
Davidson, William
Dean, Benjamin
DeLong, John
Dupue, Daniel
Doud, James
Drake, William
Duer, John Sr.
Dunlap, William Sr.
Eckman, Hieronimous
Ervin, Christopher
Evans, Edward
Everett, John
Everett, John Sr.
Fairchild, Eleazer (or Ezekiel)
Faust, Phillip
Feigle, John
Fink, Hans George

(MAHONING COUNTY—Concluded)

Fink, John
Fister, John
Fitch, Hanes
Fitch, James
Ford, Barnabas (or Bernard)
Frazee, Johnathan
Fullerton, Robert
Gault, Andrew
Gibson, James
Gibson, John
Gilbert, George
Gilson, Eleazar
Glass, Matthias
Gregory, Jacob
Grove, Windle (or Wendell)
Guthrie, John
Guthrie, William
Harding, George
Harding, Jacob
Harding, John
Harman, John
Harriff, Jacob
Heck, Peter
Hendrickson, Cornelius
Henry, Francis Sr.
Hillman, Col James
Hoffman, Detrich
Hoffman, John
Holland, William
Hull, Solomen
Huxley, Dan
Johnson, Archibald
Jordan, John
Joslyn, Darius
Ketch, Thomas
Kidd, Robert
Kincaid, John
Kindale, Joseph
Kirk, William
Kirpatrick, William
Kirtland, Turhand
Kohl, George
Kur, Robert
Launterman, William
Law, William
Leach, Abner
Lingo, Henry
Linton, Samuel
Logan, William
Love, Thomas
Loveland, Amos
Lowrey, Robert
McCombs, John Sr.
McCombs, William
McCullum, John
McGill, John
McKenzie, John
McKinsey, Samuel
McMahon, John
Marshall, James
Matthews, James
Maurer, John
May, George
May, John
May, John George
Merchant, Joseph
Miller, Daniel
Miller, Jacob
Miller, John B.
Monteith, Daniel
Moody, James
Moor, Nathan
Mowen, Belzar
Mowra, John
Mowrey, John
Musser, Daniel
Musser, Peter Sr.
Myer, Heinrich
Neff, Conrad
Newell, John
Ohle, Henry Sr.
Orr, William
Osborne, Nicholas
Oswold, Jacob
Owery, George
Pangburn, Joseph
Parshal, Samuel
Patterson, James
Patterson, William
Patton, James
Pennell, Robert
Ponteous, John
Reed, James Sr.
Reed, James Jr.
Reed, Phineas
Reed, Thomas
Reed, William
Riddle, Samuel
Riddle, William
Rilly, James
Ritter, John
Roller, Belsar
Roller, John Sr.
Rose, Jesse
Ross, Benjamin
Ross, James
Rowland, William
Rowler, Belzar (Roller)
Rudisill, John
Rush, John Sr.
Russell, James
Russell, Robert
Russell, William
Sanford, Zacheus
Schofield, Jonas (or Jonah)
Schronefeld, Von John
Scovil, Jonas (or Jonah)
Searl, Abraham
Sexton, Stephen
Shaffer, Jacob
Shehy, Daniel
Sherer, John
Shoemaker, Abraham
Shoemaker, John
Simon, Jacob
Simon, Michael
Skinner, Eli
Smith, Jonathan Sr.
Smith, Robert
Sprague, Jonathan
Stambach, Phillip
Steel, Matthew
Stevenson, James
Strain, William
Struthers, John
Stull, James
Stump, George Sr.
Sturgeon, Jeremiah
Summer, Von John
Swan, Timothy
Tanner, Tryal
Taylor, James
Taylor, William
Templeton, William
Tompson, Alexander
Trusdale, John Jr.
Turner, Adam
Van Bachman, Lawrence (or Lorentz)
Von Etton, John
Wadsworth, Elijah
Walker, Josiah
Walker, Nathaniel
Whitman, Samuel
Whitzell, Martin
Wick, William
Williamson, Joseph
Wilson, James
Winans, Jacob
Winans, James
Wise, Jacob
Wood, Charles
Woodruff, David
Yeager, Henry
Zimmerman, John
Zuck, Jacob

Capt. William Hendricks Chapter, Marion, Ohio

MARION COUNTY

Ballentine, Ebenezer
Clark, Isrial
Gillette, Joseph
Gray, Frazer
Hyde, Andrew Jr.
Irey, John
Lindsey, John
Otis, Barnabas
Potts, David
Scott, Matthew
Swinnerton, James
VanFleet, Joshua
Wyatt, Nathaniel Sr.

James Fowler Chapter, Leroy, Ohio

MEDINA COUNTY

Bartholomew, Joseph
Brouse, Se. Michel
Bates, Benjamin
Bentley, Benjamin
Brainerd, Ansel
Cotton, Benjamin
Disbrow, Henry
Dolph, Abda
Eggleston, Timothy
Flint, John
Foster, ——
Freeman, Rufus
Gifford, James
Goodwin, Seth
Gray, Nathaniel
Hain, Christopher (Hanes)
Hamilton, Eden
Hinsdale, Elisha
Hosmer, William
Hulet, John
Jones, Frederick
Kirkum, Philemon
Leland, Thomas
Nichols, David
Parker, Benjamin
Porter, Elija
Shaw, Ebenezer
Stearns, John
Taylor, Freegift
Thompson, John
Truman, Peter
Ward, John
Weard, John

Return Jonathan Meigs Chapter, Pomeroy, Ohio

MEIGS COUNTY

Carpenter, Amos
Cowdery, Jacob
Danielson, Luther
Dains, Asa
Ensminger, John
Gaston, Thomas
Graham, James
Grant, John
Higley, Brewster
Higley, Joel
Hisel, Frederick
Hysell, Frederick
Holt, Aaron
Howell, William
Hubbell, Abijah
Jones, Seth
Lowther, Joel
Niswonger, John
Parker, Hiram
Reed, David Jr.
Rockwell, Job
Roush, George
Roush, Henry
Roush, Jonas
Silvester, Joseph
Simpson, Josiah
Stivers, Daniel
Townsend, James
Townsend, Robert
Young, Robert
Whaley, James
White, John

MERCER COUNTY

Kirkwood, Robert
Leasor, Henry
McMahon, William
McMeachen, William

Miami Chapter, Troy, Ohio
Piqua Chapter, Piqua, Ohio

MIAMI COUNTY

Baily, Daniel
Barbee, William
Blue, Uriah
Boll, Joseph
Bollin, Joseph
Brandon, Benjamin
Byens, John
Caldwell, Matthew
Carroll, Charles
Cavault, ——
Counts, Jacob
Day, John
DeFress, Joseph Hutten
Deweese, Joshua
Dye, Andrew Sr.
Edwards, Thomas
Forman, Daniel
Gerard, John
Hart, Ralph
Harter, Henry
McCorkle, Joseph
Manson, David
Marshall, Henry
Meredith, John W.
Miller, Michiel
Mitchell, Samuel
Mitchell, William
Morris, David H.
Munsell, Levi
Orr, James
Pegg, Benjamin
Penny, Henry
Rollins, Josiah
Scott, William
Scudder, Mathias
Sevems, Edward
Small, Andrew
Stewart, David
Taylor, Samuel
Taylor, William
Telford, Alexander
Thomas, Abram
Tullis, Arron
Wiley, Samuel
Winnans, Samuel

Ann Rucker Chapter, Woodsfield, Ohio

MONROE COUNTY

Atkinson, Charles
Boughner, Martin
Cummings, John
Goodrich, Abner
Hollister, Nathan
Rucker, Lemuel
Wickham, William

Jonathan Dayton Chapter, Dayton, Ohio

MONTGOMERY COUNTY

Andrews, Hugh
Bacon, Richard
Barnett, John
Bigger, John
Bowman, John
Brooks, Charles
Chase, Beverly
Chevalier, Anthony
Clency, George
Collins, William
Conner, Joseph
Cox, Benjamin
Cuppy, John
Davis, John
Davis, Joseph
Davis, Thomas
Deam, Henry
Dodds, Joseph Jr.
Dodds, William
Elliot, John
Fox, Frederick
Gebhard, Nicholas
Gilliespie, James
Grimes, John
Hall, William
Hanna, James
Harp (Herb) Frederick
Haskins, Enoch
Hatfield, Thomas
Heagan, Patrick
Hegeman, Peter
Herb, Frederick
Hole, Dr. John
Huey, Robert
Huiet, Philip
Irwin, Samuel
Kellogg, Seth
Kiester, Peter
Kimmel, David
Kiser, John
LaRose, John Jacob
Lyon, Nathaniel
McConnell, Alexander
Miller, Isaac
Negley, Philip (Nagel, Neagle)
Nichols, John
Niswonger, Samuel
Nutt, Aaron
Park, Reuben
Patterson, Robert
Peirce, Isaac
Pierson, Daniel
Recher, Peter
Reed, James
Roberts, John
Rusk, James
Saylor, John
Shuey, J. Martin
Simpson, Alexander
Smith, Charles
Snyder, George
Spinning, Isaac
Sunderland (or Sunderlin), William
Watkins, William
White, William
Williamson, John
Wilson, Daniel
Witters, Conrad
Zeiglar, Maj. David

Amanda Barker Devin Chapter, McConnelsville, Ohio

MORGAN COUNTY

Anderson, Augustine
Beckwith, Benjamin
Cheadle, Asa
Clancy, John
Duvall, Jacob
Harmon, Jacob
McMurray, William
Mummey, Christopher
Murray, William
Severance, Benjamin
Shepard, Benjamin

Mt. Gilead Chapter, Mt. Gilead, Ohio

MORROW COUNTY

Ashley, Wm. S.
Buck, ———
Campbell, McDonald
Collins, Benjamin
Cook, John
Dixon, Alexander
Doty, Peter
Foust, Jakob
Gibbs, Daniel
Hardenbrook, Lodwick
Holt, Evan
Hopkins, Timothy
Iden, John
Kester, Joseph
Kingman, Alexander
Kinney, John
Lemmon, Olexis
Lester, Thomas
Lockhart, William
McCreary, George
Martin, Reuben
Matson, Reuben
Munson, Wilmot
Patee, Edmond
Schurr, Jacob
Sheward, William
Smith, John
Smith, Joseph
Smith, Simeon
Wood, Ebenezer

Muskingum Chapter, Zanesville, Ohio
Tomepomehala Chapter, New Concord, Ohio

MUSKINGUM COUNTY

Baer, Adam
Bainter, Jacob
Barr (Baer) Adam
Beale, John
Beavers, Samuel
Belknap, Samuel
Bird, George
Bodman, Scamon
Boyd, Robert
Briggs, John
Buker, Israel
Calhoun, John
Carter, Ezekiel
Cass, Jonathan
Clapper, George
Conine, Jacob
Conner, John
Culbertson, Alexander Jr.

(MUSKINGUM COUNTY—Concluded)

Davis, John
Davis, William
Deitrick, John Balsar (Johann Baltser) Sr.
Denison, William
Evans, Joseph
Ewing, Joseph
Forsythe, John
Gaumer, Jacob Sr.
Griggs, Deacon Ichabod
Huntington, John
Jackson, George
Kelly, John
Kreager, Jacob
Lane, Richard
McHenry, Richard
Marshall, Richard
Mathews, John
Mix, Amos
Peirce, Lewis
Ralston, Andrew
Remay, John
Richardson, Jesse
Richcreek, Philip
Richey, John
Riley, William
Rose, Ezekiel
Slack, John
Smith, Jesse
Spicer, John
Sprague, James
Stone, Isaac
Taylor, James
Van Horne, Isaac
Wade, Abner
Williams, Thomas
Wilson, James
Zane, Isaac

NOBLE COUNTY

Bates, Ephraim
Blake, Simeon
Caldwell, Robert
Carpenter, Joseph
Carroll, George
Dye, (Dey) Ezekiel
Enochs, Enoch
Farley, David
George, Jesse
Gray, John
Harris, Elisha
Hutchens, Hollis
Jorden, Jacob
Lowe, James
Morris, Archibald
Ross, John
Thorla, Thomas
Waller, Jesse
Walters, Peter
Wiley, William

OTTAWA COUNTY

Green, John

PAULDING COUNTY

Brown, Capt.

PERRY COUNTY

Bugh, Peter
Custard, Jacob
Dusenberry, William
Funk, Adam
Hazelton, John
Jones, William
McClure, William
Overmyer, George
Overmyer, Peter
Parkison, (Parkeson or Parkinson) Daniel
Ritchey, James
Spencer, James
Stalter, Henry
Taylor, Tom
Ward, Edward
Whitmer, Peter

Pickaway Plains Chapter, Circleville, Ohio

PICKAWAY COUNTY

Allison, William
Bailey, George
Blackwell, John
Boggs, Capt. John
Cock, Moses
Denny, Samuel
Durham, John
Ernst, Christopher
Fryback, George
Gulic, Ferdinand
Leach, Sergeant Valentine
Leist, Andrew
Loveberry, Loufbourrow) John Wade
Lutz, John Jacob
McClintock, William
Monnett, Abraham
Mourer, John (Mowery) or Maurer
Reichelsdoefer, John (Reichelderfer)
Renick, John
Rowland, John
Sage, Herleigh
Spangler, Peter
Van Dorn, Hezekiah
Ward, William
Williamson, Eleazer
Wood, John

Scioto Valley Chapter, Waverly, Ohio

PIKE COUNTY

Cook, Zachariah
Davis, William
Foster, John 1st
Gutherie, (Guthery) John
Hull, John
Lucas, William
Price, William
Sargent, James Sr.
Sargent, Snowden
Violet, John
Wolfenbarger, Philip
Wynn, William S.

Aaron Olmstead Chapter, Kent, Ohio
Old Northwest Chapter, Ravenna, Ohio

PORTAGE COUNTY

Adams, Moses
Agard, John
Alford, Elijah
Austin, Andrew
Backus, Samuel
Baldwin, David
Baldwin, Jonathan
Baldwin, Samuel
Best, Thomas
Bierce, William
Bissell, Justus
Blackman, Elijah
Bostwick, Doctor
Bostwick, Ebenezer
Bostwick, Eleazer
Bosworth, John
Bristol, Daniel
Cane, Daniel
Canfield, Elijah
Carlton, Caleb
Chapman, Constant
Coosard, Valentine
Crocker, David
Crooks, William
Daniel, David
Daniels, Amariah
Davis, Noah
Day, Lewis
Diver, Daniel
Durkee, Ebbe
Eggleston, Benjamin
Ely, Darius
Ely, Lewis
Farnum, Elisah
Freeman, Nathan
Gaylord, John
Gilbert, Truman
Goss, Ebenezer
Granger, Julius
Hartzell, John Jr.
Hickox, Ebenezer
Hobart, William
Hoskins, Ashbel
Kennedy, David
Kent, Jonas
Kent, Zenas
Lane, John
Larcum, Paul
Lord, Ichabod
Loveland, Isaac
Mather, Abner
Messinger, Bille
Mix, Josiah
Muzzy, Nathaniel
Norton, Ozias
Parks, Elijah
Payne, Soloman
Pease, Abner
Plum, Charles
Porter, Ebenezer
Prichard, Benjamin
Randall, Reuben
Riley, Julius
Rogers, Henry
Rogers, Richard
Sanford, Samuel
Seely, John
Seward, John
Sheldon, Ebenezer
Shirtliff, Noah
Smith, Noah
Spencer, John
Stevenson, Obadiah
Taylor, Elisha
Taylor, Samuel
Thompson, Job
Thurbern, Amos
Tilden, Daniel
Trowbridge, Ebenezer
Turner, Allyn
Turrell, John
Tuttle, John
Whipple, Zebulon
Williams, Ebenezer
Wolcott, David

Commodore Preble Chapter, Eaton, Ohio

PREBLE COUNTY

Ashley, William
Caughey, Thomas
Curry, John
Fleming, James
Fleming, Thomas
Gray, William
Hamilton, Alexander
Hamilton, Andrew
Harlison, Robert
Hawkins, Samuel
Haseltine, John
Horn, Henry
Klinger, Philip
McClurkin, Matthew
McDill, David
McQuiston, David
Magaw, Capt. Wm.
Morgan, Thomas
Nessle, John
Patterson, John
Potterf, Jasper
Quinn, Robert
Ramsey, Nathan
Ramsey, Wm.
Ridenour, Peter
Sellers, Nathan
Steel, Samuel
Truax, David
Van Winkle, Michael
Williams, William

PUTNAM COUNTY

Hubbard, Israel
McDermut, James

Jared Mansfield Chapter, Mansfield, Ohio
Mary Washington Chapter, Mansfield, Ohio

RICHLAND COUNTY

Bodley, William
Coffinberry, George
Cook, Noah
Ervin, Peter
Erving, Peter (Ervin)
Fleeharty, Amasa
Gamble, James
Gates, John Sr.
Heller, John
Henry, John
Jacobs, John
McDermott, James
McKelvey, William
Mann, John
Nail, Henry Sr.
Oldfield, William
Poppleton, Samuel
Post, David
Riblet, Christian
Stoner, John
Taylor, Thomas
Watson, Amariah
Willis, Thomas
Wolfe, Adam

Nathaniel Massie Chapter, Chillicothe, Ohio

ROSS COUNTY

Arnold, Norris
Ater, George
Beard, William Sr.
Beaver, Michael Sr.
Blair, Andrew
Blue, John
Brown, White
Bush, Michael
Carson, William
Cave, Benjamin
Chestnut, Daniel
Christian, William
Condon, Redman
Crouse, John Sr.
Davenport, Anthony Sims
Day, Samuel
Dean, Abraham
Depoy, Christopher
Dickey, Robert
Downs, John
Dumm, Peter
Earl, Thomas
Elliott, Reuben
Ferguson, James
Ferguson, Matthew
Flora, Abijah
Forsman, Hugh
Freshour, John
Goldsberry, John
Holliday, Robert
Hutt, John
Jackson, Peter
Jolly, David
Kent, William
Kilbourne, ——
McClean, Moses
McClelland, Cary
McKenzie, Joshua
McRoberts, Alexander
Massie, Nathaniel
May, James Sr.
Metzger, Jacob
Morton, John
Overley, Frederick
Parrett, Fred
Platter, Christian
Platter, Peter Sr.
Plyley, Casper
Poe, John
Pritchard, James
Robbins, John
Rosebroom, Henry
Shotts, David
Smith, Abraham
Sperry, Peter
Stewart, Hugh
Stimson, James
Streve, (Streevey) Paul
Taylor, William
Thomas, Michael
Vandeman, John
Waddell, James
Ward, Nathan
Waugh, Joseph
Wentworth, Benning
Wheeler, John
Will, George
Williams, Kent
Wilson, James
Wycoff, Samuel

Col. George Croghan Chapter, Fremont, Ohio

SANDUSKY COUNTY

Armstrong, George
Burkhardt, John
Dalyrymple, David
McBurney, William
Stevens, Phinehas
Waggoner, John
Watrous, Allen
Wright, Joal or Joab

Joseph Spencer Chapter, Portsmouth, Ohio

SCIOTO COUNTY

Barber, Uriah
Belli, John
Bennett, Thaddeus
Boynton, Asa
Briggs, John
Brown, John Jr.
Burt, Benjamin
Clingman, John Michael
Dever, John (Deavor)
Edwards, Jessie
Fort, Joseph
Funk, Martin
Hammitt, George
Hempstead, Hallam
Hoskinson, Josiah
Keyes, Selma
Marshall, Samuel S.
Mitchel, David
Munn, Major James
Neal, Robert

Dolly Todd Madison Chapter, Tiffin, Ohio
Jane Washington Chapter, Fostoria, Ohio

SENECA COUNTY

Carson, Robert
Dean, Aaron
Ditto, Francis
Earl, Grantham
Groscoat, Daniel
Harris, William
Heaton, Isaac
Holmes, Jedediah
Kemp, John W.
Kent, John
Miller, Jacob
Peterson, Matson
Robinson, Oliver
Robinson, ——
Shawhan, Frederick
Summerland, David
Valentine, George
Williams, Jeremiah
Wright, Eli
Wright, Joab

Lewis Boyer Chapter, Sidney, Ohio

SHELBY COUNTY

Boyer, Lewis
Cannon, Lt. James
Cecil, Zachariah
Hardin, John
Johnston, Silas
Line, John
Line, Joseph
Lyon, John
Shaw, Thomas
Stephens, Joshua
Wales, Timothy
Woodward, Samuel

Canton Chapter, Canton, Ohio
Freedom Chapter, Alliance, Ohio
Massillon Chapter, Massillon, Ohio

STARK COUNTY

Croninger, Joseph
Davidson, James
Doxsee, Thomas
Essig, Simon
Eversole, Jacob
Fisher, Adam
Hildenbrand, Michael
Houser, Martin
Kerstetler, Leonard
Koch, Adam
Kuhn, John
Mills, John
Page, Benjamin
Poe, Adam
Reed, Jacob Jr.
Shreve, John
Whipple, Zebulion
Wise, Peter

Akron Chapter, Akron, Ohio
Cuyahoga Falls Chapter, Cuyahoga Falls, Ohio
Cuyahoga-Portage Chapter, Akron, Ohio
Temperance Avery Chapter, Ellet, Ohio

SUMMIT COUNTY

Atwater, ———
Baird, George
Bates, Hinsdale
(or Henesdale)
Beach, Reuben
Bettes, Nathaniel
Boosinger, Conrad
Brouse, M.
Brown, Henry
Brown, Samuel
Butler, Stephen
Canfield, Leve
Chapman, Titus
Clark, Zelotus
Clement, Lambert
Daily, John
Davis, Nathaniel
Dewey, Oliver
Dimick, Moor
Draper, Jonathan
Dudley, Isaac
Elliott, Samuel
Ellsworth, John
Farnum, John
Galpin, Daniel
Gaylord, Joel
Gaylord, Johnathan
Gaylord, Samuel
Geer, Guerdon
Gillett, Nathaniel
Goodall, ———
Granger, Thaddeus
Granger, Thomas
Griswald, Alexander
Hammond, Jason
Hardy, Nathaniel
Harrington, Richard
Hawkins, Joseph
Hershberger, John
Humphrey, Simon
Kinney, Aaron
Lacy, Thaddeus
Lampson, William
McMillan, John
McNeil, Thomas
Mather, Eleazer
Neal, William
Newell, Norman
Norton, Peter Jr.
Powers, Gregory
Preston, David
Prior, Simeon
Ranney, Nathaniel
Reuben, Beach
Richards, Jedediah
Riley, Daniel
Steele, Isaac
Smith, Samuel
Sumner, Thomas
Thayer, Joel
Thompson, Stephen Jr.
Thompson, Stephen Sr.
Tupper, Simeon
Van Hyning, Henry
Walker, John
Waltz, Peter
Weager, John
Welton, Elijah
Weston, John
Weston, Samuel
Wilcox, Hosea
Wooden, Charles
Wright, John

Mary Chesney Chapter, Warren, Ohio

TRUMBULL COUNTY

Adams, Asahel
Adgate, John Hart
Allen, John
Anderson, William
Applegate, James
Backus, Samuel
Bailey, David
Barnes, John
Beach, Elihu
Belamy, Asa
Bellesselt (Bellesfeller), Peter
Benedict, Hezekiah
Bigelow, Timothy
Bostwick, Reuben

(TRUMBULL COUNTY—Concluded)

Bostworth, Peter
Bradford, Joshua
Bradley, James
Brockway, Edward
Brooks, David
Brooks, Oliver
Burnett, David
Burnett, Edmund
Burnham, Jedediah
Bushnell, Alexander
Bushnell, Daniel
Bushnell, Thomas
Caldwell, Robert
Carlton, Francis
Case, Meshel (Meshek)
Cherry, John
Clark, Ephraim
Clark, Isaac
Cook, James
Cox, John New
Craft, Thomas
Cramer, Frederick
Crosby, Obed
Crowell, Mathew
Dana, Dan
Davidson, Abigail
DeForest, Abraham
Denison, John
DeWolf, Joseph
Dilley, Samuel
Deake, Abraham
Drapes, Nathan Sr.
Dray, Edward
Everett, Samuel
Fight, Jacob Sr.
Finney, Josiah
Fithian, Isaac
Flower, Isaac
Frazier, George
Freeman, Robert
Frisby, Luther
Gates, Freeman
Gilbert, Henry
Gilson, Daniel Jr.
Gilson, David Sr.
Gilson, David Jr.
Gordon, John
Gotdon, Thomas
Griswold, Zacheus
Hake, Frederick
Halstead, Jacob
Hampton, Moses
Harmon, Ruben G.
Harper, John
Harsh, Henry
Hart, Bliss
Hasford, Isaac
Hassen, Hugh
Haughton, Henry
Hayes, Titus
Headley, Joseph
Hoagland, John
Holcomb, Jesse Sr.
Hood, George
Hoover, Manuel Capt.
Hover, Emanuel
Howells, Daniel Veach
Huffstetter, James
Humason, Joe
Humphrey, David
Hurlburt, Jehiel Sr.
Jacobs, Jonathan
Jones, Silas
Jones, William Clarke
Joslin, Reuben
Kimball, Jared
Kinsman, John
Laird, James Sr.
Lane, Henry Sr.
Lane, Isaac Sr.
Langley, John
Leach, Abraham
Leavitt, John
Leavitt, Samuel
Leslie, Samuel
Lindsley, (Lingsley or Linsley) Stephen
Lossee, Peter (or Loffee)
McMullen, Neil
Maltby, Benjamin
Matthews, William
Mayes, William W.
Mead, Libens
Moore, Robert
Musser, Peter Jr.
Osborn, Joshua
Oviatt, Samuel Sr.
Owery, George
Parker, Lovell
Partner, John
Peck, Jesse
Pierson, Amos
Proctor, Francis Sr.
Pruden, Joseph
Quigley, Robert
Ralston, Archibald
Ramsey, John
Rankins, Johnathan
Rawdon, Ezra
Reeder, Jacob
Reeve, Ebenezer
Reeves, Joseph
Reuben, John
Rice, Aaron
Rice, Enoch
Rice, Ephraim Sr.
Rice, Isaac
Roberts, John Sr.
Roberts, William
Rust, Aloney
Rutan, John
Rutledge, Michael
Sanderson, John
Smith, Gager
Smith, Jonathan
Smith, Martin
Sperry, Elias
Sperry, George
Stewart, Charles
Stow, Comfort
Swager, Henry
Tait, Thomas
Talcott, Elizar
Tanner, W. M.
Taylor, Simon
Tidd, ———
Tracy, Seth
Tucker, James
Ulph, Jared (see Ulp)
Ulp, Jared
Wakefield, Lyman
Wakley, Johnathan
Waldorf, John
Waters, Abner
Webb, David
Whipple, Eizra
White, Henry
Wilcox, Jeremiah (M. D.)
Wilson, James
Wilson, Samuel
Wilson, William
Winans, Isaac Sr.
Winterstein, Philip E.
Wolcott, Josiah

TUSCARAWAS COUNTY

Blickensderfer, Christian
Brehmer (Bremer), Conrad
Carr, Aquilla
Davis, Henry
Demuth, Christopher
Demuth, Gottlieb
Frantz, Adam
Ganer (Gainer, Gardner), Peter
Ginther, Peter

Hannah Emerson Dustin Chapter, Marysville, Ohio
Plain City Chapter, Plain City, Ohio

UNION COUNTY

Amrine, Abraham
Amrine, Adrian
Burdick, John
Carter, Charles
Coleman, James
Crary, Christopher
Curry, James
Edgar, William
Fisher, Enoch
Hale, Israel
Hale, P.
Hall, Peter
Hibbard, Ozias
Mitchell, Samuel
Richmond, Enoch Fisher
Robinson, James
Shover, Henry
Snodgrass, Robert
Stewart, Joseph
Thompson, James
Westlake, George
Worley, David

Isaac Van Wert Chapter, Van Wert, Ohio

VAN WERT COUNTY

Shepherd, Phineas

VINTON COUNTY

Blakely, James
Craig, James
Craig, Thomas Sr.
Darby, William
Davis, William
Dowd, Conner
Duc, Henry
Gill, Daniel
Pratt, Ephraim
Sage, Samuel
Winters, Thomas

Turtle Creek Chapter, Lebanon, Ohio

WARREN COUNTY

Anderson, Lewis
Banta, Daniel
Banta, Peter
Benham, Robert
Brant, Stephen
Campbell, John
Collett, Daniel
Crosley, Moses
Dunlevy, Francis
Fitch, Andrew
Geohegan, Anthony
Goehegan, John Edmund
Graham, William
Gray, Daniel
Gray, Robert
Gustin, Benajah
Halsey, John
Hamilton, Robert
Haynes, Daniel
Henderson, William
Holcomb, Jonathan
Jefferies, George
Kell, Samuel
Kibbey, Ephraim
Light, George
Lillie, David
McDonald, John
Mason, William
Morrell, Calvin, M. D.
Morris, Isaac
Moses, Robert
Munger, Johnathan
Pratt, Nathan (or Jonathan)
Ross, Alexander
Rue, Benjamin
Russell, William
Schenck, Garret G.
Schenck, William
Sering, Samuel
Stevens, Ephraim
Stites, Elijah
St. John, John
Stump, Daniel
Tapscott, James
Tharp, John
Tichinor, Jonathan
Troville, Johnathan
Tufts, Francis
Tullis, John
Vandeveer, Joseph
Van Note, Joseph
Zehring, Christopher (or Christian)

Marietta Chapter, Marietta, Ohio

WASHINGTON COUNTY

Backus, Elijah
Battelle, Ebenezer
Bent, Silas
Bigford, Samuel
Bosworth, Sala
Bradford, Robert
Brown, John
Burlingame, Christopher
Chapman, Herman
Coburn, Asa
Cole, John
Curtis, Eleazer
Curtis, John
Cushing, Nathaniel
Dana, William
Davis, Daniel
Deming, Simeon
Devin, Michael
Devol, Jonathan
Dickerson, Thomas
Doane, Richard
Dodge, John Jr.
Dodge, Nathaniel
Dunham, Jonathan
Dutton, James
Ellenwood, Benjamin
Evans, Nathan
Evarts, Ambrose (for record see Everets, Ambrose)
Everets, Ambrose
Fisher, Daniel
Fletcher, Sherebiah

(WASHINGTON COUNTY—Concluded)

Ford, William
Foster, Ephraim
Foster, Peregrine
Franks, Henry
Frye, Joseph
Gates, Timothy
Gilman, Joseph
Glover, James Lawrence
Goldsmith, Benoni
Goodale, Nathan
Gray, William
Green, Duty
Green, Griffin
Green, John
Greenway, Jeremiah
Hart, Josiah
Haskell, Jonathan
Hildreth, Samuel
Hill, Ira
Hovey, William
Howe, Peter
Kerr, Matthew
Kidd, Nathaniel
King, Zebulon
Knowles, James
Lankton, Levi
Leavens, John
Lincoln, Joseph
Little, Nathaniel
Loring, Daniel
McAllister, Andrew
Melvin, Isaac
Middleswart, Henry
Miles, Benjamin
Munro, Josiah
Newton, Elias
Nye, Ebenezer
Nye, Ichabod
Oliver, Alexander
Oliver, Robert
Owen, James
Palmer, Joseph Jr.
Parsons, Samuel H.
Prentiss, Stanton
Putnam, Allen
Putnam, Ezra
Putnam, Israel Jr.
Putnam, Rufus
Rice, Nathan
Rice, Oliver
Rogers, Joseph
Russell, James
Saltonstall, Nathaniel
Saunders, Abraham
Shaw, Benjamin
Shaw, Peter
Shepherd, Enoch
Sherman, Abel
Simons, Joseph
Sparhawk, Noah
Sprague, Joshua
Sproat, Ebenezer
Stacy, William Jr.
Stacy, William
Stanley, Thomas
Stone, Israel
Stone, Jonathan
Talbot, Richard
Taylor, Robert
Trew, Ephraim
True, Jabez
Tupper, Anselm
Tupper, Benjamin
Varnum, James M.
Whipple, Abraham
White, Hatfield
Wickersham, Peter
Williamson, Samuel
Woodward, Oliver

Wooster Wayne Chapter, Wooster, Ohio

WAYNE COUNTY

Barnhart, Fred S.
Brouse, Michael
Case, Augustus Sr.
Cobler, Michael
Conkey, Ezekiel
Davidson, John
Dulin, John Sr.
Fike, Henry
Franke, Henry
Fritz, Martin
McCaughey, William
Marshall, William
Metcalf, Masson
Meyer, Christian
Mitsco, Conrad
Morgan, James
Munson, Isaac
Naylor, William
Patterson, Robert
Peterson, Conrad
Rice, Frederick
Shankland, Alexander
Sharp, George
Tryon, Ezra
Walker, Nathaniel
Waltz, Michael
Waltz, Peter
Yocum, John

Black Swamp Chapter, Bowling Green, Ohio

WOOD COUNTY

Badger, Rev. Joseph
Dunlap, Robert
Howard, Thomas
Waterman, Gladding

Col. William Crawford Chapter, Upper Sandusky, Ohio

WYANDOTTE COUNTY

Crawford, William
Harper, Samuel
Reed, Alexander
Rowland, Joseph
Sheely, Ludwig
Shepherd, Jacob
Terflinger, Christopher
Welch, Felix
Young, George

REVOLUTIONARY SOLDIERS BURIED IN OHIO — COUNTY NOT STATED

Allyn, Nathan
Armstrong, Abel
Barr, Alexander
Bassett, Cornelius
Bennett, Ishmael
Butler, Ebenezer Jr.
Butler, Zebulon
Coddington, William
Cribbs, John
Culver, Solomon
Cummins, James
Davies, Marmaduke S.
Deaver, John
Falkner, John
Fish, Ebenezer
Frazee, Moses
Gibson, George
Hamilton, Jonathan
Hogue, James
Huber, Andrew
Janes, Elijah
Karr, Matthew
Kemper, Peter
Kingsbury, Samuel
Kingsley, Nathan
Letts, Nehemiah
Long, Michael
McFadden, Conley
McMillan, Robert
Morrison, Francis
Osborn, Josiah
Perry, Winslow
Piatt, Abraham
Radabach, Peter
Rhoads, Frederick
Sampson, Spaulding
Scott, Mark
Scott, Oliver
Shaw, Knowles
Sinclair, Richard Jr.
Smith, Simeon
Stephens, Jabez
Stryker, Peter
Swickhart, Martin
Taylor, Jasher
Tremain, Philip
Warth, George
Webber, Benjamin
Weir, John
Wells, Benjamin
Wright, Shadrach
Wyllys, John Palsgran
Zane, Capt. Silas

The following list was taken from Byron Williams' "History of Clermont and Brown Counties." At the time of publication of this roster there was not sufficient information to justify the publication of these records as authentic. However, there is little doubt as to their service during the American Revolution.

Alexander, Lieut. James
Aldridge, John
Apple, Andrew
Barber, Nathaniel
Buckingham, Enoch
Brannen, Daniel
Carter, James
Carter, Reece
Clarke, Judge James
Coen, Edward
Colglazer, David
Conrey, John
Conrad, John
Corbley, Rev. John
Cowen, Lt. William
Davis, Benjamin
Davis, Thomas
Day, Jeremiah
Day, John
Denune, John
Donham, Nathaniel
Durham, Daniel
English, Robert
Fitzwater, William
Fox, Jacob
Frybarger, Lewis
Hall, Capt. Richard
Hare, John
Hill, Benajah
Hoy, Adam
John, Capt. James
Johnson, James
Kain, James
Knott, Ignatius
Leeds, Hezekiah
Logston, John
Looker, Othniel
Love, Mordecai
McCollun, Ensign Cornelius
McCormick, Rev. Francis
McKay, James
McKnight, William
Mitchell, John
Mock, David
Morgan, Daniel
Morin, Edward
Murry, Neal
Murphy, James
Nelson, John
Neville, Gen. Presley
Nichols, Nathan
Niles, John
Owen, William
Payne, John
Penn, Benjamin
Porter, Eli
Ramsey, Capt. John
Reddick, William
Richardson, Joshua
Riggs, Gideon
Rose, Reuben
Ulrey, Jacob
Salt, Edward
Sargent, Elijah
Sargent, John
Sargent, James
Shaw, James
Sherwin, Elnathan
Slye, Jacob
Smith, Absalom
Smith, Obadiah
Stewart, Sergt. John
Stroup, Jacob
Thomas, Jacob
Thomas, John
Walburn, Samuel
Webster, Sergt. Samuel
Whidden, Solomon
Wilson, Samuel
Winters, Mordecai

MEN REPORTED BURIED IN PIKE COUNTY

The following men were reported to have been buried in Pike County and for further information correspondence should be carried on with the parties who furnished these names.

McMILLAN, ALEXANDER, (Pike Co.)

Fur infor Scioto Valley Chap.

CHENOWETH, ELIJAH, (Pike Co.)

Private. Fur infor Scioto Valley Chap.

CISSNA, CHARLES, (Pike Co.)

2nd Lt. Fur infor Scioto Valley Chap.

DANIELS, BENJAMIN, (Pike Co.)

Major. Fur infor Scioto Valley Chap.

LOVE, CHARLES, (Pike Co.)

Private. Fur infor Scioto Valley Chap.

BEEKMAN, WILLIAM, (Pike Co.)

Fur infor Scioto Valley Chap.

REVOLUTIONARY SOLDIERS CLAIMED BY OHIO BURIED IN OTHER STATES

Investigation of the records of the following Revolutionary soldiers reveals that although they lived or were pensioned in Ohio, for various reasons they were buried in another state.

BRANDT, ADAM

Pvt Lancaster Co Pa Mil, in Capt Henning's Co. Br Dauphin Co, Pa, Nov 29, 1751. Mar Eva Metzler Mar 28, 1775. D Dec 13, 1838 and bur in Pa where the Elizabeth Sherman Reese Chap of Lancaster, Ohio, placed a bronze marker on his grave Aug 30, 1927. Ref: Mrs Edith Brandt Henry, Lancaster, O. Fur infor Elizabeth Sherman Reese Chap.

BROOKS, DR. JOHN

Reported in records as living in Jefferson County, is bur at Florence, Pa. Fur infor Steubenville Chap.

BRYANT, DAVID

Br Springfield, N. J. D 1835, Fort Wayne, Ind. Removed to Pa 1791; thence to Knox Co, O. in 1816, where he was pensioned. Ref: Natl No 75199, Vol 76, D. A. R. Lin.

BLAIR, JAMES

Pensioned as residing in Geauga Co, 1818. Br 1763; was living in Thompson, O. 1833; in Clark Co, O, 1846; Erie Co, Pa, 1848, where he was buried. Service was in N H Continental Line. Fur infor Taylor Chap.

DURAND, ANDREW

Pvt Capt Hotchkiss' Company, Col Cook's Regt Conn Mil, Mar 1778. Capt Curtis' Company; Sapt Andrews' Company 1781. Br Cheshire, Conn, 1758. Parents were Andrew Durand and Eunice Hotchkiss. Carried package of letters to Maj Coggswell fr Fishkill, N Y to Bennington, Vt. Came to Burton, O, 1806, from Cheshire, Conn. Pensioned 1833 in Geauga Co. Later moved to Indiana. Ref: Pioneer Hist of Geauga Co, p 451. Pens Dept file 2528, Vol A, p 103. Fur infor Taylor Chap.

GARDNER, JOHNATHAN

Served in NJ State Tr. Lived at one time in Cincinnati, O. Pens while living in Geauga Co, 1833. Was 87 yrs old. Pension file 31051, Vol II, p 149. Removed to Coles, Ill.

HARRINGTON, JOHN

Pvt Mass Continental Line, Capts Thomas Francis-Heyward, and Bailey, Cols Tupper and Sprout from Mass. Br Sandisfield, Mass. In 1819 placed on the pension roll at age of 69. Transferred from New York. Ref: Pension Roll, 1st Session, 23d Congress, Vol III, Rev Pension Roll. 1833-34 Portage Co, statement. D in Hancock Co, Ill. Fur infor Cuyahoga-Portage Chap.

HOLCOMB, ELIJAH

His service record established by Margaret Holcomb, Bremen, O. He was a resident of Muskingum Co, O at the time of his death, but died while in the east, on a visit, and buried there to save travel expenses. Grave marked by Revolutionary marker, Lambertville, NJ. Fur infor Muskingum Chap.

HOUSTON, WILLIAM

See D A R Lin Vol 63, p 183, for date. Statement of Margaret Houston, Lowellville, O, Mahoning Co, locates his grave in Deer Creek cem, New Bedford, Lawrence Co, Pa. "D Dec 28, 1834, aged 77 yrs, 7 mos, after devoting his early life to the defense of his county etc" is inscribed on his stone. Ref: Houston Family, p 98.

LAKE, REUBEN

Pens as residing in Geauga Co, O, 1818, with service in the Conn Continental Army. Pens Record Natl No 35515. Removed to Peoria, Ill. Fur infor Taylor Chap.

McCLELLAN, ROBERT

Although the name appears on the tablet in the Soldiers' and Sailors' Monument at Hamilton, O, Butler Co, as a Revolutionary soldier, he died in 1914, at Cape Girardeau, Mo, where he is buried. Fur infor John Reily Chap.

PERIN, LEMUEL

Br in Mass Oct 21, 1749. D Oct 23, 1814. 1st wife, Martha Nash, mar in Mass. 2d wife, Amelia Dickinson. Children: John, Rachel, Lucy, Hannah, Samuel (br 1785, mar in Cayuga Co, NY, Mary Simpkins. He (Samuel) served in WAR 1812; d 1865; twins were Lemuel and Glover, and Amelia. Came to Miami Twp, Clermont Co, O about 1808. Family history gives burial at Connersville, Ind. Ref: Natl No 134845, D. A. R. and A. S. Abbott, Bethel, O, who fur this information.

POWERS, ———

Came to Ohio from Beaver, Pa about 1797; had lived near the border of NY, NJ, and Pa; also in Westmoreland Co, Pa. One son was Isaac. Received land for service in general. Ref: NY Men in the Rev, p 213-215. Bur in Pa. Descendant, G. M. McKelvey, Youngstown, O. Fur infor Mahoning Chap.

SMITH, JOHN

Pvt in Col Henry Jackson Regt, Capt Lyman's Company, Mass Continental Line. Br 1754, resided at Merryfield, Mass, where he returned later, and was bur. In 1818 he was pensioned as living in Burton, Geauga Co, O. See Natl No 40470, Pens Rolls. Fur infor Taylor Chap.

STONE, JONATHAN

(1725-1806.) D A R Lin, Vol 23, p 339, places burial in Auburn, O. This should be "bur in Mass" as investigation finds in the Stone genealogy he died in Mass. Fur correction, Taylor Chap.

QUINBY, SAMUEL

Revolutionary soldier who lived in Trumbull Co. He was given military funeral and taken to Oakwood cem at Sharon, Pa, where he was buried. Fur infor Mary Chesney Chap.

INDEX

www.ingramcontent.com/pod-product-compliance
Lightning Source LLC
Chambersburg PA
CBHW030233030426
42336CB00009B/83

* 9 7 8 1 6 3 9 1 4 0 4 6 6 *